CHILD ABUSE

A Multidisciplinary Survey

Series Editor
BYRGEN FINKELMAN, J.D.

A GARLAND SERIES

SERIES CONTENTS

VOLUME

3

CAUSES, PREVENTION AND REMEDIES

Edited with introductions by

BYRGEN FINKELMAN, J.D.

GARLAND PUBLISHING, Inc.
New York & London
1995

Library of Congress Cataloging-in-Publication Data

Child abuse : a multidisciplinary survey / series editor, Byrgen
Finkelman.
    p.   cm.
    Includes bibliographical references and indexes.
    Contents: v. 1. Physical and emotional abuse and neglect
— v. 2. Sexual abuse — v. 3. Causes, prevention, and remedies
— v. 4. Short- and long-term effects — v. 5. Treatment of child
and adult survivors — v. 6. Treatment of offenders and
families
    ISBN 0-8153-1813-8 (v. 1 : acid-free paper). — ISBN
0-8153-1814-6 (v. 2 : acid-free paper). — ISBN 0-8153-1815-4
(v. 3 : acid-free paper). — ISBN 0-8153-1816-2 (v. 4 : acid-
free paper). — ISBN 0-8153-1817-0 (v. 5 : acid-free paper).
— ISBN 0-8153-1818-9 (v. 6 : acid-free paper)
    1. Child abuse—United States.   I. Finkelman, Byrgen.
HV6626.52.C54   1995
362.7'62'0973—dc20   95-753
                                               CIP

Printed on acid-free, 250-year-life paper
Manufactured in the United States of America

CONTENTS

PREVENTION

REMEDIES

SERIES INTRODUCTION

In 1960 Elizabeth Elmer said of child abuse "little is known about any facet of the problem and that methods for dealing with it are random and inadequate." She spoke of a "professional blind-spot" for abuse and of "the repugnance felt by most of our society for the entire subject of abused children."[1] Two years later, Dr. C. Henry Kempe and his colleagues brought national attention to the problem of child abuse with their article, "The Battered-Child Syndrome."[2] Prior to the publication of that landmark article, the literature on child abuse was almost non-existent. In the three decades since its publication, the research and literature on child abuse have become vast and daunting.

Social workers, psychologists, psychiatrists, counselors, and doctors have studied child abuse in great detail. As a result, we know that child abuse includes physical, emotional, and sexual abuse as well as neglect. Researchers have studied the causes of abuse from both the individual and societal perspectives. There are effective interventions for tertiary remediation of the problem, and there are many prevention models that hold out hope that child abuse can be stopped before it starts. Studies of the short- and long-term effects of child abuse show a range of maladies that include infant failure-to-thrive, learning disabilities, eating disorders, borderline personality disorders, violent behavior, delinquency, and even parricide. We now recognize the need for treatment of child victims, adult survivors, and adult perpetrators of all forms of abuse. Lawyers, legislators, and judges have grappled with the profusion of legal problems raised by protective services and proceedings, foster care, and the termination of parental rights to free abused children for placement in permanent homes. Legislatures have passed and amended statutes requiring various health, education and child care professionals to report suspected abuse, and they have dealt with the difficult problem of defining abuse and determining when the state should intervene to protect children from abusive parents. They have also struggled with the legal and psychological issues that arise when the child victim becomes a witness against his or her abuser. Even the Supreme Court has been called upon to sort out the constitutional rights of victims and criminal defendants and to determine the extent of government liability for failure to adequately protect children from abuse.

The articles in this series document our passage through five of the six stages that C. Henry Kempe identified in his 1978 commentary "Recent Developments in the Field of Child Abuse" as developmental stages in addressing the problem of child abuse:

> Stage One is denial that either physical or sexual abuse exists to a significant extent . . . Stage Two is paying attention to the more lurid abuse . . . Stage Three comes when physical abuse is better handled and attention is now beginning to be paid to the infant who fails to thrive . . . Stage Four comes in recognition of emotional abuse and neglect . . . and Stage Five is the paying attention to the serious plight of the sexually abused child, including the youngster involved in incest . . .

In spite of the voluminous research and writing on child abuse, the sixth and final of Kempe's stages, "that of guaranteeing each child that he or she is truly wanted, is provided with loving care, decent shelter and food, and first class preventive and curative health care," remains elusive.[3] There are many explanations for our inability to conquer the problem of child abuse. In reality, the explanation for our continued inability to defeat this contemptible social problem is as complex as the problem itself.

We continue to sanction the use of violence in the name of discipline. We put our societal stamp of approval on "punishment inflicted by way of correction and training" and call it discipline. But discipline also means "instruction and exercise designed to train to proper conduct or action."[4] It is not difficult to see the inherent conflict in these two definitions when applied to child-rearing. How can we "train to proper conduct or action" when we use physical punishment as a means of training, punishment that we would not inflict upon an adult under the same circumstances?

The courts and legislatures have been unable to find the correct balance between a family's right to privacy and self governance and the need of children for protection. We are unable or unwilling to commit sufficient revenue to programs that combat abuse.

There is also the tendency among many professionals working with abused children and abusive parents to view the problem and solution through specialized cognitive lenses. Doctors, social workers, lawyers, psychologists, psychiatrists, counselors, and educators are all striving to defeat child abuse. However, for the most part, these professionals focus on the problem of child abuse from the perspective of their own field of expertise. The literature on child abuse is spread throughout journals from these fields and in more specialized journals within these fields. It would be impossible for any single person to remain abreast of the developments in all other disciplines working toward a solution to child abuse. But it is also patently clear that the solution to the problem of child abuse is not going to come from any one individual or discipline. It is going to take professionals and lay people from all disciplines, working with knowledge from all disciplines.

An interdisciplinary examination is important in the fight against child abuse. The more professionals know about all aspects of the problem of child sexual abuse, the better equipped they will be to do work within their area of expertise. It is important, for example, for lawyers, working in the midst of the current backlash against child sexual abuse claims, to understand that there is a long history of discovery and repression of childhood sexual abuse. With a full understanding of why this backlash is occurring, lawyers and social service professionals can continue to effectively work against child sexual abuse.

Child abuse is a complex social problem. The issues confronted in these volumes are interconnected and overlapping. It is my hope that bringing together the articles in this series will aid in the fight against child abuse by facilitating a multidisciplinary search for a solution.[5]

NOTES

1. Elizabeth Elmer, M.S.S., "Abused Young Children Seen in Hospitals," *Social Work* 5(4), pp. 98–102 (October 1960).
2. C. Henry Kempe, M.D., F.N. Silverman, M.D., Brandt F. Steele, M.D. and others, "The Battered-Child Syndrome," *JAMA* 181, pp. 17–24 (1962).
3. C. Henry Kempe, M.D., "Recent Developments in the Field of Child Abuse," *Child Abuse & Neglect* 3(1), pp. ix–xv (1979).
4. *The Random House Dictionary of the English Language*, unabridged edition.
5. The articles in this collection may give the impression that child abuse and neglect and child sexual abuse are uniquely American

phenomena. They are not. There is a wealth of similar articles from almost every country imaginable. American sources have been used mainly because of the space limitations and because understanding the American child welfare system is vital to developing a cure for the problem.

Volume Introduction

In order to prevent child abuse it is necessary to know why parents and other caregivers abuse their children. Following the "discovery" of "battered child syndrome" in 1962 researchers and scholars began the search for its cause.[1]

Initially, the blame was laid on the psychopathology of the abusive parent(s). Richard J. Gelles (1973) did a critical review of the "psychopathological model" of child abuse and found a number of deficiencies. First, Gelles found the explanation to be too narrow. Second, psychopathology theory was inconsistent with the findings of researchers that all child abusers were not psychopaths.

Furthermore, treating the psychopathology of abusing parents did not prove to be effective in stopping child abuse. Gelles stated that "one reason may be that the strategies [of intervention] are based on erroneous diagnoses of the problem."

Gelles suggested a social psychological model of child abuse that takes into account the multiple social factors that influence child abuse. Gelles further suggested that if factors such as "unemployment and social class are important contextual variables, then strategies to prevent child abuse should aim at alleviating the disastrous effect of being poor in an affluent society."[2] Third, Gelles expressed a concern that continues to be expressed today, that the literature on child abuse does not meet even the minimal standards of evidence in social science.[3]

Arthur T. Davidson (1977) confirmed that "the syndrome of physical child abuse is only the symptomatic manifestation of a complex family sickness that breaks under a societal crisis." He also found that:

> child abusers most often have a history of abuse as a child. An in depth analysis and evaluation of the psychological make-up of the child abuser reveals the following negative factors: (1) low frustration tolerance, (2) low self-esteem, (3) impulsivity, (4) dependency, (5) immaturity, (6) severe depression, and (7) role reversal.

xiii

In role reversal parents expect the children to fulfill the parents' emotional needs and tend to have age-inappropriate expectations of their children's abilities. This leads parents to be frustrated and to blame the child.[4]

William N. Freidrich and Karen K. Wheeler (1982) reviewed the findings by Spinetta and Rigler (1972)[5] in light of the research and findings of the intervening decade. They concluded that some but not all of Spinetta's and Rigler's findings withstood the test of time. The evidence supported the earlier finding that many abusing parents were abused as children. The evidence was mixed as to whether maltreating parents actually lacked adequate parenting knowledge or merely had different parenting attitudes. Freidrich and Wheeler did reiterate that stress plays a major role in child abusing families. They went on to state that "stress somehow interacts with personality and child variables to 'potentiate maltreatment by widening the discrepancy between limited parental capacities and demanding offspring.'" They also recommended further research in this area.[6]

In the same vein, David A. Wolfe (1985) reviewed studies comparing child-abusive and nonabusive parents on psychological and behavioral dimensions. Wolfe concluded that "studies have indicated that abusive parents' behavior is related to salient situational events, especially child-related phenomena. The parents' self-report of displeasure, anxiety, and attributions, in addition to physiological arousal and observed punitive behaviors, have shown a relation to contextual variables."[7]

Joel S. Milner and Kevin R. Robertson (1990) studied 150 subjects (30 physical child abusers, 15 intrafamilial child sexual abusers, 30 child neglecters, and 3 matched comparison groups). They found that "as predicted, the intrafamilial sexual child abusers were significantly below physical child abusers and child neglecters on scales indicating a negative view of child and self, and perceptions of having a child with problems." They found that "physical child abusers perceive more problems with their children . . . and have low self-esteem and poor ego strength" while "sexual child abusers view their children in a positive manner and report few problems with their children." They also found that "intrafamilial sexual child abusers also reported fewer problems from their families and others than child neglecters and physical child abusers."[8]

Prevention of child abuse has been addressed on both a macro and a micro level. David G. Gil (1976) spoke of primary prevention of child abuse as a philosophical and political issue. He defined child abuse as "waste of a child's developmental potential, or interference with a child's development due to circumstances of living that are not conducive to optimal development, irrespective of who or what causes these deficits." He pointed out that "the home rarely is an independent source of child abuse, but usually is the final link in a long chain of societal conditions and factors."[9] Gil's solution to the problem would involve a broad rethinking of our social, economic, and political order. He would replace "the now dominant inegalitarian and competitive social philosophy . . . with an egalitarian, cooperative philosophy, and with societal institutions which fit that philosophy." This would require:

> redefining childhood and the rights of all children in a manner that assures them full constitutional protection as persons and the legally enforceable right to live in conditions conducive to full development in accordance with their inherent potential.[10]

Gil admonishes that:

> if one's priority is to prevent *all* child abuse, one must be ready to part with its many causes, even when one is attached to some of them, such as the apparent blessings, advantages, and privileges of inequality. If, on the other hand, one is reluctant to give up all aspects of the causal context of child abuse, one must be content to continue living with this social problem. In that latter case, one ought to stop talking about primary prevention and face the fact that all one may be ready for is some measure of amelioration.[11]

A wholesale restructuring of society is not, of course, forthcoming, but Gil's point is well-taken. Perhaps we will have an opportunity, with the passage of a national health care reform bill providing universal health care, to examine Gil's philosophy applied to a single problem plaguing our society. Perhaps too, the benefits will convince those with political power that what benefits "the many" also, in fact, benefits "the few."

Others have focused on the problem on a micro level. Ray E. Helfer (1982) undertook the task of reviewing the literature in the area of child abuse and neglect and reporting on the "'programs or maneuvers that have been found to be successful in terms of efficacy, effectiveness, etc. . . .'" While there were some problems with the research he reviewed, most notably attempts to assess effectiveness of programs during their development and the lack of control groups, Helfer did conclude that "the prevention of child abuse and neglect is achievable if, and only if, the approach is multifaceted."[12]

N. Dickon Reppucci and Jeffrey J. Haugaard (1989) examined programs to prevent child sexual abuse and concluded that it is not possible to be sure "whether preventive programs are working, nor can we be sure that they are causing more good than harm." Reppucci and Haugaard believe that "programs may adversely affect a child's positive relationships with meaningful people in his or her life or cause the child undue worry or fear at least in the short run. However, it may also be that these programs can actually place some children at greater risk for sexual abuse if we incorrectly assume that the children are protected because of these programs and consequently become less vigilant about the problem." They fear "that parents, teachers, and others working with children will abdicate their responsibility to protect to the abuse prevention programs."[13]

Bonnie Trudell and Marianne H. Whatley (1988) discussed other unintended consequences of sexual abuse prevention programs. Prevention programs that are aimed at teaching children to avoid abuse or to say no are applying a simple solution to a complex social problem. Furthermore, "to the extent that they focus on teaching children to protect themselves, school sexual abuse prevention programs can have the unanticipated negative consequence of contributing to blaming the victim." Trudell and Whatley also discussed the simplification of the problem in the materials used, which they believe can lead to misinformation or even convey to children that their sexual organs are somehow bad. For instance, vague descriptions in materials such as "private parts" or "under your swimsuit" can lead children to believe there is something wrong with those parts since they cannot even be discussed.[14]

Carolyn Swift (1979) argued that prevention programs aimed at the potential victims do not prevent sexual assault, but rather displace it. Cautious children may be protected, but "the attacker continues to victimize the young, the weak, the vulnerable, or the uninformed." Programs teaching children to "say no or to claim the right to control their own bodies . . . raise the consciousness of the community and alert the children to their vulnerability to sexual exploitation. Even if successful, however—and their success is problematic: how successful will a child be telling Daddy no?— they would not eliminate child sexual assault." Swift believes we can only effect a substantial reduction in child sexual abuse if prevention programs are "targeted to alter the behavior of adult perpetrators."[15]

Swift set forth two causal hypotheses concerning sexual abuse. One, that a large portion of males who sexually abuse were sexually abused themselves, and two, that a large portion of males who sexually abuse are sexually ignorant and socially immature. She argues that the logical conclusion from the first hypothesis is to open our eyes to the fact that boys are sexually abused in large numbers and to attempt to break down the social stigma associated with sexual abuse of boys so that boys who are abused will report it. In this way, they may be treated for their own abuse rather than becoming abusers. She argues that the logical conclusion of the second hypothesis is to provide sex education programs in schools.

However, Swift acknowledges the difficulties this approach would encounter:

> Even if irrefutable evidence of the preventive power of sex education in reducing cases of sexual child abuse could be produced, which it cannot, it is unlikely that sex education would become a standard in school curricula in the near future. Parental fears, bureaucratic timidity and a tradition of repression of sexual information combine to obstruct the implementation of sex education programs in schools.[16]

Swift was writing in 1979, and since then many school districts have in fact adopted sex education programs. However, the recent controversy in Texas over textbooks that contain information on AIDS and AIDS prevention is a striking reminder that "parental fears, bureaucratic timidity and a tradition of repression of sexual information" even in the face of overwhelming evidence of "the preventive power of sex education" still rule the day.

The more we know about the cause of child abuse, the less likely it seems that a complete solution to this complex and devastating social problem will be found soon. The best we can hope for may be, as Gil said, "some measure of amelioration." In that regard, some strides have been made in the treatment of individual child abusers and prevention of repeated abuse.

Neil J. Hochstadt and Neil J. Harwicke (1985) undertook an evaluation of the multidisciplinary approach to handling child abuse cases. They concluded that the multidisciplinary team, which functions within highly complex and overlapping systems (medical, social service, protective service, judicial and legal), can make significant contributions to the follow-up care of abused and neglected children.[17] In the short run, this may be the best we can hope for.

NOTES

1. C. Henry Kempe, M.D., F.N. Silverman, M.D., Brandt F. Steele, M.D. and others, "The Battered-Child Syndrome," *JAMA* 181, pp. 17–24 (1962). For an historical overview and current perspective on physical and emotional abuse and neglect, see Volume 1. For an historical overview and current perspective on child sexual abuse, see Volume 2.

2. Richard J. Gelles, "Child Abuse as Psychopathology: A Sociological Critique and Reformulation,"*American Journal of Orthopsychiatry* 43(4), pp. 611–21, 620 (July 1973).

3. Id. at 611.

4. Arthur T. Davidson, "Child Abuse: Causes and Prevention," *Journal of the National Medical Association* 69(11), pp. 817–20 (Nov 1977).

5. John J. Spinetta, and D. Rigler, "The Child Abusing Parent: A Psychological Review," *Psychological Bulletin* 77, pp. 296–304, 302 (1972).

6. William N. Freidrich, and Karen K. Wheeler, "The Abusing Parent Revisited: A Decade of Psychological Research," *The Journal of Nervous and Mental Disease* 170(10), pp. 577–87, 585 (October 1982).

7. David A. Wolfe, "Child-Abusive Parents: An Empirical Review and Analysis," *Psychological Bulletin* 97(3), pp. 462–82, 479 (May 1985).

8. Joel S. Milner, and Kevin R. Robertson, "Comparison of Physical Child Abusers, Intrafamilial Sexual Child Abusers, and Child Neglecters," *Journal of Interpersonal Violence* 5(1), pp. 37–48, 45 (Mar 1990).

9. David G. Gil, "Primary Prevention of Child Abuse: A Philosophical and Political Issue," *Psychiatric Opinion* 13(2), pp. 30–34, 31 (Apr 1976).

10. Id. at 33–34.

11. David G. Gil, "Unraveling Child Abuse," *American Journal of Orthopsychiatry* 45(3), pp. 346–56, 355–56 (Apr 1975)

12. Ray E. Helfer, "A Review of the Literature on the Prevention of Child Abuse and Neglect," *Child Abuse & Neglect* 6(3), pp. 251–61 (1982).

13. N. Dickon Reppucci, and Jeffrey J. Haugaard, "Prevention of Child Abuse—Myth or Reality," *American Psychologist* 44(10), pp. 1266–75, 1274 (October 1989).

14. Bonnie Trudell, and Marianne H. Whatley, "School Sexual Abuse Prevention: Unintended Consequences and Dilemmas," *Child Abuse & Neglect* 12(1), pp. 103–113, 105 (1988).

15. Carolyn Swift, "The Prevention of Sexual Child Abuse: Focus on the Perpetrator," *Journal of Clinical Child Psychology* 8(2), pp. 133–36, 133 (Sum 1979).

16. Id. at 136.

17. Neil J. Hochstadt, and Neil J. Harwicke, "How Effective is the Multidisciplinary Approach? A Follow-up Study," *Child Abuse & Neglect* 9(3), pp. 365–72 (1985).

FURTHER READING

Conte, Jon R., et al. "An Evaluation of a Program to Prevent the Sexual Victimization of Young Children." *Child Abuse & Neglect* 9(3), pp. 319–28 (1985).

Gil, David G. "Unraveling Child Abuse." *American Journal of Orthopsychiatry* 45(3), pp. 346–56 (Apr 1975).

Milner, Joel S., and Kevin R. Robertson. "Comparison of Physical Child Abusers, Intrafamilial Sexual Child Abusers, and Child Neglecters." *Journal of Interpersonal Violence* 5(1), pp. 37–48 (Mar 1990).

Pelton, Leroy H. "Child Abuse and Neglect: The Myth of Classlessness." *American Journal of Orthopsychiatry* 48(4), pp. 608–17 (October 1978).

Salzinger, Suzanne, et al. "Risk for Physical Child Abuse and the Personal Consequences for its Victims." *Criminal Justice and Behavior* 18(1), pp. 64–81 (1991).

Taylor, Carol G., et al. "Diagnosed Intellectual and Emotional Impairment Among Parents Who Seriously Mistreat Their Children: Prevalence, Type, and Outcome in a Court Sample." *Child Abuse & Neglect* 15(4), pp. 389–401 (1991).

Wolfner, Glenn D., and Richard J. Gelles. "A Profile of Violence Toward Children: A National Study." *Child Abuse & Neglect* 17, pp. 197–212 (1993).

Causes, Prevention and Remedies

CLINICAL EVALUATION OF CHILD ABUSE - SCARRED FAMILIES: A PRELIMINARY REPORT

DR. RICHARD KOMISARUK

**Director, Clinic For Child Study
Wayne County Juvenile Court
Detroit, Michigan**

Since 1962 the Wayne County Juvenile Court Clinic for Child Study has been involved in a detailed study of the problem of child abuse. There are several reasons for doing this research. First, we have been impressed with the recentness of the recognition of child abuse as a syndrome. Reports of cases have dated only from the early 1950's. There have, evidently, been obstacles to this recognition until a few physicians were able to perceive that it is possible for parents to behave towards their children in a way which deviates from the usual benevolent and protective image.

Second, in the light of the denial of the existence of the condition which has existed for so long, studies as to the etiology of child abuse on observation of a significant number of families had not yet been accomplished. Thus, impressed with the dearth of available clinical material on child abuse, and realizing that it would be of great importance to develop an understanding of this problem in order to be able to make intelligent recommendations for disposition in these cases, we began to study each case which came to the attention of the Wayne County Juvenile Court in which child abuse was the complaint.

Cases of child abuse in which legal protection of the child seems indicated may be referred to the Juvenile Court either by the Child Care Bureau or by any other agency which comes in contact with a family in which an inflicted injury has occurred. Child abuse falls within the neglect provisions of the Juvenile Code. Children who are abused are thus entitled to the same legal protection as those who are subjected to other forms of neglect.

Because of the special nature of the child abuse problem, particularly the feelings that the phenomenon arouses in persons who are called upon to work with families in which it has occurred, the investigation of all cases of child abuse is carried out by the Clinic for Child Study. This has made it possible for the Clinic to compile data on the subject and to train personnel in the special techniques required in the management of child abuse cases. At the present, all cases of child abuse are handled by a single psychiatric social worker in the Clinic. In many instances, parents who have abused their children have already been subjected to numerous interviews with various interested agencies and persons. We consider it worthwhile that a particular individual be assigned to each case so that the families can most effectively use the services of the Court in terms of the development of a personal therapeutic relationship.

With respect to management techniques, it should be noted that cases which come to our attention have already been screened to eliminate those which do not truly represent child abuse. Thus, the authority of the Court is being used, to some extent, to evoke an improvement in the safety of the child's environment. In spite of the fact that it is implied by the court referral that outside resources have failed in safeguarding the child from abuse, we undertake as much as possible to deal with cases of child abuse on an informal level. A neglect petition in these cases is not automatically accepted by the Court, but the possible acceptance of such a petition is made known to the parents, particularly if they appear to be refractory to our efforts to intervene in the abuse.

There are several further techniques which are employed in our effort to "destigmatize" the parents who come to our attention. First, we reassure repeatedly that the investigation which is being conducted is not a criminal matter and that there is no possibility of material which is discussed in the Juvenile Court being used in an actual or potential criminal case. Second, we conduct our interviews in a manner which is designed to place the parents as much at ease as possible. To this end, we have provided a special room which is as much unlike a conventional office as our budget would allow. The empathic attitude of the interviewers, and the assurance that no accusation is being made, seem to facilitate the flow of materials which aids us in assessing the dynamics of the abusive situation for the possibility of recurrence. A third measure along these lines which is sometimes taken by the Judge, is to conduct the hearings on these cases in his chambers, rather than in the courtroom. At times, this step has proven to be of considerable value in eliminating the legal and, to the parents, presumably punitive atmosphere which might otherwise prevail.

CLINICAL DATA

Between July 1962 and the present time we have seen for study some sixty-five families. Of this group, we have sufficient data on forty-seven cases to warrant presentation at this time. The following data we feel serves to suggest a profile of the family constellation in which child abuse has occurred.

Race .... White 21
                               Negro 26
Religion .... Protestant 30
                               Catholic 14
Known mental deficiency in
  mother (I.Q. less than 75)..13
Known mental illness in mother 8
Age of abusing parent ....26 less than 25 years
Age of parents at time of
marriage ....21 married before age 20
Educational attainment of
  parents .... Half failed to graduate from
                               high school
Age of child at time of abuse....33 less than 3 years
Siblings of abused children ....116 living; 10 deceased
Abuse confined to single child
  in family 23
Sustained agency contact
  prior to abusive episode 29
Emotional loss of significant
  parental figure in early life
  of abusive parent ....mother 25/36
                               father 17/28
Disposition
  Child removed from home ...33
  Returned to parental home ..11

The above represents some of the more interesting data which has been collected in our series. Several questions are raised in regard to this data. First, we have no correlation of our cases of child abuse with a control group. One possible control group might consist of neglectful parents who were not physically abusive, in order to isolate the physical abuse factor. The selection of a control group would present considerable and obvious difficulties.

A second problem inherent in this research is the highly variable severity of injury. We are comparing, in some instances, scratches and bruises with multiple fractures—a spanking which "got out of hand" with obvious homicidal attack. The cases are grouped together only arbitrarily over the common denominator of "child abuse."

Mental deficiency and illness—We were struck by the frequency with which the parents studied exhibited a significant degree of mental retardation. The poor judgment which so commonly attends intellectual deficit undoubtedly plays an etiological role in many cases of child abuse. We were equally impressed by the relative paucity of diagnosed mental illness (psychosis) in the cases which we have studied. This may be accounted for on the basis that we would be less likely to see those cases in which hospitalization had already become necessary.

Relative youth of parents—The youth of the abusive parents and particularly the rather young age at which they were married, is probably not incompatible with a general social and cultural trend in the direction of early marriage and pregnancy. However, the marked degrees of immaturity and childishness which are an almost ubiquitous clinical observation in our cases, can probably also be correlated to some extent with the young marriages.

Age of child at time of abuse, and confinement of abuse to a particular child—The fact that the majority of children who were abused were infants at the time of the abuse is suggestive that the helpless state of the infant does not serve to protect the child against the parental need to inflict abuse. Further, it points up the fact that most abuse does not occur as an accidental extension of punishment which is inflicted as a disciplinary measure, but that the abusive parent may be responding to a demand which the young child is making which the parent feels unable to meet or to feelings aroused in the parents which are out of control of judgment. The fact that so many of the siblings of the abused children had also been abused was in contradistinction to our earlier impression that in a majority of cases a particular child was singled out from his siblings to receive abuse, although this latter was certainly true in a few cases.

GENERAL OBSERVATIONS

The most striking statistic presented in the clinical data are the figures concerning emotional loss of a significant parental figure in the early life of the abusive parent. We are fairly sure that high frequency of such losses would exceed the frequency of the same phenomenon that could be observed in neglectful, but not physically abusive parents. In those cases in which there was not an emotional loss of a parental figure, there were other psychic traumata in the early lives of the abusive parents, often of an especially devastating nature. An example is a family in which the parents had both been absconded with, in their own childhood by their grandparents.

Another general trend which we observed in these parents was that of passive dependency. More than most parents whom we see in the Clinic, these exhibited the need for sustenance and assistance to sometimes remarkable degrees. Some require assistance in budgetary planning; others have needed advice on the management of the problems of everyday living.

A third characteristic of these parents was their narcissism. The aspect of the narcissism which was most vexing from a clinical standpoint, was the tendency to evaluate problems exclusively from the standpoint of the self. In addition, the self-evaluation was often extremely and inappropriately high. Coupled with this phenomenon is the unexpected characteristic of absence of depression. Of the entire group of families that we studied, in only one case

DETROIT CLINIC FOR CHILD STUDY

could a parent be described as depressed and aggrieved in the usual sense. This one mother was the most classically neurotic of the group, and was also the most amenable to a type of treatment designed to bring about major revision in the personality structure.

An additional characteristic of the parents that we have studied is their rather marked immaturity and childishness. This is seen in a variety of ways. One mother, for example, had some of her own toys with which she actually played in her child's room. The dress and manner of many of the parents was suggestive of a lack of adaptation to usual adult standards. Explosiveness and tantrums, even during an interview in which it would be desirable to create the impression of maturity and restraint, were also sometimes seen.

Another curious clinical fact about our group of parents is that their manifest attitudes are characterized by marked degrees of reaction formation. By this is meant that they tend to see themselves, in many instances, as model parents. Their own ideals of parental benevolence are often exceedingly high. Several of the families in which abuse has occurred had, at some time, applied to be foster parents. A family in which the first child had been dispatched as a result of an "accident," and the second rather seriously injured, had a large menagerie of pets. It is our suspicion that the high ideals of parenthood serve as a sometimes futile defense against the breakthrough of the rage which results in injuries.

In the interview situation, parents who have inflicted abuse tend to show varying degrees of amnesia concerning the abuse itself. The amnesia, at times, appears to be a contrived suppression because of fear of either punishment, the removal of the child, or both. At times, this type of amnesia has been responsive to the considerable reassurance which we employ in our interviews. In many of the cases, however, the amnesia represents a largely unconscious inability to recall the events which led up to the injury. Obviously, the more time that elapses between the injury and the interview, the more repression and forgetting there will be.

SOME THEORETICAL HYPOTHESES

In our efforts to understand the child abuse problem from a theoretical standpoint, we have developed the following definition of child abuse:

It is a condition of injury to a child resulting from the lack or suspension in a nominally responsible adult of the parental protective function accompanied by a release of unrestrained instinctual drive energy toward the child. This may be differentiated from discipline or punishment in that the latter are at least rationalized as being beneficial to the child.

The weakness in the parental ego which allows the drive energy to be uninhibited could be described as a deficiency of the central governing body in the personality. Certain parallels may be seen between the eruption of aggressive drive energy and that of libidinal energy in the sexual crime. We suspect that there is a comparable ego deficiency in the controls over the two drives in individuals who become involved in either type of such behavior. In some of our child abuse cases, the injury was accompanied by the arousal of sexual feelings on the part of the abusive parent, although very few were instances of sadism in the sense of a regularly practiced or fantasied perversion. In many cases, there were sexual improprieties in the families which bore at least superficial relationship to the physical abuse.

The ego deficiency theory is related to the problem of emotional loss of a parental figure in this way. It is known that the existence of a satisfactory parental model is needed for the normal development of the ego. The gaps and distortions in the egos of the parents whom we have studied can, to some extent, be accounted for on the basis of the limited exposure to normal parenthood. Compatible and coordinate with this is the existence of other forms of ego pathology in the same parents. These forms would include paranoid traits (although rarely full-blown paranoid psychosis), infantilism as well as poor judgment and reality testing.

In addition to the ego deficiency concept, and from a somewhat different standpoint, in many of the families which we have studied, there has been a revival of the conflicts of infancy and childhood in adult life. This can be seen in a variety of ways and can be illustrated by the following example:

A twenty-nine year old man, the father of six children, became enraged at his two year old daughter at a time when he was responsible for taking care of the children during his wife's confinement. The oldest boy in the family at the time (who happened to be named after his father) was six. These facts almost exactly simulated the conditions of this father's childhood when his own mother expired during childbirth.

DR. RICHARD KOMISARUK

The massive rage which had to be held in check by this father erupted when the conditions for a revival of the conflicts of his own childhood were right. The psychological phenomenon of displacement from one object to another is also seen in the above example, and tends to be characteristic of most of the parents whom we studied.

Still another point of view with regard to the problem of child abuse, is that normally the disagreeable parts of parenthood are made more possible for the parent to carry out because the child becomes a psychological extension of the parent through a form of identification. By means of this process the parent treats the child as he himself would like to be treated. The capacity for this identification seems to be lacking, at least at times, in the abusive parent. This, too, is a sign of a deficiency in the structure of the parental ego.

MANAGEMENT TECHNIQUES

Many of the techniques which we employ in collecting information about the abuse and about the parental history are described above. Disposition and management of the case at the time of the court hearing require some further amplification.

Very few of the parents in our series were candidates for uncovering type of psychotherapy. In general, the likelihood of successful treatment on the psychoanalytic model is directly proportional to the resemblance of the parental pathology to a neurosis.

In most instances, when the child has been returned to the home, the treatment mode has been casework therapy, accompanied by some degree of environmental manipulation. A particularly useful step which we have sometimes taken is to require that a new adult be in the home to share responsibility. This may be a grandparent or any other person with or without family ties. The theoretical basis for this technique is the parental model problem which is referred to above. We have recently made arrangements with the Wayne State University College of Nursing which will provide a graduate nurse who is being trained in psychiatric nursing to be assigned to selected families for purposes of making home calls, and to assist with some of the practical problems of parenthood in which so many of our abusive parents have failed.

Removal from the home remains, unfortunately, the most commonly employed disposition as noted in our statistics. None of the children who have been removed from their homes have been made permanent wards of the Juvenile Court. It is anticipated, however, that some children who are removed will have to remain out of the parental home for extended periods if they can ever be returned. It should be mentioned that in general our effort has been to return children to the home whenever prudence permits this.

CRITERIA FOR RETURNABILITY

Obviously, the return of a child to the parental home following an abusive episode can only be safe if some modification has occurred in the parental home which would eliminate or at least substantially reduce the problems which give rise to the abuse. As noted above, the number of cases in which psychotherapeutic modification can be counted on is small. In a somewhat larger number of cases the home can be made more safe for the child by means of environmental manipulation and various other social and legal devices which can be brought to bear. In altogether too many cases, it does not become clear what the criteria are for returnability—to what extent modification in the home can be predicted. In making recommendations concerning this, we continue to rely on intuition and educated guess to some extent. Thus, it is the intent of our continuing study to become more explicit in this area, developing sound criteria for returnability which would not be so reliant on hunches based on our experience in the matter.

The problem of child abuse is one of those social issues which has come to light too late because of the kind of social repression which makes it impossible for us to examine unpalatable and unpleasant issues. It has become increasingly clear that child abuse is a genuine syndrome with specific clinical characteristics which can be studied and understood and that the resulting information can be used to be of assistance to the Court in making determinations of disposition.   ‖

The writer wishes to acknowledge the valuable assistance of Dr. Herman M. Schornstein and Mrs. Jeannette Andary in the preparation of this material.

APPENDIX
Michigan Public Acts—1964
Public Act No. 98

AN ACT to require the reporting of certain injuries to certain minors; to provide immunity for certain persons making such reports; to provide rules of evidence in certain cases and to provide a penalty for violation of this act.
The People of the State of Michigan enact:
Sec. 1. Any licensed physician who provides medical treatment or who makes a medical examination of any child under seventeen years of age who has physical injuries which were, or may have been intentionally inflicted upon him by any person responsible for his care, shall immediately cause a report to be made as required by this act. When the attending or examining physician is a member of a hospital staff he shall notify the person in charge thereof of his finding and the person in charge shall cause the report to be made.
Sec. 2. The report required by section 1 shall be made in triplicate and 1 copy shall be mailed to the prosecuting attorney and to the department of social welfare of the county where the physician believes the injury may have been inflicted. One copy shall be mailed to the Lansing office

of the State Department of Social Welfare. The report shall contain the names and addresses of the child, his parents, his guardian or the person with whom he resides, the child's age and a description of his injuries. The report shall also contain any other information available to the reporting person which might establish the cause of the injuries and the manner in which they were inflicted.
Sec. 3. Any person acting in good faith who makes a report or assists in making a report pursuant to the provisions of this act shall be immune from civil or criminal liability which might otherwise be incurred thereby. Any person making or assisting in the making of the report shall be presumed to have acted in good faith.
Sec. 4. Neither the physician-patient privilege nor the privilege between spouses shall prevail in any action, civil or criminal, which is or may have been brought because of any report made pursuant to the provisions of this act.
Sec. 5. Any person who violates the provisions of this act is guilty of a misdemeanor.

A Sociocultural Perspective On Physical Child Abuse

A broad study—on a nationwide scale— of physical child abuse, conducted by Brandeis University, stressed the sociological and cultural aspects of this phenomenon. The findings suggest a series of measures as a basis for prevention through education, legislation, elimination of poverty, and social services.

DAVID G. GIL

Throughout history children have frequently been subjected to various forms of abuse in many human societies.[1] This phenomenon, which seems to be one consequence of the inequality in physical strength and social status between children and adults, has always aroused the concern of human individuals and groups. In recent decades public and professional interest in child abuse has increased markedly in the United States and in many other countries.

David G. Gil, D.S.W., is Professor of Social Policy, Florence Heller Graduate School for Advanced Studies in Social Welfare, Brandeis University, Waltham, Massachusetts. This article is based on his book Violence Against Children *(Cambridge, Mass.: Harvard University Press, 1970). The study reported here was supported by the U.S. Children's Bureau, under grant PR-288-1.*

In this country the heightened interest goes back to the years right after World War II, when pediatric roentgenologists, psychiatrists and social workers identified violent physical attacks by parents and other caretakers as the probable cause of a frequently observed, puzzling association between multiple fractures of the long bones in very young children and subdural hematomas.[2] This discovery caused shock and dismay among professionals who had studied the phenomenon, and gradually, also among the public at large, once the news media began reporting it in gruesome detail.

In the 1950s and 1960s several books and numerous articles were written on the subject by professional authors and journalists,[3] papers were presented at conferences of physicians, social workers and lawyers, and radio and television networks outdid each other in presenting programs on child abuse. This intensive publicity and the correspondingly intensive interest of professional groups and public authorites led during the 1960s to the swift enactment throughout the country of legislation requiring physicians, and at times other professionals, to notify welfare and law-enforcement authorities of incidents of suspected physical abuse of children.[4]

This growing concern also stimulated efforts to investigate the scope and nature of the phenomenon. However, studies usually involved relatively small and

7

unrepresentative samples of cases known to hospitals, clinics and social welfare agencies.[5] The orientation and methodology of these studies was clinical, and the general conclusion suggested by their findings was that physical abuse of children resulted from psychological disorders of the abusing caretakers, or, at times, of the abused children themselves, from pathological family relationships, and from stressful environmental conditions. Students of child abuse also suggested that the phenomenon was widespread throughout all groups of the population, that it involved primarily very young children, and that it was an important cause of mortality and morbidity among children.

The implementation throughout the United States of laws on reporting child abuse opened up possibilities of conducting epidemiologic studies involving relatively large and more representative cohorts of abused children. At the initiative of the U.S. Children's Bureau and with its support, Brandeis University carried out a nationwide survey of all incidents reported through legal channels during 1967 and 1968, a total of almost 13,000 cases. The method, findings and conclusions of this survey have been reported in detail elsewhere.[6] The following observations represent highlights from this survey.

The Brandeis study attempted to transcend the clinical understanding of individual incidents of child abuse, and to unravel the underlying sociocultural dynamics of this manifestation of interpersonal violence. It was expected that such understanding would yield suggestions for primary preventive measures aimed at the configuration of forces that seem to cause this destructive phenomenon.

Systematic study of child abuse had been hampered in the past by lack of an unambiguous conceptual definition. Investigators tended to derive definitions from observable consequences of abusive attacks such as injuries inflicted upon children, rather than from the motivation and the behavior of perpetrators of abuse. Consequences of abusive attacks, however, are likely to be due to chance factors as much as to the behavior of perpetrators, and constitute thus an inappropriate basis for developing a conceptually sound definition. In view of this, physical abuse of children was defined in the Brandeis studies as "the use of physical force by a caretaker toward a child, in order to hurt, injure, or destroy the child." This conceptualization is broad, but unambiguous and free of relativism and arbitrariness. It includes every act of physical aggression directed against a child, irrespective of consequences.

The Sanctioning of Force

The foregoing conceptual definition leads to the realization that physical abuse of children is actually endemic in American society, since the cultural definition of child rearing in the United States does not exclude the use of physical force toward children by parents and other caretakers. Rather, the use of some physical force in child rearing is encouraged in subtle, and at times not so subtle, ways by communications disseminated by the press, radio and television, and by popular and professional publications. Moreover, children are subjected to physical abuse in many schools and child care facilities and even in juvenile courts.[7] Against this background of public sanction of the use of violence toward children, it should surprise no one that extreme incidents occur from time to time in the interaction between individual caretakers and children in their care.

It should be noted that adult persons in American society have legal protection against physical attack by other persons. Children are not assured such protection. This seems to be a denial of "equal protection under the law," an apparent violation of the 14th Amendment to the U.S. Constitution.

The culturally sanctioned use of force in child rearing thus constitutes the basic level of all physical abuse of children. Different social classes and ethnic and nationality groups tend to differ in their child-rearing practices, and also in the extent to which they approve of physical force as a socialization method. These variations among social classes and ethnic groups constitute a second dimension of the phenomenon. The third dimension is determined by environmental chance factors that may transform "acceptable" disciplinary measures into unacceptable outcomes. The fourth dimension is a broad range of environmental stress factors that may weaken a person's psychological mechanisms of self-control and thus contribute to the uninhibited discharge of aggressive and destructive impulses toward physically powerless children. The final dimension is a broad range of deviance in physical, social, intellectual and emotional functioning of caretakers, and at times of children in their care, as well as of entire family units to which they belong. Physical abuse of children appears thus to be a multidimensional phenomenon rather than a uniform one with a single set of causal factors.

Before presenting recommendations based on the foregoing conceptual framework, several comments seem indicated concerning major substantive findings of the nationwide surveys. In spite of its strong emotional impact and the tragic aspects of every incident, the phenomenon of child abuse needs to be put into a balanced perspective. Its true incidence rate has not been uncovered by the nationwide surveys, but the scope of physical abuse of children resulting in serious injury does not seem to constitute a major social problem, at least in comparison with several more widespread and more serious social problems that undermine the developmental opportunities of many millions of children in American society, such as poverty, racial discrimination, malnutrition, and inadequate provision for medical care and education.

Cohorts of officially reported incidents of child abuse are likely to represent the severe-injury segment of the physical child abuse spectrum, since severity of injury is an important decision criterion in reporting. If the 6000 to 7000 incidents that are reported annually through official channels are as a group an approximate representation of the severe segment of the nationwide abuse spectrum, the physical consequences of child abuse do not seem to be serious in the aggregate, for more than half these children suffered only minor injuries, and the classical "battered-child syndrome" was found to be relatively infrequent. Even if allowance is made for underreporting, especially of fatalities, physical abuse cannot be considered a "major killer and maimer" of children in the United States.

Precipitating Factors

Turning to an epidemiologic perspective, it should be noted that physical abuse of children, and especially more serious incidents, was found to be over-concentrated among the poor and among nonwhite minorities. Although it may be valid to argue that overrepresentation of the poor and nonwhites in cohorts of reported child abuse may be in part a function of reporting bias, it must not be overlooked that life in poverty and in the ghettos generates additional stressful experiences likely to become precipitating factors of child abuse. Moreover, the poor and members of ethnic minorities have fewer alternatives and escapes than the nonpoor in dealing with aggressive impulses toward their children. Finally, there is an additional factor, the tendency toward more direct, less inhibited expression and discharge of aggressive impulses, a tendency learned apparently through lower class and ghetto socialization, which differs in this respect from middle-class mores and socialization.

Of considerable interest in terms of forces contributing to child abuse are relatively high rates of deviance in areas of bio-psycho-social functioning of children and adults involved in abuse incidents. Deviance in functioning of individuals was matched by high rates of deviance in family structure, reflected in a high proportion of female-headed households and of households from which the biological fathers of abused children were absent. It is also worth noting that, as a group, families of physically abused children tend to have many more children than other American families with children under age 18.

The age distribution of abused children and their parents was found to be less skewed toward younger age groups than had been thought on the basis of earlier, mainly hospital-based, studies. This difference seems due to the fact that younger children tend to be more severely injured when abused and are, therefore, overrepresented among hospitalized abused children. More boys than girls are subjected to physical abuse, yet girls outnumber boys among adolescent abused children.

Although more mothers than fathers are reported as perpetrators of abuse, the involvement rate in incidents of child abuse is higher for fathers and stepfathers than for mothers. This important relationship is unraveled when account is taken of the fact that nearly 30 percent of reported abuse incidents occur in female-headed households. Altogether, nearly 87 percent of perpetrators are parents or parent substitutes.

Many children in the study had been abused on previous occasions. Also, siblings of many abused children were abused on the same or previous occasions. Many perpetrators were involved in incidents of abuse on previous occasions and many had been victims of abuse during their childhood. The high rate of recidivism reflected in these findings indicates that the use of physical force tends to be patterned into child-rearing practices and is usually not an isolated incident.

Recommendations

Applying a public health model · of preventive intervention to physical abuse of children, and proceeding on the foregoing conceptualization of its etiology, the following measures can be suggested:

(1) Since culturally determined permissive attitudes toward the use of physical force in child rearing seem to constitute the common core of all physical abuse of children in American society, systematic educational efforts aimed at gradually changing this aspect of child-rearing philosophy and developing clear-cut cultural prohibitions and legal sanctions against the use of physical force in

10

rearing children are likely to produce over time the strongest possible reduction of the incidence of physical abuse of children.

As a first step, the U.S. Congress and state legislatures could outlaw corporal punishment in schools, juvenile courts, correctional institutions and other child care facilities. This would assure children the same protection against physical attack outside their homes as the law provides for adult members of society. Moreover, such legislation would be likely to affect child-rearing attitudes and practices in American homes, for it would symbolize society's growing rejection of violence toward children.

Giving up the use of physical force against children may not be easy for adults who were subjected to physical force and violence in their own childhood and who have integrated the existing value system of American society. Children can sometimes be irritating and provocative in their behavior and may strain the tolerance of such adults to the limit. Yet, in spite of these realities, which must be acknowledged and faced openly, society needs to work toward the gradual reduction, and eventual elimination, of physical violence toward its young generation if it is serious about preventing the physical abuse of children.

Rejecting corporal punishment does not imply favoring unlimited permissiveness in rearing children. To grow up successfully, children require a sense of security inherent in nonarbitrary structures and limits. Understanding adults can establish such structures and limits through love, patience, firmness, consistency and rational authority. Corporal punishment seems devoid of constructive educational value, since it cannot provide that sense of security and non-arbitrary authority. Rarely, if ever, is corporal punishment administered for the benefit of the attacked child; usually it serves the needs of the attacking adult, seeking relief from anger and stress.

(2) The multiple links between poverty and physical abuse of children suggest that one important route toward reducing child abuse is the elimination of poverty from America's affluent society. No doubt this is only a part answer to the complex issue of preventing violence toward children, but perhaps it is an important part of the total answer, and certainly a part without which other preventive efforts may be utterly futile. This nation possesses the resources for eliminating poverty, assuming willingness to redistribute national wealth more equitably.

(3) Deviance and pathology in areas of physical, social, intellectual and emotional functioning of individuals and of family units were found to be another set of forces that may contribute to the incidence and prevalence of physical abuse of children. These conditions tend to be strongly associated with poverty and, therefore, the elimination of poverty is likely to reduce, though by no means to eliminate, their incidence and prevalence. The following measures should be available in every community as components of a comprehensive program for reducing physical abuse of children, and for helping individuals and families once abuse has occurred:

(a) Comprehensive family planning programs, including the repeal of all legislation limiting medical abortions. The availability of family planning resources and medical abortions is likely to reduce the number of unwanted and rejected children, known to be

11

frequent victims of severe physical abuse and infanticide. Families with many children and female-headed households are overrepresented among families involved in physical abuse of children.

(b) Family life education and counseling programs for adolescents and adults in preparation for marriage and afterward. Such programs should be developed on the assumption that there is much to learn about married life and parenthood that one does not know merely on the basis of sexual and chronological maturity.

(c) A comprehensive, high-quality, neighborhood-based, national health service, financed through general tax revenue, and geared not only to the treatment of acute and chronic illness, but to the promotion of maximum feasible physical and mental health for everyone.

(d) A range of high-quality, neighborhood-based social services geared to the reduction of environmental stresses on family life and especially on mothers who carry major responsibility for the child-rearing function. Any measure reducing these stresses would also indirectly reduce the rate of child abuse. Homemaker and housekeeping services, mothers' helpers and baby-sitting services, and family and group day care facilities for preschool and school-age children are examples of such services.

(e) A system of social services geared to assisting families and children who cannot live together because of severe relationship or reality problems. Physically abused children frequently are in this category, and in such situations the welfare of the child and of the family may require temporary or permanent separation. The first re-quirement in such situations is comprehensive diagnostic facilities capable of arriving at sound decisions that take into consideration the circumstances, needs and rights of all concerned. Next, a community requires access to a variety of facilities for the care of children away from their homes.

The measures proposed here are aimed at different levels and aspects of physical abuse of children. The first set would attack the culturally determined core of the phenomenon; the second would eliminate a major condition to which child abuse is linked; the third approaches the causes of child abuse indirectly. It would be futile to argue the relative merits of these approaches. All three are important, and a beginning should be made in utilizing them all. The basic question seems to be not which measure to select for combating child abuse, but whether American society is indeed committed to the well-being of all its children.

It is important to keep in mind that physical abuse committed by individual caretakers constitutes a relatively small problem within the array of problems affecting the nation's children. Abuse committed by society as a whole against large segments of the next generation through poverty, discrimination, malnutrition, poor housing and neighborhoods, inadequate care for health, education and general well-being are far more dangerous problems that merit the highest priority in the development of constructive social policies. ◆

References

1. J.H.S. Bossard and E.S. Boll: *The Sociology of Child Development* (New York: Harper and Brothers, 1966); S.X. Radbill: "A History of

12

Child Abuse and Infanticide," in R. E. Helfer and C.H. Kempe, eds.; *The Battered Child* (Chicago: University of Chicago, 1968).

2. J. Caffey, "Multiple Fractures in the Long Bones of Infants Suffering From Chronic Hematoma," *American Journal of Roentgenology*, LVI (1946), 163.

3. *Bibliography on the Battered Child*, U.S. Children's Bureau (Washington, D.C.: Government Printing Office, 1969).

4. *The Abused Child: Principles and Suggested Language on Reporting the Physically Abused Child*, U.S. Children's Bureau (Washington, D.C.: Government Printing Office, 1962); *The Child Abuse Reporting Laws—A Tabular View*, U.S. Children's Bureau (Washington, D.C.: Government Printing Office, 1966).

5. Elizabeth Elmer, "Abused Young Children Seen in Hospitals," *Social Work*, V, No. 4 (1960), 98; Helen E. Boardman, "A Project to Rescue Children From Inflicted Injuries, *Social Work*, VII, No. 1 (1962), 43; C.H. Kempe, F.N. Silverman, B.F. Steele, W. Droegemueller, H.K. Silver, "The Battered-Child Syndrome," *JAMA*, CXXCI (1962), 17; I. Kaufman, "Psychiatric Implications of Physical Abuse of Children," in V. DeFrancis, ed.: *Protecting the Battered Child* (Denver: American Humane Association, 1962), 17-22; H.D. Bryant *et. al.*, "Physical Abuse of Children: An Agency Study," *Child Welfare*, XLII No. 3 (1963), 125-130; M.G. Morris and R.W. Gould, "Role Reversal: A Concept in Dealing With the Neglected/Battered Child Syndrome," in *The Neglected/Battered Child Syndrome* (New York: Child Welfare League of America, 1963), 29-49, V. DeFrancis, *Child Abuse Preview of a Nationwide Survey* (Denver: American Humane Association, 1963); L.R. Young, *Wednesday's Children* (New York: McGraw-Hill, 1964), 1-195; R. Galdstone, "Observations on Children Who Have Been Physically Abused and Their Parents," *American Journal of Psychiatry*, CXXII, 440; I.D. Milowe and R.S. Lounie, "The Child's Role in the Battered-Child Syndrome, "*Abstracts of the Society for Pediatric Research* (1964), 1079.

6. David G. Gil, *Violence Against Children* (Cambridge, Mass.: Harvard University Press, 1970).

7. Jonathan Kozol, *Death at an Early Age* (Boston: Houghton Mifflin Co., 1967); Howard James, *Children in Trouble* (New York: David McKay, 1970).

13

Psychological Bulletin
1972, Vol. 77, No. 4, 296–304

THE CHILD-ABUSING PARENT:

A PSYCHOLOGICAL REVIEW

JOHN J. SPINETTA [1]   DAVID RIGLER

University of Southern California   *Childrens Hospital of Los Angeles*

Review of professional opinions in the literature reveals that (*a*) the abusing parent was himself raised with some degree of deprivation; (*b*) the abusing parent brings to his role as parent mistaken notions of child rearing; (*c*) there is present in the parent a general defect in character structure allowing aggressive impulses to be expressed too freely; and (*d*) while socioeconomic factors might sometimes place added stresses on basic personality weakness, these stresses are not of themselves sufficient or necessary causes of abuse. A critique is made of a recent demographic survey in light of the foregoing data.

Why does a parent physically abuse his or her own child? During the past 10 years, many attempts have been made to answer this question. An extensive literature has emerged on the medical and legal aspects of the problem of child abuse since the publication of an article by Kempe, Silverman, Steele, Droegemueller, and Silver (1962) and the pursuit of child-protective laws in California by Boardman (1962, 1963). Sociologists and social workers have contributed their share of insights, and a few psychiatrists have published their findings, but surprisingly little attention has been devoted to the problem of child abuse by the psychologist. One seeks with little success for well-designed studies of personality characteristics of abusing parents. What appears is a literature composed of professional opinions on the subject.

The aim of this review is to bring together professional opinions of this decade on the psychological characteristics of the abusing parent, in order to determine from the most commonly held opinions what generalizations can be induced and thus to lay the groundwork for systematic testing of hypotheses.

[1] The authors wish to thank James Kent, of the Division of Psychiatry, Childrens Hospital of Los Angeles, for his critical reading of earlier versions and for his helpful suggestions and support during the research.

Request for reprints should be sent to John J. Spinetta or David Rigler, who are now at Division of Psychiatry, Childrens Hospital of Los Angeles, 4650 Sunset Boulevard, Los Angeles, California 90054.

DEFINITION

What is child abuse? Kempe et al. (1962) limited their study to children who had received serious physical injury, in circumstances which indicated that the injury was caused willfully rather than by accident. They coined the term "battered child" to encompass their definition. Zalba (1966), after a brief review of definitions, likewise addressed himself primarily to those cases in which physical injury was willfully inflicted on a child by a parent or parent substitute.

Because of the difficulty of pinpointing what is emotional or psychological or social neglect and abuse, and because of the extent of the literature on physical abuse alone, this review, following Kempe's and Zalba's lead, limits the term "child abuse" to the concept of physical injury to the child, willfully inflicted. The review omits studies of parents who neglect their children—emotionally, socially, or psychologically—and adults who sexually molest them.

MEDICAL AND LEGAL HISTORY

Literature on the medical and legal aspects of the problem of child abuse is extensive. The edited volume of Helfer and Kempe (1968) contains a general overview, as do the articles by Paulson and Blake (1967), Silver (1968), and Zalba (1966). Legal aspects are delineated in De Francis (1970), McCoid (1965), and the various articles by Paulsen (1966a, 1966b, 1967, 1968a, 1968b). Simons and Downs (1968) gave an overview of patterns, problems, and accomplishments of the child-abuse reporting laws. A thorough bibliography on child abuse was published by the United States Department of Health, Education and Welfare (1969).

This review is not concerned with the medical and legal aspects of the problem and refers only to those articles that gave more than a passing mention to the psychological and social determinants of parental abuse of children.

REVIEW OF THE LITERATURE

Most of the studies of child abuse are subject to the same general criticism. First, the studies that set out to test specific hypotheses are few. Many start and end as broad studies with relatively untested common-sense assumptions. Second, in most studies in this area, the researchers used samples easily available from ready-at-hand local populations, and thus the samples were not truly representative. We shall have to rely on the convergence of conclusions from various types of sampling to establish generalizations. Third, practically all of the research in child abuse is ex post facto. What is left unanswered and still to be tested is whether one can determine prior to the onset of abuse which parents are most likely to abuse their children, or whether high-risk groups can only be defined after at least one incident of abuse has occurred.

In spite of these criticisms, the studies of child abuse do give general data that can furnish hypotheses for more rigorous research design, and for a more differentiated approach to the question of why parents abuse their children.

Demographic Characteristics

In an attempt to discover whether or not various social or economic stresses make abuse more likely, many of the studies have described demographic characteristics of abusing families. Kempe et al. (1962) found in the abusing families a high incidence of divorce, separation, and unstable marriages, as well as of minor criminal offenses. The children who were abused were very young, often under one year of age. In many of the families, children were born in very close succession. Often one child would be singled out for injury, the child that was the victim of an unwanted pregnancy.

Various other studies enter figures from their own samples, generally repeating Kempe's findings (Birrell & Birrell, 1968; Cameron, Johnson, & Camps, 1966; Ebbin, Gollub, Stein, & Wilson, 1969; Elmer & Gregg, 1967; Gregg & Elmer, 1969; Helfer & Pollock, 1967; Johnson & Morse, 1968; Nurse, 1964; Schloesser, 1964; Skinner & Castle, 1969).

Elmer (1967) and Young (1964) add to Kempe's findings the factors of social and economic stress, lack of family roots in the community, lack of immediate support from extended families, social isolation, high mobility, and unemployment.

While pointing to the role that economic and social stresses play in bringing out underlying personality weaknesses, the majority of the foregoing authors caution that economic and social stresses alone are neither sufficient nor necessary causes for child abuse. They point out that, although in the socially and economically deprived segments of the population there is generally a higher degree of the kinds of stress factors found in abusing families, the great majority of deprived families do not abuse their children. Why is it that most deprived families do not engage in child abuse, though subject to the same economic and social stresses as those families who do abuse their children?

A study that sheds light on the fact that social and economic factors have been overstressed as etiological factors in cases of child abuse is that of Steele and Pollock (1968), whose sample of abusers consisted mainly of middle-class and upper-middle-class families. Though social and economic difficulties may have added stress to the lives of the parents, Steele and Pollock considered these stresses as only incidental intensifiers of personality-rooted etiological factors.

Simons, Downs, Hurster, and Archer (1966) conducted a thorough study delineating abusing families as multiproblem families in which, not the socioeconomic factors alone, but the interplay of mental, physical, and emotional stresses underlay the abuse.

Allowing that child abuse in many cases may well be the expression of family stress, Adelson (1961), Allen, Ten Bensel, and Raile (1969), Fontana (1968), Holter and Friedman (1968), and Kempe et al. (1962) considered psychological factors as of prime importance in the etiology of child abuse. There is a defect in character structure which, in the presence of added stresses, gives way to uncontrolled physical expression.

Paulson and Blake (1969) referred to the deceptiveness of upper- and middle-class abusers, and cautioned against viewing abuse and neglect as completely a function of educationally, occupationally, economically, or socially disadvantaged parents, or as due to physical or health impoverishment within a family.

If it is true that the majority of parents in the socially and economically deprived segments of the population do not batter their children, while some well-to-do parents engage in child abuse, then one must look for the causes of child abuse beyond socioeconomic stresses. One of the factors to which one may look is parental history.

Parental History

One basic factor in the etiology of child abuse draws unanimity: Abusing parents were themselves abused or neglected, physically or emotionally, as children. Steele and Pollock (1968) have shown a history of parents having been raised in the same style that they have recreated in the pattern of rearing their own children. As infants and children, all of the parents in the groups were deprived both of basic mothering and of the deep sense of being cared for and cared about from the beginning of their lives.

Fontana (1968) also viewed the parents as emotionally crippled because of unfortunate circumstances in their own childhood. The parents reacted to their children in keeping with their own personal experiential history of loneliness, lack of protection, and lack of love. Many authors corroborated the hypotheses of Steele and Pollock and of Fontana.

In a study surveying 32 men and 7 women imprisoned for cruelty to their children, Gibbins and Walker (1956) concluded that it was rejection, indifference, and hostility in their own childhood that produced the cruel parents.

Ten years later, Tuteur and Glotzer (1966) studied 10 mothers who were hospitalized for murdering their children and found that all had grown up in an emotionally cold and often overtly rejecting family environment, in which parental figures were either absent or offered little opportunity for wholesome identification when present.

Komisaruk (1966) found as the most striking statistic in his study of abusing families the emotional loss of a significant parental figure in the early life of the abusive parent.

Perhaps the most systematic and well-controlled study in the area of child abuse, that of Melnick and Hurley (1969), compared two small, socioeconomically and racially matched groups on 18 personality variables. Melnick and Hurley found, among other things, a probable history of emotional deprivation in the mothers' own upbringing.

Further support for the hypothesis that the abusing parent was once an abused or neglected child is found in Bleiberg (1965), Blue (1965), Corbett (1964), Curtis (1963), Easson and Steinhilber (1961), Fairburn and Hunt (1964), Fleming (1967), Green (1965), Harper (1963), Kempe et al. (1962), McHenry, Girdany, and Elmer (1963), Morris, Gould, and Matthews (1964), Nurse (1964), Paulson and Blake (1969), Silver, Dublin, and Lourie (1969b), and Wasserman (1967).

In a summary statement, Gluckman (1968), repeating the findings of earlier observers, set up a 10-point differential diagnosis category. His main point, and the point of this section of the review, is that the child is the father of the man. The capacity to love is not inherent; it must be taught to the child. Character development depends on love, tolerance, and example. Many abusing parents were raised without this love and tolerance.

Parental Attitudes toward Child Rearing

In addition to concurring on the fact that many abusing parents were themselves raised with some degree of abuse or neglect, the authors agreed that the abusing parents share common misunderstandings with regard to the nature of child rearing, and look to the child for satisfaction of their own parental emotional needs.

Steele and Pollock (1968) found that the parents in their study group expected and demanded a great deal from their infants and children, and did so prematurely. The parents dealt with their children as if older than they really were. The parents felt insecure and unsure of being loved, and looked to their children as sources of reassurance, comfort, and loving response, as if the children were adults capable of providing grown-up comfort and love.

Melnick and Hurley (1969), in their well-controlled study of personality variables, also found in the mothers severely frustrated dependency needs, and an inability to empathize with their children.

Galdston (1965) concurred that abusing parents treated their children as adults, and he added that the parents were incapable of understanding the particular stages of development of their children.

Bain (1963), Gregg (1968), Helfer and Pollock (1967), Hiller (1969), Johnson and Morse (1968), Korsch, Christian, Gozzi, and Carlson (1965), and Morris and Gould (1963) also reported that abusing parents have a high expectation and demand for the infant's or child's performance, and a corresponding disregard for the infant's or child's own needs, limited abilities, and helplessness. Wasserman (1967) found that the parents not only considered punishment a proper disciplinary measure but strongly defended their right to use physical force.

In a 1969 study, Gregg and Elmer, comparing children accidentally injured with those abused, judged that the mother's ability to keep up the personal appearance of the child when well, and her ability to provide medical care when the child was moderately ill, sharply differentiated the abusive from the nonabusive mothers.

The authors seem to agree that abusing parents lack appropriate knowledge of child rearing, and that their attitudes, expectations, and child-rearing techniques set them apart from nonabusive parents. The abusing parents implement culturally accepted norms for raising children with an exaggerated intensity and at an inappropriately early age.

Presence of Severe Personality Disorders

There has been an evolution in thinking regarding the presence of a frank psychosis in the abusing parent. Woolley and Evans (1955) and Miller (1959) posited a high incidence of neurotic or psychotic behavior as a strong etiological factor in child abuse. Cochrane (1965), Greengard (1964), Platou, Lennox, and Beasley (1964) and Simpson (1967, 1968) concurred. Adelson (1961) and Kaufman (1962) considered only the most violent and abusive parents as having schizophrenic personalities. Kempe et al. (1962), allowing that direct murder of children betrayed a frank psychosis on the part of the parent, found that most of the abusing parents, though lacking in impulse control, were not severely psychotic. By the end of the decade, the literature seemed to support the view that only a few of the abusing parents showed severe psychotic tendencies (Fleming, 1967; Laupus, 1966; Steele & Pollock, 1968; Wasserman, 1967).

Motivational and Personality Variables: A Typology

A review of opinions on parental personality and motivational variables leads to a conglomerate picture. While the authors generally agree that there is a defect in the abusing parent's personality that allows aggressive impulses to be expressed too freely (Kempe et al., 1962; Steele & Pollock, 1968; Wasserman, 1967), disagreement comes in describing the source of the aggressive impulses.

Some authors claim that abuse is a final outburst at the end of a long period of tension (Nomura, 1966; Ten Have, 1965), or that abuse stems from an inability to face life's daily stresses (Heins, 1969). Some claim that abuse stems from deep feelings of inadequacy or from parental inability to fulfill the roles expected of parenthood (Cohen, Raphling, & Green, 1966; Court, 1969; Fontana, 1964; Johnson & Morse, 1968; Komisaruk, 1966; Silver, 1968; Steele & Pollock, 1968). Others described the parents as immature, self-centered, and impulse-ridden

(Cochrane, 1965; Delaney, 1966; Jacobziner, 1964; Ten Bensel, 1963).

Some authors consider a role reversal between the spouses as a prime factor in the etiology of child abuse. A home in which the father is unemployed and the mother has taken over the financial responsibility of the family is considered a breeding ground for abuse (Galdston, 1965; Greengard, 1964; Nathan, 1965; Nurse, 1964).

Finally, there are those authors who considered low intelligence as a prime factor in the etiology of child abuse (Fisher, 1958; Simpson, 1967, 1968), although this point is disputed in the findings of Cameron et al. (1966), Holter and Friedman (1968), Kempe et al. (1962), and Ounsted (1968).

Is there a common motivational factor behind child abuse? Is there only one "type" of abusing parent? Realization that each of the above described characteristics was found to exist at least in some individual circumstances has led some authors to group together certain characteristics in clusters, and to evolve a psychodynamic within each cluster. The first major attempt at a typology was made by Merrill (1962). Because Merrill's typology is the most often quoted, it is summarized in some detail.

Merrill identified three distinct clusters of personality characteristics that he found to be true both of abusing mothers and fathers, and a fourth that he found true of the abusing fathers alone. The first group of parents seemed to Merrill to be beset with a continual and pervasive hostility and aggressiveness, sometimes focused, sometimes directed at the world in general. This was not a controlled anger, and was continually with the parents, with the only stimulation needed for direct expression being normal daily difficulties. This angry feeling stemmed from conflicts within the parents and was often rooted in their early childhood experiences.

The second group Merrill identified by personality characteristics of rigidity, compulsiveness, lack of warmth, lack of reasonableness, and lack of pliability in thinking and in belief. These parents defended their right to act as they had in abusing their child. Mothers in this group had marked child-rejection attitudes, evidenced by their primary concern with their own pleasures, inability to feel love and protectiveness toward their children, and in feelings that the children were responsible for much of the trouble being experienced by themselves as parents. These fathers and mothers were extremely compulsive in their behavior, demanding excessive cleanliness of their children. Many of these parents had great difficulty in relaxing, in expressing themselves verbally, and in exhibiting warmth and friendliness.

Merrill's third group of parents showed strong feelings of passivity and dependence. Many of these parents were people who were unassuming, reticent about expressing their feelings and desires, and very unaggressive. They were individuals who manifested strong needs to depend on others for decisions. These mothers and fathers often competed with their own children for the love and attention of their spouses. Generally depressed, moody, unresponsive, and unhappy, many of these parents showed considerable immaturity.

Merrill's fourth grouping or cluster of personality characteristics included a significant number of abusing fathers. These fathers were generally young, intelligent men with acquired skills who, because of some physical disability, were now fully or partially unable to support their families. In most of these situations, the mothers were working, and the fathers stayed at home, caring for the children. Their frustrations led to swift and severe punishment, to angry, rigid discipline.

Two further attempts at classification, Delsordo (1963) and Zalba (1967), with slight modifications, can be reduced to Merrill's categories.

The use of categories seems simple, unifying, and time saving. If further work can be done in refining the categories, validating them in field research, perhaps they or similar clusters shown to be empirically valid can be used as an aid in the determination of high-risk parents.

In this section, we have seen a conglomerate picture of parental motivational and personality variables, with one author's attempt to cluster the characteristics into a workable unity. One basic fact of agreement emerges from the studies in this section. The authors feel that a general defect in character—from whatever source—is present in the abusing parent allowing aggressive impulses to be expressed too freely. During times of additional stress and tension, the impulses express themselves on the helpless child.

CRITIQUE OF A SURVEY

Of the studies surveying the demographic characteristics of families in which child abuse has occurred, the most extensive in scope was the national survey undertaken by Gil (1968a, 1968b, 1969).[2] In 1969, Gil reported that the phenomenon of child abuse was highly concentrated among the socioeconomically deprived segments of the population. Concluding that "physical abuse is by and large not very serious as reflected by the data on the extent and types of injury suffered by the children in the study cohort [p. 862]," Gil placed his intervention strategy in the general betterment of society. For Gil, the cultural attitude permitting the use of physical force in child rearing is the common core of all physical abuse of children in American society. Since he found the socioeconomically deprived relying more heavily on physical force in rearing children, he recommended systematic educational efforts aimed at gradually changing this cultural attitude, and the establishment of clear-cut cultural prohibitions against the use of physical force as a means of rearing children. He viewed this educational effort as likely to produce the strongest possible reduction in the incidence and prevalence of physical abuse of children.

For Gil, child abuse is ultimately the result of chance environmental factors. While admitting to various forms of physical, social, intellectual, and emotional deviance and pathology in caretakers, and in the family units to which they belong, Gil stressed a global control of environmental factors as the solution to the problem of child abuse. He suggested: (a) the elimination of poverty from the midst of America's affluent society; (b)

[2] Gil's book reporting his national findings (*Violence against children: Physical child abuse in the United States*. Cambridge, Mass.: Harvard University Press, 1970) appeared after the present review was accepted for publication. Although the book offers greater detail, the findings and conclusions are identical to those in the cited references.

the availability in every community of resources aimed at the prevention and alleviation of deviance and pathology; (c) the availability of comprehensive family planning programs and liberalized legislation concerning medical abortions, to reduce the number of unwanted children; (d) family-life education and counseling programs for adolescents and adults in preparation for and after marriage, to be offered within the public school system; (e) a comprehensive, high-quality, neighborhood-based national health service, to promote and assure maximum feasible physical and mental health for every citizen; (f) a range of social services geared to the reduction of environmental stresses on family life; and (g) a community-based system of social services geared to assisting families and children who cannot live together because of severe relationship problems. Gil's ultimate objective is "the reduction of the general level of violence, and the raising of the general level of human well-being throughout our entire society [p. 863]."

While one must praise the efforts of the Gil study in data collection, and the ultimate objective of reducing the general level of violence and raising the general level of human well-being in our entire society, one cannot help but feel that Gil did not address himself to the question of child abuse. If there really does exist as strong a link as Gil suggests between poverty and physical abuse of children, why is it that all poor parents do not batter their children, while some well-to-do parents engage in child abuse? Eliminating environmental stress factors and bettering the level of society at all stages may reduce a myriad of social ills and may even prove effective, indirectly, in reducing the amount of child abuse. But there still remains the problem, insoluble at the demographic level, of why some parents abuse their children, while others under the same stress factors do not.

Other authors throughout the decade have allowed for the types of services outlined by Gil, but less globally and in a manner less disregarding of parental personality factors. That raising the general educational and financial level of families that are socioeconomically deprived is of long-range value in the lessening of the prevalence of child abuse is generally agreed upon, and finds support throughout the literature. However, most of the authors explicitly caution against considering abuse, as does Gil, as a function solely of educational, occupational, economic, or social stresses. This point is made by Adelson (1961), Allen et al. (1969), Elmer (1967), Fontana (1968), Helfer and Pollock (1967), Holter and Friedman (1968), Kempe (1968), Kempe et al. (1962), Paulson and Blake (1967), Silver et al. (1969a, 1969b), and Steele and Pollock (1968).

The great majority of the authors cited in this review have pointed to psychological factors within the parents themselves as of prime importance in the etiology of child abuse. They see abuse as stemming from a defect in character leading to a lack of inhibition in expressing frustration and other impulsive behavior. Socioeconomic factors sometimes place added stress on the basic weakness in personality structure, but these factors are not of themselves sufficient or necessary causes of abuse.

Conclusions

The purpose of this review has been to bring together the published professional opinions on the psychological characteristics of the abusing parent, in order to determine from the most commonly held opinions what generalizations can be induced, and thus to lay the groundwork for more systematic testing of hypotheses.

The psychologist, both as a specialist in the functioning of the human as an individual, and as a scientist trained in research methodology, is in a unique position to test the hypotheses raised by professionals in the fields of medicine and social work, in the study of the personality characteristics of the abusing parent.

Certainly, one would hope that research can eventually develop criteria to distinguish those inadequate parents who, with professional help, can meet the needs of their children, from those who cannot. We need eventually to be able to identify the high-risk families prior to the onset of abuse, but should be satisfied for the time being if we can help

determine after the fact of abuse which families must receive the most attention to assure the further safety of their child.

REFERENCES

ADELSON, L. Slaughter of the innocents: A study of forty-six homicides in which the victims were children. New England Journal of Medicine, 1961. 264, 1345–1349.

ALLEN, H. D., TEN BENSEL, R. W., & RAILE, R. B. The battered child syndrome. Minnesota Medicine, 1969. 52, 155–156.

BAIN, K. Commentary: The physically abused child. Pediatrics, 1963, 31, 895–898.

BIRRELL, R. G., & BIRRELL, J. H. W. The maltreatment syndrome in children. Medical Journal of Australia, 1968. 2, 1023–1029.

BLEIBERG, N. The neglected child and the child health conference. New York State Journal of Medicine, 1965, 65, 1880–1885.

BLUE, M. T. The battered child syndrome from a social work viewpoint. Canadian Journal of Public Health, 1965, 56, 197–198.

BOARDMAN, H. E. A project to rescue children from inflicted injuries. Social Work, 1962, 7, 43–51.

BOARDMAN, H. E. Who insures the child's right to health? Child Welfare, 1963, 42, 120–124.

CAMERON, J. M., JOHNSON, H. R. M., & CAMPS, F. E. The battered child syndrome. Medicine, Science, and the Law, 1966, 6, 2–21.

COCHRANE, W. The battered child syndrome. Canadian Journal of Public Health, 1965, 56, 193–196.

COHEN, M. I., RAPHLING, D. L., & GREEN, P. E. Psychologic aspects of the maltreatment syndrome of childhood. Journal of Pediatrics, 1966, 69, 279–284.

CORBETT, J. T. A psychiatrist reviews the battered child syndrome and mandatory reporting legislation. Northwest Medicine, 1964, 63, 920–922.

COURT, J. The battered child: Historical and diagnostic reflections, reflections on treatment. Medical Social Work, 1969, 22(1), 11–20.

CURTIS, G. Violence breeds violence—perhaps. American Journal of Psychiatry, 1963, 120, 386–387.

DE FRANCIS, V. Child abuse legislation in the 1970's. Denver, Colo.: American Humane Association. 1970.

DELANEY, D. W. The physically abused child. World Medical Journal, 1966, 13, 145–147.

DELSORDO, J. D. Protective casework for abused children. Children, 1963, 10, 213–218.

EASSON, W. M., & STEINHILBER, R. M. Murderous aggression by children and adolescents. Archives of General Psychiatry, 1961, 4, 1–10.

EBBIN, A. J., GOLLUB, M. H., STEIN, A. M., & WILSON, M. G. Battered child syndrome at the Los Angeles County General Hospital. American Journal of the Diseases of Children, 1969, 118, 660–667.

ELMER, E. Children in jeopardy: A study of abused minors and their families. Pittsburgh: University of Pittsburgh Press, 1967.

ELMER, E., & GREGG, G. S. Developmental characteristics of abused children. *Pediatrics*, 1967, **40**, 596–602.

FAIRBURN, A. C., & HUNT, A. C. Caffey's 'third syndrome': A critical evaluation. *Medicine, Science, and the Law*, 1964, **4**, 123–126.

FISHER, S. H. Skeletal manifestations of parent-induced trauma in infants and children. *Southern Medical Journal*, 1958, **51**, 956–960.

FLEMING, G. M. Cruelty to children. *British Medical Journal*, 1967, **2**, 421–422.

FONTANA, V. J. *The maltreated child: The maltreatment syndrome in children*. Springfield, Ill.: Charles C Thomas, 1964.

FONTANA, V. J. Further reflections on maltreatment of children. *New York State Journal of Medicine*, 1968, **68**, 2214–2215.

GALDSTON, R. Observations on children who have been physically abused and their parents. *American Journal of Psychiatry*, 1965, **122**, 440–443.

GIBBINS, T. C. N., & WALKER, A. *Cruel parents*. London: Institute for the Study and Treatment of Delinquency, 1956.

GIL, D. G. California pilot study. In R. E. Helfer & C. H. Kempe (Eds.), *The battered child*. Chicago: University of Chicago Press, 1968. (a)

GIL, D. G. Incidence of child abuse and demographic characteristics of persons involved. In R. E. Helfer & C. H. Kempe (Eds.), *The battered child*. Chicago: University of Chicago Press, 1968. (b)

GIL, D. G. Physical abuse of children: Findings and implications of a nationwide survey. *Pediatrics*, 1969, **44**(5, Supplement), 857–864.

GLUCKMAN, L. K. Cruelty to children. *New Zealand Medical Journal*, 1968, **67**, 155–159.

GREEN, K. Diagnosing the battered child syndrome. *Maryland State Medical Journal*, 1965, **14**(9), 83–84.

GREENGARD, J. The battered-child syndrome. *American Journal of Nursing*, 1964, **64**(6), 98–100.

GREGG, G. S. Physicians, child-abuse reporting laws, and injured child: Psychosocial anatomy of childhood trauma. *Clinical Pediatrics*, 1968, **7**, 720–725.

GREGG, G. S., & ELMER, E. Infant injuries: Accident or abuse? *Pediatrics*, 1969, **44**, 434–439.

HARPER, F. V. The physician, the battered child and the law. *Pediatrics*, 1963, **31**, 899–902.

HEINS, M. Child abuse: Analysis of a current epidemic. *Michigan Medicine*, 1969, **68**, 887–891.

HELFER, R. E., & KEMPE, C. H. (Eds.) *The battered child*. Chicago: University of Chicago Press, 1968.

HELFER, R. E., & POLLOCK, C. B. The battered child syndrome. *Advances in Pediatrics*, 1967, **15**, 9–27.

HILLER, R. B. The battered child: A health visitor's point of view. *Nursing Times*, 1969, **65**, 1265–1266.

HOLTER, J. C., & FRIEDMAN, S. B. Principles of management in child abuse cases. *American Journal of Orthopsychiatry*, 1968, **38**, 127–136.

JACOBZINER, H. Rescuing the battered child. *American Journal of Nursing*, 1964, **64**(6), 92–97.

JOHNSON, B., & MORSE, H. A. Injured children and their parents. *Children*, 1968, **15**, 147–152.

KAUFMAN, I. Psychiatric implications of physical abuse of children. In V. De Francis (Ed.), *Protecting the battered child*. Denver, Colo.: American Humane Association, 1962.

KEMPE, C. H. Some problems encountered by welfare departments in the management of the battered child syndrome. In R. E. Helfer & C. H. Kempe (Eds.), *The battered child*. Chicago: University of Chicago Press, 1968.

KEMPE, C. H., SILVERMAN, F. N., STEELE, B. F., DROEGEMUELLER, W., & SILVER, H. K. The battered-child syndrome. *Journal of the American Medical Association*, 1962, **181**, 17–24.

KOMISARUK, R. Clinical evaluation of child abuse: Scarred families, a preliminary report. *Juvenile Court Judges Journal* (Wayne County, Michigan), 1966, **17**(2), 66–70.

KORSCH, B. M., CHRISTIAN, J. B., GOZZI, E. K., & CARLSON, P. V. Infant care and punishment: A pilot study. *American Journal of Public Health*, 1965, **55**, 1880–1888.

LAUPUS, W. E. Child abuse and the physician. *The Virginia Medical Monthly*, 1966, **93**(1), 1–2.

McCOID, A. H. The battered child and other assaults upon the family. *Minnesota Law Review*, 1965, **50**, 1–58.

McHENRY, T., GIRDANY, B. R., & ELMER, E. Unsuspected trauma with multiple skeletal injuries during infancy and childhood. *Pediatrics*, 1963, **31**, 903–908.

MELNICK, B., & HURLEY, J. R. Distinctive personality attributes of child-abusing mothers. *Journal of Consulting and Clinical Psychology*, 1969, **33**, 746–749.

MERRILL, E. J. Physical abuse of children: An agency study. In V. De Francis (Ed.), *Protecting the battered child*. Denver, Colo.: American Humane Association, 1962.

MILLER, D. S. Fractures among children: Parental assault as causative agent. *Minnesota Medicine*, 1959, **42**, 1209–1213.

MORRIS, M. G., & GOULD, R. W. Role reversal: A concept in dealing with the neglected/battered child syndrome. In, *The neglected battered-child syndrome: Role reversal in parents*. New York: Child Welfare League of America, 1963.

MORRIS, M. G., GOULD, R. W., & MATTHEWS, P. J. Toward prevention of child abuse. *Children*, 1964, **11**, 55–60.

NATHAN, H. Abused children. *American Journal of Psychiatry*, 1965, **122**, 443.

NOMURA, F. M. The battered child 'syndrome': A review. *Hawaii Medical Journal*, 1966, **25**, 387–394.

NURSE, S. Familial patterns of parents who abuse their children. *Smith College Studies in Social Work*, 1964, **35**, 11–25.

OUNSTED, C. Review of K. Simpson, Battered baby syndrome. *Developmental Medicine and Child Neurology*, 1968, **10**, 133–134.

PAULSEN, M. G. Legal protection against child abuse. *Children*, 1966, **13**, 43–48. (a)

PAULSEN, M. G. The legal framework for child protection. *Columbia Law Review*, 1966, **66**, 679–717. (b)

PAULSEN, M. G. Child abuse reporting laws: The shape of the legislation. *Columbia Law Review*, 1967, **67**, 1–49.

PAULSEN, M. G. A summary of child-abuse legislation. In R. E. Helfer & C. H. Kempe (Eds.), *The battered child*. Chicago: University of Chicago Press, 1968. (a)

PAULSEN, M. G. The law and abused children. In R. E. Helfer & C. H. Kempe (Eds.), *The battered child*. Chicago: University of Chicago Press, 1968. (b)

PAULSON, M. J., & BLAKE, P. R. The abused, battered and maltreated child: A review. *Trauma*, 1967, **9**(4), 3–136.

PAULSON, M. J., & BLAKE, P. R. The physically abused child: A focus on prevention. *Child Welfare*, 1969, **48**, 86–95.

PLATOU, R. V., LENNOX, R., & BEASLEY, J. D. Battering. *Bulletin of the Tulane Medical Faculty*, 1964, **23**, 157–165.

SCHLOESSER, P. T. The abused child. *Bulletin of the Menninger Clinic*, 1964, **28**, 260–268.

SILVER, L. B. Child abuse syndrome: A review. *Medical Times*, 1968, **96**, 803–820.

SILVER, L. B., DUBLIN, C. C., & LOURIE, R. S. Child abuse syndrome: The 'gray areas' in establishing a diagnosis. *Pediatrics*, 1969, **44**, 594–600. (a)

SILVER, L. B., DUBLIN, C. C., & LOURIE, R. S. Does violence breed violence? Contributions from a study of the child abuse syndrome. *American Journal of Psychiatry*, 1969, **126**, 404–407. (b)

SIMONS, B., & DOWNS, E. F. Medical reporting of child abuse: Patterns, problems and accomplishments. *New York State Journal of Medicine*, 1968, **68**, 2324–2330.

SIMONS, B., DOWNS, E. F., HURSTER, M. M., & ARCHER, M. Child abuse: Epidemiologic study of medically reported cases. *New York State Journal of Medicine*, 1966, **66**, 2783–2788.

SIMPSON, K. The battered baby problem. *Royal Society of Health Journal*, 1967, **87**, 168–170.

SIMPSON, K. The battered baby problem. *South African Medical Journal*, 1968, **42**, 661–663.

SKINNER, A. E., & CASTLE, R. L. *78 battered children: A retrospective study*. London: National Society for the Prevention of Cruelty to Children, 1969.

STEELE, B. F., & POLLOCK, C. B. A psychiatric study of parents who abuse infants and small children. In R. E. Helfer & C. H. Kempe (Eds.), *The battered child*. Chicago: University of Chicago Press, 1968.

TEN BENSEL, R. W. The battered child syndrome. *Minnesota Medicine*, 1963, **46**, 977–982.

TEN HAVE, R. A preventive approach to problems of child abuse and neglect. *Michigan Medicine*, 1965, **64**, 645–649.

TUTEUR, W., & GLOTZER, J. Further observations on murdering mothers. *Journal of Forensic Science*, 1966, **11**, 373–383.

UNITED STATES DEPARTMENT OF HEALTH, EDUCATION AND WELFARE. *Bibliography on the battered child*. Washington, D. C.: United States Government Printing Office, 1969.

WASSERMAN, S. The abused parent of the abused child. *Children*, 1967, **14**, 175–179.

WOOLLEY, P. V., & EVANS, W. A. Significance of skeletal lesions in infants resembling those of traumatic origin. *Journal of the American Medical Association*, 1955, **158**, 539–543.

YOUNG, L. *Wednesday's children: A study of child neglect and abuse*. New York: McGraw-Hill, 1964.

ZALBA, S. R. The abused child: A survey of the problem. *Social Work*, 1966, **11**(4), 3–16.

ZALBA, S. R. The abused child: A typology for classification and treatment. *Social Work*, 1967, **12**(1), 70–79.

(Received August 10, 1970)

Amer. J. Orthopsychiat. 43(4), July 1973

CHILD ABUSE AS PSYCHOPATHOLOGY:
A Sociological Critique and Reformulation

Richard J. Gelles

University of Rhode Island

Much of the current research on child abuse employs a psychopathological model, which explains child abuse as a function of a psychological pathology, or a "sickness." This paper asserts that major deficiencies of this model are its inconsistency and narrowness. It is suggested that a more dimensional approach to child abuse is possible by focusing on the sociological and contextual variables associated with abuse.

Each year in this country, thousands of children are brutally beaten, abused, and sometimes killed by their mothers and fathers. The dominant theme of research on this problem has been the use of a "psychopathological model" of child abuse—the parent who abuses suffers from a psychological pathology or sickness that accounts for abusing or battering a child.

This paper takes a critical look at the psychopathological theory of child abuse and finds a number of deficiencies with the model. First, this explanation of child abuse is too narrow. It posits a single causal variable (a presumed mental abberation or disease) to account for child abuse, while it ignores other variables that this paper will show are equally or more important causal factors. Secondly, psychopathology theory is inconsistent in stating that abuse is caused by a pathology, while many of the research reports state that all abusers are not psychopaths. Finally, close examination of the literature on child abuse shows that it is not based on research that meets even the minimal standards of evidence in social science.[20]

The purpose of this paper is to provide a more dimensional analysis of the

Presented, in a somewhat different version, at the annual meeting of the American Sociological Association, August 1972. The research was supported by NIMH grants MH–15521–04 and MH–13050–01.

611

23

generative sources of child abuse. The analysis goes beyond the uni-causal approach of the psychopathology model; it analyzes sociocultural features of the abuser such as socioeconomic status, sex, employment status, and previous experience with violence, and it relates these to such factors as the age, temper-ament, and sib-order of the abused child. In addition, the social context of child abuse is examined.

The paper concludes with a broader, social-psychological model of child abuse and discusses the implications of this approach for strategies of intervention in child abuse.

THE PSYCHOPATHOLOGICAL MODEL *

THE CHILD ABUSER: A PSYCHOPATHIC PORTRAIT

Articles on child abuse almost invariably open by asserting that a parent who would inflict serious abuse on a child is in some manner sick. This assertion ranges from the point blank statement that the child abusing parent is mentally ill[5] to the indirect statement that the abuser is the patient of the clinician.[2] In some cases, the sickness is traced to a flaw in the socialization process, where "something went haywire or was not touched in the humanization process."[26] Many articles and books begin with the assumption that the parent abuser is a psychopath. Steele and Pollack[21] announce that their first parent abuse was a "gold mine of psychopathology"; Kempe[13] describes the abuser as the "psychopathological member of the family"; while Galdston[8] mentions parents who "illustrate their psychopathology" when discussing their relations with their children.

The psychopathological model goes on to focus on specific psychological characteristics of the parent. Steele and Pollack[21] hold that child abusing parents have severe emotional problems, while Kempe[13] locates the problem in a defect of the character structure. The parent who abuses is described as impulsive, immature, and depressed.[21, 13, 2, 29] A link between sex and violence in the abusive parent is shown in the findings that abusive parents are sado-masochistic[21] and that they abuse their children to displace aggression and sadism.[2] Abusive parents are also described as having poor emotional control[2] and quick to react with poorly controlled aggression.[13] Some authors describe the child abuser as inadequate,[2] self-centered and hypersensitive,[13] having pervasive anger,[29] and dependent, egocentric, narcissistic, demanding, and insecure.[21] Abusive parents also suffer from some psychosomatic illnesses[21] and have a perverse fascination with punishment of children.[28]

Many other authors[3] could be cited as illustration that the psychopathological model views the abusing parent as having abnormal psychological traits. However, those works cited are sufficient to make clear that mental abnormality is viewed as the cause of child abuse.

PARENT AND CHILD: REVEALING THE PSYCHOPATHY

The authors advancing the psycho-pathological model of child abuse find

---

* Not *all* students of child abuse subscribe to or support the psychopathological model. Two notable exceptions, who approach child abuse with a more multi-dimensional model are David Gil[9] and Myra Blumberg.[4]

Table I

PSYCHOPATHOLOGICAL MODEL OF CHILD ABUSE

EARLY CHILDHOOD EXPERIENCE———→	PSYCHOPATHIC STATES———→	CHILD ABUSE
Abused	Personality traits	
Emotionally abandoned	Character traits	
Psychologically abandoned	Poor control	
Physical punishment	Neurological states	

the disorder manifested in the parent's relationship with his child. One form of this manifestation is the "transference psychosis." [8] Abusive parents often speak of their child as if he were an adult; they perceive the child as a hostile persecuting adult, and often see former guilt in their own child.[8] As a result of the "transference," the parental distortion of reality causes a misinterpretation of the infant child. The child is perceived as the psychotic portion of the parent, which the parent wishes to destroy.[21] The child is projected as the cause of the parent's troubles [21] and becomes a "hostility sponge" for the parent.[26]

The psychopathy of the abusive parent is conceived as manifesting itself as a transference and distortion of reality on the part of the parent. In this state, the immature, impulsive, dependent (etc.) individual lashes out at a hostile world. More specifically, he lashes out at what he projects as the source of his troubles—his child.

CAUSE OF THE PSYCHOPATHY

After identifying the abusive parent as sick, listing the traits or symptoms of the sickness, and illustrating how the sickness manifests itself in parent-child relations, the psychopathological model establishes a causal explanation for the presence of the psychopathy. Steele and Pollack [21] state that one cause is that

the parent was raised in the same style (physical punishment and abuse) he recreates in raising his own children. This position is elaborated by Reiner and Kaufman,[17] who find that an abusive parent is an imbedded depressive because he was emotionally or psychologically abandoned as a child; as a result, violent behavior becomes the child's means of communication. This establishes a life pattern of aggression and violence, which explains both the psychopathy and the abuse.[2] Thus, the cause of the pathology is the parent's early childhood experience, which included abuse and abandonment. The assumption is that the parent who was abused as a child will almost certainly pass this on to his own child.

The resulting psychopathological model is diagrammed in TABLE 1; it is an elementary linear model. Early childhood experience characterized by abuse creates psychological stress that produces certain psychopathic states. These psychopathic conditions, in turn, cause abusive acts toward the child.

PROBLEMS OF
THE PSYCHOPATHOLOGICAL MODEL

A problem of the psychopathological approach is that most of the discussions of the causes of child abuse are clearly inconsistent and contradictory. Some authors contradict themselves by first stating that the abusing parent is a psy-

25

chopath and then stating that the child abuser is no different from the rest of society. Steele and Pollack [21] state that their first patient was a "gold mine of psychopathology," and then later state that their patients were a "random cross-secion of the general population" who "would not seem much different than a group of people picked by stopping the first several dozen people one would meet on a downtown street." Zalba [29] states that child abusers do not fit easily into a psychiatric category, while Galdston [8] maintains that, aside from the "transference psychosis," there are no other symptoms of psychotic disorder. Kempe,[13] after describing the psychopathic personality of the child abuser, goes on to state that child beating is not confined to people with psychopathic disorders.

A second problem is an inability to pinpoint the personality traits that characterize the pathology. Of nineteen traits listed by the authors, there was agreement by two or more authors on only four traits. Each remaining trait was mentioned by only a single author. Thus, there is little agreement as to the make-up of the psychopathy.

A third problem is that few studies attempt to test any hypothesis concerning the phenomenon. A recent comprehensive review of the literature [20] found that most of the studies start and end with relatively untested common-sense assumpions. This, in turn, is because most of the studies are *ex post facto*.[20] When the analysis of the behavior takes place after the fact, little analytic understanding of the genesis of the behavior is offered. For instance, authors state that abusive parents have poor emotional control,[2] or that they react with poorly controlled aggression.[13] Analyzed after the fact, it seems obvious that a parent who beats his child almost to the point of death has poor emotional control and reacts with uncontrolled aggression. This type of analysis does not distinguish the behavior in question from the explanation. The drawbacks of this type of labeling are pointed out by Szasz [23, 24, 25] in his discussion of the myth of mental illness. Szasz argues that people who are labeled mentally ill are *then* thought to be suffering from mental illness. The types of after-the-fact explanation offered by the psychopathologic model offer little predictive power in the study of child abuse.

A final criticism of the psychopathological approach is the sampling technique used to gather the data. Most of the data are gathered from cases that medical or psychiatric practitioners have at hand. Thus, the sample cannot be considered truly representative of child abusers since many or most are not seen in clinics. More importantly, there is no attempt to compare samples of "patients" with any comparative group of non-child abusers. Without this comparison, we have no way of knowing whether, in fact, child abusers differ from the rest of the population in terms of the causal variables proposed by the psychopathological model.*

---

* Similar problems of the psychopathological approach to child abuse are also articulated in sociological analyses of other forms of deviancy. See, for examples, Dunham; [6] Becker; [1] and Hakeem.[11]

A SOCIOLOGICAL APPROACH TO CHILD ABUSE

It should be noted that authors advancing the psychopathological model make a special effort to point out that social variables *do not* enter into the causal scheme of child abuse. Steele and Pollack,[21] for instance, state that social, economic, and demographic factors are irrelevant to the actual act of child beating. Other researchers [4, 8, 28, 29] also argue that their cases of child abuse make up a cross-section of socioeconomic status, ethnicity, age, and education.

In examining the data presented in the research on child abuse it is apparent that, even though the authors deny the relevancy of social factors, there are patterns of sociological and contextual variables that *are* associated with child abuse.* This section re-examines the data in terms of three aspects of child abuse: the social characteristics of abusing parents, the social characteristics of the victims, and the situational or contextual properties of the act of child abuse. This section is aimed at broadening our understanding of the causes of child abuse by examining the sociological features of the abusers, abused, and acts of abuse.

THE PARENT WHO ABUSES

Even though the authors note that their case materials evidence a large number of middle-class parents, there is evidence that the working and lower classes are overrepresented among child abusers. The articles that provide data on the socioeconomic class of each abuser show an association between social class and child abuse. Gil [9] found that, in most of his cases, the perpetrator of the abuse was of low socioeconomic status. Bennie and Sclare [2] found that 80% of their cases of child abuse (ten cases) were from the lower class (unskilled workers). Factors related to socioeconomic status also support the notion of the low status of the abuser. Gil [9] reports that education, occupation, and income of child abusers are lower than those of the general population. Galdston [8] states that battering parents have limited education and financial means.

This evidence lends support to the claims that intrafamily violence occurs more often in the lower class or the working class. Blumberg [4] points out that the lower class uses "normal violence" more often than do upper classes. Steinmetz and Straus,[22] while arguing that the literature is not conclusive,**

---

* This multi-dimensional approach has been advocated by Gil [9] in his research on child abuse (see also, Gil, D., 1970, Violence Against Children, Harvard University Press, Cambridge, Mass.; and Gil, D., 1966, First steps in a nation-wide study on child abuse, *in* Social Work Practice, Columbia University Press, New York). Much of the material in this section is drawn from Gil's empirical research and theoretical formulations, which focus on social and economic factors related to child abuse.

** There are a wide range of interpretations that can be applied to statistical data on child abuse (see Steinmetz and Straus [22] footnotes #1 and #2 for detailed discussion of this). One problem in interpreting the data is that middle-class children might be overrepresented in the case literature, since their parents have more resources to draw on in obtaining medical and psychological attention for their children and themselves. On the other hand, middle-class children might be underrepresented since the act of child abuse might be more shocking to middle-class families, and lead them to use their resources to "cover up" the abuse by seeking help from a private physician or clinic.

do concede that intrafamily violence is more common among the working class. In explaining his findings, Gil [9] argues that the socioeconomic pressures on the lower class weaken the caretakers' psychological mechanisms of self-control; he feels that the poverty of the lower classes produces frustration that is released in a physical attack on the child.

Another finding in the sociological analysis of child abuse is that the sex of the abuser is often female. Resnick's [18] study of child filicide found that mothers kill more often than fathers (88–43). Of Bennie and Sclare's [2] ten cases of abuse, seven of the abusers were women. Steele and Pollack [21] report that, of their 57 cases of child abuse, the mother was the abuser 50 times. In Zalba's [29] study, the sexes split 50–50 in terms of who was the actual abusing parent. Gil's [9] analysis of cases found that the mother abused children 50% of the time, while the father abused children 40%. (Gil also determined that the reason for this might be the predominance of female headed households.)

Given the culturally defined male-aggressive/female-passive roles in our society and that men are usually more aggressive than women,[19] it might be surprising that females are so highly represented and overrepresented in cases of child abuse. One explanation for this is that the child threatens or interferes with the mother's identity and esteem more than it does the father's. (Except when the father cannot fill the provider role, and children can be seen as a threat to his identity and esteem.[16]) An illustration of this hypothesis is a case cited by Galdston,[8] in which a mother had to quit work as a result of a pregnancy and her husband's desire to return to work. Forced into closer contact with her ten-month-old child, she subse-

quently beat him because she found his cries "so demanding." Other case studies indicate that it is the mother who, through close contact with the child, experiences the frustration of trying to rear and control the child. The child who is perceived by the mother as impinging on her freedom and desires seems to be vulnerable to abuse from the frustrated mother.

THE CHILD WHO IS ABUSED

The most dangerous period for the child is from three months of age to three years. The abused, battered, or murdered child is most vulnerable during those years when he is most defenseless and least capable of meaningful social interaction. Resnick [18] found that the first six months were the most dangerous for the child. Bennie and Sclare [2] report that, in their sample, battered children were usually from two to four months old. Kempe [13] stated that the "Battered Child Syndrome" was most common in children under three years of age, while Galdston [8] found that the most frequent cases of abuse were from three months to three-and-a-half years. It is entirely possible that these data are somewhat misleading, since the vulnerability of a child to physical damage is greater the younger he is. Older children may also be subject to physical abuse, but they might not appear in medical case studies because their age-produced physical durability makes them less vulnerable to serious physical damage caused by abuse.

There are two analytic directions that can be followed. The first is that there is something about parental relations with young, sub-social children that leads some parents to abuse them; the second is that parental abuse of children is not a function of the child's age and that the data are misleading by nonrepresentative and selective gathering of cases. At this point, I would opt for the first direction. There seem to be three interrelated factors that result in the three-month to three-year-old child being particularly vulnerable to parental abuse.

First, the small infant or toddler lacks the physical durability to withstand much physical punishment or force. While an older child might absorb a great deal of physical punishment, the three-month to three-year-old is likely to be severely damaged or even killed by the same type of force. Thus, since the younger child is more likely to be harmed, he is more easily *abused*. Secondly, the fact that the infant is not capable of much meaningful social interaction may create a great deal of frustration for the parent who is trying to interact with the child. The case studies reveal that abusing parents often complain that they hit their child because they could not toilet-train him, get him to stop crying, or get him to obey their commands. Since the parent cannot "reason" with the infant, he may feel his only course of action is physical punishment.

Thirdly, the new or infant child may create stress for the parent by his birth. The new-born child may create economic hardship for the family, or may interfere with professional, occupational, educational, or other plans of the parents. Thus, the new child may create structural stress for his parents, which is responded to by abuse.

THE SOCIAL CONTEXT

Perhaps the best example of the narrowness of the psychopathological approach to child abuse is the fact that it does not examine possible social causes of the psychological stress that it sees as leading to child abuse.

One stress-producing condition is unemployment. O'Brien,[16] in his discussion of the causes of intra-family violence, argues that one should find violence most common in families whose classically dominant member (male-adult-husband) fails to possess the superior skills, talents, or resources on which his preferred superior status is supposed to be based. O'Brien's theory would support the notion that unemployment of the husband would lead to intra-family violence. This assumption is supported in the child abuse literature. Gil[9] found that nearly half of the fathers of abused children were not employed during the year preceding the abusive act, while 12% were unemployed at the time of the abusive act. Galdston[8] also found that, in abusive families, the father of the abused child was unemployed or worked part-time while the wife worked part-time and cared for the child the rest of the time.

A second contextual factor is that the abused child is usually the product of an unwanted pregnancy. The Massachusetts Society for the Prevention of Cruelty to Children reports that in 50% of 115 families studied, there was premarital conception.[29] Wasserman[26] found that, in many of the child abuse cases, the child was conceived out of wedlock. Bennie and Sclare[2] report that the abused child was often the product of an unwanted pregnancy—the pregnancy was unwanted either because it was premarital or inconvenient. In Kempe's[13] Case #1 the battered child was an unwanted one, born soon after marriage "before the parents were ready for it." One of Resnick's[18] cases of child murder reveals that a mother killed after she felt "labor pains" and was afraid she was pregnant again. The mother articulated the stress that another baby would cause by stating "how hard it is to raise even two children."

The finding that the abused child is often the product of an unwanted pregnancy ties in with the finding that the abused child is both young and usually the youngest or only child,[2] and with Gil's [9] finding that there is more abuse in families of four or more children. These findings suggest that a newborn, unwanted child may create a tremendous amount of stress in family life. The child may be a financial burden, an emotional burden, or a psychological burden to the parent or parents who did not plan or want his arrival. Thus, the unwanted child can become the receiver of a parent's aggression, not because of some fantasy or "transference psychosis," but because the unwanted child is, in fact, a source of stress for the family. The abusive parent *is not* lashing out at a *projected* source of his troubles, he is beating a concrete source of family stress—an unwanted child.

The data about unemployment and unwanted children suggest that economic conditions producing stress and frustration are important factors in explaining parental abuse of children. This is a specific example of Goode's [10] general proposition that a family that has little prestige, money, and power suffers greater frustration and bitterness and thus may resort to more violence.[10]

Economic conditions are not the only source of stress that may lead to child abuse. Bennie and Sclare [2] found that in four of seven cases of child abuse, women entered into marriage with men of different religions. The authors propose that intermarriage produced prolonged family stress, which eventually was a variable causing child abuse. Bennie and Sclare also found abusive families characterized by disrupted marital relationships. Zalba [29] also found a great deal of marital and family conflicts in families where there were cases of child abuse.

THE CAUSES OF ABUSE: TOWARD A SOCIAL PSYCHOLOGICAL MODEL

That stress in the family is associated with child abuse is not a sufficient explanation of child abuse. In order to develop a broad causal model of child abuse, one would have to explain why abuse is an adaptation to stress—as opposed to other types of responses.[14] This section extends the analysis of the causes of child abuse by examining the experience of parents with violence.

A review of the literature points out that abusive parents were raised in the same style that they have recreated in the pattern of rearing their own children.[21] Kempe [13] stated that attacking parents were subject to similar abuse as children, and that this pattern of child rearing is passed on in unchanged form. Gil's [9] survey found that 11% of parents who abuse their children were victims of abuse during childhood. Granted, as the authors articulating the psychopathological approach argue, that abuse as a child has psychological consequences, it also has sociological consequences. One factor that determines what form of adaptation a parent will use in dealing with family stress is his own childhood socialization. An individual who was raised by parents who used physical force to train children and who grows up in a violent household has had as a role model the use of force and violence as a means of family problem solving. The parent who recreates the

Figure 1
A SOCIAL PSYCHOLOGICAL MODEL OF THE CAUSES OF CHILD ABUSE

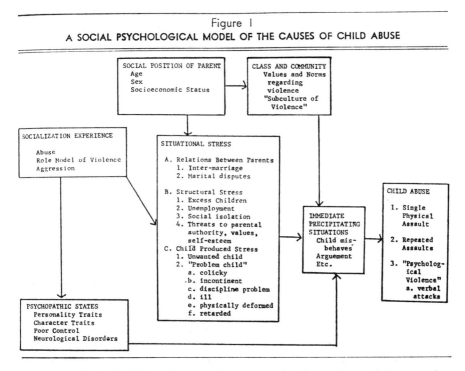

pattern of abusive child rearing may be doing this because this is the means of child rearing he learned while growing up. It is the way he knows of responding to stress and bringing up his child.

Considering this notion of child socialization and its effect on later patterns of child rearing, we may think of child abuse in terms of a social psychological model such as the one in FIGURE 1.

Some people would regard this model as the "social origins of psychopathology," and indeed the model does assume that a certain amount of child abuse is a function of psychopathic states (bottom left box). However, psychopathic states are only a possible, but not necessary, intervening variable in the explanation. The model goes beyond the unicausal approach by analyzing the sociocultural causes of abuse. The model as-

sumes that frustration and stress are important variables associated with child abuse (middle box). Therefore, child abuse can be examined using the frustration-aggression approach.[15] Certain structural conditions,[14] such as social position, family roles, and unemployment (top left box and middle box) are also associated with abusive behavior towards children. In addition, norms concerning appropriate behavior and levels of physical punishment of children are important considerations [27] (top right box). Finally, the role of the child is important (middle and middle right box). The disposition of the child, his behavior, and his demands function as both causal factors and precipitating events of child abuse.

The purpose of presenting this model of factors influencing child abuse is not to suggest an exhaustive list of approaches nor to select one that is superior to the others. Instead, the purpose is to illustrate the complexity and the interrelationships of the factors that lead to child abuse.

CONCLUSION: IMPLICATIONS FOR STRATEGIES OF INTERVENTION AND FUTURE RESEARCH

When a patient is diagnosed as sick, the treatment administered to him is designed to cure his illness. Consequently, when a child abuser is diagnosed as psychopath, the treatment is designed to cure his disease and prevent future episodes that result from the disease. Basically, the cure prescribed is psychological counseling, psychotherapy, psychoanalysis, psychiatric aid, and other psychiatric mechanisms designed to rid the patient of his disorder. So far, the treatment of psychopathic disorders of abusive parents tends to be of limited effectiveness. Psychiatrists feel that treatment of the so-called sociopath or psychopath is rarely successful.[13] With this treatment being of limited utility, the only remaining strategy of intervention is to remove the child from the parents. Even this strategy has little success, since the state cannot keep the child from the parent indefinitely. Elmer[7] reveals the case history of one family in which the child was abused, removed from the family, thrived, returned, and was again beaten.

Thus far, it seems that the existing strategies of intervention in child abuse cases hold little promise for solving the problem. This article suggests that one reason may be that the strategies are based on erroneous diagnoses of the problem. If one steps out of the psychopathological framework, it can be seen that the strategies are designed to cure

symptoms that in many cases, do not exist. If the parent is not a psychopath in any meaningful sense of the word, then how can treatment aimed at eliminating the psychopathy be of consequence?

As far as developing new strategies of intervention, it is now necessary to stop thinking of child abuse as having a single cause: the mental aberrations of the parents. As Gil[9] states, physical abuse of children is not a uniform phenomenon with one set of causal factors—but a multi-dimensional phenomenon. It is time to start thinking about the multiple social factors that influence child abuse. If unemployment and social class are important contextual variables, then strategies to prevent child abuse should aim at alleviating the disastrous effect of being poor in an affluent society. The fact that unwanted pregnancy appears so often in the cases indicates that programs ought to be designed to aid in planned parenthood, birth control devices, etc. Within this area is also a strong argument for the removal of the legal and social stigma of abortion so that unwanted children do not have to be born. And, finally, since there appears to be an association between child rearing and child abuse, programs should be developed to teach parents alternative means of bringing up their children.

The major flaw that exists in current programs and current strategies of intervention is that they amount to "an ambulance service at the bottom of the cliff." Child abuse programs now are after-the-fact treatment of parents and children. What needs to be done is to "fix the road on the cliff that causes the accidents." Strategies should be developed that can deal with the problem before the child is beaten or killed. These programs depend on a predictive theory of child abuse. The social psychological model of child abuse in this paper is a start in that direction.

REFERENCES

1. BECKER, H. 1963. Outsiders: Studies in the Sociology of Deviance. Free Press, New York.
2. BENNIE, E. AND SCLARE, A. 1969. The battered child syndrome. Amer. J. Psychiat. 125(7):975–979.
3. Bibliography on the Battered Child. 1969. U.S. Department of Health, Education, and Welfare. Social and Rehabilitation Service (July).
4. BLUMBERG, M. 1964. When parents hit out. Twentieth Century 173(Winter): 39–44.
5. COLES, R. 1964. Terror-struck children. New Republic 150(May 30):11–13.
6. DUNHAM, H. 1964. Anomie and mental disorder. *In* Anomie and Deviant Behavior, M. Clinard, ed. Free Press, New York.
7. ELMER, E. ET AL. 1967. Children in Jeopardy: A Study of Abused Minors and Their Families. University of Pittsburgh Press, Pittsburgh.
8. GALDSTON, R. 1965. Observations of Children who have been physically abused by their parents. Amer. J. Psychiat. 122(4): 440–443.
9. GIL, D. 1971. Violence against children. J. Marr. Fam. 33(Nov.):637–657.
10. GOODE, W. 1971. Force and violence in the family. J. Marr. Fam. 33(Nov.): 624–636.
11. HAKEEM, M. 1957. A critique of the psychiatric approach to the prevention of juvenile delinquency. Soc. Problems 5 (Fall):194–206.
12. HELFER, R. AND KEMPE, C., eds., 1968. The Battered Child. University of Chicago Press, Chicago.
13. KEMPE, C. ET AL. 1962. The battered-child syndrome. JAMA. 181(July 7):17–24.
14. MERTON, R. 1938. Social structure and anomie. Amer. Sociol. Rev. 3(Oct.):672– 682.
15. MILLER, N. 1941. The frustration-aggression hypothesis. Psychol. Rev. 48:337– 342.
16. O'BRIEN, J. 1971. Violence in divorce prone families. J. Marr. Fam. 33(Nov.): 692–698.
17. REINER, B. AND KAUFMAN, I. 1959. Character Disorders in Parents of Delinquents. Family Service Association of America, New York.
18. RESNICK, P. 1969. Child murder by parents: a psychiatric review of filicide. Amer. J. Psychiat. 126(3):325–334.
19. SINGER, J. 1971. The Control of Aggression and Violence. Academic Press, New York.
20. SPINETTA, J. AND RIGLER, D. 1972. The child abusing parent: a psychological review. Psychol. Bull. 77(April):296–304.
21. STEELE, B. AND POLLACK, C. 1968. A psychiatric study of parents who abuse infants and small children. *In* The Battered Child, R. Helfer and C. Kempe, eds. University of Chicago Press, Chicago.
22. STEINMETZ, S. AND STRAUS, M. 1971. Some myths about violence in the family. Paper read at the meetings of the American Sociological Association.
23. SZASZ, 1960. The myth of mental illness. Amer. Psychol. 15(Feb.):113–118.
24. SZASZ, T. 1961. The Myth of Mental Illness: Foundations of a Theory of Personal Conduct. Delta, New York.
25. SZASZ, T. 1970. The Manufacture of Madness. Harper and Row, New York.
26. WASSERMAN, S. 1967. The abused parent of the abused child. Children 14(Sept.-Oct.):175–179.
27. WOLFGANG, M. AND FERRACUTI, F. 1967. The Subculture of Violence. Tavistock Publications, London.
28. YOUNG, L. 1967. Wednesday's Child: A Study of Child Neglect and Abuse. McGraw-Hill, New York.
29. ZALBA, S. 1971. Battered children. Transaction 8(July-Aug.):68–61.

For reprints: Richard J. Gelles, Department of Sociology and Anthropology, University of Rhode Island, Kingston, R.I. 02881

Psychopathology of the Abusing Parent

MARVIN L. BLUMBERG, M.D.* | *Rego Park, N.Y.*

Child abuse has lately reached epidemic proportions, with the most severe cases occurring in children under three years of age. Psychopathology of abusing parents and contributory factors are analyzed. Many involved families can be rehabilitated. Successful treatment includes psychotherapy for parents and temporary removal of the children from the homes.

Children have been abused, neglected, and killed by ritual, accident, and malicious intent from the dawn of the human race. On the one hand, belief in the will of a deity and the rights of parents have condoned these acts. On the other hand, faith in the myth of the maternal instinct and the widespread notion that everyone loves and protects innocent children have lulled public awareness and have obscured the true extent of child abuse. Long before society took notice of maltreatment of children, it was concerned with harm to domestic animals. In fact, in 1874, when a child named Mary Ellen was found beaten and chained to her bedstead, the American Society for the Prevention of Cruelty to Animals was the only agency that could be persuaded to act in her behalf. Subsequently the first Society for the Prevention of Cruelty to Children was formed in New York City in 1875.

Sporadic medical articles appeared from time to time concerning injuries resulting from child beating. Psychoanalysis began to take hold during the early decades of this century but there was only indirect interest in the emotional aspects of adult child abusers. One of the earliest papers on the subject was written by Freud and was entitled, "A Child is Being Beaten." Significantly it dealt entirely with fantasy. Only during recent years has the abused child merited a focus of attention in medical, social, and legal contexts. A new concept, child advocacy, is now developing on the local, state, and federal levels. The emphasis is being placed on the family as the treatment unit of reference in an attempt to maintain its structural integrity.

The American Academy of Pediatrics sponsored a seminar on child abuse in 1961. In an attempt to increase the awareness and attention of physicians to this problem, the term, "battered child," was created. This has stirred up the medical and legal professions who have been using the expression as a battle cry since then. Kempe and Helfer (1) define the

* Chairman, Department of Pediatrics, Jamaica Hospital, Jamaica, N.Y. *Mailing address:* 98-120 Queens Boulevard, Rego Park, N.Y. 11374.

21

battered child as "any child who received nonaccidental physical injury (or injuries) as a result of acts (or omissions) on the part of his parents or guardians." This definition does not include physical neglect or emotional abuse that may be less obvious but equally or more devastating to the child.

It is impossible to enumerate or even to estimate the true incidence of child abuse for, like an iceberg, the hidden bulk is much greater than the revealed amount. Abusing parents often conceal less serious injuries, private physicians frequently feel constrained not to report or do not bother to report cases, and even hospitals are often negligent in documenting abused children for the authorities. Most of the collected statistics date from the late 1960's. There has been a steady annual increase of cases since then. It is difficult to conclude whether this has been the result of more children actually being abused or better reporting of cases, or both. In any event, it is apparent that child neglect and child abuse have reached epidemic proportions and are major etiologic factors in morbidity and mortality among children.

Three misconceptions must be dispelled at the outset of a psychiatric analysis of child abusing. First, there is no maternal instinct, no universal protecting mother love that endows a biologic parent with automatic cathexis toward her infant. Statistical studies show that 70 per cent or more of all cases of serious child abuse are attributable to the mothers of the children. The vast majority of the victims are under three years of age and most of these are under one year. Second, psychosis is very rarely a factor in child abuse. The number of children harmed or killed by schizophrenic parents is only a very small fraction of the total. The abusing parent is almost always aware of the nature, if not the reason, for his or her act. Alcohol is an important contributory factor in child abuse. Lately, narcotics have also entered the picture as an additional pathogenic influence. Third, as Wertham states (2), the classifying of human violence and aggression as instinctive is a rationalization rather than an explanation. Instead of being considered an ineradicable biologic instinct, violence in general and against children specifically must be viewed as rooted in culturally determined practices, such as child rearing, and cultural exposure to brutality in the public media.

The difference between discipline and punishment on the one hand and abuse on the other hand is qualitative rather than quantitative. The former may be rationalized, justified, or excused as necessary or even beneficial. The latter is inexcusable on any grounds. The motivations and mechanisms behind the two types of aggression differ. Flynn (3) notes that there is a natural attitude or temptation, at least in fantasy, to strike an offensive child. Fantasies are trial actions that have two functions. They make the person aware of what he is tempted to do and they help him to discharge some of his anger. Flynn explains further that, when the idea to hit enters one's consciousness, the pertinent ego mechanisms of reality testing and memory are activated and check the act of violence. In the psychotic or the sociopath with a deficient conscience, these mechanisms are unavailable or ineffective. The sociopath exhibits an extraordinary reliance on the ego defense mechanisms of repression, denial, and projection that produce an incapacity to learn from experience and to appreciate realistically the possible or inevitable consequences of the actions. Thus, the abusing parent tends to project her anger onto the child while denying or repressing it in herself.

Certain aspects of parenthood should be considered in connection with child abuse. Kempe (4) very practically declares that the quality of mothering is a continuum from none of it to a lot of it. By mothering he means caring for a helpless young child and giving of oneself to the child without limit by mother, father, or any other person whether related or not. Very few parents or surrogates have the ability or the capacity to mother 24 hours a day, seven days a week on a continuing basis. Those parents who can afford to hire nursemaids or to avail themselves of day care programs for their children while they pursue occupations out of the home for part of each day are usually better able to cope with parent-child problems than parents who cannot separate from their homes for part of each day. Kempe further states that parents do not mean willfully to kill their children. Most of those who batter their children are caught in a tangle of their own past, each other, the baby, and the crisis situation.

Newberger (5) defines child abuse as an illness, with or without inflicted injury, stemming from threatening situations in the home. He states, "We are coming to see that the essential element in child abuse is not the intention to destroy a child but rather the inability of a parent to nurture his offspring—a failing which can stem directly from ascertainable environmental conditions. . . ."

Coincident with the growing medical and social involvement with the problem of child battering in the early 1960's, psychiatrists became interested in the personality and psychodynamics of abusing parents. There has been continued probing into the factors behind child abuse, such as motivation, demography, psychosocial background, and personality make-up. As is characteristic of much of scientific medical investigation, there have been a number of attempts at nosological and typological classification of abusing parents. The first noteworthy typology was formulated by Merrill in 1962 (6). He described three groups of personality characteristics that applied both to abusing mothers and fathers, and a fourth group applicable only to abusing fathers. The first group of parents showed continual hostility and aggressiveness that may have been focused or generally manifested, that was uncontrollable, and that could be triggered by normal daily difficulties. Their anger stemmed from internal conflicts resulting from early childhood experiences. The second group was characterized by rigidity, compulsiveness, lack of warmth, lack of reasonableness, and lack of flexibility in thinking. Mothers in this group showed severe child rejection. The third group of parents were markedly passive, dependent, moody, and immature. They often competed with their own children for the love and attention of their spouses. The fourth group consisted of young fathers frustrated by physical or other deficiencies that prevented them from being breadwinners while their wives had to work. Their frustrations drove them to angry excessive discipline and punishment for their children.

Further study of abusing parents has demonstrated that there is no specific psychiatric diagnosis that applies to all child abusers nor can any typology like Merrill's be designated for them. There are, however, certain psychodynamic factors in their early histories and in their extant circumstances that serve as frequent common denominators in their psychopathology.

Almost without exception abusing parents were themselves abused, neglected, and deprived of love and mothering when they were children. Because of their own early rejection, they did not develop the ability to love. Thus, as adults they are narcissistic, immature, have poor ego control, and demand nurturing themselves. They have a poor self-image and low self-esteem. They cannot accept any adversity or criticism and react with impulsive violence. Marital difficulties are common among these persons because of their own inner conflicts and because of their frequent poor choice of mates, often those with similar problems.

While fathers have the same abreactive mechanisms as do mothers, mothers have more continued contact with the infants and toddlers in the home so they are by far the more frequently abusive parents. Fathers or paramours with the personality potential for battering do mistreat children when stress occasions arise while the victim is at hand. Child battering occurs at any socioeconomic level so that poverty and lack of education are not necessarily of themselves conducive to violence against children. It must be noted, however, that when underlying personality deficits exist, these conditions may add fuel to the fire.

Concerning the parent-child relationship, several specific situations may exist. Occasionally a child of an unwanted pregnancy or a defective child may be the subject of neglect or abuse. If the pregnancy was not anticipated, sexual guilt feelings may arise or even anger against the father. These will then likely be externalized and projected onto the child. A defective child may be resented and rejected as if he were to blame for his own condition. Often, in these cases, the mother or the father may feel guilty for some fantasied deed or transgression that is believed to have brought on divine retribution in the form of the defective child. The child then becomes the scapegoat for parental anger and frustration.

At other times, a mother may actually want a child with the hope and desire for comfort and love from the child for herself. Since this satisfaction is not forthcoming in a manner to satisfy the mother's unresolved dependency needs, her mechanisms of denial and projection come into play and the child is endowed with her own negative traits. As the baby, feeling rejected, demands more nurturing, the mother's need for nurturing becomes intensified. She seeks and expects gratification from the child. The child's crying is interpreted by her as rejection. This then becomes justification for excessive punishment.

Terr (7) and Green (8) both discuss the phenomenon of role reversal. When her own fragile narcissistic equilibrium is unbalanced by environmental pressures, the potentially abusing parent externalizes and projects her aggressive hostility. Her unconscious thus identifies her child with herself and her own self with her own abusing, rejecting mother. This results in aggressive violence against the child.

A poor husband-wife relationship in which there is a clash of aggressive and passive personalities resulting in an exaggerated dominant-submissive pattern can, as Terr (7) indicates, set the stage for child battering. The hostility that one parent feels toward the other but cannot express because of fear, can be displaced onto the child. A similar mechanism can play a role concerning one parent's child by a previous partner. In a stable husband-wife relationship, both parents share the responsibilities of child rearing in one way or another. Frustrations can be communicated and solutions or advice can be forthcoming. In the case of an unmarried mother or when husband or paramour deserts the home, the mother with a poor ego structure and a vulnerable personality may resort to battering her child when she is faced with stressful situations.

Interestingly, the victimized child, though logically not a prime or causal factor of the hostility that is directed against him, may be a reciprocal stimulus for the continued brutality that he receives. Conscious and subconscious mechanisms provoke him to poor feeding (which usually distresses mothers), excessive crying, overaggression, lying, stealing, and demanding more attention. An abused school-age child may develop behavior problems in class, be a fighter, and may seek to be a scapegoat. These actions add further reason and, in the parent's mind, justification for excessive physical punishment. Occasionally, the excuse of transgression against God and religion is used as a mandate for severe beatings. It can, therefore, be seen that there are cases in which there exists a vicious cycle of abuse-retaliation-abuse.

Sexual abuse of children is an act entirely apart from physical maltreatment. The psychodynamics involved are different in the two occurrences. The former, therefore, must be considered as a separate problem.

A discussion of the psychodynamics and the psychopathology of abusing parents would be incomplete without a consideration of therapy. The reaction of the average socially adjusted person to a child abuser is to demand for him or her severe retribution and to remove the child from the noxious home. It is obvious, though, on careful analysis, that this is no solution. First, there is the dilemma as to whether the harm to the child who is left in an abusive environment of his own family causes more serious consequences than the emotional trauma of separation and placement in another family or in an institution. Second, there are now over 3,000 cases of child abuse and neglect reported annually to the Central Registry in New York City alone. From 1966 to 1970 the increase was 549 per cent and the figure continues to grow (9). Sixty thousand cases were reported in 1972 for the United States as a whole according to Senator Mondale, as reported in the press. Displacing and replacing all of these children is an impossible task. There are, however, constructive suggestions. These all point in the direction of maintaining the family structural integrity by therapy and rehabilitation. Dr. Marianne Schwob, Chairman of the Child Abuse Committee of Roosevelt Hospital in New York City, was quoted in the press as claiming that 75 per cent of the city's abused children can be returned to their parents. Senator Walter Mondale, Chairman of the Senate's Subcommittee on Children and Youth, stated that his subcommittee has found the national average of possible returnees to be 90 per cent. These statements do not imply rehabilitative treatment.

Dr. Vincent J. Fontana operates a combined program at the New York Foundling Hospital for abused children (mainly infants) and their mothers where emotional therapy for the mothers supplements medical treatment for the children. The parents are mothered by selected community volunteer women, by nurses, and by psychiatric social workers under the consultative supervision of psychiatrists. While their own nurturing needs are being satisfied and their ego structures strengthened, the mothers are helped to learn how to nurture and to rear their own children. Upwards of 50 per cent of mothers have been rehabilitated since the inception of the program. This is, of course, the desirable goal rather than considering it relatively safe and expedient just to return the child to the abusing parent, under agency supervision, it may be hoped.

In view of the multiplicity and complexity of subconscious mechanisms involved in the psychodynamics and psychopathology of abusing parents, Flynn (3) advocated individual psychoanalytically oriented psychotherapy for them as the most effective treatment. With a somewhat different view,

Green (8) has gone into considerable detail about direct psychotherapy for the abusing parent with its attendant difficulties and with the need for ancillary support for the child as well as for the parent. When a case of child abuse is brought to the attention of the authorities, the investigation that ensues may well hinder the parent's relationship with the therapist. As a result of her own early rejection and poor self-image, she usually has a basic suspicion and mistrust of any authority, and finds it difficult to accept criticism and advice. This may impede the development of positive transference on her part.

Furthermore, the therapist must be on guard himself. He must control his own feelings lest he develop a negative transference toward his patient. Yet, on the contrary, he must not overidentify with the parent patient in his desire to help. The infantile character of the patient may pose the threat of role reversal on her part. The subject of the abused child must be gradually and cautiously introduced. Otherwise, the narcissistic parent will feel the threat of competition for the attention of the therapist.

Psychotherapy must be aimed at improving the patient's self-image and ego strength. She must abreact her own childhood experiences and understand the relationship with her present emotions and actions. For success, therapy must be combined with a rehabilitation program for parent and child in which the parent is mothered until she can stand alone and where she is taught proper child rearing techniques. If a child is beyond the infant stage, he too may require psychotherapy to undo the effects of the early trauma of physical abuse and emotional rejection.

Green estimates that, with proper combined therapeutic modalities and under optimum conditions, about 80 per cent of parent-child situations can be rehabilitated. Optimum is a concept that must be stressed. Nevertheless, it is a goal to be sought. Of course, the truth must be faced realistically that 20 to 50 per cent of all cases, depending upon time, place, and available facilities, are untreatable. Some parents and some family situations are irremediable under any circumstances. Here there is no choice but to remove the child, possibly to a suitable foster home, or less optimally to an institution.

Recently, group therapy sessions for abusing and potentially abusing parents have been instituted. So far they are few and scattered. Some are associated with day and night "hot lines" for frantic about-to-batter parents. The expectations and preliminary reports from these parents anonymous groups indicate a good probability of success for some participants. The example is taken from such ongoing groups as Alcoholics Anonymous and the narcotic addict rehabilitation groups. One reason for success of abusing parent groups is that the clients do not feel the threat of authority that is inherent in a one-to-one therapeutic relationship. Furthermore, the anonymity of the group suits the person with a poor self-image and low self-esteem. There is also a comforting lessening of guilt feelings in the presence of other similar miscreants. Another practical consideration must not be overlooked. The financial burden of individual psychotherapy is eliminated by the availability of community supported group therapy.

Kempe and Helfer (1) have been attempting to develop a valid simple predictive questionnaire to identify parents who may be potential child abusers. It is suggested that the questionnaire might be administered by professionals or by instructed laymen to new parents in a baby care clinic or during a home visit. High risk parents could then be involved in a supportive, supervised program. In essence this would be a form of prophylactic psychotherapy.

SUMMARY

Physical abuse of children, by parents, has reached epidemic proportions in recent years because of increased societal pressures and other factors. Recently there has been increasing awareness of the magnitude and severity of the problem by medical, psychiatric, and legal professionals.

Most of the severe cases of child abuse occur in children under three years of age and are perpetrated largely by the mothers. The abusing parents almost always were abused and neglected themselves when they were young. Personality characteristics that they possess in common are narcissism, poor self-image and self-esteem, uncontrollable hostility and aggression, rejection, denial, projection, and a strong need for mothering.

Therapeutic goals are ideally aimed at maintaining the family integrity through psychotherapy for the abusing parent and rehabilitative measures for the parent and the child. Some individuals and families are untreatable. There is no choice, then, but to remove the victimized child from the home, for the physical danger outweighs the potential emotional separation trauma. Recently, group therapy sessions for abusing and potentially abusing parents have been meeting with some success.

REFERENCES

1. Kempe, C. H. and Helfer, R. E. Helping the Battered Child and His Family. Lippincott, Philadelphia, 1972.
2. Wertham, F. Battered Children and Baffled Adults. *Bull. N.Y. Acad. Med.,* 48:887, 1972.
3. Flynn, W. R. Frontier Justice: A Contribution to the Theory of Child Battery. *Am. J. Psychiat.,* 127:375, 1970.
4. Kempe, C. H. A Practical Approach to the Protection of the Abused Child and Rehabilitation of the Abusing Parent. *Pediatrics,* Part II, 51:804, 1973.
5. Newberger, E. H. The Myth of the Battered Child Syndrome. *Current Medical Dialog,* April 1973, p. 327. Condensation of a paper presented at the 95th Anniversary Symposium, American Humane Association, October 1971.

6. Merrill, E. J. Physical Abuse of Children: An Agency Study. In *Protecting the Battered Child*. De Francis, V., Ed. American Humane Association, Denver, Colo., 1962.

7. Terr, L. C. A Family Study of Child Abuse. *Am. J. Psychiat.*, 127:125, 1970.

8. Green, A. H. Psychiatric Study and Treatment of Abusing Parents. Paper presented at the 122nd Annual Convention of the American Medical Association, June 1973.

9. Fontana, V. J. Which Parents Abuse Children? *Med. Insight*, October 1971, p. 16.

Child Abuse: Causes and Prevention

Arthur T. Davidson, MD
New York, New York

In every organized society there are certain sensitive barometers that, if properly evaluated, will indicate the state of the health and general welfare of the society in question. Perhaps the most sensitive barometer in determining the quality of the health care delivery system of a country is its infant mortality rate. In the same vein, the overall health and general welfare of a society can be rather accurately determined by the manner in which it cares for, protects, or abuses its children. Indeed, the noted psychiatrist, Noshpitz, stated that "a society succeeds or fails in direct proportion to the way it enhances or impedes the development of its children."[1]

Historical Background

An indepth historical review of the subject of child abuse in the United States reveals three major events: the first was an article appearing in the August 1946 issue of the *American Journal of Roentgenology* entitled,

"Multiple Fractures in the Long Bones of Infants Suffering from Chronic Subdural Hematoma" by the distinguished Columbia University Roentgenologist, Dr. John Caffey.[2]

Here he describes six cases of infants whose principal disease was chronic subdural hematoma and who "exhibited 23 fractures and four contusions of the long bones. In not a single case was there a history of injury to which the skeletal lesions could reasonably be attributed and in no case was there clinical or roentgen evidence of generalized or localized skeletal disease which would predispose to pathological fractures."[2]

Caffey, however, fell into the same trap as many other physicians who see child abuse cases. This was pointed out by Kempe, the second great contributor to the recognition of the problem of child abuse, who stated that "physicians have great difficulty both in believing that parents could have attacked their children and in undertaking the essential questioning of parents on this subject. Many physicians find it hard to believe that such an attack could have occurred and they attempt to obliterate such suspicions from their minds, even in the face of obvious circumstantial evidence."[3]

Caffey, after recognizing that the complete fractures in the femurs of three of his cases could not have been caused by "trivial unrecognizable trauma," gently suggested "that the question of intentional ill-treatment" must be raised.[2]

The second historial milestone

focusing mass public attention on the area of physical child abuse was the coining of the emotional term, "the battered child." This shock-effect term had its origin in a seminar sponsored by the American Academy of Pediatrics in 1961. The participants at this conference were aware that pediatricians were unduly complacent about the problem of child abuse. It was felt that something stark and dramatic had to be done to gain attention and create an impact upon society's universal conscience.[3]

It remained for another individual to create the third milestone — a sort of trilogy — in the area of awakening our nation's conscience to the problem of child abuse. Kempe published an article which outlined the major components of this heinous syndrome.[4] Its essential element was "a clinical condition in young children who have received serious physical abuse, generally from a parent or foster parent." He described, on a single day in November 1963 on the pediatric service of a Colorado General Hospital, four infants suffering from the parent-inflicted battered-child syndrome. Two of the four died of their central nervous system pathology and one died suddenly four weeks later, in an unexplained manner, after discharge from the hospital to his parents.[4] The results of Kempe's report were truly electrifying. Within a brief span of approximately five years, 1963-1968, all states passed laws dealing with the problem and mandated reporting, by health professionals to state agencies, of suspected cases of child abuse.[5,6]

Read at the Sixth Annual Convention and Scientific Assembly of Region I of the National Medical Association, Kiamesha Lake, New York, May 27-30, 1977. Requests for reprints should be addressed to Dr. Arthur T. Davidson, 1378 President Street, New York, NY 11213.

45

The initial definition of child abuse was limited to actual, willful, or intentional physical injury inflicted upon the child by the parent or foster parent. The movement now, however, is away from the narrow confines of this limited definition to a more all-embracing concept. This one includes acts of omission "or neglect" which interfere with the normal development of the child through Dr. Fontana's expanded definition in his "The Maltreated Child"[7] and the broad concepts of Alvy[8] of the Center for the Improvement of Child Caring, Los Angeles, California. The comprehensive report defines child abuse as being collective, institutional and individual in nature.

Definition

The strict definition of the phrase "child abuse" in terms of willful, intentional, physical trauma, which reaches its ultimate in the "battered child" syndrome, is too narrow a premise for this very extensive and paramount problem. In contrast to an act of commission, the almost equally shameful acts of neglect or omission are now recognized as major components of the child abuse syndrome. This confusing interchange of definitions accounts for wide discrepancies in the compilation of statistical data and clouds the overall extent of the problem. Because of the confusion of the terms abuse and neglect, the actual number of child abuse cases reported per year in the United States shows a wide range, usually from 300,000 to 600,000, of which an estimated 6,000 or 10 percent die.[9-11]

Dr. Vincent J. Fontana, Medical Director of New York Foundling Hospital and a tireless worker in the field of child abuse has grown impatient with an effort to distinguish between abuse and neglect. He has now introduced the term "maltreated child" which combines the elements of abuse and neglect but goes further to include all elements of society that affect the emotional, physical, or mental health of the child. He places the responsibility for the abuses, of whatever source, upon the community at large. Indeed he suggests what might be called a community credo which includes the following:

1. All members of the community must recognize their responsibility in the field of child welfare and care.

2. All governmental agencies must subscribe to the essential needs of children in the fields of health, food and nutrition, family and child welfare, education, vocational guidance, and training.

3. There must be a combined effort of governments, international agencies, voluntary agencies, and private citizens to eradicate conditions proving detrimental to the welfare and future of children.[7,12]

The widest dimension to the term child abuse has been given by Alvy.[8] He defines the term in a comprehensive manner consisting of three types of child abuse: (1) collective abuse; (2) institutional abuse; and (3) individual abuse.

Collective abuse has as its frame of reference all of those attitudes collectively held by our society that impede the psychological and physical development of children. This would include racial, sex, and social discrimination; substandard child-rearing environments that commonly exist in most racially segregated and economically impoverished neighborhoods in the United States. He quotes the figures from the US Bureau of Census, 1972, which state that seven million children are being raised in the abusive child-rearing conditions of poverty.

Institutional abuse includes all abusive and damaging acts perpetrated against children by such stalwart institutions as schools, juvenile courts, child welfare agencies, and correctional facilities.

Individual abuse encompasses the traditional physical and emotional abuse and neglect of children that result from willful, intentional acts of commission or deliberate acts of omission or neglect on the part of parents or other individual caretakers which result in physical and emotional trauma to the child.[8]

Causes

The syndrome of physical child abuse is only the symptomatic manifestation of a complex family sickness that breaks under a societal crisis.[13]

The vast majority of prima facie cases of physical child abuse are composed of three factors: the abusing parent or parents; the abused child; and a crisis situation.

The child abusers most often have a history of abuse as a child. An indepth analysis and evaluation of the psychological make-up of the child abuser reveals the following negative factors: (1) low frustration tolerance, (2) low self-esteem, (3) impulsivity, (4) dependency, (5) immaturity, (6) severe depression, and (7) role reversals.

The problem of role reversals is extremely interesting in that these individuals expect their children to function as adults while they, the parents, are engaged in an almost childlike preoccupation with self.[14]

The typically abused and/or neglected child has the following characteristics: (1) under three years of age, (2) more frequently a male, and (3) somewhat different. This would include the hyperactive child or seemingly apparent personality traits different from the other children.

Crisis

Given an unstable parent and the "slightly different child," another factor usually must be added to this equation which acts as the spark to ignite the powder keg. This crisis incident usually is external in origin and societal in nature. In many instances, it is the grinding, relentless, self-demeaning poverty but this, all authorities in the field unanimously agree, is not to infer that low socioeconomic status is the primary crisis problem. Since child abusers are found in all strata of our society, this crisis episode in many cases is unrelated to apparent economic difficulty.

The situational stress leading to crisis may take many forms and may be associated with economic stress, job insecurity, and alcohol and drug abuse.

46

Prevention

Comprehensive Programs

The approaches to prevention of child abuse, in general, depend on which of the etiological types of child abuse that we are dealing with. This is why I particularly favor the three-tier definition of Alvy.[8]

The commonly held but narrow view of child abuse from an individual standpoint deals primarily with physical abuse and emotional trauma to the child. Prevention takes two forms: (1) preincidence or before-the-fact intervention and (2) postincidence or after-the-fact intervention.

In the first category, the health professional is concerned with recognizing those telltale symptoms (usually in the abusing parent) that would lead to an explosive outburst. A recent report from the Colorado General Hospital and the University of Colorado Medical Center indicates that potential child abusers sometimes develop "functional" or "psychosomatic" illness to signal their need for help.[15]

One illustrative case was of a 31-year-old man who was seen in the Emergency Room complaining of chest pains and weakness in the legs. After a thorough physical examination, which was completely negative, a psychiatric evaluation was done. It was then learned that the alleged symptoms had begun two weeks after he had gained custody of a six-year-old stepson. The patient used the term "hateful" to describe the child. Recognizing the potential setting for an impending disaster, the physicians wisely chose to send the child to live with relatives and to have the patient and his wife attend the psychiatric clinic.[15]

Most authorities in the field of child abuse are of the opinion that preventive measures for individual abuses should begin by prenatal, perinatal, and postnatal observations. Prenatally, the mother's psychological profile in respect to the expected child is observed. The following questions should be considered. Is there an attempt to deny that there is a pregnancy? Is this child going to be one child too many? Could this be the 'last straw'? Is there great depression over this pregnancy? Is the mother alone and frightened, especially by the physical changes caused by the pregnancy? Do careful explanations fail to dissipate these fears? and Is support lacking from husband and/or family?

During delivery, fathers are encouraged to be present. The reaction of the parents to the child is carefully noted. Specifically, are the parents passive, showing no active interest in the baby or not holding it?

The postpartum and pediatric checkups are extremely important to note: (1) Does the mother have fun with the baby? (2) Does the mother establish eye contact with the baby? (3) Are most of her verbalizations negative?

A broader and relatively novel prevention approach was suggested by Kempe,[4] who suggested that the United States develop a system of lay health visitors, probably nurses, who visit every child during the first four years of life. He, in effect, proposes a universal health visitors system. This is patterned on the European visiting nurse system where nurses periodically visit the homes of newborn and preschool children. The unique features of Kempe's preventive report are the following two elements. First, it would be compulsory, and secondly, it would be a universal service. He aptly compares his health visitors system to the present public school system which is, of course, compulsory and universal by law. He expects the anticipated human cry that his system would certainly generate outcry similar to that of a hundred years ago, when the concept of free compulsory universal public education was first seriously suggested to an unready public. Today, of course, we recognize that basic education is the right of every child. The concept of Kempe has its parallel in the preventive programs of other dedicated workers in this field when they speak of a bill of rights for children. Kempe recognizes the basic common-law tenet of the parent/child relationship with its protected rights from intrusion by the state. However, Kempe, without apparently knowing it, is on very sound grounds when he advocates state interference based on the protection of an overriding public policy. He rightfully points out the many areas in which the state does intervene into what might be called traditional private areas of a free society. He brings up an interesting point — which is that the traditional support of pediatric care depends, in large part, on parental motivation. In effect, a willing mother brings a wanted child to the pediatrician for well-baby care. These healthy, happy people, as he pointed out, are delighted to keep their appointments. They are a joy for us to have in our offices and they make our days pleasant and fulfilling ones.

He rightfully points out that these people do deserve excellent care. But, he goes further and, as in Sinclair Lewis' *Main Street*, disturbs our complacency by treating of alien themes. Specifically he asks us to direct our attention to the isolated families — the unmotivated families, the families who break appointments — the families who are unappreciative and unresponsive. It is to these people he is asking us as health professionals to reach out to protectively. When we are rebuffed by them, instead of uttering the time honored phrase, "well we tried," he is demanding that we say instead, "this behavior is so unusual and worrisome that we must intervene actively." It is at this point he would mandate active intervention by child protective services initiated on the complaint of the physician or other health professionals.

He suggests that such a program be administered by our municipal or state health departments. However, he rightfully points out that if these antiquated and creeky bureaucratic machines are unwilling or unable to handle the task, we should utilize our hospitals as bases from which to establish a system of aftercare. He is asking that we extend our aftercare program for at least five years. He points to such countries as France and Holland where monetary stipends are given to those families with young children that seek health care. In a cost-conscious society Kempe addresses himself to the cost of such an ambitious program. He asked for a reordering of our priorities with emphasis on spending before, rather than after, the fact. He uses a lower figure of 300,000 cases of annual child abuse and neglect in the United States, with 60,000 children receiving significant injuries, 2,000 dying, and 6,000 having permanent brain damage. The cost of providing institutional care for a severely brain-damaged child in the United States is approximately $700,000 for a lifetime. He sums up his program by stating that (1) in a free society, the newborn child does not belong to the state nor to his

47

parents, but to himself in the charge of his parents; and (2) universal, egalitarian, and compulsory health supervision in the broadest sense of the term is the right of every child.[4]

Access to regular health supervision should not be left to the motivation of the parents but must be guaranteed by society.[16]

Kempe feels that even though a man's home may be his castle, that does not give him a constitutional protective right to keep his child a prisoner in this dungeon.

Present Partial Program

There are currently a number of programs of a limited scope which address themselves to the prevention of child abuse. One of these is the Education for Parenthood Program. This program, which began in 1972 as a joint venture of the US Office of Education and the Office of Child Development, has as its goal the preparation of teenage boys and girls for effective parenthood through high school-based educational experiences about child development and the role of parent, and by participatory observation experiences with young children in day care, nursery school, and kindergarten settings. This program has high potential because (1) it exposes teenagers to the various stages of human development through classroom and field experiences; and (2) it exposes these teenagers to child care workers who are particularly sensitive to the needs of children and who are capable of helping the children to channel their aggression in appropriate ways.[8] The program should be available in all high schools, probably on a compulsory basis.

A second excellent prevention program that is already in operation is the Home Start Program of the Office of Child Development. This grew out of the Headstart Program, which of itself has abuse prevention potentials. Specifically, the Home Start Program sends trained caseworkers into the homes of economically disadvantaged families who have three to five-year-old children. These home workers are able to offer counseling and help with a variety of problems. It serves as a link between the family and community services such as employment counseling, job training, drug counseling, and psychotherapy. The program should be extended to homes with children under three years of age and should be nationwide. This program is, in effect, a mini-type health visitors system of Kempe.

Although not specifically designed as a child abuse prevention program, Headstart projects, which began in the 1960s, were shown to have great primary abuse prevention potentials because their programs served as a catalyst to the communities to improve their educational, health, and social services to the poor. The programs are based in local centers rather than the home. They are directed towards poverty families and consist of one-year programs that provide health, nutritional, educational, social and psychological services to economically disadvantaged pre-schoolers. Community Mental Health Centers and children's services departments, should and could deliver mental health services to family groups. The adult education programs of the public school system could and should offer parent training programs. The early periodic screening, diagnosis, and treatment programs have excellent records in providing health care for many children. However, these programs are only for Medicaid clients and only those clients who are motivated to present their children for screening.

Another program that deserves mentioning is Parents Anonymous. This is a volunteer self-help program composed of child-abusing parents and patterned after Alcoholics Anonymous. Like AA, it provides these parents with an opportunity to talk over their common problems. However, unlike AA, The Parents Anonymous group has as its sponsor a social worker or another professional concerned with child abuse.

Conclusion

Child abuse is a symptom complex of a family sickness that has as its etiology the impact of negative societal stresses upon a psychologically inadequate parent which surfaces at a crisis point and results in intentional, willful, physical, emotional, or psychological harm to a child.

Acknowledgment

The writer wishes to acknowledge the help and contribution of Mrs. Edith A. Taub, Director of the Library, Methodist Hospital of Brooklyn, for obtaining reprints of the reference articles and Mrs. Marion Paige for the typing and researching of this manuscript.

Literature Cited

1. Noshpitz JD: Issues and approaches in child psychiatry. Hosp Community Psychiatry 25:96-97, 1974
2. Caffey J: Multiple fractures in the long bones of infants suffering from chronic subdural hematoma. Am J Roentgenol 56(2):163-173, 1946
3. Kempe C, Helfer RE: Helping the battered child and his family. In The Battered Child, (ed 2). Chicago, University of Chicago Press, 1974, pp 120-122
4. Kempe CH, Silverman FN, Steele BF, et al: The battered-child syndrome. JAMA 181:(1)17-24, 1962
5. Wilcox DP: Child abuse laws: past, present, and future. Jour Forensic Sciences 21(1):71-75, 1976
6. DeFrancis V, Lucht C: Child abuse legislation in the 1970s, rev ed. Denver, The American Humane Association Childrens Division, 1974
7. Fontana VJ: The Maltreated Child: The Maltreatment Syndrome in Children. Springfield, Illinois, Charles C Thomas, 1971, pp 32-57
8. Alvy KT: Preventing child abuse. Am Psychol, 1975, pp 921-927
9 Solomon T: History and demography of child abuse. Pediatrics, 51(2):773-776, 1973
10, Nagi S: Child abuse and neglect programs: A national overview. Child Today, May-June, 1975
11. Congressional Record-Proceedings and Debates of the 93rd Congress, First Session (Senate). USA 119(39):S4444. pp 1-9. Washington (Tuesday, March 13, 1973)
12. Polansky NA, Hally C, Polansky NF: Profile of Neglect: A Survey of the state of knowledge of child neglect. US Department of Health, Education, and Welfare, Social and Rehabilitation Service, Community Services Administration, 1975
13. Ebeling NB, Hill DA (eds): Child Abuse: Invervention and Treatment. Acton, Massachusetts, Publishing Sciences Group, Inc, 1975, pp 58-65
14. Hindman M: Child abuse and neglect: The alcohol connection. Alcohol Health and Research World, 1977, pp 3-7
15. Child Abusers Often Given Medical Signals. The New York Times, Sunday, April 17, 1977, p 8
16. Kempe CH: Approaches to preventing child abuse: The health visitors concept. Am J Dis Child 130:941-947, 1976

48

Child abusers as parents and children: a review

Srinika Jayaratne

Are the assumptions about child abuse based on valid evidence? The author analyzes the documentation in the literature concerning two widely held beliefs about child-abusing parents and suggests further study that is needed.

Srinika Jayaratne, Ph.D., is Assistant Professor of Social Work, University of Oklahoma, Norman. *The preparation of this article was facilitated by the bibliography collected under HEW Grant No. 84-P 96805/0–01, directed by Diane Green, MSW, Assistant Professor of Sociology, Washington State University, Pullman.*

CHILD ABUSE is an ugly fact of life that is difficult to understand. The dimensions of the problem are tremendous as seen in the following statistics. In 1972 alone, according to Nagi, approximately 600,000 children were reported to local protective service agencies for abuse, neglect, or both.[1] Cohen and Sussman estimate that each year an additional 325,000 cases are unreported.[2] Even though the various states use diverse reporting procedures and definitions so that the figures on which this estimate is based are somewhat inconsistent, the total is still staggering.[3]

A recurring statement in the literature is the notion that "child abuse is not committed just by them"—that is, people of the lower classes.[4] As Hopkins has indicated, "an observer would find these people to be very much like any other group of parents."[5] In one of the first and most significant studies on child abuse, Gil surveyed the attitudes and opinions of a national random sample. Nearly 23 percent of the respondents thought they could at some time injure a child.[6]

Many professionals have argued that not age, sex, race, occupation, education, or income has any direct and significant correlation with child abuse.[7] According to this position, the abuse of children and the potential for such abuse are representative characteristics of parents in the United States. Although this may be a legitimate statement, it is not substantiated by empirical evidence; furthermore, it is debated in the literature. Gil, for example, points out that "physical abuse of children . . . was found to be overconcentrated among the poor and among non-white minorities."[8] Galdston, Gelles, and Paulson and Blake have reported similar findings.[9] Others claim that these findings involve reporting biases and institutional racism.[10]

The relationship of ethnic background to child abuse is pointed up in the following statement by Blanchard: "In my nine years with the Bureau of Indian Affairs, I am not aware of a single case of child abuse among Pueblo Indians."[11] Although this statement does not indicate that child abuse is nonexistent among Pueblo Indians, it raises critical questions about the definition of abuse and about the imposition of sociocultural values and norms on different ethnic groups.

Variance in definition and in cultural values are phenomena that are little explained and researched in child abuse. Philosophically, Gil is probably right in stating that the root cause of the problem lies in the social class structure of this society and that the solution lies in the elimination of poverty and degradation.[12] Unfortunately, even those who agree with Gil's view admit that the revolutionary changes he proposes are unlikely to occur for a long time. It is perhaps, then, practicality that has led the majority of clinical workers to concentrate their interventive efforts on the psychosocial phenomena related to child abuse. Most of the writings in the area pertain to the psychological makeup of the abusing parent, and their authors probably subscribe to Steele's proposition:

> Basic and constant in the instigation of abuse is the psychologic set of the parent which creates a recognizable style or pattern of parent-child interaction in which abuse is likely to happen.[13]

Although this proposition sounds reasonable enough, the total picture of child abuse is much more complex and bewildering. For example, as Steele and Pollock note:

> Child abusers have been described as "immature," "impulse ridden," "dependent." . . . Such adjectives are essentially appropriate to those who abuse children, yet these qualities are so prevalent among people in general that they add little to specific understanding.[14]

In a sense, this is a contradictory statement, but a significant one nonetheless. The literature is replete with these and other such terms describing abusing parents, and it is an arduous task to search for their origin.

The intent of this article is to analyze the two most common sociocultural statements about abusing parents in terms of their empirical and clinical validity. The author is not concerned with the myriad definitions

"Schools and institutions in the United States provide information on family planning and birth control, but offer little assistance with the care and upbringing of progeny."

PARENTAL INADEQUACY

It is an unfortunate social reality that parenting is primarily a generational art. Schools and institutions in the United States provide information on family planning and birth control, but offer little assistance with the care and upbringing of progeny. It is therefore not surprising to find that most people rely on their "parental instincts," personal experiences, and self-selected readings and observations when it comes to child rearing.

In essence, all of us are inadequately socialized to the role of parent. Inadequacy as used in the literature is a generic term that encompasses all facets of parental incapacity. The first question, then, that emerges is this: Why do only some parents abuse their children? The generational hypothesis —that abuse leads to abuse—has been the primary answer. This is not to say that there are no other causal factors, but rather that this one is the most prominently mentioned in the literature. In pursuing this proposition two related questons emerge: Are the abusing parents more inadequate in their parenting than the nonabusing parents? If they are, how do the abusing and the nonabusing differ?

De Lissovoy studied a group of nonabusing teenage parents over a period of three years. He reported that in general his subjects tended to be impatient, irritable, and prone to use punishment in their interactions with their children. Furthermore, they were unfamiliar with developmental norms, and followed their own parents' advice of "doing what comes naturally."[15] Abusing parents have been systematically described as interacting in similar ways. This then raises the basic question of stylistic differences between abusing and nonabusing parents.

Some agencies and organizations recognize that parental inadequacy is the norm and have attempted to rec-

tify the situation by launching educational programs. In Pittsburgh, an experimental project begins parent education before the child is born; in Oklahoma City, mental health authorities distribute booklets to new parents describing the needs of the newborn.[16] These are examples of preventive efforts being directed to average parents, regardless of the potential for abuse. Such programs are particularly valuable since the basic philosophy of the laws of the United States gives parents broad freedom in child-rearing.[17] Unusual circumstances must arise before the child's rights receive attention.

Given the natural risk of inadequate parenting and the probability that among child abusers other interacting variables will compound the problems even further, those concerned with the welfare of children may well agree with Hammell that the "responsibility to assess parental capacity is inescapable and is the core of professional knowledge."[18] On the other hand, the following statements that are presented as a sine qua non in the clinical arena seem open to question:

1. "The distinguishing features of the abusing parents were their attitudes toward discipline and child-rearing."[19]

2. "Parenting is learned, and battering parents have usually been taught some very potent lessons by their own parents."[20]

In the opinion of this author, there is little or no empirical evidence to substantiate the idea that abusing parents follow parenting practices that are significantly different from those of nonabusing parents. This statement is made in view of the lack of comparison group studies to test that assumption.

Consider the following reviews of the literature or of clinical case studies of child abuse. Kaufman, reviewing the

work of Steele and his colleagues in Denver, reported that "the common denominator of all their patients who abused children was a pattern of child-rearing characterized by premature demand for high performance."[21] This is, however, an empirical question requiring the presence of a nonabusing comparison group. Similarly, Paulson and Blake, in considering studies of child abuse, point out that "inappropriate and distorted concepts of the nature and limits of discipline in child rearing are generally noted in the literature."[22] Here again, the conclusions were drawn from studies of abusing parents only, not from comparison of the abusing and the nonabusing. Nonetheless, the need for retraining in the parenting styles of abusers has been expressed vehemently by many authors.[23]

Roth presented clinical procedures for intervention with abusing parents and suggested that the teaching of parenting be a central part of the treatment regimen.[24] Burland, Andrews, and Headsten—in reviewing the record of 28 abused or severely neglected children—pointed out that inadequate parenting was expressed in a wide variety of behaviors.[25] Steele and Pollock studied 60 abusing families intensively for a period of five years and concluded that these parents made inappropriate demands and had unrealistic expectations regarding the capabilities of their children.[26] In the one control group study that the author encountered, Melnick and Hurley found that the abusing parents exhibited general difficulties with parenting, especially with regard to empathy toward their children.[27] However, the validity of this study is minimized by the small sample size.

REPARENTING

It is perhaps fair to say that the literature of child abuse agrees virtually unanimously that an educational program in reparenting is a critical factor in the treatment regimen. The two major reviews of the literature in the area by Lystad and Spinetta and Rigler essentially came to that conclusion.[28] However, three critical questions need to be answered prior to proceeding with intervention:

1. If all parents are potential abusers, how different are the child-rearing practices of the abusers and the nonabusers? Here the issues of definition and culture seem to transcend the problem. Blumenthal, Chadiha, Cole, and Jayaratne, reporting on a national study of attitudes toward violence, state that 48 percent of all respondents and 66 percent of black respondents indicated that under certain circumstances they would punish their children by hitting them with a belt or paddle.[29] Is this child abuse? If it is, does this mean that a massive national program of parent education is needed?

2. Are those involved in reparenting aware of and sensitive to cultural differences in child-rearing practices, or are they applying the middle-class yardstick as the criterion? Little is known about child-rearing practices in general, and even less is known about those of cultural and ethnic minorities. The work of Hoffman and Salzstein, among others, provides evidence that class differences exist in child rearing.[30] Similarly, Blumenthal et al note that "it is clear from the data that black respondents have very different norms about the use of physical punishment than do whites in the sample."[31] Given Gil's findings about the prevalence of abuse among the lower classes and the inherent probability of biased reporting, is a problem being created when it does not exist or a different value system being imposed when it should not be?[32]

3. What or whose child-rearing practices are being transmitted in parenting classes? Perhaps one could argue that socioemotional and affective aspects of parent-child interaction are sufficiently universal that they transcend class and culture. Also it is quite feasible to teach parents developmental norms without imposing values. What about discipline and paren-

tal expectations? Are these not affected by class and culture? Can values be dissociated from convictions in this sensitive area? Tracy and Clark maintain that, in the treatment of child abusers, similarity in racial (and possibly socioeconomic) background will engender a better therapeutic relationship.[33] Training in clinical procedures, however, should play a critical and significant role in the entire process. In the long run, the training of those conducting parent education classes, their background, and the ideas they are transmitting must be systematically evaluated.

GENERATIONAL HYPOTHESIS

The generational phenomenon of child abuse is one of the most commonly held conceptions (or misconceptions) about abusing parents. The essence of this proposition is that the victim of abuse incorporates patterns of aggression, which are then repeated from generation to generation. This position is illustrated in the works of numerous authors.[34]

Even a superficial survey of the literature reveals that many subscribe to the premise that "out of the ranks of today's maltreated children . . . will emerge tomorrow's maltreating parents."[35] In a review article, for example, Wasserman argued that battering parents felt that their own parents were punishing them when they were rejected.[36] Burland et al. in their review of 28 case records indicated that "parents who abuse their children usually themselves were abused as children."[37] Helfer, discussing the etiology of child abuse, said that abusing parents "invariably have had some kind of disastrous rearing experience when they were small."[38]

Despite the formidable array of authors and studies, Kadushin, in reviewing the literature, concluded: "There is little valid evidence to support the theory that abusive parents were themselves abused as children."[39] The need for validity in the evidence reported in the literature is an important point. A major and continuing problem with respect to validity is the lack of a normative comparison group. Also, the

findings in a significant national study by Gil show that only 14.1 percent of the mothers and 7 percent of the fathers in the abusing sample had been victims of abuse in their childhood.[40]

EMOTIONAL ABUSE

It appears, then, that Lystad's review article, concluding that the generational phenomenon is "particularly well documented in the study of child abuse," is questionable, even from a purely definitional perspective.[41] For example, Steele and Pollock found that "several" of their subjects had experienced severe abuse but "a few reported never having a hand laid on them."[42] The primary causal factor appeared to be emotional stress rather than physical abuse per se. What explanation, then, can be offered for the presence of nonabused parents in this abusing sample? Similarly, Fontana concluded that abusing parents were emotionally crippled because of unfortunate childhood experiences.[43] Young reported that approximately 51 percent of the abusing parents in her study came from homes where they were physically abused or neglected—"more from neglecting"—but that no direct attempt was made to evaluate these circumstances.[44] In both these studies, the evidence seems tangential at best.

Silver, Dublin, and Lourie studied the case records of 34 suspected and proved battered children over a period of four years. They concluded that "the child who experiences violence as a child has the potential of becoming a violent member of society in the future."[45] These authors, however, were referring to generalized violence rather than to child abuse. Similar conclusions were reached via case-record analysis by Morris, Gould, and Matthews and by McHenry, Girdnay, and Elmer.[46] All these studies are fraught with the inherent weaknesses of the analytic procedures involved, such as differential recording and differences in interpretation.

In addition to the methodological weaknesses, there appears to be confusion of definitions between the generations. Whereas the vast majority of

> *"In the opinion of this author there is little or no empirical evidence to substantiate the idea that abusing parents follow parenting practices that are significantly different from those of nonabusing parents."*

child abuse studies deal with physical injury to the child, the etiological descriptions of parental experiences is not as clear-cut. As an illustration, consider the study by Tuteur and Glotzer, which looked at ten mothers who murdered their children. Not even a hint of physical abuse is evident in the mothers' backgrounds. "All of them grew up in emotionally cold, and often directly rejecting family environments." [47] Could it not be said, then, that "emotional abuse" and "physical abuse" are being considered as a single phenomenon? If they are a single phenomenon, then the sample is biased when only hospital cases, or other cases in which physical damage was done, are being evaluated. If they are different phenomena, then equating the two in etiological analyses will result in inaccurate and unreliable data. Whether they should be considered together or separately is an issue for discussion in the literature. [48]

When variance and inconsistency in definition exist and when the validity of evidence is questionable, important clinical questions such as these are likely to arise:

■ If abuse is a generational phenomenon, what happened to the adult siblings of the abusing parents? Although physical violence could conceivably be directed at only one child in a family, some studies suggest generalized abuse of all the brothers and sisters as the norm. [49] In addition, it is known that aggressive behavior is learned through observation and modeling. This theoretical perspective, then, leads to the need to study the adult siblings of abusing parents. Could it be that these siblings also are abusing their children but have escaped detection? If the generational phenomenon is viable, such a study might lead to the detection and prevention of further child abuse. If the generational hypothesis is not valid,

significant clinical data could be gathered as to why these siblings did not grow up to be abusing parents.

■ How different are the childhood experiences of abusing parents from their nonabusing counterparts? This obviously requires experimental studies utilizing comparison groups. [50] Furthermore, if such studies are to be truly productive, they must differentiate between the concepts of emotional and physical abuse.

■ Can it really be said that childhood experience is a valid predictor of adult behavior? This is purely a methodological issue, and pertains to the temporal aspects of the generational phenomenon. Furthermore, available data do not substantiate the direct and significant correlation that —according to the generational hypothesis—exists between abuse experience and abusing behavior. It is perhaps too simplistic to argue that innumerable events occurred during the period under consideration (from the time the parents allegedly were abused until the time they were abusing their own children) and that some of these happenings might explain much of the variance. This is nonetheless true, and the simplicity of the explanation belies the complexity of the picture.

CONCLUSION

In general, the literature suggests that parental inadequacy and misinformation are major contributing factors to child abuse. Where the studies in the literature fail is in the examination and delineation of different parenting styles between abusing and nonabusing family systems. This qualitative difference should be investigated from different cultural perspectives before parent training programs are implemented. The failure to base clinical intervention on empirical data is likely to result in redundant effort and little

success. As Oettinger points out, it is imperative to discover "the factors which contribute to parental inability to provide proper care for their young." [51]

With regard to the generational hypothesis of child abuse, the author is somewhat skeptical. Although, as Zalba maintains, "the epidemiological implications are rather serious," the literature is spotted with definitional confusion, poor methodology, clinical assumptions, and a definite "Rosenthal Effect"—that is, fulfilling a priori expectations of the research. [52] Virtually every clinical study encountered in carrying out the research on which this article is based delved into the notion that abuse leads to abuse and virtually all emerged successful—that is, emerged proving the notion. There is little doubt that experiential and observational learning play a significant role in parenting practices, but the available data on the generational hypothesis do not stand the test of empiricism. If this perspective is to be clinically legitimate, it must be empirically validated.

NOTES AND REFERENCES

1. Saad Z. Nagi, "Child Abuse and Neglect Programs: A National Overview," *Children Today*, 4 (May–June 1975), pp. 13–17.
2. Stephen J. Cohen and Alan Sussman, "The Incidence of Child Abuse in the United States," *Child Welfare*, 54 (June 1975), pp. 432–443.
3. Ibid, p. 16.
4. Richard G. Farrow, "Violence," *"The National Humane Review* (September 1972), p. 13.
5. Joan Hopkins, "The Nurse and the Abused Child," *Nursing Clinics of North America*, 5 (December 1970), p. 590.
6. David G. Gil, *Violence Against Children* (Massachusetts: Harvard University Press, 1970), p. 138.
7. Brandt F. Steele, "Working With Abusive Parents: A Psychiatrist's View," *Children Today*, 4 (May–June 1975), pp. 3–5; and Sidney Wasserman, "The Abused Parent of the Abused Child," *Children*, 4 (1967), pp. 175–179.
8. David G. Gil, "A Socio-Cultural Perspective on Physical Child Abuse," *Child Welfare*, 50 (July 1971), p. 392.
9. Richard G. Galdston, "Observations on Children Who Have Been Physically Abused and Their Parents," *American*

Journal of Psychiatry, 122 (April 1965), pp. 440–443; Richard Gelles, "Child Abuse As Psychopathology: A Sociological Critique and Reformulation," *American Journal of Orthopsychiatry*, 43 (July 1973), pp. 611–621; and Morris J. Paulson and Phillip R. Blake, "The Physically Abused Child: A Focus On Prevention," *Child Welfare*, 48 (February 1969), pp. 86–95.

10. Richard J. Light, "Abused and Neglected Children in America: A Study of Alternative Policies," *Harvard Educational Review*, 43 (1975), pp. 556–596; and John J. Spinetta and David Rigler, "The Child Abusing Parent: A Psychological Review," *Psychological Bulletin*, 77 (April 1972), pp. 296–304.

11. Evelyn L. Blanchard, *The American Indian Perspective* (Albuquerque, N. M.: Bureau of Indian Affairs), p. 126. (Mimeographed.)

12. Gil, *Violence Against Children*.

13. Brandt F. Steele, "Parental Abuse of Parents and Small Children," in Elwyn J. Anthony and Therese Benedek, eds., *Parenthood* (Boston: Little, Brown & Co., 1970), p. 450.

14. Brandt F. Steele and Carl B. Pollock, "The Battered Child's Parents," in Arlene S. Skolnick and Jerome H. Skolnick, eds., *Family in Transition* (Boston: Little, Brown & Co., 1971), p. 360.

15. Vladimir De Lissovoy, "Child Care By Adolescent Parents," *Children Today*, 2 (July–August 1973), pp. 22–25.

16. *See* Stephanie Murphy, "Children's Programs: Meeting Some of the Needs," *Innovations*, 3 (Fall 1975), p. 24.

17. Michael G. Paulsen, "The Law and Abused Children," in Ray E. Helfer and C. Henry Kempe, eds., *The Battered Child* (Chicago: University of Chicago Press, 1968).

18. Charlotte L. Hammell, "Preserving Family Life for Children," *Child Welfare*, 10 (December 1969), p. 41.

19. Hopkins, op. cit., p. 590.

20. Elizabeth Davoren, "Working with Abusive Parents: A Social Worker's View," *Children Today*, 4 (May–June 1975), p. 2.

21. Irving Kaufman, "The Physically Abused Child," in Nancy B. Ebeling and Deborah A. Hill, eds., *Child Abuse Intervention and Treatment* (New York: Publishing Science, 1975), p. 81.

22. Paulson and Blake, op. cit., p. 87.

23. *See*, for example, J. Alexis Burland, Roberta G. Andrews, and Sally J. Headsten, "Child Abuse: One Tree In the Forest," *Child Welfare*, 52 (November 1973), pp. 585–592; Davoren, op. cit.;

Hammell, op. cit.; Joan C. Holter and Stanford B. Friedman, "Principles of Management In Child Abuse Cases," *American Journal of Orthopsychiatry*, 38 (January 1968), pp. 127–135; Hopkins, op. cit.; Alfred Kadushin, *Child Welfare Services* (New York: Macmillan Co., 1974); Barry Melnick and John R. Hurley, "Distinctive Personality Attributes of Child-Abusing Mothers," *Journal of Consulting and Clinical Psychology*, 33 (December 1969), pp. 746–749; Frederick Roth, "A Practice Regimen for Diagnosis and Treatment of Child Abuse," *Child Welfare*, 54 (April 1975), pp. 268–273; Steele, "Working with Abusive Parents: A Psychiatrist's View"; Steele and Pollock, op. cit.; and Wasserman, op. cit.

24. Roth, op. cit.

25. Burland, Andrews, and Headsten, op. cit.

26. Steele and Pollock, op. cit.

27. Melnick and Hurley, op. cit.

28. Mary H. Lystad, "Violence At Home: A Review of the Literature," *American Journal of Orthopsychiatry*, 45 (April 1975), pp. 328–344; and Spinetta and Rigler, op. cit., pp. 296–304.

29. *See* Monica D. Blumenthal, Letha B. Chadiha, Gerald A. Cole, and Toby E. Jayaratne, *More About Justifying Violence* (Ann Arbor: University of Michigan, Institute for Social Research, 1975).

30. *See* Martin L. Hoffman and Herbert D. Salzstein, "Parent Discipline and the Child's Moral Development," *Journal of Personality and Social Psychology*, 5 (January 1967), pp. 45–57.

31. Blumenthal et al., op. cit.

32. Gil, "A Socio-Cultural Perspective on Physical Child Abuse."

33. James J. Tracy and Elizabeth H. Clark, "Treatment for Child Abusers," *Social Work*, 19 (May 1974), p. 339.

34. *See*, for example, Burland, Andrews, and Headsten, op. cit.; James D. Delsordo, "Protective Casework for Abused Children," *Children*, 1 (November–December 1963), pp. 46–51; Vincent J. Fontana, "Further Reflections on Maltreatment of Children," *New York State Journal of Medicine*, 68 (1968), pp. 2214–2215; Galdston, op. cit.; Gil, *Violence Against Children*; Ray E. Helfer, *The Diagnostic Process and Treatment Programs* (Washington, D. C.: U.S. Department of Health, Education & Welfare, 1975); Paulson and Blake, op. cit.; Larry B. Silver, Christina C. Dublin, and Reginald S. Lourie, "Does Violence Breed Violence?" *American Journal of Psychiatry*, 126 (March 1969), pp. 404–407; Steele and Pollock, op. cit.; and Wasserman, op. cit.

35. Vincent J. Fontana, *Somewhere A Child Is Crying* (New York: Macmillan Co., 1964), p. 110.

36. Wasserman, op. cit.

37. Burland, Andrews, and Headsten, op. cit.

38. Ray E. Helfer, "The Etiology of Child Abuse," *Pediatrics*, 51 (1973), p. 777.

39. Kadushin, op. cit.

40. Gil, *Violence Against Children*; and Gil, "A Socio-Cultural Perspective on Physical Child Abuse."

41. Lystad, op. cit., p. 330.

42. Steele and Pollock, op. cit.

43. Fontana, *Somewhere a Child Is Crying*; and Fontana, "Further Reflections on Maltreatment of Children."

44. Leontine Young, *Wednesday's Children* (New York: McGraw-Hill Book Co., 1964).

45. Silver, Dublin, and Lourie, op. cit., p. 591.

46. Marian G. Morris, Robert W. Gould, and Patricia J. Matthews, "Toward Prevention of Child Abuse," *Children*, 11 (1964), pp. 55–60; and Thomas McHenry, Bertram R. Girdnay, and Elizabeth Elmer, "Suspected Trauma with Multiple Skeletal Injuries During Infancy and Childhood," *Pediatrics*, 47 (June 1963), pp. 903–908.

47. Werner Tuteur and Jacob Glotzer, "Further Observations on Murdering Mothers," *Journal of Forensic Sciences*, 11 (1966), p. 375.

48. *See* Eustace Chesser, *Cruelty to Children* (New York: Philosophical Library, 1952); Irving Kaufman, "The Contributions of Protective Services," *Child Welfare*, 36 (1957), pp. 8–13; and Young, op. cit.

49. *See*, for example, Silver, Dublin, and Lourie, op. cit.; Helen E. Boardman, "A Project to Rescue Children from Inflicted Injuries," *Social Work*, 7 (January 1962), pp. 43–51; and Serapio Richard Zalba, "The Abused Child": I and II, *Social Work*, 11 and 12 (October 1966 and January 1967), pp. 3–16 and 70–79.

50. *See*, for example, Carol Schneider, Ray E. Helfer, and Carl Pollock, "The Predictive Questionnaire: A Preliminary Report," in C. Henry Kempe and Ray E. Helfer, eds., *Helping the Battered Child and His Family* (Philadelphia: J. B. Lippincott Co., 1972). These authors have begun to study abusing and nonabusing samples in order to establish differences in specific behavioral and psychological characteristics.

51. Katherine Oettinger, as quoted in Paulson and Blake, op. cit., p. 88.

52. Zalba, op. cit.

JAYARATNE / Child Abusers

53

FAMILY CIRCUMSTANCES IN CHILD MALTREATMENT: A REVIEW OF THE LITERATURE

Michael J. Martin*

Information regarding the characteristics of families who are involved in various kinds of child maltreatment has been presented in an isolated, fragmented fashion with little attempt to integrate the information in a meaningful way. The following paper integrates current knowledge and theory relating to the physical abuse, the sexual abuse, and the neglect of children.

Every year thousands of children are subjected by their parents or caregivers to maltreatment of varying severity including physical abuse, abandonment, physical neglect, emotional abuse, and sexual abuse. The theoretical base, however, for developing hypotheses as to the causes of various forms of child maltreatment has been fragmented and largely built of data which are highly suspect (Spinetta and Rigler 1972). Neither study of factors relating to the severity of the maltreatment nor analysis of similarities or differences between the forms of child maltreatment has been systematically undertaken. In addition, even though all forms of child maltreatment tend to be dealt with in the same service systems, current literature has tended to focus on one area, i.e., child abuse, even when several types of child maltreatment are present in the same family. Clearly, there is a need for a careful integration of existing information and theory relating to the abuse and neglect of children.

PHYSICAL ABUSE

Characteristics of Parents

There has been little agreement concerning characteristics of abusing parents which cause physically abusive behavior. Indeed Gelles (1973) concluded that of nineteen personality traits commonly

*Michael J. Martin is an extension specialist in human development, part of the Cooperative Extension Service of Kansas State University, Manhattan 66506.

noted by various investigators in the area of child abuse, there was agreement by two or more authors on only four traits, with the remaining fifteen characteristics being unique to only one particular author. In addition, in a comprehensive review of the psychological approach to the study of child abuse, it was concluded that the literature is largely composed of professional opinions and that there exists little empirical research to support the opinions expressed (Spinetta and Rigler 1972).

Even with the serious limitations of the data base, however, some tentative similarities among abusive parents can be suggested from existing literature. Perhaps the most consistently found characteristic among abusive parents is that they themselves were abused or neglected as children (Kempe et al. 1962, Steele and Pollock 1968, Spinetta and Rigler 1972, Parke and Collmer 1975). In a classic study of 60 abusive families, it was found that abusive parents tended to reenact the same patterns of abusive childrearing to which they had been subjected. All the parents in the study had been deprived of basic nurturant parenting (Steele and Pollock 1968).

In addition to the generational nature of child abuse, a high incidence of divorce, separation, and unstable marriages, as well as minor criminal offenses, has been observed in abusing families (Kempe et al. 1962). Extending Kempe's findings, Young (1964) and Elmer (1967) added the factors of social and economic stress, lack of family roots in the community, lack of immediate support from extended families, social isolation, high mobility, and unemployment.

Although some psychotic persons are responsible for child abuse, it has been estimated that only 10 percent of abusive adults can be classified as psychotic (Kempe 1973). It is generally agreed, however, that there is a defect in the abu-

sive parent's personality that allows aggressive impulses to be expressed so freely (Kempe et al. 1962, Steele and Pollock 1968, Wasserman 1967, Spinetta and Rigler 1972).

Parental Expectations. An additional characteristic found in abusive parents relates to their perceptions of the development of the abused child. Parents who abused their children were found to have unrealistic expectations of their infants and children (Steele and Pollock 1968). Galdston (1965) reported that abusive parents treated their children as if they were adults. In addition, the parents appeared to be incapable of understanding normal stages of development in their children. It is easy to understand that, if parents lacked knowledge of normal stages of development and had unrealistic expectations of their children's behavior, parenting might become an unrewarding and frustrating experience, especially when additional psychopathology is present.

Discipline. One area which appears to be particularly important in the etiology of abuse is the pattern of ineffective discipline utilized by the abusing parent. For example, in one study almost all the abusing families were inconsistent in disciplining their children. All of the severe-abuse families and 91 percent of moderate-abuse families had inconsistent discipline practices. Additionally, 88 percent of the severe-abuse families and 81 percent of the moderate-abuse families failed to show consistent expectations for their children's behavior. Moreover, there was a general disintegration of parental authority within the families of those who abused their children (Young 1964).

A number of studies (e.g., Parke and Collmer 1975) have shown that, under conditions of stress and frustration, predominant responses are likely to be accentuated. For example, if physical discipline is used as the major discipline technique, under conditions of stress and frustration the intensity of the response may be escalated. Physical punishment becomes than an impulsive, angry reaction instead of a deliberate discipline technique. Parke (1969) believes that high-intensity punishment is more effective on a short-term basis than low-intensity punishment. Thus, the parent may be reinforced for the use of high-intensity tactics. If the punishment is inconsistent, however, only momentary control will be achieved, and the parent may resort to a more intense punishment on some future occasion.

Factors Eliciting Abusive Behavior

There is a growing amount of evidence that suggests that the child plays an influential role in eliciting abusive behavior. For instance, Helfer's psychodynamic model of abuse (Helfer 1975) suggests that for abuse to occur the following three conditions must be met:

1. A very special kind of child,
2. A crisis or a series of crises, and
3. The potential in the parent for abuse.

One pattern of findings that would add support to this notion is a number of clinical investigations which have pointed to the selectivity of abuse; not all children in the family are abused, but usually only a single child (Parke and Collmer 1975). Characteristics of the child which appear to enhance the likelihood of his being physically abused include irritability and soothability in infants, crying behavior in infants, birth complications and aggressive misbehavior in older children (Parke and Collmer 1975). Additionally, Friedrich and Boriskin (1976) have added the likelihood of prematurity, mental retardation, and physical handicaps as possible additions to the characteristics of children that could lead to abuse.

It has been suggested that infants who exhibit excessive and sustained crying may present particularly frequent and strong aversive stimuli to the mother and thus elicit punitive kinds of behavior (Parke and Collmer 1975). Robson and Moss (1970) noted decreases in mother-infant attachment after the first month as a result of sustained irritability of the child. Failure to control infant crying effectively and maternal withdrawal in the later part of the child's first year of life have been noted by Bell and Ainsworth (1972).

Thus, although current theory in the etiology of child abuse does not indicate that behavior in the child is sufficient cause for the development of abusive behavior in the parent or caregiver, it is suggested that particular kinds of aversive behavior characteristics in the child might be contributory factors.

A Sociological Model

Gill (1970) has suggested a sociological model for explaining physical abuse. Basic to the sociological approach in understanding child abuse are two assumptions (Parke and Collmer 1975). First, patterns of child abuse can be understood by an examination of prevailing cultural attitudes toward violence and the use of physical force as a control. Inherent in this assumption is the notion that conflict resolution strategies that are predominant at a societal level appear to be mirrored in family interaction. Second, social forces on the societal level such as unemployment, racism, poverty, overcrowding, and social isolation impact on the levels of family stress and thus increase the likelihood of the occurrence of abuse (Parke and Collmer 1975).

In support of the first assumption, a United States–Canada comparison found lower levels of intrafamilial aggression in Canada, where the levels of criminal aggressive activity are also low (Steinmetz 1974a). Additionally, similarities were found among the types of marital conflict

170

tactics, discipline techniques, and methods employed by children in settling sibling conflicts. Families who use verbal and physical aggressive tactics for the resolution of husband-wife disputes also tend to use similar types of techniques in disciplining their children. Moreover, their children tend to duplicate these tactics in their sibling relationships (Steinmetz 1974b). Stark and McEvoy (1970) reported that 93 percent of all parents sampled in their study used physical punishment, although some used it only rarely and with small children.

In support of the assumption of the impact of social forces on family stress and thus on child abuse, several investigators have documented a relationship between unemployment and physical abuse (Gil 1970, Galdston 1965, Young, 1964). Three reasons have been suggested why the father's unemployment may lead to an increase in physical abuse. First, the unemployed father may be home a greater proportion of time and thus have more contacts with his children than employed fathers. Second, the unemployed father may assume the role of disciplinarian because he is home more often. And third, status loss and loss of income may lead to the development of a higher level of stress (Parke and Collmer 1975).

SEXUAL ABUSE

Although the literature relating to family circumstances in the physical abuse of children is incomplete, it far exceeds the literature relating to circumstances in families in which sexual abuse occurs. It has been suggested that the reason for this lack of information in sexual abuse relates to societal taboos on inquiry into such sensitive subject matter (Brant and Tisza 1977). Most research in the past has focused on treatment rather than etiological investigations. Similarly, information on the total incidence of sexual abuse of children is obscure. Estimates can be found in the literature that range from a low of 4,000 cases per year in the U.S. to a high of 500,000 cases (Schultz 1973). As an indication of the number of cases that go unreported, however, in a retrospective study of 1,200 college-age women, Gagnon (1965) found that 26 percent reported a sexual experience with an adult prior to age 13. Further, only 6 percent of these incidents had ever been reported to authorities.

Females tend to be abused more often than males, and the perpetrator is usually male, although homosexual abuse and cases where females abuse male children do occur (Schechter and Roberge 1976). In a study of 250 families in which sexual abuse had occurred, it was found that 75 percent of the perpetrators of sexual abuse were known to the child or his family. In addition, 72 percent of the parents in the study actually contributed to the sexual abuse, either by committing the abusive act or by omission of parental safeguards which protect the child from exploitation (DeFrancis 1969). Schechter and Roberge (1976) reported that 75 percent of all incest involved fathers and daughters. The age of the father was usually 30–50 years, and the daughters were usually entering adolescence when the sexual abuse first occurred.

Unlike physical abuse cases, there is a wide range of difference in the direct role which the child plays in eliciting his or her own abuse. This range extends from totally random forced victimization or rape to actual seduction or active participation on the part of the child. In general, physical force used on victims plays only a small role in the offense (Schultz 1973).

A close similarity between the home situations of children who are physically abused and those who are sexually abused has been noted (Martin 1976). In addition, children are in greater danger of being abused sexually if their parent had also been sexually abused when he or she was a child (Brant and Tisza 1977). Moreover, DeFrancis (1969) found a large degree of social isolation present in sexual-abuse families. Similar to findings among physical-abuse families, 70 percent of the families in which sexual abuse had occurred indicated an absence of ties with community groups. In addition, only 4 percent of the parents had turned to public or voluntary social services for help with their many problems.

Somewhat contrary to the findings in physical-abuse families, it has been reported that although physical violence was present in some of the homes, it was by no means a universally observed phenomenon. Causes for conflict included disputes over income and its management (33%), quality of housekeeping and child care (33%), suspicions of infidelity (23%), and aggressive, abusive behavior (25%). It is interesting to note that in only 10 percent of the families was an unsatisfactory sexual relationship listed as a cause of conflict (DeFrancis 1969).

Unlike physically abused children who tend to be thought of by their parents in an unrealistically negative light, Giarretto (1976) in his work with father-daughter incest cases, found a close psychological bond between the father and the abused child. In addition, he has suggested that the roles within the family of father, mother, and daughter often become blurred over a period of time, leading to confusion and conflict among family members. Two major problems are common to most families in which incest has occurred. The first problem is a lack of impulse control, either as a result of transient stress or as a long-term characteristic of the individual. The second problem involves role confusion on the part of the family members. The child is often regarded as being more than a child, capable of being a surrogate for meeting the parent's emotional and sexual needs (Summit and Kryso 1978).

NEGLECT

Unlike physical and sexual abuse, which require an action by the parent or caregiver against the child, neglect is most often described in terms of an omission of providing for the basic needs of the child. Because of the chronic nature of neglect in many neglectful families, it is more difficult to quantify in terms of incidents of occurrence than are physical abuse and sexual abuse (Polansky et al. 1975). It is generally believed, however, that there is considerably more child neglect present in families than abuse, the ratio of parents who neglect their children to those who are abusive being at least 2:1 (AHA 1978) or 3:1 (Polansky et al. 1975).

Traditional explanations of the causes of child neglect have centered around the effects of poverty on the ability of a family to provide adequate parenting. Recently, however, this basic causal interpretation has been questioned in light of current trends which document more child neglect in middle-class families. It has been suggested that spread of child neglect to middle-class families may reflect a more pervasive trend to abdicate parental responsibility in favor of personal gratification (Polansky et al. 1975).

In a departure from traditional sociological explanations of child neglect, Young (1964) found that neglecting parents tend to be childlike in their decision-making capacities. They tend to be dependent, unable to carry continuing responsibilities, and lacking adequate inner controls, and to have poor or distorted judgment. Others have suggested alcoholism may be present in one or more parents. Neglectful families, like physical- and sexual-abusive families, are often isolated from an extended family either by lacking one, being rejected by it, or being withdrawn from it (Polansky et al. 1975).

In a major study by the American Humane Association (1978) which included 9,241 neglectful families, insufficient income was found to be a factor in 48 percent of the families. Broken families accounted for 47.3 percent of incidences of neglect, and family discord was listed as a factor in 32.3 percent. Heavy continuous child care responsibility was listed as a problem in 27.4 percent, and inadequate housing was reported in 26.2 percent of the families which neglected their children. In a study of 186 low-income mothers who were categorized as parenting adequately, potentially neglectful, and neglectful, significant differences were found between the neglectful groups and the other two groups. Neglectful mothers were more likely to have more children, to be single parents, to have had recent marital problems, and to have even worse financial and child care resources than the other low-income groups (Giovannoni and Billingsly 1970). In addition, Komarovsky (1969) found that very low-income families typically have no rationale for childrearing other than an inconsistent attempt to keep the children under minimal control.

INTEGRATING THE STUDY OF CHILD MALTREATMENT

The utility of the conceptual distinctions between the various forms of child abuse and neglect, considering the realities of a single entry service system for all maltreatment, has been seriously questioned (Giovannoni 1971). Given the overlap of family circumstances currently documented in the literature among families who engage in various forms of abuse and neglect, there is a need for research which attempts to integrate and compare family characteristics of those whose children sustain child abuse and neglect.

Toward this end several studies have been attempted although none to date have included sexually abusive families as a separate unit of comparison. In a comparison of 103 cases of abuse, 153 cases of neglect, and 242 families who were providing adequate care, Giovannoni (1971) found that abusive families had more members in higher status positions and were more likely to have higher incomes, independent sources of income, and a male head who had gone beyond a high school education. Both abusive and neglectful families showed more social disorganization with respect to community behavior than the adequate care group. Abusive families tended to have more interpersonal and intrapsychic disorders as evidenced by marital discord, drinking problems, and mental illness than neglectful families, but both abusive and neglectful families showed more of these kinds of disorders than the families that provided adequate care.

Similarly, in a study of abusive mothers, neglectful mothers, and mothers not known to mistreat their children, there was a clear distinction between abusive mothers⁻ and the other two groups in psychopathology. There was no clear difference found, however, between the neglectful mothers and the non-mistreating mothers (Griswald and Billingsley 1967).

Extending the findings of family circumstances to the observation of direct family interaction in the homes of abusing, neglectful, and control families, Burgess and Conger (1978) found that abusive and neglectful families have lower rates of overall interaction, and they are much more likely to emphasize negative aspects of their relationships with each other.

In perhaps the largest study of circumstances in abusive and neglectful families to date, the American Humane Association (1978) has found consistent differences between abusive and neglectful families among their 16,040 case reports. Although family discord was fairly common in both types of families, it was more common in abusive families (41.9%) than in neglectful families (32.8%). Lack of tolerance was considerably more common in abusive families (48.2%) than neglectful families (12.7%). Insufficient income, however, was a factor in only 25.2 percent of the abusive families whereas it was a factor in 48.0 percent of the neglectful families. Similarly, inadequate housing was a factor in only 9.25 percent of the abusive families but was a circumstance in 26.2 percent of the neglectful families. Both abusive and neglectful families showed moderate incidence of alcohol dependence (abuse—18.5%, neglect—14.0%) and social isolation (abuse—18.3%, neglect—13.1%).

SUMMARY

From this review it would appear that neglect of children seems to be more directly related to environmental factors such as poverty, whereas physical abuse of children is more closely associated with psychological and interpersonal difficulties. Like physical abuse, sexual abuse appears to be related to psychological and interpersonal difficulties in the parent, although they frequently go undiagnosed before the abusive incident. Unlike physical abuse, however, there does not appear to be a relationship between behavior problems in the child and the incidence of abuse. Finally, no clear relationship has been found between environmental factors such as poverty and the onset of sexual abuse.**

**The author would like to express his sincere appreciation to James Walters for his valuable assistance in the preparation of this paper.

REFERENCES

American Humane Association
1978 National analysis of official child neglect and abuse reporting. Denver, Colo.

Bell, S. M., and Ainsworth, M. D.
1972 Infant crying and maternal responsiveness. Child Development 43:1171-90.

Brant, R.; and Tisza, V.
1977 The sexually misused child. American Journal of Orthopsychiatry 47:80-90.

Burgess, R.; and Conger, R.
1978 Family interaction in abusive, neglectful, and normal families. In press.

DeFrancis, V.
1969 Protecting the child victim of sex crimes committed by adults. Denver, Colo.: The American Humane Association.

Elmer, E.
1967 Children in jeopardy: A study of abused minors and their families. Pittsburgh: University of Pittsburgh Press.

Friedrich, W. N.; and Boriskin, J. A.
1976 The role of the child in abuse: A review of the literature. American Journal of Orthopsychiatry 46(4):580-90.

Gagnon, J.
1965 Female child victim of child sex offenses. Social Problems 13:176-92.

Galdston, R.
1965 Observations on children who have been physically abused and their parents. American Journal of Psychiatry 122:440-43.

Gelles, R. J.
1973 Child abuse as psychopathology: A sociological critique and reformulation. American Journal of Orthopsychiatry 43:611-21.

Giarretto, H.
1976 Humanistic treatment of father-daughter incest. In Helfer, R., and Kempe, H. (eds.), Child abuse and neglect. Cambridge, Mass.: Ballinger.

174

Gil, D. G.
1970 Violence against children: Physical abuse in the United States. Cambridge, Mass.: Harvard University Press.

Giovannoni, J.
1971 Parental mistreatment: Perpetrators and victims. Journal of Marriage and the Family 33:649-57.

Giovannoni, J.; and Billingsley, A.
1970 Child neglect among the poor: A study of parental adequacy in three ethnic groups. Child Welfare 49:196-204.

Griswold, B.; and Billingsley, A.
1971 Psychological functioning of parents who mistreat their children and those who do not. Unpublished manuscript, Berkeley. Quoted in Giovannoni, J. (1971), p. 650.

Helfer, R.
1975 The diagnostic process and treatment programs. Washington, D.C.: Office of Child Development.

Kempe, C. H.
1973 A practical approach to the protection of the abused child and rehabilitation of the abusing parent. Pediatrics 51(Pt. 3):804-12.

Kempe, C. H.; Silverman, F. N.; Steele, B. B.; Droegemuller, W.; and Silver, H. K.
1962 The battered-child syndrome. Journal of the American Medical Association 181:17-24.

Komarovsky, M.
1969 Blue-collar marriages. In Roach, J. (ed.), Social stratification in the United States. Englewood Cliffs, N.J.: Prentice-Hall.

Martin, H. P.
1976 The abused child: A multidisciplinary approach to developmental issues and treatment. Cambridge, Mass.: Ballinger.

Parke, R. D.
1969 Effectiveness of punishment as an interaction of intensity, timing, agency nurturance, and cognitive structuring. Child Development 40:213-35.

Parke, R. D.; and Collmer, C. W.
1975 Child abuse: An interdisciplinary analysis. In Hetherington, E. M. (ed.), Review of child development research (vol. 5). Chicago: University of Chicago Press.

Polansky, N.; Hally, C.; and Polansky, N.
1975 Profile of neglect: A survey of the state of knowledge of child neglect. Washington, D.C.: U.S. Department of Health, Education, and Welfare.

Robson, K. S.; and Moss, H. A.
1970 Patterns and determinants of maternal attachment. Journal of Pediatrics 77:976-85.

Schechter, M.D.; and Roberge, L.
1976 Sexual exploitation. In Helfer, R. E.; and Kempe, C. H. (eds.), Child abuse and neglect: The family and the community. Cambridge, Mass.: Ballinger, pp. 127-42.

Schultz, L.
1973 The child sex victim: Social, psychological, and legal perspectives. Child Welfare 52:147-57.

Spinetta, J. J.; and Rigler, D.
1972 The abusing parent: A psychological review. Psychological Bulletin 77:296-304.

Stark, R.; and McEvoy, J.
1970 Middle class violence. Psychology Today 4:52-65.

Steele, B. F.; and Pollock, D.
1968 A psychiatric study of parents who abuse infants and small children. In Helfer, R. E., and Kempe, C. H. (eds.), The battered child. Chicago: University of Chicago Press.

Steinmetz, S. K.
1974a Intra-familial patterns of conflict resolution: United States and Canadian comparisons. Paper presented at the Annual Meeting of the Society for the Study of Social Problems, Montreal.

Steinmetz, S. K.
1974b Normal families and violence: The training ground for abuse. Paper presented at Research NIH Conference on Child Abuse and Neglect, Bethesda, MD.

Summit, R.; and Kryso, J.
1978 Sexual abuse of children: A clinical spectrum. American Journal of Orthopsychiatry 48(2):237-51.

Wasserman, S.
1967 The abused parent of the abused child. Children 14:175-79.

Young, L.
1964 Wednesday's children: A study of child neglect and abuse. New York: McGraw-Hill.

Journal of Consulting and Clinical Psychology
1978, Vol. 46, No. 6, 1409–1414

Parental Personality Factors in Child Abuse

John J. Spinetta
San Diego State University

In an attempt to demonstrate that abusing parents differ from nonabusing parents in personality variables, the Michigan Screening Profile of Parenting was administered to six groups of mothers: (a) adjudicated abusers, (b) spouses of adjudicated abusers, (c) mothers convicted of child neglect, (d) nonabusing mothers from a college student population, (e) nonabusing mothers from a middle socioeconomic level, and (f) nonabusing mothers from a lower socioeconomic level. Major differences occurred when comparison was made of one or more of the first three groups with one of the latter three groups. The groups differed significantly on six factor-analyzed cluster categories: (a) relationship to one's own parents, (b) tendency to becoming upset and angry, (c) tendency toward isolation and loneliness, (d) expectations of one's own children, (e) inability to separate parental and child feelings, and (f) fear of external threat and control. In all of the cases, the first three groups scored at levels of higher risk than did the latter three groups, whereas the abusers scored at the highest risk levels throughout. It is suggested that a therapist who helps a parent develop the ability to maintain equanimity under stress, by helping reduce deviations from the norm in characteristics related to abuse potential, is ultimately helping to reduce actual abusive behavior.

With the growing emphasis in the literature on the fact that the causes of child abuse are multiple and interactive, many therapists who deal with parental personality and attitudinal variables are made to feel as if they are engaging in a futile effort (D'Agostino, 1975; Smith, 1975). Although many new and exciting identification and treatment programs for child abuse abound throughout the country (National Center on Child Abuse and Neglect, 1975, 1976), very little encouragement has been given to the therapist who does not have easy access to the new interdisciplinary treatment programs and who, in many instances, remains the

sole therapeutic agent for a particular set of families (Steele, 1975). The problem is viewed as sufficiently complex that an individual therapist who deals solely with parental attitudes is often discouraged. It is the purpose of this study to demonstrate that parental personality and attitude are important factors in the etiology of child abuse. Such a demonstration can give hope to the therapist that efforts in dealing with the parental personality are aimed in a profitable direction and that he or she can be effective in reducing potential for abuse.

It is not my intent to suggest that factors of parental background or inadequacy are the sole determinants of child abuse. The fact is that the causes of child abuse are multiple and interactive; there is no single type of child abuser or a single causative factor as sufficient explanation of abuse (Spinetta & Rigler, 1972). Emphasis on parental personality is in no way meant to detract from these other factors. Rather, it is suggested that helping the parent to develop the ability to maintain equanimity

The author wishes to thank Richard Bourke, Esther Cardall, and Don King of the Department of Public Welfare, County of San Diego, and their social service staffs for their assistance in the administration of the questionnaires and Ruth Reinman and Richard Sprigle for their help in the coordination and analysis of the data.

Requests for reprints should be sent to John J. Spinetta, Department of Psychology, San Diego State University, San Diego, California 92182.

under stress is directly related to situational variables, and it can be of central value in the rehabilitative or preventive process.

It is in the broader context of situational variables that I ask the question, Why is it that the majority of parents do not abuse their children? Although in the socially and economically deprived segments of the population there is generally a higher degree of the kinds of stress factors found in abusing families, the great majority of deprived families do not abuse their children. Why is it that most deprived families do not engage in child abuse, though they are subject to the same economic and social stresses as those families who do abuse their children? Is there an actual difference between the types of stresses encountered by abusing parents and nonabusing parents within the same socioeconomic level (Gil, 1970, 1976), or is the difference in the parents' manner of approaching the stress situation (Kent, 1976; Smith, 1975; Spinetta & Rigler, 1972; Young, 1976)? I hold the latter position. When one takes into account the fact that some well-to-do and middle-class families also engage in child abuse, then one must look for the causes of child abuse beyond mere socioeconomic stress. The problem of etiology remains insoluble at the demographic level alone.

The present study is an attempt to demonstrate that however one might explain the particular circumstances that helped shape the parents' personality, abusing parents differ from nonabusing parents in attitudinal and personality variables.

Method

Instrument

In 1972, Schneider, Helfer, and Pollack disclosed efforts under way to design and validate a questionnaire with the goal of uncovering parents who have a potential to abuse their small children. They based their questions on their clinical experience, which suggested that parents who abuse their small children reported more severe physical punishment in their own childhood, more anxiety about dealing with their children's problems, more concern about being alone and isolated, more concern with criticism, and higher expectations for performance in their children than did nonabusers. After several

years of analysis and validation, they published first a 74-item and then a 50-item instrument, originally entitled *Survey on Bringing Up Children* (Schneider, Hoffmeister, & Helfer, 1976). The instrument has since been renamed the Michigan Screening Profile on Parenting (Helfer, Schneider, & Hoffmeister, 1977).

Although the questionnaire has not yet been sufficiently validated to be of use as a legally valid criterion in decisions regarding child placement or parental readiness to resume parenting functions, it has been shown to be capable of differentiating between attitudes regarding child rearing and regarding self-awareness and self-control functions in the parents.

With the permission of Helfer, I administered the questionnaire to several groups of parents, as discussed below, to see (a) whether abuse-potential cluster categories similar to those found by Helfer and his associates could be validated in a local sample and (b) whether scores based on the locally factor-analyzed categories could sort out abusing from nonabusing parents.

Subjects

As is typical of parents who come to the attention of public agencies (National Center on Child Abuse and Neglect, 1975), the parents referred to the participating agencies were from low socioeconomic levels. The use of such parents in the present study is not meant to suggest that abuse takes place only at low socioeconomic levels, because it does not (Spinetta & Rigler, 1972). Similarly, although more women than men have been found to abuse their children (Gelles, 1973; Gil, 1970; Smith, 1975), child abuse is not an act solely of the mother. However, the questionnaire was administered only to women to ensure nonconfounding by differences in child-rearing attitudes between men and women.

Subjects were chosen in the following manner: The participating agencies agreed to administer the questionnaire to all of the mothers currently under their jurisdiction as active cases. The questionnaire was administered to (a) adjudicated abusers, (b) spouses of adjudicated abusers, and (c) parents convicted of child neglect. The parents in these categories were chosen by the following criteria: (a) The child was under 5 years of age, and (b) court adjudication had been finalized, so that parents would not feel that their answers would affect the placement of their child or decisions regarding their own disposition. In this manner, workers were able to ensure that responses to the questionnaire were given as honestly as possible.

For purposes of comparison and contrast, the questionnaire was also administered to groups of parents who were nonabusers with children under 5 years of age. The following groups were tested: (d) nonabusing mothers from a college student population whose children were in a day-care center because one or both parents were in school, (e) nonabusing mothers from a middle socioeconomic level whose children were in a preschool not because of necessity but through express parental wish, and (f) nonabusing mothers from a lower socioeconomic level with children in a preschool because the mother was working. Group f was chosen to match as closely as possible the educational, occupational, and socioeconomic status of Groups a, b, and c. Group d was chosen because it was similar to Groups a, b, and c in financial status but not in terms of education or potential occupation. Group e, different in terms of education, occupation, and financial status, and the most representative of the population as a whole, was chosen to test possible class differences in responding.

The samples consisted of the following numbers: (a) adjudicated abusers, 7; (b) spouses of abusers, 9; (c) parents convicted of neglect, 13; (d) nonabusing mothers from a college population, 15; (e) nonabusing mothers from a middle socioeconomic level, 15; and (f) nonabusing mothers from a lower socioeconomic level, 41.

The purpose of the study was explained in detail to the respective supervisors, the agency officials in Groups a–c, and the day-care administrators and teachers in Groups d–f. Because of the sensitive nature of the accusation of child abuse and neglect, and to prevent socially desirable responses, parents were not told specifically that the survey's ultimate purpose was to differentiate abuse potential. Rather, parents were asked if they wished to take part in a survey on attitudes in bringing up children, conducted by the university to learn how parents viewed child rearing. In accord with U.S. Department of Health, Education, and Welfare guidelines, parents were promised that the results would remain anonymous, and that any parent who wished would be given the overall results on completion of the study.

All of the parents who were approached in Groups d and e, without exception, filled out the survey as requested. Of the parents approached in Group f, all but three (93%) filled out the survey. The parents in Groups a–c were approached by assigned workers who had established rapport with them and were told that this survey would not only aid the university but that it might be of therapeutic aid to the specific worker in each case. Each worker was asked to screen out those parents who would be unduly threatened by the questionnaire, those who might be tempted to answer with socially desirable responses, and those whose cases were still pending court completion. The workers did not receive any refusals from the selected cases. The final small sample thus represents responses from parents who were motivated to fill out the questionnaires as honestly as possible. Comments from each worker on each case attested to the honest efforts of the parents who made up the final samples in Groups a–c. It is my belief that the final sample represents the cases most amenable to treatment. There is no reason to suspect that the sample represents the most severe of the abusers. On the contrary, workers' case records show that the final sample is on the conservative side of the abuse-potential continuum in the agencies' overall abuser population. Thus, any differences that appear between the abuser and nonabuser groups would appear at least equally as strong in the general abuser population of the agencies in question. With the questionnaire aimed at being of eventual use as an aid to the therapist in sorting out areas of weakness, honest cooperation of the parents was deemed essential. In addition, honest cooperation in each of the six groups minimized confounding that would appear if the groups differed in willingness to participate.

Results

A varimax rotated factor analysis of the responses to the questionnaires was conducted by the experimenter. The six clusters of variables closely resemble the high-abuse potential categories of Helfer et al. (1977). The six resultant clusters of the present analysis are (a) relationship to one's own parents, (b) tendency to becoming upset and angry, (c) tendency toward isolation and loneliness, (d) expectations of one's own children, (e) inability to separate parental and child feelings, and (f) fear of external threat and control.

With these six factor-analyzed cluster categories as a basis, a six-column scoring form was devised, with direction of scoring set so that the higher score on each cluster represented abuse potential. Total raw scores for each subject were determined for each of the six cluster categories.

A 1×6 analysis of variance was performed for the six groups for each of the six abuse-potential categories. Table 1 gives the means and standard deviations for scores in each of the abuse-potential categories for each subject group. Table 2 gives the results of the analysis of variance for each of the six categories.

Scores on each of the six abuse-potential categories showed that significant differences existed among the six groups ($df = 5, 90$ in all cases). The resultant F on the first abuse-potential category, relationship to one's own parents, was 4.55, significant at the .001 level. The resultant F of 6.70 on the second abuse potential category, tendency to becoming upset and angry, was significant at the .001 level. The resultant F on the third category, tendency toward isolation and lone-

Table 1
Means and Standard Deviations in Each Abuse Potential Category

	1: Abusers		2: Spouses		3: Neglect		4: College		5: Middle		6: Lower	
Cluster	M	SD	M	SD	M	SD	M	SD	M	SD	M	SD
1 (Parents)	57.4	14.7	48.7	9.4	53.3	10.3	44.9	11.6	37.7	10.2	44.3	10.3
2 (Control)	25.4	9.6	22.2	7.6	22.8	7.3	17.7	4.0	14.1	3.8	16.7	4.7
3 (Affiliation)	31.9	8.2	26.9	5.3	25.9	4.0	22.5	4.2	19.9	3.8	22.5	4.8
4 (Expectations)	39.1	18.6	37.3	11.7	34.3	10.7	28.7	7.8	22.3	6.3	30.0	8.8
5 (Symbiosis)	17.3	5.1	16.2	2.3	19.2	2.9	14.9	2.1	14.5	2.7	16.2	3.3
6 (Threat)	61.3	16.5	52.6	12.9	57.4	10.8	40.7	8.7	29.3	5.7	43.9	10.5

liness, was 7.53, significant at the .001 level. The resultant F on the fourth category, expectations of one's own children, was 4.20, significant at the .001 level. The resultant F on the fifth category, inability to separate parental and child feelings, was 3.79, significant at the .01 level. The resultant F of 13.92 on the sixth abuse-potential category, fear of external threat and control, was significant at the .001 level.

A posteriori tests using the Scheffé method were conducted for each of the abuse-potential clusters. Significant differences were found as follows: Group a (abusers) sig-

Table 2
Analysis of Variance

Cluster	MS	F
1		
Between	527.5	4.55**
Within	116.1	
2		
Between	213.5	6.79**
Within	31.5	
3		
Between	177.3	7.53**
Within	23.5	
4		
Between	409.3	4.20**
Within	97.5	
5		
Between	35.9	3.79*
Within	9.5	
6		
Between	1,546.3	13.92**
Within	11.1	

Note. $df = 5, 90$.
* $p < .01$.
** $p < .001$.

nificantly differed from Group e (middle-class nonabusers) in Abuse-Potential Clusters 1, 2, 3, 4, and 6. Group a significantly differed from Groups d and f in Abuse-Potential Clusters 2, 3, and 6.

Group b (spouses of abusers) significantly differed from Group e in Abuse-Potential Clusters 2, 3, 4, and 6.

Group c (neglecters) significantly differed from Group e in Abuse-Potential Clusters 1, 2, 5, and 6. Group c significantly differed from groups d and f in Abuse-Potential Clusters 2, 5, and 6.

The Scheffé a posteriori test showed that the major differences in each of the six abuse-potential categories occurred when comparison was made of one or more of the first three groups (abusers, abusers' spouses, and neglecters) with one of the latter three groups (nonabusers). The greatest differences occurred when each of the first three groups was compared to the fifth group (middle-class nonabusers). In each of the abuse-potential categories, Group e scored at the lowest level. Group d (college student nonabusers) and Group f (lower socioeconomic level nonabusers) were the next lowest in abuse potential, scoring almost identically throughout. Although the fifth group scored lowest on all of the categories, the other two nonabuser groups scored at a level not significantly higher. In contrast, the abusers scored at the highest risk level in all but one of the abuse-potential categories.

Discussion

The Michigan Screening Profile on Parenting was able to differentiate between abusing and nonabusing mothers on personality and attitudinal variables. The empirically derived set of abuse-potential categories proved useful in significantly differentiating between abusing and nonabusing mothers within the same socioeconomic level in three areas: the tendency to becoming upset and angry, feelings of isolation and loneliness, and the fear of external threat and control. The abusing mothers differed significantly from nonabusing mothers in a middle socioeconomic level in the same categories; in their relationship to their own parents, both past and present; in having higher than normal expectations for their young children's performance; and in failing to separate their own feelings from those of their children. Although not at a significant level, abusing mothers differed from nonabusing mothers in the same socioeconomic level in the latter categories as well. Neglecting parents and spouses of abusers were also shown to be weak in the six abuse-potential categories.

Personality and attitudinal factors do make a difference. Abusing mothers differ from nonabusing mothers in areas of attitude and personality that have been clinically related to potential for abuse (Colman, 1975; Corey, Miller, & Widlack, 1975; Kent, 1976; Paulson et al., 1974; Smith, 1975; Spinetta & Rigler, 1972; Steele, 1975; Tracy & Clark, 1974; Walters, 1975). The fact that neglecting mothers and spouses of abusers also scored high on the abuse-potential categories demonstrates the power of the test in pointing to weaknesses in parental personality and attitudes that can affect the parenting role itself, regardless of whether the result is actual physical abuse, neglect of the child, or passively allowing one's spouse to abuse the child. Intervention and direction is called for in each case.

As stated above, there is no suggestion made that factors of parental inadequacy and personality weakness are the sole determinants of child abuse. Certainly, those involved in the care of the abusing parent must continue to relieve the family as much as possible of overwhelming situational stresses. However, personality does play a role. The therapist who helps the parent develop the ability to maintain equanimity under stress can be of immense aid in the rehabilitative or preventive effort.

One must caution that the questionnaire cannot be used as a legally valid criterion for sorting out abusing from nonabusing parents, since false positives have been shown on occasion (Schneider et al., 1976) and since false negatives can appear with those parents who refuse to answer the questions honestly. It is possible to fake answers by giving socially desirable responses. However, for those parents in a therapeutic situation who respond to the questionnaire with an honest desire to be helped, the responses can help point to weaknesses in areas that have been clinically shown to relate to potential for abuse. A therapist who directs interventional and preventive efforts toward the amelioration of parental attitudes, both attitudes toward the self and toward the child, is not, as Alby (1975) suggested, misdirecting energies, but is rather helping reduce deviations from the norm in characteristics related to abuse potential and, hopefully, is ultimately helping reduce the actual abusive behavior.

References

Alby, K. T. Preventing child abuse. *American Psychologist*, 1975, *30*, 921–928.

Colman, W. Occupational therapy and child abuse. *American Journal of Occupational Therapy*, 1975, *29*, 412–417.

Corey, E. J., Miller, C. L., & Widlack, F. W. Factors contributing to child abuse. *Nursing Research*, 1975, *24*, 293–295.

D'Agostino, P. Strains and stresses in protective services. In N. B. Ebeling & D. A. Hill (Eds.), *Child abuse: Intervention and treatment*. Acton, Mass.: Publishing Sciences Group, 1975.

Gelles, R. J. Child abuse as psychopathology: A sociological critique and reformulation. *American Journal of Orthopsychiatry*, 1973, *43*, 612–621.

Gil, D. G. *Violence against children: Physical abuse in the United States*. Cambridge, Mass.: Harvard University Press, 1970.

Gil, D. G. Primary prevention of child abuse: A philosophical and political issue. *Pediatric Psychology*, 1976, *1*(2), 54–57.

Helfer, R. E., Schneider, C., & Hoffmeister, J. K. *Manual for use of the Michigan Screening Profile of Parenting*. East Lansing: Michigan State University Press, 1977.

Kent, J. T. A follow-up study of abused children. *Pediatric Psychology*, 1976, *1*(2), 24–27.

National Center on Child Abuse and Neglect. *Child abuse and neglect: The problem and its management* (3 vols) (DHEW Publ. No. OHD 75-30073). Washington, D.C.: U.S. Govt. Printing Office, 1975.

National Center on Child Abuse and Neglect. *Federally funded child abuse and neglect projects 1975* (DHEW publ. No. OHD 76-30076). Washington, D.C.: U.S. Government Printing Office, 1976.

Paulson, M. J., et al. Parents of the battered child: A multidisciplinary group therapy approach to life-threatening behavior. *Life-Threatening Behavior,* 1974, *4,* 18–31.

Schneider, C., Helfer, R. E., & Pollack, C. The predictive questionnaire: Preliminary report. In C. H. Kempe & R. E. Helfer (Eds.), *Helping the battered child and his family.* Philadelphia: Lippincott, 1972.

Schneider, C., Hoffmeister, J. K., & Helfer, R. E. A predictive screening questionnaire for potential problems in mother-child interaction. In R. E. Helfer & C. H. Kempe (Eds.), *Child abuse and neglect: The family and the community.* Cambridge, Mass.: Ballinger, 1976.

Smith, S. M. *The battered child syndrome.* London: Butterworth, 1975.

Spinetta, J. J., & Rigler, D. The child-abusing parent: A psychological review. *Psychological Bulletin,* 1972, *77,* 296–304.

Steele, B. F. *Child abuse and neglect: The problem and its management* (Vol. 3, chap. 3, pp. 65–114) (DHEW Publ. No. OHD 75-30073). Washington, D.C.: U.S. Govt. Printing Office, 1975.

Tracy, J. J., & Clark, E. J. Treatment for child abusers. *Social Work,* 1974, *19,* 338–342.

Walters, D. R. *Physical and sexual abuse of children: Causes and treatment.* Bloomington: Indiana University Press, 1975.

Young, M. Multiple correlates of abuse: A systems approach to the etiology of child abuse. *Pediatric Psychology,* 1976, *1*(2), 57–61.

Received November 29, 1977 ∎

The Child Victim's Role in Sexual Assault by Adults

KENNETH J. GRUBER

Although children are sometimes accused of complying with adults' demands for sexual relationships, emotional and situational factors force them to become willing victims. Understanding these factors is a better treatment approach than assigning blame.

An adult's sexual assault or involvement with a minor is generally considered an act of sexual abuse. But the degree of responsibility the victim is perceived to have had in initiating or encouraging the relationship affects how conclusively it is labeled an act of child sex abuse [9; 13] and may also determine whether persons close to the victim give her understanding and support. Most young sex victims are female adolescents. If the girl is perceived as an "active" participant in a sexual relationship with an adult, she may not be considered a "real" victim, and she may even be blamed. Because blame often leads to rejection [12], the child may suffer more harm from the reactions of those close to her than from the sexual experience itself [17]. In such cases the victim is virtually assured of lasting emotional scars.

Kenneth J. Gruber, M.A., is Special Projects Director with the BIABH Study Center of Appalachian State University, Morganton, NC. He thanks Robert J. Jones, Gary D. Timbers, and E. Elaine Talbert for their helpful comments during the preparation of this manuscript.

0009-4021/81/050305-07 $01.25 © Child Welfare League of America

But how can the victim be blamed? Are not children considered legally incapable of consenting to sexual relations with an adult? And what of the common belief in the innocence of childhood? Laws protect children, particularly when an adult is involved.

> Reactions against sexual contacts between adults and children stem from several assumptions about the nature of childhood and about sexual behavior in general. Childhood is considered a state of innocence characterized by a lack of experience, an inability to perceive consequences and an inclination to absorb indiscriminately all events impinging on the senses. In short, there is an absence of responsibility because children lack judgment and moral sense. The state recognizes this deficiency of responsibility when it deems that children can neither enter into contracts nor commit crimes, that they should be the objects of solicitude, not targets of retribution [13:18].

Society has decided that children need protection because they have not yet achieved adult levels of social and emotional development; should it hold them responsible when their actions result in a potentially harmful encounter with an adult?

The fact that society does hold some child sex victims responsible suggests that in those situations the difference in age or maturation level between the adult and the child may not be important and raises doubts whether an act of sex abuse has indeed occurred. Therefore the child's role must be considered carefully. This paper will examine the child's role and consider the social implications of blaming the victim.

The Child Victim as Participant

The belief that children may not be innocent victims of adult-child sexual relations stems from some of the early research on the effects of sexual abuse and incestuous relationships of children with adults. Relying heavily on psychiatric clinical samples, much of that research concluded that most children who were involved in incestuous relationships or who were victims of sexual assault consciously or unconsciously encouraged such acts. In many cases, particularly those involving incest, the child victim was presumed to have solicited or seduced the adult. Bender and Blau [1], for example, asserted that incestuous daughters often play an active and initiating role in establishing a sexual relationship that continues until it is discovered, and even then they rarely act like injured parties. Bender and Blau argued further that a child's indifference to this kind of sexual relationship can indicate desire for its continuation.

More recent research has also attributed collaborative or participant roles to young victims. Girls were described as "seducers" in 21% of 185 offenses investigated by Glueck [7], as "fully participating" in 60% of 73 cases reported by Weiss, Rogers, Darwin and Dutton [20], as "non-objecting" in 40% of 1944 offenses in a study by Radinowicz [15], as "encouraging" to the offender in 66% to 95% of all sex offenses investigated by Gebhard, Gagnon, Pomeroy, and Christenson [6], and as "precipitating" the offenses in 48% of 64 cases reported by Virkkunen [18].

Most of these studies based their conclusions on the offender's report of the victim's contributory role (the Weiss et al. study is an exception), which may have been self-serving. For example, Revitch and Weiss, basing their conclusions on a sample of sex offenders, said it was their ". . .clinical impression that quite often the child is aggressive and seductive and quite often induces the adult offenders to commit the offense" [16:74].

From the victim's perspective, however, seductive or collaborative behavior may be less frequent than is generally reported. Gagnon [5], for example, in a reanalysis of a portion of Kinsey et al.'s 1953 data [10], found that of 333 adult women who recalled a sexual experience with an adult before the age of 13, fewer than 10% described themselves as having a "collaborative" role in the offense.

Often, children participate in sexual relations with adults because they are promised favors or because they believe the adult will not hurt them [2, 3, 14]. In a study of 263 child sex victims, DeFrancis [4:45] found that in approximately 15% of the cases the adult obtained the child's consent by offering her "a sum of money, from small coins to large bills; or a gift, from pieces of candy to some rather expensive items."

Because most offenders are related to or acquainted with the victim [3, 4, 11], the child may comply with the adult's instructions simply from a desire not to displease the adult. As DeFrancis [4:46] notes:

> A subtle threat underlies the compliance of the child in these circumstances. The child not only wishes to prevent causing displeasure to this person in whom she has faith and for whom she has affection, but also, his position of authority in their relationship carries an implied threat of possible punishment for incurring displeasure by a refusal.

> It would not be correct, therefore, to consider these children as true participants. Their seeming willingness to conform in most

cases stems from a combination of subtle pressures too obscure for the children to know or identify.

Furthermore, even if a child is perceived as the initiator of a sexual liaison, her intent may not be to enter into a sexual relationship per se. Children often actively seek out or willingly receive affectionate behavior from adults and in their attempts to attract adult attention they may naively engage in what appears to be seductive behavior [13]. And, as a result of this naivety, an adult may perceive the child as desiring or willing to engage in intimate sexual activity [17].

> It is normal for children to be sexually provocative, seductive, and curious about sexual matters. This makes the young child a vulnerable target for adults to perpetrate their immature, perverse, or revengeful sexual drives, especially if those children are not properly supervised or protected. Children who are rejected and unloved in the home are often involved in sexual incidents. They are seeking love and acceptance, and they unwittingly invite sexual exploitation. [Weeks, 19:609]

Hence, close examination of a child victim's contributory role in a sexual relationship with an adult may reveal that the child is not acting as systematically and purposefully as the adult thinks. Often the child does not get away from the situation or offers too little resistance to an adult's sexual advances. For example, in the study by DeFrancis [4] in which 263 child sex victims were interviewed, 36% were judged to have directly or indirectly contributed to their victimization. In the bulk of these, however, a child placed herself in a position that provided the offender time and opportunity—accepting a car ride with the offender or going to his residence or elsewhere.

Factors Motivating the Child's Compliance

Few studies have considered the circumstances involved in the commission of sex offenses (e.g., the relationship of the victim to the offender, the use of bribes or threats) or the child's inability to avoid or escape from unwanted sexual encounters. In blaming the child for her own sexual molestation, past research has not given equal consideration to the factors behind the child's compliance. Since children tend to believe adults and often do not initially recognize the sexual relationship as exploitation, their failure to resist or act like victims does not mean that they participate voluntarily or encourage the sexual encounter. In any case, the emphasis on guilt merely obscures the real question: What factors led to the victim's "culpability" in the first place?

The Need for Affection

First, children normally seek affection from adults out of a need for nurturance. Because of previous experience or a lack of discrimination, some children may make inappropriate overtures to receive this affection. As a result, their behavior may unintentionally invite intimate sexual contact.

Offenders' Self-Serving Defenses

Second, in judging whether a child has actively participated in a sex offense, more than the offender's report must be considered. Since the offender has much at stake if he is found guilty, he may predictably offer the defense that the victim consented or had an active part in the encounter. In their now classic study of sex offenders, Gebhard et al. [6] found ample evidence of this practice. Often an offender will claim that the victim seduced him and that she seemed older than she really was.

Situational Pressures

Third and perhaps most important are the situational pressures. The situation may force her to comply with the adult's demands, but she is nonetheless sexually abused. The stronger the pressures, the more severe may be the abuse and its impact on the victim [2, 17]. Because of the personal relationship between the victim and the offender, some children have no choice but to participate in sexual relations. Sexual abuse may be an unfortunate part of their emotional world.

> A woman who has been raped can cope with the experience in the same way that she would react to any other intentionally cruel and harmful attack. She is not socially or psychologically dependent on the rapist. She is free to hate him. But the daughter who has been molested is dependent on her father for protection and care. Her mother is not an ally. She has no recourse. She dares not express or even feel the depths of her anger at being used. She must comply with her father's demands or risk losing the parental love that she needs. She is not an adult. She cannot walk out of the situation (although she may

try to run away). She must endure it, and find in it what compensations she can. [8:48]

Conclusion: Replacing Blame with Help

Because the victim may be at considerable risk of long-term psychological harm, whether the offender is innocent or the victim guilty should be a minor consideration. Both offender and victim need help. It should not matter that some incidents of adult-child sexual activity are not "true" cases of assault or molestation but that the child participated willingly. The important thing is to assess what factors led to the victim's culpability in the first place.

The laws protecting children show society's abhorrence of adult sexual activity with children. Regardless of who is at fault, the recognition that a child has been potentially traumatized should be the primary concern of all involved. Moreover, whatever role the child may have had should not in any way be used to determine how seriously harmed she may be. As a child and an individual, she should be recognized as a victim who needs assurance and support from those who care about her. This approach will help ensure that the victim is minimally affected by an abusive or inappropriate sexual relationship. In short, the victim of sexual abuse will benefit least from being blamed and most from being treated supportively.   ♦

References

1. Bender, L., and Blau, A. "The Reactions of Children to Sexual Relations With Adults." American Journal of Orthopsychiatry 7 (1937).
2. Burgess, A. W., and Holstrom, L. L. "Rape: Its Effect on Task Performance at Varying Stages in the Life Cycle," in Sexual Assault: The Victim and the Rapist, edited by M. J. Walker and S. L. Brodsky. Lexington, MA: D.C. Heath, 1976.
3. Chaneles, S. "Child Victims of Sexual Offenses." Federal Probation 31 (1967).
4. DeFrancis, V. Protecting the Child Victim of Sex Crimes Committed by Adults. Final Report. Denver, CO.: The American Humane Association, Children's Division (1969).
5. Gagnon, J. H. "Female Child Victims of Sex Offenses." Social Problems 13 (1965).
6. Gebhard, P.H.; Gagnon, J.H.; Pomeroy, W. B.; and Christenson, C. V. Sex Offenders: An Analysis of Types. New York: Harper and Row, 1965.
7. Glueck, B. Research Project for the Study and Treatment of Persons Convicted of Crimes Involving Sexual Aberrations, Final Report. New York: New York Department of Mental Hygiene, 1956.
8. Herman, J., and Hirschman, L. "Father-Daughter Incest." Signs: Journal of Woman in Culture and Society 2 (1977).

9. Johnston, M.S. "The Sexually Mistreated Child: Diagnostic Evaluation." Child Abuse and Neglect 3 (1979).

10. Kinsey, A. C.; Pomeroy, W. B.; Martin, C. E.; and Gebhard, P. H. Sexual Behavior in the Human Female. Philadelphia: W. B. Saunders, 1953.

11. Krasner, W.; Meyer, L. C.; and Carroll, N. E. Victims of Rape. U.S. Department of Health, Education and Welfare. DHEW Publication No. (Adm) 77-485 (1977).

12. Lerner, M. J.; Miller, D. T.; and Holmes, J.G. Deserving and the Emergence of Forms of Justice, in Advances in Experimental Social Psychology, edited by L. Berkowitz. New York: Academic Press, 1976.

13. McCaghy, C. H. "Child Molesting." Sexual Behavior 1 (1971).

14. Peters, J. J. "Children Who Are Victims of Sexual Assault and the Psychology of Offenders." American Journal of Psychotherapy 30 (1976).

15. Radinowicz, L. Sexual Offenses. New York: Macmillan, 1957.

16. Revitch, E., and Weiss, R. G. "The Pedophiliac Offender." Diseases of the Nervous System 23 (1962).

17. Schultz, L. G. "The Child Sex Victim: Social, Psychological and Legal Perspectives." Child Welfare 52 (1973).

18. Virkkunen, M. "Victim-Precipitated Pedophilia Offenses." British Journal of Criminology 14 (1975).

19. Weeks, R. B. "The Sexually Exploited Child." Southern Medical Journal 69 (1976).

20. Weiss, J.; Rogers, E.; Darwin, M.R.; and Dutton, C. E. "A Study of Girl Sex Victims." Psychiatric Quarterly 29 (1955).

(Address requests for a reprint to Kenneth J. Gruber, BIABH Study Center, 204 Avery Avenue, Morganton, NC 28655.)

THE JOURNAL OF

NERVOUS AND
MENTAL DISEASE

VOL. 170, NO. 10
October 1982
SERIAL NO. 1199

The Abusing Parent Revisited

A Decade of Psychological Research

WILLIAM N. FRIEDRICH, Ph.D., and KAREN K. WHEELER, B.A.[1]

In 1972, a major review paper by Spinetta and Rigler (Spinetta, J. J., and Rigler, D. The child abusing parent: A psychological review. Psychol. Bull., 77: 296–304, 1972) was published. This paper examined the largely clinical literature that existed up to that time on the psychological characteristics of the abusing parent. The authors concluded that abusive parents were abused as children, lacked accurate parenting knowledge, and were characterologically impulsive, and that socioeconomic stressors were neither necessary nor sufficient causal factors in the abuse cycle. In the last decade, a considerable number of controlled empirical studies on the abusive parent have been published. This paper critically investigates these studies with respect to the four conclusions offered by Spinetta and Rigler and suggests future areas of research need.

Spinetta and Rigler (56) summarized the literature on abusing parents that existed up until 1969. At that time, psychologists had largely neglected this area of research, and few well designed studies of personality characteristics of abusing parents had been published. The literature in the area consisted primarily of discussions of the medical and legal aspects of abuse and neglect. The intent of that review was to examine the largely clinical studies that existed at the time on the psychological characteristics of abusing parents and to posit some hypotheses that could be subjected to empirical examination. Essentially four conclusions were reached: a) the abusing parent was deprived as a child; b) the abusing parent lacks accurate knowledge concerning childrearing; c) these parents have a character defect which allows aggressive impulses to be expressed too freely; and d) socioeconomic stresses are neither necessary nor sufficient causes of physical abuse.

These four conclusions by Spinetta and Rigler (56) have served to organize and direct much of the research that has been done in this area in the past decade. It is necessary at this time to review the findings of over 10 years of controlled research in these four areas, i.e., child abusers as children, child abusers' knowledge of parenting, personality of child abusers, and stress and the child abuser. The empirical literature pertinent to each of these areas is now presented.

[1] Department of Psychology, University of Washington, Seattle, Washington 98195. Send reprint requests to Dr. Friedrich.

Child Abusers as Children

Behavioral scientists from several disciplines agree that children are more often than not similar along personality dimensions to their parents, and utilize childrearing methods similar to those used by their parents. Whether these similarities between parent and child result from genetic and/or social learning mechanisms is still being debated. The existence of similarities has prompted considerable research that examines adults' perceptions of their childhood experiences. Spinetta and Rigler (56) report that a history of emotional deprivation and/or loss of a significant parental figure early in life was a unanimous finding in the various clinical reports about abusing parents that they reviewed. How well has this conclusion fared under the impact of further research?

Disbrow et al. (11) compared an abusive-neglectful group of parents with a matched control group of parents and discovered that the two groups differed in whether they were abused as children, with the abusive-neglectful group reporting a greater incidence of abuse as children. However, no differences in early rearing were noted between the abusive and neglectful parents. Both groups reported similar amounts of abuse as children. The authors used path analysis to statistically interpret the data and suggested that a direct connection existed between the parent's background of abuse as a child and the personality, social resources, ways of handling irritating child behaviors, parental attitudes, and physiological response the parents had in response to their child's behavior.

Loveland (30) found that neglectful mothers reported experiencing as children a significantly higher level of physical punishment for aggressive and non-aggressive acts than a reference group of mothers similar in socioeconomic and educational variables. He measured a variety of variables, including self-esteem and discipline practices, and found that the mothers' reported level of receiving physical punishment for aggressive behavior as a child was the most highly intercorrelated measure with all of the other variables. Wolock and Horowitz (62) reported differences in the parent's background even when the maltreating parents and the control parents were all on public assistance. The former group was less likely to have been raised by both parents and more likely to report having been beaten as young children. Conger (9) discovered that abusive parents were more likely to report severe physical punishment as part of their own upbringing than either neglectful or control parents. He was able to find differences between abusive and neglectful mothers in terms of upbringing, with 47 per cent of the abusive parents agreeing that they or a sibling were severely punished as a child and only 6 per cent of the control sample responding in a similar fashion (10). In a British study, Smith and Hanson (50) found a significantly greater percentage of abusive parents reporting impaired relationships with their parents than did members of a control group. The abusive parents described their parents as harsh, rejecting, and unreasonable in their discipline and given to frequent use of physical punishment.

The Michigan Screening Profile of Parenting (MSPP) (22), which was developed to detect parents at risk for abuse, has a number of factors, including one entitled relationship with parents. Gaines et al. (19) used the MSPP with abusive, neglectful, and control parents and were unable to find differences between groups on the factor relationship with parents, which measured how the parent viewed his own parents and upbringing. The authors then independently derived a number of factors. One, which consisted primarily of items on the factor relationship with parents, was a significant contributor to a discriminant analysis of these three groups of parents, with the control parents reporting the most satisfactory relationship with their parents. The MSPP was also used by Spinetta (55) with six groups of mothers: adjudicated abusers, spouses of adjudicated abusers, mothers convicted of child neglect, and three control groups of nonabusing mothers, differing in levels of education and income. Significant between-group differences were found on the factor relationship with parents, with the first three groups being very similar to one another.

The finding of differences between abusive and control parents in their history of abuse as children has not been unanimous. Ceresnie (7) failed to find differences between matched samples of abusive and non-abusive mothers on reports of whether they were abused as children, and attributed this to the face-valid nature of the scale used to measure this dimension. This failure was duplicated in another study which did not find significant differences in self-reports of abuse and neglect in the life histories of abusive and control mothers of similar socioeconomic status (20). Hagenau (21) was unable to find differences in reported upbringing between abusive women and nonabusive women who had been convicted of assault of an adult. Straus and Gelles (57) did find differences between individuals who admitted using physically abusive treatment with their children and their history of physical punishment as a child. However, they dichotomized their sample ($N = 1146$) into those individuals who had been physically punished twice or more a year as a teenager (with 17.6 per cent of this group reporting that they had abused a child) and those who had been physically punished less than twice a year as a teenager (with 12.5 per cent of this group reporting that they had abused a child). Although valuable in pointing out that the relationship between physical punishment and abuser status is not directly linear, this study does not address abuse history as a child per se.

A number of factors may contribute to the failure to find differences between abusive, neglectful, and control groups in their reports of their parents' behavior. For example, agencies which investigate abuse and neglect differ widely in their operational definitions of these two phenomena. In addition, in many cases, abuse and neglect are both present, but the parent is charged with what is most easily substantiated (15). It is also important to determine whether the research utilized test data from a presentencing investigation of the parents or whether the parents suspected that the information gathered would be used against them. Finally, the reading level of these parents is not always determined, even in those studies relying heavily or solely on pencil and paper tests (19).

The uncertainty with regard to concluding that there is a direct connection between abuse history and abusive behavior as a parent does define a problem with research in this area. Most studies end up treating abusive parents as a homogeneous sample to be contrasted with a "homogeneous" control sample. That is far from the reality of the situation.

Several authors have taken issue with the common assumption that child abusers experienced abuse themselves as children. Jayaratne (24) cites several authors who report that abuse was common, but not universal, in the childhood of abusive parents. In addition, the lack of a normative comparison group is seen as a recurring problem. He also reports that emotional abuse and physical abuse are considered as single phenomena in studies reporting abuse in the background of abusive parents. Whether or not this is valid needs to be examined empirically. He proposes three other areas of research that need to be investigated before the generational hypothesis of child abuse can be considered valid. For example, given that abuse affects all the children in a family, it would be important to determine whether the adult siblings of abusive parents are also abusive. In addition, research is needed to determine whether abusive and control parents differ not only on reported childhood experiences but also in terms of actual experiences as children. No research has yet been done that examines differential effects of emotional vs. physical abuse experiences. Finally, since there is still considerable debate as to what small portion of adult behavior is predicted by childhood experiences, the utility and validity of reports of childhood experiences are still in question. Potts and Herzberger (44) also point out that a simple hypothesis, in this case that abused children become abusive parents, is suspect in behavioral research, since single variables rarely explain global patterns of behavior.

These are valid criticisms and need to be addressed. The current literature has several investigations of the reports of the childhood experiences of abusive parents. There is a common but disputed finding (7, 20) of greater amounts of physical abuse in these individuals' background, but no explanations are offered for abusive parents who do not report this phenomenon, and no longitudinal study has yet reported the extent of this relationship. In addition, no study has yet been reported that examined nonabusive parents who had been abused as children.

Child Abusers as Parents

Spinetta and Rigler (56) concluded that the primarily clinical, noncontrolled studies that they reviewed indicated a lack of appropriate knowledge of childrearing in abusive parents. In addition, these parents had aberrant attitudes, expectations, and childrearing techniques resulting in their expecting "too much, too fast" from their children. An issue that needs to be addressed, however, is whether samples of abusers, who are most often drawn from low socioeconomic categories, differ in their knowledge and attitudes when compared with a similarly deprived sample. Abusers who are facing court involvement or who recently were adjudicated may be able to respond in a socially desirable manner, thus eliminating any between-group differences. And finally, attitudes and

knowledge of childrearing do not necessarily predict behavior. In the final analysis, actual behavior needs to be analyzed, in addition to attitudes.

The results of studies examining parental reports of attitudes and knowledge are somewhat equivocal. Ceresnie (7) found that measures of maternal childrearing interaction were the most powerful discriminators between abusive and control families. However, no differences were demonstrated in parental knowledge of developmental norms. Loveland (30) found that neglectful mothers reported significantly greater usage of physical punishment for both aggressive and common misbehaviors than did mothers from a matched control group. However, the two groups did not differ on their knowledge of discipline options, the reported effectiveness of their discipline procedures, and the reported ease with which their children are disciplined. Disbrow et al. (11) found that abusers, neglectors, and spouses of abusers differed from control parents in greater use of physical and withholding types of punishment, and were less likely to reason with the child or consider the behavior as normal on the part of the child. Stultz (58) noted that abusive mothers valued the use of parental power with their children and were less able to empathize with them. However, no differences between abusive mothers and two control groups of mothers were found on a measure of what parents could expect at different ages in terms of their child's behavior. Egeland and Brunquell (13) attempted to differentiate good from inadequate mothers based on data prior to the occurrence of any abuse or neglect and found that a factor based on the mother's understanding of the psychological complexity of the infant and her relationship with the infant contributed most to a correct discrimination. However, when using data including mother's knowledge of childrearing, personality, behavior during feeding with the child, infant temperament, etc., interaction between mother and child during feeding was the best discriminator. In this case, behavior accounted for more variance than childrearing knowledge and attitudes. The longitudinal nature of the study lends further credence to the finding of the primacy of behavior, rather than knowledge or attitudes.

Gaines et al. (19) found that responses to a childrearing questionnaire were not significantly different between abusive, neglectful, and control parents, and failed to contribute significantly to the discrimination between the two groups. However, Spinetta (55) did find significant differences in expectations of one's child between abusive mothers, spouses of abusers, neglectful mothers, and three other control groups of mothers. The difference was most significant, however, between the low-income abusers and a middle-income control group, and it seems obvious that cultural and educational differences influenced this finding. Wolock and Horowitz (62) did not find consistent differences in childrearing knowledge or attitudes between abusers and nonabusers, all of whom were on public assistance.

Popular measures of childrearing attitudes, particularly the Parent Attitude Research Instrument (PARI), have not demonstrated a relationship to actual parent behavior or to the child's later development, and are particularly invalid with parents from low-income brackets (2). However, this has not prevented the PARI from being used, with mixed success, with abusing parents. Hagenau (21) used the PARI to successfully discriminate abusers from a control group of assaultive women, and Rosenblatt (48) noted that abusive parents were found to be more punitive and authoritarian on the PARI. Thompson (59) reported that objective parenting attitudes (on the PARI) were inversely related to the incidence of child abuse. Another study was able to correctly classify abusive and control parents with only 65 per cent accuracy when using the PARI, which is 15 per cent above chance (40), and Berg (4) failed to find either the PARI or a parental expectations survey to be useful discriminators between abusing and control parents.

Several studies of maternal-child and family interaction in abusive families have been reported. One large study investigated 10 abuse, 10 neglect, and 12 control families, and found that the abuse and neglect families were more negative, less positive, and spoke less than the controls (9). These differences resulted largely from the mother's behavior in the abuse families, whereas both father and mother contributed in neglect families. In addition, the abuse families showed a distinctly lower rate of physical interaction than either of the other family types. Another large study of 17 abuse, 17 neglect, and 19 control families supported these findings (6). They concluded that the lower rate of positive, negative, or neutral physical interaction in the abuse families indicates that the parents, particularly the mothers, are unskilled in the use of physical contacts, so that when they do employ physical behavior, they tend to do so inappropriately or excessively. Reid and Taplin (45) examined 27 control families, 27 abusive families, and 61 distressed but nonabusive families in the home environment. A composite of behaviors called total aversive behavior, which consists of 14 categories of highly aversive behaviors, e.g., destructiveness, humiliation, physical negative, etc., was examined. The mean rates of total aversive behavior were higher for all members of abusive families in comparison to their counterparts in the other groups, with mothers and index children revealing significant between-group differences. Two

other categories were examined, and both physical negative behaviors and command negatives were also higher for mothers and index children in the abuse group. The fact that the index child was as high in total aversive behavior as the abusive mother suggests that the child is not a passive participant in the abuse process and often behaves in a way that perpetuates the abusive cycle. In addition, the abuse families were characterized by an overall tendency to handle problems in a physical, aggressive manner. Walker (61) compared two groups of 14 mother-child dyads (one abusive, one control) across a variety of tasks, including an unstructured period, free play, a story period, and a structured task period. Rating from observers blind to the status of the parents indicated that, on all measures of maternal warmth and supportiveness, the abusive mothers differed significantly from the nonabusive mothers. The abused children were also much more hesitant in initiating play with their mothers than the nonabused children. Further support for the contention of disrupted parental behavior in abusive families comes from a recent study comparing a sample of college students who reported having been abused ($N = 38$) with a matched, nonabused sample of college students ($N = 38$) on the Family Environment Scale developed by Moos (8, 34). The two groups differed considerably in how they described their family, with the abused group reporting significantly more conflict and control issues present.

Jayaratne (24) has taken issue with the common assumption of parental inadequacy in abusive parents. He reports that a longitudinal study has shown that nonabusing teenage parents tend to interact with their children in a manner similar to abusive parents, and calls for studies using comparison groups. However, his research was completed prior to the publication of some very adequately controlled studies which did report parental inadequacy in neglectful and abusive parents (6, 9, 45, 61). Although self-reports of parental attitudes are suspect as far as discriminating maltreating from control parents, behavioral ratings discriminate much more convincingly and argue for differences in parenting between these groups.

Personality of Child Abusers

The majority of the authors cited in the review by Spinetta and Rigler (56) pointed to psychological factors within the parents as prime etiological variables in child abuse. Socioeconomic factors could aggravate these personality weaknesses, but by themselves were neither necessary nor sufficient causes of abuse. This has been an active area of research since the 1972 review. Other than two studies (20, 32), all of the controlled research has been published since 1970.

The Minnesota Multiphasic Personality Inventory (MMPI) Scales

The MMPI and its special scales have been used considerably in an effort to examine personality characteristics of child-abusing parents. Griswold and Billingsley (20) reported that MMPI scales F, Pt, and Sc differed significantly between 12 abusive and 27 nonmaltreating mothers, and MMPI scales Hs, D, and Hy differed significantly between 8 neglectful and 27 nonmaltreating mothers. The 12 abusive and eight neglectful mothers also differed significantly between each other on the MMPI scales Pt and Sc, with the abusing mothers having greater elevations on these scales.

Wright (63) presented MMPI data on 15 abusive parents and reported that the profile was generally elevated and had significantly higher than average scores on the Pd and Sc scales. Kaleita and Wise (26) also noted that the Pd and Sc scales were the most elevated scales in 25 battering parents, lending some support to this finding. Wright (64) also reported MMPI data on 13 convicted abusing parents and 13 nonabusive control parents. Significant differences on the L and K ($p < .05$) scales were noted and differences on the Pd scale just missed significance. The author coined the term "sick but slick" to describe abusive parents. It appears that Wright combined the results of his two studies to arrive at this label; *i.e.*, the "slickness" is derived from the elevated L and K scales in the 1976 study and "sickness" is derived from the elevated Pd and Ma scales in the 1970 study.

This is a questionable tactic, and the defensiveness manifested in the 1976 study seems understandable in light of the fact that the MMPI was administered after the abuse episode as part of court proceedings.

Paulson *et al.* (39) found significant differences on the MMPI between abusive fathers and mothers and on the L, F, Mf, Pa, and Ma scales of the MMPI across abusers, passive abusers, absolute nonabusers, and control parents who were similar in socioeconomic level. However, none of the mean scores for any of the MMPI scales exceeded a *T*-score of 70, but the Pd-Ma (4-9) profile and the Ma-Pd (9-4) profile had the highest mean *T*-score values for abusive females and abusive males, respectively.

Gabinet (18) used the MMPI with three groups of mothers: abusing mothers in a parenting program (*N* = 22), the nonabusive mothers in the parenting program (*N* = 90), and mothers who were patients in an outpatient psychiatry clinic (*N* = 90). The mean profiles for the three groups were surprisingly similar, with Ma differing significantly ($p < .05$) between abusers and the outpatient psychiatry group. However,

the peak scores for the abusive mothers composite profile was Pa-Sc, with *T*-scores above 70 for both points.

Paulson *et al.* (37) item analyzed the scores of the 60 index subjects and 10 control subjects from his 1974 experiment to devise male, female, and combined male and female abuser scales from the MMPI. Paulson *et al.* (38) then used a subsample (*N* = 33) of the 60 index subjects from his 1974 study to include only active abusers. The same control sample was used (which was self-referred and older than the index subjects) and a discriminant analysis procedure was used to devise six more brief scales of the MMPI for the identification of abusive males and females. Furlong and Leton (17) used an independent (*N* = 19) sample to determine the validity of Paulson's three scales derived from item analysis and six scales derived by discriminant analysis. They correctly classified anywhere from 10 to 78 per cent of their abusing parents, depending on the scale. However, these 19 subjects were characterized by a diverse ethnic mix, lower education, and lower age than Paulson's sample. Consequently, the validity of these derived, abuse-specific scales has yet to be determined.

Paulson *et al.* (41) have also used published, experimental subscales of the Pd and Ma MMPI scales and Megargee's Over-controlled Hostility (OH) scale (31), with 53 abusive and 113 control parents of similar socioeconomic status. The control parents had a child receiving outpatient services from a psychiatric clinic. Results indicated a significantly greater degree of psychosocial pathology and a significantly greater impulse predispositions in the abusive parents as a group, compared to nonabusive mothers and fathers of children receiving outpatient psychiatric services. In addition, females, both abusive and control, scored significantly higher than females on two of the Ma scales.

A variant of the MMPI, the Mini-Mult (29), is a 71-item short form of the MMPI which has considerable comparability to the full-scale MMPI. It has been used in one study of abusive (*N* = 13), neglectful (*N* = 14), and low-income control (*N* = 15) mothers.[2] The results found significant differences between groups on the F, D, Pd, Pt, and Sc scales from the Mini-Mult, with the neglect group appearing the most deviant of the three groups and the control groups appearing the least deviant.

Other General Personality Measures

A variety of other personality measures has been used with abusive parents. Hyman (23) examined 40

---

[2] Friedrich, W. N. Personality and psychophysiological variables in abusive, neglectful, and low-income control mothers. Unpublished doctoral dissertation, University of North Dakota, Grand Forks, North Dakota, 1980.

abusive and 37 control subjects and reported average intelligence in the abusive parents along with significantly greater immature impetuosity in the abusive mothers and introversion in the abusive fathers, as measured by the 16PF. Smith et al. (51) found significantly lower intelligence and greater neuroticism (as measured by the Eysenck Personality Inventory) in abusive mothers. Smith et al. (53) found an abnormal EEG in eight of 35 parents who had abused their children. This subgroup also appeared to be more psychopathic and of lower intelligence. Smith and Hanson (50) reported significantly greater amounts of hostility and neuroticism (as measured by the Eysenck Personality Inventory) in both abusive mothers and fathers when compared with nonabusive parents.

Melnick and Hurley (32) compared 10 abusive and 10 carefully matched control mothers on 18 personality variables, largely from the Thematic Apperception Test and the California Test of Personality. Abusive mothers seemed less able to empathize with their children, had a probable history of emotional deprivation, and had severely frustrated dependency needs. Evans (14) compared 20 abusive and 20 carefully matched control mothers all on Aid to Families with Dependent Children and was able to discriminate 97.5 per cent of the mothers. The best discriminators were four scales derived from the Thematic Apperception Test, including frustrated independence, aggression pathogenesis, and frustrated dominance. The author interpreted this as indicative of the pervasiveness of the abusive mother's psychopathology, and concluded that basic character traits are involved.

The adequacy of maternal care in mothers at high risk for child abuse and neglect has been studied longitudinally in a large group of low-income primiparous mothers (5). A variable defined as level of personal integration was the best discriminator of mothers who provided excellent care from mothers who provided inadequate care. Although this variable was derived through factor analysis, and was not a personality measure per se, it was comprised of such variables as intelligence, positive response to pregnancy, positive expectations regarding their children, and a better understanding of their relationship with their children.

Specific Personality Variables

Rosen (47) found significant differences between 30 abusive and 30 control mothers in that the former mothers had lower and more inconsistent self-concepts, and expressed greater incongruence between the way they viewed themselves and the way they would like to be. Using the same sample, she also found on a measure of interpersonal values that abusive mothers valued conformity and benevolence less

and authority over others more than did nonabusive mothers (46). Loveland (30) compared 10 neglectful and 10 carefully matched control mothers, and although no significant differences were found between groups in self-esteem, the neglect group possessed a significantly higher number of deviant signs, a higher level of psychosis, and less personality integration as measured by clinical interview than the reference group. Kertzman (28) found that 40 abusers differed from 40 matched nonabusers in greater dependency and lower frustration tolerance in the former group. In addition, in an experimental setting, he noted that abusers responded primarily to frustration and only secondarily to gratification, with the reverse being true for the nonabusers. Ceresnie (7) found significantly more alienation and social nonconformity in 20 abusive mothers when compared with 20 nonabusive control mothers.

Kenel (27) compared 43 child abusers, 43 nonabusers, and 50 aggressive offenders, and failed to find differences between groups on impulsivity, although the abusers and aggressive offenders reported significantly more mistrust, guilt, and willingness to express anger. A later study compared 15 low-income control mothers with 13 abusive and 14 neglectful mothers on measures of repression-sensitization, field dependence, socialization, and anxiety, hostility, and depression.[2] The control mothers were significantly less anxious and hostile, more socialized, and less field dependent than the other two groups.

Social isolation and interpersonal withdrawal are commonly reported behaviors of abusive and neglectful mothers (43, 52, 62). Apparently, a mother must possess some sense of inner effectiveness in order to involve herself in support systems around her.

The MSPP has been used recently (19, 55) in several very important studies which elucidate personality characteristics of maltreating parents. Gaines et al. (19) found significant differences between a large group (N = 240) of abusive, neglectful, and low-income control mothers on two MSPP factors, emotional needs met and coping. Neglectful mothers, followed by abusive mothers, appeared as the least healthy on these two factors. Spinetta (55) independently derived six factors from the MSPP and found significant differences between adjudicated abusers and nonabusers on the factors of a) tendency to become upset and angry, b) tendency toward isolation and loneliness, and c) fear of external threat and control. Neglectful mothers differed significantly from the same control group on two of these same factors, i.e., a and c, and also on another factor labeled inability to separate parental and child feelings.

Milner and Wimberley (33) devised a Child Abuse Potential Inventory with four factors, loneliness, rigidity, problems, and control, that was successful in discriminating a small group of abusive from nonabusive mothers. Independent validation of this measure comes from a study which found that college students who reported having been abused as children scored significantly higher on the Child Abuse Potential Inventory than a matched sample of nonabused college students (8).

Most of the above reports have focused on mothers. However, several studies have focused solely on fathers. Amberg (1) found that 15 male inmates of the psychiatric unit of a state prision who had admitted in the course of psychotherapy that they had abused their children were compared on the Rorschach Test with 15 inmates who had not voluntarily acknowledged abusing their children and 15 nonabusing fathers from the community. The protocols were independently evaluated, and abusive fathers seemed less able to integrate emotion effectively with realistic thinking and appeared less integrated with regard to personality structure. However, this is not surprising in that the fathers who voluntarily admitted abusing a child apparently were ready to disclose damning things about themselves. O'Hearn (35) compared 23 abusive fathers with 23 carefully matched nonabusive fathers, and found significantly less self-esteem, ego strength, assertiveness, and greater feelings of powerlessness in the abusive fathers.

How similar are abuse and neglect? Since many studies do not differentiate these two, it would be very important to determine whether they are similar or diverse manifestations of inadequate parenting. Sourkes (54) attempted to discriminate abuse and neglect in the child care characteristics of 30 mothers whose infants were enrolled in a primary prevention mental health program. The mother's behaviors were rated as abusive or neglectful, and the author examined what maternal variables predicted this behavior. Abuse and neglect shared some common variance, but in the main seemed unique. Socioeconomic status, internal resources, and external resources were important in predicting ratings of neglect. The findings were less clear for abuse, but both emerged as complex, psychosocial phenomena, with potentially different etiologies. Some evidence also suggests that neglectful mothers appear more disturbed on standardized measures of pathology than abusive mothers.[2]

There is a considerable amount of evidence that personality does play a role as a determinant of child abuse, although there is no suggestion that factors of personality weakness and parental inadequacy are the sole determinants of child abuse. In addition, only a very small percentage of abusive parents are thought to be psychotic. However, in the last several years, increasingly well designed research has been published

which adds to our awareness of the personality problems existing in this group. Some characteristics which have been found across several studies indicate that abusive parents have difficulty with impulse control, lowered self-esteem, an impaired capacity for empathy, and are isolated interpersonally. Kertzman (28) also suggested that abusive parents appear to be motivated differently from nonabusive parents, in that the former respond primarily to frustration and only secondarily to gratification. Interpreted broadly, this suggests that abusive parents tend to seek frustration-inducing and frustration-perpetuating interactions. This would clearly exacerbate the childrearing situation even further and make the parent even more prone to abuse.

But, as Gabinet (18) has suggested, the MMPIs of abusive mothers are very similar to other nonabusive mothers seeking outpatient therapy. This suggests that a determination of the mediating influences that make one person abuse and make an individual with a similar personality type not abuse would be critical to understanding this phenomenon.

Stress and the Child Abuser

Spinetta and Rigler (56) concluded that socioeconomic stresses are neither necessary nor sufficient causes of child abuse. They stated that, if it was indeed true that abuse occurred in only a minority of socially and economically deprived families, and also did occur in other, less deprived families, the cause of child abuse had to lie beyond socioeconomic stresses.

This conclusion has been challenged (42). While allowing that child abuse and neglect have indeed been found among all socioeconomic classes, Pelton states that very clear evidence exists to show that abuse and neglect are not distributed proportionately among the total population, and that socioeconomic class variables are very important. Data from the national studies completed annually by the American Humane Association indicate that, in 1975 and 1976, between 11 and 15 per cent of abusive and neglectful families had incomes exceeding $11,000. The median family income in 1976 for these families was $5,051, as compared to $13,900 for all American families in the same year. Pelton also reports that child abuse and neglect are related to degrees of poverty, with the highest level of child maltreatment occurring in families living in the most extreme poverty.

Pelton's arguments have support in other studies which have shown that stress, although not exclusively socioeconomic, is related to child abuse and neglect. For example, Justice and Duncan (25) were able to show a relationship between life change and child abuse when they compared 35 abusing parents with a control sample of 35 nonabusing parents on the Social Readjustment Rating Scale. The mean score on the rating scale was 234 for the abusing parents and 124 for the nonabusing parents. Rather than economic or environmental stress, the distinguishing factor between the groups was change, which was requiring constant readjustment. These authors state that, when life events occur too rapidly, people become so exhausted by the strain of coping that they lose control over their situation and the chances for their acting out in an abusive manner increases. Another study used a similar measure of stress and found that 20 abusive parents had significantly greater life stress than 20 matched control parents (10). In addition, the abuse parents reported a significantly greater number of physical and emotional health problems on the Cornell Medical Index. This suggests a variety of other stressors that are affecting parental functioning in the abuse sample.

Further support for the role of stress comes from Gaines et al. (19) who performed a stepwise multiple discriminant analysis between 80 abusive, 80 neglectful, and 80 control mothers. The 12 independent variables measured types of stress, parenting factors, some personality dimensions, and a measure of infant risk. Two of the six significantly discriminating variables were related to stress, the first measuring negative life experiences typically encountered by very poor families and the other one similar to the scale used by Justice and Duncan (25). Neglectful mothers were discriminated from abusive and control mothers on the basis of the first stress variable, a factor from the MSPP called emotional needs met, and on a dimension related to coping and stress. This study is limited because of its reliance on a large number of paper and pencil surveys that were difficult for many of the mothers to fill out, 88 per cent of the variance was left unexplained, and parent category could be predicted only 15 per cent better than chance. Regardless of these deficiencies in the Gaines et al. (19) study, it is increasingly questionable whether maltreatment can be primarily attributed to childrearing attitudes or specific personality variables. Rather, stress and the ability to cope with stress seem to be more important.

A recent study examined the complex relationship of socioeconomic stress and quality of mother-child attachment (60). They determined that improvement in mother-child attachment over a 6-month period was best predicted in these low-income mothers by a decrement in stressful events experienced by the mother.

This is an important finding and underscores the interaction between stress and parenting and personality variables, which needs to be more closely and systematically examined. For example, do maltreating mothers respond similarly to all types of stress, or is the response exclusively to socioeconomic stressors? It would seem that a well designed, ego-specific stressor should be able to elicit a similar interaction in mothers for whom child abuse reports have been substantiated.

Several recent studies have utilized specific stressors to further examine the nature of psychophysiological responding in maltreating parents (12, 16).[2] These studies were designed to examine abuse as a consequence of the interaction of stress and parent characteristics. In one large study ($N = 169$, with 84 controls, 33 abusive, 18 spouses of abusers, and 34 neglectful), subjects were asked to observe videotapes of three stressful and three pleasant scenes of parent-child behavior, while heart rate, blood volume, and skin conductance were measured (12). The results quite clearly demonstrated strong differences among the physiological response patterns of these subjects. The authors interpreted the pattern of results as showing abusive and neglectful parents as being less in tune with their environment, failing to differentiate between stimulus scenes, with abusive parents having generally elevated physiological measures throughout and neglectful parents with lower physiological levels throughout. This differed markedly from the control subjects, who differentiated between stimulus scenes, showed regular habituation patterns, and were described as in tune with their environment.

Frodi and Lamb (16) examined 14 child abusers and a matched group of nonabusers while watching videotapes of smiling and crying infants. In addition to measuring skin conductance, heart rate, and blood pressure, the authors had the parents rate their emotional responses on a mood adjective checklist. The abusers responded to the cry with greater heart and skin conductance arousal and rated it as more aversive than the nonabusers. This group did not seem to be able to discriminate crying from smiling scenes, reminiscent of the Doerr et al. (12) finding of abusers being less in tune with their environment.

An audiotape of a crying infant, interspersed with segments of white noise or a tone, was utilized in another study of the psychophysiological responses of maltreating parents.[2] Three matched groups were used: control ($N = 15$), abuse ($N = 13$), and neglect ($N = 14$); and heart rate, finger blood volume, and skin resistance measures were recorded. In addition, the mothers rated six dimensions of the infant's cry: age, length, loudness, irritating, anger, and demanding. The groups differed on skin resistance measures, but not on the cardiovascular measures. The pattern of results from the measures of skin resistance suggested that both neglectful and abusive mothers were more easily aroused and remained aroused for longer periods of time than did the control mothers, who habituated more rapidly. The neglectful mothers also showed even less ability to differentiate the various auditory stimuli, responding with greater arousal across all stimuli. In addition, the maltreating mothers labeled the cry as significantly more demanding, angry, and irritating.

Several analogue studies have recently been completed which further elucidate some of the mediating influences of stress (36).[3] Both of these studies used nonabusive mothers as their subjects. Doran[3] utilized a stress × control design in which four randomly assigned groups of mothers, differing in the degree of stress (presence or absence of intermittent bursts of loud white noise) and the degree of control (presence or absence of a button which could "turn the noise off" at the discretion of the subject) responded to vignettes depicting children's misbehavior by describing how they would intervene. The high stress-low control group was significantly more punitive than any of the other groups. In the other analogue study, Passmann and Mulhern (36) had mothers "punish" their child by taking away candy when informed by buzzer their child, in another room, had made an error on a task. Stress was manipulated in two ways. Child-independent stress entailed increasing the number of buzzers which interrupted the mother while she worked. Both forms of stress increased maternal punitiveness.

The results of these studies on the role of stress in the maltreatment cycle have added some understanding of the complex interactional process that occurs between the person and the actual stressor. Abusive parents have a much more difficult time habituating to stress and, in addition, have a cognitive labeling process that interferes with the habituation response. For example, if a parent labels a particular child response as more irritating than another parent, the former will feel more stressed. And, as the analogue research demonstrates, mothers who feel in control are less punitive than those who feel less control or who are feeling overwhelmed, with no end in sight. (These studies suggest that therapy focused on changing the labeling process, or cognitions, involved with regards to feeling of control, the aversive features of the child, etc. may be useful in helping the parent stop the abuse cycle [49].)

Granted, environmental stress is neither a necessary nor sufficient cause of child abuse. The interaction is much more complex than that. Stress, coupled with a deficiency in parental capacity, a stress-heightening

[3] Doran, L. D. Mothers' disciplinary responses under controllable and uncontrollable stress: A child abuse analogue. Unpublished doctoral dissertation. University of Washington, Seattle, Washington, 1981.

attributional process, and chronic feelings of having little or no control, seems to describe quite accurately the parent that is investigated for child abuse.

Discussion and Conclusions

At present, it appears that the conclusions concerning the four areas of research reviewed by Spinetta and Rigler (56) have not all withstood the brunt of careful research. The evidence seems to support the earlier hypotheses that many abusing parents were maltreated as children and the existence of some personality variables that discriminate abusive from nonabusive parents, e.g., self-esteem, impulsivity, hostility, and abusive from neglectful parents, with evidence for greater pathology in the neglectful parents. However, the evidence is rather mixed with regard to whether maltreating parents lack adequate parenting knowledge. Rather, evidence points to actual differences in parenting and not to differences in childrearing attitudes. For example, studies of the family interaction of abusive families clearly demonstrate much more aversive behavior in these families (9, 45). Walker (61) too has shown that dyadic interaction research shows much lower maternal warmth and support in the abusive group. In addition, it appears that stress, and particularly socioeconomic stress, is an extremely important variable to consider in future research. The most comprehensive study to date (19) has indicated that stress overshadows personality variables in importance when discriminating between neglectful, abusive, and control mothers. Yet, at the same time, stress somehow interacts with personality and child variables to "potentiate maltreatment by widening the discrepancy between limited parental capacities and demanding offspring" (19, p. 532). Many families experience high levels of stress and the vast majority of children in these families are not neglected or abused.

It seems that it is here that future research efforts needs to be expended. Stress is mediated by a variety of variables, and it seems that the further delineation of those variables which discriminate those parents who do abuse from those parents who do not abuse, despite the presence of socioeconomic, medical, and other stressors, is needed. Child abuse is truly a problem of our society, and intervention is required at that level, although as Belsky (3) points out, for intervention to be effective, it must address problems of the abuser, the victim of the abuse, as well as his family, and the community and society in which they reside. However, research into what mediates stress can make such intervention more immediately useful, particularly when social intervention of this magnitude is an area from which the government is backing away.

References

1. Amberg, E. C. A projective assessment of fathers who abuse their children (Doctoral dissertation, Michigan State University, 1977). (University Microfilms No. 77-18, 449.) Diss. Abstr. Int., 38: 1392-B, 1977.

2. Becker, W. C., and Krug, R. S. Parent Attitude Research Instrument: A research review. Child Dev., 36: 329-365, 1965.

3. Belsky, J. A theoretical analysis of child abuse remediation strategies. J. Clin. Child Psychol., 7: 117-121, 1978.

4. Berg, T. I. Parental expectations and attitudes in child abusing families (Doctoral dissertation, University of Southern California, 1976). Diss. Abstr. Int., 37: 1889-B, 1976.

5. Brunnquell, D., Crichton, L., and Egeland, B. Maternal personality and attitude in disturbances of child rearing. Am. J. Orthopsychiatry, 51: 680-691, 1981.

6. Burgess, R. L., and Conger, R. D. Family Interaction in Abusive, Neglectful, and Normal Families. Paper presented at the Biennial Meeting of the Society for Research in Child Development, New Orleans, 1977.

7. Ceresnie, S. J. Child abuse: A controlled study of social and family factors (Doctoral dissertation, University of Washington, 1976). (University Microfilms No. 77-9378.) Diss. Abstr. Int., 37: 5826-B, 1977.

8. Chan, D. A., and Perry, M. A. Child Abuse: Discriminating Factors Toward a Positive Outcome. Paper presented at the Biennial Meeting of the Society for Research in Child Development, Boston, 1981.

9. Conger, R. D. A comparative study of interaction patterns between deviant and non-deviant families (Doctoral dissertation, University of Washington, 1976). (University Microfilms No. 77-18, 325.) Diss. Abstr. Int., 38: 1660-A, 1977.

10. Conger, R. D., Burgess, R. L., and Barrett, C. Child abuse related to life change and perceptions of illness: Some preliminary findings. Fam. Coordinator, 28: 73-77, 1979.

11. Disbrow, M. A., Doerr, H., and Caulfield, C. Measures to Predict Child Abuse. Paper presented at the Biennial Meeting of the Society for Research in Child Development, New Orleans, 1977.

12. Doerr, H. O., Disbrow, M. A., and Caulfield, C. Psychophysiological Response Patterns in Child Abuse. Paper presented at the Meeting of the Society for Psychophysiological Research, Philadelphia, 1977.

13. Egeland, B., and Brunnquell, D. An at-risk approach to the study of child abuse: Some preliminary findings. J. Am. Acad. Child Psychiatry, 18: 219-352, 1979.

14. Evans, A. L. Personality characteristics of child-abusing mothers (Doctoral dissertation, Michigan State University, 1976). (University Microfilms No. 77-11, 642.) Diss. Abstr. Int., 37: 6322-6323-B, 1977.

15. Friedrich, W. N., and Boriskin, J. A. Child abuse and neglect in North Dakota: Psychological and legal aspects. N. D. Law Rev., 53: 197-224, 1976.

16. Frodi, A. M., and Lamb, M. E. Child abusers' responses to infant smiles and cries. Child Dev., 51: 238-241, 1980.

17. Furlong, M. J., and Leton, D. A. The validity of MMPI scales to identify potential child abusers. J. Clin. Child Psychol., 6: 55-57, 1977.

18. Gabinet, L. MMPI profiles of high-risk and outpatient mothers. Child Abuse Neglect, 3: 373-379, 1979.

19. Gaines, R., Sandgrund, A., Green, A. H., and Power, E. Etiological factors in child maltreatment: A multivariate study of abusing, neglecting and normal mothers. J. Abnorm. Psychol., 87: 531-540, 1978.

20. Griswold, B. B., and Billingsley, A. Personality and social characteristics of low-income mothers who neglect or abuse their children. (In Final Report: Grant No. PR11001R.) Children's Bureau, Welfare Administration, U. S. Department of Health, Education, and Welfare, Washington, D. C., 1969.

21. Hagenau, H. R. Parental attitudes, perceptions of parents, and some personality characteristics of child abusing women (Doctoral dissertation, Catholic University of America, 1977).

(University Microfilms No. 77-19, 971). Diss. Abstr. Int., 38: 1402-1403-B, 1977.

22. Helfer, R. E., Schneider, C., and Hoffmeister, J. Manual for the Use of the Michigan Screening Profile of Parenting. Department of Human Development, Michigan State University, East Lansing, Mich., 1977.

23. Hyman, C. A. A report on the psychological test results of battering parents. Br. J. Soc. Clin. Psychol., 16: 221-224, 1977.

24. Jayaratne, S. Child abusers as parents and children: A review. Soc. Work, 22: 5-9, 1977.

25. Justice, B., and Duncan, D. F. Life crisis as a precursor to child abuse. Public Health Rep., 91: 110-115, 1976.

26. Kaleita, T., and Wise, J. H. An MMPI comparison of child abusers with two groups of criminal offenders. Clin. Proc. Child. Hosp. Natl. Med. Cent., 32: 180-184, 1976.

27. Kenel, M. E. A study of the cognitive dimension of impulsivity reflectivity and aggression in female child abusers (Doctoral dissertation, Catholic University of America, 1976). (University Microfilms No. 76-20, 229.) Diss. Abstr. Int., 37: 1438-B, 1976.

28. Kertzman, D. Dependency, frustration tolerance, and impulse control in child abusers (Doctoral dissertation, State University of New York at Buffalo, 1978). (University Microfilms No. 78-17050.) Diss. Abstr. Int., 38: 1484-B, 1978.

29. Kincannon, J. C. Prediction of the standard MMPI scale scores from 71 items: The Mini-Mult. J. Consult. Clin. Psychol., 32: 319-325, 1968.

30. Loveland, R. J. Distinctive personality and discipline characteristics of child-neglecting mothers (Doctoral dissertation, University of North Dakota, 1976). (University Microfilms No. 77-14, 569.) Diss. Abstr. Int., 33: 368-B, 1977.

31. Megargee, E. I., Cook, P. E., and Mendelsohn, G. A. The development and validation of an MMPI scale of assaultiveness in overcontrolled individuals. J. Abnorm. Psychol., 72: 519-528, 1967.

32. Melnick, B., and Hurley, J. R. Distinctive personality attributes of child-abusing mothers. J. Consult. Clin. Psychol., 33: 746-749, 1969.

33. Milner, J. S., and Wimberley, R. C. An inventory for the identification of child abusers. J. Clin. Psychol., 35: 95-100, 1979.

34. Moos, R. Preliminary Manual for the Family Environment Scale. Consulting Psychologists Press, Palo Alto, Calif., 1974.

35. O'Hearn, T. A comparison of fathers in abusive situations with fathers in non-abusive situation (Doctoral dissertation, University of Denver, 1974). (University Microfilms No. 75-1872.) Diss. Abstr. Int., 35: 3591-B, 1975.

36. Passman, R. H., and Mulhern, R. K. Maternal punitiveness as affected by situational stress: An experimental analogue of child abuse. J. Abnorm. Psychol., 86: 565-569, 1977.

37. Paulson, M. J., Afifi, A. A., Chaleff, A., et al. A discriminant function procedure for identifying abusive parents. Suicide, 5: 104-114, 1975.

38. Paulson, M. J., Afifi, A. A., Chaleff, A., et al. An MMPI scale for identifying "at risk" abusive parents. J. Clin. Child Psychol., 4: 22-24, 1975.

39. Paulson, M. J., Afifi, A. A., Thomason, M. L., and Chaleff, A. The MMPI: A descriptive measure of psychopathology in abusive parents. J. Clin. Psychol., 30: 387-390, 1974.

40. Paulson, M. J., Schwemer, G. T., Afifi, A. A., and Bendel, R. B. Parent Attitude Research Instrument (PARI): Clinical vs. statistical inferences in understanding abusive mothers. J. Clin. Psychol., 33: 848-854, 1977.

41. Paulson, M. J., Schwemer, G. T., and Bendel, R. B. Clinical application of the Pd, Ma, and (OH) experimental MMPI scales to further understanding of abusive parents. J. Clin. Psychol., 32: 558-564, 1976.

42. Pelton, L. H. Child abuse and neglect: The myth of classlessness. Am. J. Orthopsychiatry, 48: 608-617, 1978.

43. Polansky, N. A., Chalmers, M. A., Buttenweiser, E., and Williams, D. P. Isolation of the neglectful family. Am. J. Orthopsychiatry, 49: 149-152, 1979.

44. Potts, D., and Herzberger, S. Child Abuse: A Cross-Generational Pattern of Child-rearing. Paper read at Midwestern Psychological Association Convention, Chicago, 1979.

45. Reid, J. B., and Taplin, P. S. A Social Interactional Approach to the Treatment of Abusive Families. Paper read at the American Psychological Association Convention, Washington, D. C., 1976.

46. Rosen, B. Interpersonal values among child abusive women. Psychol. Rep., 45: 819–822, 1979.

47. Rosen, B. Self-concept disturbance among mothers who abuse their children. Psychol. Rep., 43: 323–326, 1978.

48. Rosenblatt, G. C. Parental expectations and attitudes about child-rearing in high-risk vs. low-risk child-abusing families (Doctoral dissertation, University of Southern California, 1978). Diss. Abstr. Int., 39: 3537-B, 1979.

49. Sanders, R. W. Systematic desensitization in the treatment of child abuse. Am. J. Psychiatry, 135: 483–484, 1978.

50. Smith, S. M., and Hanson, R. Interpersonal relationships and child-rearing practices in 214 parents of battered children. Br. J. Psychiatry, 127: 513–525, 1975.

51. Smith, S. M., Hanson, R., and Noble, S. Parents of battered babies: A controlled study. Br. Med. J., 4: 388–391, 1973.

52. Smith, S. M., Hanson, R., and Noble, S. Social aspects of the battered baby syndrome. Br. J. Psychiatry, 125: 568–582, 1974.

53. Smith, S. M., Honigsberger, L., and Smith, C. A. E.E.G. and personality factors in baby batterers. Br. Med. J., 2: 20–22, 1973.

54. Sourkes, B. M. Parental neglect and lashing out: Maladaptive styles of coping (Doctoral dissertation, University of Pittsburgh, 1976). (University Microfilms No. 77-3040.) Diss. Abstr. Int., 37: 4170–4171-B, 1977.

55. Spinetta, J. J. Parental personality factors in child abuse. J. Consult. Clin. Psychol., 46: 1409–1414, 1978.

56. Spinetta, J. J., and Rigler, D. The child abusing parent: A psychological review. Psychol. Bull., 77: 296–304, 1972.

57. Straus, M. A., and Gelles, R. J. Behind Closed Doors: Violence in the American Family. Anchor Press, New York, 1980.

58. Stultz, S. L. Child rearing attitudes of abusive mothers: A controlled study (Doctoral dissertation, Cornell University, 1976). (University Microfilms No. 76-21, 124.) Diss. Abstr. Int., 37: 1419-B, 1976.

59. Thompson, J. W. Frustration tolerance, parenting attitudes, and perceptions of parenting behavior as factors in the incidence of child abuse (Doctoral dissertation, Georgia State University, 1977). (University Microfilms No. 78-04940.) Diss. Abstr. Int., 38: 5598-B, 1978.

60. Vaughn, B., Egeland, B., Sroufe, L. A., and Waters, E. Individual differences in infant-mother attachment at twelve and eighteen months: Stability and change in families under stress. Child Dev., 50: 971–975, 1979.

61. Walker, L. M. Patterns of affective communication in abusive and nonabusive mothers (Doctoral dissertation, Michigan State University, 1977). (University Microfilms No. 78-03575.) Diss. Abstr. Int., 38: 5049–5050-B, 1978.

62. Wolock, I., and Horowitz, B. Factors Relating to Levels of Child Care Among Families Receiving Public Assistance in New Jersey. (ERIC Document Reproduction Service No. ED 144 336) Rutgers University, New Brunswick, N. J., 1977.

63. Wright, L. Psychological aspects of the battered child syndrome. South. Med. J., 58: 56–60, 1970.

64. Wright, L. The "sick but slick" syndrome as a personality component of parents of battered children. J. Clin. Psychol., 32: 41–45, 1976.

Journal of Clinical Child Psychology
1983, Vol. 12, No. 3, 244-256

The Abused Child: A Psychological Review

William N. Friedrich and Alison J. Einbender

University of Washington

The clinical-research literature relating to the abused child is critically review-ed. Included are demographic and epidemiological studies, behavioral studies, and studies of the cognitive/intellectual functioning of these children. Research which suggests that characteristics of the child contribute to abuse is also presented, along with suggestions for further research and preven-tion/treatment.

Spinetta and Rigler (1972) published a review of the literature pertaining to abusive parents. To a large degree, this seminal paper made the psychological community aware of this phenomenon and precipitated a considerable amount of research that has complemented the highly clinical literature that existed up to that time.

However, abuse is a parent-child phenomenon. It is appropriate that the literature relating to the abused child be reviewed at this time, given both the interactive nature of abuse and the need for direction in this area of research.

Physical abuse will be the primary focus of this review, since physical neglect is seldom research-ed. However, some studies reviewed in this paper will have examined both physically abused and neglected children, and in those instances, neglect will also be addressed.

Several questions will be addressed in this review. First, what are the demographic characteristics of abused children? Secondly, do abused children differ from nonabused children, and to what degree is this a function of the abuse? Finally, the interactive nature of abuse needs to be addressed further. Some recent research on abusive-parent child interaction has been publish-ed. Additionally, there are suggestions that some

Bill Friedrich is an assistant professor at the University of Washington. His research interests include child abuse, pediatric psychology and familial coping with chronic childhood illness.

Alison J. Einbender is a graduate student in clinical child psychology at the University of Washington. Her interests in-clude divorce and child abuse research.

Reprint requests and other correspondence should be ad-dressed to William N. Friedrich, Ph.D., Department of Psychology, NI-25, University of Washington, Seattle, Washington, 98195.

children are more stressful than others, and this results in a greater-than average abuse rate (Friedrich & Boriskin, 1976). Both clinical and comparison group research will be reviewed.

Demographic Characteristics

Several sources of data are available concerning demographic characteristics of abused children. These include early hospital-based research (Simons, Downs, Hurster, & Archer, 1966; Zuckerman, Ambuel, & Bandman, 1972), a na-tionwide survey done prior to changes in the child abuse reporting laws (Gil, 1970), as well as annual reports from the American Human Association. This agency collects child abuse data from all over the United States on a standard reporting form completed by child protective workers at the time the initial abuse report is filed (American Humane Association, 1981). The data from nationwide studies differs from hospital-based data not only in that a larger sample size is available, but also that a broader spectrum of abuse is reported in the national studies, whereas the hospital settings tend to see the more severe and medically involved types of abuse. These factors complicate the inter-pretation of demographic statistics.

Incidence

An important variable in abuse is the incidence of child maltreatment. Gil (1970) examined reports of physical abuse forwarded by central registries in the years 1967 and 1968. A total of 12,610 reports were studied with a resultant na-tionwide reporting rate of 8.4 reports per 100,000 children for 1967 and 9.3 reports for 1968. He reported that shifts in reporting patterns were due in large measure to changes in legal, professional, and administrative factors, suggesting that these variables are important determinants of reporting level. Recent data, available from the National Center on Child Neglect and Abuse Reporting, covers the year 1979 (American Humane Association, 1981). They received over 711,000 reports from 53 states and territories, for a 15.7% increase over the previous year. Their analysis of individual case data suggested a 40% substantiation rate for abuse and neglect, with neglect reports outnumbering abuse reports at a rate of 2:1. Whether this represents a real increase in abuse and neglect from 10 years earlier is impossible to determine. It does, however, present an idea of the extent of the problem.

Age

A second variable is the age of the child. Studies based on emergency room admissions generally show that at least two-thirds of the abused children in their samples are under 6 years of age (Simons, et. al, 1966; Zuckerman, et. al, 1972). Some hospital based studies have reported that as many as 60% of abused children are less than two years old (Ebbin, Gollub, Stein & Wilson, 1969; Lauer, Broeck & Grossman, 1974; Smith & Hanson, 1974). Smith and Hanson (1974) compared 134 abused children under 5 years of age with 53 nonabused children of similar sex and age breakdowns, who were emergency room admissions and noted that the younger the child, the more likely they had been abused. These studies have concluded that young children, particularly infants, are especially vulnerable to abuse for several reasons: 1) infants and preschoolers require more care and attention and hence, are more frustrating; 2) they are less able to defend themselves or evade punishment, and 3) younger children are physically more fragile.

However, data from Gil (1970) and the American Humane Association (1981) suggest that physical abuse is by no means limited to small children. Gil (1970) noted that more than three-quarters of the children in his nationwide sample were over two years of age, and nearly half of the children were over six years. Approximately one-fifth of the abused children in the sample were teenagers. This is supported by data from the American Humane Association (1981), reporting that approximately 40% of abused and neglected children in their sample were less than six years of age. Gil (1970) does report, however, that 65% of children under age three, as opposed to 35% of the children older than age three, were either severely or fatally injured. These data suggest that a source of bias may exist in emergency room studies; and so younger children may be overrepresented, due to their more severe injuries.

Sex Differences

Most studies report no significant difference between the proportion of males and females in their samples (American Humane Association, 1981; Simons, et al., 1966; Smith & Hanson, 1974; Ebbin, et al., 1969). Gil (1970) found that boys outnumbered girls in every age group below 12, when thereafter almost twice as many girls are abused as boys. This shift is supported, but not nearly as pronounced, by several other nationwide studies (American Humane Association, 1981). Gil (1970) proposed that the increase in physical abuse of girls as they enter adolescence may reflect parent-child conflicts over the daughter's developing sexuality.

Classification

It is possible to categorize the specific types of abuse that children most frequently incur. Common types of injuries that abused children receive are bruises, abrasions, and lacerations, and to a lesser extent burns and fractures (Gil, 1970). A sizable percentage of abused children seen in emergency room settings have been found to suffer from the "battered child syndrome," which is characterized by subdural hematoma, long bone fractures, and soft-tissue swelling. One hospital based study (Simons, et al., 1966) found that this syndrome characterized 22% of a sample of 313 abuse cases, and 100% of this sample was less than one year of age. However, national reporting data generally indicates that minor physical abuse occurs approximately 10 times more frequently than either major physical injury or burns (American Humane Association, 1981).

Reoccurrence

Research has reported that half of the abused children in sampled populations have had previous abuse or are reabused (Ebbin et al., 1969; Herrenkohl, & Herrenkohl, 1979; Lauer et al., 1974; Simons, et al., 1966; and Zuckerman et al., 1972). One recent study directly addressed the issue of recidivism (Herrenkohl, Herrenkohl, Egolf, & Seech, 1979). They examined the case records of 286 families who were verified to have abused their children, and found 67% of these families had a second recorded abuse incident, and 54% of them had between two and five additional recorded incidents. They also noted a significant association between age of child and recidivism, with younger children at greater risk than older children for experiencing recurrent abuse. Gil (1970) suggested that the high rate of recurrent abuse episodes indicates that the use of physical force tends to be part of a general pattern of child rearing, rather than just one isolated incident.

Single vs. Miltiple Children

A sixth variable, which is related to the conceptualization of abuse as a means of parenting, is the extent to which the abuse of one child is generalized to other children in the family. Gil (1970) noted that abuse of more than one child occurred in almost 30% of families in his study. Herrenkohl, et al. (1979) examined case records in 328 families and found that half of the families had more than one target of abuse. Findings from these two studies are contrary to the idea that abuse represents the scapegoating of one child.

Ethnic Differences

The rate of abuse in white vs. non-white families is the seventh domographic variable considered. Most studies have found that non-white children are abused at a rate exceeding their representation in the U.S. population (American Humane Association, 1981; Gil, 1970). Factors cited to explain a higher level of abuse in non-white families are: 1) discriminatory attitudes and reporting practices; 2) lower socioeconomic conditions among non-whites; and 3) different ethnic child rearing practices (Gil, 1970).

Family Intactness

A final variable concerns the intactness of abusive families. Research has found that between 30 - 42% of abused children come from single-parent households, which is a rate double that of the normal frequency of single-parent households in the U.S. (Gil, 1970; American Humane Association, 1981). Several studies also suggest that abused children are more frequently part of larger families (Gil, 1970). Despite initial reports to the contrary, which claimed that child abuse was a phenomenon evenly distributed across all SES categories, low SES characterizes the largest proportion of abuse families (Pelton, 1978). A related finding is that increases in child abuse in two large urban areas were preceded by high periods of job loss (Steinberg, Catalano, & Dooley, 1981). Lennington (1981) analyzed the data collected by American Humane Association and Gil (1970) and contrasted this data to census information. She concluded that rates of child abuse are highest for young male children from poor families. Further variables related to the rate of abuse were large family size, family breakdown, and defects in the child.

Intellectual and Cognitive Status of Abused Children

The general impression is that physical abuse results in lowered intelligence (Lynch, 1978) and delays in language (Blager & Martin, 1976). For example, Martin and Rodeheffer (1976) state that "abused children are handicapped in learning and intelligence" (p. 93). However, as is usually the case, at least two divergent opinions exist with regard to the relationship of abuse to the child's learning abulity and intelligence level. A second opinion is provided by Elmer (1977), who did an eight year follow-up of a small sample of abused and accidentally injured low-income children and found multiple developmental problems in both groups. She concluded that abuse per se was not as important as the pervasive neglect that characterizes low-income families. If true, this finding would deemphasize the specific impact of physical abuse. In this section, we will examine those studies which address the issue of the cognitive status of abused children.

Clinical Research

Early research, using no comparison groups, indicated that abused children did poorly in formal IQ testing. For example, 57% of one sample of 22 severely abused children has WISC IQ's below 80 (Elmer & Gregg, 1967), 42% of another sample of 21 abused children were judged to be mentally retarded (Morse, Sahler, & Friedman, 1970), 35% of 58 abused children had IQ's below 85 (Martin, Beezley, Conway & Kempe, 1974), 33% of 42 abused children were judged to be mentally retarded (Martin, 1972), the Baylay and Stanford-Binet scores for 25 children in another sample were very negatively skewed (Hyman & Mitchell, 1975), and 26% of 138 abused and neglected children were in special classes (Kline, 1977). The absence of appropriate comparison groups hampers the generalizability of these findings, but they do suggest that groups of abused children score lower than the norm on IQ tests.

Comparison Group Research

More recently, studies have been published that compare abused children with an appropriate comparison group. This has been done most often with infants. Gregg and Elmer (1969) compared 30 children with suspected abuse, with 83 children who were judged to have accidental injuries. All infants were under 13 months of age and generally from low SES categories. With standardized developmental screening, 42% of the abused children, as compared to 18% of the accidentally injured children, were judged retarded. A subset of each of these groups (2 groups of 17) were followed up after 8 years and were found not to differ in intellectual standing (as measured by ratings of school files) (Elmer, 1977; 1978). Appelbaum (1977) compared 30 infants with verified physical abuse to 30 nonabused infants, matched for age, sex, race and SES on the Baylay and the Denver Developmental Screening Test (Frankenburg, Dodds & Fandal, 1970). The mean age of the infants was just over one year and highly significant differences were found on the Baylay Mental Scale, with the abused children on the average, approximately 4 months below the controls. On the Motor Scale, the abused children on the average, scored 5-6 months below the controls. In addition, on 3 of the Denver Scales, personal-social, language, and gross motor, the abused infants were significantly lower, with no differences on the fine-motor subscale.

Koski and Ingram (1977) also used the Baylay Scales with three groups of infants: control (N = 38), abuse (N = 46), and failure-to-thrive (neglect) (N = 38). Abused infants had significantly lower Mental Scale scores, and failure-to-thrive infants were lower on both Mental and Motor Scales, than the controls.

Another study using the Bayley (Dietrich, Starr & Kaplan, 1980) compared abused (N = 14) with control (N = 14) infants, who were similar in SES, age, sex, race, and birth variables. Although the mean scores for both samples were within the normal range, 42% of the abused sample were more than one standard deviation below the mean on both Motor and Mental Scales, while this was true for only 14% of the control group. In addition, the mean score on the Mental Scale differed significantly with the abused children scoring lower as a group.

Another study (Fitch, Cadol, Goldson, Wendell, Swartz & Jackson, 1976) compared 49 abused children two years old and younger on the Bayley Scales. They were contrasted with 14 control infants (matched n age, sex, SES) and found to differ significantly on both Mental and Motor Scales, with the abused group having the lower mean score.

Abused children, other than infants, have not been studied in a similarly well controlled and systematic fashion. Fitch et al. (1976) compared a small sample of abused children (N = 9) between 2-½ and 8 years of age with a matched control sample (N = 5) on the McCarthy Scale of Children's Abilities. On two evaluations six months apart, these two groups differed significantly (p < .05) on the General Cognitive Index and the five scales, i.e., Verbal, Perceptual-Performance, Quantitative, Memory, and Motor, with the abused group scoring lower overall. A recent study, which also used the McCarthy, found significant differences on the Verbal and Memory Scales between two well-matched groups of male preschoolers, one severely physically abused (N = 11) and the other a low-income control group (N = 10) (Friedrich, Einbender & Lueke, 1983).

The two groups also differed on the General Cognitive Index (M = 83.0 vs M = 97.6) in favor of the control group. Kent (1976) compared 217 abused children with 159 neglected children and 185 low income control children (many of whom were from disrupted families). Age ranges were not reported for these samples. Caseworkers for the children completed a questionnaire for each of these children and found that 53% of the abuse group, 82% of the neglect group, and 28% of the control group were rated as doing below average or failing work in school. I.Q. scores were available for the abuse and neglect groups, with 78% of the neglect group having I.Q.'s less than or equal to 89 (39% below 70), and 44% of the abuse group having I.Q.'s less than or equal to 89 (24% below 70). Perry (1981) studied two groups of carefully matched children, one abused (N = 21), and the other low income control (N = 21) (range 2-11 years). Pairwise comparisons of their performances on the Peabody Picture Vocabulary Test and the Alpern-Boll Developmental Profile indicated that the abused children scored significantly lower (p < .01) on both measures, i.e., 89.2 vs. 108.5 on the PPVT, and 80.0 vs. 97.5 on the Developmental Profile.

As part of a larger study on the social-cognitive styles of abused children between the ages of 6-8 (Barahal, Waterman & Martin, 1981), the investigators used the Slosson Intelligence Test for Children to compare two groups, an abused group (N = 17) and a control group (N = 16), matched on age, sex, family background and SES. Although abused children obtained I.Q.'s well within the average range (M = 102), as a group they scored significantly lower than the controls (M = 112). Morgan (1979) compared 42 abused children with 57 nonabused children on the Illinois Test of Psycholinguistic Abilities (ITPA). All of the children were between 6-10 years of age and were in special classes for the emotionally disturbed. The children were all of at least average intelligence and were matched along age, sex, intelligence, and diagnostic category variables. She noted that while the control group's mean ITPA profile was within normal limits, the abused group had mean scores suggesting differences on five subtests: Auditory Closure, Auditory Reception, Visual Reception, Verbal Expression, and Grammatic Closure. Abused males scored generally lower than abused females.

Clearly, many of the studies presented here suffer from small sample sizes and questionable methodology. The studies of Appelbaum (1977), Koski and Ingram (1977), Barahal, et al. (1981), Friedrich, et al. (1983), and Perry (1981) are clearly the most sound and their findings of highly significant differences between abused and nonabused children suggest that a contributor to these differences may be, in part, the abuse. Barahal, et al. (1981) concluded that "diminished intellectual achievements may be a pervasive consequence of abused child care (p. 512)." Their findings are even more suggestive in that the abused children in their sample were without neurological impairment, and were not typically from economically disadvantaged families.

Elmer (1977) suggests that the oppressive, impoverished environment is the primary factor in determining outcome. Some support for this comes from two related studies (Starr, 1982; Starr, Ceresnie, Dietrich, Fischoff, Schumann, & Demorest, 1982) which failed to find differences between predominantly low income abused children ($N=87$) and a matched comparison group ($N=87$) on either the Bayley or McCarthy, or between 54 abused children and their nonabused sibling on the same measures. Chronic neglect was evident in both the abused and comparison children, however, as were significant health problems. Starr (1982) indicated that the two groups of children "were more alike than different" (p. 132) and this clearly obscured any differences. However, it does illustrate the pervasive and depressing consequences of an impoverished environment.

Summary

Research in this area generally reports lowered intellectual abilities and impaired cognitive status in abused children. The findings are particularly strong for abused infants, and further research is needed with older abused children, e.g., preschoolers. It is important to examine these children prospectively and longitudinally along neuropsychological and academic dimensions, to determine whether the differences persist with time.

Neurological Sequelae

It has been suggested that neurological problems in abused children may have preceded the abuse or be the result of abuse (Sandgrund, Gaines, & Green, 1974). Data in this area come from case studies and retrospective screening of hospital records. For example, Buchanan and Oliver (1977) surveyed the records of 140 children in two hospitals for the mentally retarded and found that at least 3% (and possibly as many as 11%) of these children had been rendered mentally retarded as a result of abuse. Caffey (1972) reported that shaking infants led to whip lash, chronic subdural hematomas, and possibly retardation. Indeed, Oliver (1975) reported on three cases of microcephaly following the rough handl-

ing of very young infants. Baron, Bejar, and Sheaff (1970) report a case of an infant with diffuse and nonfocal neurologic signs, where it was later found that she had been chronically abused.

Martin, et al. (1974) reported that over 50% of their abused sample had neurologic findings, including hypotonia, perceptual-motor dysfunction, dyspraxia, and other "soft signs." Children from that sample and another abused sample had neurological abnormalities even without a history of head trauma (Green, Voeller, Gaines & Kubie, 1981).

It is not surprising that some abused children are impaired neurologically as a result of head trauma. Martin (1972) reports that 64% of the 13 children in his study with major physical injury, i.e., skull fracture accompanied by subdural hematoma, were in the retarded range, based on standardized intelligence testing. At present, however, the connection between abuse, neurological damage, and subsequent retardation has not been systematically documented or elaborated.

Behavior and Personality Characteristics

The literature on the behavior and personality characteristics of abused children is comprised of widely divergent studies which have used a variety of methods of assessment. Many of these studies suffer from the lack of comparison groups against which to evaluate their findings. These studies also tend to be confounded by the fact that physical abuse often occurs in conjunction with other deleterious conditions, such as neglect, maternal/parental deprivation, sexual abuse, parental psychiatric disturbance, social isolation, and economic disadvantage. Researchers have had difficulty differentiating the separate effects of each of these factors.

Clinical Impressions

Maltreated children are described clinically as extremely dependent, overly compliant, exhibiting ineffective and anxious efforts to please others at the expense of self-enjoyment, slow to develop self-confidence, and hypervigilant to external cues (Martin & Beezley, 1977). These authors observed 50 abused children, ages 2-13 years. Nine dimensions seemed to characterize the children and include: 1) an impaired ability to enjoy life; 2) low self-esteem; 3) symptoms indicative of emotional turmoil, such as enuresis, poor peer relations, tantrums, sleep disturbances, hyperactivity, and socially inappropriate behaviors; 4)withdrawal; 5) oppositional behavior; 6) hypervigilance; 7) compulsivity; 8) pseudo-adult behavior, and 9) learning problems. However, their failure to include a comparison group, and to operationalize their definition of "self concept," compromises the validity and generalizability of their findings.

A similar constellation of behaviors was found in a different sample of abused children ($N = 138$) (Kline, 1977). Additionally, a significant and positive relationship between a history of physical abuse and the degree of violent behavior has also been noted in incarcerated juvenile delinquents (Lewis, Shanok, Pincus, & Glaser, 1979).

Other clinical observations of abused children have noted an increase in negative and ambivalent affect, i.e. unreadable facial expressions and indirect means of seeking contact (Elmer & Gregg, 1967; Gaensbauer & Sands, 1979). Galdston (1965) noted that abused children will initially exhibit terror at physical contact, severe anxiety, apathy, withdrawal, and a marked loss of appetite. We now turn to comparison studies to see to what degree the clinical impressions are reliably seen.

Comparison Studies

A variety of comparison studies examining personality/behavioral dimensions in abused children have been published. Green (1978a; 1978b) used psychiatric interviews and psychological testing with abused ($N = 60$), neglected ($N = 30$), and control ($N = 30$) children, ages 5-12. Abused and neglected children were significantly more impaired than comparison children on a variety of dimensions, e.g. thought process, anxiety, depression, etc. Abused children differed from neglected children in that the former were more aggressive, and the latter were more passive and apathetic (Green, 1978a). Abused children were also more self-destructive than either of the other two groups (Green, 1978b). The high incidence noted is atypical of this age group, and the self-destructiveness seemed to follow parental assault or threatened/actual separation from caregivers. The self-destructiveness noted seemed to reflect an imitation of their parents own aggressiveness and an internalization of parental hostility/rejection.

Barahal et al. (1981) compared the social-cognitive styles of abused children ($N = 17$) with a carefully matched (age, sex, family backgrounds, parent SES) control group ($N = 16$). These children were assessed on locus of control, social sensitivity, perspective taking, social role concepts, and moral judgment. Because the two groups differed in mean I.Q., data was compared with analysis of covariance. Significant differences were noted on locus of control and understanding social roles, with abused children having little confidence in their power to shape their experiences and appearing less able to understand subtle and complex interpersonal relationships.

Another recent study measured fantasy aggression, emotional maladjustment, and empathy in 19 abused children between 5-10 years of age (Straker, & Jacobson, 1981). These children were contrasted with 19 control children similar to each other on age, sex. socioeconomic status, I.Q., language, and race. The abused children were significantly less empathic and more emotionally maladjusted. However, a more recent and similar investigation of empathy in 3-5 year old children failed to identify differences in empathy between abused ($N = 8$), neglected ($N = 12$), and comparison children ($N = 40$) when IQ was covaried out (Frodi, 1983).

Reidy (1977) has investigated both behavioral and fantasy aggression in abused ($N = 20$), neglected ($N = 16$), and control children ($N = 22$), in free-play and on TAT stories. Abused children express significantly more fantasy aggression and behavioral aggression in a free-play setting than the other groups. Abused and neglected children were also rated as significantly more aggressive on a behavior checklist completed by teachers than control children, with no differences between the abused and neglected groups.

Kinard (1980) contrasted 30 abused children between 5 and 12 years old, with a matched sample of 30 nonabused children on tests measuring self-concept, aggression, socialization with peers, establishment of trust, and separation from the child's mother. The abused children were significantly more extrapunitive and less impunitive on a frustration task than the nonabused children, yet did not differ on total self-concept, as measured by a paper-pencil self-concept questionnaire. In addition, abused children showed a significant decrease in their motivation for socialization. In a later paper with the same sample, Kinard (1982) found that the severity of abuse was directly related to the degree of aggression seen in psychological testing.

A variety of other studies have found that abused adolescents have a significantly more impaired body image than normal adolescents (Hjorth & Harway, 1981), that abused children could be discriminated from nonabused children on the House-Tree-Person Test (Blain, Bergner, Lewis, & Goldstein, 1981), and that no significant differences existed between abused and nonabused preschoolers on a persistence/frustration task (Friedrich, et al., 1983). Two studies have found differences on the Bayley Infant Behavior Record with abused and nonabused infants. These have included immature object attachment (Appelbaum, 1977), and decreased attention span and cooperativeness (Koski & Ingram, 1977).

The abused child's perspective of his family has been focus of several recent studies. The Family Relations Test has been used with two small samples of abused children. These children differed from nonabused children in that they perceived the abusive parent as significantly more negative (Hyman & Mitchell, 1975; Einbender & Friedrich, 1983). In a more direct fashion, Herzberger, Potts, and Dillon (1981) interviewed abused ($N = 14$) and nonabused ($N = 10$) boys, ages 8-12, who were residents in a group home. The interviews focused upon the child's perceptions of parental characteristics, disciplinary techniques, etc. While most of the abused boys reported feeling loved and cared for by the abusive parent, the abused sample generally felt that they had been punished excessively.

Dyadic Studies

In contrast to normal infants, abused/neglected infants were found to exhibit a variety of distorted affective communications which serve to disrupt the caregiver-infant interaction (Gaensbauer & Sands, 1979). They observed 48 abused children, (age range = 6-36 months) and 100 control children in a structured play situation. The abused children demonstrated a lack of pleasure, withdrawal form social contact, and inconsistency and unpredictableness in their affective communication. "Indiscriminate attachment" (Martin, 1976), wherein a child will not be specific in their affection seeking or giving, was also apparent in these abused infants. The researchers concluded that the distorted affective communications that they observed resulted from and contributed to the abuse and neglect these children experienced. However, they do not clearly describe how the children's behavior was rated and analyzed and these methodological limitations affect the generalizability and validity of their findings.

These shortcomings are not found in an elegant study which specifically investigated the social interactions of abused preschoolers with their peers and teachers (George & Main, 1979). Ten abused toddlers, ages 1-3 years, and 10 matched control children, who belonged to stressed families, but had not been abused were studied. Abused children approached the teachers only half as often as the control children, and when they did approach, they would approach from the side or by back stepping. This deviated from the controls, who generally approached the teacher directly. Avoidance of affiliative encounters comprised 25% and 6% of the abused and control children's responses, respectively. It was anecdotally noted that abused children seemed to show more gaze aversion than control children. All of the abused children, but none of the controls, were observed to respond to peer affiliations with approach-avoidance behavior. Surprisingly, the investigators found that the aggression of the abused children exceeded that of the control children only when the teachers were considered as targets; the incidence of peer directed aggresssion was comparable in both groups. Over half of the abused sample physically assaulted or threatened to assault the teachers, whereas no control children exhibited these harassing behaviors towards the teachers.

Several other studies of parent-maltreated child interaction have been published. Neglectful mothers ($N = 9$) were rated as significantly more negative and controlling than low-income comparison mothers ($N = 9$), but no description of the child's behavior was reported (Aragona & Eyberg, 1981). In another study, 12 abusing and 12 matched comparison mothers were observed during free play with their infant. Abusive mothers were more negative and less positive, and abused infants complied less with their mothers' attempts to direct their play (Wasserman, Green & Allen, 1983). Eighteen abusive and 18 nonabusive mothers and their preschoolers were observed interacting in both a structured and unstructured task in a third study (Mash, Johnston, & Kovitz, 1983). Abusive mothers were observed to be more directive and controlling of their children, but this was true only in the structured task situation, which was seen as more stressful and required the mother to be more controlling. Again, no description of reciprocal aversive child behaviors was reported. Finally, abused children were observed to display significantly more negative behavior than nonabused children in a family setting (Kimball, Stewart, Conger & Burgess, 1980). The overall rate was greater in single-parent families than in intact families, and appeared related to the overall high rate of parental aversive behavior.

A recent mother-child interaction study focused on measuring the quality of attachment in a prospective study of 267 low-income mothers (Egeland & Sroufe, 1981a; 1981b). Mother-infant pairs where abuse was present were compared on a variety of behaviors, including attachment outcome with control mother-infant pairs at 3,6,9,12,18, and 24 months. This is a very rich, complex, and extremely important study in this area, and results are only briefly presented here. The abused infants were characterized by a significantly lower proportion of secure attachment, and evidenced declines in psychological functioning over time. Particular patterns of maltreatment seemed related to particular patterns of outcome in the child. Improvement in mother-child attachment over time appeared to be primarily related to the mother increasing her social support network. The children of psychologically unavailable mothers seemed to have the most malignant and pervasively negative outcome, and it appeared that the addition of physical abuse to the psychological unavailability actually resulted in a less negative outcome. Apparently, some contact, even if aversive, was better than no contact at all. The authors stated that one of the important findings of the study was the pattern of declining functioning in maltreated children. From relatively normal developmental levels at 9 months, these children appeared very delayed at 24 months. Clearly, the noxious emotional rearing environment had a very deleterious impact on these children above and beyond the low-income status of the mothers.

Summary

The results of these studies strongly suggest that abused children manifest serious problems in emotional development that appear to be a function of the abuse. Clinical impressions of low self-esteem, behavioral problems, and poor social relationships have been supported by comparison-group research. Although there is no one unique behavioral style that is characteristic of an abused child, the high incidence of emotional problems is consistently documented. Children of divergent developmental levels will differ widely in their ways of responding to physical abuse, which is multi-dimensional, of varying duration, and of differential impact. Their development will be further mediated by the quality of their subsequent home environment. The efforts of researchers to investigate this incredibly difficult research area have met, however, with some success in providing directions, both for future research and treatment.

Child's Contribution to the Abuse Cycle

Friedrich and Boriskin (1976) published a review suggesting that the prevalent notion of abuse as exclusively a function of a parental defect, ignored the fact that some groups of children had a greater incidence of abuse. It was suggested that a variety of child-related factors may increase the child's risk of abuse. These included prematurity, mental retardation, physical handicaps, temperament, and the fact that some children are seen clearly difficult and deviant by the parents. A transactional model in which infant and caregiver responses are viewed as mutually influential appears to be the most appropriate (Sameroff & Chandler, 1975). In addition to the parent-child interaction studies reviewed earlier, a variety of studies have either supported or failed to support this transactional model. Abused children were compared with their nonabuse siblings and it was reported that 6.9% of abused children were born prematurely, compared to 1.5% of their nonabused siblings (Herrenkohl & Herrenkohl, 1979). While no relationship was found between physical abnormalities at birth and subsequent abuse, the presence of physical problems at the birth of the child (e.g., low Apgar scores, "birth defects," slow development) was insignificantly related to life-threatening neglect. Starr, et al. (1982), also found that abused children had a significantly lower birth weight than their nonabused sibling.

A prospective study of 255 premature and ill newborns found that the incidence of reported child maltreatment in this group, after one year, was 4% (Hunter, Kilstrom, Kraybill & Loda, 1978). This high incidence of maltreatment supports the findings of retrospective studies indicating that premature and ill babies are at greater risk for parenting failure in the form of abuse (Oliver, Cox, Taylor & Baldwin, 1974; Murphy, Jenkins, Necombe & Silbert, 1981; Kotelchuck & Newberger, 1983). However, in a prospective study of a large group of young mothers, no differences were noted in pregnancy, delivery, and infant data for two groups of mothers: those that were rated as providing optimal care ($N = 33$) and those whose child was identified as not receiving adequate care, e.g., abuse, neglect. Variables that were examined include prematurity, delivery complications, and the presence of physical anomalies, none of which were related to later disorders of mothering (Egeland & Vaughn, 1981). In addition, a study of 240 low income mothers (80 abusive, 80 neglectful, 80 control) failed to find a relation between post-natal risk or deviancy (determined by the number of days each infant spent in the hospital following birth) (Gaines, Sandgrund, Green & Power, 1978). The authors did conclude, however, that this was a very gross measure that may have been inadequate at measuring this particular aspect of abuse vulnerability.

Why might a premature child be more vulnerable to abuse? Research in this area has noted that the premature child's physical characteristics are deviant from parental expectations, they typically require special care, parent-infant bonding may be disrupted by parent-infant separation and isolation, and they have high-pitched cries (Frodi, 1981). For example, the cry of a premature infant elicits greater autonomic arousal and more negative emotions than does the cry of a term infant. It appeared that premature infants "trig-

97

gered a response pattern consistent with a readiness to aggress" (Frodi, 1981, p. 345).

Summary

It is likely that certain temperamental, illness, and birth-related characteristics contribute to the abuse cycle. This is supported by the data and in turn is supportive of a transactional model. At the same time, Egeland and Sroufe's (1981b) finding of no differences at birth, 3 and 6 months and major differences at 24 months clearly indicate that for physical abuse, the impact of the maltreatment overshadows any contribution from the child. This is echoed by Starr (1982) who found that child variables contributed little to the overall prediction of abuse. In fact, it is probable that the characteristics that make one child vulnerable over another activate an abusive pattern primarily in those parents who have, for one reason or another, difficulty in dealing with child-related stress and a proclivity for physical punishment.

Discussion and Conclusions

Research on the physically abused child has benefitted considerably from the use of comparison groups, and the several research findings taht continue to emerge can be noted, particularly those findings related to the characteristics of children that are abused. For example, neglected children outnumber abused children by a ratio of 2:1. The "unbattered child," or the child who incurs severe physical injury, is considerably more unusual, than the child who has incurred minor physical injuries, with the latter outnumbering the former by a ratio of 10:1. The ratios do change considerably, depending upon whether the study is done in a hospital emergency room, but data from a nationwide clearing house is assumed by these authors to be more representative. However, data from emergency room studies do suggest that a considerable percentage of young children seen in emergency rooms with physical trauma are victims of abuse. Indeed,, many hospital-based child protection teams "red-flag" these cases as soon as they arrive.

The severity of abuse does certainly seem to be related to the age of the child, with the younger child more likely to receive more severe abuse. Whether physical abuse is a phenomenon that is relatively evenly distrubuted across childhood and adolescence is still debated, and seems to be differentially motivated, depending on the age and sex of the child. The male: female ratio is even overall, although males are more likely to incur abuse at a younger age, and females more frequently reported as victims during adolescence.

Abused children also come largely from families which are low-income, larger than average, and more frequently with a single parent. These families are conflicted and tend to use rather harsh methods of discipline as part of a child-rearing style, which could explain the high rate of recurrent abuse episodes and the fact that anywhere from 30-50% of abused children have another sibling that has also been abused.

It is much more difficult to address the issue of the outcome of abuse. Data from Egeland and Sroufe's (1981a, 1981b) prospective study has found that maltreatment differs in type and that each type can be related to different outcomes. In general, the impact is clearly and markedly deleterious, and by 24 months, abused children differed from comparison children along a variety of attachment, behavioral, and cognitive dimensions.

Child maltreatment is a highly complex, heterogeneous phenomenon, with a wide variety of different manifestations, etiologies, and developmental sequelae (Cicchetti & Rizley, 1981). Applied research is difficult to do, and research in the area of child abuse and neglect is even more difficult given the typical defensiveness of the parents, and the service orientation of the agencies that serve the parents. These children also often have medical problems (e.g., severe chronic ear infections, anemia, malnutrition) that interfere both with assessment and determination of the impact of abuse. Given that these children most often have a history of conflicted relations with adults, personality and cognitive asessment must be delayed considerably until trust is somewhat established. Blager and Martin (1976) acknowledge their use of repeated testing, reinforcers, and trust-building in their evaluation of abused children. One begins to readily see that the abuse is but one insult with which these children need to deal, and that the disordered settings in which many of these children are raised make them caretaking casualties (Sameroff & Chandler, 1975). Elmer's (1977) conclusion that the unmitigating poverty, depression, and understimulation that characterize their environment exerts such an influence that the contribution of abuse is difficult or impossible to ascertain, and thus becomes difficult to deny.

Further complicating the question of outcome is the fact that child maltreatment is highly heterogeneous. Currently, data is practically nonexistent on whether different types of maltreatment have different consequences, antecedents, or treatment responses (expecting Egeland & Sroufe, 1981b). The Harvard Child Maltreatment Project (Cicchetti & Rizley, 1981), which is currently underway, will be delineating different types of child maltreatment and examining their differential effects on the child's social, emotional, cognitive, and physical development. In addition they plan on examining the mediation factors which either buffer or render these children more vulnerable to the negative consequences of abuse. This study is extremely well-designed and promises to add immeasureably to our understanding of the phenomenon of child maltreatment.

Studies on the cognitive and behavioral characteristics of abused children should be interpreted as highlighting potential areas of intervention. Studies that have examined young infants (Appelbaum, 1977; Koski & Ingram, 1977; Dietrich, et al., 1980) are particularly valuable in that very young abused children differ significantly from nonabused children on the Baylay Scales. What this suggests is that in very young children, abuse is related to a degree of lag in the cognitive competence of these children. The results cannot be interpreted as cause-and-effect, but do suggest that early on, there are some indications that these children are not processing as efficiently as groups of well-matched infants. The degree to which these differences show up in older children is much less clear, and is only now being systematically addressed. Data from a study that examined 6-8 year old abused children found them to differ significantly on a standardized I.Q. measure from a well-matched comparison group (Barahal, et al., 1981). A younger sample (3-5 years) of more severely abused males were below the average range of intelligence and were significantly lower than a carefully matched comparison group on the General Cognitive Index of the McCarthy Scales of Children's Abilities (Friedrich, et al., 1983). Elmer's (1977) finding not withstanding, it appears that intellectual assessment of abused children very frequently finds impaired performance.

However, little research has adequately examined these children to determine whether abused children have a generalized lowering of test scores, or whether the impact is less uniform, (e.g. language disorders being more common, etc.). For example, Blager and Martin (1976) state that abused children's lowered language performance could be related to the child's learning that it is dangerous to talk. This reduces the child's verbal output, and the practice and feedback necessary to learn this important skill are often not a part of the abused child's environment. Alternatively, abuse may have occured throughout the initial stages of language acquisition and, consequently, delayed the acquisition of language. It may be that rather than a generalized lowering of test scores, these children may be more prone to specific learning problems. This represents an important area

of future investigation.

Clinical observations have long suggested that abused children differ from nonabused children in their behavior and interactional style, with the former being more aggressive, having a reduced capacity to enjoy life, demonstrating low self-esteem and a greater incidence of psychiatric symptoms (Martin & Beezley, 1977). However, no classical profile for abused children has been noted. George and Main (1979) have added considerably to the understanding of the behavior of the abused child with their explication of the approach-avoidant and "harassing" behavior young abused children demonstrate. Whether this behavior alters as the child develops is unclear. What does seem clear is that adults are viewed with suspicion and seen as unpredictable sources of nurturing and support, the very same characteristics which mark the interpersonal stance of many abusive parents. Related to this is a study of college students with a history of abuse ($N = 72$) (Chan, 1983).These were compared to college students without an abuse history ($N = 87$). The abused group reported a significantly lower self-esteem and a significantly higher score on a child abuse potential screening measure.

This behavior on the part of the abused child is quite likely a product of the interaction with aggressive, unpredictable parents. Yet, research continues to suggest that there are a variety of child characteristics that contribute to an abusive relationship, e.g., prematurity, other medical problems. The interactive nature of abuse certainly needs further clarification.

What does the research say that can be related to intervention? How does one best intervene in the abuse cycle? It should be clear that single acts of abuse in relatively stable families are a rarity. This characteristically is an ongoing world of abnormal rearing where the stressors on the various family members are many and unrelenting. Despite the real questions about the basis for Elmer's (1977) conclusions that abuse per se is only one component of the deprived world these children live in, it seems clear that appropriate intervention is going to require, to a large degree, community and society wide changes in the manner in which parents rear their children and mental health professionals deliver services.

These interventions require governmental support. The nature of support, and whether that type of support is available, is uncertain. Pelton (1978) revealed how Congress agonized over funding for child abuse research and intervention in the early 1970's. It was necessary at that time to propagate the "myth of classlessness," or the idea that physical child abuse was evenly distributed across all SES classes, since Congress was seen as reluctant to fund more programs for poor people. At this time of cutbacks on the federal level, the nature of societal intervention needs to be rethought. Yet research supports that abused children are at greater risk for medical, cognitive, academic, and behavioral problems than their low-income, nonabused counter-parts. The large number of children involved suggests that a wide variety of programmatic interventions are needed that address this problem as a societal problem. The published research is suggesting how this intervention may be tailored (e.g., provisions of social support to the mother [Egeland & Sroufe, 1981a;], parent training [Reid, 1982]), but increasing research on risk factors, mediating factors, and outcome are very much needed.

References

American Humane Association (1981). *Highlights of the 1979 National Data.* Englewood, Colorado.

Appelbaum, A.S. (1977). Developmental retardation in infants as a concomitant of physical child abuse. *Journal of Abnormal Child Psychology, 5,* 417-423.

Aragona, J.A., & Eyberg, S.M. (1981). Neglected children: Mothers' report of child behavior problems and observed verbal behavior. *Child Development, 52,* 596-602.

Barahal, R.M., Waterman, J. & Martin, H.P. (1981). The social cognitive-development of abused children. *Journal of Consulting and Clinical Psychology, 49,* 508-516.

Baron, M.A., Bejar, R.L., & Sheaff, P.J. (1970). Neurologic manifestations of battered child syndrome. *Pediatrics, 45,* 1003-1007.

Blager, F., & Martin, H.P. (1976). Speech and language of abused children. In H.P. Martin (Ed.), *The abused child: A multidisciplinary approach to developmental issues and treatment.* Cambridge, Mass.: Ballinger.

Blain, G.H., Bergner, R.M., Lewis, M.L., & Goldstein, M.A. (1981). The use of the objectively scored House-Tree-Person indicators to establish child abuse. *Journal of Clinical Psychology, 37,* 667-673.

Buchanan, A., & Oliver, J.E. (1977). Abuse and neglect as a cause of mental retardation: A study of 140 children admitted to subnormality hospitals in Wiltshire. *British Journal of Psychiatry, 131,* 458-467.

Caffey, J. (1972). On the theory and practice of shaking infants. *American Journal of Diseases of Children, 124,* 161-169.

Chan, D. (1983). Mediating factors in the long-term effects of physical child abuse. Unpublished manuscript. Department of Psychology, University of Washington. Seattle, WA. 98195.

Cicchetti, D., & Rizley, R. (1981). Developmental perspectives on the etiology, intergenerational transmission, and sequelae of child maltreatment. In R. Rizley and D. Cicchetti (Ed.), *New directions for child development: Developmental perspectives on child maltreatment (No. 11).* San Francisco: Jossey-Bass, Inc.

Dietrich, K.N., Starr, R.H., & Kaplan, M.G. (1980). Maternal stimulation and care of abused infants. In T.M. Field, S. Goldberg, D. Stern, and A.M. Sostek (Eds.), *High-risk infants and children.* New Yor: Academic Press.

Ebbin, A.J., Gollub, M.H., Stein, A.M., & Wilson, M.G. (1969). Battered child syndrome at the Los Angeles County General Hospital. *American Journal of Diseases of Children, 118,* 660-667.

Egeland, B., & Sroufe, L.A. (1981). Attachment and early mal treatment. *Child Development, 52,* 44-52.

Egeland, B., & Sroufe, L.A. (1981). Developmental sequelae of maltreatment in infancy. *New Directions for Child Development, 11,* 77-92.

Egeland, B., & Vaughn, B. (1981). Failure of "bond formation" as a cause of abuse, neglect, and maltreatment. *American Journal of Orthopsychiatry, 51,* 78-84.

Einbender, A.J., & Friedrich, W.N. (1983). A validational study of the Family Relations Test with physically and sexually abused children. Unpublished manuscript. Department of Psychology, University of Washington. Seattle, WA. 98195.

Elmer, E. (1977). A follow-up study of traumatized children. *Pediatrics, 59,* 273-279.

Elmer, E. (1978). Effects of early neglect and abuse on latency age children. *Journal of Pediatric Psychology, 3,* 14-19.

Elmer, E., & Gregg, G.S. (1967). Developmental characteristics of abused children. *Pediatrics, 40,* 596-602.

Fitch, M.J., Cadol, R.V., Goldson, E., Wendell, T., Swartz, D. & Jackson, E. (1976). Cognitive development of abused and failure-to-thrive children. *Journal of Pediatric Psychology, 1*(2), 32-37.

Frankenburg, W.K., Dodds, J.B., & Fandal, A. (1970). *Manual for the revised Denver Developmental Screening Test.* Denver: University of Colorado Press.

Friedrich, W.N., & Boriskin, J.A. (1976). The role of the child in abuse: A review of the literature. *American Journal of Orthopsychiatry, 46,* 580-590.

Friedrich, W.N., Einbender, A.J., & Luecke, W.J. (1983). Cognitive and behavioral characteristics of physically abused children. *Journal of Consulting and Clinical Psychology, 51,* 313-314.

Frodi, A.M. (1981). Contribution of infant characteristics to child abuse. *American Journal of Mental Deficiency, 85,* 341-349.

Frodi, A.M. (1983). The effects of IQ: Maltreated preschoolers' ability to discriminate other's emotions. Paper presented at the Society for Research in Child Development, Detroit, March.

Gaensbauer, T.J., & Sands, K. (1979). Distorted affective communications in abused/neglected infants and their potential impact on caretakers. *Journal of the American Academy of Child Psychiatry, 18,* 236-250.

Gaines, R., Sandgrund, A., Green, A.H., & Power, E. (1978). Etiological factors in child maltreatment: A multivariate study of abusing, neglecting, and normal mothers. *Journal of Abnormal Psychology, 87,* 531-540.

Galdston, R. (1965). Observations on children who have been physically abused and their parents. *American Journal of Psychiatry, 122,* 440-443.

George, C., & Main, M. (1979). Social interactions of young abused children: Approach, avoidance, and aggression. *Child Development, 50,* 306-318.

Gil, D.G. (1970). *Violence against children.* Cambridge, Mass.: Harvard University Press.

Green, A.H. (1978). Psychopathology of abused children. *Journal of the American Academy of Child Psychiatry, 17,* 92-103.

Green, A.H. (1978b). Self-destructive behavior in battered children. *American Journal of Psychiatry, 135,* 579-582.

Green, A.H., Voeller, K., Gaines, R.W., & Kubie, J. (1981). Neurological impairment in maltreated children. *Child Abuse and Neglect, 5,* 129-134.

Gregg, C.S., & Elmer, E. (1969). Infant injuries: Accident or abuse. *Pediatrics, 44,* 434-439.

Herrenkohl, E.C., & Herrenkohl, R.C. (1979). A comparison of abused children and their nonabused siblings. *Journal of the American Academy of Child Psychiatry, 18,* 260-269.

Herrenkohl, R.C., Herrenkohl, E.C., Egolf, B., & Seech, M. (1979). The repetition of child abuse: How frequently does it occur. *International Journal of Child Abuse and Neglect, 3,* 67-72.

Herzberger, S.D., Potts, D.A., & Dillon, M. (1981). Abusive and nonabusive parental treatment from the child's perspective. *Journal of Consulting and Clinical Psychology, 49,* 81-90.

Hjorth, C.W., & Harway, M. (1981). The body-image of phy sically abused and normal adolescents. *Journal of Clinical Psychology, 37,* 863-866.

Hunter, R.S., Kilstrom, N., Kraybill, E.N., & Loda, F. (1978). Antecedents of child abuse and neglect in premature infants: A prospective study in a newborn intensive care unit. *Pediatrics, 61,* 629-635.

Hyman, C.A., & Mitchell, R. (1975). A psychological study of child battering. *Health Visitor, 48,* 294-296.

Kent, J.T. (1976). A follow-up study of abused children. *Journal of Pediatric Psychology, 1,* 25-31.

Kimball, W.H., Stewart, R.B., Conger, R.D., & Burgess, R.L. (1980). A comparison of family interaction in single- versus two-parent abusive, neglectful, and control families. In T. Field (Ed.) *High-risk infants and 'children.* New York: Academic Press.

Kinard, E.M. (1980). Emotional development in physically abused children. *American Journal of Orthopsychiatry, 50,* 686-696.

Kinard, E.M. (1982). Experiencing child abuse; Effects on emotional adjustment. *American Journal of Orthopsychiatry, 52,* 82-91.

Kline, D.F. (1977). Educational and psychological problems of abused children. *International Journal of Child Abuse and Neglect, 1,* 301-307.

Koski, M.A., & Ingram, E.M. (1977). Child abuse and neglect: Effects on Bayley Scale Scores. *Journal of Abnormal Child Psychology, 5,* 79-91.

Kotelchuck, M., & Newberger, E.H. (1983). Failure to thrive: A controlled study of familial characteristics. *Journal of the American Academy of Child Psychiatry, 22,* 322-328.

Lauer, B., Broeck, E., & Grossman, M. (1974). Battered child syndrome: Review of 130 patients with controls. *Pediatrics, 54,* 67-70.

Lenington, S. (1981). Child abuse: The limits of sociobiology. *Ethology and Sociobiology, 2,* 17-29.

Lewis, D.O., Shanok, S.S., Pincus, J.H., & Glaser, G.H. (1979). Violent juvenile delinquents. *Journal of the American Academy of Child Psychiatry, 18,* 307-319.

Lynch, M.A. (1978). The prognosis of child abuse. *Journal of Child Psychology and Psychiatry, 19,* 175-180.

Martin, H.P. (1972). The child and his development. In C.H. Kempe and R.E. Helfer (Eds.), *Helping the battered child and his family.* Philadelphia: Lippincott.

Martin, H.P. (1976). (Ed.), *The abused child: a multidisciplinary approach to developmental issues and treatment.* Cambridge, Mass.: Ballinger.

Martin, H.P., & Beezley, (1977). Behavioral observations of abused children. *Developmental Medicine and Child Neurology, 19,* 373-387.

Martin, H.P., Beezley, P., Conway, E., & Kempe, C.H. (1974). The development of abused children. *Advances in Pediatrics, 21,* 25-73.

Martin, H.P., & Rodeheffer, M. (1976). Learning and intelli-

gence. In H.P. Martin (Ed.), *The abused child: a multidisciplinary approach to developmental issues and treatment.* Cambridge, Mass.: Ballinger.

Mash, E.J., Johnston, C., & Kovitz, K. (1983). A comparison of the mother-child interactions of physically abused and non-abused children during play and task situations. *Journal of Clinical Child Psychology,* (in press).

Morgan, S.R. (1979). Psychoeducational profile of emotionally disturbed abused children. *Journal of Clinical Psychology, 8,* 3-6.

Morse, C.W., Sahler, O.J., & Friedman, S.B. (1970). A three-year follow-up study of abused and neglected children. *American Journal of Diseases of Children, 120,* 439-446.

Murphy, J.K., Jenkins, J., Newcombe, R.G., & Sibert, J.R. (1981). Objective birth data and the prediction of child abuse. *Archives of Disease in Childhood, 56,* 295-297.

Oliver, J.E. (1975). Microcephaly following baby battering and shaking. *British Medical Journal, 2,* 262-264.

Oliver, J.E., Cox, J., Taylor, A. & Baldwin, J.A. (1974). Severely ill-treated young children in northeast Wiltshire. Oxford University Unit of Clinical Epidemiology, Research Report No. 4.

Pelton, L.H. (1978). Child abuse and neglect: The myth of classlessness. *American Journal of Orthopsychiatry, 48,* 608-617.

Perry, M.A. (1981). Behavioral and cognitive status of abused children. Unpublished manuscript. Department of Psychology, University of Washington. Seattle, WA. 98195.

Reid, J.B. (1982). Social interactional patterns in families of nondistressed, oppositional, and abused children. Unpublished manuscript. Oregon Social Learning Center. Eugene, OR 97401.

Reidy, T.J. (1977). the aggressive characteristic of abused and neglected children. *Journal of Clinical Psychology, 33,* 1140-1145.

Sameroff, A.J. & Chandler, M. (1975). Reproductive risk and the continuum of caretaking casuality. In F.D. Horowitz (Ed.), *Review of child development research,* Vol. 4. Chicago: University of Chicago Press.

Sandgrund, A., Gaines, R.W., & Green, A.H. (1974). Child abuse and mental retardation: A problem of cause and effect. *American Journal of Mental Deficiency, 79,* 327-330.

Simons, B., Downs, E.F., Hurster, M.M., & Archer, M. (1966). Child abuse: Epidemiologic study of medically reported cases. *New York State Journal of Medicine, 66,* 2783-2788.

Smith, S.M., & Hanson, R. (1974). 134 battered children: A medical and psychological study. *British Medical Journal, 3,* 666-670.

Spinetta, J.J., & Rigler, D. (1972). The child abusing parent: A psychological review. *Psychological Bulletin, 77,* 296-304.

Starr, R.H. (1982). A research-based approach to the prediction of child abuse. In Starr, R.H. (Ed.) *Child abuse prediction: Policy implications.* Cambridge, MA.: Ballinger Publishing Company.

Starr, R.H., Ceresnie, S.J., Dietrich, K.N., Fischoff, J., Schumann, B., & Demorest, M. (1982). Child abuse: A case-sibling assessment of child factors. Paper presented at the American Psychological Association Meeting, Washington, D.C., August.

Steinberg, L.D., Catalano, R., & Dooley, D. (1981). Economic antecedents of child abuse and neglect. *Child Development, 52,* 975-985.

Straker, G., & Jacobson, R.S. (1981). Aggression, emotional maljustment, and empathy in the abused child. *Developmental Psychology, 17,* 762-765.

101

Wasserman, G.A., Green, A., & Allen, R. (1983). Going beyond abuse: Maladaptive patterns of interaction in abusing mother-infant pairs. *Journal of the American Academy of Child Psychiatry, 22,* 245-252.

Zuckerman, K., Ambuel, J., & Bandman, R. (1972). Child neglect and abuse: A study of cases evaluated at Columbia Children's Hospital in 1968-1969. *Ohio State Medical Journal, 68,* 629-632.

Received: 11/17/81
Revised: 10/18/83

102

Psychological Bulletin
1985, Vol. 97, No. 3, 462–482

Child-Abusive Parents: An Empirical Review and Analysis

David A. Wolfe
University of Western Ontario

Studies comparing child-abusive and nonabusive parents on psychological and behavioral dimensions are reviewed to determine relevant distinctions between these populations. Whereas few studies found significant differences between abusers and nonabusers on traditional psychological dimensions, abusers are more likely to report stress-related symptoms, such as depression and health problems, that are linked to the parenting role. Comparative studies of family interactions have also indicated that abusers display reciprocal patterns of behavior with their children and spouses that are proportionately more aversive and less prosocial than nonabusers. Child abuse is viewed as an interactive process involving both parental competence and situational demands. Attention is given to methodological refinement and prevention efforts derived from these findings.

Public awareness of the incidence and severity of child abuse has changed dramatically over the last decade. For example, *Time* magazine reported that in 1976 only 10% of the American population considered child abuse to be a serious national problem, whereas a recent Louis Harris survey found the concern had risen to 90% (Magnuson, 1983). Despite greater awareness, an unfortunate roadblock to the public's understanding and prevention of child abuse may now exist, in part due to the successful campaigns that shocked the public and lawmakers into first realizing the problem. The communications media (Magnuson, 1983), documentary films (Mary Jane Harper Cried Last Night), and articles in professional journals continue to propagate alarming macabre images of the abusive parent as a seriously disturbed individual, despite the widely held consensus among researchers that perhaps 5% of abusers evidence such extreme symptomatology (Friedman, Sandler, Hernandez, & Wolfe, 1981; Kempe, 1973; Parke & Collmer, 1975; Spinetta & Rigler, 1972). Viewing child abuse as a grossly aberrant characteristic of the

parent may seriously restrict both our research and prevention directions, as well as impede efforts to involve more communities in providing important family support services (Alvy, 1975; Garbarino, 1982; Ross & Zigler, 1980).

The significance of child abuse is underscored by both incidence figures and projections of long-term consequences. The National Center on Child Abuse and Neglect (1981) recently estimated that 351,100 children (5.7 per 1,000) are physically, sexually, or emotionally abused by their caregivers each year, on the basis of substantiated reports nationwide. In contrast to this conservative estimate, Straus, Gelles, and Steinmetz (1980) estimated, on the basis of extrapolated data from a representative nationwide survey, that between 1.4 and 1.9 million children each year are at risk of serious injury from a family member. In reference to nonaccidental injury to children, a 1976 report to the Parliament of the United Kingdom (cited in Standing Senate Committee on Health, Welfare, & Science, 1980) stated that such acts are the fourth most common cause of death in the first 5 years of life. The significance of the problem, further, may be far greater than physical injuries. Child abuse has been implicated in the etiology of serious antisocial behavior occurring later in life and the perpetuation of family violence through generations (Straus et al., 1980). Alfaro (1981), for example, found that an average of 50% of

Preparation of this review was supported in part by Medical Research Council Grant MA-7807. The author gratefully acknowledges the assistance of Gary Austin, Peter Jaffe, Cathy Koverola, Alan Leschied, Ian Manion, Louise Sas, and Vicky Wolfe in preparing this article.

Requests for reprints should be sent to David A. Wolfe, Department of Psychology, University of Western Ontario, London, Ontario N6A 5C2, Canada.

the families reported for abuse and neglect in New York State had at least one child who was later taken to court for delinquency or being ungovernable. A child who is exposed to the use of violence as a conflict-resolution technique may fail to develop adequate controls of aggression, anger, and tension (Emery, 1982; Welsh, 1976). Therefore, child abuse is a concern not only because of physical harm to the child, but because it may have a significant impact upon the child's competence and future behavior.

This article presents a brief overview of research models, definitions, and methodology, followed by a critical review of research studies comparing physically abusive and nonabusive families.

Child-Abuse Research Issues

Conceptual Models

Theoretical views of personality functioning led to the early development of a child-abuse model that assumed a distinct personality syndrome or disorder (Melnick & Hurley, 1969; Steele & Pollock, 1968). This supported the assessment of personality attributes indicative of a characterological fault that might cause parents to lose control, isolate themselves from others, distort their children's problems or abilities, or harbor anger and resentment from their own childhood experiences.

The initial conceptualization (often referred to as the Psychiatric Model; cf. Parke & Collmer, 1975) assigns a primacy to cognitive, affective, and motivational factors (Merrill, 1962; Oates, 1979; Sloan & Meier, 1983; Zalba, 1967) inherent in the individual adult and relegates contemporaneous, controlling variables to lesser importance. Thus, comparative studies of abusers and nonabusers, following this psychiatric model, have involved measures of psychological problems such as self-esteem, depression, and impulse control, to distinguish etiological features of the parent that may be responsible for child abuse. In particular, case reports and controlled studies have addressed hypotheses related to abusive parents' early childhood experiences, coping and defense mechanisms, personality profiles, and similar characteristics

to support the contention that parental psychopathology is responsible for child abuse.

A contrasting viewpoint of child abuse—the social interactional model—places heavy emphasis on bidirectional influences of behavior among family members, antecedent events that may precipitate abuse, and consequences that may maintain the use of excessive punishment with the child (cf. Parke & Collmer, 1975; Burgess, 1978; Burgess & Richardson, 1984). These theorists are concerned primarily with the current behavior of the abusive parent in the context of the family and community. In addition, the parents' learning history, interpersonal experiences, and intrinsic capabilities are regarded as predisposing characteristics presumed to be important contributors to an abusive episode or pattern (Friedman et al., 1981).

Research instigated by the social interactional model has focused on a microanalysis of interactions between members in abusive and nonabusive families. Parents who abuse their children, according to this analysis, should display rates and patterns of aversive behaviors (i.e., behaviors belonging to the same general response class as aggression) that distinguish them from nonabusers. In return, other family members, especially the target child, are viewed as active participants in an escalating cycle of coercion (Patterson, 1982; Reid, Taplin, & Lorber, 1981). One parent may become abusive and another may not as a function of their aggregate child-rearing and interpersonal skills and the frequency and intensity of aversive stimulation impinging on family members from outside or within the family unit (Burgess, 1978).

As a corollary to this model, conditions commonly associated with child abuse are viewed as predisposing factors which in themselves do not produce abusive behavior (Vasta, 1982). The presence of child-aversive behavior and a stress-filled environment are precipitating conditions that interact with parental experience and competence. In response to these events, the parent may experience conditioned arousal and/or negative attributions that serve to mediate an aggressive retaliation (Knutson, 1978; Vasta, 1982). Therefore, social interactional researchers have attempted to measure abusive parents' emotional and cognitive reactions to aversive child stimuli and to investigate the interactional patterns of abusive families.

Although these two conceptual models differ on several dimensions, they share important commonalities and do not necessarily represent radically opposed viewpoints of the abusive parent. Both models represent attempts to understand individual characteristics of abusive parents in relation to prior experience and current demands. The major distinction between these two models is the amount of significance each places on the parent as the principal cause of the abuse. This distinction, in turn, is expressed in the types of questions being addressed by researchers and their choices of assessment devices.

Methodological Considerations

Defining child abuse. The broadest definition of child abuse places it within a continuum of parental behaviors that includes affectionate interactions at one end and extreme abuse at the other (Burgess, 1978; Zigler, 1980). However, for more specific intervention and research purposes the commonly used definition is "non-accidental physical injury (or injuries) that are the result of acts (or omissions) on the part of parents or guardians that violate the community standards concerning the treatment of children" (Parke & Collmer, 1975, p. 513; see Kempe & Helfer, 1972). Nevertheless, studies have been criticized for using definitions that lack comparability, reliability, and operational standards (Besharov, 1981; Friedman, 1975; Plotkin, Azar, Twentyman, & Perri, 1981). In response to these concerns, recent investigators have typically adopted a two-fold procedure for defining and selecting physically abusive parents: (a) due to evidence known to the protective service agency, the parent was considered to meet the statutory and community criteria for abuse, and (b) the research staff, in consideration of the protective service report and clinical interview information, judged the parent to have committed an abusive act. This approach has led to consistencies in research studies that reflect an acceptable degree of operational validity (Gelles, 1982). This definitional consensus, however, does not attempt to distinguish

chronicity, severity, or complexity of the problem. Child abuse is a notoriously multifaceted disorder, and abusive parents differ considerably from one another. Such heterogeneity and multicausality continue to pose a challenge to research endeavors.

Measurement and design restraints. Child abuse does not lend itself to direct observation, and thus the task of assessing all of the problem areas is difficult. Several investigators have relied upon psychological tests, specialty questionnaires, collateral report, and clinical interviews to diagnose parents and evaluate their psychological adjustment. Investigators interested in family interactions, in contrast, have emphasized direct observations of abuse-analog behaviors, such as negative verbal and physical acts between family members.

Child-abuse researchers are not free to manipulate independent variables or to assign subjects randomly to groups, and consequently must rely primarily upon ex post facto designs (Friedman, 1975). The limitations of such designs require several precautions which unfortunately have not been well heeded. A priori predictions of both significant and nonsignificant relations that are expected to occur, as well as careful matching of comparison groups on extraneous variables, are necessary to avoid overinterpretation of findings (Campbell & Stanley, 1966; Plotkin et al., 1981). Further, if the purpose of a study is to discriminate between abusers and nonabusers on particular dimensions, it is essential that background variables that might confound interpretation be controlled (Friedman, 1975). Most child-abuse researchers have been careful to match families on important demographic factors, such as socioeconomic status (SES), sex and age of child, and marital status. Few, however, have adequately controlled for other forms of family distress, such as neglect or child behavior problems, that would allow for a more specific understanding of how abusive families differ from nonabusive, problem families. Finally, empirical findings on the characteristics of abusive parents have been almost entirely based upon parents who have been reported to authorities. Sampling and selection biases may occur at several stages of research enquiry and restrict the external validity of the results. These problems notwithstanding, recent investigators have been careful to provide complete information about characteristics of their sample, and the percentage of studies that use comparison groups and inferential statistics has shown a clear positive trend over the past decade (Plotkin et al., 1981).

Selection Criteria for Review

The current review covers empirical studies that compare samples of physically abusive parents with one or more control samples on psychological and behavioral dimensions. The selection criteria were: (a) a definition of the child-abuse sample indicating that parents and children were under the supervision of a child-protection agency due to alleged or confirmed physical abuse, (b) observational or self-report measures of known or reported psychometric properties; (c) research design that controlled for major demographic factors, and (d) complete presentation of results which enables reviewers to evaluate and interpret the findings. The presentation and discussion of comparative findings have been organized into two sections that correspond to the conceptual models previously delineated.

Child Abuse and Parental Attributes

Interest in child abusers' psychological functioning has been strong throughout 2 decades of research, despite a lack of consensus regarding distinct personality attributes among abusive parents (e.g., Friedman, 1975; Parke & Collmer, 1975; Starr, 1979). This interest may be due, in part, to the clinical impressions of abusing parents reported in the first decade of research (Spinetta & Rigler, 1972; Steele & Pollock, 1968) as well as clinical significance derived from the approach (Kempe & Helfer, 1972). Although abusing parents rarely show severe psychological disturbance (Spinetta & Rigler, 1972; Starr, 1979; Steele & Pollock, 1968), professional opinion reported by Spinetta and Rigler (1972) converged on the general assumption that abusers have a "defect in personality that allows aggressive impulses to be expressed too freely" (p. 299). The concept of a *severe disorder* was then replaced by such terms as inadequate, poor impulse control, immature, and related personality constructs. Recent data challenges assumptions of significant character

disorder. Instead, behavioral differences that are situation specific have emerged in recent studies comparing abusive and nonabusive parents.

Studies of abusers' psychological characteristics have typically attempted to determine whether preexisting traits can account for a significant aspect of abusive behavior without reference to current concrete events. Investigators have focused primarily on two global indexes of emotional and cognitive functioning: the parents' stable personality traits and their perceptions and expectations related to children. The relation between psychological symptoms and stressful life events emerges as well from these efforts.

Psychological Traits Versus Reactive Symptoms

Studies comparing abusive and nonabusive parents on psychological variables are presented in the first part of Table 1. Because these studies have involved a number of different questionnaires and factor labels, comparability of findings is questionable; therefore, the present review focuses upon the general outcome of these studies. Studies are presented chronologically to emphasize the recent surge of investigations.

Overall, the results indicate that studies using measures of underlying personality attributes or traits have been unable to detect any patterns associated with child abuse beyond general descriptions of displeasure in the parenting role and stress-related complaints. Studies conducted by Wright (1976), Gaines, Sandgrund, Green, and Power (1978), and Starr (1982) failed to find significant group differences on multiple measures of personality functioning. Only two studies (Milner & Wimberley, 1980; Spinetta, 1978), using separate instruments designed to discriminate abusive from nonabusive parents, found more reported psychological symptoms among abusers (e.g., anger, unhappiness, rigidity). Interestingly, both instruments included a majority of questions related specifically to the parenting role, which could account for these findings. Abusers did not differ on any dimension from members of other problem families (Spinetta, 1978) and did not reveal consistent or interpretable patterns in these studies.

107

In contrast to these findings, three investigations have found elevated reports of affective and somatic distress among abusive samples, as shown in Table 1. Conger, Burgess, and Barrett (1979) reported that abusers were more likely to reveal physical health problems than were controls, which they interpreted in relation to greater life changes in abusive families. In a related study, Lahey, Conger, Atkeson, and Treiber (1984) found abusers to report more symptoms of depression and physical and emotional distress than low-SES and mid-SES control groups. Moreover, correlational analyses revealed that higher scores on distress measures were associated with

(text continues on page 470)

Table 1
Comparative Studies of Abusive Parents

Study	Comparison groups (N)	Assessment situation	Target of assessment	Results
		Studies of abusers' psychological characteristics and child perceptions		
Wright (1976)	Abuse (13), control (13)	Questionnaire	Personality functioning	Personal adjustment: No significant differences on 9 clinical MMPI scales
Gaines et al. (1978)	Abuse (80), neglect (80), control (80)	Questionnaires	Personal adjustment; child rearing attitudes	Personal adjustment: No differences between A or C on any variable (stress, emotional needs, denial of problems, relationship with own parents, coping); N greater life stress and emotional needs than A or C; perceptions of child: No significant differences
Spinetta (1978)	Abuse (7), neglect (13), abuser's spouse (9), Control: low SES, high education (15); mid SES (15); low SES (41)	Questionnaire	Parental personality and child rearing attitudes	Personal adjustment: 3 high-risk groups (abuse, neglect, abuser's spouse) more anger, isolation, fear of external control, poor family history than three control groups; no significant differences between 3 high-risk groups; perceptions of child: Abusers and their spouses had poorer expectations of child than did mid-SES group; no other significant group differences
Conger et al. (1979)	Abuse (20), control (20)	Questionnaires	Perceptions of physical and emotional health, life change	Personal adjustment: A more physical health problems than C, and no significant differences in reported emotional problems; A more life change units than C, corresponding to major life stress

Table 1 (*continued*)

Study	Comparison groups (N)	Assessment situation	Target of assessment	Results
	Studies of abusers' psychological characteristics and child perceptions (*continued*)			
Milner & Wimberley (1980)	Abuse (65), control (65)	Questionnaire	Child abuse potential	Personal adjustment: A more unhappy, rigid, and distressed than C; no group differences on loneliness, self-concept, and interpersonal factors; perceptions of child: No differences
Starr (1982)	Abuse (87), control (87)	Questionnaires	(a) Personality and social factors associated with abuse; (b) parents' perceptions of child	Personal adjustment: No significant differences[a]; perceptions of child: No significant differences on child perceptions and discipline choices
Lahey et al. (1984)	Abuse (8); control: low-SES (8), mid-SES (8)	Questionnaires	Depression, anxiety, and somatic complaints	Personal adjustment: A more depressed, more physical and emotional distress than C; A more anxious than mid- but not low-SES controls
Larrance & Twentyman (1983)	Abuse (10), neglect (10), control (10)	Presentation of 6 sequences of photographic stimuli of their own child and another child	(a) Causal attributions of child behavior; (b) expectations of child	Perceptions of child: A and N more negative expectations of child than C; attributions of child transgression: A more internal and stable than N or C when own child transgressed; attributions of positive child behavior: A and N more external and unstable than C; attributions of negative child behavior: A more internal and stable than N or C
Mash et al. (1983)	Abuse (18)[b], control (18)	Questionnaires	(a) Parenting stress and competence; (b) ratings of child behavior	Personal adjustment: A more problems than C in stress related to child, mother–child relationship, mother and situational characteristics, and lower sense of competence; perceptions of child: A more internalizing and externalizing child problems than C
Rosenberg & Reppucci (1983)	Abuse (12), distress (12)	(a) Presentation of 3 vignettes of problem child	Perceptions and interpretations of child behavior	Perceptions of child: No group differences on perceptions of intent or disposition of child; no differences on use of (*table continued*)

Table 1 (*continued*)

Study	Comparison groups (N)	Assessment situation	Target of assessment	Results

Studies of abusers' psychological characteristics and child perceptions (*continued*)

| | | behavior; (b) parent description of 3 experiences with own child | | intent statements to explain child behavior |

Studies of abusers' behavior with family members

Study	Comparison groups (N)	Assessment situation	Target of assessment	Results
Disbrow, Doerr, & Caulfield (1977)	Abuse (22), neglect (24), control (50)	(a) One structured home observation; (b) presentation of stressful and nonstressful family interactions on videotape	(a) Behavior ratings of parenting skills in the home (b) Psychophysio-logical changes in the lab	Interactions with child: A and N less communication and less facilitating behavior than C; no group differences in parents' use of physical and verbal directives; response to stressful scenes: A higher heart rate and GSR responses than C; no differences for N group
Burgess & Conger (1978)	Abuse (17)ᶜ, neglect (17), control (19)	Four 1-hr structured home observations	Rates of positive and negative behaviors among family members	Interactions with spouse: No group differences; interactions with child: A less physical and less positive than C; no significant differences in rates of negative behaviors; N more negative and less positive than C; A and N groups showed lower rates of family inter-action overall than C
Dietrich, Starr, & Kaplan (1980)	Abuse (14), control (14)	Unstructured free-play with child in clinic	Duration and type of maternal stimulation with child	Interactions with child: A fewer tactile and auditory modes of stimulation than C; no differences on visual and vestibular modes of stimulation
Frodi & Lamb (1980)	Abuse (14), control (14)	Presentation of stressful and nonstressful infant stimuli on videotape	(a) Psychophysio-logical changes in the lab; (b) parental mood ratings	Response to stressful scenes: A more heart rate and skin conductance responses than C; no significant differences in blood pressure; A more annoyed, less sympathetic than C; response to nonstressful scenes: A more blood pressure changes than C; A less attentive and happy, more indifferent, less

Table 1 (*continued*)

Study	Comparison groups (N)	Assessment situation	Target of assessment	Results
		Studies of abusers' behavior with family members (*continued*)		
Reid et al. (1981)	Abuse (27), distress (61), control (27)	6–10 unstruc-tured home observations	Rates of total aversive behavior among family members	willing to interact with infant than C Interactions with other family members: A higher rates of aversives than C or D; mothers in A higher rates of physical negatives than C or D; interactions with spouse: A more aversive than C or D; interactions with child: A and D more aversive than C
Mash et al. (1983)	Abuse (18)[b], control (18)	One 30–40 min struc-tured and unstructured clinic obser-vation	Percentage of positive and negative parent behaviors	Interactions with child: A more directive than C during structured task; no significant differences across situations on question, interaction, praise, negative, and no response categories
Wolfe et al. (1983)	Abuse (7), control (7)	Presentation of stressful and nonstress-ful Parent × Child interactions on videotape	Psychophysiological changes in the lab	Response to stressful scenes: A more skin conductance and respiration changes than C; no differences in heart rate
Bousha & Twentyman (1984)	Abuse (12), neglect (12), control (12)	Three 90-min unstructured home obser-vations	Rates of positive and negative behaviors	Interactions with child: A less social interaction, initiation, verbal and nonverbal instruction and affection, play behavior than C; A more physical and verbal aggression than C and N; no significant differences on vocal negative; N less social interaction and verbal instruction than A or C; A and N similar on rates of prosocial behavior
Lahey et al. (1984)	Abuse (8), control: low SES (8); mid SES (8)	Six 45-min structured home obser-vations	Rates of positive and negative behaviors among family members	Interactions with other family members: A more physically negative than both C groups; A less positive affect than mid-SES but not low-SES controls; no significant differences on verbal and physical positives, verbal negatives

(*table continued*)

Table 1 (*continued*)

Study	Comparison groups (*N*)	Assessment situation	Target of assessment	Results
			Studies of abusers' behavior with family members (*continued*)	
Lorber, Felton, & Reid (1984)	Abuse (9), distress (9), control (9)	Three 20-min unstructured home observations	Rates of parent and child aversive interactions; parenting skills	Interactions with other family members: A and D more aversive than C; no differences between A and D in overall rates of aversives or extremely aversive behaviors; A reciprocated aversives with spouse ($r = .94$) more than D or C; interactions with child: A and D equally effective in terminating aversive child behavior; A more inappropriate than D in response to unprovoked (prosocial) child behavior (no C comparison due to low rates of aversives)

Note. A = abuse family; C = control family; D = distressed family (referred for child-behavior problems); N = neglect; MMPI = Minnesota Multiphasic Personality Inventory; SES = socioeconomic status; GSR = galvanic skin response.
[a] In this study 249 variables across social, demographic, and individual factors were analyzed and could not be reduced by factor analysis. Although 16 variables were significant at $p < .05$, Starr (1982) stressed that these findings do not exceed chance.
[b] Abuse groups were significantly lower in SES than controls.
[c] Analyses were conducted with both target parent and spouse. *N* reflects number of families in study.

relatively less positive and more negative interactions of both mothers and children. Similarly, Mash, Johnston, and Kovitz (1983) found that abusers reported more problems related to stressful child rearing when responding to their sense of competence and frustration in the parenting role.

These latter findings suggest an alternative to the psychiatric viewpoint of the importance of the parents' psychological functioning in the etiology or maintenance of child maltreatment. Parental ability may be significantly influenced by events within and outside of the family (cf. Belsky, 1980). Thus, one would expect to see some signs of emotional distress in persons who are exposed to a large number of uncontrollable, aversive demands (Johnson & Sarason, 1978; Justice & Duncan, 1976). Moreover, these signs or symptoms could be expressed by the individual in relation to the situational context, such as child rearing or family conflict, without being of such magnitude as to be evident without reference to specific problem events (Mischel, 1973). These studies suggested that both overcontrol (e.g., depression, physical complaints) and undercontrol (e.g., aggression, verbal abuse) parental behaviors and symptoms are possible reactions to child- and family-mediated stress. Individual characteristics that have received less attention from researchers, such as low tolerance for stress, inappropriate and inadequate models and learning opportunities, and a poor repertoire of life skills, may be precursors to these reactions to stressful life events (Kelly, 1983).

Evidence that abusive parents perceive their environment to be unpredictable and stressful has also been reported in several comparative studies. The results suggest that, in the aggregate, abusers may not be subjected to significantly more socioeconomic disadvantage and life changes than matched control families (Gaines et al., 1978; Starr, 1982). Yet, the type and degree of life change associated with abusive families is more often perceived by these parents as aversive and debilitating (Conger et al., 1979; Mash et al., 1983; Rosenberg & Reppucci, 1983). Further, these perceptions of adverse family and environmental conditions are strongly associated with abusers' failure to use social supports (Garbarino, 1976, 1982; Salzinger, Kaplan, & Artemyeff, 1983; Turner, 1982).

These findings linking social influences and parental behavior have also been reported among nonabusive populations similar in social characteristics to abusive samples. In a recent observational study of 74 mothers and their children, Conger, McCarty, Yang, Lahey, and Kropp (in press) reported that social factors (income, family structure, education, and age at birth of first child) accounted for as much as 36% of the variance in a measure of psychological risk for maladaptive parenting. Similarly, stress and social supports were found to be important predictors of mother-child interaction (Weinraub & Wolf, 1983), maternal attitudes and behavior with young infants (Crnic, Greenberg, Ragozin, Robinson, & Basham, 1983), and pediatric social illnesses (Morse, Hyde, Newberger, & Reed, 1977).

In sum, these studies suggested that although abusive parents do not reveal symptoms indicative of a psychological disorder, they display stress-related symptoms such as depression and health problems that likely impair their parental competence. The bidirectional relation between psychological functioning and adaptation to stressful life events appears to be the most parsimonious explanation of these findings. Child abuse can be considered as an attempt by parents to gain control over multiple aversive events present in their environments. According to this argument, parents who possess the capability for handling these events would be less likely to respond to their child in an aggressive fashion.

Perceptions and Expectations of Children

A second major dimension suspected to engender inappropriate parent behavior involves the parents' unusually high demands or distorted perceptions of their child's be-

havior. The parents' lack of awareness of children's needs has been linked by earlier investigators (Spinetta & Rigler, 1972; Steele & Pollock, 1968) to their own immaturity, self-centeredness, projection, history of deprivation, and similar intrinsic and acquired characteristics.

As shown in Table 1, four studies exploring this issue using questionnaires failed to differentiate abusers from controls on attitudinal/perceptual dimensions. Using the factor termed "Expectations of Children" from the Michigan Screening Profile of Parenting, Gaines et al. (1978) reported no overall differences between groups, and Spinetta (1978) found that abusers and their spouses differed only from one of their comparison groups (mid-SES parents). Milner and Wimberley (1980), using the Child Abuse Potential Inventory, reported that the two factors on this scale that are related to child-behavior problems and negative concept of the child did not distinguish between abusing and nonabusing parents. The large-scale study reported by Starr (1982) likewise found no group differences on any measure of child perceptions or discipline choices from a questionnaire.

Recent studies have approached the issue of child perception through improved methodology that has included samples of real or simulated child behavior. The study by Mash et al. (1983) found a discrepancy between parental report and direct observation of child behavior. Abusive mothers in the study reported more behavior problems with their children, yet observations of each child with their respective parent failed to reveal significant differences in child behavior in comparison to controls. This issue was further explored by two studies in Table 1 that presented abusive and nonabusive parents with easily recognizable, unpleasant child stimuli in the laboratory. Abusers reported more annoyance and lack of sympathy to a crying infant (Frodi & Lamb, 1980) and more negative expectations and more internal and stable attributions of their child when the child apparently misbehaved (Larrance & Twentyman, 1983). These latter two studies presented the parent with highly salient child cues; no group differences were found in a third laboratory study that relied upon parental recall of child bahavior and less salient cues (i.e., taped vignettes of child behavior; Rosenberg & Reppucci, 1983).

The available findings regarding parental perceptions and expectations of children suggest that causal inferences of child abuse based on preexisting characteristics are misleading. An alternative explanation involves a learning process whereby salient child characteristics (e.g., noncompliance, voice tone, facial expressions) are associated with parental frustration, poor coping, and low self-efficacy (Kadushin & Martin, 1981; Vasta, 1982). Thus, an abuser's perceptual/cognitive style with a child may be a learned pattern that serves to perpetuate conflict and disharmony. Moreover, the parent may fail to acknowledge improvements in child behavior and to modify their behavior accordingly (Bell & Harper, 1977; Egeland & Sroufe, 1981). This pattern or style can be best revealed during realistic child situations. This issue is further explored in studies investigating parents' behavioral (as opposed to self-report) responses vis-à-vis child behavior in the family.

Child Abuse and Dysfunctional Family Interactions

For many years, child-abuse and family-violence researchers and practitioners have reported more hitting, overt conflict, and disharmony among family members, although efforts at measuring family interactions have lagged behind self-report assessments. Ascribed roles, lack of privacy, high levels of stress, and the legitimate acceptance of physical aggression are several important factors that may be responsible for higher rates of violence in the family in comparison to other social groups (Gelles & Straus, 1979). This line of research focuses on the amount and type of aversive behavior among family members as well as possible antecedents that provoke and maintain child abuse. In particular, researchers are interested in whether abusive parents are more harsh toward their children, less positive or affectionate, and whether they respond to child-related events with signs of arousal and agitation.

The interactional orientation of these investigations is accompanied by an emphasis upon behavioral observations, in contrast to

self-report measures. Investigators have generally narrowed their focus to allow for more detailed analyses of specific concerns, such as a parent's reactions to the child's demands at home. Observation periods may be structured to increase family activity (such as a teaching or compliance task) or unstructured to observe the families with only a minimum amount of interference. Although the reactive effects of observers are not precisely known, the consensus among researchers is that naturalistic observations provide a close approximation of family life (Christensen & Hazzard, 1983; Friedman et al., 1981; Patterson, Reid, Jones, & Conger, 1975). These interactional data enable the researchers to investigate sequential behaviors and conditional probabilities, and to combine several related codes to form an index of positive and negative interactions.

Instead of observing family members directly, three investigations reviewed below have approached the study of parent–child interactions by presenting child stimuli to the parent in a laboratory setting and measuring their psychophysiological responses, as an analog of problems at home. Audio–visual cues of stressful child behavior (e.g., crying infant, defiant preschooler) are used to simulate common child rearing situations to determine whether abusive parents display more conditioned arousal and displeasure under controlled stimulus conditions than nonabusive controls.

Levels of Conflict in Abusive Families

A significant advancement in one's understanding of child abuse was the confirmation of a link between abusive behavior and other forms of severe family conflict. Interviews conducted with a nationwide sample of 1,146 persons living with a partner and children revealed that previous exposure to harsh physical punishment as a child and marital disharmony and violence as an adult were significantly associated with higher rates of severe violence toward children (Straus, 1980a, 1980b). The explanation proffered for this association contends that violence in one sphere of life tends to carry over into other spheres. These interview data also showed that mothers tend to use more physical punishment with children than do fathers, and that the amount of violence toward a child was associated with marital violence, more so for women than for men (Straus, 1980b).[1] These initial empirical findings directed researchers' attention to the importance of aversive encounters with others in the family that may evoke aggression.

As shown in the second section of Table 1, abusive parents emit aversive behaviors (such as physical negatives, threats, yelling) toward others in the family at a rate that significantly differs from nonabusive controls. Burgess and Conger (1978) found family members in abusive homes to interact with one another at a much lower rate than nonproblem families, and such interactions were proportionately more negative in tone. Similarly, Reid et al. (1981), Lahey et al. (1984), and Lorber, Felton, and Reid (1984) reported that abusive parents in their samples emitted higher rates of aversive behavior toward other family members than did control families. In comparing abusive parents with a distressed group of parents (i.e., clinic referred for child-behavior problems) it should be noted that abusers are not necessarily unique in their patterns of family conflict. Whereas Reid et al. (1981) reported that their abuse sample was significantly more aversive than a distressed sample of nonabusing parents, Lorber et al. (1984), using a similar methodology and coding system, did not replicate this finding. Nonetheless, these studies clearly indicated that child abuse is significantly associated with observable levels of conflict and problem behavior in the home, and that the tone of family interactions is less positive than in nonproblem families (Burgess & Conger, 1978; Lahey et al., 1984).

Turning more specifically to interactions between adult partners, two out of three research studies have found evidence that the abusive parent is more likely than controls to engage in aversive interactions with a partner. Reid et al. (1981) reported that abusers displayed higher rates of aversive behavior toward their spouses than did parents from distressed (i.e., experiencing child-behavior problems) or normal families. Interestingly, in a replication of the Reid study, Lorber et al. (1984) did not find differences in rate of aversive interactions with a partner,

yet they found these aversive behaviors to be highly correlated ($r = .94$) among abusive families only. The investigators interpreted this finding as evidence for reciprocation of aversive behavior in aggressive families, which is theorized as an important contributor to the coercive family process (Patterson, 1982). Moreover, these findings provide further empirical support for the position that adult conflict is associated with inappropriate behavior toward children (Emery, 1982; Straus, 1980a, 1980b).

Common Child Rearing Situations

The most widely investigated issue related to interactions in abusive families is the suspicion that such parents are significantly more punitive and harsh toward their children during common child rearing situations. If supported by empirical findings, one could interpret such aversive interactions as indicative of a pronounced impulse disorder or characterological defect, because they would be using excessive punishment and force that is far out of proportion to the situation or cultural norms (Spinetta & Rigler, 1972). Alternatively, social interaction theorists have argued that abusive parents fail to use effective contingencies that would serve to reduce problems with their child and fail to use positive methods to teach their child desirable behaviors (Burgess & Richardson, 1984; Friedman et al., 1981). As a result of such indiscriminant methods, the parent and child engage in a cycle of aversive behavior that may culminate in harm to the child (Kelly, 1983; Wolfe, Kaufman, Aragona, & Sandler, 1981).

Several studies in Table 1 reveal that abusive parents rely on ineffective child-management techniques as opposed to excessively aversive or punitive methods. Investigators reporting a measure of positive behavior toward the child have demonstrated that abusive parents use fewer communicative and facili-

---

[1] The reader is referred to the original papers by Straus (1980a, 1980b) for a full discussion of possible explanations regarding family violence and mother–child conflict, as well as discussions by Lorber et al. (1984) and Burgess and Conger (1978).

tating behaviors (Disbrow, Doerr, & Caulfield, 1977), use fewer physical and positive behaviors (Bousha & Twentyman, 1984; Burgess & Conger, 1978), use tactile and auditory modes of stimulation less frequently (Dietrich, Starr, & Kaplan, 1980), and display less positive affect (Lahey et al., 1984) during interactions with their children relative to control families. In contrast, investigations of abusers' rates of aversive behavior toward their children have produced equivocal findings. Burgess and Conger (1978) and Mash et al. (1983) found no differences between abusive and nonabusive families on rate of negative behaviors. Reid et al. (1981) and Lorber et al. (1984) reported that abusive and distressed parents were more aversive toward their children than were parents in nonproblem families, but the two problem groups did not differ from each other on this measure. Two studies, however, found abusers to be significantly more physically negative or aggressive toward their children than are controls (Bousha & Twentyman, 1984; Lahey et al., 1984).

One possible explanation for the findings that abusers are less positive but not necessarily more negative toward their child than nonabusers has been suggested by Lorber et al. (1984). These researchers studied separately the parents' behavior following an episode of child-aversive or child-prosocial behavior. Whereas abusive parents were similar to nonabusive parents with problem children in terminating aversive child-behavior episodes, abusive parents often responded negatively to prosocial child behavior. Moreover, these authors found a significant correlation only for the abuse sample ($r = .77$, $p < .01$) between mother and child in terms of aversive behavior directed toward each other. Lahey et al. (1984) similarly reported a significant correlation ($r = .47$, $p < .01$) between abusive parents' and children's percentage of positive affect expressed during interactions. These findings suggest that the actual rates of negative or aversive behavior shown by parents toward their children may not be as important in distinguishing abusive and nonabusive parenting as was once assumed. Instead, the reciprocal manner by which they emit such behavior, the manner in which aversive behavior is negatively reinforced, and the relatively infrequent use of positive statements

seem to characterize parent/child interactions in abusive homes. According to Lorber et al. (1984), "not only do abusive mothers and abused children reciprocate one another's aversive behavior, but they seem to respond in a fashion which *actively maintains it*" (p. 38).

In sum, observations of parent–child interactions in abusive and nonabusive families have revealed an imbalance in the proportion of negative to positive behavior. Abusive parents do not necessarily emit a significantly higher frequency of aversive behaviors with their children than other parents (especially those having child problems); however, abusers are more likely to engage in aversive as opposed to prosocial behaviors when they do choose to interact with the child. The reliance upon aversive control may result in an escalation of coercive behavior (Reid et al., 1981). Such qualitative differences in patterns of interaction seem to be a significant factor in the differentiation of abusive from nonabusive families (Crittenden, 1981).

Difficult Child Rearing Situations

Behavior problems among abused children. The influence of child behavior upon adult caregiving behavior has been recognized as a potential factor in child abuse (Bell & Harper, 1977; Friedman et al., 1981; Friedrich & Boriskin, 1976). Because several studies included in this review of abusive parents also reported data regarding child behavior, a brief discussion of the child's role in abuse is presented in conjunction with the parents' responses.

Comparisons of the rate and type of behavior problems shown by abused and nonabused children suggest that abused children display more disruptive behaviors than children in nonproblem families. Moreover, their behavior patterns resemble those often displayed by behavior-problem children from distressed families (Lahey et al., 1984; Lorber et al., 1984; Wolfe & Mosk, 1983). Reid et al. (1981) reported that abused children in their sample displayed the highest rates per minute (rpm) of Total Aversive Behavior of any family member (.83 rpm), which also exceeded the rates of clinic-referred, behavior-problem (.52 rpm) and nonproblem (.28 rpm) children. Lahey et al. (1984) reported that an average of 4% of the behaviors emitted by abused children involve a physical negative (pushing, hitting, or grabbing), as compared with 1.5% of low-SES and 0.5% of middle-SES control children. Similarly, Bousha and Twentyman (1984) found that abused and neglected children emitted significantly higher rates of physical and verbal aggression than nonproblem children. Two other observational studies investigating child behavior (Burgess & Conger, 1978; Mash et al., 1983) did not find the rates of negative behaviors shown by abused children to differ significantly from those of controls.

As suggested by these data, the abused child is likely to present the parent with a high frequency of problematic situations due to dispositional characteristics, learned reactions to family members, or both (George & Main, 1979; Toro, 1982). As discussed previously, one noteworthy explanation for the relation between child behavior and abuse was suggested by the significant correlation between aversive parent and child behavior in abusive families (Lorber et al., 1984). The parent and child engage in the reciprocation of coercive behavior that increases conflict.

Arousal and reactivity to aversive child stimuli. Most incidents of child abuse involve a great deal more than the use of corporal punishment with a child during a "coercive battle." The potential for injury to the child dramatically increases as the parent loses control and accelerates from low- to high-intensity punitive behavior (Vasta, 1982). As in related areas of aggression research, this transition from anger to aggression is viewed as a key factor in explaining interpersonal violence (Berkowitz, 1983). A brief look at the theoretical process of aggressive responding, followed by data from abusive parents, will allow a parallel understanding of child abuse.

Hostile aggression in humans appears to be highly attributable to situational cues and characteristics of the individual (Averill, 1983; Berkowitz, 1983; Zillman, 1979). In the case of abusive parents, the situational cues involve aversive behavior or features of the child, and the presumed individual characteristics include such factors as oversensitivity (Knutson,

1978), disinhibition of aggression (Zillman, 1979), poor skill repertoire (Novaco, 1978), and related characteristics of the adult. Experiments with normal subjects have determined that anger, a precursor to aggression, is a highly interpersonal emotion that typically involves a close affectional relationship between the angry person and the target (Averill, 1983). To explain how anger may lead to aggression, Berkowitz (1983) maintained that the paired association of noxious events (such as child tantrums) with otherwise neutral stimuli (such as child's facial expression) can evoke aggressive responding in the adult in subsequent interactions. Presumably, the adult is responding to cues that have previously been associated with frustration or anger, and the adult's behavior toward the child may be potentiated by these conditioning experiences (Berkowitz, 1983; Vasta, 1982).

Theoretical interpretations and findings from related aggression research have sparked investigators to measure abusive parents' emotional reactivity to aversive child behavior. Child abusers, according to this model, would display conditioned arousal to child events that resemble previous situations they have encountered. To address this concern, three studies in Table 1 used a laboratory analog of aversive child behavior using videotaped stimuli and measured parental psychophysiological responses. Results from a comparison of the arousal of abusers with that of matched controls support the contention that abusers show more emotional reactivity to child behavior (Disbrow et al., 1977; Frodi & Lamb, 1980; Wolfe, Fairbank, Kelly, & Bradlyn, 1983). Such arousal can be a significant mediator of aggression when it takes the form of anger (Rule & Nesdale, 1976), and it may explain why abusive parents have difficulty controlling their reactions toward their children despite their intentions (Spinetta & Rigler, 1972).

Abuse Versus Neglect: Psychological and Behavioral Distinctions

Parental and situational factors associated with child neglect may be considerably different from those discussed in reference to child abuse (Aragona & Eyberg, 1981; Polansky, Hally, & Polansky, 1975). In particular, researchers have generally not found child-related reasons associated with neglect (Polansky et al., 1975), whereas child abuse appears to be significantly linked to child behavior (Kadushin & Martin, 1981). A study of case records describing the circumstances surrounding the occurrence of child abuse and neglect illustrates this distinction (Herrenkohl, Herrenkohl, & Egolf, 1983). Physical abuse was associated most often with oppositional child behaviors, whereas neglect was characterized by adult inadequacy and failure to assume basic responsibilities. The neglecting parent, therefore, may show a more chronic pattern of interpersonal conflict, irresponsibility, and apathy than the abusive parent.

Six studies reviewed in Table 1 involved samples of neglecting parents in comparisons that illustrate the behavioral and psychological factors that may distinguish abusing and neglecting parents. In their multivariate study examining large samples of abusing, neglecting, and normal parents, Gaines et al. (1978) found neglectors to differ significantly from abusers and normals on a measure of life stress and emotional needs. These investigators reported in their discussion that the neglect group was functioning more poorly on all 12 measures than either of the comparison groups. Two additional studies using self-report measures and smaller samples generally did not report significant differences between abusing and neglecting parents on child rearing knowledge or attributions (Larrance & Twentyman, 1983; Spinetta, 1978). However, neglect samples differed from normal controls in both studies.

Differences in family interactions are reflected in observational data from abusing, neglecting, and normal families. As shown in Table 1, Burgess and Conger (1978) found not only that neglectors interacted less frequently in the family than did normals, but they also were more negative in their total interaction and in their interaction with their children than were abusers. Bousha and Twentyman (1984) also reported that neglectors had low rates of social interaction and prosocial behavior toward their children, although neglectors were not more aversive than abusers. Data presented by Disbrow et

al. (1977) similarly support the conclusion that neglecting parents tend to ignore child behavior and, further, do not show changes in psychological measures when presented with stressful situations with their children. These findings require additional support to clarify more precisely the behavioral and situational correlates of neglect and abuse. It would be especially useful to investigate a wide range of psychological and behavioral variables that may pinpoint the different aspects of these forms of maltreatment. It is conceivable that neglect and abuse have substantially different etiologies and may require different treatments (Aragona & Eyberg, 1981; Bousha & Twentyman, 1984; Herrenkohl et al., 1983).

To summarize, the review on child abuse and dysfunctional family interactions has pinpointed several important distinguishing features of the behavior of family members in abusive versus nonabusive families. Observations of family interactions have supported clinical and theoretical statements regarding the negative and coercive style prevalent in abusive families. Moreover, the results of separate analyses of mother and father conflict are highly suggestive of excessive coercion and disharmony accompanying marital interactions, which may serve to precipitate or exacerbate child rearing problems. The data also link together important findings concerning parental behavior with the child that are contrary to earlier unidirectional theories of abuse. Both the parent and child are more likely to reciprocate aversive behavior and to maintain a higher level of conflict. In combination with a relatively low rate of positive or neutral exchanges, a pattern of behavior with their child is displayed by abusers that is proportionately more aversive than for nonabusers. Similarly, it has been shown that the abused child is likely to display rates of aversive behavior that are comparable with clinic-referred, behavior-problem children. In response to a child's problem behavior, the abusive parent may develop an idiosyncratic arousal pattern that is governed by situational factors and child cues and which serves to evoke aggressive reactions. Finally, findings comparing abusing and neglecting parents support the argument that these two forms of parental dysfunction may be distinguished on the basis of parent–child interactions and parent symptomatology.

Child Abuse Prevention and Research

Enhancing Parental Competence and Family Functioning

Several authors have called for a multidisciplinary prevention approach that attacks child abuse at all levels (e.g., Belsky, 1980; Cohn, 1982; Helfer, 1982; Lutzker, 1983). Community support (Garbarino, 1982) and training programs (Wolfe, Sandler, & Kaufman, 1981) designed to improve the quality of child rearing are clearly more desirable than recrimination and blame. On the basis of the present review, several practical methods are suggested for reducing situational demands and increasing the parent's ability to withstand adversity.

Methods for reducing situational demands should be a high priority in any child-abuse prevention program. Child-related demands, perhaps the most significant factor associated with abuse, can be eased temporarily through the availability of respite homes and relief parents. More stable and adequate provisions for reducing child distress, however, should be the goal of every community. These include (a) subsidized day care and preschool for families, (b) volunteer homemaker programs that provide nonthreatening, paraprofessional assistance, and (c) early stimulation programs to enhance the child's abilities in such areas as language and social interaction, because delays in adaptive and prosocial behavior can lead to parental rejection, inattention, or abuse (Friedman et al., 1981; Wolfe, in press).

It has become increasingly apparent that abuse is precipitated by or associated with other forms of family conflict and stress in addition to child-related demands. Conflict between adult partners places the child in jeopardy of injury and impaired emotional development (Emery, 1982). Child abuse appears to be enmeshed in hierarchical levels of family distress and disadvantage, and thus any effort directed toward ameliorating family dysfunction (e.g., Jaffe, Thompson, & Wolfe, 1984) should have compensatory benefits to the child.

Methods for increasing the parent's adaptive skills are also desirable, because these efforts will better prepare the parent for diverse role demands. There are several behavioral dimensions that merit assessment and evaluation. First, the parent's skills and complaints related to teaching and disciplining the child should be determined by observation and interview. Problems in these areas may be approached by training procedures that approximate naturalistic conditions for skill rehearsal (e.g., Forehand & McMahon, 1981; Wolfe et al., 1981), as well as by counseling and volunteer services (Kempe & Helfer, 1972). Second, the parents' level of conditioned arousal (i.e., expressions of tension, anger, being out of control, and concomitant physiological changes) can be assessed by prompting the parents to recall aversive situations with their children. A parent who admits or noticeably displays emotional arousal to problems with a child may be taught coping strategies, such as relaxation, stress management, or in vivo desensitization (Denicola & Sandler, 1980; Koverola, Elliott-Faust, & Wolfe, 1984). Third, some parents who avoid or dislike social contacts may be assisted by services that are culturally familiar and nonthreatening (Kelly, 1983; Turner, 1982). Neighborhood child care, religious and cultural activities, and interest groups that provide some compatible incentives for the parent to participate offer low-cost alternatives to child-welfare agencies. Fourth, conflict resolution and marital problem-solving approaches that address particular concerns may reduce verbal and physical aggression between family members.

The abusive parent often lacks skills for handling life events, personal relationships, and child rearing responsibilities due to insufficient learning opportunities and psychological characteristics more than to personality disturbances. Approaches to intervention should emphasize education and guidance in a format that is flexible and responsive to individual needs (Blechman, 1981; Cohn, 1982; Lutzker, 1983).

Research Needs

In view of the interactive, multivariate nature of child abuse, innovative correlational and experimental studies are warranted. The behavior of abusive parents is strongly affected by situational demands; yet our understanding of individual factors and the critical events that interact with them remains primarily speculative and is based almost entirely on research with mothers only. To narrow these gaps, researchers can consider large- or small-scale investigative projects that study the relations among several variables simultaneously.

Prospective and descriptive studies may be pursued to investigate the individual and situational factors associated with high- versus low-competence parents. An exemplary study was begun by Egeland and his colleagues (Brunnquell, Crichton, & Egeland, 1981; Egeland, Breitenbucher, & Rosenberg, 1980) which has helped to clarify the relation between maternal characteristics and the later emergence of caretaking patterns. Mothers in their Excellent Care group, for example, were found to be of higher intelligence, reacted positively to pregnancy, and had more positive expectations and understanding of their parental role than parents in their Inadequate Care group. Moreover, they have shown that parental competence (defined as sensitivity and responsiveness to infant cues, quality of verbalization and physical contact, and related skills) and adjustment (e.g., low anxiety and adequate flexibility) were distinguishing abilities that moderated the impact of aversive life events. Our understanding of child abuse could profit from additional studies that explore theoretical predictions over time or between well-defined comparison groups.

Extended baseline studies and home-based intervention studies offer additional evaluation strategies for exploring the relations among a complex array of variables. The study of the behavior of family members over an extended time period affords a more thorough understanding of parental functioning in relation to important contextual variables. The correlation between negative parent behavior and chronic, yet relatively low-rate, events can be studied on an individual-case basis to determine patterns and predictors of deviant behavior within the family (Koverola, Manion & Wolfe, in press). Self-report and collateral report measures of daily hassles (Kanner, Coyne, Schaefer, & Lazarus, 1981), crises

(Patterson, 1982), contacts with nonfamily members (Wahler, 1980), perceived social supports (Turner, 1982), and fluctuations in mood, energy, and physical health (Conger et al., 1979) merit more detailed investigation for the assessment and treatment of abusive families.

Experimental studies have been viewed as premature, because the nature and complexity of child abuse precluded the feasibility of controlled experiments. However, experimental studies of certain components are possible (Bell, 1981). For example, an experimental manipulation could investigate interaction effects between parental behavior and typical stimulus events, such as child behavior and competing activity, which are important for formulating theoretical relations, treatment programs, and guiding the selection of behaviors and situations for naturalistic studies (Bates & Pettit, 1981).

Recent studies have used laboratory analogs that simulate difficult parent/child situations (Mulhern & Passman, 1979; Passman & Mulhern, 1977; Vasta & Copitch, 1981; Zussman, 1980). These investigations, using nonabusive subjects, were successful in demonstrating that maternal punitiveness toward the child varied as a function of environmental and child-related stress imposed on the mother, the effectiveness of the punishment delivered, and competing activity. In a similar manner, naturalistic observational methods could be expanded to quasi-experimental designs. Experimenter-controlled competing activity (for example, parents' involvement in a problem-solving task) could be introduced to observe changes in both parental and child behavior.

A final comment on the assessment of multidimensional factors associated with abuse is warranted in view of the conclusions presented herein. Home- and clinic-based behavioral observations of family interactions are sensitive and comprehensive research methods. This approach allows for an analysis of bidirectional effects and sequential interactions, and has been valuable in the discrimination of specific problem areas (Friedman et al., 1981; Wolfe & Sandler, 1981). Behavioral observations, however, do not reveal the significance of many contextual factors that may dramatically influence parent and child behavior, such as marital, social, or financial problems (Griest & Wells, 1983; Wahler & Graves, 1983). Indirect assessment procedures that are tailored to the parental role are necessary for determining stable behavior patterns and qualitative factors that affect or are affected by parental competence. In addition, measures that reflect processes involved in family interactions may lead to clarification of distinct etiological or moderating variables involved in abuse and neglect. A taxonomic framework for treatment, epidemiology, and research may result from such efforts.

Conclusions

Studies have indicated that abusive parents' behavior is related to salient situational events, especially child-related phenomena. The parents' self-report of displeasure, anxiety, and attributions, in addition to physiological arousal and observed punitive behaviors, have each shown a relation to contextual variables. This relation between child abuse and situational events argues for a better understanding and assessment of psychological variables that exert an influence on parental competence, as opposed to psychopathology. Studies of psychological processes such as cognitive abilities, family roles, standards, expectations, and child-related experiences may lead to the conceptualization of differences in situationally defined competence among diverse parent populations. These findings will guide prevention efforts aimed at reducing situational demands and providing compensatory learning experiences for disadvantaged families.

References

Alfaro, J. D. (1981). Report on the relationship between child abuse and neglect and later socially deviant behavior. In R. J. Hunner & Y. E. Walker (Eds.), *Exploring the relationship between child abuse and delinquency* (pp. 175–219). Monteclair, NJ: Allanheld, Osmun.

Alvy, K. T. (1975). Preventing child abuse. *American Psychologist, 30,* 921–928.

Aragona, J. A., & Eyberg, S. M. (1981). Neglected children: Mothers' report of child behavior problems and observed verbal behavior. *Child Development, 52,* 596–602.

Averill, J. R. (1983). Studies on anger and aggression: Implications for theories of emotion. *American Psychologist, 38,* 1145–1160.

Bates, J. E., & Pettit, G. S. (1981). Adult individual differences as moderators of child effects. *Journal of Abnormal Child Psychology, 9,* 329–340.

Bell, R. Q. (1981). Introduction to symposium on parent, child, and reciprocal influences: New experimental approaches. *Journal of Abnormal Child Psychology, 9,* 299–301.

Bell, R. Q., & Harper, L. (1977). *Child effects on adults.* Hillsdale, NJ: Erlbaum.

Belsky, J. (1980). Child maltreatment: An ecological integration. *American Psychologist, 35,* 320–335.

Berkowitz, L. (1983). Aversively stimulated aggression: Some parallels and differences in research with animals and humans. *American Psychologist, 38,* 1135–1144.

Besharov, D. J. (1981). Toward better research on child abuse and neglect: Making definitional issues an explicit methodological concern. *Child Abuse and Neglect, 5,* 383–390.

Blechman, E. A. (1981). Toward comprehensive behavioral family intervention: An algorithm for matching families and interventions. *Behavior Modification, 5,* 221–236.

Bousha, D. M., & Twentyman, C. T. (1984). Mother-child interactional style in abuse, neglect, and control groups: Naturalistic observations in the home. *Journal of Abnormal Psychology, 93,* 106–114.

Brunnquell, D., Crichton, L., & Egeland, B. (1981). Maternal personality and attitude in disturbances of child rearing. *American Journal of Orthopsychiatry, 51,* 680–691.

Burgess, R. L. (1978). Child abuse: A social-interactional analysis. In B. B. Lahey & A. E. Kazdin (Eds.), *Advances in clincial child psychology* (Vol. 2, pp. 142–172). New York: Plenum.

Burgess, R. L., & Conger, R. (1978). Family interactions in abusive, neglectful, and normal families. *Child Development, 49,* 1163–1173.

Burgess, R. L., & Richardson, R. A. (1984). Coercive interpersonal contingencies as determinants of child abuse: Implications for treatment and prevention. In R. F. Dangel & R. A. Polster (Eds.), *Behavioral parent training: Issues in research and practice* (pp. 239–259). New York: Guilford.

Campbell, D. T., & Stanley, J. C. (1966). *Experimental and quasi-experimental designs for research.* Chicago: Rand McNally.

Christensen, A., & Hazzard, A. (1983). Reactive effects during naturalistic observation of families. *Behavioral Assessment, 5,* 349–362.

Cohn, A. H. (1982). Stopping abuse before it occurs: Different solutions for different population groups. *Child Abuse and Neglect, 6,* 473–483.

Conger, R. D., McCarty, J. A., Yang, R. K., Lahey, B. B., & Kropp, J. P. (in press). Perception of child, childrearing values, and emotional distress as mediating links between environmental stressors and observed maternal behavior. *Child Development.*

Conger, R., Burgess, R., & Barrett, C. (1979). Child abuse related to life change and perceptions of illness: Some preliminary findings. *Family Coordinator, 28,* 73–78.

Crittenden, P. M. (1981). Abusing, neglecting, problematic, and adequate dyads: Differentiating by patterns of interaction. *Merrill-Palmer Quarterly, 27,* 201–208.

Crnic, K. A., Greenberg, M. T., Ragozin, A. S., Robinson, N. M., & Basham, R. B. (1983). Effects of stress and social support on mothers and premature and full-term infants. *Child Development, 54,* 209–217.

Denicola, J., & Sandler, J. (1980). Training abusive parents in cognitive-behavioral techniques. *Behavior Therapy, 11,* 263–270.

Dietrich, K. N., Starr, R. H., & Kaplan, M. G. (1980). Maternal stimulation and care of abused infants. In T. M. Field, S. Goldberg, D. Stern, & A. M. Sostek (Eds.), *High-risk infants and children: Adult and peer interactions* (pp. 25–41). New York: Academic Press.

Disbrow, M. A., Doerr, H., & Caulfield, C. (1977). Measuring the components of parents' potential for child abuse and neglect. *Child Abuse and Neglect, 1,* 279–296.

Egeland, B., Breitenbucher, M., & Rosenberg, D. (1980). Prospective study of the significance of life stress in the etiology of child abuse. *Journal of Consulting and Clinical Psychology, 48,* 195–205.

Egeland, B., & Sroufe, L. A. (1981). Attachment and early maltreatment. *Child Development, 52,* 44–52.

Emery, R. E. (1982). Interparental conflict and the children of discord and divorce. *Psychological Bulletin, 92,* 310–330.

Forehand, R. L., & McMahon, R. J. (1981). *Helping the noncompliant child: A clinician's guide to parent training.* New York: Guilford.

Friedman, R., Sandler, J., Hernandez, M., & Wolfe, D. (1981). Child abuse. In E. Mash & L. Terdal (Eds.), *Behavioral assessment of childhood disorders* (pp. 221–255). New York: Guilford.

Friedman, R. M. (1975). Child abuse: A review of the psychosocial research. In Herner Co. (Eds.), *Four perspectives of child abuse and neglect research.* Springfield, VA: National Technical Information Service (NTIS No. PB-250-852AS).

Friedrich, W. N., & Boriskin, J. A. (1976). The role of the child in abuse: A review of the literature. *American Journal of Orthopsychiatry, 46,* 580–590.

Frodi, A. M., & Lamb, M. E. (1980). Child abusers' responses to infant smiles and cries. *Child Development, 51,* 238–241.

Gaines, R., Sandgrund, A., Green, A. H., & Power, E. (1978). Etiological factors in child maltreatment: A multivariate study of abusing, neglecting and normal mothers. *Journal of Abnormal Psychology, 87,* 531–540.

Garbarino, J. (1976). A preliminary study of some ecological correlates of child abuse: The impact of socioeconomic stress on mothers. *Child Development, 47,* 178–185.

Garbarino, J. (1982). *Children and families in the social environment.* Hawthorne, NY: Aldine.

Gelles, R. J. (1982). Toward better research on child abuse and neglect: A response to Besharov. *Child Abuse and Neglect, 6,* 495–496.

Gelles, R. J., & Straus, M. A. (1979). Determinants of violence in the family: Toward a theoretical integration. In W. R. Burr, R. Hill, F. I. Nye, & I. L. Reiss (Eds.), *Contemporary theories about the family* (pp. 549–581). New York: Free Press.

George, C., & Main, M. (1979). Social interactions of young abused children: Approach, avoidance, and aggression. *Child Development, 50,* 306–318.

Griest, D. L., & Wells, K. C. (1983). Behavioral family therapy with conduct disorders in children. *Behavior Therapy, 13,* 37–53.

Helfer, R. E. (1982). A review of the literature on the prevention of child abuse and neglect. *Child Abuse and Neglect, 6,* 251–261.

Herrenkohl, R. C., Herrenkohl, E. C., & Egolf, B. P. (1983). Circumstances surrounding the occurrence of child maltreatment. *Journal of Consulting and Clinical Psychology, 51,* 424–431.

Jaffe, P., Thompson, J., & Wolfe, D. A. (1984). Evaluating the impact of a specialized civilian family crisis unit within a police force on the resolution of family conflicts. *Journal of Preventive Psychiatry, 2,* 63–69.

Johnson, J. H., & Sarason, I. G. (1978). Life stress, depression, and anxiety: Internal–external control as a moderator variable. *Journal of Psychosomatic Research, 22,* 205–208.

Justice, B., & Duncan, D. F. (1976). Life crisis as a precursor to child abuse. *Public Health Reports, 91,* 110–115.

Kadushin, A., & Martin, J. (1981). *Child abuse: An interactional event.* New York: Columbia University.

Kanner, A. D., Coyne, S. C., Schaefer, C., & Lazarus, R. S. (1981). Comparison of two modes of stress measurement: Daily hassles and uplifts vs. major life events. *Journal of Behavioral Measurement, 4,* 1–39.

Kelly, J. A. (1983). *Treating child abusive families: Intervention based on skills training principles.* New York: Plenum.

Kempe, C. H. (1973). A practical approach to the protection of the abused child and the rehabilitation of the abusing parent. *Pediatrics, 51,* 804–812.

Kempe, C. H., & Helfer, R. E. (1972). *Helping the battered child and his family.* Philadelphia: Lippincott.

Knutson, J. F. (1978). Child abuse as an area of aggression research. *Journal of Pediatric Psychology, 3,* 20–27.

Koverola, C., Elliott-Faust, D., & Wolfe, D. (1984). Clinical issues in the behavioral treatment of a child abusive mother experiencing multiple life stresses. *Journal of Clinical Child Psychology, 13,* 187–191.

Koverola, C., Manion, I., & Wolfe, D. A. (in press). A microanalysis of factors associated with child abusive families. *Behavioral Research and Therapy.*

Lahey, B. B., Conger, R. D., Atkeson, B. M., & Treiber, F. A. (1984). Parenting behavior and emotional status of physically abusive mothers. *Journal of Consulting & Clinical Psychology, 52,* 1062–1071.

Larrance, D. T., & Twentyman, C. T. (1983). Maternal attributions and child abuse. *Journal of Abnormal Psychology, 92,* 449–457.

Lorber, R., Felton, D. K., & Reid, J. B. (1984). A social learning approach to the reduction of coercive processes in child abusive families: A molecular analysis. *Advances in Behavior Research and Therapy, 6,* 29–45.

Lutzker, J. R. (1983). Project 12-Ways: Treating child abuse and neglect from an ecobehavioral perspective. In R. F. Dangel & R. A. Polster (Eds.), *Parent training: Foundations of research and practice* (pp. 260–297). New York: Guilford.

Magnuson, E. (1983, Sept. 5). Child abuse: The ultimate betrayal. *Time,* pp. 16–18.

Mash, E. J., Johnston, C., & Kovitz, K. (1983). A comparison of the mother–child interactions of physically abused and non-abused children during play and task situations. *Journal of Clinical Child Psychology, 12*, 337–346.

Melnick, B., & Hurley, J. R. (1969). Distinctive personality attributes of child-abusing mothers. *Journals of Consulting and Clinical Psychology, 33*, 746–749.

Merrill, E. J. (1962). Physical abuse of children: An agency study. In V. DeFrancis (Ed.), *Protecting the battered child.* Denver, CO: American Humane Association.

Milner, J. S., & Wimberley, R. C. (1980). Prediction and explanation of child abuse. *Journal of Clinical Psychology, 36*, 875–884.

Mischel, W. (1973). Toward a cognitive social learning reconceptualization of personality. *Psychological Review, 80*, 252–283.

Morse, A. E., Hyde, J. N., Newberger, E. H., & Reed, R. B. (1977). Environmental correlates of pediatric social illness: Preventive implications of an advocacy approach. *American Journal of Public Health, 67*, 612–615.

Mulhern, R. K., Jr., & Passman, R. H. (1979). The child's behavioral pattern as a determinant of maternal punitiveness. *Child Development, 50*, 815–820.

National Center on Child Abuse and Neglect. (1981). *Executive summary: National study of the incidence and severity of child abuse and neglect* (DHHS Publication No. OHDS 81-30329). Washington, DC: U.S. Government Printing Office.

Novaco, R. W. (1978). Anger and coping with stress. In J. Foreyt & D. Rathjen (Eds.), *Cognitive behavior therapy: Research and applications* (pp. 135–173). New York: Plenum.

Oates, R. M. (1979). A classification of child abuse and its relation to treatment and prognosis. *Child Abuse and Neglect, 3*, 907–915.

Parke, R. D., & Collmer, C. W. (1975). Child abuse: An interdisciplinary analysis. In E. M. Hetherington (Ed.), *Review of child development research* (Vol. 5, pp. 509–590). Chicago: University of Chicago Press.

Passman, R. H., & Mulhern, R. K., Jr. (1977). Maternal punitiveness as affected by situational stress: An experimental analogue of child abuse. *Journal of Abnormal Psychology, 86*, 565–569.

Patterson, G. R. (1982). *Coercive family process.* Eugene, OR: Castalia.

Patterson, G. R., Reid, J. B., Jones, R. R., & Conger, R. E. (1975). *A social learning approach to family intervention* (Vol. 1). Eugene, OR: Castalia.

Plotkin, R. C., Azar, S., Twentyman, C. T., & Perri, M. G. (1981). A critical evaluation of the research methodology employed in the investigation of causative factors of child abuse and neglect. *Child Abuse and Neglect, 5*, 449–455.

Polansky, N. A., Hally, C., & Polansky, N. F. (1975). *Profile of neglect: A survey of the state of knowledge of child neglect.* Washington, DC: Community Services Administration, Social and Rehabilitation Services, DHEW.

Reid, J. B., Taplin, P. S., & Lorber, R. (1981). A social interactional approach to the treatment of abusive families. In R. B. Stuart (Ed.), *Violent behavior: Social learning approaches to prediction, management, and treatment* (pp. 83–101). New York: Brunner/Mazel.

Rosenberg, M. S., & Reppucci, N. D. (1983). Abusive mothers: Perceptions of their own children's behavior. *Journal of Consulting and Clinical Psychology, 51*, 674–682.

Ross, C. J., & Zigler, E. (1980). An agenda for action. In G. Gerbner, C. J. Ross, & E. Zigler (Eds.), *Child abuse: An agenda for action.* (pp. 293–304). New York: Oxford.

Rule, B. G., & Nesdale, A. R. (1976). Emotional arousal and aggressive behavior. *Psychological Bulletin, 83*, 851–863.

Salzinger, S., Kaplan, S., & Artemyeff, C. (1983). Mothers' personal social networks and child maltreatment. *Journal of Abnormal Psychology, 92*, 68–76.

Sloan, M. P., & Meier, J. H. (1983). Typology for parents of abused children. *Child Abuse and Neglect, 7*, 443–450.

Sloan, M. P., & Meier, J. H. (1983). Typology for parents of abused children. *Child Abuse and Neglect, 7*, 443–450.

Spinetta, J. J. (1978). Parental personality factors in child abuse. *Journal of Consulting and Clinical Psychology, 46*, 1409–1414.

Spinetta, J. J., & Rigler, D. (1972). The child-abusing parent: A psychological review. *Psychological Bulletin, 77*, 296–304.

Standing Senate Committee on Health, Welfare, and Science. (1980). *Child at risk* (Cat. No. YC17-304/2-DIE). Hull, Quebec: Canadian Government Publishing Centre.

Starr, R. H., Jr. (1979). Child abuse. *American Psychologist, 34*, 872–878.

Starr, R. H., Jr. (1982). A research-based approach to the prediction of child abuse. In R. H. Starr, Jr. (Ed.), *Child abuse prediction: Policy implications.* Cambridge, MA: Ballinger.

Steele, B. F., & Pollock, C. (1968). A psychiatric study of parents who abuse infants and small children. In R. Helfer & C. Kempe (Eds.), *The battered child* (pp. 89–133). Chicago: University of Chicago Press.

Straus, M. A. (1980a). Stress and child abuse. In C. H. Kempe & R. E. Helfer (Eds.), *The battered child* (3rd ed., pp. 86–102). Chicago: University of Chicago Press.

Straus, M. A. (1980b). Victims and aggressors in marital violence. *American Behavioral Scientist, 23*, 681–704.

Straus, M. A., Gelles, R. J., & Steinmetz, S. K. (1980). *Behind closed doors: Violence in the American family.* Grand City, NY: Doubleday/Anchor.

Toro, P. A. (1982). Developmental effects of child abuse: A review. *Child Abuse and Neglect, 6*, 423–431.

Turner, R. J. (1982). *Risk and prevention for maladaptive parenting: The family volunteer study.* Toronto, Ontario: Ontario Ministry of Community and Social Services, Child Abuse Program.

Vasta, R. (1982). Physical child abuse: A dual-component analysis. *Developmental Review, 2*, 125–149.

Vasta, R., & Copitch, P. (1981). Simulating conditions of child abuse in the laboratory. *Child Development, 52*, 164–170.

Wahler, R. G. (1980). The insular mother: Her problems in parent–child treatment. *Journal of Applied Behavior Analysis, 13*, 207–219.

Wahler, R. G., & Graves, M. G. (1983). Setting events in social networks: Ally or enemy in child behavior therapy? *Behavior Therapy, 14*, 19–36.

Weinraub, M., & Wolf, B. M. (1983). Effects of stress

and social supports on mother–child interactions in single- and two-parent families. *Child Development, 54,* 1297–1311.

Welsh, R. S. (1976). Severe parental punishment and delinquency: A developmental theory. *Journal of Clinical Child Psychology, 5,* 17–21.

Wolfe, D. A. (in press). Prevention of child abuse through the development of parent and child competencies. In R. J. McMahon & R. Peters (Eds.), *Childhood disorders: Behavioral–development approaches.* New York: Brunner/Mazel.

Wolfe, D. A., Fairbank, J., Kelly, J. A., & Bradlyn, A. S. (1983). Child abusive parents' physiological responses to stressful and non-stressful behavior in children. *Behavioral Assessment, 5,* 363–371.

Wolfe, D. A., Kaufman, K., Aragona, J., & Sandler, J. (1981). *The child management program for abusive parents.* Winter Park, FL: Anna.

Wolfe, D. A., & Mosk, M. D. (1983). Behavioral comparisons of children from abusive and distressed families. *Journal of Consulting and Clinical Psychology, 51,* 702–708.

Wolfe, D. A., & Sandler, J. (1981). Training abusive parents in effective child management. *Behavior Modification, 5,* 320–335.

Wolfe, D. A., Sandler, J., & Kaufman, K. (1981). A competency-based parent training program for child abusers. *Journal of Consulting and Clinical Psychology, 49,* 633–640.

Wright, L. (1976). The "sick but slick" syndrome as a personality component of parents of battered children. *Journal of Clinical Psychology, 32,* 41–45.

Zalba, S. R. (1967). The abused child: A typology for classification and treatment. *Social Work, 12,* 70–79.

Zigler, E. (1980). Controlling child abuse: Do we have the knowledge and/or the will? In G. Gerbner, C. J. Ross, & E. Zigler (Eds.), *Child abuse: An agenda for action* (pp. 3–32). New York: Oxford.

Zillman, D. (1979). *Hostility and aggression.* Hillsdale, NJ: Erlbaum.

Zussman, J. U. (1980). Situational determinants of parental behavior: Effects of competing cognitive activity. *Child Development, 51,* 792–800.

Received March 26, 1984
Revision received August 9, 1984 ∎

The Family and Its Role in the Abuse of Children

By RICHARD J. GELLES, PhD

The first people to identify a problem often shape how others will perceive it.[1] Nowhere is this truer than in the study of child abuse. The effort to understand, explain, predict, treat, and prevent the physical abuse of children has been strongly influenced by an individual level, medical/psychiatric perspective employed by those who first identified the problem of child abuse.

Although children have probably been the victims of parental physical abuse for centuries,[2-5] it was not until C. Henry Kempe and his colleagues[6] wrote about the "clinical condition in young children who receive serious physical abuse, generally from a parent or foster parent," that the problem of child abuse received serious public and professional attention.

The fact that child abuse was "discovered" by the medical community has had profound implications for research and intervention. The first research articles on abuse characterized offenders as suffering from various forms of psychopathology.[7-9] Thus, for many years researchers applied a "kind of person" model to research and sought to identify the hypothesized personality and character disorders associated with abusers.

Although numerous articles attempted to present the psychological profiles of abusers, the research efforts were limited by methodological design problems, includ-

ing small, non-representative samples and lack of appropriate comparison groups.[10,11] "Kind of person" explanations failed to provide a consistent profile of abusers and failed to explain a significant amount of the variance in the abusive behavior of caretakers.

Current theoretical approaches to child abuse tend to recognize the multi-dimensional nature of abuse and locate the roots of physical abuse in the structure of the family and/or society. It is noteworthy that a sociologist and psychiatrist independently writing on family violence agree that social factors explain as much as 90% of the variance in family violence.[12,13]

In this article, the major social and family factors related to the physical abuse of children are reviewed. One of the great difficulties in the study of child abuse has been to develop precise definitions of abusive behavior. The term "abuse" has been applied to a wide range of acts of commission and omission including emotional abuse, medical neglect, willful mal-

nourishment, and sexual victimization of children.[14,15] For purposes of clarity, we confine our examination only to acts of physical violence that injure children or have great potential of causing injury.

Five major social and family factors that have been consistently found to be related to the physical abuse of children are reviewed. The factors are:

- The cycle of violence—the intergenerational transmission of physical abuse;
- Low socioeconomic status;
- Social and structural stress;
- Social isolation and low community embedment;
- Family structure.

The article concludes with a brief review of some sociological theoretical frameworks that have been applied to the physical abuse of children.

THE CYCLE OF VIOLENCE

The single, most consistent finding reported in the child abuse literature is that experiencing abuse as a child

> *The single, most consistent finding reported in the child abuse literature is that experiencing abuse as a child increases the likelihood of becoming an abusive caretaker.*

increases the likelihood of becoming an abusive caretaker.[6,10,11,16-18] However, this is not a perfect association. Potts and Herzberger point out that the relationship between being abused and becoming the abuser is probabalistic, not deterministic.[19] Kaufman and Zigler reviewed the major research studies on the cycle of physical abuse (Kaufman J, Zigler E, unpublished data). They note that data come from four primary sources—case study materials, social agency records, clinical interviews, and self-report questionnaire data. Kaufman and Zigler dismiss the evidence derived from case histories, agency data, and clinical interviews. Such studies are almost always limited by the use of small, non-representative samples. Few of the investigators include comparison groups in their studies. Data from self-report questionnaires and interviews find that between 17% and 70% of abused children grow up to become abusive caretakers.

Kaufman and Zigler reason that the best estimate is that some 30% of abused children grow up to be abusive (Kaufman J, Zigler E, unpublished data). They conclude that the link between being maltreated and becoming abusive is far from inevitable, and they advocate abandoning the notion that abused children grow up to be abusers. Yet, the 30% rate of abusive behavior is far greater than the rate of less than 4% of abusive behavior found among the general population.[18,20] Exposure to violence does appear to be a significant factor related to the likelihood of later abusive behavior, even if less than half of abused children grow up to become abusers.

Kaufman and Zigler suggest that the most appropriate question to ask is not, "Do abused children grow up to be abusers?" (Kaufman J, Zigler E, unpublished data). Rather, they say researchers ought to ask, "Under what conditions do abused children grow up to be abusive?"

Egeland, Jacobvitz, and Papatola have followed 267 high risk mothers from the last three months of their pregnancies to the time when their

Abusive and neglectful families are reported as experiencing more stressful life events than non-maltreating families.

children were in kindergarten.[21] Seventy percent of the mothers who were seriously abused were abusive to their children. Those mothers who were seriously abused but who did not become abusive shared a number of characteristics, including having at least one parent or foster parent who provided love and support when they were children. As adults, these mothers had husbands who provided a supportive home environment and a stable source of income. Hunter and Kilstrom report that parents who broke the cycle of abuse had more extensive social supports, fewer ambivalent feelings about their pregnancies, and healthier babies.[22] The non-abusive, abused parents displayed more open anger about their abusive experiences and were able to describe these experiences freely. They were typically abused by only one parent while the other parent provided support.

Both studies that have examined the condition under which violence and abuse is repeated point to the fact that the link can be broken if present support—both psychological and social—is available.

LOW SOCIOECONOMIC STATUS

The first researchers who studied child abuse thought that social, economic, and demographic factors were irrelevant to the actual act of abuse.[9] Indeed, child abuse may be found among all socioeconomic groups. Yet, a disproportionate number of cases of abuse come from low income families.[10,16-18,23-25]

There is a need for caution in interpreting data on the relationship between child abuse and social class. The caution stems from the fact that lower class families are much more vulnerable to being publically recorded for abusive behavior. A variety of investigators and experiments have demonstrated that, given the same injury or condition, children from lower class homes are much more likely to be reported as being abused than children from middle or upper class families.[26-28]

Data collected directly by questionnaire or interview are less subject to the biases of official report data, and these data do confirm the higher rates of abuse among the lower class. The difference between social classes, however, is not nearly as great as it would seem from the data collected from official agency or case study sources.

SOCIAL STRESS

Researchers agree that the mechanism through which low socioeconomic status works to bring about child abuse is social stress. Abusive and neglectful families are reported as experiencing more stressful life events than non-maltreating families.[16,18,23-26]

One of the more significant social stressors that is related to abuse and neglect is unemployment. Among families in which the father is unemployed or employed part-time, the risk of abuse is higher than in other households where the father has full-time work.[8,16,18]

Poor housing conditions and larger than average family size are also risk factors for maltreatment.[16,18,29] Other stressful life conditions found related to abuse include a new baby present in the home, presence of a handicapped person in the home, illness, death of a family member, and child care problems.

Stress produced by child-related factors can also lead to abuse. Low

230

birth weight babies, premature children, and handicapped, retarded, or developmentally disabled children are at higher risk for abuse than children without these conditions.[16,17,23,27,30]

SOCIAL ISOLATION AND LOW COMMUNITY EMBEDMENT

Parents who abuse their children tend to be socially isolated from both formal and informal social networks.[23,31] Smith found that abusive mothers have fewer contacts with their parents, relatives, neighbors, or friends, and engaged in fewer social or recreational activities.[32]

The lack of formal or informal social networks deprives abusive parents of support systems that would aid them in dealing with social or family stress. Moreover, the lack of community contacts makes these families less likely to change their behavior to conform with community values and standards.[33] Thus, they are particularly vulnerable to violent responses to stress while not perceiving their behavior as deviant.

FAMILY STRUCTURE

Certain family structures are common among abusive and neglectful families. There is a general belief that single parents are at higher risk to abuse their children. Unfortunately, it is difficult to partial out the effects of youth and poverty from the impact of the single parent family structure—many single parent homes are those of young mothers who live in poverty.

Within intact homes, a major structural feature found related to the use of abusive violence toward children is inequality. Straus and colleagues found that the rate of severe violence toward children was highest in homes where there was little shared decision making.[18] Those homes in which either the husband or wife dominated the decision making and where little family equality existed were among the most violent.

EXPLAINING THE ABUSE OF CHILDREN

The study of child abuse abounds

> It is difficult to partial out the effects of youth and poverty from the impact of the single parent family structure.

with simplistic models. The earliest research advanced a psychopathological model—mental illness caused people to abuse their children. Other intra-individual models proposed that abuse was caused by alcohol and/or drugs.

The major theoretical approaches to child abuse have been reviewed extensively elsewhere.[14,34] This section reviews some of the more complex theories that have been applied to examining the family and its role in the abuse of children. These theories include an economic model, a sociocultural explanation, an ecological model, and an exchange theory approach.

AN ECONOMIC MODEL

The economic or social-structural model explains that violence and abuse arise out of socially structured stress. Stress, such as low income, unemployment, and illness, is unevenly distributed in the social structure. When violence is the accepted response or adaptation to stress, stress leads to violence and abuse.[35]

A SOCIOCULTURAL EXPLANATION

Students of violence have explained the occurrence of family violence, including child abuse, by drawing on sociocultural attitudes and norms concerning violent

behavior. Societies, cultures, and subcultures that approve the use of violence are thought to have the highest rates of domestic violence and abuse of children.[13]

AN ECOLOGICAL MODEL

Garbarino has proposed an ecological model of child maltreatment.[36] The model rests on three levels of analysis: the relationship between organism and environment, the interacting and overlapping system in which human development occurs, and environmental quality. Garbarino proposes that maltreatment arises out of a mismatch between parent, children, and family to neighborhood and community.

EXCHANGE THEORY

Exchange theory proposes that family violence and child abuse are governed by the principle of costs and rewards.[37] Abuse is used when the rewards are higher than the costs. The private nature of the family, the reluctance of social institutions and agencies to intervene—in spite of mandatory child abuse reporting laws—and the low risk of other interventions reduce the costs of abuse and violence. The cultural approval of violence as both expressive behavior and, in the case of disciplining children, instrumental behavior, raises the potential rewards for violence.

SUMMARY

The comparative recency of child abuse as an area of study and the fact that the first decade of research was dominated by the psychopathology model has resulted in the limited level of theoretical development of the field. Yet, despite the rather primitive level of theory building and theory testing, one conclusion is inescapable. Researchers have found that no one factor can explain the presence or absence of child abuse. Characteristics of the child, parent, family, social situation, and community are related to which children are abused and under what conditions. Individual states of caretakers and community factors are moderated and influenced by family struc-

127

ture and family situations. Although there are indeed multiple factors related to abuse of children, all operate through the structure and function of the family group.

REFERENCES

1. Nelson BJ: *Making an Issue of Child Abuse: Political Agenda Setting for Social Problems.* Chicago, University of Chicago Press, 1984.
2. De Mause L (ed): *The History of Childhood.* New York, Psychohistory Press, 1974.
3. De Mause L: Our forebears made childhood a nightmare. *Psychology Today* 1975; 8:85-87.
4. Radbill S: A history of child abuse and infanticide, in Helfer R, Kempe C (eds): *The Battered Child,* ed 2. Chicago, University of Chicago Press. 1974, pp 3-21.
5. Robin M: Historical introduction: Sheltering arms: The roots of child protection, in Newberger EH (ed): *Child Abuse.* Boston, Little Brown, 1983, pp 1-14.
6. Kempe CH, Silverman FN, Steele BF, et al: The battered-child syndrome. *JAMA* 1962; 181:17-24.
7. Bennie E, Sclare A: The battered child syndrome. *Am J Psychiatry* 1969; 125:975-979.
8. Galdston R: Observations of children who have been physically abused by their parents. *Am J Psychiatry* 1965; 122:440-443.
9. Steele B, Pollock C: A psychiatric study of parents who abuse infants and small children, in Helfer R, Kempe C (eds): *The Battered Child,* ed 2. Chicago, University of Chicago Press, 1974.
10. Gelles R: Child abuse as psychopathology: A sociological critique and reformulation. *Am J Orthopsychiatry* 1973; 43:611-621.
11. Spinetta J, Rigler D: The child abusing parent: A psychological review. *Psychol Bull* 1972; 77:296-304.
12. Steele B: The child abuser, in Kutash IL, Kutash SB, Schlesinger LB, et al (eds): *Violence: Perspectives on Murder and Aggression.* San Francisco, Jossey-Bass, 1978, pp 285-300.
13. Straus M: A sociological perspective on family violence, in Green M (ed): *Violence and the Family.* Boulder, Colorado, Westview Press, 1980.
14. Gelles R, Straus M: Determinants of violence in the family: Toward a theoretical integration, in Burr W, et al (eds): *Contemporary Theories About the Family.*

New York, Free Press, 1979, vol 1, pp 549-581.
15. Gelles R: Family violence, in Turner RH, Short JF, Jr (eds): *Annual Review of Sociology.* Palo Alto, California, Annual Reviews, Inc., 1985, vol 11, pp 347-367.
16. Gil D: *Violence Against Children: Physical Child Abuse in the United States.* Cambridge, Massachusetts, Harvard University Press, 1970.
17. Parke RD, Collmer CW: Child abuse: An interdisciplinary analysis, in Hetherington M (ed): *Review of Child Development Research.* Chicago, University of Chicago Press, 1975, vol 5, pp 1-102.
18. Straus M, Gelles R, Steinmetz S: *Behind Closed Doors: Violence in the American Family.* New York, Doubleday/Anchor, 1980.
19. Potts D, Herzberger S: *Child Abuse: A Cross Generational Pattern of Child Rearing?* Presented at the Annual Meeting of the Midwest Psychological Association, Chicago, 1979.
20. Burgdorf K: *Recognition and Reporting of Child Maltreatment.* Rockville, Maryland, Westat, 1980.
21. Egeland B, Jacobvitz D, Papatola K: Intergenerational continuity of abuse, in Gelles R, Lancaster J (eds): *Child Abuse and Neglect: Biosocial Dimensions.* Hawthorne, New Jersey, Aldine de Gruyter, 1987, to be published.
22. Hunter R, Kilstrom N: Breaking the cycle in abusive families. *Am J Psychiatry* 1979; 136:1320-1322.
23. Elmer E: *Children in Jeopardy: A Study of Abused Minors and Their Families.* Pittsburgh, University of Pittsburgh Press, 1967.
24. Maden MF, Wrench DF: Significant findings in child abuse research. *Victimology* 1977; 2:196-224.
25. Pelton L: Child abuse and neglect: The myth of classlessness. *Am J Orthopsychiatry* 1978; 48:608-617.
26. Gelles R: On the association of sex and violence in the fantasy production of college students. *Suicide* 1975; 5:78-85.
27. Newberger EH, Reed RB, Daniel JH, et al: Pediatric social illness: Toward an etiologic classification. *Pediatrics* 1977; 60:178-185.
28. Turbett JP, O'Toole R: *Physician's Recognition of Child Abuse.* Presented at Annual Meeting of American Sociological Association, New York, 1980.
29. Johnson B, Morse H: Injured children and their parents. *Children* 1968; 15:147-152.
30. Friedrich W, Boriskin J: The role of the child in abuse: A review of literature. *Am*

J Orthopsychiatry 1976; 46:580-590.
31. Garbarino J, Gilliam G: *Understanding Abusive Families.* Lexington, Massachusetts, D.C. Heath, 1980.
32. Smith S: *The Battered Child Syndrome.* London, Buttersworth, 1975.
33. Steinmetz S: Violence between family members. *Marriage Fam Rev* 1978; 1(3):1-16.
34. Gelles R: Violence in the family: A review of research in the seventies. *J Marriage Fam* 1980; 42:873-885.
35. Coser LA: *Continuities in the Study of Social Conflict.* New York, Free Press, 1967.
36. Garbarino J: The human ecology of child maltreatment. *J Marriage Fam* 1977; 39:721-735.
37. Gelles R: An exchange/social control theory, in Finkelhor D, Gelles R, Straus M, et al: *The Dark Side of Families: Current Family Violence Research.* Beverly Hills, California, Sage, 1983, pp 151-165.

Dr. Gelles is Dean, College of Arts and Sciences, University of Rhode Island. Kingston. Address reprint requests to Richard J. Gelles, PhD, Office of the Dean, College of Arts and Sciences, University of Rhode Island, Kingston, RI 02881.

This research is part of the University of Rhode Island Family Violence Program. A complete list of program publications and reports is available on request. Support for the writing of this paper was provided by NIMH grant MH 40027.

Family Violence in Stable Middle-Class Homes

Cyrus Stewart, Mary Margaret Senger, David Kallen, and Susan Scheurer

Only in the past 10 years has abuse within the family been recognized as a national problem. Typically, the recognition of deviance in a society begins with its manifestations in lower classes. Consequently, abuse within the family was considered generated by the personal trauma and social stress often characteristic of life in the lower class. Recently, it has become common knowledge, especially among professionals, that abuse and neglect exist across all social classes.[1] The social worker therefore is placed in the difficult position of dealing not only with the problem of lower-class abuse, but with middle-class abuse as well. Causes of abuse and therapeutic strategies are well formulated for handling lower-class abuse. However, similar information is unavailable on the middle class. Social workers therefore have no alternative but to apply what is known about lower-class problems to middle-class situations.

Research consistently has found significant associations between child abuse and neglect and various social conditions that produce a high vulnerability or risk to the child.[2] Newberger suggests that child abuse and neglect have been almost exclusively studied in working-class communities, particularly in those agencies that handle socially marginal families.[3] Although Nixon et al. investigated the socioeconomic correlates of violent nonaccidental deaths during childhood, they did not investigate any other aspects of abuse or neglect in the middle class.[4]

Regardless of how accessible sample populations may be, they do not address the social class distributions of child abuse and neglect. Newberger concludes that studies that address the class distribution of these aspects of violence are needed urgently.[5] This article therefore reports data on the extent of abuse and neglect (both physical and emotional) in a population of middle-class families.

METHODS

The data for this study were derived from undergraduate social science students (n = 570) at Michigan State University by means of a survey (120 forced-choice questions). Because social science courses were required of all students for graduation, the range of student characteristics adequately reflected the general characteristics of the university population. Family violence and neglect were measured by answers to six questions that inquired about physical abuse of one's self and one's siblings, and spouse abuse. Emotional and physical neglect of children and emotional neglect of one spouse by the other also were measured (Table 1). Responses were obtained on a seven-point scale that ranged from strongly agree to strongly disagree. The data were analyzed through frequency distributions and Pearson product-moment intercorrelations.

FINDINGS

Demographic analysis of the respondents revealed that the sample was uniformly middle class. The ethnic group identification of the sample produced a highly skewed distribution: only 9 percent reported a nonwhite (for example, black, Latin, Asian, or native American) group membership. Of the sample, 40 percent reported that the combined yearly income of their parents was more than $50,000. More than 30 percent reported parental income between $30,000 and $50,000.

The income distribution was consistent with student reports of the educational and occupational status of their parents. Approximately three of every 10 mothers (28 percent) were employed as professionals or managers. An additional 24 percent were employed in white collar (that is, sales and clerical) positions, whereas 33 percent of the total sample was not employed outside the home (that is, homemakers). Of the mothers of the respondents, 40 percent currently were employed full-time. The educational level data conveys the same impression. Of the mothers of the respondents, 56 percent had attended college. Of these, 43 percent had earned undergraduate degrees and 20 percent had graduate degrees.

The educational and occupational status of the fathers was congruent with the data reported for mothers. Approximately 60 percent of the fathers of the respondents were employed in professional and managerial occupations, whereas 16 percent were in clerical or sales positions. Of the fathers, 87 percent were employed full-time. More than half of the sample (55 per-

cent) reported their fathers possessed graduate or undergraduate degrees.

Clearly, the sample was consistently middle class, as indicated by income, education, and occupation. The sample also came from stable home environments. Divorce or separation occurred moderately, affecting only 17 percent of the sample. Of the respondents, 93 percent did not experience significant separation from their mothers before the age of 11 years. The same percentage were raised in a two-parent home environment. In 10 percent of the sample, the two-parent homes represented a blended family. These data consistently indicated that our sample population was a stable middle-class group.

The frequency distribution of family abuse and neglect responses across aggregated agree and disagree categories clearly demonstrates a substantial majority of the sample had not experienced physical abuse or witnessed physical abuse of siblings or parents. The percentages revealed only minor variations across abuse categories. The response frequency ranged from a low of less than 1 percent who agreed that "Sometimes my parents beat me so badly that I needed to see a doctor," to a high of 6 percent who agreed that "There were times when my father beat my mother."

The data on physical and emotional neglect were consistent with the literature, which implies that in a middle-class setting neglect is more typical than abuse.[6] In addition, the emotional aspects of neglect are expected to occur more frequently than physical neglect. The reported frequency for emotional neglect was more than four times greater than that reported for physical neglect (9 percent as compared with 2 percent). Respondents reported that their parents neglected each other's emotional needs twice as frequently (18 percent) as they neglected the needs of their children.

Given the findings on family violence in the lower class, the authors anticipate that middle-class family violence, will present a highly unified pattern. Specifically, when one form of abuse occurs within a family, there is a high probability that other forms of violence also will occur. For example, when a child reports having been physically abused

CCC Code: 0037-8046/87 $1.00 © 1987, National Association of Social Workers, Inc.

Table 1.
Percentage Distribution of Family Violence and Neglect

Category	Statement	Agree	Disagree	Uncertain	n^a
1. Child abuse by parents	1. I have been beaten so badly that it left marks on my body.	18 (3.17)	542 (95.59)	7 (1.24)	567
	2. My parents have beaten me so badly that I was ashamed to be seen by others.	9 (1.58)	555 (97.88)	3 (0.54)	567
	3. Sometimes my parents beat me so badly that I needed to see a doctor.	2 (0.35)	564 (99.47)	1 (0.18)	567
2. Spouse and sibling abuse	4. There were times when my father beat my mother.	36 (6.35)	524 (92.42)	7 (1.23)	567
	5. There were times when my mother beat my father.	17 (3.00)	546 (96.30)	4 (0.70)	567
	6. There were times when my parents beat my brothers and/or sisters so badly that it left marks on their body.	19 (3.36)	541 (95.75)	5 (0.89)	565
3. Neglect in the family	7. While I was growing up my parents neglected my physical needs.	14 (2.49)	527 (93.77)	21 (3.74)	562
	8. While I was growing up my parents neglected me emotionally.	52 (9.26)	493 (87.88)	16 (2.86)	561
	9. My parents neglected each other's emotional needs.	105 (18.72)	417 (74.33)	39 (6.95)	561

Response Categories

^{a}Fluctuation in numbers due to random patterns of response.

by parents, the parents will be found to have been aggressive toward each other, as well as toward other siblings. Moreover, we anticipate that each type of abuse also would be associated with both emotional and physical neglect. Consequently, the guiding hypothesis can be stated as follows: Family violence and neglect represent an integrated behavior in which diverse forms of interpersonal aggression are present and intercorrelated.

The integrated nature of the entire matrix of associations is indicated because the average correlation for the matrix is statistically significant ($\bar{r} = .36, p < .001$). Conceptually, the matrix in Table 2 can be subdivided into three categories: (1) child abuse by parents (questions 1–3); (2) spousal and sibling abuse (questions 4–6); and (3) neglect in the family (questions 7–9). To appreciate the information given in the matrix, both within-group and between-group variations should be observed. The highest average correlation is found among the questions that measure child abuse ($\bar{r} = .63, p < .001$). Other within-group analyses revealed a similar response pattern. Category 2, for example, has an average within-group correlation of $\bar{r} = .48$ ($p < .001$).

Between-group comparisons also revealed a series of significant associations. The strongest of the associations ($\bar{r} = .45, p < .001$) is between category 1 and category 2. This means that reports by respondents that they were physically abused are strongly associated with reports that both

their siblings and parents were physically abused. Significant correlations also are found between category 3 and categories 1 and 2, indicating that if neglect occurs, various forms of violence also are present.

FINAL THOUGHTS

One of the most important results of this study is the generation of data concerning family violence and neglect from a sample of stable, middle-class respondents. It is well-known that middle-class individuals socialize their children and interact personally in ways that minimize physical aggression. Despite these prohibitions, 6 percent of the sample reported fathers beating mothers. A comparison of spouse abuse at 6 percent with emotional neglect of spouses at 18 percent illustrates what would be expected of middle-class behavior patterns (that is, more neglect than abuse). This is understandable. The middle class has been socialized to inhibit displays of violence, and emotional neglect would be easier to "neutralize," (to perceive as justified) in the context of the individual's value systems.[8] In addition, emotional neglect is not as visible; it is easier to hide, and there are no discernible marks on the child. Also neglectful relationships are difficult to establish in a court of law.

Emotional neglect has been less vigorously defined than physical abuse. While physical abuse does show variations in content and severity, there are, nevertheless, objective physical criteria that are em-

ployed in its identification.[9] Physical neglect also is specified by legal criteria. Nonetheless, as many caseworkers are aware, applying these criteria may be difficult.

On the continuum of specificity of abuse, physical neglect, and emotional neglect, the latter is least specifically definable. What constitutes emotional neglect is strongly affected by variations in situations, social class status, and family interaction patterns. It seems clear that a parent who verbally assaults a child's self-esteem, security, and sense of adequacy is engaging in emotional abuse. The extent of alternative reinforcements available to the child will affect the child's reaction to parental verbal assaults. For example, when a parent tells a child he is worthless and incapable, but the child knows that his academic performance is excellent and his social relationships are rewarding, that child may be able to weather the effects of parental verbal assaults. However, many children, especially younger ones and those otherwise socially isolated, are vulnerable to negative remarks and judgments that may not appear to be outright emotional assaults.

In the final analysis, emotional neglect is defined through the eye of the beholder. What is real in its consequences is real for the child. Therefore, when a child reports emotional neglect, it is real for that child and must be attended to. Until a concept akin to the "battered child syndrome" emerges in the identification of emotional neglect, social workers are forced to rely on a victim's report of emotional neglect, even

130

Table 2.
Intercorrelation of Family Violence and Neglect (n = 570)

Statement	Category 1. Child Abuse by Parents			Category 2. Spouse and Sibling Abuse			Category 3. Neglect in the Family		
	1	2	3	4	5	6	7	8	9
1. I have been beaten so badly that it left marks on my body.	1.0	.77	.47	.30	.38	.62	.28	.33	.24
2. My parents have beaten me so badly that I was ashamed to be seen by others.		1.0	.66	.35	.46	.61	.33	.27	.20
3. Sometimes my parents beat me so badly that I needed to see a doctor.			1.0	.36	.46	.48	.28	.18	.11 *
4. There were times when my father beat my mother.				1.0	.59	.38	.32	.28	.38
5. There were times when my mother beat my father.					1.0	.46	.28	.23	.31
6. There were times when my parents beat my brothers and/or sisters so badly that it left marks on their body.						1.0	.26	.33	.29
7. While I was growing up my parents neglected my physical needs.							1.0	.46	.29
8. While I was growing up my parents neglected me emotionally.								1.0	.53
9. My parents neglected each other's emotional needs.									1.0

All correlations $p < .001$, except as indicated by an asterisk.

though such methodology creates problems of reliability and validity.

The social worker, therefore, is faced with knowing the neglect exists while being able to do little about it. The task of social workers is easier where abuse exists, however. In situations where official action is indicated, the social worker should be aware that family violence appears in diverse forms. In families where children are physically abused there will be a strong likelihood that the siblings will be abused and for spouse abuse to be present. In these families emotional neglect also will be found.

It is clear that in cases of family violence and neglect, social workers are dealing with more than a lower-class phenomenon. While emotional neglect may be the presenting problem in middle-class families, the social worker is well-advised to examine family dynamics for more covert forms of family violence. Only in this way will professionals become sensitive to the realities of abuse and neglect among middle-class families.

Cyrus Stewart, PhD, is Professor of Social Science, Michigan State University, Vice President of Meridian Professional Psychological Consultants, 5031 Park Lake Drive, East Lansing, MI 48824. Mary Margaret Senger, PhD, is Director of Behavioral Medicine, Department of Family Practice, College of Human Medicine, Michigan State University. David Kallen, PhD, is Professor and Susan Scheurer, MD, is Assistant Professor,

Department of Pediatrics, College of Human Medicine, Michigan State University.

Notes and References

1. D. Elkind, *The Hurried Child* (Reading, Mass.: Addison-Wesley, 1981).

2. J. Garbino and D. Sherman, "High-Risk Neighborhoods and High-Risk Families," *Child Development*, 51 (1980), pp. 181–198; R. Helfer and C. Kempe, *The Battered Child* (Chicago: University of Chicago Press, 1980); J. Jason and N. Anerick, "Fatal Child Abuse in Georgia," *Child Abuse and Neglect*, 7 (1983), pp. 1–9; D. Lagaerberg, "Child Abuse: A Literature Review," *Acta Paediatrician Scandanavia*, 67 (1978), pp. 68; M. Lynch, "Recognizing a Child at Increased Risk of Abuse," *Paediatrician*, 8 (1979), pp. 188–199.

3. E. Newberger, "Child Abuse and Neglect: Toward a Firmer Foundation for Practice and Policy," *American Journal of Orthopsychiatry*, 47 (1977), pp. 374–375.

4. J. Nixon, et al., "Social Class and Violent Child Death," *Child Abuse and Neglect*, 5 (1981), pp. 111–116.

5. Newberger, "Child Abuse and Neglect: Toward a Firmer Foundation for Practice and Policy."

6. D. Gill, *Violence Against Children* (Cambridge, Mass.: Harvard University Press, 1970); and R. Gelles, *The Violent Home* (Beverly Hills, Calif.: Sage Publications, 1974).

7. R. Elkin and G. Handel, *The Child and Society* (New York: Random House, 1978).

8. G. Sykes and D. Matza, "Techniques of Neutralization: A Theory of Delinquency,"

American Sociological Review, 22 (1957), pp. 664–670.

9. F. N. Silverman, "Radiologic and Special Diagnostic Procedures," pp. 215–240, and J. T. Watson, "The Pathology of Child Abuse and Neglect," in R. Helfer and C. Kempe, eds., *The Battered Child* (Chicago: University of Chicago Press, 1980), pp. 241–271.

Accepted November 26, 1985

Children and Youth Services Review, Vol. 11, pp. 2__–2___, 1989.
Printed in the USA. All rights reserved.

0190-7409/89 $3.00 + .00

Toward A Causal Typology of Child Neglect

Rebecca L. Hegar
University of Maryland at Baltimore

Jeffrey J. Yungman
Covenant House, New Orleans, LA

This article represents part of the authors' ongoing review of research concerning the whole range of child maltreatment, including physical abuse, neglect, and sexual abuse. The typology presented in this article includes the following categories: physical neglect; developmental neglect; and emotional neglect, which is divided into a general type and nonorganic failure-to-thrive. Within this typology, the authors examine the research literature to discover relationships between each type of neglect and etiological factors, including: stressors; cultural patterns or beliefs; lack of skills or supports; problems in family roles or relationships; and personality characteristics of parents and adult caretakers.

This analysis of the etiology of child neglect is part of the authors' ongoing review of research in the whole range of abusive and

An earlier version of this article was presented by the authors at the World Congress of Victimology, Orlando, FL, July 10–12, 1986.
Requests for reprints should be addressed to Rebecca Hegar, School of Social Work, University of Maryland at Baltimore, 525 W. Redwood St., Baltimore, MD 21201.

neglectful behavior. The complete typology explores etiological factors related to the following major categories of child maltreatment: abuse (battering, over-discipline, and torture); neglect (physical, developmental, and emotional); and sexual abuse (sadistic abuse, incest, violent-onset abuse, and other sexual misuse).

Within this typology, the authors review the research literature for primary and contributing factors associated with different types of abuse and neglect. The broad groups of factors considered include: cultural patterns or beliefs; lack of skills or supports; problems in family roles or relationships; personality characteristics of parents and adult caretakers; and stressors.

Overview of Factors Associated with Child Maltreatment

This review and analysis of the literature focuses on factors related to the parents and family unit. The primary reason for building the analysis around parents is that it is consistent with the need to keep responsibility for child maltreatment focused on adults. While it is useful to know that a premature child or one with abnormalities may be at special risk, it is even more important to assess whether the caretakers of a particular child-at-risk are potential perpetrators. In this analysis, the special needs of children are considered as stressors to parents and as demands for particular child-care skills.

In evaluating each factor that may contribute to child neglect, it is a long step from noting that research shows some association to maintaining that a cause-and-effect relationship exists. Keeping in mind the complex etiology of child maltreatment, what follows is presented as a step toward a *causal typology*. It will require much more study, perhaps even new theoretical approaches to causality, before any discussion of etiology in child maltreatment will be complete. Each group of etiological factors included in this exploratory analysis is defined briefly below.

Stress

The first group of factors relates to stress and its sources, which have been studied rather extensively as contributors to or precipitants of child maltreatment. This discussion uses Barth and Blythe's (1983) terminology for three types of stressors. The first is the *phenomenological* stressor that leads to the feeling of loss of control for a particular individual. Such stressors may be symbolic or concrete events, or have elements of both. An example might be an angry spouse who walks out of the house, leaving behind the baby and the other parent who, from earlier family experiences, has a great fear of abandonment. Although stress of this type may be triggered by an event in the environment, the history that makes it stressful is peculiar to the individual.

Life change is another form of stressor that has been studied extensively by Justice and others (Justice & Calvert, 1985; Justice & Duncan, 1976; Justice & Justice, 1976; Straus & Kantor, 1987). These stressors include marital and employment changes, losses of significant people, legal and financial difficulties, and role changes, many of which may be seen by those affected as either positive or negative. Generally, this type of stressor originates in the interaction between an individual and the family or environmental system.

The third type of stressor discussed by Barth and Blythe (1983) includes poverty, difficult living conditions, and environmental insecurity. These *social* stressors result primarily from problems in the community (i.e., high levels of unemployment) and in the wider social environment (i.e., racism, sexism).

As explanations for maltreatment, Barth and Blythe (1983) find shortcomings in each stress model and call for research exploring the conditions under which specific stressors influence individual parents.

Personality

In discussing the second set of etiological factors, based on the personality or psychological make-up of parents, this section draws some terminology from the *Diagnostic and Statistical Manual* (DSM III-R) of the American Psychiatric Association (1987). This brings a standard set of nomenclature to the consideration of parental personality. However, this group of factors includes not only diagnosable pathology, but also personality traits such as authoritarianism.

Lack of Skill

The third group of etiological factors considered here includes gaps in parental knowledge, skill, or experience concerning child care or other matters relating to child rearing. An example of this factor at work is the maltreatment that sometimes occurs when parents do not known enough about the nutritional needs and feeding patterns of infants. Gaps in parents' experiential backgrounds may be related to poor self-esteem and to lack of role models for parenting.

Culture and Belief

Culture and belief, which constitute the fourth set of factors, may be individual, subcultural, or culture-wide. An example is the belief that consistent attentiveness to the needs and wants of young children spoils them, while allowing them to cry unattended builds self-sufficiency.

Role and Relationship Problems

Finally, the fifth set of factors is grouped under the label of role and relationship problems. These include difficulties such as parent/child role reversal, scapegoating of one child, marital discord, and absent parents.

The sections that follow present a beginning causal typology that draws from the research to link specific etiological factors from these five categories to various types of child neglect.

Etiological Factors in Child Neglect

In general, neglect involves inattention to a child's needs by parents or caretakers in any of the following areas: health, education, stimulation, physical care, discipline, nutrition, safety, and emotional nurture (Cantwell, 1980). This typology groups these areas into three major categories of child neglect: physical, developmental, and emotional. The last includes both general emotional neglect and nonorganic failure-to-thrive. These categories of the typology are represented in Table 1, along with a summary of the etiological factors associated with each one. It should be noted that in any given family, more than one type of neglect may occur over time or at the same time, just as abuse or sexual abuse also may be present in neglecting families. Maltreatment also has degrees of severity that are not reflected in this beginning typology.

Physical Neglect

Physical neglect of children involves deprivation of basic necessities, including food, clothing, shelter, and hygiene. Although most data compiled from reported incidents of child neglect do not specify the type of neglect, this category is the most common. The American Humane Association (1987) reports that 56% of 1985 child protection reports involved deprivation of necessities.

In the past two decades, many studies have found stress,

TABLE 1
Etiological Factors in Child Neglect

	Physical	Developmental	Emotional	
			General	Failure-to-thrive
Stress	Social	Social Life-change	Social	Social Life-change
Person-ality	Alcohol abuse Depression Anxiety Immaturity	Depression Antisocial personality	Depression Alcohol abuse	Depression Antisocial personality Neurosis Psychosis
Lack of skill, etc.	Lack of child care skill/ knowledge Lack of motivation Isolation	Insufficient knowledge of child development	Lack of role models for nurturing/ showing affection	Lack of skill in parenting Social isolation
Culture belief	Expectations of children	Religious or ethnic patterns Expectations of children	Sex roles that limit emotional expression by males Beliefs about spoiling	Sex roles that limit emotional expression by males Beliefs about spoiling
Relation-ship or role prob-lem	Marital discord Parental absence Parent/child role-reversal	Failure to assume parental role	Poor parent/ child relationship Marital discord Parental absence	Lack of parent/ infant bonding Disengagement Marital discord

particularly from social stressors often associated with poverty, to be related to child neglect (Giovannoni, 1971; Martin & Walters, 1982; Russell & Trainor, 1984). Based on neglect referrals to child protective agencies, American Humane Association studies report that insufficient income and inadequate housing are associated more commonly with child neglect than with any other type of child maltreatment (American Humane Association, 1978; Russell & Trainor, 1984). Martin and Walters (1982), also comparing different types of child maltreatment, found neglecting families to have the most difficulty with finances, income, and family size. Zuravin (1988), who investigated three measures of sociodemographic stress as mediating factors for teenage mothers at risk for child maltreatment, found the most important mediator, number of live births, to have a stronger relationship to neglect than to abuse.

Unlike some types of child abuse, physical neglect has not been shown to have a clear relationship to high levels of life-change stress. Egeland, Breitenbucher, and Rosenberg (1980) compared maltreating (primarily neglecting) mothers with other mothers whose life-change scores were similarly high. Their findings suggest that personality variables may be more influential than stress. Another group of researchers studied the effects of high job loss in two communities on the rate of referral for abuse and neglect. While abuse reports increased following loss of jobs, the effect on reports of neglect was less clear, findings the authors attribute to the more chronic nature of neglect (Steinberg, Catalano, & Dooley, 1981).

In addition to factors related to stress, several parental personality factors have been found to be associated with neglect. Meier (1985) identifies a relationship between child neglect and alcoholism, and other authors report similar findings for use of both alcohol and other substances (Famularo, Stone, Barnum, & Wharton, 1986; Herrenkohl, Herrenkohl, & Egolf, 1983). Black and Mayer's (1980) Boston study of alcoholics and opiate addicts assessed children as being neglected in 30.5% of the families. However, research conducted by Kameen and Thompson (1983) found no significant differences in the types of child abuse and neglect found in families of substance abusers.

Other personality variables identified in the literature as related to neglectful behavior include anxiety (Egeland et al., 1980; Meier, 1985), depression (Famularo et al., 1986; Kinard, 1982; Zuravin, in press), intellectual inadequacy (Martin & Walters, 1982), and gross immaturity (Polansky, Ammons, & Gaudin, 1985). Most studies of personality factors have focused on the mother, with comparatively little attention to the fathers of neglected children. The study of alcoholism and depression by Famularo and others (1986) is an exception that reports data for both parents.

The general exclusion of fathers also applies to studies of parental skill and knowledge in child rearing. Together with social stress, gaps in parental experience are among the most frequently identified factors in the etiology of physical neglect, contributing to lack of child rearing skills, limited knowledge of growth and development, inability to anticipate the difficulties of parenthood, social isolation, and problems with making behavioral changes.

A New York study of 32 mothers in a program for abusing and neglecting parents found them to be isolated, with smaller peer networks than the control group (Salzinger, Kaplan, & Artemyeff,

1983). The authors concluded that neglectful behavior was reinforced by the mothers' limited contact with "normal" models for child rearing. Polansky et al. (1985) and Garbarino and Sherman (1980) also found social isolation to be a factor in child neglect.

Together with the lack of a social network, "neglectful parenting can be attributed to lack of knowledge, lack of judgement, and lack of motivation," according to Cantwell (1980, p. 184). In Pennsylvania, Herrenkohl and others (1983) examined 799 occurrences of neglect and found a high incidence of poor parenting skills and insufficient knowledge of children's needs.

The expectations of parents for their children's behavior and development have also been the focus of substantial research. Azar and others (1984) conclude that neglecting mothers, when compared with controls, showed significantly more unrealistic expectations of their children, a conclusion supported by Steele (1987). However, findings about differences in expectations have been questioned by Kravitz and Driscoll (1983), whose research does not confirm the conclusions of other authors.

Parental difficulties with interpersonal relationships and family roles are mentioned frequently in the literature concerning physical neglect of children. Isolation from others, which has already been discussed in the context of lack of social supports and role models, is regarded by some authors as the result of problems forming interpersonal relationships (Polansky et al., 1985).

Other evidence of relationship and role problems in neglecting families is found in the high incidence of marital discord and inability to assume parental responsibilities, reported by Giovannoni (1971) and Herrenkohl and others (1983). Although the latter researchers did not find parental desertion or the presence of a single parent to be more highly associated with neglect than with other forms of child maltreatment, many authors do see it as contributing to the neglect of children. Biller and Solomon (1986) offer an extensive review of research into the relationship between child maltreatment and paternal absence or lack of involvement with family. They make an impressive case for the role of parental absence in child neglect.

Finally, some of the role and relationship problems in neglecting families concern parents' relationships with the victim child or children. Larrance and Twentyman (1983) report that neglecting mothers, while not as negative about their children as abusers, expected more negative behavior than controls. Steele (1987) describes the phenomenon of role-reversal, where the child is expected to meet the parent's physical or emotional needs, and Cantwell (1980) notes that role-reversal in neglecting families can involve children as young as one or two years of age. However, empirical evidence of the reversal dynamic is lacking.

Developmental Neglect

Developmental neglect deprives children of experiences necessary for growth and development, including supervision and services or care to promote education, health, and mental health. This is among the most culture-bound categories of abuse and neglect, because definitions of what is necessary for healthy development vary widely with group norms. For example, there is little consensus concerning when children can leave school without suffering educational neglect or when they are old enough to be left alone at home.

Incidence of developmental neglect is difficult to determine, again because reporting statistics are rarely broken down by specific type of neglect. Also, physical and developmental neglect often occur in the same families. For example, in an extensive study of 328 maltreating families, Herrenkohl and others (1983) found problems with use of medical facilities were a significant component of the neglect cases, but not of those experiencing physical or emotional abuse.

What research is available suggests some similarities in the etiologies of physical and developmental neglect. Social stressors probably play a comparable role in both types of neglect. The "poverty-induced, low-living situation" found by Martin and Walters (1982) to be related to neglect in general would certainly inhibit parents' abilities to meet consistently their children's developmental needs. For example, children's education may be interrupted by parents' needs for their services as baby sitters, interpreters, or wage earners.

Personality factors may interact with social stress to create problems of developmental neglect. The *Diagnostic and Statistical Manual* (DSM III-R) of the American Psychiatric Association lists among the diagnostic criteria for Antisocial Personality Disorder that the individual:

Lacks ability to function as a responsible parent, as indicated by one or more of the following: (a) malnutrition of a child, (b) child's illness resulting from lack of minimal hygiene, (c) failure to obtain medical care for a seriously ill child, (d) child's dependence on neighbors or nonresident relatives for food or shelter, (e) failure to arrange for a caretaker for a young child when parent is away from home...(APA, 1987, p. 345)

Several of these criteria specify types of developmental neglect, which can also be exacerbated by depression. Kinard (1982) cites "considerable evidence that depressed mothers show significant impairments in their parenting abilities and that these impairments are often manifested in neglect, rejection, or hostility toward their children" (p. 404). Because depressed adults frequently neglect their own health, work, or education, it is probable that depression is also related to some cases of developmental neglect of children.

Parents' lack of knowledge about child development or health is also mentioned in the literature as contributing to this type of neglect (Cantwell, 1980; Herrenkohl et al., 1983). Twentyman and Plotkin (1982) write that

data clearly support the view that informational deficits exist. Moreover, a model that stresses educational deficits is intuitively appealing given that parents who have been reported for abusing and neglecting their children are often young and have not been provided with adequate professional counseling during pregnancy and their children's early development. (p. 501)

More than in some other types of neglect, it appears that lack of child care knowledge or skill may be sufficient to bring about developmental neglect. This is because not having a critical piece of information (i.e., babies with diarrhea may develop life-threatening dehydration) can lead otherwise well-functioning people to neglect a child's needs.

This is also a problem in which the culture or belief patterns of the family may play a critical role. Religion and folk healing practices are particularly influential in leading parents to try to meet children's health or educational needs outside of generally accepted channels. Although this is not necessarily neglectful, in extreme cases it can threaten a child's health or welfare, as when a court must intervene to authorize life-saving treatment for the child of parents whose religion forbids blood transfusions. In addition to legal cases, there has been some attention in the literature, but little research, concerning parental belief systems and child welfare (Beavers, 1986; Garbarino & Ebata, 1983).

Other children are developmentally neglected because their parents fail to assume parental responsibilities due to absence, apathy, lack of motivation, or outright rejection of the parental role. Herrenkohl et al. (1983) found these role or relationship problems to be related to "inadequate or inappropriate provision of medical care... and inadequate child supervision" (p. 430).

Unlike physical neglect, which the research suggests is due most often to multiple causes, it appears than developmental neglect can be brought about by a single parental attitude, belief, or behavior.

Emotional Neglect

This typology groups two phenomena under the category of emotional neglect. The first is a general type of emotional neglect that may affect children of any age, and the second is the discrete syndrome of nonorganic failure-to-thrive, primarily a condition of very young children. Each subcategory is defined and discussed in the balance of this article.

General Emotional Neglect. As used here, this term refers to parental failure to meet children's needs for attention, security, self-esteem, and emotional nurture. Of all types of child abuse and neglect, Cantwell (1980) characterizes this as the most difficult to define and the most likely to arouse controversy. Indeed, some advocates of legal reform in child protection would prefer that statutes omit references to emotional neglect on the basis that it is both difficult to prove and uncertain in its effect on children (Goldstein, Freud, & Solnit, 1979; Wald, 1976). Others would include only situations where demonstrable harm to the child can be established (Besharov, 1988).

Despite this controversy, general emotional neglect is included here as one of the types of maltreatment to which children are subjected. However, definitional and measurement problems have hindered researchers' efforts to study the phenomenon. American Humane Association (1987) classifies 8.9% of referrals in 1985 as involving "emotional maltreatment," although that category overlaps only partially with the neglect discussed here.

There is little controversy about the definition or seriousness of an extreme manifestation of this type of neglect, the abandonment of a child. Abandonment is not usually thought of as a type of emotional neglect, and it typically is named separately in child protection statutes. However, there is no doubt that it represents the ultimate parental withdrawal from nurturing and meeting the child's needs for emotional security. Physical neglect is not equally present in abandonment, because children frequently are left in settings where their needs for physical care are met, for example with a neighbor, in a hospital, or where they will be found promptly. This type of abandonment is different from leaving a baby in a trash dumpster and other attempts at infanticide.

Martin and Walters (1982) are among the few researchers to consider how the etiology of abandonment differs from other forms of maltreatment. On the basis of their study of 489 Tennessee and Georgia cases, including 65 involving abandonment, they suggest that parent characteristics rather than child or environmental factors were the best predictors of abandonment when these cases were compared with other types of child abuse and neglect. Mothers who evidenced sexual promiscuity and/or alcoholism, temporary financial problems, and relative health, were the most likely to abandon their biological children. (p. 269)

They go on to suggest that this avoidance of parental responsibility is similar to that described in the literature about child neglect. Elsewhere they note that abandoned children were somewhat more likely than other neglected children to have mothers who were single but living with a man (p. 273).

The characteristics of abandoning mothers identified by Martin and Walters (1982) appear in this typology as personality characteristics of the parent, social stressors, and role and relationship problems. Several authors support the conclusion that other manifestations of emotional neglect are also influenced by parental personality. Kinard's (1982) study of depression as an antecedent of maltreatment identifies rejection of the child as one result. Although Zuravin's comprehensive review of the literature concerning maternal depression and child maltreatment notes that research findings have been contradictory or inconclusive, her own findings show that the risk of neglect, but not abuse, increases with severity of the maternal depression (Zuravin, in press).

Emotional nurture of children may also be affected by the parents' lack of knowledge or skill in meeting their needs. Parents who lack aptitude for meeting their children's emotional needs have been described in the literature as emotionally deprived, lacking role models for parenting, and nondemonstrative (Cantwell, 1980; Meier, 1985, Polansky, Gaudin, Ammons, & Davis, 1985).

Behaviors that indicate lack of knowledge about the emotional needs of children may also have cultural or belief components. For example, attitudes about appropriate sex roles influence parenting when adults believe that boys should not be shown physical affection or allowed to express feelings, or when they reject the father's role in providing emotional nurture for children. Although these beliefs are not inherently neglectful, they may become part of a pattern of neglect when other predisposing factors are also present.

Problems with family roles and relationships are among the predisposing factors identified by Cantwell (1980) and by Herrenkohl and others (1983). The later authors found conflict between parents, especially about child-rearing issues, in emotionally neglecting families, while the former discusses the role of negative messages about the child, lack of attention, and other indications of a disturbed parent/child relationship.

The sparse research into what is called general emotional neglect here makes it difficult to draw conclusions about its etiology. However, there is substantial research into the characteristics of families where infants fail to thrive, and the differences between these two types of emotional neglect may be matters of degree and age of the children affected. Therefore, the following final section also may provide some insight into families where children are emotionally neglected, but not so severely or at such a young age that they show retardation in growth and development as a result.

Failure-to-Thrive. Failure-to-thrive (FTT), characterized by Kempe, Culter and Dean (1980) as "a marked retardation or cessation of growth" during the first three years of life (p.164), is usually defined as weight gain below the third percentile on a growth curve of expected development. It can have many contributing causes. Organic FTT is due to physiological problems of the infant, while nonorganic FTT results from environmental factors relating to feeding and nurture. Kempe et al. (1980) note the central importance of nurture and care:

Surprisingly, until recently, neglect was often considered last, although it is now apparent that it is probably the most common cause of FTT. Indeed, the term *FTT syndrome* is often used to describe the growth failure due to "psychosocial deprivation," or maternal deprivation. (p. 166).

It is in this sense of lack of involved, personal care that nonorganic failure-to-thrive is considered here as a manifestation of emotional child neglect. Including FTT is consistent with the conclusions of Garbarino, Guttman, and Seeley (1986) in their major exploration of psychological maltreatment.

Recently, Kempe and Goldbloom (1987) advocate that the term nonorganic failure-to-thrive be replaced by "malnutrition due to neglect." Other authors question whether FTT implies neglect at all (Ayoub & Miller, 1985). This concern with the classification of failure-to-thrive is not new; over twenty years ago Bullard and others (1967) contributed a particularly insightful discussion of the concepts of neglect and FTT to the literature. Despite the debate over terminology and classification, failure-to-thrive due to emotional deprivation is included in this typology because it is the best-known term for what Steele (1987) calls "the most clearcut clinical syndrome" within the larger problem of child neglect (p. 95).

Many of the etiological factors associated with FTT are stressors to parents, particularly the social stressors of poverty. For example, Blehar and Kent (1979) note that of 32 families with hospitalized FTT children in a California study, all had low incomes and few had telephones. Several types of life-change stress are also identified with failure-to-thrive, particularly losses and family separations health problems, unplanned pregnancy, and complications during pregnancy and birth (Gagan, Cupoli, & Watkins, 1984; Jacobs & Kent, 1977; Kempe & Goldbloom, 1987; Steele, 1987). Two studies also identify a problem with the law as another life-change stressor associated with some FTT cases (Bullard et al., 1967; Jacobs & Kent, 1977).

Stress of various types appears to be the unifying concept in the cases that Kent and his team label as families showing a "sociology of neglect," one of three groups in their typology of FTT cases (Blehar & Kent, 1979; Jacobs & Kent, 1977). While that group of families is described as having chronic problems, Kempe and colleagues (1980, 1987), who also divide the families of FTT infants into tentative categories, report that the syndrome can also be precipitated by a single serious life-change stressor, such as death or divorce.

Personality characteristics of parents that contribute to a child's failure-to-thrive also have been identified in several studies. Depression of one or both parents is identified by Alderette and deGraffenried (1986), Kempe et al. (1980), and Leonard, Rhymers, and Solnit (1966). Leonard and colleagues also implicate alcoholism in many failure-to-thrive cases, as do a number of other researchers (Bullard et al., 1967; Kempe, et al. 1980; Jacobs & Kent, 1977). In addition to depression and possible substance abuse, Kempe and colleagues (1980, 1987) note antisocial and aggressive behavior in a subgroup of families, and Kent's research team (Jacobs & Kent, 1977) describes certain neurotic or psychotic parents as showing a "psychology of neglect." Although subject to some stressors, this group did not have the same high exposure to social stress as the group of families discussed above (Blehar & Kent, 1979).

Most studies conclude that parents of FTT infants have serious problems with stress, personality, or both. Some families may lack knowledge or skill in child care, either as the central problem or in combination with other serious difficulties. Kent's team describes a lack of "mothercraft" skill in feeding and caring physically for infants, sometimes related to mental retardation of the parent (Jacobs & Kent, 1977). Kempe and Goldbloom (1987) also identify a lack of child care skills in the most disturbed parent/child relationships:

Some mothers were more hostile and tended to see their babies as demanding or "bad." They denied any feeding problems or need for medical help. Their approach to their babies lacked empathy, and they seemed very unskilled in relating to their babies both physically and socially. Their care occasionally become aggressive or even abusive. (p. 324)

Although some families with FTT infants have difficulties in one or more of the three areas of stress, personality, and skill, a fourth area of this typology highlights a basic commonality of most cases. Role and relationship problems between parents, their families and support systems, and their children appear to be more basic to the problem of nonorganic failure-to-thrive than are the other types of problems presented here. Originally, most of the emphasis on relationship focused on the mother and infant, and much of the understanding of this syndrome derives from the concept of "maternal deprivation." Although that term first was used in cases of children who literally lacked a mother figure, it came to be applied to cases where the mother, although present, was unresponsive to the child. Iwaniec and Herbert (1982) describe this phenomenon as follows: "the child can be thought of as physically with the mother, but emotionally, it is as if he does not belong to her" (p. 10). Other authors note "a lack of warmth, nurturance and caring expressed toward the child" (Ayoub & Milner, 1985, p. 497).

Several authors have taken issue with the notion that lack of a mother's care is exclusively responsible for a child's failure to thrive, and Gagan and others (1984) suggest the broader concept of "parental deprivation." Support for this reframing of the problem can be found in the research identifying physically absent or emotionally unsupportive fathers in many families where children fail to thrive (Blehar & Kent, 1979; Jacobs & Kent, 1977; Gagan et al., 1984; Kempe & Goldbloom, 1987). This perspective illustrates how culture and belief, in this case about sex roles, can contribute to family relationship difficulties and to child neglect. If family members do not see it as appropriate for a father to feed or cuddle the baby, then the child may suffer from parental deprivation if, for some reason, the mother also is unable to meet the child's needs.

Alderette and deGraffenried (1986) go beyond the concept of a disordered parent/child relationship by identifying a pattern of family disengagement in FTT cases. Drawing from the work of Minuchin (1974), they explain:

Disengagement is characterized by difficulty in communication among family members .... The disengaged family tends to have rules that allow only minimal interaction between its members, thereby negating interdependence and endorcing the separateness of members. Thus, the family, as a system, does not develop loyalty, unity, or a strong sense of family identity and belonging. (1986, p. 207–208)

146

Disengagement appears to involve lack of bonding on a grand scale, not just between mother and child, but between each family member and every other.

Sometimes family problems are extreme, reaching the level of outright rejection of or hostility toward the FTT child. Kempe and others (1980) refer to extreme rejection by a subgroup of families "in whom the baby is not seen just as another burden, but as a bad or defective child, often one who deliberately behaves so as to cause the mother problems" (p. 174). These families resemble to those whose children are battered, and several authors identify a substantial risk of serious physical abuse of FTT children (Kempe et al., 1980; Koel, 1969).

In summary, parents of children who fail to thrive due to emotional neglect may show different constellations of problems involving stress, personality, and lack of skill. However, relationship problems between parents, infant, and other key members appear to be core etiological characteristics of families where a child suffers nonorganic failure-to-thrive.

Implications

Ultimately, the importance of understanding etiology in child maltreatment is tied to the application of that knowledge. When those empowered to intervene lack tools for distinguishing between types of maltreatment, problems with different causes and dynamics are treated as similar by police, medical personnel, child protection staff, and the courts.

Intervention to prevent child abuse and neglect or to help when maltreatment has occurred needs to be based on sound differential assessment of the problem at hand. Understanding the differences among the many forms of maltreatment sometimes makes it unnecessary to expend scarce resources on exhaustive assessment workups or on the most extreme steps to protect children. In the assessment phase, few neglecting parents require psychiatric evaluations, and few abused children need routine longbone x-ray series, although those diagnostic measures are absolutely essential when particular types of neglect or abuse are suspected. In the intervention phase, parenting education is a potential benefit to only a subgroup of families, and arrest and prosecution have potential to change the behavior of some but not others.

This article, part of the authors' ongoing work to explore the etiology of child maltreatment, provides an overview of research into a broad range of neglectful phenomena. The article presents a beginning framework to assist those who deal with child maltreatment to meet the challenge of differential assessment and intervention.

References

Alderette, P., & deGraffenried, D.F. (1986). Nonorganic failure-to-thrive syndrome and the family system. *Social Work, 31,* 207–211.

American Humane Association. (1978). *National Analysis of Official Child Neglect and Abuse Reporting.* Englewood, CO: Author.

American Humane Association. (1987) *Highlights of Official Child Neglect and Abuse Reporting, 1985.* Denver, CO: Author.

American Psychiatric Association. (1987). *Diagnostic and Statistical Manual of Mental Disorders.* 3rd ed, revised. Washington: Author.

Ayoub, C.C., & Miller, J.S. (1985). Failure to thrive: Parental indicators, types, and outcomes. *Child Abuse and Neglect, 9,* 491–499.

Azar, S.T., Robinson, D.R., Hekimian, E., & Twentyman, C.T. (1984). Unrealistic expectations and problem-solving ability in maltreating and comparison mothers. *Journal of Consulting and Clinical Psychology, 52,* 687–690.

Barth, R.P., & Blythe, B.J. The contribution of stress to child abuse. (1983). *Social Service Review, 57,* 477–489.

Beavers, C. (1986). A cross-cultural look at child abuse. *Public Welfare, 44* (4), 18–22.

Besharov, D.J. (1988). *Child abuse and neglect reporting and investigation: Policy guidelines for decision making.* Washington: American Bar Association.

Biller, H.B., & Solomon, R.S. (1986). *Child maltreatment and paternal deprivation: A manifesto for research, prevention, and treatment.* Lexington, MA: Lexington.

Black, R., & Mayer, J. (1980). Parents with special problems: Alcoholism and opiate addiction. *Child Abuse and Neglect, 4,* 45–54.

Blehar, M.C., & Kent, J. (1979). Helping abused children and their parents. In E. Corfman (Ed.), *Families today — A research sampler on families and children,* NIMH Science Monograph 1. Washington: U.S. Government Printing Office.

Bullard, D.M., Glaser, H.H., Heagarty, M.C., & Pivchik, E.C. (1967). Failure to thrive in the 'neglected' child. *American Journal of Orthopsychiatry, 37,* 680–690.

Cantwell, H.B. (1980). Child neglect. In H.C. Kempe & R.E. Helfer (Eds.), *The battered child,* 3rd edition (pp. 183–197). Chicago: University of Chicago Press.

Egeland, B., Breitenbucher, M., & Rosenberg, D. (1980). Prospective study of the significance of life stress in the etiology of child abuse. *Journal of Consulting and Clinical Psychology, 48,* 195–205.

Famularo, R., Stone, K., Barnum, R., & Wharton, R. (1986). Alcoholism and severe child maltreatment. *American Journal of Orthopsychiatry, 56,* 481–485.

Gagan, R.J., Cupoli, J.M., & Watkins, A.H. (1984). The families of children who fail to thrive: Preliminary investigations of parental deprivation among organic and nonorganic cases. *Child Abuse and Neglect, 8,* 93–103.

Garbarino, J., & Ebata, A. (1983). The significance of ethnic and cultural differences in child maltreatment. *Journal of Marriage and the Family, 45,* 773–783.

Garbarino, J., & Sherman, D. (1980). High-risk neighborhoods and high-risk families: The human ecology of child maltreatment. *Child Development, 51,* 188–198.

Garbarino, J., Guttmann, E., & Seeley, J.W. (1986). *The psychologically battered child.* San Francisco: Jossey–Bass.

Giovannoni, J.M. (1971). Parental mistreatment: Perpetrators and victims. *Journal of Marriage and the Family, 33,* 649–657.

Goldstein J., Freud, A., & Solnit, A. (1979). *Before the best interests of the child.* New York: Free Press.

Herrenkohl, R.C., Herrenkohl, E.C., & Egolf, B.P. (1983). Circumstances surrounding the occurrence of child maltreatment. *Journal of Consulting and Clinical Psychology, 51,* 424–431.

Iwaniec, D., & Herbert, M. (1982). The assessment and treatment of children who fail to thrive. *Social Work Today, 13,* 8–12.

Jacobs, R.A., & Kent, J.T. (1977). Psychosocial profiles of families of failure-to-thrive infants — Preliminary report. *Child Abuse and Neglect, 1,* 469–473.

Justice, B., & Calvert, A. (1985). Factors mediating child abuse as a response to stress. *Child Abuse and Neglect, 9,* 359–363.

Justice, B., & Duncan, D.F. (1976). Life crisis as a precursor to child abuse. *Public Health Reports, 91,* 110–115.

Justice, B., & Justice, R. (1976). *The abusing family.* New York: Human Sciences Press.

Kameen, M., & Thompson, D.L. (1983). Substance abuse and child abuse–neglect: Implications for direct-service providers. *Personnel and Guidance Journal, 61,* 269–273.

Kempe, R.S., & Goldbloom, R.B. (1987). Malnutrition and growth retardation ("failure to thrive") in the context of child abuse and neglect. In R.E. Helfer & R.S. Kempe (Eds.), *The battered child, 4th ed.* (pp. 312–335). Chicago: University of Chicago Press.

Kempe, R.S., Cutler, C., & Dean, J. (1980). The infant with failure-to-thrive. In C.H. Kempe & R.E. Helfer (Eds.), *The battered child,* 3rd. ed. (pp. 163–182). Chicago: University of Chicago Press.

Kinard, E.M. (1982). Child abuse and depression: Cause or consequence? *Child Welfare, 7,* 403–413.

Koel, B. (1969). Failure to thrive and fatal injury as a continuum. *American Journal of Diseases of Children, 118,* 565–567.

Kravitz, R.I., & Driscoll, J.M. (1983). Expectations for childhood development among child-abusing and nonabusing parents. *American Journal of Orthopsychiatry, 53,* 345–352.

Larrance, D.T., & Twentyman, C.T. (1983). Maternal attributions and child abuse. *Journal of Abnormal Psychology, 92,* 449–457.

Leonard, M.F., Rhymers, J.P., & Solnit, A.J. (1966). Failure to thrive in infants: A family problem. *American Journal of Diseases of Children, 111,* 600–612.

Martin, M.J., & Walters, J. (1982). Familial correlates of selected types of child abuse and neglect. *Journal of Marriage and the Family, 44,* 267–276.

Meier, J.H. (1985). *Assault against children: Why it happens how to stop it.* San Diego, CA: College-Hill Press.

Minuchin, S. (1974). *Families and family therapy.* Cambridge, MA: Harvard.

Polansky, N.A., Ammons, P.W., & Gaudin, J.M. (1985). Loneliness and isolation in child neglect. *Social Casework, 66,* 38–47.

Polansky, N.A., Gaudin, J.M., Ammons, P.W., & Davis, K.B. (1985). The psychological ecology of the neglectful mother. *Child Abuse and Neglect, 9,* 265–275.

Russell, A.B., & Trainor, C.M. (1984). *Trends in child abuse reporting.* Denver, CO: American Humane Association.

Salzinger, S., Kaplan, S., & Artemyeff, C. (1983). Mothers' personal social networks and child maltreatment. *Journal of Abnormal Psychology, 92,* 68–76.

Steele, B. (1987). Psychodynamic factors in child abuse. In R.E. Helfer & R.S. Kempe (Eds.), *The battered child,* 4th ed. (pp. 81–114). Chicago: University of Chicago Press.

Steinberg, L.D., Catalano, R., & Dooley, D. (1981). Economic antecedents of child abuse and neglect. *Child Development, 52,* 975–985.

Straus, M.A., & Kantor, G.K. (1987). Stress and child abuse. In R.E. Helfer & R.S. Kempe (Eds.), *The battered child,* 4th ed. (pp. 42–59). Chicago: University of Chicago Press.

Twentyman, C.T., & Plotkin, R.C. (1982). Unrealistic expectations of parents who maltreat their children: An educational deficit that pertains to child development. *Journal of Clinical Psychology, 38,* 497–503.

Wald, M.S. (1976). State intervention on behalf of 'neglected children': Standards for removal of children from their homes, monitoring the status of children in foster care, and termination of parental rights. *Stanford Law Review, 28,* 623–703.

Zuravin, S.J. (1988). Child maltreatment and teenage first births: A relationship mediated by chronic sociodemographic stress? *American Journal of Orthopsychiatry, 58,* 91–103.

Zuravin, S.J. (in press). Maternal depression and child maltreatment. In A. Cowan (Ed.), *Current research in child neglect.* Washington: U.S. Government Printing Office.

RISK FOR PHYSICAL CHILD
ABUSE AND THE PERSONAL
CONSEQUENCES FOR ITS VICTIMS

SUZANNE SALZINGER
RICHARD S. FELDMAN
MURIEL HAMMER
New York State Psychiatric Institute
Columbia University

MARGARET ROSARIO
New York State Psychiatric Institute

This article summarizes the recent literature on the effects of physical abuse on children in the domains of neurological impairment, intellectual functioning, socioemotional functioning, social behavior, and social cognition. New empirical data are presented on dysfunctional peer relationships in school-age children. The findings are interpreted within a theoretical framework composed of three elements: the conceptualization of abusive parenting as on a continuum with the parenting process in general, the effect of abuse-attributable changes in children's behavior on their future behavior, and the continuing interaction between children's dysfunctional behavior and their social environment. In addition, a multivariate family risk model for child abuse is offered and tested using a path analysis.

What puts children at risk for being abused? What kind of households and family situations do they live in? In some recent work on a nonreferred confirmed sample of physically abused school-age children ($n = 106$) and nonmaltreated classmate control children ($n =$

AUTHOR'S NOTE: *This research has been partly supported by Research Grant #R01MH38814 and Clinical Research Center MH30906 from the National Institutes of Mental Health. Grateful acknowledgement is made to Luz Alvarado, Louis Caraballo, and Albert Ortega for the excellent work they contributed to the research. Requests for reprints should be sent to the Suzanne Salzinger at Box 114, New York State Psychiatric Institute, 722 W. 168 St., New York, NY 10032.*

CRIMINAL JUSTICE AND BEHAVIOR, Vol. 18 No. 1, March 1991 64-81

85) in New York City, we examined some familial risk factors for physical abuse to determine how they combined to put a child at risk for being abused (Salzinger, Rosario, Feldman, & Hammer, in press).

Using the children's mothers as informants and supplementing the abuse mothers' information with Protective Services records, we examined a set of family factors that, based on our current reading of the literature, we believed would function to increase the probability that physical child abuse would occur in a child's household. These factors include behavior in the child's mother's household during the years that she lived with her own parents as well as behavior in the child's household. Comparisons of the proportions of abusive and nonabusive families showing these characteristics reveal that partner abuse in the child's household was found in a significantly higher proportion of abusive families ($\chi^2 = 7.857$, $df = 1$, $p = .005$); dysfunctional family life in the child's household, where the adults engage in substance abuse and severe discord, was found in a marginally larger number of abusive families ($\chi^2 = 3.834$, $df = 1$, $.05 < p < .06$); substance abuse by the mother's parents and severe beating of the mother when she was a child do *not* differentiate between the families in any simple manner (although there is a strong presumption among many practitioners that parents who have themselves been abused tend to have abused children). A breakdown of the types of family dysfunction in the child's household shows only discord to differentiate singly between the groups ($\chi^2 = 5.085$, $df = 1$, $p = .025$). Drugs and alcohol may be taken as exacerbating factors, as other investigators have found (Famularo, Stone, Barnum, & Wharton, 1986).

These simple comparisons of the risk factors taken one at a time, however, do not do justice to the complexity of the process that results in physical child abuse. If we consider all the risk factors together, we derive a clearer picture of how abusive behavior in one generation gets transmitted to the next, and we see how some variables act in concert with others to produce a higher probability of abuse than would be the case for each of the variables alone. Figure 1 illustrates the interrelationships in the form of a path model. It can be seen that there are two significantly likely paths to child abuse. Note that both involve behaviors in the mother's family of origin (substance abuse by the mother's parents and severe beating of the mother), although as can be seen in

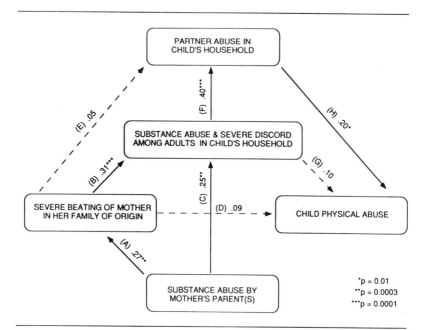

Figure 1: Path model describing the relationship between family violence and child physical abuse.

Figure 1, these behaviors do not necessarily and singly predict child abuse. One of the paths — A, B, F, H — begins with substance abuse in the mother's family, either accompanied by or followed by severe beating by her parents. This is followed by substance abuse and discord among the adults in her child's household, leading to partner abuse in her child's household, and finally culminating in physical abuse of her child. The other path — C, F, H — also begins with substance abuse in the mother's family, followed by substance abuse and discord in her child's household, leading to partner abuse and finally to child abuse.

To summarize these findings, it can be appreciated that all these contextual family variables are implicated in raising the risk for physical abuse of children even though, singly, none of them except for partner abuse is directly and significantly related to child abuse.

A number of junctures in this cycle can be seen to be pivotal in the sense that if specific interventions were initiated at these points, the probability of child abuse would be lessened. The first is, of course, partner abuse. Households where physical violence occurs among the adults are risky for children — not only in the sense that the children witness the violence, which has its own detrimental effects on them (Rosenberg, 1987), but because the children are likely to be targeted as well. Discordant households, particularly those with the exacerbating behaviors of alcohol and drug abuse, are likely also to show partner abuse and subsequently child abuse. Such families need to be identified before that happens and helped to resolve their disputes in less violent ways and to reduce their dependence on alcohol and drugs. Therefore, even in suspected cases of abuse where it appears that substance abuse and violence were present in the mother's family during her own childhood, therapeutic family intervention with the members of her current household is strongly indicated. Our data clearly show that in these cases the child's family is likely also to be severely discordant, with possible violence occurring among the adult members of the family as well. For such families, a range of specific family therapeutic interventions needs to be made available, including not only parent training, although that is clearly needed in confirmed cases of abuse, but training in problem solving, conflict resolution, anger control, and other relevant techniques available for dealing with family discord. The preventive services component of our child protective systems should be augmented by expanded mental health services targeted at families and family functioning, rather than just at individuals, if we want to prevent abuse against children.

Intervention aimed at preventing or stopping child abuse is, however, not enough, because abuse and the witnessing of family violence may both have immediate and long-term detrimental effects on children that need to be remedied as well.

The rest of this article summarizes the effects of physical abuse on children, drawing on both those studies from the literature, mostly recent, that use appropriate control procedures and standardized data collection techniques and some additional recent work of our own on abused school-age children. Although most of the studies report on the effects of violence directed at the child, it is clear that in many, if not most, cases the abuse itself is only part of a pattern of family violence and discord, and the effects on the children are often the effects of these combined factors. Witnessing violence itself has been found to independently cause adverse effects such as difficulty in social problem solving for children (Rosenberg, 1987), and the combined effect of both abuse and associated family discord is found to produce even poorer adjustment in children than either alone (Hershorn & Rosenbaum, 1985; Hughes, Parkinson, & Vargo, 1989). Many studies do not explicitly state that witnessing violence is part of the pattern of abusive behavior the child is exposed to, but judging from our own data, it seem likely that often the effects on children are due to both types of violence.

Physical abuse of children by caretakers has an immediate negative impact on children. In order to understand its full or enduring impact, it is necessary to set forth a conceptual framework in which its effects can be better examined and understood. In recent years we have seen a more sophisticated view of child abuse evolving, and although there are many differences among investigators in the field, there seems to be agreement on the importance of three elements of such a framework. All three elements are critical in evaluating both the immediate and the enduring effects of abuse on children.

The first is the consideration of physical child abuse not as a separate pathological entity, as earlier work tended to portray it, but as an extension of the range of parenting behavior. This view of abuse, based on a continuum model of parenting (Burgess, 1979), has led us to quantify abusive parental behavior along dimensions that have a long history in the research literature on parenting and parent-child relationships. Wolfe, for example, conceptualizes abusive parenting as "the degree to which a parent uses negative, inappropriate control strategies with his or her child" (Wolfe, 1987, p. 25). In much the same way that Sameroff and Chandler (1975) first put forth the notion that biological risk could only be adequately assessed by considering its intricate association with the "continuum of caretaking casualty," so must the evaluation of the impact of child abusive behavior include an account of the entire context in which abused children are raised. In abusive families, abuse is not the only cause of developmental problems; they are also caused by associated familial and environmental factors.

A second element in such a framework is the consideration of the effects of abuse within a developmental perspective. Insofar as development is hierarchically structured and behaviors which are acquired earlier in the child's life provide the basis for future development, the effect of abuse on any specific type of behavior (e.g., physical, emotional, cognitive, social) at a given age must be considered not only for its effect on that behavior, but also for how the changed behavior determines the way the child will react to new situations which call forth responses in that or a related behavioral domain. It is, for example, not difficult to understand how punishing social approach could condition a fear response that results in later generalized social avoidance.

A third element critical to this conceptual framework views development as a transactional process in which the child's behavior acts on the environment, particularly the social environment, to change it, thereby influencing the way in which it will in the future respond to the child. The coercive behavior processes documented by Patterson (1980), where both the parent's and the child's aversive behavior escalates, are clear examples of such transactions. A child's immediate attempt to cope with abuse — as, for example, responding with extreme compliance or aggressive behavior — may well call forth inadequate or negative responses from other people, resulting in the long run in what Sroufe and Rutter (1984) call "adaptational failure."

In reporting the findings of the specific effects of physical abuse on children, we will try to draw attention to their implications for a developmental picture of abuse based on the three elements of the conceptual framework set forth above. To gain a truly comprehensive picture of how abuse affects development, requires good longitudinal data (e.g., Erickson, Egeland, & Pianta, 1989). However, the literature is still too young to yield a clear picture of all the developmental domains that would be expected to be seriously affected by abuse, and there is very little longitudinal research available. What we have now are greatly improved cross-sectional studies which utilize proper control procedures and standard methods, unlike many of the earlier studies which based their work on clinically referred convenience samples and clinical assessments.

157

Findings in five behavioral domains will be reported: neurological functioning; intellectual functioning; affective or socioemotional behavior; social behavior; and social cognition.

Neurological functioning. Neurological or physical impairment is the most immediate and direct effect of physical abuse. Evidence for such impairment comes from Lynch and Roberts (1982), who found greater impairment among abused children than their siblings; from Lewis, Mallouh, and Webb's (1989) review of the association between child abuse, delinquency, and violent criminality, in which many of their own studies showed evidence of elevated rates of neurological impairment; from Martin (1976), who estimated that 20% to 50% of physically abused children had a neurological system severely enough impaired to hamper everyday functioning; and from Frank, Zimmerman, and Leeds (1985), who found that vigorous shaking by parents (headshaking) produced neurological impairment.

Intellectual functioning. Aside from the obvious pervasive effects that severe neurological impairment entails for all aspects of a child's life, it may also be the case that the intellectual and learning problems that appear to be found at a higher rate in physically abused children, are at least in part due to minor neurological deficits. A number of studies have shown developmental status and intellectual competence to be retarded in abused children. The Minnesota Mother-Child Interaction Project found lower Bayley scores at 24 months and lower Wechsler Preschool-Primary Scale of Intelligence (WPPSI) scores at 5 years (Erickson et al., 1989); Perry, Doran, and Wells (1983) found that physically abused lower socioeconomic status Caucasian children between 2 and 12 years of age performed poorly on the Peabody Picture Vocabulary Test (PPVT), a measure of receptive vocabulary; Hoffman-Plotkin and Twentyman (1984) found that the IQs of abused 3- to 6-year-olds were about 20 points lower than the IQs of nonabused preschoolers using the Stanford Binet Intelligence Scale and the PPVT; Oates and Peacock (1984) reported that children averaging 9 years of age who had been hospitalized as a result of physical abuse, scored significantly lower than nonabused children on both the Verbal and Performance subscales of the revised Wechsler Intelligence

Scale for Children and the WPPSI; Barahal, Waterman, and Martin (1981) also found IQ differences. Salzinger, Kaplan, Pelcovitz, Samit, and Krieger (1984) found that significantly more abused and neglected children than control children were 2 years below grade level in reading and mathematics, were failing in academic subjects, and were placed in special education classrooms.

The dysfunctional intellectual behavior of abused children certainly cannot all be attributed to neurological deficit. A developmental perspective would suggest that we look at other aspects of the child's caretaking environment and its effects on the children's behavior to see where their learning problems stem from (Azar, Barnes, & Twentyman, 1988). If learning is construed as an active process, then children who do not seek to achieve intellectual mastery and who show poor motivation will eventually have problems in meeting normal age-appropriate intellectual demands. Crittenden's work with abused infants has uncovered a parenting process which seems to contribute both to low levels of infant motivation and to lower developmental quotients than normally reared babies. She has observed that physically abused babies, whose parents do not attend to their behavioral cues and who are out of synchrony with their behavior, are at first difficult babies, but in time learn to adapt by ceasing to complain, and by becoming passive, fearful, vigilant, and compliant (Crittenden, 1981, 1985, 1988; Crittenden & DiLalla, 1988). Egeland's group (Erickson et al., 1989) found that 2-year-olds who had been physically abused exhibited less enthusiasm for a tool-use task than control toddlers. Oates and Peacock (1984) suggest that their subjects' persistent intellectual deficit and other adverse effects are due to the fact that the children have remained within a disturbed family environment for 5 years after battering. In assessing children's "secure readiness to learn," Aber, Allen, Carlson, and Cicchetti (1989) found, in a study that systematically examined the behavior of mothers and children in a series of tasks, that maltreated 4- to 8-year-olds engage in more verbal attention seeking and compliant behavior during learning-type tasks than lower-class control children, who, in turn, show more curiosity and less dependency. They also found that parental discouragement of autonomy in abused children was significantly correlated with lower cognitive maturity as assessed by PPVT scores. In general, then, abused children's inability to function as well as other children in the tasks of learning and school achievement, as well as in other areas discussed below, may be taken as an example of Sroufe and Rutter's (1984) "adaptational failure."

Affective and socioemotional behavior. Documentation of the early emotional and affective effects of abuse comes largely from the well-studied area of the quality of child-parent attachment. Insofar as secure attachment with caretakers provides the basis for the ability to form and maintain positive affective ties with other people (Bowlby, 1977a, 1977b), insecure attachment should put children at risk for socioemotional disorder. Results based on the behavior of infants and toddlers in the strange situation paradigm (Ainsworth, Blehar, Waters, & Wall, 1978), where children are observed with their parents and others during separation and reunion, have shown that infants and toddlers who have been abused show insecure patterns of attachment to their mothers and other adults in contrast to normally reared children, who show secure patterns of attachment (Carlson, Cicchetti, Barnett, & Braunwald, 1989; Crittenden & Ainsworth, 1989; Egeland & Sroufe, 1981; Schneider-Rosen, Braunwald, Carlson, & Cicchetti, 1985). Not all the insecure patterns which have been identified are the same but all predispose a child to difficulty in affiliative behavior.

Data consistent with the relationship between insecure attachment in abused children and later socioemotional problems are found in a number of studies. Summarizing the results of the Minnesota longitudinal study with respect to socioemotional development of high-risk children from 18 to 54 months of age, Erickson et al. (1989) found anxious patterns of attachment in the children at 18 months; by 24 months, they showed angry noncompliant behavior and more frustration with their mothers; by 42 months, they were nonaffectionate with and avoidant of their mothers, more hyperactive and distractible, lacking in self-control and assertiveness, lower in self-esteem, and less creative in their approach to coping with mild frustration; by 54 months, they were more impulsive, showed more negative affect, continued to lack self-control, and were more dependent. Howes, in her UCLA Project (Howes, 1984; Howes & Eldredge, 1985; Howes & Espinosa, 1985), found that abused toddlers showed less positive emotion and engaged in less initiation of social interactions with peers than nonabused children, and that these differences became more pronounced with age.

In addition to the very early parental behavior that results in insecure attachment, Cicchetti (1989) discusses the possibility that the continuing disapproval by maltreating mothers of the expression of affect in their children results in the "overcontrol" of their children's emotions. Evidence which is consistent with this hypothesis comes from Burgess and Conger's (1978) observations of family interaction, which showed that abusive mothers conversed less and were more negative and overcontrolling; from Cicchetti and Beeghly's study (1987), which found that maltreated toddlers used fewer internal state words, particularly for negative emotions, than nonmaltreated children; and from Coster, Gersten, Beeghly, and Cicchetti's (in press) study, which found differences in 31-month-old maltreated toddlers' expressive language. As children grow older, the results of early deficits in emotional behavior begin to show themselves in a lack of social competence and deficiencies in communicative competence. Blager and Martin (1976) found deficiencies in the discourse skills of maltreated children as did Salzinger, Wondolowski, Kaplan, and Kaplan (1987), in a study which showed that maltreating mothers and their maltreated children engaged in more prolonged runs of negative verbal interchanges than control pairs.

Another consequence of early socioemotional problems might well be later affective psychopathology. Kazdin, Moser, Colbus, and Bell (1985), in a study of 6- to 13-year-old psychiatric inpatients, found that physically abused children showed significantly higher rates of depressive behavior and lower self-esteem. In another study of 6- to 18-year-old maltreated children referred for treatment with their families to a hospital-based family crisis intervention program, significantly higher rates of diagnosed psychopathology, especially depression in girls, were found for maltreated than for control children (Kaplan, Montero, Pelcovitz, & Kaplan, 1988). Other studies, using standardized behavior ratings by parents and teachers, have found emotional problems as evidenced in increased rates of internalizing behaviors (Reid, Kavanagh, & Baldwin, 1987; Salzinger et al., 1984; Salzinger, Feldman, Hammer, & Rosario, 1989; Reid et al., 1987) and in a lack of social competence (Kravic, 1987; Salzinger et al., 1984, 1989; Vondra & Garbarino, 1988; Wolfe & Mosk, 1983).

Social behavior. Parental maltreatment of children is essentially an interpersonal phenomenon and, as such, it would be expected to have major effects on children's social behavior and their understanding of social relationships. Given the child's exposure to parental violence as a legitimate means of interacting with other people, it is not surprising to find that the behavioral effect most well documented by both direct observation and parent and teacher ratings is that abused children are more aggressive, showing more hostile, externalizing and negative social behavior with other people than nonabused children (Bousha & Twentyman, 1984; Burgess & Conger, 1978; Egeland & Sroufe, 1981; George & Main, 1979; Hoffman-Plotkin & Twentyman, 1984; Howes, 1984; Howes & Eldredge, 1985; Howes & Espinosa, 1985; Kravic, 1987; Lahey, Conger, Atkeson, & Treiber, 1984; Lewis & Schaeffer, 1981; Reid et al., 1987; Reid, Taplan, & Lorber, 1981; Reidy, 1977; Wolfe & Mosk, 1983). The majority of these studies have been concerned with young children — toddlers, preschoolers, and beginning school-age children. It is especially important to note that the effects on social interaction are found in such young children (Aber et al., 1989; Cicchetti, 1989; Crittenden, 1985; George & Main, 1979; Howes & Espinosa, 1985) because it implies that these effects and others based on these problems are probably well established by the time the children reach school age. Studies of school-age children themselves are more rare. However, it is essential that we study the problem in older preadolescent school-age children because the literature on delinquents (Garbarino & Platz, 1984; Gray, 1988; Lewis et al., 1989) and on adults abused as children (McCord, 1983) strongly suggests not only a robust association between early abuse and continuing aggressive and antisocial behavior, but a quantitative relationship between abuse and the violence of later delinquent behavior as well. Garbarino and Platz (1984) conclude their review of the association between maltreatment and delinquency by stating that it appears "that child maltreatment (particularly when defined broadly) is associated with juvenile delinquency (particularly when defined narrowly)." They consider that delinquency and abuse may both be the result of a "common etiology in disrupted, ineffectual families, and culturally based practices that legitimize family violence, decrease social control in adolescence, and support institutional practices that respond punitively to adolescent reactions to family disruptions."

Social cognition. Because of abused children's social history, one might expect distortions in the way they appraise others' behavior, intentions and feelings. Although there is not a great deal of direct evidence, there are reports in the literature of abused children being deficient in some aspects of social cognition (Smetana & Kelly, 1989). Dean, Malik, Richards, and Stringer (1986) found that abused children's descriptions of child-adult and child-child reciprocal behavior differed from those of nonabused children. Howes and Espinosa (1985) found that physically abused preschool children have difficulty in role-taking or perspective-taking skills. Rieder and Cicchetti (in press), in a study of preschool and early school-age children, found that maltreated children assimilated aggressive stimuli more easily and with less distortion than nonmaltreated children, suggesting that a maltreating environment might encourage hypervigilance and the "ready assimilation of aggressive stimuli as an adaptive coping strategy." Smetana, Kelly, and Twentyman (1984), in a study of preschoolers, found that maltreated children appraised moral and social transgressions differently from nonmaltreated youngsters and that the history of maltreatment determined the type of appraisals they gave. Barahal et al. (1981) found that 6- to 8-year-old abused children were poorer than nonabused children in identifying appropriate emotions in others and in perspective-taking skills. Main and George (1985), in an observational study of abused preschoolers, found abused children to be less concerned with the distress of peers than were nonabused classmates. And Straker and Jacobson (1981) found that 5- to 10-year-old abused children were less empathic than nonabused children.

A number of the findings listed above for young children, especially with respect to disturbed socioemotional development, social behavior, and distortions of social cognition, might well be expected to predispose abused children to difficulty with peer relationships. Consistent with this expectation, we found, in recently completed work with a sample of disadvantaged urban children in New York City, that abused school children were significantly lower in sociometric status than demographically matched control classmates and that their social behavior, as rated by peers, accounted for a significant portion of their diminished social status.

Using a peer nomination procedure (Coie, Dodge, & Coppotelli, 1982) in each of 87 classrooms to identify the two classmates each child most liked to be with, the two they least liked to be with, and their best friend in the class, abused children were found to have significantly lower social status than nonabused matched control classmates. Their standardized social preference scores were more negative ($p = .0003$); they received fewer positive choices ($p = .01$), more negative choices ($p = .0004$), and fewer best friend nominations ($p = .003$). When the children's peer status was categorized in terms of popular, rejected, neglected, controversial, and average status, a significantly higher percentage of the abused children were found to be rejected (38.8% vs. 25.9%, $p = .035$) and a lower percentage were found to be popular (14.1% vs. 28.2%, $p = .01$). Although there were very few sociometrically neglected children in the sample overall, and therefore no significant difference between groups, twice as many abused as control children were so classified. There were no differences between the proportions of average status and controversial status children.

To determine why the abused children were less preferred, shyness, leadership, fighting, sharing, verbal meanness, and attention getting were selected as behaviors on which all the same gender children in the class rated each other. Matched t tests between the groups showed that the abused children were rated significantly lower than control children on leadership and sharing and higher on fighting, meanness and attention getting.

Taking social preference as a summary index of sociometric status, our results showed that it accounted for 14% of the variance ($R^2 = .14$, $F1/84 = 14.00$, $p = .0003$) between abused and control children. The extent to which the behavior of the children, as assessed by peers, accounted for this relationship was determined by a stepwise regression procedure in which the dependent variable was that portion of the abuse/nonabuse variance that was attributable to the social status of the children, and the 6 social behaviors rated by same gender classmates (shyness, leadership, sharing, starting fights, meanness, and attention getting) were entered into the analysis as predictors. Leadership, sharing, and starting fights all contributed independently to the prediction. Combined, they accounted for 45% of the variance (R^2 = .45, $F3/170$ = 47.18, p = .0001), suggesting that abused children's own social behavior accounts for almost half of their lower sociometric status.

To better understand the abused children's social dysfunction, we examined the characteristics of the children they designated as their best friends. Because most "best friends" named by both samples of children turned out to be classmates, we were able to examine those classmates' evaluations of our children to obtain a measure of reciprocity of the relationships. We found that abused children, more than nonabused children, tended to choose as their best friends children who did not necessarily choose them positively and even children to whom they assigned a negative or neutral evaluation when asked to characterize the way they felt about the relationship.

CONCLUSION

As this article documents, physical abuse of children has disturbing and far-reaching consequences for them. Despite this, it is disconcerting to realize that within the past few years, even bombarded as we are by the media and our own personal observations of community life with images of violent and aggressive behavior (often among teenagers and especially, although certainly not exclusively, in poor and underserved neighborhoods), support for research, and consequently the amount of research conducted, on aggressive behavior and physical abuse has declined. However, the problem of violence has not declined, with national yearly estimates of violence between adults in families at about 16% and between parents and children at about 10% (Straus & Gelles, 1988). It deserves our continuing study of its basic parameters and its effects, with an eye to determining where, in the longitudinal cycle of abuse and in the present context of children's lives, we can intervene most effectively to prevent the immediate and long-range behavioral and emotional consequences that not only affect the children themselves but which lead subsequently to disruption in the communities in which such children become adults.

REFERENCES

Aber, J. L., Allen, J. P., Carlson, V., & Cicchetti, D. (1989). The effects of maltreatment on development during early childhood: Recent studies and their theoretical, clinical, and policy implications. In D. Cicchetti & V. Carlson (Eds.), *Child maltreatment* (pp. 579-619). Cambridge: Cambridge University Press.

Ainsworth, M.D.S., Blehar, M., Waters, E., & Wall, S. (1978). *Patterns of attachment: A psychological study of the strange situation.* Hillsdale, NJ: Lawrence Erlbaum.

Azar, S. T., Barnes, K. T., & Twentyman, C. T. (1988). Developmental outcomes in physically abused children: Consequences of parental abuse or the effects of a more general breakdown in caregiving behaviors? *Behavior Therapist, 11,* 27-32.

Barahal, R. M., Waterman, J., & Martin, H. P. (1981). The social cognitive development of abused children. *Journal of Consulting and Clinical Psychology, 49,* 508-516.

Blager, F. , & Martin, H. P. (1976). Speech and language of abused children. In H. P. Martin (Ed.), *The abused child.* Cambridge, MA: Ballinger.

Bousha, D. M., & Twentyman, C. T. (1984). Child interactional style in abuse, neglect, and control groups: Naturalistic observations in the home. *Journal of Abnormal Psychology, 93,* 106-114.

Bowlby, J. (1977a). The making and breaking of affectional bonds. *British Journal of Psychiatry, 130,* 201-210.

Bowlby, J. (1977b). The making and breaking of affectional bonds. *British Journal of Psychiatry, 130,* 421-431.

Burgess, R. L. (1979). Child abuse: A social interactional analysis. In B. B. Lahey & A. E. Kazdin (Eds.), *Advances in clinical child psychology* (pp. 142-172). New York: Plenum.

Burgess, R. L., & Conger, R. D. (1978). Family interaction in abusive, neglectful and normal families. *Child Development, 49,* 1163-1173.

Carlson, V., Cicchetti, D., Barnett, D., & Braunwald, K. (1989). Finding order in disorganization: Lessons from research on maltreated infants' attachments to their caregivers. In D. Cicchetti & V. Carlson (Eds.), *Child maltreatment* (pp. 494-528). Cambridge: Cambridge University Press.

Cicchetti, D. (1989). How research on child maltreatment has informed the study of child development: perspectives from developmental psychopathology. In D. Cicchetti & V. Carlson (Eds.), *Child maltreatment* (pp. 377-431). Cambridge: Cambridge University Press.

Cicchetti, D., & Beeghly, M. (1987). Symbolic development in maltreated youngsters: An organizational perspective. In D. Cicchetti & M. Beeghly (Eds.), *Atypical symbolic development.* San Francisco: Jossey-Bass.

Coie, J. D., Dodge, K. A., & Coppotelli, H. (1982). Dimensions and types of social status: A cross-age perspective. *Developmental Psychology, 18,* 557-570.

Coster, W., Gersten, M., Beeghly, M., & Cicchetti, D. (in press). Communicative functioning in maltreated toddlers. *Developmental Psychology.*

Crittenden, P. M. (1981). Abusing, neglecting, problematic, and adequate dyads: Differentiating by patterns of interaction. *Merrill-Palmer Quarterly, 27,* 1-18.

Crittenden, P. M. (1985). Maltreated infants: Vulnerability and resilience. *Journal of Child Psychology and Psychiatry, 26,* 85-96.

Crittenden, P. M. (1988). Relationships at risk. In J. Belsky & T. Nezworski (Eds.), *Clinical implications of attachment* (pp. 136-174). Hillside, NJ: Lawrence Erlbaum.

Crittenden, P. M., & Ainsworth, M.D.S. (1989). Child maltreatment and attachment theory. In D. Cicchetti & V. Carlson (Eds.), *Child maltreatment* (pp. 432-463). Cambridge: Cambridge University Press.

Crittenden, P. M., & DiLalla, D. L. (1988). Compulsive compliance: The development of an inhibitory coping strategy in infancy. *Journal of Abnormal Child Psychology, 16*, 585-599.

Dean, A. L., Malik, M. M., Richards, W., & Stringer, S. A. (1986). Effects of parental maltreatment on children's conceptions of interpersonal relationships. *Developmental Psychology, 22*, 617-626.

Egeland, B., & Sroufe, L. A. (1981). Attachment and early maltreatment. *Child Development, 52*, 44-52.

Erickson, M. F., Egeland, B., & Pianta, R. (1989). The effects of maltreatment on the development of young children. In D. Cicchetti & V. Carlson (Eds.), *Child maltreatment* (pp. 647-684). Cambridge: Cambridge University Press.

Famularo, R., Stone, K., Barnum, R., & Wharton, R. (1986). Alcoholism and severe child maltreatment. *American Journal of Orthopsychiatry, 56*, 481-485.

Frank, Y., Zimmerman, R., & Leeds, M. D. (1985). Neurological manifestations in abused children who have been shaken. *Developmental Medicine and Child Neurology, 27*, 312-316.

Garbarino, J., & Platz, M. (1984). Child abuse and juvenile delinquency: What are the links? In E. Gray (Ed.), *Child abuse: Prelude to delinquency? Final report.* Chicago, IL: National Committee for Prevention of Child Abuse.

George, C., & Main, M. (1979). Social interactions of young abused children: Approach, avoidance, and aggression. *Child Development, 50*, 306-318.

Gray, E. (1988). The link between child abuse and juvenile delinquency: What we know and recommendations for policy and research. In G. Hotaling, D. Finkelhor, J. T. Kirkpatrick, & M. A. Straus (Eds.), *Family abuse and its consequences* (pp. 109-123). Newbury Park, CA: Sage.

Hershorn, M., & Rosenbaum, A. (1985). Children of marital violence: A closer look at the unintended victims. *American Journal of Orthopsychiatry, 55*, 260-266.

Hoffman-Plotkin, D., & Twentyman, C. T. (1984). A multimodal assessment of behavioral and cognitive deficits in abused and neglected preschoolers. *Child Development, 55*, 794-802.

Howes, C. (1984). Social interactions in patterns of friendships in normal and emotionally disturbed children. In T. Field, J. Roopnarine, & M. Segal (Eds.), *Friendships in normal and handicapped children.* Norwood, NJ: Ablex.

Howes, C., & Eldredge, R. (1985). Responses of abused, neglected, and non-maltreated children to the behaviors of their peers. *Journal of Applied Developmental Psychology, 6*, 261-270.

Howes, C., & Espinosa, M. P. (1985). The consequences of child abuse for the formation of relationships with peers. *Child Abuse and Neglect, 9*, 397-404.

Hughes, H. M., Parkinson, D., & Vargo, M. (1989). Witnessing spouse abuse and experiencing physical abuse: A "double whammy"? *Journal of Family Violence, 4*, 197-209.

Kaplan, S., Montero, J., Pelcovitz, D., & Kaplan, T. (1988, October). *Psychopathology of abused and neglected children.* Paper presented at the 35th Annual Meeting of the American Academy of Child and Adolescent Psychiatry, Seattle, WA.

Kazdin, A. E., Moser, J., Colbus, D., & Bell, R. (1985). Depressive symptoms among physically abused and psychiatrically disturbed children. *Journal of Abnormal Psychology, 94*, 298-307.

Kravic, J. N. (1987). Behavior problems and social competence of clinic-referred abused children. *Journal of Family Violence, 2*, 111-120.

Lahey, B. B., Conger, R. D., Atkeson, B. M., & Treiber, F. A. (1984). Parenting behavior and emotional status of physically abusive mothers. *Journal of Consulting and Clinical Psychology, 52*, 1062-1071.

Lewis, D. O., Mallouh, C., & Webb, V. (1989). Child abuse, delinquency, and violent criminality. In D. Cicchetti & V. Carlson (Eds.), *Child maltreatment* (pp. 707-721). Cambridge: Cambridge University Press.

Lewis, M. L., & Schaeffer, S. (1981). Peer behavior and mother-infant interaction. In M. L. Lewis & S. Schaeffer (Eds.), *The uncommon child* (pp. 193-223). New York: Plenum.

Lynch, M. A., & Roberts, J. (1982). *Consequences of child abuse.* New York: Academic Press.

Main, M., & George, C. (1985). Responses of abused and disadvantaged toddlers to distress in agemates: A study in the day care setting. *Developmental Psychology, 21*, 407-412.

Martin, H. P. (1976). *The abused child: A multidisciplinary approach to developmental issues and treatment.* Cambridge, MA: Ballinger.

McCord, J. (1983). A forty year perspective on effects of child abuse and neglect. *Child Abuse and Neglect, 7*, 265-270.

Oates, R. K., & Peacock, A. (1984). Intellectual development of battered children. *Australia and New Zealand Journal of Developmental Disabilities, 10*, 27-29.

Patterson, G. R. (1980). Mothers: The unacknowledged victims. *Monographs of the Society for Research in Child Development, 45*, (5, Serial No. 186).

Perry, M. A., Doran, L. D., & Wells, E. A. (1983). Developmental and behavioral characteristics of the physically abused child. *Journal of Clinical Child Psychology, 12*, 320-324.

Reid, J. B., Kavanagh, K., & Baldwin, D. V. (1987). Abusive parents' perceptions of child problem behaviors: An example of parental bias. *Journal of Abnormal Child Psychology, 15*, 457-466.

Reid, J. B., Taplan, P., & Lorber, R. (1981). A social interactional approach to the treatment of abusive families. In R. B. Stuart (Ed.), *Violent behavior: Social learning approaches to prediction, management and treatment* (pp. 83-101). New York: Brunner/Mazel.

Rieder, C., & Cicchetti, D. (in press). An organizational perspective on cognitive control functioning and cognitive-affective balance in maltreated children. *Developmental Psychology.*

Reidy, T. J. (1977). The aggressive characteristics of abused and neglected children. *Journal of Clinical Psychology, 33*, 1140-1145.

Rosenberg, M. S. (1987). Children of battered women: The effects of witnessing violence on their social problem-solving abilities. *Behavior Therapist, 4*, 85-89.

Salzinger, S., Feldman, R. S., Hammer, M., & Rosario, M. (1989, December). *Peer status, behavioral disturbance, and family background factors in child physical abuse.* Paper presented at the 2nd Annual Research Conference of the New York State Office of Mental Health, Albany, NY.

Salzinger, S., Kaplan, S., Pelcovitz, D., Samit, C., & Krieger, R. (1984). Parent and teacher assessment of children's behavior in child maltreating families. *Journal of the American Academy of Child Psychiatry, 23*, 458-464.

Salzinger, S., Rosario, M., Feldman, R. S., & Hammer, M. (in press). Constellations of family violence and their differential effects on children's behavioral disturbance. In E. Viano (Ed.), *Violence among intimates.* Papers prepared for the Fifth International Institute on Victimology, 1989.

Salzinger, S., Wondolowski, S., Kaplan, S., & Kaplan, T. (1987, April). *A discourse analysis of the conversations between maltreated children and their mothers.* Paper presented at the meetings of the Society for Research in Child Development, Baltimore, MD.

Sameroff, A. J., & Chandler, M. J. (1975). Reproductive risk and the continuum of caretaking casualty. In F. D. Horowitz (Ed.), *Review of child development research* (Vol. 4., pp. 187-244). Chicago: University of Chicago Press.

Schneider-Rosen, K., Braunwald, K. G., Carlson, V., & Cicchetti, D. (1985). Current perspectives in attachment theory: Illustration from the study of maltreated infants. In L. Bretherton & E. Waters (Eds.), Growing points of attachment theory and research. *Monographs of the Society for Research in Child Development, 50,* (1,2, Serial No. 209).

Smetana, J. G., & Kelly, M. (1989). Social cognition in maltreated children. In D. Cicchetti & V. Carlson (Eds.), *Child maltreatment* (pp. 620-646). Cambridge: Cambridge University Press.

Smetana, J. G., Kelly, M., & Twentyman, C. (1984). Abused, neglected and nonmaltreated children's conceptions of moral and social-conventional transgressions. *Child Development, 55,* 277-287.

Straker, G., & Jacobson, R. S. (1981). Aggression, emotional maladjustment and empathy in the abused child. *Developmental Psychology, 17,* 762-765.

Straus, M. A., & Gelles, R. J. (1988). How violent are American families?: Estimates from the National Family Violence Resurvey and other studies. In G. T. Hotaling, D. Finkelhor, J. T. Kirkpatrick, & M. A. Straus (Eds.), *Family abuse and its consequences* (pp. 14-36). Beverly Hills, CA: Sage.

Sroufe, L. A., & Rutter, M. (1984). The domain of developmental psychopathology. *Child Development, 55,* 17-29.

Vondra, J., & Garbarino, J. (1988). Social influences on adolescent behavior problems. In S. Salzinger, J. Antrobus & M. Hammer (Eds.), *Social networks of children, adolescents and college students* (pp. 195-224). Hillsdale, NJ: Lawrence Erlbaum.

Wolfe, D. A. (1987). *Child abuse: Implications for child development and psychopathology.* Newbury Park, CA: Sage.

Wolfe, D. A., & Mosk, M. D. (1983). Behavioral comparisons of children from abusive and distressed families. *Journal of Consulting and Clinical Psychology, 51,* 702-708.

Child: care, health and development, 1991, **17**, 243–258

The abuse of disabled children: a review of the literature

HELEN WESTCOTT *Public Policy Department, National Society for the Prevention of Cruelty to Children (NSPCC), 67 Saffron Hill, London EC1N 8RS, England*

Accepted for publication 5 March 1991

Summary Literature concerning the abuse of disabled children is examined with a view to elucidating why it is that this problem has not received full attention from professionals to date. Two contributing factors emerge: the limits of studies that have been conducted and the failure of society to address the needs of disabled children. It is concluded that disabled children are at increased risk of abuse, and that new policy and research initiatives are required in this area.

Investigations into the abuse of disabled children have been taking place for the last 3 decades (e.g. Benedict *et al.* 1990, Glaser & Bentovim 1979, Johnson & Morse 1968, Morgan 1987) and recently, professionals working in the child abuse field have come to realize the additional difficulties facing disabled children who are victimized, including the need to evaluate current policies and practices with respect to this particular group of children (e.g. Brown & Craft 1989, Kennedy 1989). So why has it taken so long for the problem to be widely recognized?

There are no easy answers to this question, but a review of the available literature may provide some insights. Specifically, two underlying issues may be identified: the limits of studies conducted to date (including methodological shortcomings and failure to address the key issues), and the failure of society to respond to the needs of disabled children. The role of each of these factors will be discussed in turn.

THE LIMITS OF STUDIES CONDUCTED TO DATE

Generally, the limits of studies conducted to date may be grouped into two categories. The first category consists of methodological constraints, whereas the second deals with limits arising from the lack of theory available to provide both a framework for the results and for the role of aetiological variables. Methodologically, the question of abuse of disabled children can be approached in two ways. First, the authors can select an abused sample of children and see what percentage of these children was known to be disabled before the abuse. Alternatively, the authors can study a disabled population and try to establish what proportion of these children have been abused.

The problem besetting either approach is that in many cases it might have been abuse (particularly physical) which initially caused the child's disability. Table 1 presents a summary of those studies which have tried to study the prevalence of abuse in disabled populations. Table 2 presents studies which have looked at abused populations to locate pre-existing disability amongst victims.

The most serious criticism of these studies is their failure to employ a control group of non-abused and/or able-bodied children which is matched for sex, race, socio-economic status, etc., to the subject children (see Tables 1 and 2). Thus, apparently significant findings regarding the incidence of abuse in disabled populations, or regarding characteristics of an abused sample of children, are severely compromised. Related to this, only a few studies have provided comparison abuse and/or disability statistics for the general child population (Ammerman et al. 1989, Benedict et al. 1990, Frisch & Rhoads 1982, Sullivan et al. 1987).

A second shortcoming concerns the retrospective method of data collection employed by the majority of studies which results in a lack of control over the type and quality of information collected. Few authors appear to have measured inter-rater reliability in examining these records (with the exceptions of Ammerman et al. 1989 and Benedict et al. 1990), nor report rating the records 'blind' (but see Benedict et al. 1990).

The issue of definitions is particularly pertinent when attempting to obtain an overall view of the studies, as in many cases these are unclear, although abuse is generally better defined than disability. More recent studies have adopted quite stringent criteria in specifying their subjects' characteristics so that it is easier to identify those populations to which the findings apply (e.g. Ammerman et al. 1989, Benedict et al. 1990).

One of the most serious problems with existing studies is their failure to expound and develop a guiding theory or specific hypotheses. This results in the confused nature of some findings and uncertainty as to the implications. The one theory that has been discussed is that of the 'frustration model' of abuse, where a combination of (a) social/familial stress or crises, (b) parental inadequacy/weakness and (c) characteristics of the child result in the child being abused (e.g. Birrell & Birrell 1968, Zirpoli 1986; see also reviews by Ammerman *et al.* 1988, Starr *et al.* 1984, White *et al.* 1987).

Some authors have suggested why disabled children are more vulnerable to abuse (e.g. Brown & Craft 1989, Craft 1987, Krents *et al.* 1987, Martin & Martin 1990, Schor 1987, Trevelyan 1988, Walmsley 1989). However, they fail to produce any empirical studies to support their claims. While these theories may therefore be borne out by experience, there still remains the need for research designed specifically to evaluate the characteristics of disabled children that increase vulnerability to abuse.

Characteristics said to make disabled children more vulnerable include the following: dependency on others for basic and social needs; lack of control or choice over their own life; compliance and obedience 'instilled' as good behaviour; lack of knowledge about sex, and the misunderstanding of sexual advances; isolation and rejection by others which increases responsiveness to attention and affection (accompanied by an increased desire to please); inability to communicate experiences; and inability to distinguish between different types of touching (Brown & Craft 1989, Craft 1987). Additionally, the apparent 'childishness' of many learning-disabled children may attract potential abusers (Trevelyan 1988). Kempton (1975) argues that learning-disabled children's problems in reasoning, lack of impulse control and inability to predict the consequences of their actions also heighten vulnerability.

Great care is necessary in considering these characteristics, so that, for example, children with physical disabilities (e.g. deafness) are not automatically ascribed the attributes of children with learning difficulties. Each disabled child will have his or her own needs as a result of his or her disability, which will in turn make the child vulnerable to abuse. Further research is therefore necessary to document the precise mechanisms through which this occurs.

The lack of a coherent underlying theory found in research concerning the abuse of disabled children suppresses examination of fundamental issues in two ways. First, it permits the casual application of aetiological variables derived from the abuse of able-bodied

TABLE 1. Summary of studies examining the prevalence of abuse in disabled populations

Authors	Date	Country	Size	Subject characteristics (disability)	Is a control or comparison group available?	Source of information	Results (i.e. records of abuse)
Ammerman et al.	1989	USA	148 children 3–19 years	Psychiatrically referred, multi-disabilities, number of different physical and learning disabilities of varying severity	Yes (non-maltreated disabled children)	Medical, psychiatric, nursing and social-work records	1. 39% of children shared evidence of past or current abuse or neglect (19% definite, 9% probable and 11% possible). 2. Of these 39%, 69% were physical abuse, 45% neglect and 36% sexual abuse.
Benedict et al.	1990	USA	500 children	Mutliply disabled children with physical and mental impairments including cerebral palsy, seizure disorder and moderate to profound 'mental retardation'	No (but DSS statistics used for comparison)	Medical, nursing, social-work and clinical records	1. Reports of maltreatment had been filed in 10·6% cases. Of these cases, 64% were abuse, 26% neglect. 2. Physical abuse was the most prevalent form of abuse (67·6%), sexual abuse in 8·8% cases. Other abuse in 17·7% cases, 5·9% 'unknown'. 3. Authors conclude no over-representation of abuse in their sample.
Buchanan & Oliver	1977	Great Britain	140 children under 16 years	Children with learning disabilities to differing degrees (mild to profound), located in 'subnormality' hospital	No	Medical and social records and clinical assessments	1. 22% of children were victims of physical abuse, 10% 'at risk'. 11% of children could have been rendered learning disabled as a result of abuse (3%... definitely)

cont.

Chamberlain et al.	1984	USA	87 females, mean age 16·7 years	Adolescents suffering learning difficulties to differing degrees (mild–severe)	No	Records and interviews with parents	1. 25% of subjects had a known history of sexual assault, narrowly defined as 'attempted or successful coerced intercourse'. Mean age at time of assault was 14 years.
Diamond & Jaudes	1983	USA	86 children: 42 boys, 44 families	Children suffering from cerebral palsy and some degree of learning disability	No	Hospital records and psycho-social assessments	1. For 8 children, child abuse was cause of disability. 2. 8 children abused after caretaker aware of disability: 19 children at risk of abuse.
Doucette	1986	USA	30 disabled and 32 non-disabled women	Disabled women	Yes	Self-reports of childhood experience	1. 67% of disabled women experienced physical abuse compared to 34% of able-bodied women (1·97 times more likely). 2. 47% of disabled women sexually victimized, compared to 34% non-disabled women (1·38 times as likely).
Frisch & Rhoads	1982	USA	30+ children	Students referred for an evaluation of learning problems	No	Assessment records	1. 6·7% of children reported to state child abuse agency. This was 3·5 times higher than reported child abuse rate for all other children of same age

TABLE 1. cont.

Authors	Date	Country	Size	Subject characteristics (disability)	Is a control or comparison group available?	Source of information	Results (i.e. records of abuse)
Glaser & Bentovim	1979	Great Britain	174 children aged 0–10 years	Moderately-severely physically or learning-disabled children and chronically sick children	Yes	Records	1. 46% of children with pre-existing disability or sickness showed signs of abuse, compared to 75% of non-disabled children. 2. Disabled children: 71% neglect, 29% physical abuse. Able-bodied children: 60% physical abuse, 40% neglect.
Green	1986	USA	70 school-age children	Schizophrenic children	No	Case histories and treatment records	1. 33% of children had suffered abuse.
Hard (cited in Mayer & Brenner 1989)	1986	USA	95 adults	Developmentally disabled adults	No	Not known	1. 83% of females and 32% of males had suffered abuse. 2. In 45% cases, this was prior to victim's 18th birthday.
Jaudes & Diamond	1985	USA	37 children	Children suffering from cerebral palsy	No	Records	1. In 14 children, abuse caused cerebral palsy (CP). 2. 23 children were abused or neglected following diagnosis of CP (15 neglect, 8 abuse)

Kennedy	1989	Great Britain	156 teachers and social workers for the deaf	Deaf children known to teachers and social workers for the deaf	No	Survey	1. 136 deaf children were 'confirmed' abused and 262 children were suspected victims.
Sullivan *et al.*	1987	USA	1. All members of 9th grade at residential school for deaf.	Deaf children	No	Questionnaire survey	1. 50% of students reported they had been sexually victimized.
			2. 150 children at residential school for deaf	Deaf children	No	Individual interviews	2. 50% of children reported sexual abuse.
			3. 322 students at further education college	Hearing-impaired students	No	Questionnaire survey	3. 53 students indicated they had been physically abused. 13 reported sexual abuse. 24 reported both physical and sexual abuse.
			4. 100 children	Deaf children attending either residential or mainstream placements	No	Individual interviews	4. Of children attending residential schools, 40 were abused at school, 10 at home and 15 at both school and home. Of children attending mainstream schools, 21 reported abuse at home, 9 at school and 5 at both home and school.
Welbourne *et al.*	1983	USA	39 women	Women blind from birth or prior to the age of 10 years	No	Interviews	1. Over 50% of women had experienced at least one incident of forced sexual contact.

TABLE 2. Summary of studies examining abused populations to locate pre-existing disability amongst victims

Authors	Date	Country	Size	Subject characteristics (abuse)	Is a control or comparison group available?	Source of information	Results (i.e. records of abuse)
Birrell & Birrell	1968	Australia	42 children (24 boys, 18 girls) under age 3 years	Victims of physical abuse and/or neglect	No	Nursing and social work records and personal experience of some cases	1. Congenital anomalies ('disabilities') in over 25% of children. 2. 10 children suffering 'marked retardation' as a result of abuse.
Gil	1970	USA	12 610 children (more boys than girls) 6 months to 15 years	Physically abused and neglected children	No	Survey	1. 29% of children suffered deviations in social interaction and functioning in year prior to abuse. 2. 22% suffered some deviations in physical or mental functioning.
Johnson & Morse	1968	USA	101 children (0–14 years)	Physically abused or neglected children	No	Case records	1. Nearly 70% of children showed physical or developmental disability before injury reported. 2. 16% were physically or learning disabled as a result of abuse.
Lebsack (cited in Soeffing 1975)	1975	USA	14 083	Abused and neglected children	No	Home interviews	1. 12% of children were reported as having one or more 'distinguishing characteristic'. 2. Learning disability = 2%, physical disability = 1·6%, congenital disability = 1·2%, emotional disturbance = 1·8%

	Year	Country	Sample	Population		Method	Findings
Lightcap *et al.*	1982	USA	24 abusive families	Abused children and their siblings (non-abused)	No	Questionnaire	1. 22% of children in these families were disabled. 2. 43% of *abused* children were disabled.
Martin *et al.*	1974	USA	37	Abused children (with no history of head trauma)	No	Psychological testing, interview of parent(s) by social worker including questionnaire and observation	1. 43% displayed slight to severe neurological dysfunctions.
Morse *et al.*	1970	USA	25 (aged 33–90 months)	Physically abused and neglected children	No	Family interviews, agency contacts, patient records	1. At time of study, only 29% of children were judged to be within normal intellectual and emotional limits. 2. 8/9 learning disabled children were disabled prior to abuse.
Sandgrund *et al.*	1974	USA	60 abused; 30 neglected and 30 non-abused (aged 5–13 years)	Abused, neglected and non-abused children	Yes	Interviews by psychiatrist and psychologist	1. Significant differences in IQ between the three groups, with disproportionate frequency of IQs below 70 ('mental retardation') among abused and neglected children: 25% abused, 20 neglected, 3% non-abused.

children to those cases in which a disabled child has been abused. Ammerman *et al.* (1988) comment:

> Most studies associating child characteristics and abuse and neglect do not include handicapped children. Thus, findings from these investigations are only tangentially relevant to handicapped populations. While these efforts have a relevant bearing on handicapped children they are unable to address the fundamental question: *Do characteristics of handicapped children contribute to their maltreatment?*
> (p. 62, own emphasis)

For example, several studies have suggested that the *degree* of disability may be important in influencing the response of parents to their child's behaviour (e.g. Benedict *et al.* 1990, Chamberlain *et al.* 1984, Starr *et al.* 1984). Thus parents' expectations of their child may affect whether a child's failure to show affection, for example, results in increased stress and frustration for the parents (and thus possible abuse) or whether it is accepted as the norm. Benedict *et al.* (1990), Chamberlain *et al.* (1984) and Starr *et al.* (1984) suggest that less severely disabled children may be at greater risk (c.f. Klopping 1984). The important point, here, is that this 'degree of disability' factor will not be relevant to an able-bodied population, and so will be 'lost' if aetiological theories for the abuse of disabled children are simply derived from the existing able-bodied abuse literature.

In the same way, children with disability may be put in unique situations as a result of their disability, which increases their vulnerability to abuse. For example, possibly long periods of time unaccompanied in buses travelling to and from school (Cohen & Warren 1990, Sullivan *et al.* 1987). Again, this possible risk factor will be lost if the abuse of disabled children is considered to be simply the same as the abuse of able-bodied children.

The second area in which underlying theory could play an important role is in clarifying the problem of 'cause and effect'. As noted earlier, it is difficult in some cases to establish whether disability pre-dated the abuse or resulted from it. There is always the possibility that an unidentified abusive episode may have caused the child's disability, which in turn makes him or her vulnerable to further abuse (Garbarino 1987, Morgan 1987, Sandgrund *et al.* 1974).

Frodi (1981) comments that some children may acquire behaviour patterns typical of disabled children as a means of reducing attention they would otherwise attract from abusive parents. Sinason (1986) refers to 'secondary handicap' as a disability used by the child as a psychotic defence to cope with sexual abuse. The existence of such a defence could further complicate the issue of cause and effect.

Whether disability serves to increase the likelihood of abuse, or abuse leads to disability in children, the precise nature of this relationship ought to be explored on a case-by-case basis. Only careful documentation of the disability–abuse relationship will lead to a better understanding of the role of disabling characteristics in abuse (see White *et al.* 1987 for further discussion of this issue). In failing to address these issues, the fundamental question of why disabled children should be vulnerable to abuse remains unanswered.

SOCIETY'S FAILURE TO ADDRESS THE NEEDS OF DISABLED CHILDREN

The factor of society's failure to address the needs of disabled children underlies the others in that research is not, and cannot be, conducted in a social or political vacuum. In reviewing literature about the abuse of disabled children, the fundamental issue that emerges is the need to consider society's response to disability and disabled children.

The application of the 'frustration hypothesis' helpfully serves to stress the need for supportive counselling and guidance to be available to the parents of disabled children. Much advice offered to these parents at present focuses on the negative aspects of the child's disability — what he or she will not be able to do — instead of fostering positive, realistic expectations of the child and his or her future achievements (e.g. Dunst *et al.* 1987).

The converse situation has also been noted by some authors (Buchanan & Oliver 1977). Here, collusion (whether 'conscious' or 'unconscious') can take place between the agency and the caretaker(s) so that possible abuse is overlooked. This further increases the problems of identifying abuse in disabled children.

Sullivan *et al.* (1987) argue that depersonalization of deaf children plays a role in their abuse, an argument which extends to the abuse of any child with disabilities. These authors contend that when deaf children are assumed to be 'less human' because of their deafness, it then follows that their abuse is 'not that inhumane'. Similarly, Garbarino (1987) discusses a 'license' to abuse disabled children in a society within which they are repeatedly stigmatized.

It is therefore society's response to disability that may lead to increased abuse and vulnerability of disabled people, more than the disability or any other attribute of the abuse victim (Sobsey & Varnhagen 1988). This is reflected in the unequal power relationships which encourage children, and especially disabled children, to comply with the instructions of any adult. Special efforts are needed to equalize existing power inequities in society and to employ empowering techniques for children, particularly disabled children (Craft 1987, Walmsley 1989).

Thus, professionals repeatedly call for the provision of training on assertiveness, empowerment, discrimination of appropriate and inappropriate requests from others and improved sex education within the educational curriculum for disabled children (Brookhauser 1987, Craft 1987, Craft & Hitching 1989, Hames 1990, Kennedy 1989, 1990, Krents et al. 1987, Martin & Martin 1990, Shaul 1981, Sobsey & Varnhagen 1988, Sullivan et al. 1987, Trevelyan 1988). Several have begun to develop sex education materials specifically designed for learning disabled children (e.g. Craft & Hitching 1989, Shaul 1981) and have adapted available abuse prevention programmes (most notably 'Kidscape') for learning-disabled pupils (e.g. Hames 1990, Trevelyan 1988).

The issue of communication is relevant here. Kennedy (1989) and Sullivan et al. (1987) argue that communication channels for and with disabled children and adults need to be improved so that disclosure of abuse is facilitated and, more generally, mutual understanding between able-bodied and disabled people develops. Deficits in communication affect the quality of interactions as well as the quantity (Sobsey & Varnhagen 1988). Children with communication problems show very little initiation of discourse, and often only communicate in response to others' enquiries. They would be unlikely to report abuse, especially if not questioned directly. This problem may be exacerbated for children in residential institutions who are unable to locate potential help (Sobsey & Varnhagen 1988).

Problems in communication relate also to the difficulty in *identifying* abuse in disabled children. The studies reviewed here have relied on hospital records to document abuse in most cases, and a few have elicited self-reports. Identifying abuse (especially sexual abuse) in able-bodied children is a complex and difficult task, and the problem is greatly exacerbated where the child suffers a physical or learning disability. Reliance on personal disclosure is likely to be less reliable and to give more of an underestimate of the actual incidence. Learning-disabled children are at a disadvantage since they may suffer comprehension difficulties (i.e. they may not recognize that they are being abused), as well as communication difficulties.

Many of these difficulties could be overcome if attempts were made to reduce the isolation of disabled children, whether they are living in the community or (more seriously) in institutions (Schor 1987, Shaul 1981). The increased vulnerability to abuse that accompanies a child's move to group residential accommodation or educational institutions has been documented (e.g. Brookhauser 1987, Garbarino 1987, Klopping 1984).

CONCLUSIONS AND POSSIBILITIES FOR FUTURE RESEARCH

In conclusion, disappointment remains with the majority of existing research that in focusing so narrowly on the documentation of abuse of disabled children it has failed to address the wider issues raised above.

Disabled children are at risk from abuse. Given the large differences in subject populations and definitions used by the various authors, it is impossible to provide an accurate incidence figure. The apparently increased risk of abuse in some studies could be the result of methodological biases. Professionals may select the sample from populations they have been working with, where the high incidence of abuse of disabled persons was what prompted their research in the first place. Additionally, editors of journals are unlikely to publish studies that do not show 'interesting effects' (Sobsey & Varnhagen 1988). Sobsey concludes from his review that disabled people suffer an increased risk of about 50% for abuse, controlling for age, sex and other factors. This review suggests that disabled children *are* at increased risk of abuse, but the specific percentage increase is impossible to determine given the generally poor quality of existing studies.

As Ammerman *et al.* (1988) have stated, no study has specifically investigated the relationship between the attributes of disabled children and child abuse. The fundamental question of what aspects of their disability render them vulnerable to abuse has not been addressed.

There is an urgent need for careful sensitive research to be carried out within Great Britain which includes matched control groups and information input from the children themselves whenever possible.

Operational definitions of disability and abuse should be developed, and investigations carried out into the extent to which a child's disability precipitated his or her abuse, and the role of his or her disabling characteristics in that abuse. The services provided for disabled children need to be evaluated, and the methods by which professionals identify abuse in disabled children examined.

To conclude, this review has highlighted factors which may have contributed to the relative lack of interest to date in the abuse of disabled children. The development of good quality research and sensitive policies is urged both to increase understanding of the problem and to rectify it.

REFERENCES

Ammerman R.T., Hersen M., Van Hasselt V.B., McConigle J.J. & Lubetsky M.J. (1989) Abuse and neglect in psychiatrically hospitalised multihandicapped children. *Child Abuse and Neglect* **13**(3), 335–343

Ammerman R.T., Van Hasselt V.B. & Hersen M. (1988) Maltreatment of handicapped children: a critical review. *Journal of Family Violence* **3**(1), 53–72

Benedict M.I., White R.B., Wulff L.M. & Hall B.J. (1990) Reported maltreatment in children with multiple disabilities. *Child Abuse and Neglect* **14**(2), 207–215

Birrell R. & Birrell J. (1968) The maltreatment syndrome in children: a hospital survey. *Medical Journal of Australia* **2**, 1023–1029

Brookhauser P.E. (1987) Ensuring the safety of deaf children in residential schools. *Otolaryngology* **97**, 361–368

Brown H. & Craft A. (1989) *Thinking the Unthinkable: Papers on Sexual Abuse and People with Learning Difficulties.* Family Planning Association Education Unit, London

Buchanan A. & Oliver J.E. (1977) Abuse and neglect as cause of mental retardation: a study of 140 children admitted to sub-normality hospitals in Wiltshire. *British Journal of Psychiatry* **131**, 458–467

Chamberlain A., Rauh J., Passer A., McGrath M. & Burket R. (1984) Issues in fertility control for mentally retarded female adolescents: 1. Sexual activity, sexual abuse, and contraception. *Pediatrics* **73**, 445–450

Cohen S. & Warren R.D. (1990) The intersection of disability and child abuse in England and the United States. *Child Welfare* **LXIX**, 253–262

Craft A. (1987) *Mental Handicap and Sexuality: Issues and Perspectives.* Costello Publishers Ltd, Kent

Craft A. & Hitching G.M. (1989) Keeping safe: sex education and assertiveness skills. In *Thinking the Unthinkable: Papers on Sexual Abuse and People with Learning Difficulties,* eds H. Brown & A. Craft. Family Planning Association Education Unit, London

Diamond L.J. & Jaudes P.K. (1983) Child abuse in a cerebral-palsied population. *Developmental Medicine and Child Neurology* **25**, 169–174

Dunst C.J., Cooper C.S. & Bolick F.A. (1987) Supporting families of handicapped children. In *Special Children — Special Risks. The Maltreatment of Children with Disabilities,* eds J. Garbarino, P. E. Brookhauser & K. J. Authier. De Gruyter, New York

Doucette J. (1986) *Violent Acts Against Disabled Women*. DAWN Canada, Toronto

Frisch L.E. & Rhoads F.A. (1982) Child abuse and neglect in children referred for learning evaluation. *Journal of Learning Disabilities* 15(10), 583–586

Frodi A.M. (1981) Contribution of infant characteristics to child abuse. *American Journal of Mental Deficiency* 85, 341–349

Garbarino J. (1987) The abuse and neglect of special children: an introduction to the issues. In *Special Children — Special Risks. The Maltreatment of Children with Disabilities*, eds J. Garbarino, P. E. Brookhauser & J. Authier. De Gruyter, New York

Gil D. (1970) *Violence Against Children: Physical Child Abuse*. Harvard University Press, Cambridge, Massachusetts

Glaser D. & Bentovim A. (1979) Abuse and risk to handicapped and chronically ill children. *Child Abuse and Neglect* 3, 565–575

Green A. (1968) Self-destruction in physically abused schizophrenic children: report of cases. *Archives of General Psychiatry* 19, 171–197

Hames A. (1990) To be on the safe side. *Community Care* 799, 22–23

Hard S. (1986) Sexual abuse of the developmentally disabled: a case study. Paper presented at the National Conference of Executives of Associations for Retarded Citizens, Omaha, Nebraska, 22 October. Cited in Mayer P. & Brenner S. (1989) Abuse of children with disabilities. *Children's Legal Rights Journal* 10(4), 16–20

Jaudes P.K. & Diamond L.J. (1985) The handicapped child and child abuse. *Child Abuse and Neglect* 9, 341–347

Johnson B. & Morse H. (1968) Injured children and their parents. *Children* 15, 147–152

Kempton W. (1975) *Sex Education for Persons with Disabilities that Hinder Learning*. Danbury Press, North Scituate, Massachusetts

Kennedy M. (1989) The abuse of deaf children. *Child Abuse Review* 3(1), 3–7

Kennedy M. (1990) The deaf child who is sexually abused. *Child Abuse Review* 4(2), 3–6

Klopping H. (1984) The deaf adolescent: abuse and abusers. In *Habilitation and Rehabilitation of Deaf Adolescents — Proceedings of the National Conference*. National Academy of Gallaudet College, Washington DC

Krents E., Schulman V. & Brenner S. (1987) Child abuse and the disabled child: prospectives for parents. *Volta Review* 89, 78–95

Lebsack J.R. (1975) Cited in Soeffing M. Abused children are exceptional children. *Exceptional Children* 42, 126–133

Lightcap J.L., Kurland J.A. & Burgess R.L. (1982) Child abuse: a test of some predictions from evolutionary theory. *Ethology and Sociobiology* 3, 61–67

Martin H.P., Beezley P., Conway E.F. & Kempe C.H. (1974) The development of abused children: a review of the literature and physical, neurologic, and intellectual findings. *Advances in Pediatrics* 21, 25–73

Martin N. & Martin B. (1990) Sexual abuse: special considerations when teaching children who have severe learning difficulties. *Mental Handicap* 18, 69–74

Morgan S.R. (1987) *Abuse and Neglect of Handicapped Children*. College-Hill Press, Boston, Massachusetts

Morse C.W., Sahler O.Z. & Friedman S.B. (1970) A three-year follow-up study of abused and neglected children. *American Journal of Diseases of Children* 120, 439–446

Sandgrund H., Gaines R. & Green A. (1974) Child abuse and mental retardation: a problem of cause and effect. *American Journal of Mental Deficiency* 79, 327–330

Schor D.P. (1987) Sex and sexual abuse in developmentally disabled adolescents. *Seminars in Adolescent Medicine* 3, 1–7

Shaul S. (1981) Deafness and human sexuality: a developmental review. *American Annals of the Deaf* June, 432–439

Sinason V. (1986) Secondary mental handicap and its relationship to trauma. *Psychoanalytic Psychotherapy* 2, 131–154

Sobsey D. & Varnhagen C. (1988) Sexual abuse and exploitation of people with disabilities: a study of the victims. Unpublished manuscript. Department of Educational Psychology. University of Alberta, Edmonton

Starr R.H., Dietrich K.N., Fischoff J., Ceresnie S. & Zweier D. (1984) The contribution of handicapping conditions to child abuse. *Topics Early Childhood Special Education* **1**, 55–59

Sullivan P.M., Vernon M. & Scanlan J.M. (1987) Sexual abuse of deaf youth. *American Annals of the Deaf* **3**, 256–262

Trevelyan J. (1988) When it's difficult to say No. *Nursing Times* **84**, 16–17

Walmsley S. (1989) The need for safeguards. In *Thinking the Unthinkable. Papers on Sexual Abuse and People with Learning Difficulties*, eds H. Brown & A. Craft. Family Planning Association Education Unit, London

Welbourne A., Lipschitz S., Selvin H. & Green R. (1983) A comparison of the sexual learning experiences of unusually visually impaired and sighted women. *Journal of Visual Impairment* June, 256–259

White R.B., Benedict M.I., Wulff L.M. & Kelley M. (1987) Physical disabilities as risk factors for child maltreatment: a selected review. *American Journal of Orthopsychiatry* **57**(1), 93–101

Zirpoli T.J. (1986) Child abuse and children with handicaps. *Remedial and Special Education* **7**, 39–48

PRACTICE UPDATE

Physical child abuse continues to be a major social concern, particularly because the sequelae of physical child abuse can persist long after the experience of abuse. This article presents the practitioner with a representative, albeit not an exhaustive, review of perpetrator characteristics. Perpetrator variables are discussed under four major headings: social, biological, cognitive/affective, and behavioral factors. Each section contains a review of selected variables and a discussion of their possible roles in the occurrence of physical child abuse. Finally, implications for assessment and intervention programs are discussed. Given that no physical child abuse perpetrator typology has been adequately validated, it is underscored that interventions should be tailored to individual perpetrator characteristics with a consideration of factors from other ecological levels.

Physical Child Abuse Perpetrator Characteristics

A Review of the Literature

JOEL S. MILNER
CHINNI CHILAMKURTI
Northern Illinois University

Interest in physical child abuse perpetrator characteristics began with the recognition of the battered child syndrome (Kempe, Silverman, Steele, Droegemueller, & Silver, 1962). Abusive parents were seen as suffering from psychopathology, and clinicians were told to assess parents for personality traits thought to be associated with physical child abuse. As a consequence, psychiatric models of physical child abuse were developed. Following these early efforts, a number of investigators developed multidimensional, bidirectional models of physical child abuse that include perpetrator, familial, and sociological factors (e.g., see Azar, 1991, for a review).

Authors' Note: This review was supported in part by National Institute of Mental Health Grant MH34252 to Joel S. Milner. Correspondence concerning this article should be addressed to Joel S. Milner, Family Violence Research Program, Department of Psychology, Northern Illinois University, DeKalb, IL 60115-2892.

JOURNAL OF INTERPERSONAL VIOLENCE, Vol. 6 No. 3, September 1991 345-366

In many interactional models, child characteristics are viewed as especially important (e.g., Friedrich & Boriskin, 1976). The child is given a significant role in coercive parent-child exchanges that are believed to lead to violence (e.g., Trickett & Kuczynski, 1986). However, the view that child factors are major contributors to physical child abuse has been questioned (e.g., Ammerman, in press). For example, although abusive parents relative to comparison parents report more child behavior problems (e.g., Milner & Robertson, 1990; Wolfe & Mosk, 1983), differences in child behaviors have not been found in studies where independent observations of child behavior have been made (e.g., Mash, Johnston, & Kovitz, 1983; Reid, Kavanagh, & Baldwin, 1987). These studies suggest that some abusive parents may merely perceive more behavior problems in their children.

As a consequence of these and other findings, such as the tendency of abusers to perceive more social isolation and stress, there has been an increased interest in the role of perpetrator cognitive factors (e.g., Twentyman, Rohrbeck, & Amish, 1984). Perpetrator characteristics, however, are still seen as contributing to physical child abuse in a context of dysfunctional familial interactions and poor sociological conditions. Further, the role of buffering factors (both perpetrator and familial) are beginning to receive increased attention (e.g., Caliso & Milner, in press; Egeland, Jacobvitz, & Sroufe, 1988; Milner, Robertson, & Rogers, 1990).

The literature on physical child abuse perpetrator characteristics is large and variable in quality. Reviews of methodological problems in physical child abuse research are available elsewhere (e.g., Geffner, Rosenbaum, & Hughes, 1988; Mash & Wolfe, 1991; Plotkin, Azar, Twentyman, & Perri, 1981). The purpose of this article is to present the practitioner with a representative, albeit not exhaustive, review of perpetrator characteristics found in the literature. An overview of these perpetrator characteristics is provided in Table 1. It is hoped that an increased practitioner awareness of the wide array of perpetrator characteristics, coupled with a knowledge of contributing factors from other ecological levels, will enhance the assessment and treatment of physical child abusers.

SOCIALIZATION FACTORS

Demographics

Although some demographic factors (e.g., income level, location of residence, number of children) are external to the perpetrator, other factors

TABLE 1:   Perpetrator Variables Associated With Physical Child Abuse

Socialization factors
  Demographics
  Childhood history of abuse

Biological factors
  Neurological and neuropsychological characteristics
  Physiological reactivity
  Physical health problems

Cognitive and affective factors
  Self-esteem and ego-strength
  Locus of control
  Perceptions, attributions, and evaluations of child behavior
  Expectations of child behavior
  Life stress/distress
  Depression
  Other personality factors

Behavioral factors
  Alcohol and drug use
  Social isolation
  Parent-child interactions
  Parental discipline strategies

NOTE: Many of these categories overlap.

(e.g., gender, ethnic background, age, educational level) directly represent perpetrator characteristics. Gil (1970) provided the first comprehensive study of sociological variables that included a description of the relationship between perpetrator demographic factors and child abuse. Although still debated, certain demographic factors are believed to contribute to the development of negative perpetrator characteristics (e.g., see Gelles & Cornell, 1990). For example, previous reports indicated that females abuse more often than males, although a recent national survey indicated no gender differences (Wauchope & Straus, 1990). Herrenkohl, Herrenkohl, Toedter, and Yanushefski (1984) reported that higher family income was related to higher levels of affectionate behavior, communication, and positive parent-child interactions. Covariates of lower income included lower perpetrator intelligence, lower educational level, single parent status, lower levels of personal health, and higher levels of personal distress and psychopathology. Gabinet (1983) suggests that demographic-related conditions set the stage for the intergenerational transmission of abuse because it is difficult for the parent to teach the child how to function appropriately.

Childhood History of Abuse

In the child abuse literature, probably the most frequently mentioned perpetrator characteristic is a childhood history of physical abuse. Over the past quarter of a century, explanatory models and clinical and empirical research have repeatedly suggested a relationship between a childhood history of physical assault and adult physical child abuse (e.g., Altemeier, O'Conner, Vietz, Sandler, & Sherrod, 1982; Baldwin & Oliver, 1975; Cappell & Heiner, 1990; Cohen, Raphling, & Green, 1966; Friedrich & Wheeler, 1982; Gil, 1970; Helfer, 1987; Spinetta & Rigler, 1972; Steele, 1987). In addition, studies have reported a relationship between a reported childhood history of physical abuse and adults' scores on the Conflict Tactics Scale (Straus, Gelles, & Steinmetz, 1980) and on the Child Abuse Potential Inventory (Caliso & Milner, in press; Milner et al., 1990). Relationships between the seriousness and chronicity of childhood abuse and measures of adult child abuse have been reported (Milner et al., 1990; Straus et al., 1980), as well as a relationship between the childhood observation of physical child abuse and adult child abuse potential (Milner et al., 1990).

From a social learning perspective, parents may physically abuse their children because of the receipt or observation of physical abuse during their childhood or because of the effects of other aversive social interactions in their family of origin. In the latter case, a childhood history of assault would be only a marker variable for the presence of other family problems that are more directly related to the transmission of abuse. Thus factors such as inappropriate parental expectations, poor parental communication, and lack of parental emotional support that are associated with physical child abuse may mediate the intergenerational transmission of physical child abuse.

However, as Widom (1989) points out in a review of the intergenerational transmission of child abuse literature, the quality of most of the research can be criticized; and, we do not fully understand the nature and extent of the relationship between a childhood history of abuse and adult child abuse. As noted by Milner et al. (1990), additional data are needed on the relationship between different types of childhood assault at different ages (i.e., developmental stages) and later parental physical child abuse. Likewise, the effects of buffering factors, such as supportive childhood and adult relationships, on the intergenerational transmission of abuse need further investigation because buffering factors may explain why some individuals who experience childhood physical abuse do not abuse their children when they become parents (e.g., Caliso & Milner, in press; Egeland et al., 1988; Milner et al., 1990).

BIOLOGICAL FACTORS

Neurological and Neuropsychological Characteristics

At present, the extent that perpetrator neuropsychological factors contribute to physical child abuse is unclear. There is a paucity of research on neuropsychological factors, and no research has established a causal relationship between neuropsychological conditions and physical child abuse. Nevertheless, Elliott (1988) stated that we have generally overlooked the abuser's "neurological handicaps" in both our research and treatment efforts. Further, Milner and McCanne (in press) speculate that a childhood history of physical abuse may result in victim neurological and neuropsychological problems that in some cases may contribute to the intergenerational transmission of abuse.

In several early articles, investigators reported that low perpetrator intelligence was related to physical child abuse (e.g., Fisher, 1958; Simpson, 1967). Subsequent reports also indicated that mentally retarded parents were more likely to maltreat their children (Schilling, Schinke, Blythe, & Barth, 1982; Seagull & Scheurer, 1986). Recently, however, the role of mental retardation as a factor in child abuse has been questioned (Tymchuk & Andron, 1990; Tymchuk, Andron, & Unger, 1987). Although the role of general intelligence in physical child abuse remains under debate, there is evidence that abusers have problems in specific cognitive areas, such as abstract reasoning ability, flexibility in understanding children's behavior, and ability to generate appropriate child management strategies (e.g., Hansen, Pallotta, Tishelman, Conaway, & MacMillan, 1989; Walker, Bonner, & Kaufman, 1988).

Elliott (1988) has proposed that several neuropsychologically related clinical disorders contribute to child abuse. These disorders include episodic dyscontrol, antisocial personality disorder, and attention deficit disorder. Elliott (1988) also suggested that "patchy" cognitive deficits, such as limited vocabulary and slowness of thought related to minimal brain dysfunction, reduces the parents' ability to effectively communicate, which decreases their ability to adequately cope with family problems. Thus neuropsychological difficulties are believed to increase the likelihood of inappropriate parental behavior, including physical child abuse.

If the proposed neuropsychological problems are shown to be related to abuse, it is likely that the relationships will be complex. For example, different types of cognitive deficits may be related to different types of physical assault. The effects of variables from other ecological levels, including buffering variables (e.g., supportive family), on possible neuropsychological deficits will also need to be determined. More complete discussions of the possible role of neurological and neuropsychological factors in physical child abuse are available elsewhere (Elliott, 1988; Milner & McCanne, 1991).

Physiological Reactivity

It has been suggested that physical child abusers have a hyperreactive trait (Knutson, 1978) and are hyperresponsive to stimuli (Bauer & Twentyman, 1985). Disbrow, Doerr, and Caulfield (1977) were the first to report physiological differences between abusers/neglecters and comparison subjects in response to pleasant and unpleasant family interactions. On the basis of physiological responding, Disbrow et al. concluded that comparison parents distinguished between pleasant and unpleasant scenes, whereas abusers/neglecters did not. Wolfe, Fairbanks, Kelly, and Bradlyn (1983) measured abusive and nonabusive mothers' physiological responses to stressful and nonstressful mother-child interaction scenes. They found that abusers had larger increases in skin conductance and respiration rates in response to both scenes.

Frodi and Lamb (1980) reported that abusive mothers, relative to comparison mothers, showed more physiological reactivity to a crying child. Abusive mothers also showed physiological reactivity to a smiling infant, whereas no change was observed in comparison mothers. Abusers reported more irritation and annoyance and less sympathy in response to the crying infant and more annoyance in response to the smiling infant. Frodi and Lamb concluded that the abusive mothers appeared to find aversive any social response (i.e., crying or smiling) of the infant. Extending the work of Frodi and Lamb (1980), Pruitt and Erickson (1985) investigated physiological responses to a crying and a smiling infant in at-risk and low-risk childless adults. At-risk adults showed higher peak heart rates across both crying and smiling presentations. Self-report measures indicated that the at-risk subjects were more moody, touchy, emotionally labile, overactive, restless, and aggressive (Pruitt, 1983). Because these data were obtained from at-risk childless adults, it appears that some adults enter the parenting role with relatively high levels of autonomic and emotional reactivity to children's positive and negative affective states. A remaining question is do abusers and at-risk parents show autonomic reactivity to stressful nonchild-related stimuli?

Several recent studies have attempted to answer this question. Friedrich, Tyler, and Clark (1985) investigated physiological reactivity in abusive, neglectful, and nonabusing parents to a nonnoxious white noise, a noxious tone, and a crying infant. Although no differences were found between groups for heart rate and finger blood volume for non-child-related stimuli, abusive and neglectful mothers showed higher levels of skin conductance in response to the crying infant and required more time to return to prestimulus levels. However, in a subsequent study, Casanova, Domanic, McCanne, and Milner (in press) used at-risk and matched low-risk parents and found that at-risk mothers showed greater autonomic reactivity to non-child-related stimuli. The stimuli included a cold pressor task, a stressful film, a car horn, and unsolvable anagrams. At-risk mothers showed greater and more prolonged sympathetic activation in response to the cold pressor task and the stressful film, the two stimuli rated as the most stressful.

A critical review of studies on the physiological reactivity of abusive and at-risk individuals is available elsewhere (McCanne & Milner, 1991). Despite study limitations and inconsistent results, most investigators have concluded that abusive and at-risk subjects show greater autonomic reactivity to child-related stimuli. Further, some evidence suggests that abusers and at-risk subjects are more reactive to nonchild-related stimuli and are slower to return to prestimulus arousal levels. However, even if increased levels of physiological reactivity are confirmed, it will be necessary to demonstrate a causal relationship between autonomic reactivity and physical child abuse and to determine how this reactivity interacts with other variables.

Physical Health Problems

Although not frequently studied, several researchers report that physical child abusers have more physical handicaps and health problems (Conger, Burgess, & Barrett, 1979; Lahey, Conger, Atkeson, & Treiber, 1984). For example, Lahey et al. found that abusive mothers reported more physical symptoms than two matched comparison groups. In addition, physically abusive parents, relative to matched comparison parents, indicate on the Child Abuse Potential Inventory that they have more physical handicaps and health problems (Milner, 1986). These findings are based on self-reports, and their accuracy needs verification. Independent confirmation is also needed because Steele and Pollock (1974) report that abusers suffer from more psychosomatic illnesses. Thus abusive parents may simply have more somatoform disorders, which involve a variety of self-reported physical symptoms suggesting physical health problems for which there is no identifiable physiological basis.

COGNITIVE/AFFECTIVE FACTORS

Self-Esteem and Ego-Strength

Clinical and empirical child abuse literature indicates that physical child abuse perpetrators lack self-esteem and have poor ego-strength (e.g., Anderson & Lauderdale, 1982; Evans, 1980; Friedrich & Wheeler, 1982; Rosen, 1978; Steele, 1987). Recently, Milner (1988) reported expected ego-strength differences between parent groups in the following descending order: nurturing parents, general population parents, and physical child abusers. Further, low self-esteem has been related to negative parental perceptions of child behavior (e.g., Mash et al., 1983) and to an inability to cope with stress (e.g., McCubbin, Cauble, & Patterson, 1982).

Although the research is uniform in demonstrating a general relationship between self-concept and physical child abuse, many self-concept models are hierarchical (i.e., a global construct with subdivisions) and multifaceted, including academic, physical, social, and affective components (e.g., Shavelson, Hubner, & Stanton, 1976). To the extent that self-concept measures used to assess child physical abusers are global, they lack specificity and may fail to provide useful information about perpetrators.

Locus of Control

At-risk parents and physical child abusers appear to have an external locus of control (e.g., Ellis & Milner, 1981; Stringer & LaGreca, 1985) that includes control by powerful others and chance factors. These data support clinical observations that abusive parents often project responsibility for their abusive behavior onto external factors, including the child. Parental perceptions that external factors control their behavior coupled with perceptions that their child has many behavior problems (see next section) may set the foundation for negative parent-child interactions that lead to physical assault.

Overall, external individuals are described as less competent, more anxious, and more depressed (e.g., Lefcourt, 1976), characteristics that are frequently used to describe physical child abusers. Phares (1976) indicated that the antecedents of externality include parental behavior such as "rejection, hostile control, lack of warmth, withdrawal," and inconsistency in the subject's family of origin. This suggests the possibility of a linkage between externality and a childhood history of abuse.

194

Perceptions, Attributions, and Evaluations of Child Behavior

Clinical studies indicate that physically abusive parents have negative perceptions of their children and perceive their children as intentionally disruptive and disobedient (e.g., Helfer, McKinney, & Kempe, 1976; Pollock & Steele, 1972). Although there are exceptions (Rosenberg & Repucci, 1983), most studies that use comparison groups and examine abusive mothers' perceptions and attributions of children's behavior report similar findings. Wood-Shuman and Cone (1986) found that at-risk and abusive mothers rated more child behavior as negative than comparison mothers. Mash et al. (1983) found that abusive mothers rated their children as more problematic and as showing less social involvement than comparison mothers. Blind observers, however, rated the behavior of abused and nonabused children as similar. Reid et al. (1987) also studied the behavior of children in abusive and matched nonabusive families. Physically abusive parents perceived their children as being more aggressive, as having more conduct disorders, as being more hyperactive, and as having less intellectual ability. Independent observers, however, reported no differences on these measures.

With respect to attributions for children's behavior, physically abusive mothers perceive their own child's positive behavior as due to external and unstable factors and perceive their child's negative behavior as due to internal and stable factors (Larrance & Twentyman, 1983). Nonabusive comparison mothers make the opposite attributions for their child's positive and negative behaviors. Physically abusive mothers also view their child's behavior as more intentionally annoying (Bauer & Twentyman, 1985).

In addition to making different attributions for their children's behavior, abusive and at-risk mothers may differ in their evaluations of children's transgressions. Chilamkurti and Milner (1991) found that high-risk mothers, compared to matched low-risk mothers, assigned a greater degree of wrongness to child transgressions that lend themselves to more subjective appraisal.

Collectively, these studies suggest that abusive and at-risk mothers tend to ignore their children's positive behaviors and focus on their children's negative behaviors. Cognitive differences in abusers' perceptions, attributions, and evaluations of their children's behavior may serve as mediating variables for their use of physical aggression.

Expectations of Child Behavior

Although there is evidence that differences exist between abusive and nonabusive parents' perceptions and evaluations of children's behaviors, there is less conclusive evidence regarding abusive parents' expectations of children's behavior. An early view that still persists is that abusive parents lack awareness of and/or have unrealistically high expectations of child development (Kempe et al., 1962). Role reversal, where the parent expects care from the child, was believed to provide a basis for the abuser's unrealistic expectations regarding child development.

This view received support from Steele and Pollock (1974) who reported that abusive parents have high expectations of their children. However, subsequent studies have reported other findings. Perry, Wells, and Doran (1983) found that mothers and fathers in abusive families expected slower development of their children. Other studies have reported that abusive parents have inappropriate expectations that in some cases are too high and in other cases are too low (Kravitz & Driscoll, 1983; Twentyman & Plotkin, 1982). To some extent, the conflicting findings may be due to the different ways in which parental expectations are defined and measured. For example, Azar, Robinson, Hekimian, and Twentyman (1984) assessed abusive, neglectful, and comparison mothers' expectations of their children's behavior and problem-solving ability. The Child Development Questionnaire (CDQ) and the Parent Opinion Questionnaire (POQ) were used to measure maternal expectations. No group differences were found on the CDQ, which measures knowledge of developmental milestones. However, on the POQ, which asks about complex sequences of child behaviors, abusive mothers reported more unrealistic expectations.

Most of the expectations research has focused on parental expectations related to child development. A recent study assessed mothers' expectations of their children's compliance following different types of child transgressions and found that high-risk mothers, relative to low-risk mothers, expected less compliance for moral transgressions and more compliance for personal transgressions (Chilamkurti & Milner, 1991). Thus high-risk mothers had relatively lower expectations that their children would not continue to engage in more serious misbehavior (e.g., stealing), as well as relatively high expectations that their children would not engage in more common child misbehavior (e.g., writing on the hand with a pen).

Life Stress/Distress

Stress is often viewed as a central etiologic factor in physical child abuse (e.g., Wolfe, 1987). Stress is seen as increasing the likelihood that the parent with limited resources will react with aggressive behavior. Most often, researchers indicate that perpetrators live in stressful environments (e.g.,

Straus, 1980), albeit some researchers indicate that the amount of stress in abusers' environments is not different from that of matched comparison parents (Gaines, Sandgrund, Green, & Power, 1978). Further, many parents who live in stressful environments do not abuse. Because individuals respond differently to the same stressors, the subjective level of distress may more accurately represent the internal state of the parent, and physical child abusers report higher levels of distress (Milner, 1986). High levels of self-reported perpetrator distress are congruent with studies reporting higher levels of physiological reactivity to stressful stimuli in abusers, which suggests a decreased level of stress tolerance. Abusers' hyperreactivity may be exacerbated by the lack of stress management skills. High levels of distress are also related to health-related disorders and depression (Brown & Harris, 1978).

Depression

In an early study, Gil (1970) reported that maternal depression was common in families at risk for child abuse. Subsequently, a number of investigators have indicated that depression is a characteristic of the physically abusive parent (e.g., Lahey et al., 1984; Paulson, Afifi, Thomason, & Chaleff, 1974; Spinetta & Rigler, 1972). Congruent with these findings are reports that depression is correlated with scores on the Child Abuse Potential Inventory (Kirkham, Schinke, Schilling, Meltzer, & Norelius, 1986; Milner, Charlesworth, Gold, Gold, & Friesen, 1988).

Although depression appears to be associated with physical child abuse, the nature of the relationship is unclear. Additional study is needed to understand which aspects of the cognitive style and the affective state typical of the depressed parent contribute to child abuse. For example, some research suggests that depressed mothers are unaffectionate, distant, irritable, and punitive, resulting in a lower threshold for perceived child misbehavior and more punitive reactions to it (Lahey et al., 1984).

Other Personality Factors

A variety of other personality factors have been mentioned as representative of abusers and/or at-risk parents. Abusers are reported to have higher levels of state and trait anxiety (e.g., Aragona, 1983). They appear to display more anger and less assertiveness (e.g., Mee, 1983). Abusive parents are rigid (e.g., Milner & Wimberley, 1980), are unable to form attachments (e.g., Pollock & Steele, 1972), and have less empathy (e.g., Steele, 1987) than comparison parents. Not surprisingly, therefore, they report less family cohesion (e.g., Caliso & Milner, in press), more family conflict (e.g., Caliso & Milner, in press; Reid, Taplin, & Lorber, 1981), and more loneliness (e.g., Milner & Wimberley, 1980).

Finally, a recent study indicates that physical child abusers often deny any knowledge of how their child's injuries occurred. Rivara, Kamitsuka, and Quan (1988) report that 36% of abusers, compared to none of the comparison parents, had no explanation of their child's injury. Thus, although clinical lore indicates that abusers often attempt to mislead others about the causes of their child's injury, Rivara et al. indicated that abusers often simply deny knowledge of how the injury occurred.

BEHAVIORAL FACTORS

Alcohol and Drug Use

The general aggression literature (e.g., Taylor & Leonard, 1983) indicates that alcohol use, especially at high levels, is related to the likelihood and severity of aggression. Alcohol use has also been implicated in spouse abuse and sexual child abuse. Somewhat surprising, therefore, is the fact that few studies have investigated the association between substance abuse and physical child abuse. Most of the published literature consists of survey studies on the use of alcohol by physical child abusers. Collectively, studies suggest that alcohol consumption is modestly related to physical child abuse. For example, Gil (1971) reported that 13% of abusers were intoxicated at the time of the abuse. Black and Mayer (1980) studied alcoholic and opiate-addicted parents and reported that abuse was more common in the alcoholic group (27%) than in the opiate-addicted group (19%). Steele (1987) suggests that alcohol and drug abuse occurs more often in abusers who exhibit severe patterns of physical assault. Stasiewicz and Lisman (1989) studied at-risk and low-risk male college students and found that at-risk males consumed more alcohol following the presentation of stressful stimuli. However, Smith, Hanson, and Noble (1973) studied abusers and matched comparison subjects in England and failed to find a high rate of alcoholism in either group.

Existing studies have numerous methodological problems. Not only are the definitions of child abuse variable, but a variety of definitions are used to define alcohol consumption. Few distinctions are made among Alcohol Use (the occasional consumption of alcohol), Alcohol Abuse (a pattern of pathological use with impairment of social or occupational functioning), and Alcohol Dependence (a pattern of pathological use or impairment in functioning and tolerance or withdrawal problems). Because most studies do not use adequate comparison subjects, the results are difficult to interpret. That is, we do not know if the reported alcohol consumption is associated with physical child abuse or is simply representative of population base rates. Leonard and Jacob (1988) provide an excellent discussion of methodological problems in this research area. They indicate that the research problems are so extensive as to preclude any firm conclusions. Nevertheless, they conclude that if alcohol use or alcoholism is related to child abuse that it "will not account for major portions of variance in child abuse" (p. 387). Given the lack of data, it is possible that the conclusions of Leonard and Jacob (1988) are premature. For example, as Steel (1987) suggests, alcohol use may have a stronger association in cases involving severe physical assault.

Josephs and Steele (1990), in a general discussion of alcohol, indicate that the effects of alcohol may be mediated by its negative effects on cognitive processing abilities and its reduction of the subject's abilities to focus on any stimuli other than the most immediate stimuli. Further, the effect may be moderated by the degree of neuropsychological deficits, so that cognitive disruption is greater in parents with neuropsychological impairment. In cases where alcohol use and depression coexist, Bland and Orn (1986) indicate that the level of dysfunction is increased. Thus it appears that the relationship between alcohol, other contributing factors, and physical child abuse is complex. Finally, although Gelles and Cornell (1990) conclude that amphetamine use is related to physical child abuse, the degree to which the use of drugs (e.g., amphetamine, crack and cocaine) other than alcohol is associated with physical child abuse remains to be explicated.

Social Isolation

Early research indicated that abusers are isolated, lack family and peer support networks (e.g., Gil, 1970), retreat from society (e.g., Elmer, 1977), and are not involved in community activities (e.g., Young, 1964). Other research indicates that abusers do not trust others, perceive more social isolation, and are less likely to use community or mental health resources when available (e.g., Starr, 1988). These characteristics may be associated with reports that abusers, especially more serious abusers, are more likely to drop out of treatment programs (e.g., Wolfe, Edwards, Manion, & Koverola, 1988). Social support is important because it is believed to moderate the effects of stress and enhance self-esteem. Social support also increases the likelihood that a parent will develop additional parenting skills and will receive assistance in child care.

Parent-Child Interactions

Evidence indicates that abusive parents display highly aversive patterns of parent-child interactions. Burgess and Conger (1978) found that abusive mothers interacted less often and in a less supportive manner with their children and engaged in a higher proportion of negative interactions than nonabusive mothers. Reid et al. (1981) also found that abusive mothers engaged in more negative interactions with their children and suggested that the abusive families were characterized by an overall tendency to handle problems in a coercive, physically aggressive manner.

Bousha and Twentyman (1984) found that abusive mothers showed more verbal and nonverbal aggression and less positive verbal and nonverbal behavior with their children. Schindler and Arkowitz (1986) reported that abusive mothers were less active overall with their children. Kavanagh, Youngblade, Reid, and Fagot (1988) found that abusive parents spent less time in positive interactions (e.g., instructing, positive comments, joining in play, and talking to the child) and responded less often to the child's initiations of interactions. Egeland, Breitenbucher, and Rosenburg (1980) reported that abusers display less emotional responsiveness. Dietrich, Starr, and Kaplan (1980) indicated that abusers spend less time with their children and use less age-appropriate stimulation (auditory and tactile) strategies. Crittenden (1981) reported that abusers fail to modify behavior in relation to their child's behavior. Similarly, Aragona (1983) reported that at-risk parents were less responsive to temporal changes in their child's behavior.

Research is consistent in suggesting that abusive mothers have lower rates of interaction with their children and are more negative than positive in their interactions. Further, it may be the relative absence of positive interactions (e.g., cohesion, expressiveness) that more clearly sets members of abusive families apart from matched nonabusive controls, rather than observed differences in negative interactions (e.g., conflict) (Caliso & Milner, in press).

Parental Discipline Strategies

The majority of studies indicate that abusive mothers resort to physical punishment as a means of control more often than nonabusive comparison parents. Lahey et al. (1984) reported that abusive mothers used more physical negatives (hitting, grabbing, and pushing) than nonabusive mothers. Trickett and Kuczynski (1986) found that abusive parents reported using punitive strategies more often and reasoning strategies less frequently. Similarly,

Oldershaw, Walters, and Hall (1986) and Chilamkurti and Milner (1991) found that abusive and at-risk mothers relied heavily on power-assertion strategies (e.g., threats, disapproval, negative demands), whereas comparison mothers used predominantly positively oriented strategies (e.g., reasoning). Trickett and Susman (1988) reported that abusive parents used reasoning less often and used verbal prohibitions and removal of privileges more often. Abusive mothers also perceived punishment to be more effective than reasoning. The reverse pattern was found for nonabusive mothers. Finally, Kelly, Grace, and Elliot (1990) found that abusive parents viewed time-out, time-out with spanking, and spanking as more acceptable than comparison parents.

A remaining question is do physically abusive parents, relative to matched comparison parents, simply have fewer parenting skills or do they elect to use more severe discipline strategies because of other factors (e.g., attributions regarding the child's behavior, evaluation of wrongness of the child's transgressions, and expectations of the effectiveness of the discipline strategy)? A recent study investigated this question. Chilamkurti and Milner (1991) found that both high and low-risk mothers used a variety of disciplinary strategies, and both groups' choice of discipline technique was influenced by the nature of the child's transgression. However, high-risk mothers evaluated minor child transgressions as more wrong, and high-risk mothers used more power assertion (i.e., verbal and physical force) and less reasoning than low-risk mothers. High-risk mothers predicted greater compliance than low-risk mothers following use of power assertion. These findings suggest that high-risk mothers used power assertion more frequently because they evaluate minor transgressions as serious and perceive power assertion as effective. Finally, Chilamkurti and Milner (1991) found that the children of the high and low-risk parents were similar to their parents on most of the measures, suggesting that the children were already internalizing many of the parental perceptions and expectations.

In summary, recent research suggests that at-risk and abusive parents' more frequent reliance on power assertion (i.e., verbal and physical force) techniques may not reflect simply a skill deficit. Albeit their absolute level of knowledge may be modest, at-risk, abusive, and matched comparison parents appear similar in their awareness of different discipline techniques. The more frequent use of physically punitive techniques by at-risk and abusive parents appears to reflect their perceptions of the wrongness of child transgressions and their belief that power assertion is effective in gaining control of their children's behavior.

IMPLICATIONS FOR ASSESSMENT AND INTERVENTION

This literature review indicates that there is an array of physical child abuse perpetrator characteristics. This has been previously recognized, and several authors have attempted to develop physical child abuse perpetrator typologies (e.g., Merrill, 1962; Sloan & Meier, 1983) or behavioral clusters (Oldershaw, Walters, & Hall, 1989). However, no perpetrator typology has been adequately validated. Interest in abuser typologies appears to have been limited by the view of many family violence researchers that perpetrator-based typologies do not adequately include factors (e.g., social support) from other ecological levels and possible interactional patterns.

Nevertheless, the fact that there are a large number of perpetrator personality factors suggests that careful evaluation of each perpetrator is needed. Although the aforementioned characteristics are descriptive of abusers on a group basis, all physical child abusers will not have all of the characteristics. For example, although many abusers have a childhood history of abuse, some will not. Others will have neuropsychological problems and/or higher levels of physiological reactivity, whereas others will not. The types and degree of cognitive, affective, and behavioral problems will vary. Until more adequate models and empirically validated intervention approaches are available (see Kaufman & Rudy, 1991, for a recent review), the practitioner should carefully assess each perpetrator for individual characteristics and design interventions based on this assessment. Thus, if neurological problems exist, educational and behavioral approaches, shown to be effective with cognitively low functioning parents, might be employed. If autonomic reactivity to stressful stimuli and poor stress management skills are problems, then relaxation techniques and other stress management skills may be important considerations in treatment. Likewise, if cognitive problems exist in parents' perceptions, attributions, evaluations, and expectations of their child's behavior, then cognitive and cognitive/behavioral interventions should be considered. For isolated parents, home-based interventions and, in some cases, group interventions might be useful to decrease isolation and to build social skills. If parenting skill deficits or drug use are found, intervention should be tailored to include treatment of these problems. Further, research suggests that there are benefits from modifying interventions to include ethnic and cultural factors (Kaufman & Rudy, 1991).

In summary, the literature clearly indicates that multimodal interventions tailored to the subjects' deficits should be implemented rather than the provision of one type of program (e.g., parent education) that emphasizes

202

one or two factors for all abusers. Finally, the development of appropriate interventions should also consider factors from other ecological levels (e.g., family and community) as well as the use of possible buffering factors (e.g., social support).

REFERENCES

Altemeier, W. A., O'Conner, S., Vietz, P. M., Sandler, H. M., & Sherrod, K. B. (1982). Antecedents of child abuse. *Journal of Pediatrics, 100*, 823-829.

Ammerman, R. T. (in press). The role of the child in physical abuse: A reappraisal. *Violence and Victims.*

Anderson, S. C., & Lauderdale, M. L. (1982). Characteristics of abusive parents: A look at self-esteem. *Child Abuse & Neglect, 6*, 285-293.

Aragona, J. A. (1983). Physical child abuse: An interactional analysis (Doctoral dissertation, University of South Florida, 1983). *Dissertation Abstracts International, 44*, 1225B.

Azar, S. T. (1991). Models of child abuse: A metatheoretical analysis. *Criminal Justice and Behavior, 18*, 30-46.

Azar, S. T., Robinson, R. R., Hekimian, E., & Twentyman, C. T. (1984). Unrealistic expectations and problem-solving ability in maltreating and comparison mothers. *Journal of Consulting and Clinical Psychology, 52*, 687-691.

Baldwin, J. A., & Oliver, J. E. (1975). Epidemiology and family characteristics of severely abused children. *British Journal of Preventive Medicine, 29*, 205-211.

Bauer, W. D., & Twentyman, C. T. (1985). Abusing, neglectful, and comparison mothers' responses to child-related and non-child-related stressors. *Journal of Consulting and Clinical Psychology, 53*, 335-343.

Black, R., & Mayer, J. (1980). Parents with special problems: Alcoholism and opiate addiction. *Child Abuse & Neglect, 4*, 45-54.

Bland, R. C., & Orn, H. (1986). Psychiatric disorders, spouse abuse, and child abuse. *Acta Psychiatrica Belgica, 86*, 444-449.

Bousha, D. M., & Twentyman, C. T. (1984). Mother-child interactional style in abuse, neglect, and control groups: Naturalistic observations in the home. *Journal of Abnormal Psychology, 93*, 106-114.

Brown, G. W., & Harris, T. (1978). *Social origins of depression: A study of psychiatric disorder in women.* London: Tavistock.

Burgess, R. L., & Conger, R. D. (1978). Family interaction in abusive, neglectful, and normal families. *Child Development, 49*, 1163-1173.

Caliso, J. A., & Milner, J. S. (in press). Childhood history of abuse and child abuse screening. *Child Abuse & Neglect.*

Cappell, C., & Heiner, R. B. (1990). The intergenerational transmission of family aggression. *Journal of Family Violence, 5*, 135-152.

Casanova, G. M., Domanic, J., McCanne, T. R., & Milner, J. S. (in press). Physiological responses to non-child-related stressors in mothers at risk for child abuse. *Child Abuse & Neglect.*

Chilamkurti, C., & Milner, J. S. (1991, April). *Evaluations of child transgressions and disciplinary responses in high and low-risk mothers and their children.* Paper presented at the biennial meeting of the Society for Research in Child Development, Seattle, WA.

Cohen, M. I., Raphling, D. L., & Green, P. E. (1966). Psychological aspects of the maltreatment syndrome in childhood. *Journal of Pediatrics, 69*, 279-284.

Conger, R. D., Burgess, R., & Barrett, C. (1979). Child abuse related to life changes and perceptions of illness: Some preliminary findings. *Family Coordinator, 28*, 73-78.

Crittenden, P. M. (1981). Abusing, neglecting, problematic, and adequate dyads: Differentiating by patterns of interactions. *Merrill-Palmer Quarterly, 27*, 201-218.

Dietrick, K. N., Starr, R. H., & Kaplan, M. G. (1980). Maternal stimulation and care of abused infants. In T. M. Field, S. Goldberg, D. Stern, & A. M. Sostek (Eds.), *High-risk infants and children: Adult and peer interactions* (pp. 25-41). New York: Academic.

Disbrow, M. A., Doerr, H., & Caulfield, C. (1977). Measuring the components of parents' potential for child abuse and neglect. *Child Abuse & Neglect, 1*, 279-296.

Egeland, B., Breitenbucher, M., & Rosenberg, D. (1980). Prospective study of the significance of life stress in the etiology of child abuse. *Journal of Consulting and Clinical Psychology, 48*, 195-205.

Egeland, B., Jacobvitz, D., & Sroufe, L. A. (1988). Breaking the cycle of abuse. *Child Development, 59*, 1080-1088.

Elliott, F. A. (1988). Neurological factors. In V. B. Van Hasselt, R. L. Morrison, A. S. Bellack, & M. Hersen (Eds.), *Handbook of family violence* (pp. 359-382). New York: Plenum.

Ellis, R. H., & Milner, J. S. (1981). Child abuse and locus of control. *Psychological Reports, 48*, 507-510.

Elmer, E. (1977). *Fragile families, troubled children*. Pittsburgh, PA: University of Pittsburgh.

Evans, A. L. (1980). Personality characteristics and disciplinary attitudes of child-abusing mothers. *Child Abuse & Neglect, 4*, 179-187.

Fisher, S. H. (1958). Skeletal manifestations of parent-induced trauma in infants and children. *Southern Medical Journal, 51*, 956-960.

Friedrich, W. N., & Boriskin, J. A. (1976). The role of the child in abuse: A review of the literature. *American Journal of Orthopsychiatry, 46*, 580-590.

Friedrich, W. N., Tyler, J. D., & Clark, J. A. (1985). Personality and psychophysiological variables in abusive, neglectful, and low-income control mothers. *Journal of Nervous and Mental Disease, 170*, 577-587.

Friedrich, W. N., & Wheeler, K. K. (1982). The abusing parent revisited: A decade of psychological research. *Journal of Nervous and Mental Disease, 10*, 577-587.

Frodi, A. M., & Lamb, M. E. (1980). Child abusers' responses to infant smiles and cries. *Child Development, 51*, 238-241.

Gabinet, L. (1983). Child abuse treatment failures reveal need for redefinition of the problem. *Child Abuse & Neglect, 7*, 395-402.

Gaines, R., Sandgrund, A., Green, A. H., & Power, E. (1978). Etiological factors in child maltreatment: A multivariate study of abusing, neglecting, and normal mothers. *Journal of Abnormal Psychology, 87*, 531-540.

Geffner, R., Rosenbaum, A., & Hughes, H. (1988). Research issues concerning family violence. In V. B. Van Hasselt, R. L. Morrison, A. S. Bellack, & M. Hersen (Eds.), *Handbook of family violence* (pp. 457-481). New York: Plenum.

Gelles, R. J., & Cornell, C. P. (1990). *Intimate violence in families* (2nd ed.). Newbury Park, CA: Sage.

Gil, D. G. (1970). *Violence against children*. Cambridge, MA: Harvard University Press.

Gil, D. G. (1971). Violence against children. *Journal of Marriage and the Family, 33*, 637-698.

Hansen, D. J., Pallotta, G. M., Tishelman, A. C., Conaway, L. P., & MacMillan, V. M. (1989). Parental problem-solving skills and child behavior problems: A comparison of physically abusive, neglectful, clinic, and community families. *Journal of Family Violence, 4*, 353-368.

Helfer, R. E. (1987). The developmental basis of child abuse and neglect: An epidemiological approach. In R. E. Helfer & C. H. Kempe (Eds.), *The battered child* (4th ed., pp. 60-80). Chicago: University of Chicago Press.

Helfer, R. E., McKinney, J., & Kempe, R. (1976). Arresting or freezing the developmental process. In R. E. Helfer & C. H. Kempe (Eds.), *Child abuse and neglect: The family and the community* (pp. 134-163). Cambridge, MA: Ballinger.

Herrenkohl, E. C., Herrenkohl, R. C., Toedter, L., & Yanushefski, A. M. (1984). Parent-child interaction in abusive and non-abusive families. *Journal of the American Academy of Child Psychiatry, 23,* 641-648.

Josephs, R. A., & Steele, C. M. (1990). The two faces of alcohol myopia: Attentional mediation of psychological stress. *Journal of Abnormal Psychology, 99,* 115-126.

Kaufman, K. L., & Rudy, L. (1991). Future directions in the treatment of physical child abuse. *Criminal Justice and Behavior, 18,* 82-97.

Kavanagh, K. A., Youngblade, L., Reid, J. B., & Fagot, B. L. (1988). Interactions between children and abusive versus control parents. *Journal of Clinical Child Psychology, 17,* 137-142.

Kelly, M. L., Grace, N., & Elliot, S. N. (1990). Acceptability of positive and punitive discipline methods: Comparisons among abusive, potentially abusive, and nonabusive parents. *Child Abuse & Neglect, 14,* 219-226.

Kempe, C. H., Silverman, F. N., Steele, B. F., Droegemueller, W., & Silver, H. K. (1962). The battered child syndrome. *Journal of the American Medical Association, 181,* 105-112.

Kirkham, M. A., Schinke, S. P., Schilling, R. F., Meltzer, N. J., & Norelius, K. L. (1986). Cognitive-behavioral skills, social supports, and child abuse potential among mothers of handicapped children. *Journal of Family Violence, 1,* 235-245.

Knutson, J. F. (1978). Child abuse as an area of aggression research. *Journal of Pediatric Psychology, 3,* 20-27.

Kravitz, M. A., & Driscoll, J. M. (1983). Expectations for childhood development among child-abusing and nonabusing parents. *American Journal of Orthopsychiatry, 53,* 336-344.

Lahey, B. B., Conger, R. D., Atkeson, B. M., & Treiber, F. A. (1984). Parenting behavior and emotional status of physically abusive mothers. *Journal of Consulting and Clinical Psychology, 52,* 1062-1071.

Larrance, D. T., & Twentyman, C. T. (1983). Maternal attributions and child abuse. *Journal of Abnormal Psychology, 92,* 449-457.

Lefcourt, H. M. (1976). *Locus of control.* New York: Wiley.

Leonard, K. E., & Jacob, T. (1988). Alcohol, alcoholism, and family violence. In V. B. Van Hasselt, R. L. Morrison, A. S. Bellack, & M. Hersen (Eds.), *Handbook of family violence* (pp. 383-406). New York: Plenum.

Mash, E. J., Johnston, C., & Kovitz, K. (1983). A comparison of the mother-child interactions of physically abused and nonabused children during play and task situations. *Journal of Clinical Child Psychology, 12,* 337-346.

Mash, E. J., & Wolfe, D. A. (1991). Methodological issues in research on physical child abuse. *Criminal Justice and Behavior, 18,* 8-29.

McCanne, T. R., & Milner, J. S. (1991). Physiological reactivity of physically abusive and at-risk subjects to child-related stimuli. In J. S. Milner (Ed.), *Neuropsychology of aggression.* (pp. 147-166). Norwell, MA: Kluwer.

McCubbin, H. I., Cauble, A. E., & Patterson, J. M. (1982). *Family stress, coping, and social support.* Springfield, IL: Charles C. Thomas.

Mee, J. (1983). *The relationship between stress and the potential for child abuse.* Unpublished thesis, Macquarie University, Australia.

Merrill, E. J. (1962). Physical abuse of children: An agency study. In V. DeFrancis (Ed.), *Protecting the battered child*. Denver, CO: American Humane Association.

Milner, J. S. (1986). *The Child Abuse Potential Inventory: Manual* (2nd ed.). Webster, NC: Psytec.

Milner, J. S. (1988). An ego-strength scale for the Child Abuse Potential Inventory. *Journal of Family Violence, 3*, 151-162.

Milner, J. S., Charlesworth, J. R., Gold, R. G., Gold, S. R., & Friesen, M. R. (1988). Convergent validity of the Child Abuse Potential Inventory. *Journal of Clinical Psychology, 44*, 281-285.

Milner, J. S., & McCanne, T. R. (1991). Neuropsychological correlates of physical child abuse. In J. S. Milner (Ed.), *Neuropsychology of aggression* (pp. 131-146). Norwell, MA: Kluwer.

Milner, J. S., & Robertson, K. R. (1990). Comparison of physical child abusers, intrafamilial sexual child abusers, and child neglecters. *Journal of Inerpersonal Violence, 5*, 37-48.

Milner, J. S., Robertson, K. R., & Rogers, D. L. (1990). Childhood history of abuse and adult child abuse potential. *Journal of Family Violence, 5*, 15-34.

Milner, J. S., & Wimberley, R. C. (1980). Prediction and explanation of child abuse. *Journal of Clinical Psychology, 36*, 875-884.

Oldershaw, L., Walters, G. C., & Hall, D. K. (1986). Control strategies and noncompliance in abusive mother-child dyads: An observational study. *Child Development, 57*, 722-732.

Oldershaw, L., Walters, G. C., & Hall, D. K. (1989). A behavioral approach to the classification of different types of physically abusive mothers. *Merrill-Palmer Quarterly, 35*, 255-279.

Paulson, M. J., Afifi, A. A., Thomason, M. L., & Chaleff, A. (1974). The MMPI: A descriptive measure of psychopathology in abusive parents. *Journal of Clinical Psychology, 30*, 387-390.

Perry, M. A., Wells, E. A., & Doran, L. D. (1983). Parent characteristics in abusing and nonabusing families. *Journal of Clinical Child Psychology, 12*, 329-336.

Phares, E. J. (1976). *Locus of control in personality*. Morristown, NJ: General Learning Press.

Plotkin, R., Azar, S., Twentyman, C., & Perri, M. (1981). A critical evaluation of the research methodology employed in the investigation of causative factors of child abuse and neglect. *Child Abuse & Neglect, 5*, 449-455.

Pollock, C., & Steele, B. (1972). A therapeutic approach to the parents. In C. H. Kempe & R. E. Helfer (Eds.), *Helping the battered child and his family* (pp. 3-21). Philadelphia: Lippincot.

Pruitt, D. L. (1983). A predictive model of child abuse: A preliminary investigation (Doctoral dissertation, Virginia Commonwealth University, 1983). *Dissertation Abstracts International, 44*, 3206B.

Pruitt, D. L., & Erickson, M. T. (1985). The Child Abuse Potential Inventory: A study of concurrent validity. *Journal of Clinical Psychology, 41*, 104-111.

Reid, J. B., Kavanagh, K., & Baldwin, D. V. (1987). Abusive parents' perceptions of child problem behaviors: An example of parental bias. *Journal of Abnormal Child Psychology, 15*, 457-466.

Reid, J. B., Taplin, P. S., & Lorber, R. (1981). A social interactional approach to the treatment of abusive families. In R. B. Stuart (Ed.), *Violent behavior: Social learning approaches to prediction, management, and treatment* (pp. 83-101). New York: Brunner/Mazel.

Rivara, F. P., Kamitsuka, M. D., & Quan, L. (1988). Injuries to children younger than 1 year of age. *Pediatrics, 81*, 93-97.

Rosen, B. (1978). Self-concept disturbance among mothers who abuse their children. *Psychological Reports, 43*, 323-326.

Rosenberg, M., & Repucci, N. (1983). Abusive mothers: Perceptions of their own children's behavior. *Journal of Consulting and Clinical Psychology, 51*, 674-682.

Schilling, R., Schinke, S., Blythe, B., & Barth, R. (1982). Child maltreatment and mentally retarded parents. Is there a relationship? *Mental Retardation, 20*, 201-209.

Schindler, F., & Arkowitz, H. (1986). The assessment of mother-child interactions in physically abusive and nonabusive families. *Journal of Family Violence, 1,* 247-257.

Seagull, E., & Scheurer, S. (1986). Neglected and abused children of mentally retarded parents. *Child Abuse & Neglect, 10,* 493-500.

Shavelson, R. J., Hubner, J. J., & Stanton, G. C. (1976). Self-concept: Validation of construct interpretations. *Review of Educational Research, 46,* 407-441.

Simpson, K. (1967). The battered baby problem. *Royal Society of Health Journal, 87,* 168-170.

Sloan, M. P., & Meier, J. H. (1983). Typology for parents of abused children. *Child Abuse & Neglect, 7,* 443-450.

Smith, S. M., Hanson, R., & Noble, S. (1973). Parents of battered babies: A controlled study. *British Medical Journal, 4,* 388-391.

Spinetta, J. J., & Rigler, D. (1972). The child abusing parent: A psychological review. *Psychological Bulletin, 77,* 296-394.

Starr, R. H., Jr. (1988). Physical Abuse of Children. In V. B. Van Hasselt, R. L. Morrison, A. S. Bellack, & M. Hersen (Eds.). *Handbook of family violence* (pp. 119-155). New York: Plenum.

Stasiewicz, P. R., & Lisman, S. A. (1989). Effects of infant cries on alcohol consumption in college males at risk for child abuse. *Child Abuse & Neglect, 14,* 313-323.

Steele, B. F. (1987). Psychodynamic factors in child abuse. In R. E. Helfer & C. H. Kempe (Eds.), *The battered child* (4th ed., pp. 81-114). Chicago: University of Chicago Press.

Steele, B. F., & Pollock, C. B. (1974). A psychiatric study of parents who abuse infants and small children. In R. E. Helfer & C. H. Kempe (Eds.), *The battered child* (2nd ed., pp. 92-139). Chicago: University of Chicago Press.

Straus, M. A. (1980). Stress and child abuse. In C. H. Kempe, & R. E. Helfer (Eds.), *The battered child* (3rd ed., pp. 86-103). Chicago: University of Chicago Press.

Straus, M. A., Gelles, R. J., & Steinmetz, S. K. (1980). *Behind closed doors.* New York: Doubleday.

Stringer, S. A., & LaGreca, A. M. (1985). Child abuse potential. *Journal of Abnormal Child Psychology, 13,* 217-226.

Taylor, S., & Leonard, K. (1983). Alcohol and human physical aggression. In R. Geen & E. Donnerstein (Eds.), *Aggression: Theoretical and empirical reviews.* New York: Academic.

Trickett, P. K., & Kuczynski, L. (1986). Children's misbehaviors and parental discipline strategies in abusive and nonabusive families. *Developmental Psychology, 22,* 115-123.

Trickett, P. K., & Susman, E. J. (1988). Parental perceptions of child-rearing practices in physically abusive and nonabusive families. *Developmental Psychology, 24,* 270-276.

Twentyman, C. T., & Plotkin, R. C. (1982). Unrealistic expectations of parents who maltreat their children: An educational deficit pertaining to child development. *Journal of Clinical Psychology, 38,* 497-503.

Twentyman, C. T., Rohrbeck, C. A., & Amish, P. L. (1984). A cognitive-behavioral approach to child abuse: Implications for treatment. In S. Saunders, A. M. Anderson, C. A. Hart, & G. M. Rubenstein (Eds.), *Violent individuals and families: A handbook for practitioners* (pp. 87-111). Springfield, IL: Charles C. Thomas.

Tymchuk, A., & Andron, L. (1990). Mothers with mental retardation who do or do not abuse and neglect their children. *Child Abuse & Neglect, 14,* 313-323.

Tymchuk, A. Andron, L., & Unger, O. (1987). Parents with mental handicaps and adequate child care: A review. *Mental Handicap, 15,* 49-54.

Walker, C. E., Bonner, B. L., & Kaufman, K. L. (1988). *The physically and sexually abused child: Evaluation and treatment.* New York: Pergamon.

Wauchope, B., & Straus, M. (1990). Age, gender and class differences in physical punishment and physical abuse of American children. In M. Straus & R. J. Gelles (Eds.), *Physical violence in American families: Risk factors and adaptations in 8,145 families* (pp. 133-148). New Brunswick, NJ: Transaction.

Widom, C. S. (1989). Does violence beget violence? A critical examination of the literature. *Psychological Bulletin, 106*, 3-28.

Wolfe, D. A. (1987). *Child abuse: Implications for child development and psychopathology.* Newbury Park, CA: Sage.

Wolfe, D. A., Edwards, B., Manion, I., & Koverola, C. (1988). Early interventions for parents at risk of child abuse and neglect: A preliminary investigation. *Journal of Consulting and Clinical Psychology, 56*, 40-47.

Wolfe, D. A., Fairbanks, J. A., Kelly, J. A., & Bradlyn, A. S. (1983). Child abusive parents' physiological responses to stressful and non-stressful behavior in children. *Behavioral Assessment, 5*, 363-371.

Wolfe, D. A., & Mosk, M. D. (1983). Behavioral comparisons of children from abusive and distressed families. *Journal of Consulting and Clinical Psychology, 51*, 702-708.

Wood-Shuman, S., & Cone, J. D. (1986). Differences in abusive, at-risk for abuse, and control mothers' descriptions of normal child behavior. *Child Abuse & Neglect, 10*, 397-405.

Young, L. (1964). *Wednesday's children: A study of child abuse and neglect.* New York: McGraw-Hill.

Joel S. Milner is a professor of psychology and coordinator of the Family Violence Research Program at Northern Illinois University. He is author of the Child Abuse Potential Inventory *and has written a number of research articles and book chapters about family violence. Much of his research has investigated physical and sexual child abuse perpetrator characteristics.*

Chinni Chilamkurti received her Ph.D. in clinical psychology from Northern Illinois University in 1990. Her doctoral research focused on at-risk mothers' and their children's perceptions and evaluations of child transgressions and disciplinary responses. She is currently in private practice, specializing in child, adolescent, and family therapy.

208

INCEST: FAMILY DYSFUNCTION
OR SEXUAL PREFERENCE?

Janet L. Menard and Genevieve M. Johnson

ABSTRACT

Traditionally, incest has been conceptualized as something very different from pedophilia. That is, the etiology of incest is believed to be related to family dynamics, while the etiology of pedophilia is believed to be related to personal sexual preference. Since the outward manifestations of both sexual offenses are identical (i.e., child molestation), this dichotomization of etiological assumptions seems questionable. In the present paper, research which establishes, at least for some offenders, that incest may indeed be the consequence of sexual preference, as opposed to dysfunctional family interactions, is reviewed. Thus, from this point of view, classification systems and therapeutic interventions require reconsideration.

The therapeutic treatment of men who sexually molest children is complicated by the heterogeneous nature of child molesters as a group. As Quinsey (1983) points out, differences among child molesters "must be taken into account both in assessment for treatment or disposition and in the evaluation of treatment programs" (p. 29). Equally, differentiating *types* of child molesters is vital for predicting recidivism (Barbaree & Marshall, 1988; Earls & Quinsey, 1985). Unfortunately, while it is important to establish and understand differences between offenders, such distinctions have traditionally been based on a limited and empirically weak set of therapeutic concepts (Conte, 1985).

This paper identifies two interrelated systems typically employed to classify child molesters: incest versus pedophile and fixated versus regressed. Discussion centers on the popular assumption that incest is generally a response to dysfunctional family dynamics, as opposed to a deviant sexual need. Given the lack of empirical validation of this assumption, however, it is not at all clear that dysfunctional family intractions are necessarily etiological of incest offenses. In fact, recent changes to the American Psychiatric Association's (1987) *Diagnostic and Statistical Manual of Mental Disorders* (DSM-III-R) suggest that

Reprint requests to Genevieve M. Johnson, Ph.D., Department of Educational Psychology, University of Alberta, Edmonton, Alberta, Canada T6G 2G5.

Family Therapy, Volume 19, Number 2, 1992
Libra Publishers, Inc., 3089C Clairemont Dr., Suite 383, San Diego, CA 92117

traditional notions of incest and pedophilia are in the process of reconceptualization.

A distinction often made between types of child molesters revolves around the family relationships of the offender and the victim (Conte, 1985). That is, incest offenders are related to their victims by blood or marriage, while pedophilic offenders are generally thought to abuse children other than their own (Marshall, 1983). However, not all child molesters fit into these two apparently mutually exclusive categories. For example, individuals who sexually molest children that are not related to them would not be classified as pedophiles if they did not have a relatively enduring sexual arousal for children (Barnard, Fuller, Robbins, & Shaw, 1989).

A more inclusive typology was developed by Groth (1978), who described two types of child molesters, the fixated and the regressed. The fixated offender has a primary sexual orientation toward children that began in adolescence and has persisted throughout his life, regardless of other sexual experiences. According to Groth, Hobson, and Gary (1982), fixated offenders have few or no sexual encounters with adults and commit premeditated offenses that are typically directed toward male victims. Precipitating stress is not seen as a factor in the fixated offender's sexual behavior. In contrast to the fixated offender, the regressed offender sexually prefers adults, with sexual interest in children having a relatively late onset (i.e., adulthood). Typically, the regressed offender targets female victims. For regressed offenders, the child constitutes a substitute for the sexually preferred adult. Offenses may be episodic depending on the presence of life stressors which, in the regressed case, are thought to be a precipitating factor. It is generally assumed that pedophiles are fixated offenders, while incest offenders fit into the regressed category (Lang, Pugh, & Langevin, 1988; Murphy, Haynes, Stalgaitis, & Flanagan, 1986).

In the case of incest, characteristics of the regressed offender are typically conceptualized in terms of family dynamics. For example, Quinsey (1977) hypothesized that "incestuous child molesters are a special case of situational [i.e., regressed] offenders whose offenses are related to family dynamics and opportunism rather than inappropriate

116

sexual preferences" (p. 207). Within the family dynamics approach, "incest is seen as a symptom of a family system that had become dysfunctional before the incest began" (Haugaard, 1988, p. 224). deChesnay (1985) provides a more specific example of family dysfunction apparently related to incest. She claims that "mother-daughter role reversal clearly places a family at risk for incest" (p. 399). Such views illustrate the assumption that the incest offender's sexual behavior is not a product of deviant sexual preference, but rather, it is a personal response to a dysfunctional family system. This position coincides with Groth's (1978) assertion that regressed offenders sexually prefer adults and that their sexual offenses represent a mechanism for coping with stress.

However, it has been suggested that Groth's (1978) typology is based on clinical impressions that have not been empirically established or validated (Barnard et al., 1989; Murphy et al., 1986). Additionally, incestuous families do not consistently possess obvious and distinct characteristics. For example, Conte (1985) failed to find empirical support for the contention and mother-daughter role reversal is a salient feature of families in which incest occurs or has occurred. Herman and Hirschman (1981) did find a high rate of mother-daughter role reversal and thus suggested that "rehabilitation of incestuous families should place major emphasis on strengthening the role of the mother" (p. 969). Curiously, this suggestion was made despite the finding that "as the daughter advanced into adolescence . . . the father often moved on to the younger sisters" (p. 969). Although this may have occurred for any number of reasons, the sexual preference of the father was not considered a possible factor, perhaps because it had been decided a priori that sexual motivation does not exist in cases of incest. However, an equally reasonable explanation of the father's sexual gravitation toward his younger daughters would be that as the eldest daughter matured, she no longer satisfied her father's sexual preference.

Phelan (1986) found that 80% of the biological fathers he studied abused more than one daughter. The implications of multiple-daughter abuse were further investigated by Fruend, Watson, Rienze and Blanchard (1988) who concluded that "incest offenders who sexually offended against more than one female child in their own biological or adopted family had a much higher percentage of true pedophilia than did incest offenders against only one female child in the family" (cited in Stermac & Hucker, 1988, p. 259). Although this investigation was not available for detailed examination, two further points require clarification. First, the study indicates the need to investigate possible differences within the incest group itself. If practitioners believe that incest offenders constitute a somewhat homogeneous group (i.e., that

117

they do not have a sexual preference for children), then important differences within the group may be overlooked. As Marshall (1983) claims, when classifications based on the choice of sexual object (i.e., familial vs. nonfamilial victims) "are used alone, they can obscure important relationships, and at times force an uncomfortably exclusive categorization" (p. 3). Second, although multiple-daughter offenders were shown to have phallometric measures identical to a group of pedophilic offenders, this assessment technique is not without limitations.

PHALLOMETRIC MEASURES OF INCEST OFFENDERS

The use of penile plethysmography as an objective measure of sexual arousal preference can be problematic. First, some individuals, presumably due to anxiety, do not respond to either appropriate or nonappropriate stimuli. Second, some individuals are able to conceal their sexual preferences by preventing arousal to inappropriate stimuli or by faking arousal to appropriate stimuli (Barnard et al., 1989). However, despite these limitations, some experts feel that "when erectile measures demonstrate a clear preference for deviant acts that match the offender's history, we can feel assured that deviant arousal is a problem, whether or not he admits the offense" (Marshall, Abel, & Quinsey, 1983, p. 47).

Studies using penile plethysmography have yielded results which suggest that at least some incest offenders have deviant arousal patterns. Abel, Becker, Murphy, and Flanagan (1981), for example, found no differences between incest offenders and pedophiles in erectile responses to audiotapes depicting sexual activity with children. In addition, the two groups of child molesters responded more to the stimuli than did a group of sex offenders that had not molested children. Quinsey, Chaplin, and Carrigan (1979) measured penile responses to slides depicting females ranging from age 5 years to adulthood. In this study, two groups of pedophiles were matched to either a group of daughter-incest offenders or a group of nondaughter (i.e., sister, cousins, niece) incest offenders. While the daughter-incest offenders "showed more appropriate age preferences than their matched controls" (p. 564), this was not the case with the incest offenders that chose sisters, cousins or nieces as victims. Murphy and colleagues (1986) used both slides and audiotapes in their study and obtained results which supported both of the above findings. Although pedophiles and incest offenders responded similarly to the audiotapes, the pedophiles responded more to slides depicting children than to slides depicting adults, while the

118

incest offenders showed an opposite pattern. These researchers point out, however, that "even with the slide stimuli, 40% of the incest cases had sexual responding to child stimuli which was equal to or greater than sexual responding to adult stimuli" (p. 352). They further suggest that "regardless of the patient's relationship to the victim, from a clinical standpoint, any subject who shows significant deviant sexual arousal probably needs treatment to reduce or control that arousal pattern regardless of whether family conflict is present or not" (p. 352).

Unfortunately, as Conte (1985) suggests, "there is a widespread notion that incest . . . is the sexual expression of nonsexual needs, needs which then often become the focus of treatment by many incest-oriented therapists" (p. 348). Incest, however, may occur in different families for very different reasons, and thus treatment must reflect the specific needs of each family. For example, Haugaard (1988) states that although belief in the "family systems perspective" may result in "appropriate interventions to some perpetrators and families . . . it may not provide needed treatment to a father with a true sexual deviance" (p. 229). Stermac and Hucker (1988) also point out that although pedophilic incest offenders have unique treatment needs, these needs have traditionally been ignored. This may be the consequence of the perception that the percentage of pedophilic incest offenders is too small to be of clinical concern.

It would be foolish to suggest that if the father's offenses were primarily motivated by sexual preferences, then the family unit is not in need of therapy. Even in cases where disclosure results in the dissolution of the *marriage*, the mother and her children may require support to deal with the emotional repercussions of the incest and to strengthen the remaining family unit. However, if the family expresses the desire to remain intact, family therapy alone may not be sufficient to address the offender's deviant sexual arousal. For example, family therapy that focuses on strengthening the role of the mother may provide little long-term help to a father who is sexually aroused by children, especially if he subsequently joins a new family unit.

Conte (1985) suggests that ignoring sexual aspects of incest by treating it as a *family problem* may encourage *continued denial* on the part of the offender. Conte is referring to instances where the topic of the abuse was specifically avoided in therapy "because the [offender's] ego was too fragile to handle the topic" (p. 348). However, even if the abuse is discussed, denial may be a problem when a family dynamics

119

approach is inappropriately used with pedophilic incest offenders. For example, an offender may readily agree with, and actually believe, the suggestion that he offends in response to the emotional distance between himself and his spouse, as this belief allows him to avoid the possibly painful disclosure that he is sexually attracted to children.

According to Langevin and Lang (1985), "a critical factor in all sexual anomalies is the reluctance of clients to admit their sexual preferences" (p. 405). However, they suggest that "in order to help the pedophile to want to change his behavior," initial therapy should include efforts for "moving the offender to admit his sexual preferences and . . . the actual extent of his sexual involvement with children" (p. 411). Given the typical resistance encountered when offenders are actively encouraged to acknowledge their sexual preferences, it seems likely that when the focus of therapy is on family dynamics, deviant sexual preferences will not be revealed. In other words, if it is assumed that deviant preferences do not exist in cases of incest, then information that contradicts this assumption is unlikely to surface. As Search (1988) suggests, "we really don't know . . . , because we haven't been asking the right question, how many incest offenders have a hobby of pedophilia?" (p. 61).

We are in no way suggesting that traditional classification systems should be discarded. On the contrary, "typologies can be clinically useful if clinicians remember that 'pure types' rarely, if ever, are found in practice" (Barnard et al., 1989, p. 37). Certainly an offender who has, since adolescence, had a persistent and exclusive sexual preference for children will have different treatment needs than an offender who engages in sexual activity with both adults and children. However, it does not necessarily follow that incest offenders, as a group, are not primarily motivated by sexual needs. Similarly, simply because an offender sexually abuses his own child, it does not necessarily follow that his sexual interest in children has not existed since adolescence.

Recent diagnostic criteria amendments for pedophilia reflect current reconceptualizations of the child molester. In the American Psychiatric Association's 1980 edition of the *Diagnostic and Statistical Manual of Mental Disorders* (DSM-III), a diagnosis of pedophilia required the act or fantasy of engaging in sexual activity with a prepubertal child as a repeatedly preferred or exclusive method of achieving sexual excitement. The American Psychiatric Association's (1987) most recent revision of its *Diagnostic and Statistical Manual of Mental Disorders* (DSM-III-R), however, has dropped the requirement that a client's sexual interest in children has to be preferred to other forms of sexual activity. Currently, diagnosis requires recurrent, intense, sexual urges and sex-

120

ually arousing fantasies, of at last six months' duration, involving sexual activity with a prepubescent child and that the person has acted on the urges, or is markedly distressed by them.

Revised criteria also include efforts to distinguish between types of offenders. The clinician must specify the gender of the offender's victim(s), if the offense is limited to incest and if the offender has an exclusive or nonexclusive sexual arousal toward children. A pertinent strength of the current DSM-III-R classification system is that it "attempts to classify disorders that people may be experiencing rather than the people themselves" (Barnard et al., 1989, p. 58). The benefits of this type of system can be contrasted with the problems created by the traditional manner in which incest offenders have been conceptualized—that is, their behavior has been used as a sign from which to make inferences. As the research suggests, however, these inferences may not be applicable to all incest offenders.

REFERENCES

Abel, G. G., Becker, J. V., Murphy, W. D., & Flanagan, B. (1981). Identifying dangerous child molesters. In R. B. Stuart (Ed.), *Violent behavior: Social learning approaches to prediction, management, and treatment* (pp. 116–137). New York: Brunner/Mazel.

American Psychiatric Association. (1980). *Diagnostic and statistical manual of mental disorders, third edition* (DSM-III). Washington, DC: American Psychiatric Association.

American Psychiatric Association. (1987). *Diagnostic and statistical manual of mental disorders, third edition, revised* (DSM-III-R). Washington, DC: American Psychiatric Association.

Barbaree, H. E., & Marshall, W. L. (1988). Deviant sexual arousal, offense history, and demographic variables as predictors of reoffense among child molesters. *Behavioral Sciences and the Law, 6,* 267–280.

Barnard, G. W., Fuller, A. K., Robbins, L., & Shaw, T. (1989). *The child molester.* New York: Brunner/Mazel.

Conte, J. R. (1985). Clinical dimensions of adult sexual abuse of children. *Behavioral Sciences and the Law, 3,* 341–354.

deChesnay, M. (1985). Father-daughter incest: An overview. *Behavioral Sciences and the Law, 3,* 391–402.

Earls, C. M., & Quinsey, V. L. (1985). What is to be done? Future research on the assessment and behavioral treatment of sex offenders. *Behavioral Sciences and the Law, 3,* 377–390.

Groth, A. N. (1978). Patterns of sexual assault against children and adolescents. In A. W. Burgess, A. N. Groth, L. L. Holmstrom, & S. M. Sgroi (Eds.), *Sexual assault of children and adolescents.* Lexington, MA: Lexington.

Groth, A. N., Hobson, W. F., & Gary, T. S. (1982). The child molester: Clinical observations. In J. Conte & D. A. Shore (Eds.), *Social work and child sexual abuse* (pp. 129–144). New York: Haworth.

121

Haugaard, J. J. (1988). The use of theories about the etiology of incest as guidelines for legal and therapeutic interventions. *Behavioral Sciences and the Law, 6,* 221–238.

Herman, F., & Hirschman, L. (1981). Families at risk for father-daughter incest. *American Journal of Psychiatry, 138,* 967–970.

Lang, R. A., Pugh, G. M., & Langevin, R. (1988). Treatment of incest offenders: A pilot study. *Behavioral Sciences and the Law, 6,* 239–255.

Langevin, R., & Lang, R. A. (1985). Psychological treatment of pedophiles. *Behavioral Sciences and the Law, 3,* 403–419.

Marshall, W. L. (1983). The classification of sexual aggressives and their associated demographic, social, developmental and psychological features. In S. N. Verdun-Jones & A. A. Keltner (Eds.), *Sexual aggression and the law* (pp. 1–13). Vancouver, Canada: Simon Fraser University Criminology Research Center.

Marshall, W. L., Abel, G. G., & Quinsey, V. L. (1983). The assessment and treatment of sexual offenders. In S. N. Verdun-Jones & A. A. Keltner (Eds.), *Sexual aggression and the law* (pp. 41–52). Vancouver, Canada: Simon Fraser University Criminology Research Center.

Murphy, W. D., Haynes, M. R., Stalgaitis, S. J., & Flanagan, B. (1986). Differential sexual responding among four groups of sexual offenders against children. *Journal of Psychopathology and Behavioral Assessment, 8,* 339–353.

Phelan, P. (1986). The process of incest: Biologic father and stepfather families. *Child Abuse and Neglect, 10,* 531–539.

Quinsey, V. L. (1977). The assessment and treatment of child molesters: A review. *Canadian Psychological Review, 18,* 204–220.

Quinsey, V. L. (1983). Prediction of recidivism and the evaluation of treatment programs for sex offenders. In S. N. Verdun-Jones & A. A. Keltner (Eds.), *Sexual aggression and the law* (pp. 27–40). Vancouver, Canada: Simon Fraser University Criminology Research Center.

Quinsey, V. L., Chaplin, T. C., & Carrigan, W. F. (1979). Sexual preferences among incestuous and nonincestuous child molesters. *Behavior Therapy, 10,* 562–565.

Search, G. (1988). *The last taboo: Sexual abuse of children.* New York: Penguin.

Stermac, L., & Hucker, S. (1988). Combining cognitive-behavioral therapy and pharmacotherapy in the treatment of pedophilic incest offenders. *Behavioral Sciences and the Law, 6,* 257–266.

122

Causes of Child Abuse and Neglect*

PHILIP G. NEY M.D.[1], TAK FUNG Ph.D.[2], ADELE ROSE WICKETT B.S.N.[3]

This paper is a study of child abuse and neglect from the perspective of the child. Generally, the mistreatment of children was associated with "poor care" from parents, attributed mainly to immaturity, marital problems, alcohol abuse, unemployment, drug abuse and lack of money. Differences in attribution are noted between males and females, and some differences are noted by the age of the child. When factors other than the causes given by the children were taken into account, mistreatment was significantly related to family break-up, as well as long-term disinterest and lack of affection from the parents. When the children were asked for their "worst experience in life," the most common responses were "abuse" "family break-up," and for the juvenile offenders "getting charged with a crime".

There have been many studies of the possible causes of child abuse and neglect, but very few that have actually examined them from a child's point of view. This study quantifies and analyzes factors which, according to children who were victims, explain early mistreatment. Children may have a more accurate view of what is going on in their own mind than adults who try to perceive it. Many articles record expressions of pain and grief that are more in accord with adults' memories of their own mistreatment. Clinical interviews and research interviews are often structured in such a way that the child must respond to the expectations imposed upon him by the adult.

In this study we examine the correlations between the children's estimate of their abuse and neglect and the causes the child feels are important. We have identified five types of mistreatment: physical abuse, physical neglect, verbal abuse, emotional neglect and sexual abuse. We asked respondents to estimate the frequency and severity of the abuse they suffered in each category.

Literature Review

Although there is no absolute agreement on the basic causes of child abuse and neglect, there is a reasonable

Manuscript received December 1991, revised June 1992.
[1]Clinical Professor, Department of Family Practice, Faculty of Medicine, University of British Columbia, Vancouver, B.C.
[2]Biostatistician, University of Calgary, Calgary, Alberta.
[3]Research Assistant
Address reprint requests to: Dr. Philip G. Ney, Box 24003, 4440 West, Saanich Rd., Victoria, B.C. V8Z 7E7

Can. J. Psychiatry Vol. 37, August 1992

concensus on the etiological categories of child mistreatment. These include parental psychopathy, parents' childhood experiences of abuse and neglect, substance abuse, privation, marital turmoil, lack of parenting skills, poor bonding, ignorance of the child's needs and unrealistic expectations of the child. In previous studies we found strong correlations between the mistreatment of children and spousal abuse (1), the abuse and neglect of parents as children (2), unresolved losses, and abnormal responses to the children crying (3).

A search of the recent literature shows far more research and clinical investigation into the apparent causes of childhood injuries than into considerations of root causes, and little from the child's perspective. There are some notable exceptions. Crittenden (4) observed the behaviour of abusive mothers and their children, and found that: 1. siblings of abused children learned their mother's parenting style and 2. some abused children develop behaviours that help maintain their mother's maltreating responses (5). Azar and her colleagues (6) found that parents most likely to be maladapted parents have unrealistic expectations of their children. Parents with unrealistic expectations blame their children more frequently, and use more punishment and less explanation (7).

There are many explanations of child abuse and neglect which are based on psychopathology. These include identification with the aggressor (8), wounding and neglecting the inner child (9), and the parents' desire for medical attention which is achieved by inducing illness in the child (10). Mothers' mental illnesses have been singled out as causative factors for various social and mental disorders in their children (11). As was previously suggested by Ney (12) parents who mistreat children may be attempting to understand the conflicts engendered as a result of abuse they suffered as children, by recreating similar experiences.

We wondered if children could detect the reasons they were abused or neglected. There appeared to be few studies of the children's explanations of their own mistreatment. However, one study found that college students are more likely to blame their behaviours on their mother's emotional problems, shyness, and dependency than they are to blame their father's abusing and alcoholism (13).

Method

As part of an ongoing study of child abuse and neglect, we collected data from 167 children and adolescents who completed the Child Experience questionnaire. These children were from two psychiatric units for children and adolescents (n = 107), a young offender's centre (n = 23), a private

Table I

Extent of Mistreatment Correlated with Quality of Parental Care

	Extent of Mistreatment*				
	Physical Abuse n = 106	Physical Neglect n = 67	Verbal Abuse n = 100	Emotional Neglect n = 91	Sexual Abuse n = 34
Poor care by mother	0.33 (p = 0.001)	0.34 (p = 0.006)	0.26 (p = 0.009)	0.20 (p = 0.057)	-0.10 (p = 0.568)
Poor care by father	0.31 (p = 0.002)	0.30 (p = 0.019)	0.20 (p = 0.052)	0.21 (p = 0.043)	0.18 (p = 0.299)

*Expressed as Pearson correlation coefficients

psychiatric practice (n = 11) and a local high school (n = 26). These numbers represent over 85% of the patients and young offenders who were asked to participate. The computing services of the University of Calgary analyzed the data.

The Child Experience Questionnaire, a device that has been used for a number of years and appears to have good reliability and validity, was administered to our sample (14). To make it easier for the children and adolescents, we used a number of visual analog scales with extreme responses on either end. The respondents were asked to make a mark on the lines to estimate of the degree abuse or neglect they suffered. There were scales for frequency, severity, abnormality, whose fault it was and how damaging it was to their lives. Other questions determined the age of onset, duration and specific types of abuse. We asked how well they were looked after, their worst experiences in life, what their parents expected them to become and the reasons for each type of mistreatment.

Subjects were asked to check one or more of the eight possible causes of their maltreatment, or to suggest other reasons for it. The eight choices were derived from a review of the literature on the etiology of child abuse and neglect. The choices were: alcohol abuse, drug abuse, immature parents, professional interference, too many children, not enough money, unemployment and marital problems. While there were a few other reasons cited by individuals, these were not numerous or significant enough to affect the given data.

For 65 of the respondents who were receiving treatment on a psychiatric unit, the staff, as well as the parents, were asked to fill out questionnaires on the extent of abuse to corroborate the patients' self-reports. There was an 0.85 Pearson correlation between the parents' and children's estimation of abuse. In addition, the parents' and staff's estimates had a 0.60 correlation with each other on the severity of abuse, and a 0.75 correlation on the frequency of abuse.

Results

We found that physical abuse, verbal abuse, physical neglect, emotional neglect, intellectual neglect or sexual abuse seldom occur alone; in less than five percent of the cases, a child was mistreated in only one way (14). We also found that a significant percentage of children were mistreated in all five ways, and that some combinations of mistreatments had a more detrimental effect than others (15). One of the volunteer high school students reported no abuse or neglect of any kind.

Table I indicates the children's perceptions of how well they were looked after by either their mother or father, corre-

lated with their estimate of the extent of abuse they experienced. The extent of abuse is a multiple of the frequency and severity. According to the children, physical abuse and neglect appear to be most strongly related to poor care by the parents.

Table II indicates what this population considered to be their worst experiences in life. It appears that being abused or neglected by their parents, family breakup, getting charged with a crime and a death in the family were considered to be the worst life experience by the largest number of children. (Some respondents indicated more than one "worst experience," leading to figures which total more than 100%.)

Table III indicates the strong correlation between what the children believe their parents expect them to become and what the children themselves expect. Of the children who expected to become criminals, for example, 72% perceived that their parents expected the same.

Table IV shows the relationship between the various causes of abuse and neglect described by the young people and the various types of abuse or neglect. It appears that children ascribe most types of abuse to their parents' immaturity, lack of money and marital problems. Alcoholism strongly correlated with physical neglect and sexual abuse. When we asked the same questions of adults abused as children, we had similar responses, with somewhat heavier weighting on the "too many children" factor.

About one-half of the respondents were below the age of 15. The respondents who were 16 and over gave roughly twice the number of reasons for their abuse per person, on average, than was given by the younger group. Older

Table II

Worst Life Experiences of Abused Children

Types of Abuse	% (n = 162)*
Abused by parents or others	37.0%
Family breakup	32.7%
Charged with a crime	32.7%
Death of family member	29.6%
Beaten up by peers	16.7%
Failing school	15.4%
Moving	12.3%
Friend's death	9.9%
Accident	5.6%
Adopted	1.9%
Crime committed by relative	1.1%

*because the subjects were not limited to only one choice, the total is more than 100%.

Table III

Children's Expectations of What They Will Become and Their Understanding of Their Parents' Expectations*

Child's Expectations	n	Criminal	Bum	Successful Business Person	Financial Failure	Good Parent	Ordinary Working Person	Prostitute
Criminal	18	72.2	16.7	5.6				5.6
Bum	5	20.0	40.0			20.0	20.0	
Successful business person	41	26.8	7.3	42.5	4.9	2.4	17.1	
Financial failure	2	50.0				50.0		
Good parent	23	34.8	4.3	8.7		43.5	4.3	4.3
Ordinary working person	43	23.3	14.0	9.3	4.7	4.6	39.5	4.7
Prostitute	2		50.0					50.0

*57 out of 64 of the valid cells have expected cell frequency of less than 5.0. Minimum expected cell frequency = 0.060.
Chi square = 125.363 with 49 degrees of freedom, significance = 0.0000; Pearson's R = 0.38850, significance = 0.0000.

children attributed their physical abuse to the immaturity of their parents ten times more often than the younger children did. The older teens were four times as likely as the younger ones to attribute their emotional neglect and physical abuse to the perpetrator's drug abuse. In all other areas, the older and younger groups gave similar responses to the causes of their abuse.

There were about twice as many boys as girls in the sample. When we examined the differences in attributing the causes for their abuse, we found that alcohol abuse and unemployment were cited about equally by boys and girls. Drug abuse, professional interference and marital problems were cited proportionally more often by girls. Boys attributed their abuse proportionally more often to "too many children" and "not enough money." Immature parents was cited more often by the girls, although boys who had been physically neglected cited parental immaturity quite often.

When we examined the differences in attributing cause of the abuse between the various groups in the sample, we found that the young offender group produced the largest number of citations of cause — for physical abuse, an average of 2.4 causes was given by each child in the young offender group. The private practice patients gave an average of 1.7 reasons for their mistreatment. The inpatients on the child psychiatric unit offered an average of 1.1 reasons. The local high school

children, most of whom suffered significantly less abuse than the other groups, gave an average of only 0.2 causes per subject. Sixty-nine percent of the young offenders blamed alcohol abuse for their physical abuse, and 48% of them pointed to marital problems. The young offender group tended to finger alcohol abuse proportionally more frequently than other groups for all types of mistreatment. Private patients and young offenders also blamed drug abuse more frequently than others did.

When a stepwise regression analysis was performed with the self-ascribed causes left out, strong correlations appear between mistreatment, family break-up, and lack of affection. Table V indicates the correlations and most significant causes of abuse identified by this analysis. When a stepwise regression analysis was used to determine the factors that correlate with less abuse, good parental care is the only significant factor to emerge.

Discussion

It appears that children attribute their mistreatment to causes that might surprise adults. If their perceptions are accurate, it seems that even young people can detect their parents' immaturity and are aware of how their marital conflict affects their treatment. They show remarkable insight

Table IV

Causes of Mistreatment as Identified by the Children Correlated with More Extensive Abuse

Major Causes Ascribed by Abused Children	Physical Abuse n = 134		Physical Neglect n = 84		Verbal Abuse n = 121		Emotional Neglect n = 105		Sexual Abuse n = 46	
Immature parents	0.315	(p < 0.000)	0.372	(p < 0.000)	0.372	(p < 0.000)	0.334	(p < 0.000)	0.013	(n.s.)
Not enough money	0.311	(p < 0.000)	0.202	(n.s.)	0.272	(p < 0.002)	0.206	(p < 0.000)	0.048	(n.s.)
Unemployment	0.301	(p < 0.000)	0.174	(n.s.)	0.232	(p < 0.010)	0.084	(n.s.)	0.196	(n.s.)
Marital problems	0.287	(p < 0.001)	0.408	(p < 0.000)	0.338	(p < 0.000)	0.298	(p < 0.002)	0.132	(n.s.)
Alcohol abuse	0.235	(p < 0.006)	0.340	(p < 0.002)	0.091	(n.s.)	0.040	(n.s.)	0.313	(p < 0.034)
Too many children	0.097	(n.s.)	0.153	(n.s.)	0.099	(n.s.)	0.162	(n.s.)	0.104	(n.s.)
Drug abuse	0.156	(n.s.)	0.275	(p < 0.011)	0.093	(n.s.)	0.071	(n.s.)	0.179	(p < 0.034)

*expressed as Pearson correlation coefficients

into the nature of the problems that result in their mistreatment. We need to validate these findings, but it may be difficult to measure such subjective responses in any other way. The same questions asked of adults regarding the causes of their own mistreatment have similar answers. The differences between children's and adults' perceptions may indicate a more mature outlook on the part of the adults, but may also reflect the influence of the media and culture.

From our data, it appears that the young people know that alcoholism, parental conflict and immaturity contribute to their neglect. We have found that neglect increases a child's propensity to be mistreated and vulnerability to abuse (3). Too often neglected children seek what they need in the wrong places at wrong times and from the wrong people. The neglect damages their self-esteem and they cannot face the bleak realization that their parents are unable or unwilling to nurture them. It seems easier for children to believe they are mistreated because of some defect or deficiency in themselves, because if that were so, they might correct the whole problem by being better children, or loving their parents more intensely. When they realize nothing they can do will stop the neglect, they search elsewhere, but always with a conviction that they don't really deserve anything better. With tragic consequences, adults who were neglected children may try to correct the effects of a neglected childhood by seeking sustenance from neglecting or abusing partners.

The evidence seems to indicate that there is an association between what some young people perceive to be their parents'

expectations regarding their future and their own expectations of their future. How can children know what is expected of them? Probably they absorb the repeated phrases, both derogatory ("You're going to be a bum, just like your old man"), or encouraging ("Keep it up; someday you'll be very successful") spoken by their parents. The children may misperceive these but, whether real or imagined, there is a connection between how the child expects his future will turn out and what he thinks his parents expect of him. This connection may also give us a clue to the frequently observed phenomenon of abuse which is passed down from generation to generation. The causes of abuse become effects in the children, and then cause mistreatment when the children become parents themselves.

There may be more difficult experiences than the ones we have considered, but, of these, mistreatment by parents and family break-up are the worst from the child's point of view. Children must be aware that a broken family leaves them vulnerable to the vagaries of their environment. Do children intuitively perceive that for their fuller development they require the nurturing and guidance of two parents? Like most research, this study raises more questions than it answers. It does, however, illustrate the necessity of carefully considering abuse and neglect from a child's point of view. The child may be wiser about these matters than we are.

Table V

Factors Associated with More Abuse

Associated Factors	n	T	Significance of T [*]
Physical abuse	134		
• Family break up		– 3.343	p = 0.001
• Less affection		–2.230	p = 0.028
Physical neglect	84		
• Neglected longer		– 4.525	p < 0.000
• Parents not interested		– 2.385	p = 0.020
• Less affection		– 2.408	p = 0.019
Verbal abuse	121		
• Abused longer		– 4.715	p < 0.000
• Immature parents		– 2.326	p = 0.022
Emotional neglect	105		
• Neglected longer		– 5.314	p < 0.000
• Less affection		– 3.730	p = 0.000
• Marital problems		– 2.688	p = 0.008
Sexual abuse	46		
• Abused longer		–2.323	p = 0.026

[*] This stepwise regression analysis does not include causes ascribed by the children, but looks at other factors, such as quality of parenting, failing school, getting charged with a crime, family breakup, moving, accidents, getting beaten up, deaths of family members or friends, early or long-term abuse, missing out on travel, challenges, money, clothes or education.

References

1. Ney PG. Transgenerational child abuse. Child Psychiatry Hum Dev 1988; 18(3): 151-168.
2. Ney PG. Child abuse: a study of the child's perspective. Child Abuse Negl 1986; 10: 511-518.
3. Ney PG. Child neglect and aggression. Paper given to Canadian Academy of Child Psychiatry, Western Branch, Vancouver, BC, March 1992.
4. Crittenden PM. Sibling interaction: evidence of a generational effect in maltreating infants. Child Abuse Negl 1984; 8(4): 433-438.
5. Crittenden PM. Maltreated infants: vulnerability and resilience. J Child Psychol Psychiatry 1985; 26(1): 85-96.
6. Azar ST, Robinson DR, Hekimian E, et al. Unrealistic expectations and problem-solving ability in maltreating and comparison mothers. J Consult Clin Psychology 1984; 52(4): 687-691.
7. Azar ST, Twentyman CT. Cognitive-behavioral perspectives on the assessment and treatment of child abuse. Advances in Cognitive-Behavioral Research and Therapy 1986; 5: 237-267.
8. Sugar M. Sexual abuse of children and adolescents. Adolesc Psychiatry 1983; 11: 199-211.
9. Kneisl CR. Healing the wounded, neglected inner child of the past. Nurs Clin North Am 1991; 26(3): 745-755.
10. Yorker BC, Kahan BB. Munchausen's syndrome by proxy as a form of child abuse. Arch Psychiatr Nurs 1990; 4(5): 313-318.
11. Bagedahl-Strindlund M, Rosencrantz-Larsson L, Wilkner-Svanfeldt P. Children of mentally ill mothers: social situation and psychometric testing of mental development. Scand J Soc Med 1989; 17(2): 171-179.
12. Ney PG. Child mistreatment: possible reasons for its transgenerational transmission. Can J Psychiatry 1989; 34(6): 594-601.
13. Der-Karabetian A, Preciado M. Mother-blaming among college students. Percept Mot Skills 1989; 68(2): 453-454.

14. Ney PG. Does verbal abuse leave deeper scars: a study of children and parents. Can J Psychiatry 1987; 32(5): 371-378.
15. Ney PG. Child abuse and neglect: the worst combinations. Presented to the Annual Meeting of the Canadian Academy of Child Psychiatry, Saskatoon, Saskatchewan, October 1991.

Résumé

Une étude effectuée auprès d'un groupe d'enfants sur la violence et la négligence à leur égard permet de les examiner de la perspective des enfants. Généralement, ils associent la violence dont ils font l'objet à des «mauvais soins» que prodiguent les parents principalement en raison de leur immaturité, de difficultés conjugales, de l'alcoolisme, du chômage, de la toxicomanie et du manque d'argent. Les raisons avancées diffèrent selon le sex et, dans une certaine mesure, l'âge de l'enfant. En tenant compte de paramètres non mentionnés par les enfants, on note une corrélation significative entre la violence à l'égard de l'enfant et la dislocation de la famille, ainsi que le désintérêt et le manque d'affection manifestés à long terme par les parents. Pour décrire la «plus mauvaise expérience de leur vie», la plupart des enfants mentionnent les «mauvais traitements» et la «dislocation de la famille»; le groupe des délinquants juvéniles indique également «le fait d'être inculpé».

Amer. J. Orthopsychiat., 45(3), April 1975

UNRAVELING CHILD ABUSE

David G. Gil, D.S.W.

Professor of Social Policy, Brandeis University, Waltham, Mass.

This paper attempts to clarify the dynamics of child abuse, and to suggest approaches to primary prevention. Child abuse is redefined, within egalitarian value premises, as inflicted gaps in children's circumstances that prevent actualization of inherent potential. Levels of manifestation and causal dimensions of child abuse are identified, and their multiple interactions are traced. Primary prevention is shown to be essentially a political, rather than a purely technical or professional, issue.

This paper is an attempt to clarify the sources and dynamics of child abuse and to suggest approaches to its primary prevention. To gain understanding of any social problem one needs to view it in the total societal context within which it evolves, rather than, as is so often done, as an isolated, fragmented phenomenon. Furthermore, one needs to avoid the fallacious tendency of interpreting its dynamics along single causal dimensions such as biological, psychological, social, economic, etc., a tendency which in our society is usually weighted in favor of individual interpretations and which thus leads to ameliorative programs designed to change individuals rather than pathogenic aspects of the social order.

A VALUE-BASED DEFINITION OF CHILD ABUSE

Understanding and overcoming the dynamics of social problems also requires specification of, and a societal commitment to, certain value premises, and a definition logically linked to such premises. I have suggested such a value-based definition of child abuse at hearings on the *Child Abuse Prevention Act* (S. 1191 of 1973) before the Sub-Committee on Children and Youth of the U. S. Senate. This definition views child abuse as inflicted gaps or deficits be-

A modified version of a paper presented at a conference on child abuse at the National Institute of Child Health and Human Development, in June 1974.

tween circumstances of living which would facilitate the optimal development of children, to which they should be entitled, and their actual circumstances, irrespective of the sources or agents of the deficit:

Every child, despite his individual differences and uniqueness is to be considered of equal intrinsic worth, and hence should be entitled to equal social, economic, civil, and political rights, so that he may fully realize his inherent potential and share equally in life, liberty, and happiness. Obviously, these value premises are rooted in the humanistic philosophy of our Declaration of Independence.

In accordance with these value premises then, any act of commission or omission by individuals, institutions, or society as a whole, and any conditions resulting from such acts or inaction, which deprive children of equal rights and liberties, and/or interfere with their optimal development, constitute, by definition, abusive or neglectful acts or conditions.

ANALYTIC CONCEPTS

The definition of child abuse presented above suggests the use of two related analytic concepts for studying the nature of child abuse and for developing effective policies and programs for its prevention. These concepts will be referred to here as "levels of manifestation" and "levels of causation" or "causal dimensions." The levels of manifestation identify the agents and the settings in which children may experience abuse. The levels of causation unravel the several causal dimensions, the interactions of which result in abusive acts and abusive conditions at the levels of manifestation. The distinction implicit in these analytic concepts, between the levels at which abuse occurs and the forces that underlie the occurrences, is important, for these levels and forces are not the same.

They do, however, complement each other and interact with each other in multiple ways. Moreover, interaction also takes place among the levels themselves, and among the forces. Clarifying the nature of child abuse means, essentially, tracing these multiple interactions among the levels of manifestation and the causal dimensions.

LEVELS OF MANIFESTATION

Three levels of manifestation of child abuse may be distinguished. The most familiar one is abusive conditions in the home, and abusive interaction between children and their caretakers. Abuse on this level consists of acts of commission or omission by individuals which inhibit a child's development. The perpetrators are parents, permanent or temporary parent substitutes, or others living in a child's home regularly or temporarily. Abuse in the home may be intentional and conscious or unintentional and also unconscious. Abuse may result from supposedly constructive, disciplinary, educational attitudes and measures, or from negative and hostile feelings toward children. Abusive acts in the home may be one-time events, occasional incidents, or regular patterns. So far, child abuse at this level of manifestation has been the dominant focus of scholarly, professional, and public concern with this destructive phenomenon.

A second level at which child abuse occurs is the institutional level. This includes such settings as day care centers, schools, courts, child care agencies, welfare departments, and correctional and other residential child care settings. In such settings, acts and policies of commission or omission that inhibit, or insufficiently promote, the development of children, or that deprive children of, or fail to provide them with, material, emotional, and symbolic means needed for their optimal development, constitute abusive acts or conditions. Such acts or policies may originate with an individual employee of an institution, such as a teacher, child care worker, judge, probation officer, or social worker, or they may be implicit in the standard practices and policies of given agencies and institutions. In the same way as in the home, abusive acts and conditions in institutional settings may also result from supposedly constructive, or from negative and hostile attitudes toward children, and they may be one-time or occasional events or regular patterns.

Institutional child care settings such as schools are often perceived by parents as bearers of cultural norms concerning child rearing practices and discipline. Hence, when schools and other child care settings employ practices that are not conducive to optimal child development, *e.g.,* corporal punishment and other demeaning and threatening, negative disciplinary measures, they convey a subtle message to parents— namely, that such measures are appropriate, as they are sanctioned by educational authorities and "experts." Influence also flows in the other direction, from the home to the institutional level. Teachers and child care personnel will frequently adopt child rearing practices and disciplinary measures similar to those practiced in the homes of children in their care, on the assumption that this is what the children are used to, what they expect, and to what they respond. In this way, methods conducive or not conducive to optimal child de-

velopment tend to be transmitted back and forth, and reinforced, through interaction between the home and the institution.

When child abuse is viewed as inflicted deficits between a child's actual circumstances and circumstances that would assure his optimal development, it seems to be endemic in most existing institutional settings for the care and education of children, since these settings usually do not facilitate the full actualization of the human potential of all children in their care. Analysis of institutional child abuse reveals that this form of abuse is not distributed randomly throughout the population. Schools and institutions serving children of minority groups, children from deprived socioeconomic backgrounds, handicapped children, and socially deviant children are less likely to facilitate optimal development of children's inherent potential than are schools and institutions serving children of majority groups, "normal" children, and children from affluent families and neighborhoods. However, even settings serving children from privileged backgrounds rarely encourage the optimal development of all children in their care. They, too, tend to inhibit the children's spontaneity and creativity, and to promote conformity rather than critical, independent thought. Only rarely will children in these settings develop all their inherent faculties and their unique individuality.

Worse, though, than the educational system, with its mind-stifling practices and its widespread use of corporal punishment and other demeaning and threatening forms of discipline, is the legally sanctioned, massive abuse of children under the policies and practices of the public welfare system, especially the "Aid to Families with Dependent Children" (AFDC) program. This system of grossly inadequate income maintenance—inadequate even by measures of minimal needs as published by the US Bureau of Labor Statistics—virtually condemns millions of children to conditions of existence under which physical, social, emotional, and intellectual development are likely to be severely handicapped.

Similarly destructive versions of legally sanctioned abuse on the institutional level are experienced by several hundred thousands of children living in foster care, in training and correctional institutions, and in institutions for children defined as mentally retarded. That these settings of substitute child care usually fail to assure optimum development for the children entrusted to them has been amply demonstrated,[1, 5] and does not require further documentation here.

The massive manifestations of institutional child abuse tend to arouse much less public concern and indignation than child abuse in the home, although the abusive conditions and practices of public education, public welfare, and child placement are endemic to these systems, and are visible to all who care to see. Perhaps the enormity of institutional abuse dulls our sensibilities in the same way in which the fate of inmates of concentration camps tends to arouse a lesser response than does the killing of a single individual with whom we are able to identify.

Institutional child abuse is linked, intimately, to the third level at which child abuse is manifested, namely, the societal level. On this level originate social policies which sanction, or cause, severe deficits between the actual circumstances of children and conditions needed for their optimal development. As direct or indirect consequences of such social policies, millions of children in our society live in poverty and are inadequately nourished, clothed, housed, and educated; their health is not assured because of substandard medical care; their neighborhoods decay; meaningful occupational opportunities are not available to them; and alienation is widespread among them. No doubt, these destructive conditions which result, inevitably, from the normal workings of the prevailing social, economic, and political order, and from the value premises which shape that order and its human dynamics, cannot fail to inhibit severely the development of children exposed to them.

Of the three levels of child abuse sketched here, the societal level is certainly the most severe. For what happens at this level determines not only how children fare on the institutional level, but also, by way of complex interactions, how they fare in their own homes.

LEVELS OF CAUSATION

Before discussing the causal dimensions of child abuse, it should be reiterated that the conventional dichotomy between individual and societal causation of social problems distorts the multidimensional reality of human phenomena. We know that psychological forces which shape individual behavior evolve out of the totality of life experiences in specific historical, cultural, social, economic, and political contexts. Individual motivation and behavior are thus always rooted in a societal force field. Yet societal forces are always expressed, or mediated, through the behavior of individuals, for societies cannot act except through their individual members. Clearly, then, any human phenomenon, at any moment, involves both social and individual elements. In real life, these elements are inseparable. Their separation in theory is merely a product of scholarly, or rather pseudoscholarly, abstraction.

Based on this reasoning, child abuse, at any level of manifestation, may be understood as acts or inactions of individuals, on their own or as institutional agents, whose behavior reflects societal forces mediated through their unique personalities.

The most fundamental causal level of child abuse consists of a cluster of interacting elements, to wit, a society's basic social philosophy, its dominant value premises, its concept of humans; the nature of its social, economic, and political institutions, which are shaped by its philosophy and value premises, and which in turn reinforce that philosophy and these values; and, finally, the particular quality of human relations prevailing in the society, which derives from its philosophy, values, and institutions. For, in the final analysis, it is the philosophy and value premises of a society, the nature of its major institutions, and the quality of its human relations that determine whether or not individual members of that society will develop freely and fully in accordance with their inherent potentialities.

To discern a society's basic social philosophy and values and its concept of humans, one needs to ascertain whether it considers everyone to be intrinsically of equal worth in spite of his or her uniqueness and, hence, entitled to the same social, economic, and political rights; or whether everyone in the society considers himself, and those close to himself, of greater worth than anyone else, and hence entitled to more desirable or privileged circumstances. The former, egalitarian philosophy would be reflected in institutional arrangements involving cooperative actions in pursuit of common existential interests. Every individual, and that includes every child, would be considered an equally entitled subject, who could not be exploited and dominated by any other individual or group, and whose right to fully and freely develop his individuality would be assured and respected, subject to the same right of all others. The latter, non-egalitarian philosophy, on the other hand, as we know so well from our own existence, is reflected in institutional structures which encourage competitive behavior in pursuit of narrowly perceived, egotistical interests. Everyone strives to get ahead of others, considers himself entitled to privileged conditions and positions, and views and treats others as potential means to be used, exploited, and dominated in pursuit of his egotistical goals.

Analysis of these contrasting social philosophies, societal institutions, and modes of human relations suggests that full and free development of every child's inherent potential may be possible only in a society organized consistently around egalitarian and cooperative value premises, since the equal right to self-actualization is implicit in an egalitarian philosophy, while such a right is incompatible with a non-egalitarian philosophy. In a society organized on non-egalitarian and competitive principles, full and free development for all children is simply impossible, as, by definition, there must always be losers in such societies, whose chances to realize their inherent potential will be severely limited. Hence, significant developmental deficits for large segments of the population or high levels of socially structured and sanctioned abuse of children, are endemic in such societies.

A second, more specific, level of causation of child abuse may be intrinsic to the social construction, or definition, of childhood prevalent in a society. Obviously, this level is closely related to the first level. How does a society view its children, all its children, and how does it define their rights? How much obedience, submission, and conformity does it expect of children? Does it process children through caste-like channels of socialization into relatively closed and inflexible social and occupational structures, or does it encourage them, within limits of reason, to discover and develop their individuality and uniqueness, and to shape their lives accordingly? Obviously, optimal development of the inherent potential of all children is a function of the extent to which a society's processes of socialization are permeated with a commitment to such self-actualization for all. When this commitment is lacking altogether, or when it varies with such factors as sex, race, and social and economic position of a family, then different children will experience varying deficits in realizing their potential. Presently, in our society, social policies that sustain different levels of rights for children from different social and economic backgrounds are a major, direct cause of many forms of child abuse on the societal and institutional levels, and an indirect cause of abuse on the family level.

A further causal dimension of child abuse is a society's attitude toward the use of force as a legitimate means for attaining ends, especially in imbalanced, interpersonal relations such as master-slave, male-female, guard-prisoner, and adult-child. The tendency to resort to the use of force for dealing with conflicts in our society seems to require no documentation here, nor does it seem necessary to document the specific readiness to use force, or the threat of it, as a means to maintain authority and discipline in adult-child relations in the public domain, such as schools and other child care settings, and in the private domain of the family. The readiness to use physical force for disciplinary objectives is certainly endemic in our society.

It should be noted that the readiness to use force in general, and in adult-child relations in particular, is intimately linked to a society's basic philosophy and value premises, and to its concept of humans and their rights. A non-egalitarian philosophy is much more likely to sanction the use of force than is an egalitarian one, since the use of force against other humans constitutes the strongest possible negation of equality. The use of force toward children is also related to the manner in which childhood, and the rights of children are defined by a society, and in turn tends to reinforce that definition.

As mentioned earlier, the use of force toward children is widespread in our society on the institutional and family levels. Attempts to limit and outlaw it in public institutions have had only limited success so far. It may be noted, in this context, that because of the compatibility between the use of physical force on the one hand, and an inegalitarian philosophy and competitive social, economic, and political institutions on the other, corporal punishment and the threat of it may actually be highly functional in preparing children for adult roles in an inegalitarian and competitive social order. For, were our children reared in a harmonious fashion without threats, insults, and physical force, they might not be adequately prepared and conditioned for adult roles in our inegalitarian, competitive reality.

Whenever corporal punishment in child rearing is sanctioned, and even subtly encouraged by a society, incidents of serious physical abuse and injury are bound to happen, either as a result of deliberate, systematic, and conscious action on the part of perpetrators, or under conditions of loss of self-control. In either case, but especially in the latter, physical attacks on children tend to relieve tensions and frustrations experienced by the perpetrators. Clearly, then, these attacks are carried out to meet emotional needs of the perpetrators rather than educational needs of the victims, as is often claimed by advocates of corporal punishment.

The next causal dimension may be referred to as "triggering contexts." These contexts operate jointly with the societal sanction of the use of physical force in adult-child relations. Adults who use force toward children do not do so all the time, but only under specific circumstances which serve as triggers for their abusive behavior. In gen-eral, abusive attacks tend to be triggered by stress and frustration which may cause reduction or loss of self-control. Stress and frustration may facilitate abusive attacks even without causing a reduction or loss of self-control, as long as the appropriateness of the use of force in child rearing is accepted.

One major source of stress and frustration for adults in our society are the multi-faceted deprivations of poverty and its correlates, high density in overcrowded, dilapidated, inadequately served neighborhoods; large numbers of children, especially in one-parent, mainly female-headed households; and the absence of child care alternatives. Having identified poverty and its correlates as an important triggering context of child abuse in the home, we may now note that social policies which sanction and perpetuate the existence of poverty among large segments of the population, including millions of children, are thus indirect sources of child abuse in the home. It should be emphasized, though, that poverty, per se, is not a direct cause of child abuse in the home, but operates through an intervening variable, namely, concrete and psychological stress and frustration experienced by individuals in the context of culturally sanctioned use of physical force in child rearing.

Poverty is not the only source of stress and frustration triggering child abuse in the home. Such abuse is known to occur frequently in many homes in adequate, and even affluent, economic circumstances. One other, important source of stress and frustration in our society is the alienating circumstances in most workplaces, be the work manual labor, skilled and unskilled occupations, or administrative, managerial, and professional work through all levels and sectors of business, academic, and government bureaucracies. A recent report by a task force of the U. S. Department of Health, Education, and Welfare [6] documented the seriousness of work alienation experienced by constantly growing segments of the working population. This government report reached conclusions similar to those voiced by many severe critics of our economic system in recent years—that the prevailing competitive and exploitative human relations in the work place, and its hierarchical and authoritarian structures, tend to cause psychological stress and alienation for nearly every working person. These pressures may lead to various forms of deviant behavior, such as alcoholism, drug addiction, mental illness, white collar crime, etc. Perhaps the most frequent locus for discharging feelings of stress and frustration originating in the formal world of work is the informal world of primary relations, the home and the family. Conflicts between spouses are one form this discharge may take. Child abuse in the form of violent physical outbursts is another.

Here, then, we identify once again a triggering context for child abuse on the interpersonal level, which is rooted deeply in societal forces, namely, the alienating quality of our society's economic and productive system complemented by the culturally sanctioned use of physical force in child rearing.

The final causal dimension of child abuse on the interpersonal level in the home and in child care settings is made up of intrapsychic conflicts and various forms of psychopathology on the part of perpetrators. Child abuse literature is largely focused on this dimension and thus little needs to be said here to document it. What needs to be stressed, however, is that psychological disturbances and their manner of expression are not independent factors but are deeply rooted in, and constantly interact with, forces in the social environment of the disturbed individual. To the extent that psychopathology is not rooted in genetic and biochemical processes, it derives from the totality of the life experiences of the individual, which are shaped by continuous interactions between the person and his social setting, his informal and formal relations in primary and secondary contexts. However, it is not only the etiology of intrapsychic conflicts and disturbances that is conditioned, in part, by social forces, but also the manner in which these conflicts and disturbances are expressed in social relations. The symptoms of emotional disturbance and mental illness are not randomly generated phenomena, but derive from normal behavioral traits in a culture. These normal traits appear in exaggerated or negated forms in behavior which is considered deviant, neurotic, and psychotic. Hence, one may assume that in a society in which the use of physical force in general, and toward children in particular, is not sanctioned, intrapsychic conflicts and psychopathology would less often be expressed through violence against children. It follows from these considerations that the "battered baby" syndrome,[3, 4] and other forms of child abuse associated with psychological disturbances of one kind or another, are not independent of societal forces, although the perpetrators of these acts may be emotionally ill individuals. We are thus again led to the conclusion that abusive acts and conditions, irrespective of the level of manifestation, cannot be understood in terms of one specific causal dimension, but only in terms of complex interactions among the several causal dimensions sketched here.

PRIMARY PREVENTION

According to a general conceptual model, primary prevention proceeds from identification toward elimination of the causal contexts from which specified, undesired phenomena derive. It needs to be realized that the prevention of undesired phenomena may also result in the elimination of other phenomena whenever such other phenomena derive from, or are part of, the same causal context. The likelihood of simultaneous prevention of several phenomena could lead to serious dilemmas if some of the phenomena are desired, while others are considered undesirable, or when groups in a society differ in their respective evaluation of the desirability of the several phenomena. Decisions concerning primary prevention of social phenomena and of "social problems" are thus essentially political choices.[2]

Turning now to the primary prevention of child abuse, we may begin by summarizing our conclusions so far. Child abuse, conceived of as inflicted deficits on a child's right to develop freely and fully, irrespective of the source and agents of the deficit, was found to occur on several related levels: on the interpersonal level in the home and in child-care settings; on the institutional level through the policies and practices of a broad array of child care, educational, welfare, and correctional institutions and agencies; and on the societal level, where the interplay of values and social, economic, and political institutions and processes shapes the social policies by which the rights and lives of all children, and of specific groups of children, are determined. The causal dimensions of child abuse are, first of all, the dominant social philosophy and value premises of a society, its social, economic, and political institutions, and the quality of human relations to which these institutions, philosophy, and values give rise; other causal dimensions are the social construction of childhood and the social definition of children's rights, the extent to which a society sanctions the use of force in general and, more specifically, in the child rearing context, stress and frustration resulting from poverty and from alienation in the workplace which may trigger abusive acts, and expressions of intrapsychic conflicts and psychopathology which, in turn, are rooted in the social fabric. While child abuse, at any particular level, may be more closely related to one rather than another causal dimension, none of these dimensions are independent, and they exert their influence through multiple interactions with each other.

This analysis suggests that primary prevention of child abuse, on all levels, would require fundamental changes in social philosophy and value premises, in societal institutions, and in human relations. It would also require a reconceptualization of childhood, of children's rights, and of child rearing. It would necessitate rejecting the use of force as a means for achieving societal ends, especially in dealing with children. It would require the elimination of poverty and of alienating conditions of production, major sources of stress and frustration which tend to trigger abusive acts toward children in adult-child interaction. And, finally, it would necessitate the elimination of psychological illness. Because of the multiple interactions among the several causal dimensions, progress in overcoming the more fundamental dimensions would also reduce the force of other dimensions. Thus, transforming the prevailing inegalitarian social philosophy, value premises, and institutions, and the kind of human relations they generate, into egalitarian ones would also result in corresponding modifications of children's rights, elimination of poverty and alienation at work, and rejection of the use of force. It would indirectly influence psychological well-being, and would thus eliminate the processes that now trigger child abuse in interpersonal relations.

Effective primary prevention requires working simultaneously toward the transformation of all the causal dimensions. Fragmented approaches focused on one or the other causal dimension may bring some amelioration, but one should entertain no illusions as to the effectiveness of such piecemeal efforts. Even such important and necessary steps as outlawing corporal punishment in schools and other child care settings would have only limited, though highly desirable, results. There simply is no way of escaping the conclusion that the complete elimination of child abuse on all levels of manifestation requires a radical transformation of the prevailing unjust, inegalitarian, irrational, competitive, alienating, and hierarchical social order into a just, egalitarian, rational, cooperative, humane, and truly democratic, decentralized one. Obviously, this realization implies that primary prevention of child abuse is a political issue which cannot be resolved through professional and administrative measures.

Primary prevention of child abuse would bring with it the prevention of other equally undesirable and inevitable consequences or symptoms of the same causal context, including many manifestations of social deviance. However, it would also result in the complete transformation of the prevailing social, economic, and political order with which large segments of our society are either identified or drifting along, because this order conforms to their accustomed mental sets, and because they seem reluctant, due to inertia, to search actively for alternative social, economic, and political institutions that might be more conducive to human fulfillment for all. Some or many members of our society may even be consciously committed to the perpetuation of the existing order, not realizing how destructive that order may be to their own real interests.

Whatever one's attitude may be toward these fundamental political issues, one needs to recognize and face the dilemmas implicit in them and, hence, in primary prevention of child abuse. If one's priority is to prevent all child abuse, one must be ready to part with its many causes, even when one is attached to some of them, such as the apparent blessings, advantages, and privileges of inequality. If, on the other hand, one is reluctant to give up all aspects of the causal context of child abuse, one must be content to continue living with this social problem. In that latter case, one ought to stop talking about primary prevention and face the fact that all one may be ready for is some measure of amelioration.

REFERENCES

1. GIL, D. 1970. Violence Against Children. Harvard University Press, Cambridge, Mass.
2. GIL, D. 1973. Unravelling Social Policy. Schenkman Publishing Co., Cambridge, Mass.
3. HELFER, R. AND KEMPE, C., eds. 1968. The Battered Child. University of Chicago Press, Chicago.
4. KEMPE, C. AND HELFER, R., eds. 1972. Helping the Battered Child and His Family. Lippincott, Philadelphia.
5. SCHORR, A., ed. 1974. Children and Decent People. Basic Books, New York.
6. TASK FORCE TO THE SECRETARY OF HEW. 1973. Work in America. MIT Press, Cambridge, Mass.

For reprints: David G. Gil, Florence Heller Graduate School, Brandeis University, Waltham, Mass. 02154

PRIMARY PREVENTION OF CHILD ABUSE: A PHILOSOPHICAL AND POLITICAL ISSUE

DAVID G. GIL, D.S.W.

While amelioration of child abuse may involve important professional, administrative, and legal elements, the primary prevention of this destructive phenomenon, like that of any other serious social problem, is essentially a philosophical and political issue. To test the validity of this admittedly unconventional proposition, one must examine the nature and dynamics of child abuse. The place to begin such an examination is a specification of what the term actually means.

Defining Child Abuse

Scholars, professionals, administrators, and legal experts tend to define child abuse as intentional acts of commission or omission, on the part of individual caretakers of children, which result in physical and psychological injury or damage to the children. While this may be a useful working definition for the purpose of service programs under prevailing conditions, closer scrutiny reveals serious limitations along at least two important dimensions. The definition lacks a frame of reference against which injury and damage may be identified and measured; and it is biased against individuals as sole agents of child abuse. It may be noted parenthetically that these shortcomings of the definition are not unusual for social science problem definitions in our culture. We tend to view problems descriptively rather than analytically, as isolated fragments, without a frame of reference that specifies desired conditions against which each problem can be identified and measured. Also, we tend to see them in a manner that leads to blaming individuals as agents rather than societal factors.

An alternative approach to defining child abuse would spell out a value position concerning the desired state of childhood or the rights of children in society, and would consider as abusive any act or condition that interfered with children attaining that desired state or exercising these rights, irrespective of the sources and agents of these acts and conditions. There are difficulties with this conceptualization, since society may be forced to confront the existence of covert disagreements concerning the desired state of childhood and the rights of children, especially children of different population segments. However, these difficulties are also an advantage, since integrating value premises into problem definitions would force these types of conflicts out of covertness and into public consciousness.

In a democratic, egalitarian society, which we claim to be, every child ought to be deemed of intrinsically equal worth and, hence, entitled to equal rights, so that he or she may develop freely and fully in accordance with innate potential. When using this value position as frame of reference, child abuse means waste of a child's developmental potential, or interference with a child's development due to circumstances of living that are not conducive to optimal development, irrespective of who or what causes these deficits.

Levels of Manifestation of Child Abuse

Our definition permits us to transcend the conventional notion that the sole locus of child abuse is his/her home, and that the sole agents of abuse are individual caretakers. Nothing could be further from the actual situation than this widespread myth. These comments are not meant to suggest that child abuse does not occur in children's homes at the hand of caretakers, but only to put these cases into proper perspective. While interference with children's optimal development does in fact occur in all too many homes, the home rarely is an independent source of child abuse, but usually is the final link in a long chain of societal conditions and factors. For homes do not exist in a social vacuum.

Quantitatively and qualitatively, more significant loci of child abuse can be identified at the institutional level, where abuse of children is practiced through the policies, programs, and procedures of public settings and agencies such as nursery schools, day-care centers, schools, foster homes, child-care institutions, juvenile courts and correctional facilities, health-care delivery systems, and, last but not least, public welfare and food support programs. Very few of these settings, when scrutinized closely, can be cleared of charges of child abuse as it is here conceived. It is an undisputed fact that assistance levels provided by the public welfare system fall far below levels defined as minimal even by the U.S. Government. Few children in families existing on AFDC or similar programs may

be assumed to live under conditions conducive to full and free development of inherent potential, and to the exercise of equal rights. And several million children in our affluent nation are forced, by circumstances not of their making, to exist under the depriving and degrading policies of this system.

" . . . Every child ought to be deemed of . . . equal worth and, hence, entitled to equal rights . . . "

The food support programs of the U.S. Department of Agriculture recently were cited in a congressional investigation as not meeting minimal expectations for a survival diet as a result of flagrant bureaucratic disregard of congressional intent. The utterly inadequate dietary levels of many expectant mothers and infants are known to be contributing factors to mental retardation, clearly a case of preventable developmental deficit. The dismal level of performance of our health-care system is reflected in such well-known indices as high infant mortality and (of particular concern to readers of this journal) the severe shortage of mental health provisions for children.

Most juvenile courts and correctional institutions may be more adequately described as gatekeepers to adult criminal careers. Many child-care institutions and foster-care programs for neglected, abused, disturbed and homeless children rarely provide these children with all that is necessary for free and full development; frequently they offer conditions that are hardly an improvement over the children's home circumstances.

Schools, from nursery school through graduate school, usually are neither designed nor equipped to bring out the true potential or the intrinsic creativity of students. Rather, they are designed to process cohorts after cohorts of conforming, well adjusted "organization men and women" who will fit without too much trouble into the existing occupational structure which, being concerned primarily with production for profit rather than for the satisfaction of human needs, leaves little room for indivual self-direction, self-expression or self-actualization.

There are significant differences in the intensity of abuse between institutional settings serving children from economically deprived and "minority" backgrounds and those caring for children from economically adequate and affluent circumstances and "majority" background. In general, abusive and handicapping conditions increase in scope and intensity as the economic circumstances of the children's families decrease, and as the proportion of children from minority backgrounds increases among the population served.

The phenomena of institutional child abuse are by no means accidental or random. They can only be understood as intentional and systemic, inevitable consequences of prevailing social policies in the domains of health, education, child rearing and human welfare. In turn, these policies reflect the dominant values of society. Shaped by these values, they also reflect the prevailing organization of processes of production of goods and services, of distribution of wealth and products, of civil and political rights, and of social prestige.

Causal Dimensions of Child Abuse

The deepest layer of causation of child abuse is a society's philosophy, its values and its concept of humans. Whether or not individuals live in conditions conducive to the full development of their potential is largely determined by the nature of institutional order and the quality of human relations hence — by the social philosophy.

A society's philosophy may be either egalitarian and cooperative or inegalitarian and competitive. In an egalitarian context, all humans in spite of their uniqueness are considered to be of equal worth and, thus, are equally entitled to develop freely and fully. Under such a philosophy people tend to cooperate to enhance collective well-being and, through it, individual fulfillment. Under an inegalitarian philosophy, competition and self-centeredness are encouraged, and with them disregard for humanness, integrity, and the needs of nearly everyone else.

Obviously only an egalitarian philosophy and an institutional order shaped by it can be conducive to the self-actualization of every individual and, hence, to systemic conditions that preclude institutional forms of child abuse. An inegalitarian philosophy and the stratified institutional order derived from it, on the other hand, render institutional child abuse almost inevitable.

A related causal dimension of child abuse is the way in which a society defines childhood and children's rights. When children are defined by law as parental property, as was the case in ancient Rome, the potential for abuse is structured into the very definition. Only when children are defined as persons in their own rights, entitled within the limits of reason to the same constitutional protection (individual civil rights and due process) as adults, does society overcome what amounts to a legal sanction of — or inducement to — child abuse. Another aspect which must be considered is whether the definition of children's legally enforcible rights is universal or whether it varies, as it does in inegalitarian societies, with the sex, ethnic origin, and family circumstances of a child. Only when the rights of all children are defined on equal terms will each have an equal opportunity to develop, and thus equal protection against abusive conditions.

Obviously, of prime importance is a society's attitude towards the use of force and coercion in general as a legitimate means in pursuing ends, and especially as an accepted measure in rearing and disciplining children. It does not seem necessary to document the all-pervasive readiness in our culture to resort to force and violence at home and abroad, and the equally widespread sanction of corporal punishment of children in the home and in the public domain. Such disciplinary measures usually are not conducive to children's development and they are often the immediate cause of physical injury and death.

The remaining causal dimensions to be noted here concern child abuse on the interpersonal level. Situational and existential stress often trigger the loss of self-control on the part of caretakers and lead to abusive attacks on children. Industrialization, bureaucratization, and competition have brought widespread, intense dissatisfaction and alienation in many work settings and for most types of occupations, whether the work is physical or mental. The tensions that build throughout the workday tend to be discharged after work in the home, where they may trigger conflicts among spouses and abusive, violent outbursts towards children.

Another source of severe stress in daily existence is poverty and its multiple social and economic correlates, such as overcrowding, inadequate public services, inefficient transportation, poor shopping facilities, etc. Thus, the strains generated by such conditions in urban and rural slums are additional factors that may trigger abuse in the home. Poverty is a central aspect of societal abuse of all children exposed to it.

Psychological disturbances often are expressed through abusive attitudes and acts toward children. This is the causal factor most frequently noted in discussions of child abuse. What is often overlooked is the fact that individual psychopatholoy is not an independent, internally generated phenomenon, but instead is a function of an individual's life experiences in a social context. We are thus led back to recognizing the multiple social and personal sources of abusive acts on any level.

It is essential to note that abusive incidents cannot be understood as a result of single dimensions, but always must be seen as consequences of complex interactions among several of the dimensions discussed here.

Primary Prevention

We are now ready to take up the discussion of primary prevention of child abuse and the proposition, stated earlier, that primary prevention is a political issue rather than a professional one. According to the general conceptual model of primary prevention, a social problem can be prevented only when its causes are identified and eliminated or modified. Accordingly, primary prevention of child abuse is predicated upon elimination or appropriate transformation of the causal dimensions identified in the preceding pages. More specifically, this means replacing the now dominant inegalitarian and competitive social philosophy — and the social, economic, and political order shaped by it — with an egalitarian, cooperative philosophy, and with societal institutions which fit that philosophy. Next, it requires redefining childhood and the rights of all children in a manner that assures them full constitutional protection as persons and the legally enforceable right to live in conditions conducive to full developement in accordance with their inherent potential. Further requirements of primary prevention of child abuse are the prohibition of the use of force and coercion in adult-child relations, the elimination of poverty, the transformation of work into a meaningful experience and a source of creative expression and self-actualization rather than of alienation, and, finally, the elimination of all sources of psychological disturbance.

It is immediately obvious that the requirements of primary prevention of child abuse amount to fundamental philosophical and structural changes of the prevailing social, economic, and political order. In concrete terms, these transformations require the establishment of a truly democratic, humanistic, cooperative and egalitarian social system in place of the existing inegalitarian, selfish and competitive one. It needs hardly to be restated that this is a political issue par excellence. *Quod erat demonstrandum.*

DAVID G. GIL — Dr. Gil is Professor of Social Policy at the Florence Heller Graduate School for Advanced Studies in Social Welfare, Brandeis University, Waltham, Massachusetts. He is Visiting Professor at Tufts University, Harvard University Extension and Washington University.

The Prevention of Sexual Child Abuse: Focus on the Perpetrator

Carolyn Swift

The author, is Director of Prevention Projects at the Wyandot Mental Health Center in Kansas City, Kansas. She Chairs the Council on Prevention for the National Council of Community Mental Health Centers. Currently she is Principal Investigator of a research project to train professionals in the identification and treatment of sexual child abuse.

ABSTRACT

Conventional approaches to the prevention of sexual assault focus on the victim. This paper presents two hypotheses relating to the development of the behavior of sexual child abuse in males, reviews empirical evidence supporting these hypotheses and projects approaches to the prevention of sexual child abuse based on these hypotheses. The hypotheses are that a large proportion of males who abuse children sexually 1) have been sexually abused themselves as children, and 2) are sexually ignorant and socially immature.

Only recently has it become scientifically respectable to accumulate data about sexual behavior. Attempts to investigate sexual behavior through experimental manipulation are blocked by legitimate concerns for risks to human subjects compounded by entrenched taboos. Nowhere is this more evident than in the field of sexual child abuse, with the result that research in this area is limited. It is estimated that 336,200 children are sexually victimized annually in the United States (Sarafino, 1979). However, no broad empirical studies of children have established the frequency or variety of their sexual experiences, nor correlated these with outcome measures in adult life. Until a decade ago there were less than 500 children for whom a usable body of data was available for study of adult-child sexual interactions (Gagnon, 1970 pp. 398-419). In the last ten years there has been a virtual explosion of information in the area of sexual child abuse. Bibliographies published within the last two years cite over 250 works produced on this subject from 1969 through 1978 (Midlarsky, 1978; Schultz, 1979). Most of the studies, however, are not experimental, and those that are, raise serious questions of reliability and validity. Case studies and anecdotal reports far outnumber systematic studies of the variables involved.

Comparisons among studies are hampered by different definitions of sexual abuse. While there is no consensus among investigators as to whether or not certain acts are sexually abusive (i.e., exhibitionism, culturally variable demonstrations of affection), there is agreement that acts of penetration — genital, oral and anal intercourse — and manipulation of genitals are acts from which children should be protected. The discussion of prevention of sexual child abuse in this paper is directed to the reduction of the incidence of these acts.

Conventionally the prevention of sexual assault has focused on altering the behavior of the victim. Through self-defense training, proscriptions of behavior resulting in vulnerability to attack (don't accept rides from strangers, don't go out alone at night, don't walk through parks alone, etc.) women and children are cautioned to restrict their activities to make themselves less accessible to sexual assault. The result of these measures is not the prevention of sexual assault, but the prevention of sexual assault of cautious women and children, and those proficient in the physical martial arts. The attacker continues to victimize the young, the weak, the vulnerable or the uninformed. Sexual assault is not prevented by this approach, but rather displaced.

Few efforts have been directed to preventing the development of the behavior of sexual assault in males, who account for over 90 percent of the perpetrators (Kinsey, Pomeroy, Martin & Gebhard, 1953; Landis, 1956). Failure to use this approach is rooted primarily in the difficulties in identifying the variables of which sexual assault is a function. Conventional efforts have identified the offender after the fact and focused futile efforts on treatment at that point. Psychotherapy, behavior modification, fines and prison sentences have been unsuccessful in altering the behavior of sexual offenders.

While blaming the victim is not as common in cases of sexual child abuse as it is in adult rape, prevention approaches still tend to focus on the child. Hot lines for victims and potential victims exemplify this focus. Programs teaching children how to say no, or to claim the right to control their own bodies are variations of assertiveness training transferred to the field of sexual behavior. These programs are not trivial. They raise the consciousness of the community and alert children to their vulnerability to sexual exploitation. Even if successful, however — and their success is problematic: how successful will a child be telling Daddy no?[1] — they would not eliminate child sexual assault. To effect substantial reduction in this phenomenon, prevention programs must be targeted to alter the behavior of adult perpetrators.

Causal Hypothesis

A variety of causal hypotheses to explain sexual child abuse have been advanced in the literature. Most identify variables associated with the victim, the perpetrator or the family of the victim. While it is recognized that causes are multiple and complex, the focus of this paper is limited to two relatively unexplored conditions believed to contribute to the development of the behavior of sexual child abuse in males.

Hypothesis One

A large proportion of males who abuse children sexually have themselves been sexually abused as children. According to this hypothesis, sexual child abuse, like other forms of child abuse, participates in the cyclical pattern of generational repetition. Without intervention the cycle of abuse can be expected to continue. Prevention programs based on this hypothesis emphasize identification and intervention with sexually abused boys to prevent the victimization of children in subsequent generations.

Hypothesis Two

A large proportion of males who abuse children sexually are sexually ignorant and socially immature. According to this hypothesis, their choice of child instead of adult partners is rooted in fears of inadequacy and rejection. Prevention programs based on this hypothesis target children, particularly boys, for sex education programs.

239

Generational Repetition

Two lines of evidence bear on the hypothesis that the perpetrator was himself sexually abused as a child, and that this experience predisposes him to commit sexually abusive acts as an adult. Recent research indicates that substantially more boys are victimized sexually than has previously been believed, and a high proportion of sex offenders were themselves sexually abused as children. Landis (1956) in a survey of 1,800 college students, found that roughly one-third of the students, both male and female, reported having been sexually victimized as children. Eighty-four percent of the victimization experiences of the males involved homosexual advances, although it is not clear whether such advances were physical, verbal or both.

Examination of the types of experiences reported suggests the startling possibility that boys may in fact be at higher risk for sexual victimization than girls. Over half of the victimization experiences reported by girls were encounters with exhibitionists, as compared with only five percent for boys. If victimization from exhibitionism were eliminated from Landis' data, the percentage of females in the sample could drop in half (from 5 to 17 percent), still leaving essentially the same percentage of male victims (30 percent).

Attempts to corroborate these data through a search of the literature have yielded provocative but inconclusive results, in part because few controlled studies have been done in this field. However, a classic study conducted in 1937 by Bender and Blau used as subjects 16 "unselected successive admissions of prepuberty children" admitted to Bellevue Hospital in New York City for observation following sexual relations with adults (Bender & Blau, 1937, p. 501). A third of the victims were boys. There appears to have been little attempt to follow with appropriate research the possibility suggested by this early study that a substantial proportion of sexual victims are young males.

Failure to pursue this lead stems in part from differential reporting rates of boys and girls, compounded by reluctance to acknowledge the reality of sexual victimization of boys. Several studies indicate that boys report sexual child abuse less frequently than girls. In Landis' survey, of the males reporting sexual victimization as children, only 16.5 percent had reported the incident to their parents, compared with 43 percent of the victimized girls. Kutchinsky (1971) found that three times as many female as male victims of sex crimes reported the incident to police. Homosexual attacks on children carry a double stigma since they violate the heterosexual norm as well as the prohibition of the use of a child as a sexual partner. The message to boys in our culture is that homosexual attacks are unspeakable events, more humiliating than the female "fate worse than death." Obviously, unreported attacks cannot be routed into the treatment system. In a paradoxical reversal of the adult double standard, boys are discriminated against in the area of protection from and treatment of sexual exploitation. A conspiracy of silence surrounds the boy who is sexually victimized. His victimization is proof that he has failed in one of the primary mandates of the masculine role — to defend himself. To share his trauma is to advertise his defeat and invite not only immediate humiliation, but continuing stigmatization. If distress overcomes reticence and he does report the incident, he is likely to be disbelieved or told to keep quiet about it. The effort and pain required to break through this conspiracy of silence functions to insure that only the more traumatic acts, such as those involving penetration, surface in the reporting system.

In a survey of the clinical staff of an urban mental health center (Swift, 1977), boys constituted a third of the child caseload reporting sexual abuse. Kutchinsky (1971) found that 30 percent of an adult sample admitting to sexual victimization were male. More recent evidence comes from data collected through Operation Lure, part of an investigation of child sexual assault undertaken by a task force of the Michigan State Police (Groth, 1979 a). Of approximately 1,000 reports of attempted sexual assaults from children between 10 and 12 years of age in selected communities over a one-year period, 49 percent came from boys, 51 percent from girls.

A study of the victims of child sexual assault reported to the San Francisco Police Department's Youth Services Division for the one year period of July 1, 1975, through June 30, 1976, showed a third to be boys. An analysis of their data[2] reveals striking differences between the severity of acts suffered by boy and girl victims. Significantly more male than female victims suffered completed acts of all kinds, including acts of penetration and completed acts of fondling (Harrer, Copeland, Brody, & Watkins, 1976).

Percentage of Sexual Child Abuse in Male and Female Victims: San Francisco Study

Acts Involved	Percent of Victimized Males	Percent of Victimized Females	Probability
Fondling of genital area (victims under 14)	42%	35%	p. < .0014
Acts of penetration (victims under 14), including oral copulation, sodomy, rape	39%	29%	p. < .001
Acts of penetration (total sample Male N = 42, Female N = 89)	43%	24%	p. < .001
Completed acts, including fondling breasts, fondling genitals, oral copulation, sodomy and rape. (there were no male victims for fondling breasts or rape).	81%	70%	p. < .001

Adapted from Blalock (1979, p. 333). Analysis of the data utilized the statistical difference of a proportion.

Since boys are considered to better equipped by physique and training to defend themselves, how can these data be explained? If it is assumed that girls are more likely than boys to report attempted as well as completed acts, then the percentage of female victims suffering completed acts will be diluted by the inclusion of the less serious offenses in the reporting sample. In fact, almost seven times as many girls as boys reported attempted acts (27 vs. 4). These data are consistent with findings cited above that boys are more reluctant than girls to report sexual victimization. Another explanation is that boys are likely to be more seriously assaulted than girls in cases of sexual child assault. Some authorities (Largen, 1978) have suggested that sexually victimized boys are murdered more often than girls. If this speculation is accurate, it may be that the perpetrator so fears public exposure of his homosexual child abuse that he kills his victim to silence him. Or boys may offer more physical resistance than girls, and in the ensuing struggle may suffer serious injury or death. In the Landis study (1956), four times as many boy as girl victims actively resisted sexual approaches (28 percent and seven percent, respectively). The sensational Corll case in Texas and the current Gacy case in Illinois involving mass sex murders of young boys demonstrate not only the perpetrator's sadism but his horror of discovery as well.

A study similar to the San Francisco study was conducted in Kansas City, covering much the same time period (Swift, 1976). Data on reports of sex crimes against children were collected in the Kansas City, Missouri, and the Kansas City, Kansas, Police Departments from January, 1976, through April, 1977. While the research is ongoing and data have not been fully analyzed, preliminary results confirm the San Francisco results. Out of 176 victims under the age of 18, 30 percent were male. The reporting categories for sex acts were not the same in both studies — in the Kansas City study sodomy includes both oral and anal intercourse. However, percent of completed acts calculated for male and female victims in the Kansas City study, shows the same differences by

240

sex as the San Francisco sample. Male victims suffered significantly more completed acts than female victims, where completed acts were rape and sodomy. Analysis of variance for completed act by sex yielded a probability of less than .001. Girls in the Kansas City study, like their San Francisco counterparts, were also significantly more likely than boys to report the less serous acts. Girls reported being molested and forced to disrobe significantly more often than boys. Chi square analysis yielded probabilities of less than .001 and .005, respectively.

Prevention

The importance for prevention of establishing empirically the incidence of sexual abuse of young males and the reporting of these events lies in the possibility that it is this group that constitutes a high risk for committing sexual offenses later in life. The phenomenon of the repetitive cycle of child abuse is a familiar theme in the literature. Studies of convicted sex offenders provide evidence of such repetitive victimization. Serrill (1974) reports that 75 percent of a group of 150 male sex offenders in Rahway State Prison in New Jersey were sexually abused as children. In a more recent study, a third of a sample of 348 males convicted of sexual assault (rape or child molestation) spontaneously mentioned, in the course of an interview, that they had themselves been sexually victimized as children (Groth, 1979b). Since these offenders were not systematically asked about possible sexual victimization, this figure is considered an underestimate.

Gebhard, Gagnon, Pomeroy & Christenson (1965) also noted that sexual offenders who molested children had often been sexually molested themselves as children. A sample of convicted pedophiles preferring boys as partners reported their first homosexual intercourse before they were 14 years old (Goldstein, 1973). Goldstein suggests that these are "second generation pedophiles," first initiated into homosexual pedophilia as victims, later reliving the pedophilic experience as adult perpetrators. Meiselman (1979) discusses intergenerational incest, in which the child incest victim carries the incest to the next generation as parent.

If these studies are valid, i.e., if a large proportion of males who sexually abuse children were themselves sexually abused as children, then prevention efforts directed toward identification of victimized males, followed by early intervention and treatment, have the potential for reducing the incidence of sexual child assault in the next generation. However, assuming it were possible to elicit prompt, accurate reporting by the male victims of sexual attacks, it is likely that these reports would meet with inappropriate responses on the part of the adult community. The silence of the 84 percent of the victimized males in Landis' study testifies to the efficacy of the taboo attached to the doubly stigmatized act of homosexual attack of a child. Therefore, direct attempts to increase reporting by sexually abused boys are premature, since it could not be guaranteed that their reports would be met with support and empathy. It would first be desirable to change the attitudes of the public to create a climate which would sanction equally reports of sexual assault by both boys and girls.

A prevention effort based on the above rationale would require a series of steps for implementation:

1. The adult community of professionals in contact with sexually abused children and their families must be educated to the reality of sexual assaults on boys as well as girls, and trained to be receptive to taking such reports from children without further traumatizing the child for reporting the incident. The Michigan study demonstrates that increased reporting from boys can be elicited by professional encouragement and direction (Groth, 1979a). Professionals to be included in educational efforts are law enforcement, mental health, medical, clergy, child protective agency and school personnel.

2. Once the professional community is prepared to deal with reports of homosexual assaults on boys, parents should be educated to the fact that their male, as well as their female children, are at risk for sexual abuse.

3. Children themselves, particularly boys, should be encouraged to report incidents in which they have been sexually abused to parents and helping authorities.

4. Early intervention and treatment with sexually abused boys would, hopefully, result in the prevention of sexual offenses by this population later in life.

Sexual Ignorance

Ethical considerations prohibit most direct experimental interventions in this field. No researcher could justify creating conditions that would place children at risk for abuse. However, the larger society has in this instance created conditions which permit a rough test of the second hypothesis — that many sexual child abusers are sexually ignorant and socially immature. In the decade between 1959 and 1969, pornographic materials beame increasingly available in Denmark (Kutchinsky, 1971). In 1967, legal sanctions against pornographic literature were removed. In 1969, it became legal to produce and commercially distribute graphic pornography. Studies of the correlation between the incidence of sex crimes in Copenhagen and the availability of pornography demonstrate that sex crimes against children dropped sharply during this period. No such drop occurred in the incidence of rape of adult women. As shown below, the relative decreases in the more serious sex crimes against children were substantial. The percentages below were derived from data supplied by Ben-Veniste (1971).

Relative Decreases in Sex Crime Against Children in Copenhagen Between 1959 and 1969

Sex Crime	Relative Decrease 1959-1969
Coitus with a child under 15	62%
Unlawful interference with children (homosexual)	74%
Unlawful interference with children short of rape	69%
Honosexual relationship with children (two age categories were collapsed)	86%
Total sex offenses against children	69%
Total sex crimes	65%

While interpretation of these data is hampered by the lack of definition of some of the crime categories, it is clear that "coitus with a child under 15" and "unlawful interference with children short of rape" are heterosexual offenses involving female victims, while homosexual offenses involve male victims.

Kutchinsky (1971) argues that the ready availability of pornography in Denmark during the Sixties is responsible for the decrease in sexual child abuse. He considers and discards several alternative explanations. The first is that public attitudes toward sexual behavior may have led to changes in the way adult-child sexual interactions were viewed. What was labeled as a sex crime in 1959 may not have been considered criminal ten years later. To assess possible attitudinal change, Kutchinsky surveyed a representative sample of 400 adults in Copenhagen in 1969. He found that while attitudes toward some sex crimes appeared to have undergone liberalization, 93 percent of the respondents labeled child molestation as a criminal act. His survey results seem to rule out any change in public attitudes as a causal factor in the noted reduction of reported cases of sex crimes against children.

A second explanation considered is that the readiness of victims and their families to report such crimes to the police may have declined over the ten year period. This possibility was not tested for child victims, since survey participants were adults. Based on the adult responses, however, Kutchinsky estimates that change in readiness to report such cases could account for no more than 20 percent of the 69 percent decrease. By surveying police officers and reviewing both police procedures for filing reports and recent legislation,

241

Kutchinsky rules out these factors as having any influence in the documented decrease. He concludes that the observed 69 percent reduction represents an actual decrease in the number of children sexually victimized over the decade of the Sixties in Copenhagen, and cites the increasing availability of pornography during this period as the operative variable in effecting the reduction. He suggests that pornography, by providing sexual release when used as a stimulant to masturbation, may be substituted for the sexual gratification these men previously found in illegal sexual interactions with children.

Pornography may also function as a source of sex education for men deprived of such information from other sources. A recurring theme in the literature is that the sexual ignorance of many child molesters contributes to their choice of children as sexual partners. According to this view, many such offenders select children not from preference, but from expediency. The child is less likely to refuse, less likely to know that the sought after sexual contacts are socially forbidden, less likely to ridicule or note the offender's sexual inadequacies, less likely to tell anybody or to be believed if s/he does tell. Pornography, then, with its graphic depiction of sex organs and acts, may serve the function of providing sex information to sexually ignorant men, facilitating their graduation to adult sexual partners.

Empirical support for the educative effects of pornography is found in a study by Goldstein and his associates (1973). They compared convicted sex offenders (rapists and pedophiles) with homosexuals, transsexuals, and a group of "normal" controls with regard to the relationship between exposure to pornography and the development of sexual pathology. The control group reported more exposure to pornography during adolescence than any of the other groups tested. The pedophiles reported the least exposure. No evidence was found that the use of pornography in childhood or adolescence leads to sexual pathology.

In response to questions about attitudes toward sex, sex education and current practices, the pedophiles reported less parental tolerance toward nudity in the home than controls, and little or no discussion of sex in the home. They reported the most discomfort of all the groups in talking about sex, and the most conservative attitudes toward premarital sexual relations. Controls were twice as likely as pedophiles to have received sex information through the schools. Pedophiles received less education about sexual matters during their childhood than any of the other groups.

Assuming that responsible sex education programs could indeed reduce the incidence of sexual child abuse, formidable problems of program implementation would still remain. One of the most frustrating barriers to prevention programs in general is the public's documented reluctance, in the face of strong empirical evidence, to take the steps necessary to prevent negative outcomes. The current public health push to insure that all children in this country are inoculated against the common childhood diseases is a reminder that many parents are willing to gamble with their childrens' health and lives. Even if irrefutable evidence of the preventive power of sex education in reducing cases of sexual child abuse could be produced, which it cannot, it is unlikely that sex education would become a standard in school curricula in the near future. Parental fears, bureaucratic timidity and a tradition of repression of sexual information combine to obstruct the implementation of sex education programs in the schools.

Kutchinsky's study makes a compelling argument for responsible sex education as a preventive measure for sexual child abuse. If the widespread provision of sexual information is instrumental in reducing sexual child abuse, then our society, through its failure to provide adequate sex information to today's children, functionally sanctions the production of child molesters, and insures the continued victimization of tomorrow's children.

REFERENCES

Ben-Veniste, R. *Pornography and sex crime: The Danish experience.* Technical reports of the Commission on Obscenity and Pornography, U.S. Government Printing Office, Washington, D.C., 1971, 7, 245-310.

Bender, L. & Blau, A. The reaction of children to sexual relationships with adults. *American Journal Orthopsychiatry,* 1937, 7, 500-518.

Blalock, J., Jr. *Social Statistics, rev. ed.* McGraw-Hill, 1979.

De Francis, V. Protecting the child victim of sex crimes committed by adults. *Federal Probation,* 1971, 35, p. 17.

Gagnon, J. Female child victims of sex offenses. In *Studies in Human Behavior: The American Scene,* Ailon Shiloh, Ed. Springfield, Ill. Chas. C. Thomas, Publisher, 1970.

Gebhard, P., Gagnon, J., Pomeroy, W. & Christenson, C. *Sex Offenders: An Analysis of Types.* New York: Harper & Row, 1965.

Gigeroff, A., Mohr, J. & Turner, R. Sex offenders on probation: heterosexual pedophiles. *Federal Probation,* December, 1968, 17-21.

Goldstein, M. Exposure to erotic stimuli and sexual deviance. *Journal of Social Issues,* 1973, 29, 197-219.

Groth, N. *Men Who Rape: the Psychology of the Offender.* New York: Plenum Publishing Corp., 1979a, in press.

Groth, N. Sexual trauma in the life histories of rapists and child molesters. *Victimology: an International Journal,* 1979b, 4:1.

Harrer, M., Copeland, L., Brody, J. & Watkins, S. *Sexual Abuse of Children.* Queen's Bench Foundation, San Francisco, 1976.

Kinsey, A., Pomeroy, W., Martin, C. and Gebhard, P. *Sexual Behavior in the Human Female,* Philadelphia: Saunders, 1953.

Krasner, W., Meyer, L. & Carroll, N. *Victims of Rape.* United States DHEW Publication No. (ADM) 77-485, 1977.

Kutchinsky, B. *Towards an explanation of the decrease in registered sex crimes in Copenhagen.* Washington, D.C.: U.S. Government Printing Office, Technical reports of the Commission on Obscenity and Pornography, 1971, 7, 263-310.

Landis, J. Experiences of 500 children with adult sexual deviation. *Psychiatric Quarterly Supplement,* 1956, 30, 91-109.

Largen, M. Personal Communication, 1978.

Meiselman, K. *Incest: a Psychological Study of Causes and Treatment Recommendations.* San Francisco: Josey-Bass, Inc., 1978.

Midlarsky, E. Child sexual assault and incest: A bibliography. *Journal Supplement Abstract Service: Catalog of Selected Documents in Psychology,* 1978, 8, 65.

Sarafino, E. An estimate of nationwide incidence of sexual offenses against children. *Child Welfare,* 1979, 58, 127-134.

Schultz, L. The sexual abuse of children and minors: a bibliography. *Child Welfare,* 1979, 58, 147-163.

Serrill, M. Treating sex offenders in New Jersey. *Corrections,* 1974, 1, 13-24.

Swift, C. Consultation in the area of sexual child abuse. NIMH grant uMH-29038-01, 1976.

Swift, C. Sexual victimization of children: An urban mental health center survey. *Victimology: an International Journal,* 1977, 2, 322-327.

Walters, D. *Physical and Sexual Abuse of Children – Causes and Treatment.* Bloomington, Indiana: Indiana University Press, 1975.

Weiss, J., Rogers, E., Darwin, M. & Dutton D. A study of girl sex victims. *Psychiatric Quarterly,* 1955, 29, 1-26.

FOOTNOTES

1. In approximately 80 percent of the cases of sexual child abuse the perpetrator is known to the child (Weiss, Rogers, Darwin & Dutton, 1955; Gigeroff, Mohr & Turner, 1968; De Francis, 1971; Walters, 1975). In at least 25 percent of the cases, the perpetrator is a family member (De Francis, 1971; Walters, 1975; Krasner, Meyer & Carrolll, 1977; Swift, 1977).

2. Grateful acknowledgment is made to Connie Osgood, Ph.D., and Chris Kukuk, Ph.D. of the Institute of Community Studies in Kansas City for their consultation in data analysis.

Requests for reprints should be sent to: Carolyn Swift, Ph.D., Wyandot Mental Health Center, Eaton at 36th Avenue, Kansas City, Kansas 66103.

242

Child Abuse and Neglect. Vol. 6, pp. 251-261. 1982
Printed in the U.S.A. All rights reserved

A REVIEW OF THE LITERATURE
ON THE
PREVENTION OF CHILD ABUSE AND NEGLECT

RAY E. HELFER, M.D.

Department of Pediatrics and Human Development
Michigan State University
East Lansing, Michigan 48824

INTRODUCTION (OBJECTIVE)

IN THE SPRING of 1981, the Children's Services Division of the Ministry of Community and Social Services, Province of Ontario, Canada, provided funds for the establishment of an epidemiological unit at the Child and Family Center, in conjunction with MacMaster University in Hamilton, Ontario. The major aim of this unit is "the provision of basic information necessary for the successful launching of primary prevention endeavors...." The overall goal is to develop "programs aimed at reducing the incidence of disorders, in the area of childhood emotional problems."

The aims are to be accomplished in several ways, one of which is, "to provide an up-to-date and ongoing review of the literature on the primary prevention of major childhood emotional disorders."

The charge provided to this reviewer indicated that the literature in the area of child abuse and neglect should be reviewed and reported by summarizing the "programs or maneuvers that have been found to be successful in term of efficacy, effectiveness, etc...." A final charge was to "rate the scientific rigors of the evidence supporting the report of success or failure."

With this charge this reviewer was given a free hand to proceed with the literature search in a manner which he felt would accomplish these objectives. Specifically, there are two areas which are *not* intended to be covered by this review; one is the literature that deals with early identification methods of high risk individuals. This is to be covered in a different section of the epidemiological unit's tasks. Secondly, this review is not intended to be an all-inclusive worldwide literature search, rather a large representative sample of the English literature.

DEFINITIONS

The United States government has spent literally hundreds of thousands of dollars on projects and grants trying to develop a working definition of child abuse and neglect. Even though this literature review was not undertaken for the purpose of searching for a resolution of this dilemma, a working definition had to be established in order to proceed with the primary objective of this project. For these reasons, the writer used a definition which was developed a number of years ago and used quite effectively since that time. The definition of child abuse and neglect that is

243

used in this review is as follows: "Any interaction or lack of interaction between a child and his or her caregiver which results in non-accidental harm to the child's physical and/or developmental state."

The key words or phrases in this definition are "interaction or lack of interaction" between two people, thereby referring to a two-way happening occurring between the child and his or her caregiver. The word "non-accidental" is of primary importance, since it does not imply motivation, rather the absence of an accident. The phrase "harm to the child's physical or developmental state" is to be taken very literally to mean that if the body is indeed harmed or the child's normal and expected developmental state is harmed or interfered with by the interaction or lack of interaction, this would classify the incident as having been abusive and/or neglectful. This definition also considers the importance of time, i.e., a single event may well injure the physical state much more significantly than the developmental state, and a prolonged event might seriously harm both the physical and the developmental state of the child. The purpose of this section is not to dwell on the definition, rather to state it, explain it and to move on to the task at hand.

In regard to the definition of prevention, this writer has reviewed the literature with the following definition in mind: "Any maneuver or program which has as its intent the prevention of child abuse and/or neglect as defined above."

There are, however, some limitations that were set forth prior to undertaking this review. These are best understood by classifying prevention into three subsets, which are as follows:

1. *Primary prevention*: any maneuver that occurs to or around an *individual* (primarily infants), the stated purpose of which is to prevent child abuse and neglect from ever occurring to that individual. A second subset of primary prevention can be stated as a *socially* defined subset, whereby a program or maneuver is proposed or initiated to change the whole societal structure, thereby preventing abuse and/or neglect from ever occurring. An example might be to rid society of poverty or, on a smaller scale, to change a program within a given segment of our society, such as a hospital or a public health department. These changes would affect large numbers of people, rather than an individual.

2. *Secondary prevention*: any program or maneuver that is implemented to or for an individual or group of individuals, who have been identified as coming from a very high risk environment, which has as its intent the prevention of the abuse and/or neglect from occurring to that individual's offspring. An example, the identifying of a child or young adult who has been abused and neglected and implementing a program in the school system or college that would prevent the occurrence of the abuse and neglect in the next generation.

3. *Tertiary prevention*: any after-the-fact program initiated after abuse and neglect has occurred, the intent of which is to keep the abuse and/or neglect from happening again. Such a program might be traditional protective services that wait for a report of abuse and neglect and implement some type of maneuver to prevent it from happening to the child or children in question a second time.

An example of these three definitions might be clearer if the medical model of tuberculosis is given. Tertiary prevention program would be the identification of a man who has tuberculosis and initiating treatment so he does not have a recurrence. A secondary prevention program would be the identification of all of his children who have been exposed to this particular individual and starting them on a drug to prevent the occurrence of tuberculosis in any of these exposed individuals. A primary prevention program for this same family would be the injection of BCG vaccine in the newborn baby of this man's wife to prevent tuberculosis from occurring in the infant.

One final condition, in this review of the literature on child abuse and neglect prevention programs no attention has been given to the voluminous literature dealing with tertiary programs, i.e., after-the-fact services for children and/or their families who have already been identified as having been abused and/or neglected. This review will center entirely on primary and secondary prevention maneuvers.

INCIDENCE

The incidence of child abuse and neglect will depend entirely on how one defines it and how extensive one searches for it. Like the definition, the United States Government has spent hundreds of thousands of dollars on trying to define the incidence of this malady of families. If one looks only at the number of reports of *suspected* abuse and neglect from the 50 states, it is clear that the incidence is, on an annual basis, between 1–1½% of all *children*. Realizing that there is an over-reporting of false cases, and an under-reporting of unknown cases, these two may be considered to "balance" one another out, giving an overall annual incidence of children who are abused and/or neglected at the approximate rate of 10–15/1,000 children per year.*

COMMENTS ON PREVENTION

Prior to undertaking the description of the methods of the review and its findings, there are a number of key elements about the prevention of child abuse and neglect that warrant mention when considering programs that are specifically intended for this purpose. These comments appeared in the literature in 1976 and should be reviewed for emphasis, as they are still very pertinent to this field [34]. As these points are read, one should keep in mind that a decision must be made by any individual wishing to implement a prevention program in the area of child abuse and neglect. This decision is to determine whether or not the ultimate purpose is to prevent something harmful, i.e., abuse and/or neglect to a child, or to enhance something positive, i.e., an improved interaction between a parent and a child. If one agrees with the above stated definition, then child abuse and neglect prevention programs could well be thought of as programs that are aimed primarily at improving or enhancing the interactional system between a parent and his/her child. This issue is discussed in greater detail later in this review.

The excerpts from the 1976 article on prevention also provided comments on the ethical issues raised [11].

METHOD OF REVIEW

The process used in searching the literature to accomplish this review was as follows: A sample run of the computer service "Medline," was done to determine the extent of the literature when the computer was given the key words "child abuse and neglect," "sexual abuse" *and* "prevention." Each of these words or phrases had to, in some way, appear in either the title and/or the abstract. Sixty-three citations were obtained. The same question, with the same criteria, was asked the computer for the search of the *Psych* abstracts. This yielded 78 citations. Finally, the mental health abstracts from the National Institute of Mental Health were searched and yielded 444 citations. With very few exceptions, the mental health citations included those also obtained from the *Psych* and "Medline" computer abstracts.

Each of the citations were then reviewed by title and a decision made as to which were most likely to give information regarding programs in primary or secondary prevention, as defined above. A total of 134 abstracts were requested, 19 from *Psych* abstracts, 97 from "Mental Health," and 18 from "Medline." The computer balked at this request, since it was not able to individually search separate titles or abstracts without very significant cost.

---

*The reader must not lose sight of the importance of the phrase *"per year."* Since abuse and neglect harm the child's developmental state, which does not "heal" in the same manner as do many physical injuries, these figures are cumulative, 10–15/1000 children *each year*; an alarming statistic.

The next request limited the computer search to provide abstracts from "Medline" and the National Institute of Mental Health on the already identified citations which contained the words "prevention" within the *title*. Eighty-seven such abstracts were obtained. Each abstract was reviewed and 30 were rejected as not meeting the primary or secondary criteria (most actually falling into the tertiary classification). Of the 57 abstracts remaining, 10 articles were found which dealt with a research methodology and 47 fell into the category of proposals only, or proposals with clinical trials. This search included the years 1970 through the present. Finally, a hand review was conducted from 1975 to present from the *Journal of Pediatrics, Pediatrics* and from Volume 1 through the present of *Child Abuse and Neglect, The International Journal*. While this review is not intended to be worldwide or all inclusive, it is representative of the "state of the art" as it currently is reported in a wide expanse of the literature. Non-English articles were not included.

A final comment should be made as to the criteria used for defining an article as "research." If the abstract indicated that there was some type of methodological approach, a control or comparison group, or a hypothesis tested, this article was found, reviewed in detail and summarized as a "research" project. Ten articles fell in this category (see below).

FINDINGS

Proposals Only or Proposals with Clinical Trials

The articles which presented proposals only or proposals with clinical trials and discussed maneuvers or programs for prevention were classified into one of ten basic areas. They are listed below (in no particular order or priority) and briefly discussed with appropriate references provided.

1. *The treatment of the child.* There is general consensus in the literature that programs that are directed toward the treatment of the child, either a child who has been abused or might be abused, should be considered in the prevention category. These fall into either the primary or secondary prevention classification. Programs that are proposed for child-centered therapy include such endeavors as play therapy, visitors in the home, infant developmental approaches, group therapy for children, special programs for adolescents and the like. There are many more articles which proposed programs only [5, 14, 17, 48, 52, 54, 64], than those which actually discuss the trial of a given program [31, 41, 44, 56].

2. *Family-oriented programs and family advocacy.* These programs are not dissimilar to the many that are in existence for what might be termed "after-the-fact" tertiary prevention programs, but are classified in these particular articles as preventive endeavors for families who were, for some reason, considered high risk. These include primarily the outreach endeavors that are family-oriented [8, 49, 51, 53, 57].

3. *Expansion of existing programs.* There are a number of authors who propose that the major method to increase preventive services is to enhance and expand existing after-the-fact services. These include such programs as increasing Protective Services in various communities and modifying the role of after-the-fact therapist in one way or another, such as the mental health worker and/or the therapist working in a private agency [2, 45, 61, 62].

4. *Early childhood education programs.* While programs to enhance the use of early childhood education programs such as Head Start and Upstart programs might be seen as a subcategory of maneuver number one (listed above) this category is separated here because of the emphasis given to it by several authors in the literature. The proposal is that existing early child development programs, nursery schools, day care, etc., be expanded to include special children with particular problems who come from abusive and neglectful environments [6, 10, 46, 63].

5. *The development of multidisciplinary teams or SCAN teams (Suspected Child Abuse and Neglect).* There is wide acceptance in the literature that the use of multidisciplinary teams not only enhances the after-the-fact tertiary prevention services, but have the potential of preventing child abuse and neglect. Most of the articles present not only a proposal but also indicate results from an actual trial of such an endeavor [7, 12, 13, 15, 22, 58, 70]. These multidisciplinary teams include a variety of professionals such as nurses, social workers, psychologists, psychiatrists, law enforcement officers, pediatricians and protective service workers from the community. Detailed discussion of the development of multidisciplinary teams within a community is provided in the literature as well [33, 59].

6. *Training of paraprofessionals and parents.* Several authors propose that a major approach to the prevention of child abuse and neglect is through the increasing education of paraprofessionals, including both volunteers and parents. Parents are seen as the frontline paraprofessional in dealing with the child. Certain innovative approaches are proposed in the literature, such as the use of television for adult education [19], a "crash course" in childhood for adults [36], and a "warm line" for the education of young parents [1]. Further suggestions are made by other authors [16, 40, 47].

7. *Increasing the role of public education.* Several articles propose the use of the public schools as a primary modality for teaching children basic interpersonal skills, as well as content information about child rearing and child abuse and neglect [9, 35, 38, 55]. The mandate to the school system is quite clear in the literature.

8. *Enhancing the mother/baby bond in the newborn period.* Increasing attention is now being given to the importance of the mother/baby, father/baby interaction with the newborn infant. Several articles not only make specific proposals [18, 21, 32] but also report on specific trial programs that are discussed in some detail [3, 20, 39].

9. *Organization of the community.* There is an underlying message that comes forth from this review which indicates that the foundation of prevention of child abuse and neglect is laid upon the organization of a given community, particularly as it relates to the services provided to families. There is extensive discussion in the literature regarding these community structures [33, 40, 59, 68].

10. *Changes within the society and the political structure.* Finally, there crops up in every review of this nature proposals that the societal structure and political framework could, if changed, make a major difference in the method in which children are dealt with in our communities [26, 27]. These are proposals only, not accompanied by specific recommendations or trials.

There is one additional article which falls into the category of proposal and trial that warrants specific mention [69]. It is highlighted, in part, because of its uniqueness but more important, because of the country from which it was reported, i.e., Russia. In all of the reports from this review and others that have been read in the past 15 years, this writer has never come across any article from the U.S.S.R. There have been no attendees from Russia at any of the three International Congresses, in Geneva (1977), London (1978), or Amsterdam (1981). Victorov reported, in 1969, in the "International Review of Criminal Policy," a program developed by their law enforcement division on a reduction in crime in the Soviet Union because of the work of the Juvenile Affairs Board [69]. He suggests that "a considerable contribution to the prevention of child neglect in juvenile delinquency is also being made by the police through their special juvenile affairs officers and through the Children's Chamber of the Police. The police work in close cooperation with the public." This program is not only unique by its involvement of the police department but is worthy of special notice because of the year in which it was written and the country from which it was reported.

247

Research Projects

The classic study in preventive methodology was performed in the mid 1970s by Gray, Cutler, Dean and Kempe. Using a screening system consisting of labor and delivery observations and parent interviews and observations in the nursery, these investigators identified high and low risk parenting groups. A population of 350 mothers having their first or second delivery were selected. They randomly assigned 50 high risk mothers to an intervene group and 50 to a non-intervene group. A third group of 50 low risk mothers were controls. Intervention consisting of comprehensive health care by a single physician and a lay health visitor or a public health nurse was provided for two years. Ten percent of the high risk, non-intervene group required hospitalization for serious injury resulting from abnormal parenting practices. None of the other two groups required hospitalization for similar injuries. Other differences were also noted. This study was reported on three separate occasions by these researchers [28, 29, 30; also see 42].

O'Connor and her colleagues studied this affect of rooming-in on the parent child interaction after the delivery of a first-born child. Random samples of 134 mothers were assigned to rooming-in and 148 to the regular routine nursery care. A seventeen month follow-up revealed eight children in the non-rooming-in group and one child in the rooming-in group required hospitalization for inadequate parenting [50].

The study of the affect of extended mother-infant contact and for home visits by a lay volunteer on attachment behavior and child abuse and neglect was completed by Siegel and his co-workers [60]. He demonstrated minimal affect of these maneuvers on his outcome variables. Unfortunately his study suffered from two serious methodological errors: first, no follow-up was attempted on any of the 201 women (from a total of 525) who did not participate; second, they made no attempt to determine the presence or absence of abusive potential in either the study or the control groups (see discussion of this error below).

Bailey advocates three separate maneuvers to evaluate the causes, effect and prevention of child abuse and neglect [4]. These include use of MMPI to describe psychopathology, case study to identify predisposing factors to abuse and the usefulness that increased knowledge has in the area of child abuse. These are preliminary studies with assumptions only, dealing with the relationship of these maneuvers to prevention.

The Gabinet study in metropolitan Cleveland was most energetic. She and her specially trained psychology assistants worked on the parenting skill of young, truly hard core, adolescent, single mothers. A total of 180 parents were referred, 103 seen five times or less and 77 were seen six or more times. Subsequent measures were used to determine the effectiveness of the parenting program. There were no controls or behavioral outcomes measured which related to child abuse and/or neglect [23].

Gladston has two reports on the Parent Center Project at Howard Medical School [24, 25]. While this is not a research study and technically does not meet the prevention definition provided, it does deal directly with abused children in an attempt to improve their plight, growth and development. Literally, to qualify this project as prevention one would have to project the treatment of children to decrease abuse of their off-spring in the next generation (i.e., a secondary prevention maneuver). Their work is of significant enough importance, however, to warrant mention as a serious study of this mode of intervention. The inbreeding of violence within the family permeates the children in this study.

Comment: The reader must keep in mind that this is a review of significant *research* done in the field of child abuse and neglect prevention. Of the hundreds of articles originally surveyed only 10 were found which were "felt," by title and abstract, to meet the criteria established for both prevention and research. When these 10 articles were actually found and read, the following was revealed:

1. Three articles were reported on the same research study [28, 29, 30] and one was a commentary on that study among other things [42].

2. One was a report on a research project done during the newborn period [50].
3. One was an infant hospital/home contact and service program which made no effort to follow 38% of the population and had no assessment of abuse potential in their control or study groups [60].
4. A seventh was a discussion of three maneuvers and provided minimal data [54].
5. The eighth was an energetic study of high risk young mothers with no controls [23].
6. The ninth and tenth were descriptions of progress made working with abused preschool children [24, 25].

In summary, only three studies were found [28, 50, 60] which truly dealt with the subject of *research* in the *prevention* of child abuse and neglect.

DISCUSSION

The natural history of the process of problem resolution for any serious malady that affects our society, or those individuals who make up our social system, is very similar regardless of the social disorder. Whether it be a disease entity such as smallpox, an economic crisis such as inflation and/or a depression, or an even more eroding dysfunction such as family violence as manifest by child and spouse abuse, the process of resolution usually progresses along an orderly, predefined pathway. Occasionally, shortcuts are forthcoming, but often what seems to be such is only a stop-gap measure, in retrospect.

The process is this: a major problem is recognized, usually by the presentation of its worst form (e.g., the truly battered and tortured child). Tolerance often ensues with a "what-can-we-do" attitude. Gradually, a few individuals appear who insist something must be done, studies are formulated, funding gained and the problem is further assessed and delineated. Other forms of the manifestation are then recognized, e.g., bruised and burned children, and eventually the entity is better understood to include variants of the problem such as overt neglect and failure to thrive. Eventually we even admit to the presence of social taboos, i.e., sexual abuse of children and the use of small children used for pornographic purposes.

As the dynamics of a malady are better understood, causation is searched for and often found. In the case of child abuse and neglect, a cause as we understand that word has not been delineated, rather many very consistent precursors and associations identified. Violence does indeed breed violence—if one is willing to define that term very broadly.

As these interrelationships are recognized, "causations" are assumed (sometimes correctly and sometimes incorrectly). From the assumptions formulated, the movement, in this natural history of problem resolution, toward preventive maneuvers begins. In the late 1940s, for example, swimming pools and theaters were closed to prevent polio from spreading—a logical maneuver, at least prior to the isolation of the polio virus and the development of a preventive vaccine. Other correlations and proposed "solutions" were not so logical, as it turned out, such as the curtailment of ice cream sales in the summer (for ice cream sales and polio incidence were highly correlated).

As one reviews the literature which deals with programs, or maneuvers, to prevent child abuse and neglect, this natural history of problem resolution is easily delineated. If this review is done with objectivity, a certain similarity to the swimming pool/ice cream days of the polio epidemics is noted. Some programs for the prevention of family violence are, indeed, built upon a logical base, while others seems to be a "shot in the dark," that is, if "X" seems good, "4X" must be four times better.

Over 85% of the articles reviewed on prevention dealt with proposals and/or trials of programs which were built upon an experiential base. Many, in fact most, are founded upon true face validity. None of this group, however, have yet been carried to the next stage of development to

249

justify the acceptance of the underlying hypothesis (usually not stated) that program "X" results in less abuse/neglect than the absence of program "X."

The few true research endeavors that have been reported have yielded most encouraging results. O'Connor's work with newborns and their mothers [50], Kempe's and Gray's reports on home care [28, 29, 30], Galdston's studies on parent education [24, 25], Bailey's work in family violence [4] and Gabinet's inner city [23] studies all indicate that the movement toward prevention is indeed underway.

Special mention should be made that many who attempt to do scientific research in this field have made serious methodological errors. The two errors made most frequently are:

1. Trying to assess the effectiveness of a program at the same time that one is trying to develop the program. The program must be developed *before* the evaluation begins.

2. Inadequate selection of comparison or control groups. Since the effects of family violence is so prevalent in our society, one cannot *randomly* select a control group and expect it to be *free* from these effects. The "wet lab" researcher understands the need to run "blanks" and adjust his/her machines accordingly, but social researchers often seem unaware of this basic methodology.

Those who struggle with research studies in this field are constantly plagued with the problem of defining terminal behaviors which can be measured. When one is looking for the *absence* of a behavior, e.g., no abuse or neglect, the task becomes even harder. If, on the other hand, one is trying to improve the interpersonal skills of interaction between parent and child, does the end point become the presence of improved skills or the absence of negative interactions, such as those resulting in abuse and neglect? Even if these questions are resolved, an added issue arises, how long must one follow his/her study and comparison (control) group to demonstrate the affect of the program under study? The literature suggests that family violence in childhood results in adverse behaviors seen in adolescence, adulthood and on to the next generation. Should one accept that the absence of abuse/neglect in the first year of life as the criteria for demonstrating the benefit, later in life, of a given maneuver or program?

Certainly, those who were the true believers in the advantages of Head Start for poor children were dismayed by short term studies, but were buoyed 15 years later as the yield finally is being shown and accepted.

Gil suggests that "the requirements of primary prevention of child abuse amount to fundamental philosophical and structural changes of the prevailing social, economic and political order" [26]. Kempe, on the other hand, states:

I continue to be very hopeful about the Society. All of us are united in wanting to give each child the very best start in life; our educational programs reflect this wish, as do our resarch efforts—all are designed to benefit children the world over. But global concerns can overwhelm and immobilize the best of us. It is just not possible to worry about all the needs of all the children all the time. There lies frustration and total inaction as well. For each of us there must be only one child at a time, and, generally, only one major research theme at a time. Thus, one keeps one's sanity and does the very best job. At the same time, all of us who are devoting our professional life to the cause of children must engage our minds and our hearts on their behalf, each one of us, and wherever we can, by the quality of our work, by being the child's advocate in our towns, in our states, and by influencing the national policy to our best ability. Do so with passion! Don't worry about being labeled a do-gooder, just DO GOOD! Only thus will our children receive their due share of all we have to give. [43]

Kempe's philosophy (the writer readily admits his bias) leads to a type of research in this field that has yet to be adequately explored, i.e., the extensive case study. Steele is a master at this form of clinical research [65, 66, 67]. His method of investigation permits acceptable scientific exploration without having to confront the many obstacles discussed above. This is not to say that controlled, long-term research studies are to be dismissed; by no means. Rather, the comprehensive long-term study of individual cases is to be encouraged.

This reviewer must conclude that the prevention of many forms of child abuse and neglect is achievable if, and only if, the approach is multifaceted. *Concurrent* maneuvers must include some combination of:

1. a community consortium committed to the dictum that family violence in their community is unacceptable [33, 40, 59, 68];
2. a mass media, never-ending campaign to educate the public on this dictum [16, 19, 40, 47];
3. a major change in our health services to include some form of training for *all* new parents in the art of communicating with one's new baby [1, 19, 39];
4. a home health visitor program for *all* new parents for the one to two years after the birth of their firstborn child [31, 41];
5. an early child development program for all preschool children run by churches, schools, community colleges or whomever [6, 10, 46];
6. an interpersonal skills program (how-to-get-along curriculum) in the public schools (K–12) built upon simple skills in grade school, advancing to courses in sexuality and parenting in high school [9, 35, 38, 55, 63]; and
7. an adult education program for two levels of young adults—those who had a positive rearing and want a refresher course in childhood before they become parents [19]; and those whose childhood was very minimal who need a "crash course in childhood" before parenting is undertaken [36].

With such a community-oriented multifaceted program, the individual child will be helped, i.e., Kempe's philosophy, and eventually the social, economic and political structure will change, a la Gil. Similar successful attacks on a seemingly unconquerable malady, such as leukemia and small pox, with multifaceted programs have been made. The destructive forces of family violence likewise can be diminished.

REFERENCES

1. ADKINS, P. G. and AINSA, T. D. The warm line: A primary prevention service. *Research Communications in Psychology, Psychiatry and Behavior* 3(2):173–176 (1978).
2. ALVY-KERBY, T. Preventing child abuse. *American Psychologist* 30(9):921–928 (1975).
3. AYOUB, C. and PFEIFER, D. R. An approach to primary prevention: The at-risk program. *Children Today* 6(3):14–17 (1977).
4. BAILEY, B. Child abuse: Causes, effect, and prevention. *Victimology: An International Journal* 2(2):337–342 (1977).
5. BAVOLEK, S. J., KLINE, D. F., McLAUGHLIN, J. A. and PUBLICOVER, P. R. Primary prevention of child abuse and neglect: Identification of high-risk adolescents. *Child Abuse and Neglect* 3(3/4):1071–1080 (1979).
6. BEAN, S. L. The parent's center project: A multiservice approach to the prevention of child abuse. *Child Welfare* 50(5):277–282 (1971).
7. BESWICK, K. Prevention of child abuse by the primary care team. *Child Abuse and Neglect* 3(3/4):1023–1026 (1979).
8. BIRENBAUM, A. The pediatric nurse practitioner and preventive community mental health. *Journal of Psychiatric Nursing and Mental Health Servies* 12(5):14–19 (1974).
9. BROADHURST, D. D. Project protection: A school program to detect and prevent child abuse and neglect. *Children Today* 4(3):22–25 (1975).
10. BROADHURST, D. D., EDMUNDS, M. and MAC DICKEN, R. A. Early childhood programs and the prevention and treatment of child abuse and neglect. *Child Abuse and Neglect User Manual Series,* DHEW Publication No. (OHDS) 79-30198 (1979).
11. BRODY, H. and GAISS, B. Ethical issues in early identification and prevention of unusual child rearing practices. In: *Child Abuse and Neglect: The Family and the Community,* Helfer and Kempe (Eds.), pp. 372–375. Ballinger Publisher, Cambridge, MA 1976.
12. CAFFO, E. and GUARALDI, G. P. An assumption for the organization of the social and sanitary services for the prevention and the management of ill-treatment of children in Italy. *Child Abuse and Neglect* 3(3/4):1051–1053 (1979).
13. CARMODY, F. J., LANIER, D., JR., and BARDILL, D. R. Prevention of child abuse and neglect in military families. *Children Today* 8(2):16, 21–23, 35 (1979).
14. CASTLE, R. L. On the prevention of child abuse and neglect. *Child Abuse and Neglect* 1(2–4):505 (1977).
15. COHN, A. The pediatrician role in the treatment of child abuse. *Pediatrics* 65:358–360 (1980).

16. COSTELLO, G. and ALGER, M. A program for secondary prevention of child abuse and neglect. *Child Abuse and Neglect* 3(3/4):1055–1058 (1979).

17. DEMBITZ, N. Preventing youth crime by preventing child neglect. *American Bar Association Journal* 65:(June): 920–923 (1979).

18. FIELDS, S. Prevention of child abuse and neglect: III. Screening can be the mother of success. *Innovations* 3(2):19–22 (1976).

19. FLANNERY, R. B., JR. Primary prevention and adult television viewing: methodological extension. *Psychological Reports* 46(2):578 (1980).

20. FONTANA, V. J. Child abuse: Prevention in teen-age parent. *New York State Journal of Medicine* 80(1):53–56 (1980).

21. FRIEDRICH, W. N. and BORISKIN, J. A. Primary prevention of child abuse: Focus on the special child. *Hospital and Community Psychiatry* 29(4):248–251 (1978).

22. FROMMER, E. A. Predictive/preventive work in vulnerable families of young children. *Child Abuse and Neglect* 3(3/4):777–780 (1979).

23. GABINET. L. Prevention of child abuse and neglect in an inner-city population: II. The program and the results. *Child Abuse and Neglect* 3(3/4):809–817 (1979).

24. GALDSTON, R. Preventing the abuse of little children: The parent's center project for the study and prevention of child abuse. *American Journal of Orthopsychiatry* 45(3):372–381 (1975).

25. GALDSTON, R. Violence begins at home: The parents' center project for the study and prevention of child abuse. *Journal of the American Academy of Child Psychiatry* 10(2):336–350 (1971).

26. GIL, D. G. Primary prevention of child abuse: A philosophical and political issue. *Psychiatric Opinion* 13(2):30–34 (1976).

27. Gil, D. G. Child abuse: Levels of manifestation, causal dimensions and primary prevention. *Victimology: An International Journal* 2(2):186–194 (1977).

28. GRAY, J. D., CUTLER, C. A., DEAN, J. G. and Kempe, C. H. Prediction and prevention of child abuse and neglect. *Child Abuse and Neglect: The International Journal* 1(1):45–58 (1977).

29. GRAY, J. D., CUTLER, D. A., DEAN, J. G., and KEMPE, C. H. Prediction and prevention of child abuse and neglect. *Journal of Social Issues* 35(2):127–139 (1979).

30. GRAY, J. D., CUTLER, C. A., DEAN, J. G. and KEMPE, C. H. Prediction and prevention of child abuse and neglect. *Seminars of Perinatology* 3:85–90 (1979).

31. GRAY, J. and KAPLAN, B. The lay health visitor program, and 18 month experience. In: *The Battered Child* (3rd ed.), Kempe and Helfer (Eds.), University of Chicago Press, Chicago (1980).

32. GURRY, D. L. Child abuse: Thoughts on doctors, nurses and prevention. *Child Abuse and Neglect* 1(2–4):435–443 (1977).

33. HELFER, R. E. and SCHMIDT. R. The community-based child abuse and neglect program. In: *Child Abuse and Neglect: The Family and the Community*, R. E. Helfer and C. H. Kempe (Eds.), Ballinger, Cambridge 1976.

34. HELFER, R. E. Basic issues concerning prediction. In: *Child Abuse and Neglect: The Family and the Community*, R. E. Helfer and C. H. Kempe (Eds.), Ballinger, Cambridge 1976.

35. HELFER, R. E. On the prevention of child abuse and neglect. *Child Abuse and Neglect* 1(2–4):502–504 (1977).

36. HELFER, R. E. *Childhood Comes First: A Crash Course in Childhood for Adults.* Published by R. E. Helfer, East Lansing, MI, 1978.

37. HELFER, R. E. An overview of prevention. In: *The Battered Child* (3rd ed.), C. H. Kempe and R. E. Helfer (Eds.), University of Chicago Press, Chicago, 1980.

38. HELFER, R. E. Developmental deficits which limit interpersonal skills (Chapter 3) and Retraining and relearning (Chapter 24). In: *The Battered Child* (3rd ed.), C. H. Kempe and R. E. Helfer (Eds.), University of Chicago Press, Chicago, 1980.

39. HELFER, R. E. and WILSON, A. L. Promoting a positive beginning: Enhancing parent-infant communications through perinatal coaching. In: *Ped. Cl. N. A.*, Christopherson (Ed.), April 1982.

40. HILL, D. Communication and collaboration in developing approaches to child abuse prevention and treatment. *Fifth National Symposium on Child Abuse, Denver*, American Humane Association, *151* p. 63–67 1976.

41. KEMPE, C. H. Approaches to preventing child abuse: The health visitors concept. *American Journal of Diseases of Children* 130(9):941–947 (1976).

42. KEMPE, C. H. Child abuse: The pediatrician's role in child advocacy and preventive pediatrics. *American Journal of Diseases of Children* 132(3):255–260 (1978).

43. KEMPE, C. H. Personal communication, 1981.

44. KEMPE, R., CUTLER, C., and DEAN, J. The infant with failure to thrive. In: *The Battered Child* (3rd ed.), C. H. Kempe and R. E. Helfer (Eds.), University of Chicago Press, 1980.

45. LAUER, J. W., LOURIE, I. S., SALUS, M. K. and BROADHURST, D. D. The role of the mental health professional in the prevention and treatment of child abuse and neglect. *User Manual Series.* DHEW Publication No. (OHDS) 79-30194, 1979.

46. LEHR, D. E. Child abuse and neglect prevention and treatment programs in Lehigh County, Pennsylvania. *Challenge* (Harrisburg) 19(2):15–17 (1976).

47. LUPTON, G. C. M. Prevention recognition management and treatment of cases of non-accidental injury to children: Arrangements in the United Kingdom. *Child Abuse and Neglect* 1(1):203–209 (1977).

48. MARTIN, H. P. and BEEZLEY, P. Prevention and the consequences of child abuse. *Journal of Operational Psychiatry* 6(1):68–77 (1974).

49. MORSE, A. E., HYDE, J. N., Jr., NEWBERGER, E. H. and REED, R. B. Environmental correlates of pediatric

social illness: Preventive implications of an advocacy approach. *American Journal of Public Health* **67**(7):612–615 (1977).

50. O'CONNOR, S., VIETZE, P. M., SHERROD, K. B., SANDLER, H. M., and ALTEMEIER, W. A. Reduced incidence of parenting inadequacy following rooming-in. *Ped.* **66**:176–182 (1980).

51. OSHEA, J. S. Child abuse and neglect update: The prevention of neglect or abuse is obvious goal. *Rhode Island Medical Journal* **61**(10):376–377 (1978).

52. PALMERI, R. Child abuse and the ounce of prevention. *Connecticut Health Bulletin* **84**(11):289–293 (1970).

53. POLLACK, C. B. Early case finding as a means of prevention of child abuse. In: *The Battered Child*, R. Helfer (Ed.), (p. 149–152) University of Chicago Press, Chicago (1968).

54. PRINGLE, M. K. Towards the prediction and prevention of abuse. *Bulletin of the British Psychological Society* (London) **31**:185 (1978).

55. RIGGS, R. S. and EVANS, D. W. Child abuse prevention: Implementation within the curriculum. *Journal of School Health* **49**(5):255–259 (1979).

56. ROBERTS, J., BESWICK, K., LEVERTON, B. and LYNCH, M. A. Prevention of Child Abuse. Group Therapy for Mothers and Children in the Community. *Child Abuse and Neglect: The International Journal* **1**(2–4):487–488 (1977).

57. ROBERTS, J., BESWICK, K., LEVERTON, B. and LYNCH, M. A. Prevention of child abuse: Group therapy for mothers and children. *The Practitioner (London)* **219**:111–115 (1977).

58. ROSENSTEIN, P. J. Family outreach: A program for the prevention of child neglect and abuse. *Child Welfare* **57**(8):519–525 (1978).

59. SHAY, S. W. Community Council for Child Abuse Prevention. In: *The Battered Child* (3rd ed.), C. H. Kempe and R. E. Helfer (Eds.), University of Chicago Press, Chicago (1980).

60. SIEGEL, E., BAUMAN, K. E., SCHAFER, E. S., SAUNDERS, M. M. and INGRAM, D. D. Hospital and home support during infancy: Impact on maternal attachment, child abuse and neglect and health care utilization. *Ped.* **66**:183–190 (1980).

61. SMITH, C. Preventative services which provide early intervention for families experiencing problems which could become crises. *Challenge* (Harrisburg) **19**(2):23–25 (1976).

62. SMITH, J. An examination of the effectiveness of social services and the law in the prevention of child abuse. *Health and Social Service Journal* (London) **86**(4513):1899 (1976).

63. SPIVACK, G., PRATT, J. and SHURE, M. *The Problem Solving Approach to Adjustment.* Jossey Bass, San Francisco (1976).

64. SMITH, S. M. The prevention of child abuse. *Canadian Journal of Public Health* **70**(2):108–110 (1979).

65. STEELE, B. F. and POLLACK, C. A psychiatric study of parents who abuse infants and small children. In: *The Battered Child* (1st ed.), R. E. Helfer and C. H. Kempe (Eds.), University of Chicago Press, Chicago (1968).

66. STEELE, B. F. Psychology of infanticide from maltreatment. In: *Infanticide and the Value of Life*, M. Kahl (Ed.), Prometheus Books, Buffalo (1978).

67. STEELE, B. F. Psychodynamic factors in child abuse. In: *The Battered Child* (3rd ed.), C. H. Kempe and R. E. Helfer (Eds.), University of Chicago Press, Chicago (1980).

68. U.S. OFFICE OF HUMAN DEVELOPMENT, OFFICE OF CHILD DEVELOPMENT. Child abuse and neglect: The problem and its management. *The Community Team: An Approach to Case Management and Prevention* (Vol. 3). U.S. Government Printing Office (1976).

69. VICTOROV, B. A. Public participation and crime prevention in the Union of Soviet Socialist Republics. *International Review of Criminal Policy* **27**:38–39 (1969).

70. ZUCKERKANDEL, D. The Supportive Child/Adult Network (SCAN) for the prevention of child abuse among families coming to West Philadelphia hospitals. *Challenge* (Harrisburg) **19**(2):19–20 (1976).

253

Secondary Prevention of Child Maltreatment: A Review

Steven L. McMurtry

Secondary prevention of child maltreatment involves identifying potential abusers and treating them before the abuse takes place. This article reviews research on attempts to screen parents to identify those who are at risk of maltreating their children. The author concludes that although accurate identification of such parents may eventually be possible, more research is needed to establish identifying criteria and to determine effective means of intervention to prevent abuse.

THE TOPIC OF prevention has received a great deal of attention in the human services literature—to the point, in fact, that this attention itself has become something of a matter for discussion (Gilbert, 1982). The logic of prevention is hard to deny, and arguments in its behalf also serve as a reminder that the existing service structure is still predominantly treatment oriented. In the vernacular of prevention, the present system may be said to be geared toward tertiary programs—those that attempt to avert further occurrence of a problem already manifested (Sundel and Homan, 1979). Much recent writing has urged the development of primary prevention strategies, which seek to affect social factors that contribute to the appearance of a problem. Somewhat lost in the shuffle has been the issue of secondary prevention, which is also before the fact in its timing but which attempts to direct services toward specific individuals or groups identified as having a high potential for experiencing a problem.

PREVENTION APPROACHES

Although not always identified as secondary prevention, suggestions for this approach have been commonly addressed to the problem of child abuse and neglect. The notion that at-risk parents may be identified and treated prior to the act of maltreatment has proven attractive. Helfer (1976) has proposed that a "disease model" may be applied, according to which the goal would be to "inoculate" susceptible parents against abusing or neglecting their children. The important difference between this approach and primary prevention is that the latter has as its point of intervention broad segments of society and many or all of its members.

Examples in public health illustrate the contrasts between the two prevention designs. Primary prevention is demonstrated by the widespread efforts of the polio vaccination programs of the 1950s and early 1960s that sought to immunize large numbers of people. Secondary prevention is exemplified by programs that try to identify individuals at risk of heart disease (on the basis of weight, eating and drinking habits, and so forth) and then prescribe remedial activities (such as dieting or reduction of smoking) to avert the onset of the disease. Although presumably everyone can benefit from maintaining proper weight and refraining from smoking, it also seems obvious that by no means should everyone be subjected to the sort of regimen required of a high-risk heart disease patient. In this sense, secondary preventive approaches to child maltreatment may offer certain advantages in efficiency of service, particularly since only a comparatively small number of parents are considered likely to maltreat their children.

As might be expected, the medical analogy does eventually break down, leaving behind some formidable difficulties. One of these stems from the fact that, unlike polio, heart disease, and other organic dysfunctions, child maltreatment escapes clear definition; it is not a discrete phenomenon that a parent clearly demonstrates or does not but instead consists of an amorphous group of behaviors that, when manifested to a different degree, might be considered characteristic of good parenting (Giovannoni and Becerra, 1979). The profession is faced, therefore, with predicting the development of a problem whose very existence is often a matter of subjective interpretation. More important, a clear and useful etiology of the problem is not known. Rigorously conducted research on the origins of abuse and neglect has been considerably scarcer than suppositions (Plotkin et al., 1981), and, as a number of reviews point out, the creditable findings available indicate a bewildering and often conflicting array of possible causal factors (Spinetta and Rigler, 1972; Martin and Beezley, 1974; Starr, 1979; Schmitt, 1980; Garbarino, 1980a; and Vietze et al., 1982).

This article reviews and summarizes the published research on secondary prevention of child maltreatment. Particular attention is given to attempts to devise measures to identify parents at risk of abusing or neglecting their children. As can be seen, these attempts have been important efforts in filling the void of research on predisposing factors and have produced some of the most carefully controlled results available. At the same time, however, they present a variety of dilemmas regarding the possibility of realistic and humane prevention of abuse and neglect. To provide a clear contrast between styles of preventive intervention, the review is preceded by a brief presentation of the major types of primary prevention designs, and is followed by discussion of the ramifications of existing knowledge for subsequent planning.

PRIMARY PREVENTION

The diversity of variables associated with the potential for child maltreatment has fed a growing array of suggestions for primary prevention programs. One approach has been concerned with the effects on the societal level of inegalitarian social organization and economic inequities (Gil, 1976), insufficient identification and protection of children's rights (Fraser, 1976), social acceptance of parental use of force (Garbarino, 1980b), rapid social change (Usdan, 1978), a rigid Judeo-Christian moral structure (D. L. Williams, 1978), and the interaction of sexism and radical "pronatalism" (G. J. Williams, 1980). The sorts of preventive interventions suggested by these writers include legislation to protect children's rights, abandonment of corporal punishment, advocacy for abortion, redistributive economic policies, and similar widely focused social reforms.

A second group of authors has been more directly concerned with the operation of intrafamilial variables in the appearance of abuse or neglect and has argued for social programs to assist families. Prominent in this literature have been proposals for various systems utilizing homemaker and home visitor services to provide support and crisis assistance to families with young children. According to these schemes, the visitors could be hospital-based personnel (Paulson and Blake, 1969), day care or other child support workers (Hammell, 1969), or community volunteers (Rosenstein, 1978). The most ambitious strategies have suggested the development of a nationwide system of health visitors fashioned after existing European models (Kempe, 1976; *Wingspread Report*, 1978).

A third group of suggested primary prevention programs has consisted of intensive educational interventions aimed at a variety of audiences. One model emphasized the potential benefits of attempting to sensitize society to basic issues of maltreatment and its deterrents on a more general level than in a simple public awareness campaign (Grazio, 1981). Another proposed the use of newsletters and "crash courses" to provide helpful information to young families (Helfer, 1978a). Probably the most frequently discussed strategy suggested making broad use of the public schools to teach adolescents essential skills likely to be required in their future parental roles (Spinetta and Rigler, 1972; *Education for Parenthood*, 1976).

EARLY CASE FINDING

In an argument that sets the stage for differentiating between primary and secondary preventive approaches, Helfer (1976) noted that, realistically, people are accessible to meaningful efforts at preventing abuse and neglect during only two periods in their lives. The first, as already mentioned, is during their careers as public school pupils. The second is when they seek medical care as parents or parents-to-be. The school setting is appropriate for many of the primary prevention programs that have been suggested. The medical setting, according to Helfer, is ideally suited for screening and intervention programs of a secondary prevention nature. As can be seen, a growing body of literature supports this idea.

In an early work, Pollock (1968) presented a series of questions to be incorporated in standard pediatric interviews when medical attention is sought under unusual circumstances. The questions would assist in identifying parents at risk of maltreatment and cover such topics as the parents' means of coping with various behaviors of the child and their general perceptions of the child's needs. Similar approaches suggested the review of cases by multidisciplinary groups trained to identify abusive or preabusive dynamics in families (Lovens and Rako, 1975; and Ayoub and Pfeifer, 1977). Martin and Beezley (1974) surveyed existing literature on abusive and neglectful families and developed categories of variables for consideration in screening that emphasize identifying characteristics that make particular children at risk

of being maltreated. These, they suggested, can be applied in postnatal, in-home, and substitute-care settings. Olson (1976) formulated an "index of suspicion" for use by maternity nurses. The index consists of a checklist of variables that indicate various types of family problem areas and referral sources for remedial services associated with these problems.

PREDICTIVE SCREENING

Much needed empirical tests of screening programs have begun to offer some validation of these efforts. Rowan (1979) examined the hospital records of 54 children, including such information as abnormalities of pregnancy and child, quality of postnatal care, whether the parents had conferred with a hospital social worker during pregnancy, and other data available on an ex post facto basis. Her results indicated that the combination of variables could distinguish between mothers who later abused their children and a matched comparison group of nonabusive mothers. Hunter et al. (1978) reasoned that infants requiring intensive care after birth presented the sort of unusual early childhood characteristics that might be associated with a higher incidence of maltreatment. Using an admissions interview to assess a range of family psychosocial characteristics among infants admitted for intensive care, they identified 41 such infants in families they believed to be at high risk. Ten of these children were later reported to authorities as victims of abuse or neglect, whereas none were reported from the comparison group of 214 infants whose scores on the psychosocial inventory suggested that they were at low risk. Another hospital program involved postnatal administration of an interview and questionnaire (Geddis et al., 1979). Parents identified as high risk and a control group were followed for up to 12 months to determine the number of families in each group experiencing sufficient parenting difficulties to result in the child being separated from the parents. By the end of the follow-up period, 32.4 percent of the at-risk mothers were no longer the primary caretakers of their children, compared to 2.8 percent of the mothers in the control group.

Altemeier et al. (1979) interviewed 1,400 pregnant women seeking care at a city hospital. Data were collected on the women's attitudes, experiences, and general knowledge of child rearing. In a 12-month follow-up, 273 mothers identified as high risk were compared to 225 randomly selected controls. The results showed a significantly greater incidence of abuse, neglect, failure to thrive, and separation of mother and child in the high-risk group. Another study on the same sample (Vietze et al., 1980) examined the cohorts of subjects over a longer period and focused additional attention on such variables as patterns of mother-infant interaction and the child's birth weight. The association between these factors and the quality of the children's care prompted the authors to advocate a "transactional" approach to prediction, in which the interaction of mother and child is a key element. Gray et al. (1977) used a questionnaire, interview, and observational measure to identify 50 of 350 new mothers at a community hospital as high risk. Half the 50 received special pediatric attention over the next several months, and both groups were compared to 25 control mothers when each child reached 17 months of age. In all, 22 of the 50 high-risk mothers showed "abnormal parenting practices," as compared to two of those in the control group. On the follow-up measures, the high-risk mothers receiving special pediatric attention differed significantly from the other 25 high-risk mothers only in terms of the number of injuries to the child requiring hospitalization.

ACCURACY OF PREDICTION

Continued work on screening procedures has been fueled by a desire to improve the accuracy of the predictive measures utilized. Accuracy, in this context, involves two dimensions: sensitivity and specificity. Sensitivity refers to the ability of the screening procedure to identify correctly all at-risk respondents, and specificity refers to its ability to include in this group only those who truly belong. Effective prediction requires high sensitivity and specificity, but an examination of results of the efforts reviewed thus far revealed that high rates of one often come at the expense of the other. For example, results of the 1977 study by Gray and her colleagues showed a fairly high

sensitivity of 92 percent (two of the 25 control group mothers were erroneously considered to be low risk) but a specificity of only 44 percent (that is, 28 of the 50 mothers identified as high risk were false positives).

The next group of studies to be reviewed are characterized by use of statistical tools such as discriminant function analysis specifically aimed at determining and optimizing the predictive ability of the procedure. One study utilized a battery of questionnaires, interviews, videotaped observations, and physiological measures to attempt to distinguish among 56 abusive parents, 11 neglectful parents, and 84 nonproblem parents (Disbrow, Doerr, and Caulfield, 1977a). The authors found that 17 variables describing personal history, personality, antecedents to early attachment, social network resources, parental attitudes toward child rearing, ways of handling children's irritating behaviors, and parent-child interactions were able to account for 43 percent of the variance among the three groups. Sensitivity and specificity over all the measures were 84 percent and 91 percent, respectively. A discriminant function fitted to some members of each group and then applied prospectively to the remainder produced a sensitivity of 79 percent and a specificity of 74 percent, figures more applicable to predictive screening. Results of a second discriminant function analysis involving a smaller sample of families showed an improvement in sensitivity and specificity to 85 percent and 89 percent, respectively (Disbrow, Doerr, and Caulfield, 1977b).

Another group of researchers (Egeland, 1979; Egeland and Brunnquell, 1979) utilized a set of screening measures consisting of prenatally administered personality and attitudinal scales, an assessment of the infant's characteristics at birth and at 3 months of age, and observations of mother-infant interactions at 3 and 6 months. A 20-month follow-up compared 26 infants found to be receiving inadequate or inappropriate

parenting to children of 25 mothers providing "high-quality care." The best combination of factors achieved an 85 percent correct classification rate, with the three-month measure of mother-child interaction and a group of prenatal questionnaire items accounting for the greatest percentage of variance in group membership. One subsequent study (Egeland, Breitenbucher, and Rosenberg, 1980) found that the addition of a "life stress" factor elevated the correct classification rate to 92 percent. Another follow-up applied a discriminant function to attempt to predict membership in abusive or nonabusive categories (Brunnquell, Crichton, and Egeland, 1981). Personality factors from the prenatal measures showed a correct classification rate of 49.6 percent, while the three-month observation factors achieved a 52.4 percent rate—discouraging figures in that they hardly improve on chance.

Other studies using combinations of existing scales and self-developed questionnaires have had similarly limited success. One effort compared information on families of children in hospital care for injuries with information on children with problems not related to injuries (Kotelchuck, 1982). Eight somewhat disparate factors, ranging from maternal history to the physical development of the child, were able to account for 47 percent of the variance of the children in a physical abuse group. Analyses of the results of a similar study by Starr (1982) also "failed to indicate any consistent interrelationships among logically similar variables" (p. 110). Ultimately, nine distinct variables that significantly distinguished between parents of accidentally and nonaccidentally injured children were used to derive a discriminant function for half the families in each group, which was then applied to the other half. An overall correct classification rate of 69.5 percent resulted, with a specificity of 66.7 percent and a sensitivity of 73.2 percent.

The most intensive examination of

44

the predictive applicability of a single existing instrument was a series of studies using the Minnesota Multiphasic Personality Inventory (MMPI). The first report demonstrated that new subscales derived from the inventory could distinguish between known abusers and nonabusers (Paulson et al., 1975b). Another study reported that the established Psychopathic Deviate and Hypomania scales could also identify abusive parents (Paulson, Schwemer, and Bendel, 1976). A third study utilized predictive functions specific to the sex of the parents that were derived from the initial results (Paulson et al., 1975a). These were applied to a different sample of known abusive and nonabusive parents to attempt to predict group membership. The functions correctly assigned 100 percent of the males, 94 percent of the females, and 89 percent of the males and females combined to the abusive or nonabusive groups. The promise of these findings is tempered, however, by at least one subsequent independent failure to replicate the results (Gabinet, 1979a).

Other researchers have applied their efforts to the development of a single written screening instrument. The initial report of one group detailed the results of the administration of an 82-item questionnaire to 30 parents known to be abusive and 30 matched nonabusers (Schneider, Helfer, and Pollock, 1972). The measure demonstrated a 93 percent sensitivity and 80 percent specificity in identifying the members of each group. A second study administered a revised 74-item instrument to 267 mothers divided into four groups: known abusers, high-risk potential abusers (as identified by the use of the criteria developed by Gray et al., 1977), low-risk potential abusers, and "model mothers" (Schneider, Hoffmeister, and Helfer, 1976). Three clusters of items that accounted for the greatest variance among the groups showed both a specificity and sensitivity of 78 percent in separating model mothers from known abusers. In the most recent reported refinement, the questionnaire was reduced to 50 items constituting five clusters: emotional needs met, relationship with parents, dealing with others, expectations of child, and coping (Helfer, Schneider, and Hoffmeister, 1978b). The instrument was administered to parents

known to be abusers or nonabusers in seven states and one Canadian province and demonstrated levels of sensitivity ranging from 78 percent to 90 percent and specificity from 80 percent to 83 percent.

In another attempt to construct such an instrument, Milner and Wimberley (1979) administered 334 items to 19 abusive and 19 matched nonabusive parents. They identified 25 items that accounted for 96 percent of the variance in group membership. In a second, larger study (Milner and Wimberley, 1980), they gave a revised 160-item scale to 65 abusive parents and 65 nonabusive controls. The 77 items that best identified group membership (again accounting for 96 percent of the variance) were subjected to factor analysis and were found to constitute seven dimensions: rigidity, distress or unhappiness, loneliness, problems with family and others, negative concept of child and self, and child with problems. A discriminant function analysis indicated that 96 percent of the respondents could be correctly classified using the scale. In a third study, the inventory was administered to 64 parents in an existing screening program (Ayoub and Pfeifer, 1977) who had already been identified as at-risk of abusing their children by the program's screening criteria (Milner and Ayoub, 1980). In comparison to a norm group, the at-risk parents scored significantly higher on the inventory. This was a useful attempt at criterion validation of the instrument but, as the authors pointed out, must be viewed judiciously in light of the extreme variability of the scores of the at-risk parents. Lacking another comparison measure, it is impossible to determine whether the screening criteria included too many parents in the at-risk group or the inventory included too few.

ISSUES IN SECONDARY PREVENTION

The crucial decisions for prevention programs in child maltreatment are whether sufficient information is available to proceed with broader implementation of secondary prevention programs and, if so, what form these programs should assume. The conclusions must ultimately rest on the ability of the research just surveyed to resolve the critical questions per-

taining to screening, prediction, and prevention, including:

1. Is the etiology of the problem such that individually focused screening and treatment are possible?
2. Can screening procedures be generalized for broad application?
3. Will results of screening instruments be sufficiently accurate to allow ethical prediction?
4. Can useful and feasible treatment programs be formulated from the results of such screening?

Individual Screening

The research provides no clear answer to the first question, partly because variables found to be useful discriminators of parents who will later abuse their children often defy combination into conceptually sound orderings (Kotelchuck, 1982; Starr, 1982). Also, each study seems to add new variables to the list, occasionally in conflict with other results. For example, the self-concept of the parent was found to be a useful predictor by some researchers (Schneider, Hoffmeister, and Helfer, 1976; and Disbrow, Doerr, and Caulfield, 1977b), but showed little discriminative ability in other studies (Milner and Wimberley, 1979). Egeland (1979, p. 275) believed his findings "support the notion that there is no particular abusing personality," yet other investigations showed that item clusters and standard scales on the MMPI may be able to distinguish abusers from nonabusers (Paulson et al., 1975b; Paulson, Schwemer, and Bendel, 1976). Still, some variables, such as maternal history, parents' expectations of the child, parental stress and isolation, and special characteristics of the child, were significant predictors in several studies. This and the fact that every study was able to identify at least some useful predictors mitigates against the argument that the etiology of abuse can never be sufficiently elaborated to make screening a feasible procedure.

Applicability

The breadth of applicability of study results is an important issue in terms of both the characteristics of the samples on which the research has been based and the dimensions of child care that have been addressed. In the first instance, a great many of the studies reviewed obtained their sample from the population served by metropolitan general hospitals. These centers provide care to a disproportionate number of patients who are unable to afford the services of private hospitals. Several authors confirmed, in fact, that their subjects tend to come from lower-middle or lower socioeconomic strata (Paulson, Schwemer, and Bendel, 1976; Altemeier et al., 1979; Egeland, 1979; and Starr, 1982). The generalizability of these findings to different populations is thus open to question.

A related matter involves the high incidence of abuse and neglect among subjects in some of the studies. For example, Egeland (1979) noted that almost 10 percent of the children in his sample were maltreated. Altemeier et al. (1979) reported rates of roughly 5 percent for abuse and 9.5 percent for abuse and neglect, and Schneider, Hoffmeister, and Helfer (1976) reported a rate of 3.5 percent for abuse only. These are substantially higher than the 1 percent rate suggested as the general norm (Light, 1973).

Finally, the exact dimensions of child care being measured vary from study to study. One study, for instance, measured "inadequate parenting practices" (Gray et al., 1977); another examined quality of care (Egeland, 1979); another looked at abuse, neglect, failure to thrive, and ingestion injuries (Kotelchuck, 1982); and so on. This variation in dependent measures results in problems for broader application of the procedures tested.

Accuracy

The problem of the accuracy of screening measures remains a central concern. A number of authors have discussed the relationship between the prevalence of a problem and the sensitivity and specificity of its measures (Daniel et al., 1978; Garbarino, 1980b; Kotelchuck, 1982), but a brief illustration should help to clarify the point. Assume the administration of a screening instrument to a sample of 1,000 parents drawn from a population in which 10 percent of all parents are abusive. If the sample is representative, one would expect that 100 parents abuse their children. Given both a sensitivity and specificity of 90 percent for the instrument, the instrument would fail to identify 10 of the 100 abusive parents (false negatives), correctly iden-

tify 90 of the 100 abusive parents (true positives), and incorrectly identify an additional 90 of the parents (10 percent of the remaining 900) as being abusers (false positives). One would therefore have to provide services to as many parents who do not require intervention as to those who do. This is certainly not maximally efficient. Moreover, if the prevalence of maltreatment in the population is only 2 percent, a figure closer to the estimate of most writers, 18 true positives, two false negatives, and 98 false positives would be expected. Services would have to be rendered to more than five parents who did not need them for every one who did.

Feasibility of Prevention Programs

Because of the combination of the limited effectiveness of existing instruments and the low incidence of child maltreatment, Garbarino (1980b, p. 68), asserted not only that "individually oriented prevention programs will prove ineffective, that they are 'doomed to failure,' " but also that attempts to predict child maltreatment would even "run the risk of pushing families into abuse merely by falsely 'accusing' them of it." Daniel et al. (1978, p. 257) presented an equally doleful scenario in which "misclassification toward abuse and neglect may lead to reflexive *separation* of a child from its family where local practices are zealously child-serving." Schmitt (1980, p. 172) acknowledged the problems of misidentification but suggested that their solution lies merely in avoiding labels such as "preabusive" or "potentially abusive." In his view, predictive screening may simply be thought of as pointing out "dysfunctional families" generally in need of assistance, even if not specifically for inchoate maltreatment.

These opposing arguments both miss the point. That a child might be removed from its home on the basis of parental responses to an assessment device is too Orwellian a notion for even the most conservative protective services practitioners. Moreover, despite the muddled etiology of abuse, the idea that it may be fostered simply through the power of suggestion seems highly doubtful. At the other extreme, the ethical problems of telling parents that their childrearing skills are in need of remedial attention will not be solved simply by

avoiding a "preabusive" label. This is especially true if, as in the example cited, the odds are more than five to one that parents are not abusive.

The reality, of course, is that professionals do not know precisely what dimensions are being tapped by these measures, but the findings to date are not entirely useless. Although respondents identified as high risk are unlikely to constitute a uniform group of future "dysfunctional families," it seems plausible that a large number of them represent a population different from that of other prospective parents. The findings that maltreatment may be more prevalent than usual in populations tested up to this point may indicate that, at least for similar populations, the proportion of false positives might not be as high as in the worst-case scenario. Finally, Paulson et al. (1975a) and Schneider, Hoffmeister, and Helfer (1976) reported that the predictive capabilities of screening instruments may be improved by such procedures as weighting items and examining the variability of responses across similar items.

One suggestion for handling some of the important ethical problems involved in preventive intervention came from Brody and Gaiss (1976), who advocated requiring informed consent from respondents prior to screening. Specific details would be provided about the limitations of the instrument and the possibility of misidentification. Still, the key issue in reporting positive results is not how to define for parents their potential problem but how to offer to them a program from which they may legitimately expect to benefit.

The predominant concern of the research to date on prediction makes sense in that identification of the potential for a problem must logically precede attempts to avoid its occurrence. However, the value of screening programs is ultimately to rest on the efficacy of their associated preventive measures, the development of such measures must assume equal importance. At present, the literature reflects only a handful of empirical attempts to validate preventive programs, and these tend to report negative or equivocal results. For example, Gray et al. (1977) found that a group of mothers receiving special pediatric attention showed significant change on only one of 13 outcome measures. Gabinet (1979b, p. 811) reported an attempt to provide outreach psychological services aimed at "treatment of the patients' emotional problems...based on [a] dynamic personality theory." The follow-up assessment (which utilized descriptive statistics to evaluate scores on a Parental Behavior Scale) suggested that the longer the parents were treated, past a three-month minimum, the greater their improvement. This study is the only one to support the use of personality-oriented interventions, but it is subject to too many methodological weaknesses to be entirely convincing. Finally, Thomasson et al. (1981) used an "ecological model" of child abuse to devise a preventive program for rural parents. Using the Child Abuse Potential Inventory devised by Milner and Wimberley (1980) as a dependent measure, they were able to show a significant improvement in the subjects' scores over time. The difficulty with their results is that changes in presumed potential for abuse may not necessarily portend changes in actual behavior.

As can be surmised, establishing the effectiveness of strategies to prevent child maltreatment remains the principal task for advocates of primary prevention programs and for those associated with developing predictive screening methods. As one author noted, "measuring prevention —the number of times something has not happened—is a difficult, if not impossible, task" (Rosenstein, 1978, p. 524). Yet, in an era of scarce resources, preventive programs can expect to have to present reasonable evidence of their efficacy and to compete for support from the same sources as established treatment services (Miller, 1981; and Sundel and Homan, 1979). Given that existing remedial efforts have by no means fully demonstrated their utility, the task facing preventive programs is indeed prodigious. Over the short term, the established treatment-oriented approach seems unlikely to change. For the long term, continued small-scale research efforts to demonstrate the ability of preventive programs to achieve their goals offers the possibility that preventive approaches may achieve wider implementation in the future.

Steven L. McMurtry, MSSW, is a doctoral candidate, School of Social Work, University of Wisconsin–Madison.

Bibliography

Readers will note that bibliographic style has been used for references in this article. This style is used only for reviews of the literature.

Altemeier, W. A.; Vietze, P. M.; Sherrod, K. B.; Sandler, H. M.; Falsey, S.; and O'Connor, S. "Prediction of Child Maltreatment During Pregnancy," *Journal of the American Academy of Child Psychiatry*, 17 (Spring 1979), pp. 205–218.

Ayoub, C., and Pfeifer, D. R. "An Approach to Primary Prevention: The At-Risk Program," *Children Today*, 6 (May/June 1977), pp. 14–17.

Brody, H., and Gaiss, B. "Ethical Issues in Early Identification and Prevention of Unusual Child-Rearing Practices," in R. E. Helfer and C. H. Kempe, eds., *Child Abuse and Neglect: The Family and Community*. Cambridge, Mass.: Ballinger Publishing Co., 1976, pp. 372–375.

Brunnquell, D.; Crichton, L.; and Egeland, B. "Maternal Personality and Attitude in Disturbances of Child Rearing," *American Journal of Orthopsychiatry*, 51 (October 1981), pp. 680–691.

Daniel, J. H.; Newberger, E. H.; Reed, R. B.; and Kotelchuck, M. " Child Abuse Screening: Implications of the Limited Predictive Power of Abuse Discriminants from a Controlled Family Study of Pediatric Social Illness," *Child Abuse and Neglect*, 2 (Summer 1978), pp. 247–259.

Disbrow, M. A.; Doerr, H. A.; and Caulfield, C. "Measures to Predict Child Abuse." Paper presented at the annual meeting of the Society for Research in Child Development, New Orleans, La., March 1977a.

————. "Measuring the Components of Parents' Potential for Child Abuse and Neglect," *Child Abuse and Neglect*, 1 (Summer 1977b), pp. 279–296.

Education for Parenthood: A Primary Prevention Strategy for Child Abuse and Neglect. Denver, Colo.: Education Commission for the States, 1976.

Egeland, B. "Preliminary Results of a Prospective Study of the Antecedents of Child Abuse," *Child Abuse and Neglect*, 3, (Fall 1979), pp. 269–278.

Egeland, B.; Breitenbucher, M.; and Rosenberg, D. "Prospective Study of Significance of Life Stress in the Etiology of Child Abuse," *Journal of Consulting and Clinical Psychology*, 48 (April 1980), pp. 195–205.

Egeland, B., and Brunnquell, D. "An At-Risk Approach to the Study of Child Abuse," *Journal of the American Academy of Child Psychiatry*, 17 (April 1979), pp. 219–235.

Fraser, B. G. "The Child and His Parents: A Delicate Balance of Rights," in R. E. Helfer and C. H. Kempe, eds., *Child Abuse and Neglect: The Family and Community*. Cambridge, Mass.: Ballinger Publishing Co., 1976.

Gabinet, L. "MMPI Profiles of High-Risk and Outpatient Mothers," *Child Abuse and Neglect*, 3 (Spring 1979a), pp. 373– 379.

————. "Prevention of Child Abuse and Neglect in an Inner-City Population: II. The Program and the Results," *Child Abuse and Neglect*, 3 (Fall 1979b), pp. 809–817.

Garbarino, J. "An Ecological Perspective on Child Maltreatment," in R. Pelton, ed., *The Social Context of Child Abuse and Neglect*. New York: Human Services Press, 1980a, pp. 228–267.

————. "Preventing Child Maltreatment," in R. Price et al., eds., *Prevention in Mental Health*, Vol. 1. Beverly Hills: Sage Publications, 1980b, pp. 63–79.

Geddis, D. C.; Monaghan, S. M.; Muir, R. C.; and Jones, C. J. "Early Prediction in the Maternity Hospital: The Queen Mary Child Care Unit," *Child Abuse and Neglect*, 3 (Fall 1979), pp. 757–766.

Gil, D. G. "Primary Prevention of Child Abuse: A Philosophical and Political Issue," *Psychiatric Opinion*, 13 (April 1976), pp. 31–34.

Gilbert, N. "Policy Issues in Primary Prevention," *Social Work*, 27 (July 1982), pp. 293–297.

Giovannoni, J. M., and Becerra, R. M. *Defining Child Abuse*. New York: Free Press, 1979.

Gray, J. D.; Cutler, C. A.; Dean, J. G.; and Kempe, C. H. "Prediction and Prevention of Child Abuse and Neglect," *Child Abuse and Neglect*, 1 (Spring 1977), pp. 45–58.

Grazio, T. F. "New Perspectives on Child Abuse/Neglect Community Education," *Child Welfare*, 60 (May 1981), pp. 343–353.

Hammell, C. "Preserving Family Life for Children," *Child Welfare*, 48 (December 1969), pp. 591–594.

Helfer, R. E. "Basic Issues Concerning Prediction," in Helfer and C. H. Kempe, eds., *Child Abuse and Neglect: The Family and Community*. Cambridge, Mass.: Ballinger Publishing Co., 1976, pp. 363–372.

————. "Childhood Comes First: A Crash Course in Childhood for Adults," Lansing, Mich.: Ray E. Helfer, 1978a.

Helfer, R. E.; Schneider, C. J.; and Hoffmeister, J. K. *Report on the Research Using the Michigan Screening Profile of Parenting*. East Lansing: Michigan State University, 1978b.

Hunter, R. E.; Kilstrom, N.; Kraybill, E. N.; and Loda, F. "Antecedents of Child Abuse and Neglect in Premature Infants: A Prospective Study in a Newborn Intensive Care Unit," *Pediatrics*, 61 (April 1978), pp. 629–635.

Kempe, C. H. "Approaches to Preventing Child Abuse," *American Journal of Diseases of Children*, 130 (September 1976), pp. 941–947.

Kotelchuck, M. "Child Abuse and Neglect: Prediction and Misclassification," in R. H. Starr, Jr., ed., *Child Abuse Prediction*. Cambridge, Mass.: Ballinger Publishing Co., 1982, pp. 67–104.

Light, R. J. "Abused and Neglected Children in America: A Study of Alternative Policies," *Harvard Educational Review*, 43 (November 1973), pp. 556–597.

Lovens, H. D., and Rako, J. A. "A Community Approach to the Prevention of Child Abuse," *Child Welfare*, 56 (February 1975), pp. 83–87.

Martin, H. P., and Beezley, P. "Prevention and Consequences of Child Abuse," *Journal of Operational Psychiatry*, 6 (Fall–Winter 1974), pp. 68–77.

Miller, C. C. "Primary Prevention of Child Maltreatment: Meeting a National Need," *Child Welfare*, 60 (January 1981), pp. 11–22.

Milner, J. S., and Ayoub, C. "Evaluation of 'At-Risk' Parents Using the Child Abuse Potential Inventory," *Journal of Clinical Psychology*, 36 (October 1980), pp. 945–948.

Milner, J. S., and Wimberley, R. C. "An Inventory for the Identification of Child Abusers," *Journal of Clinical Psychology*, 35 (January 1979), pp. 95–100.

———. "Prediction and Explanation of Child Abuse," *Journal of Clinical Psychology*, 36 (October 1980), pp. 875–884.

Olson, R. J. "Index of Suspicion: Screening for Child Abusers," *American Journal of Nursing*, 76 (January 1976), pp. 108–110.

Paulson, M. J.; Afifi, A. A.; Chaleff, A.; Liu, V. Y.; and Thomason, M. L. "A Discriminant Function Procedure for Identifying Abusive Parents, *Suicide*, 5 (Summer 1975a), pp. 104–114.

Paulson, M. J.; Afifi, A. A.; Chaleff, A.; Thomason, M. L.; and Liu, V. Y. "An MMPI Scale for Identifying 'At-Risk' Abusive Parents," *Journal of Clinical Child Psychology*, 4 (January 1975b), pp. 22–24.

Paulson, M. J., and Blake, P. R. "The Physically Abused Child: A Focus on Prevention," *Child Welfare*, 48 (February 1969), pp. 86–95.

Paulson, M. J.; Schwemer, G. T., and Bendel, R. B. "Clinical Application of the Pd, Ma, and (OH) Experimental MMPI Scales to Further Understanding of Abusive Parents," *Journal of Clinical Psychology*, 32 (July 1976), pp. 558–564.

Plotkin, R. C.; Azar, S.; Twentyman, C. T.; and Perri, M. G. "A Critical Evaluation of the Research Methodology Employed in the Investigation of Causative Factors of Child Abuse and Neglect," *Child Abuse and Neglect*, 5 (Winter 1981), pp. 449–455.

Pollock, C. B. "Early Case Finding as a Means of Prevention of Child Abuse," in R. E. Helfer and C. H. Kempe, eds., *The Battered Child*. Chicago: University of Chicago Press, 1968, pp. 149–152.

Rosenstein, P. J. "Family Outreach: A Program for the Prevention of Child Neglect and Abuse," *Child Welfare*, 57 (September–October 1978), pp. 519–525.

Rowan, J. M. "Possible Early Warning Signs of Non-accidental Injury to Children," *Child Abuse and Neglect*, 3 (Winter 1979), pp. 767–776.

Schmitt, B. D. "The Prevention of Child Abuse and Neglect: A Review of the Literature with Recommendations for Application," *Child Abuse and Neglect*, 4 (Winter 1980), pp. 171–177.

Schneider, C.; Helfer, R. E.; and Pollock, C. "The Predictive Questionnaire: A Preliminary Report," in C. H. Kempe and R. E. Helfer, eds., *Helping the Battered Child and His Family*. Philadelphia: J. B. Lippincott Co., 1972, pp. 271–282.

Schneider, C.; Hoffmeister, J. K.; and Helfer, R. E. "A Predictive Screening Questionnaire for Potential Problems in Mother-Child Interaction," in R. E. Helfer and C. H. Kempe, eds., *Child Abuse and Neglect: The Family and Community*. Cambridge, Mass.: Ballinger Publishing Co., 1976, pp. 393–407.

Spinetta, J. J., and Rigler, D. "The Child-Abusing Parent: A Psychological Review," *Psychological Bulletin*, 77 (April 1972), pp. 296–304.

Starr, R. H., Jr. "Child Abuse," *American Psychologist*, 34 (1979), pp. 872–878.

———. "A Research-Based Approach to the Prediction of Child Abuse," in Starr, ed., *Child Abuse Prediction*. Cambridge, Mass.: Ballinger Publishing Co., 1982, pp. 105–134.

Sundel, M., and Homan, C. C. "Prevention in Child Welfare: A Framework for Management and Practice," *Child Welfare*, 58 (September–October 1979), pp. 510–521.

Thomasson, E.; Berkowitz, T.; Minor, S.; Cassie, G.; McCord, D.; and Milner, J. S. "Evaluation of a Family Life Education Program for Rural High-Risk Families: A Research Note," *Journal of Community Psychology*, 9 (July 1981), pp. 246–249.

Usdan, M. D. "The Future of Training/Education for the Prevention of Child Abuse and Neglect," in M. L. Lauderdale, R. N. Anderson, and S. E. Cramer, eds., *Child Abuse and Neglect: Issues of Innovation and Implementation*, DHEW Publication No. (OHDS) 78-30147. Washington, D.C.: U.S. Government Printing Office, 1978.

Vietze, P.; Falsey, S.; Sandler, H.; O'Connor, S.; and Altemeier, W. "A Transactional Approach to Prediction of Child Maltreatment," *Infant Mental Health Journal*, 14 (Winter 1980), pp. 248–256.

Vietze, P.; O'Connor, S.; Hopkins, J. B.; Sandler, H. M.; and Altemeier, W. A. "Prospective Study of Child Maltreatment from a Transactional Perspective," in R. H. Starr, Jr., ed., *Child Abuse Prediction*. Cambridge, Mass.: Ballinger Publishing Co., 1982, pp. 21–66.

Williams, D. L. "Perspectives on the Prevention of Child Abuse: Can It Be Done? in M. L. Lauderdale, R. N. Anderson, and S. E. Cramer, eds., *Child Abuse and Neglect: Issues of Innovation and Implementation*, DHEW Publication No. (OHDS) 78-30147. Washington, D.C.: U.S. Government Printing Office, 1978, pp. 225–234.

Williams, G. J. "Toward the Eradication of Child Abuse and Neglect at Home," in Williams and J. Money, eds., *Traumatic Abuse and Neglect of Children at Home*. Baltimore, Md.: Johns Hopkins University Press, 1980, pp. 588–605.

Wingspread Report. A Community Plan for Preventing Child Abuse. Racine, Wisc.: Johnson Foundation, 1978.

Accepted September 28, 1983

THE STREETLIGHT OVER THE COURTHOUSE

JOHN E.B. MYERS*

There is a childhood story that goes something like this: One night a man was walking down the street. He saw a friend crawling about on the sidewalk at the corner of Main and Elm. The friend was obviously looking for something. A streetlight immediately overhead illuminated the area and made the search easier. As the man approached, he said, "What are you looking for Tom?" Tom replied, "I'm looking for my watch. I lost it over at the corner of Main and Peach Street." On hearing this surprising reply, the man said, "But Tom, if you lost your watch at Main and Peach, why are you searching for it way over here at Main and Elm?" The friend's matter-of-fact answer was, "Because the light's better over here."

As is true with many anecdotes enjoyed by children, adults may not find much humor in the story of a man searching for his watch in the wrong place, but for those interested in the enigma of child abuse, the *non sequitur* that drives the story illuminates an important point: society is looking in the wrong place for the solutions to child abuse.

Today, society places increasing reliance on the legal system to deal with various forms of deviant behavior, including child abuse. The hope is that by punishing abusers, society can somehow force a reduction in maltreatment. Reliance on law as a primary defense against child abuse expanded in earnest during the late 1970s and '80's as the nation turned away from the therapeutic approach to deviance which held sway up to that time. Influential scholars such as James Q. Wilson and Andrew von Hirsch wrote that in the context of criminal behavior, rehabilitation is a bankrupt theory that does not work and that the appropriate response is usually retribution and incarceration. The so-called "retribution movement" gained center stage, and the opinion emerged that the proper response to most adults who hurt or molest children is prosecution.

While there is unquestionably an important role for the law in the response to child abuse, there is growing evidence that when society

---

* Associate Professor of Law, University of the Pacific, McGeorge School of Law, Sacramento, California. Copyright 1986 by John E.B. Myers. Reprinted by permission of the Author.

seeks the solution to maltreatment in the legal system, it makes a mistake akin to looking for something in the wrong place simply because the light is better. No doubt, the light is good in the courthouse. Society can see clearly what goes on in the justice system and can bolster itself in the belief that "something" is being done. Statistics on the number of cases adjudicated are held out as "proof" that progress is under way. And yet, the more one studies child abuse, the less sanguine one becomes about the ability of the legal system to cope with the problem. A strong argument can be made that processing child abuse cases through the legal system often does more harm than good, especially for the children. This writer recently summarized the disadvantages of the legal response to child abuse in another publication as follows:

> [T]he legal response to child abuse has disadvantages which sometimes outweigh the benefits derived from litigation. The legal approach tends to ignore, or at least downplay, the deep social and psychological roots of child abuse. Additionally, since the threat of legal action attaches the moment abuse comes to official attention, it is unlikely that the problem will surface voluntarily. The consequences of involvement with the criminal justice system are simply too drastic to encourage self-reporting in the relatively small percentage of cases where it might otherwise occur. Furthermore, the Draconian societal response to a report of child abuse causes victims and other family members to remain silent. So too with professionals, many of whom feel that reporting sometimes does more harm than good. In the end, the fact that child abuse reports are routed to prosecutorial authorities may exacerbate the already serious problem of underreporting.
>
> The blaming, accusatory, punitive approach of the criminal justice system is, in a sense, inherently destructive. Families caught up in criminal litigation are torn apart, causing loss of financial support, divorce, and lasting trauma. Family dissolution is unavoidable and even desirable in some cases. In a significant percentage of cases, however, families could be salvaged if society responded with a therapeutic approach rather than with retribution.
>
> From a child advocate's perspective, one of the most disturbing consequences of the legal approach to abuse is the trauma visited on children involved in prosecutorial proceedings. The embarrassment associated with repeating the excruciatingly private details of abuse—especially sexual abuse—to professionals such as police, social workers, psychologists, and attorneys is real and serious. The difficulty of pretrial proceedings is compounded by what some have called the "second victimization" of litigation, including testimony at the grand jury, preliminary hearing, and trial stages, where the child must once again repeat the details of the abuse, this time before a room full of strangers. There are the additional traumas of cross-examination designed to paint the child an unbelievable witness or an outright liar, and face-to-face confrontation with the defendant who sits just a few feet away. The latter experience is especially difficult when the defend-

ant is known to the child. It is not hard to imagine the difficulty, ambivalence, and anguish experienced by children who must testify against a close family member or parent.

A final and important disadvantage of the legal approach to child maltreatment deserves mention. Abuse is often very difficult to prove. So difficult in fact that a substantial number of cases are simply not prosecuted. The result of lack of proof is that in many cases the state lacks authority to intervene to protect the child. While advances are being made to ease the evidentiary problems which plague child abuse litigation, the difficulties are so intractable that it is unlikely significant progress can be made. This is especially so with regard to children age five and under who may not be able to participate in the legal system by taking the witness stand.

In addition to the disadvantages inherent in the legal response to child abuse, litigation is little more than a band-aid solution which ignores the underlying social ills that generate abuse. If one accepts for the moment that in looking to the legal system for solutions to child abuse, society is looking in the wrong place, then one must ask, where are the answers?

Before suggesting what may be the best hope for reducing maltreatment of children, it is important to chart the dimensions of the problem. In 1962, the American Humane Association conducted the first national survey of the incidence of abuse. The study, which was conducted prior to enactment of child abuse reporting laws, revealed a total of six hundred sixty-two cases. This relatively small number of reported cases indicated a problem - but a problem of manageable proportions. By 1983, however, when child abuse reporting statutes had been on the books for nearly twenty years, the number of reported cases exceeded one million each year! As for sexual abuse, no one knows how many children are victimized each year. Estimates range from 100,000 to 500,000 cases although the actual number is probably higher. These numbers are shocking, but there is more. Experts on child abuse agree that maltreatment is underreported. Cases that come to light are merely the tip of the iceberg.

Given the enormity of the problem, it is important to discover where abuse occurs so that resources can be focuses appropriately. Child abuse is not the exclusive province of a particular group. Vincent Fontana writes that "[t]he problem of child abuse is not limited to any particular economic, social, or intellectual level, race or religion." Many believe that abuse is a classless phenomenon; an unfortunate social malady found in roughly equal proportions throughout society. Evidence is mounting, however, that what Leroy Pelton calls the "myth of classlessness" hides the cruel truth. Pelton writes that "[t]here is substantial evidence of a strong relationship between poverty and child abuse and neglect. [Furthermore], poverty is not merely 'associated' with child abuse and neglect; there is good reason to believe that the problems of poverty are causative agents in parents' abusive and negligent behaviors."

Pelton's disturbing observation that abuse and neglect are concentrated among the poorest members of American society is born out by his own research and that of others. In its 1984 report titled *Trends in Child Abuse and Neglect: A National Perspective*, the American Humane Association writes that "[t]he overwhelming characteristic which the data point to is economic hardship: [T]he families are composed heavily of female-headed households, they are on public assistance, and they have younger caretakers and more children than families in the general population." Bernard Horowitz and Isabel Wolock summarize their research on child abuse by stating that "[m]aterial and social deprivation . . . were central factors leading to child maltreatment. . . . [M]altreating families were the poorest of the poor." Finally, James Garbarino remarks that "the principal threat to family life is impoverishment." All of the researchers are quick to remark that the vast majority of poor parents do not abuse their children. Their point is that the social and economic deprivation of poverty creates the stresses that lead to maltreatment.

Assuming that child abuse occurs with disproportionate frequency among the poor and that poverty plays a causative role in maltreatment, it becomes important to ask whether meaningful progress is made to reduce poverty. The answer is no. Figures from the Bureau of the Census reveal that the "War on Poverty" of the 1960s substantially reduced the number of people living in poverty. Beginning in the early 1980s, however, the numbers of poor began to creep upward again. The tremendous cutbacks in social spending imposed by the Reagan Administration, coupled with high levels of unemployment, especially among Black Americans, forced large numbers of people into poverty. Statistics from the Census bureau indicate that in 1984 there were in excess of thirty-three million people below the poverty line. Another twelve million live perilously close to the line. Michael Harrington estimates that the number living in poverty may actually be as high as fifty million, roughly the same number as existed twenty years ago.

During the past two decades, a confluence of economic and social factors has emerged that promises to make the reality of American poverty even more stark and painful. Society may be witnessing the emergence of a *permanent* underclass; a huge cohort of people locked in a grinding cycle of poverty. In its issue of March 17, 1986, *U.S. News and World Report* described the growth of a "seemingly hopeless underclass," many of whom are destined to languish in poverty all their lives, and for whom the traditional paths out of poverty are rapidly disappearing. Harrington devotes an entire volume to what he calls "the new American poverty;" a poverty so intransigent and debilitating that it threatens the very foundations of the family. In a pair of articles in *The Atlantic* titled "The Origins of the Underclass," Nicholas Lemann details the steadily worsening conditions in America's ghettos. Life in the ghetto has become sadly reminiscent of conditions described by Thomas Hobbes more than three centuries ago: "nasty, mean, brutish and short." The emergence of an entire class of hopeless people raises the frightening spectre of widespread abuse and neglect for thousands, and eventually, millions of children born into the underclass.

There is an aspect of the emerging underclass which poses an immediate threat to children. More and more children live in single-parent families. In 1965, 24% of Black and 9% of White families were headed by women. By 1985, the numbers rose to 44% for Blacks and 13% for Whites. Vast numbers of these single-parent families live in the most degrading poverty; precisely the conditions that cause abuse. *U.S. News & World Report* states that in 1984 there were 1,878,000 female-headed families living in poverty. More than twenty million children were poor. A striking number of unmarried teenagers are having children. In some cities, "80 to 90 percent of births to black teenagers are out of wedlock." Shelby Miller reports that "teenage mothers are more likely to maltreat their children," a finding that is supported by the National Urban League.

Having examined the sobering facts about poverty and its relationship to child abuse, it is time to return to the tale of the search for the lost watch. When the quest for solutions to child abuse results primarily in harsher laws and increased litigation against adults who mistreat children, society is searching on the wrong street corner. The temptation to seek solutions in the law is understandable. The streetlight is bright over the courthouse, and middle-class America feels comfortable searching for answers in the safety of the law.

Concrete results emerge from the justice system and show results that assuage the guilty collective conscience about millions of abused children: results from which we build a fragile delusion that society is taking effective steps to stp the maiming and killing of innocents. In the end, however, the truth will come out, and the hard truth is that when society focuses its efforts on the legal system it ignores one of the primary sources of the problem and, at the same time, one of the most effective solutions. If we want to find answers to abuse, we must face reality. We must relocate our search from the well-lit environs of the legal system to the festering darkness of poverty. For it is there, in the ghetto, the barrio, and the central city of a hundred cities that the answer lies.

If the search for ways to reduce child abuse moves from the courthouse to the communities that breed abuse, what role, if any, is there for lawyers? The answer is that the legal profession can play a decisive role in reducing child abuse. First, there is no question that some cases of abuse must be prosecuted and punished. Naturally, this task falls to the legal system and lawyers. But litigation in the context of criminal and juvenile court is a relatively straightforward, simple and unimportant aspect of the solution to abuse. If lawyers want to participate in the search for *solutions* to the enigma of child abuse, they must shift their focus from after-the-fact litigation intended to punish what has already occurred to before-the-fact action designed to eliminate the social conditions that lead to abuse. There are at least three concrete steps that can be taken to reach that goal.

If substantially increased numbers of lawyers become involved in enforcing the civil rights, public benefits, and fair housing laws that are presently on the books, important gains will be realized in the fight against poverty. Sar Leviathan writes in his book *Programs in Aid of the Poor* that "[t]he Civil Rights Act of 1964, the Voting Rights Act of 1965, and related executive orders, if properly enforced, could prove to be more important tools to combat poverty than federal legislation involving massive investments of public funds."

The second method by which the legal profession can become part of the solution is to stimulate the bar to think seriously about the legal, social, and political issues surrounding poverty. Beyond scattered efforts to encourage uncompensated legal services for the poor, bar associations pay little or no attention to the larger issues of poverty. When the intellectual, political, legal, and experiential resources of the organized bar are brought to bear on a problem, things happen. If bar associations address the social ills rising from the miasma of poverty, progress will be made, and the direct beneficiaries will be children.

For their part, the law schools must shake off their complacency about the pressing social issues of the day. Only a handful of schools offer courses on poverty law, and most law students are never introduced to the subject. A concrete step in the right direction would be the creation and whole-hearted support of courses on poverty law and related social problems. Today's students need a good dose of reality about the tremendous social problems awaiting them after graduation. Of equal importance, law students need to hear from their teachers that they can play an important role in solving social problems. Many students are surprised and delighted when they learn that lawyering can be a helping profession akin to social work or medicine. There is more to law school than preparing students to find comfortable jobs at which they can make as much money as possible, and law professors cheat their students and their profession when they fail to expose students to the role lawyers can play in the creation of positive social change.

In addition to injecting an agenda of social issues into the classroom, law teachers must realize and convey to their students that litigation is not a panacea. By the time the average law student finishes her training, the only thing she knows how to do is sue somebody. Surely there is more to legal problem solving than that. Litigation plays a role in ameliorating the conditions that lead to abuse of children, but a relatively small role. The best hope for meaningful progress lies in coordinated political efforts to empower the people directly affected by poverty. Only when the poor themselves organize to resist the forces keeping them in poverty does society change. Witness the civil rights movement of the 1960s, a movement made up primarily of poor people. Thus, much of the answer to poverty and its attendant ills such as child abuse lies in community organizing. Indeed, James Garbarino writes that "community organizing is inseparable from child protection." And it is here, in the non-litigation domain of community organizing, that law students and lawyers can make an invaluable contribution.

Eschewing the traditional lawyer's role, in which the attorney is confined within the narrow limits of the adversary system, the lawyer as community organizer employs his knowledge of government and the legal system to assist those working for change. Not as an "attorney" representing a "client," a dyad in which the lawyer too often becomes the primary decision-maker and power figure, but as an equal among the cadre of skilled individuals serving a community of individuals seeking better conditions for themselves and their children.

Finally, lawyers in practice and in academia must realize that they do not have all or most of the answers to poverty and child abuse. Such problems lie at the interface among psychology, sociology, economics, and law. The only realistic way to achieve solutions is for lawyers to abandon the professional elitism to which they sometimes fall prey and join forces with their colleagues in other helping professions. By working together, solutions will emerge.

The scourge of child abuse can be reduced. Concrete measures are available for the taking if society possesses the strength of will to take them. But before progress is possible, society at large, and the legal profession in particular, must come to grips with the nature of the problem. The search for solutions must be squarely focused on the causes of abuse. We must face the fact that answers do not lie in the legal system but in the dim netherworld of poverty.

REFERENCES

American Humane Association, Children's Division, *Trends in Child Abuse and Neglect: A National Perspective* (1984).

Bureau of the Census, U.S. Department of Commerce, *Statistical Abstract of the United States* 1986 (1985).

J. Garbarino, *An Ecological Approach to Child Maltreatment*, THE SOCIAL CONTEXT OF CHILD ABUSE AND NEGLECT 228 (L. Pelton ed. 1981, 1985).

M. Harrington, *The New American Poverty* (1984).

B. Horowitz & I. Wolock, *Material Deprivation, Child Maltreatment, and Agency Interventions Among Poor Families*, THE SOCIAL CONTEXT OF CHILD ABUSE AND NEGLECT 137 (L. Pelton ed. 1981, 1985).

N. Lemann, *The Origins of the Underclass*, THE ATLANTIC, vol. 257(6) and (7) June and July, 1986.

S. Levitan, *Programs in Aid of the Poor* (1985).

S. Miller, *The Relationship Between Adolescent Childbearing and Child Maltreatment*, 58(6) CHILD WELFARE 553 (1984).

J. Myers, Brief Communication, 2(3) PROTECTING CHILDREN 16 (1985) (A publication of the American Human Association.). *See also* J. Myers, *The Legal Response to Child Abuse: In the Best Interest of Children?* 24 JOURNAL OF FAMILY LAW 149 (1985-86).

L. Pelton, *Child Abuse and Neglect: The Myth of Classlessness*, THE SOCIAL CONTEXT OF CHILD ABUSE AND NEGLECT 23 (L. Pelton ed. 1981, 1985).

The Growing Black Underclass—A Lost Nation Within a Land of Comfort, U.S. News & World Report, vol. 100(10), March 17, 1986.

Child Abuse & Neglect, Vol. 12, pp. 103-113, 1988
Printed in the U.S.A. All rights reserved.

SCHOOL SEXUAL ABUSE PREVENTION: UNINTENDED CONSEQUENCES AND DILEMMAS

BONNIE TRUDELL, M.S., PH.D. CANDIDATE AND MARIAMNE H. WHATLEY, PH.D.

Department of Curriculum and Instruction and Women's Studies Program, University of Wisconsin-Madison

Abstract—In view of the recent proliferation of school sexual abuse prevention programs and materials, this article critically examines current assumptions about the role of elementary school personnel in prevention and possible unintended consequences of such assumptions. These unintended consequences include emphasizing a simple solution to a complex social problem and contributing to victim blaming. Some dilemmas that arise for classroom teachers around predeveloped curricular materials and mandatory reporting are also explored. Teacher use of predeveloped materials may mean a diminishing of wider teaching skills and reduction of complex concepts to brief, noncontroversial interventions that may serve to mystify sexuality and unduly frighten students. Mandatory reporting, as it is frequently presented to teachers, can create further dilemmas by obscuring the ethical decisions inherent in the process, assuming consistently positive outcomes after reporting, and neglecting the context in which teachers work. The authors suggest that educators should be aware of these possible unintended consequences and dilemmas in order to maintain a broad perspective on child sexual abuse and to focus their efforts more effectively within a larger network addressing the problem.

BACKGROUND

DURING THE LAST TEN YEARS, the issue of childhood sexual abuse has gained an increasingly prominent place among pressing social concerns. Prevalence studies suggest that from 19 to 64% of females may have experienced some form of sexual abuse before age 18 [1-4], and definitions of sexual abuse used in these studies have been compared by Wyatt and Peters [5]. Although sexual abuse among males has been less extensively investigated, estimates are that around 10% of young males may have been similarly victimized [1, 6]. Child welfare professionals, educators, physicians, and legislators are all involved in seeking ways to cope with this heretofore "hidden epidemic" [7]. Etiology, identification, treatment, and prevention are all being discussed and debated at length in the professional journals, as well as the popular media. Most experts agree that early detection/intervention and prevention education can contribute significantly to a solution to this serious social problem.

Because of their close and ongoing contact with young children, school personnel are increasingly seen as key figures in detection and prevention efforts [7-11]. All 50 states currently encourage or mandate reporting of child sexual abuse by school personnel [11]. There are sexual abuse prevention programs in every state of the United States [9]; some states, such as Wisconsin, have passed legislation mandating "protective behavior" programs for elementary school students [12]. Programs for young children have been identified as essential because 60% of sexual abuse victims are under age 12 when the abuse first occurs [13]; the average age of a victim of intrafamilial sexual abuse in 10.8 years [8].

Reprint requests to Mariamne H. Whatley, Department of Curriculum and Instruction, 225 North Mills St., Madison, WI 53706.

Programs at the preschool and elementary level are designed primarily to assist children in preventing their own sexual victimization. Over the last five years, a staggering array of materials along these lines has proliferated, including books, audiovisuals, puppet shows, an estimated 400-500 curricula, about 40 plays, and hundreds of coloring books [9].

Although there are many competing viewpoints about specific approaches, the general parameters of elementary school sexual abuse prevention programs can be briefly delineated as follows [6, 14]. First, most programs are formulated around the "best guesses" [14:127] of professionals about what children will find useful in preventing their own sexual abuse. There has been a distinct movement from "stranger danger" to an awareness that a family member or other trusted person may be the perpetrator of sexual abuse. Although different terms may be used to describe the concepts, most programs stress a child's right to body privacy and to say no if someone touches her/him in a way that does not feel okay to the child. Many curricula incorporate a version of the "Touch Continuum" [15] to help children discriminate among good, bad, and confusing touch. The degree of explicitness about precisely where "bad" and "not okay" touch may occur varies from "private parts" or "under your swimsuit" to explicit names such as penis, vulva, etc. Most programs also stress that children should tell someone in their support network who can help if they experience such touch and that they should be persistent until they are believed [6] or feel safe again [16]. Some programs involve actual role play of assertiveness and other behavioral skills useful in preventing or escaping potentially abusive situations. Most attempt to convey the idea that sexual abuse, if it occurs, is not the fault of the child.

Given the recent upsurge in school prevention programs and materials, several proponents have suggested that a critical rethinking of this effort is needed [14, 17-19]. In light of these suggestions, the purpose of this paper is to examine some of the assumptions about the school's role in preventing sexual abuse and the possible unintended negative consequences inherent in these assumptions. It will also explore some of the dilemmas around implementation and reporting that elementary school sexual abuse prevention programs raise for classroom teachers. Pointing out the possibility of these unintended consequences is not to suggest that efforts to empower children through school prevention programs are worthless or should be abandoned. Instead, being aware of these possibilities and potential problems should help those of us involved in sexual abuse prevention focus our efforts more effectively. This paper is intended to highlight potential negative consequences so that programs can take steps to avoid them. Some programs have few, if any, problems, while some are in serious need of complete evaluation and restructuring. By drawing on specific examples, we in no way mean to imply that all programs share these errors.

UNINTENDED CONSEQUENCES OF SCHOOL PREVENTION PROGRAMS

Applying a Simple Solution to a Complex Social Problem

Childhood sexual abuse is a complex problem thought to be affected by such varied social factors as patriarchal family structure, erosion of traditional external controls over sexual behavior, changing sexual expectations, family isolation, and increased divorce rates and subsequent recoupling [20]; differences in patterns of male/female socialization, growing portrayal of children as sex objects in pornography and the popular media [4, 21, 22]; norms of child obedience to all adults; and low conviction and identification rates for offenders [17]. More specifically, David Finkelhor has identified four preconditions necessary for the occurrence of child sexual abuse: (1) sexual attraction to a child; (2) lack of internal controls; (3) lack of external controls; and (4) availability of or access to a child [2]. School prevention programs, since they are clearly directed at the fourth precondition while leaving the other three unaddressed [9], are at best a partial solution to a many faceted problem. Simply put, prevention programs in every classroom in every school would not eliminate child sexual abuse. Unfortunately, however, in the zeal to convince others of the worth of prevention programs, the school's role may be inflated. For example:

The aim of prevention is to see that child abuse and neglect do not occur at all, and the educator is in a unique position to achieve this aim [23:11].

Other proponents are less direct, but they imply the same position by neglecting to point out the complexity of the sexual abuse problem [8, 10, 24, 25]. Instead of fostering a simple solution mentality to a complicated social problem, it is the responsibility of prevention proponents to articulate more realistic goals, e.g., ". . . we adults believe children can be empowered to *help* avoid or interrupt their own victimization *sometimes*" [9:4]. We must not convey the erroneous message—either explicitly or implicitly—that school prevention efforts will solve the problem of child sexual abuse.

In fact, a single-minded pursuit of school sexual abuse prevention programs as the solution can turn attention away from other, perhaps more effective, ways to address the problem. For example, since three of Finkelhor's four preconditions relate to the offender, we might reasonably question why the major focus of sexual abuse prevention has been on training the children (the victims) to protect themselves rather than on preventing offenders from engaging in these behaviors [26, 27]. Ultimately, all of the wider social factors mentioned above, and possibly others not yet identified, must be considered if we are to effectively stop child sexual abuse.

Blaming the Victim

To the extent that they focus on teaching children to protect themselves, school sexual abuse prevention programs can have the unanticipated negative consequence of contributing to blaming the victim. This is a dynamic that has long operated in our society whereby certain individuals (those with least power) are blamed for their own victimization [28]. On an individual level, the moral and factual responsibility for instances of sexual abuse belong to the offender, not the child. Furthermore, on a societal level, it is the responsibility of adults to protect children "by not preying on them and by being alert for signs that others are" [29:105].

Nevertheless, the impression that children are responsible for preventing their own victimization can be unintentionally reinforced by trying to convince others of the potential value of a school program's efforts. For example, the following unreferenced research finding appears in one school district's letter to parents regarding an upcoming protective behaviors unit [30]:

When interviewing people who have sexually assaulted children, it has been determined that in 80% of the cases, the abuser would have stopped the assault if the child had said "No."

Thus, in an effort to convince parents of the program's effectiveness, the letter suggests that the victim, not the offender, is actually responsible for stopping sexual abuse.

Additionally, because of the egocentrism that characterizes young children's developmental level, teaching self-protection strategies to them may actually reinforce rather than counter their tendency to blame themselves should sexual abuse occur [15]. Cordelia Anderson, one of the pioneers in the school sexual abuse prevention movement and developer of the "Touch Continuum," states:

People tell children to say no and say no and say no and sometimes I see this exaggerated in a dangerous way that puts all the responsibility on children. The implication is, if you couldn't say no, it's your fault. Or if you say no and it didn't work, there's something wrong with you [15:23].

DILEMMAS FOR CLASSROOM TEACHERS

With increased focus on child sexual abuse as a social problem and the school prevention program as a solution, classroom teachers find themselves the target of both community pressure (particularly from child welfare professionals) and legal mandates. To read the exhortations by prevention proponents, one could reasonably conclude that the implementation of such programs is a straightforward matter of teachers assuming their legal and moral obligation. Most articles advocating elementary school sexual prevention programs or describing the various curricular offerings either mention only briefly or fail to discuss at all the kinds of dilemmas that such programs can raise for classroom teachers [8, 10, 23-25, 31-33]. Even articles that explicitly acknowledge at some length the possible barriers for teachers—available time and materials, teacher fear, lack of administrative support—suggest that these can be overcome rather simplistically by "proper teacher training, adequate classroom material, and good planning at the district level" [34:82]. In examining both the unintended consequences and dilemmas these sexual abuse prevention materials raise for classroom teachers, this paper focuses specifically on issues surrounding predeveloped curricular materials and mandatory reporting.

Use of Predeveloped Curricular Materials

Deskilling teachers. The vast array of sexual abuse prevention curricula appearing over the past five years is, at one level, a well-intentioned attempt to assist teachers in their expanded role in preventing child sexual abuse. However, these materials should also be examined as part of a wider trend in education toward prepackaged curricular products. One characteristic of such educational products is that planning is separated from execution. Planning occurs at the level of production by those outside the classroom, while implementation of the plan is carried out by the teacher, an arrangement that can have an unintended impact on teachers. Michael Apple, a curriculum theorist, has used the term "deskilling" to describe one such consequence of the increased use of prepackaged curricular materials:

Skills that teachers used to need, that were deemed essential to the craft of working with children—such as curriculum deliberation and planning, designing teaching and curricular strategies for specific groups and individuals based on intimate knowledge of these people—are no longer necessary. . . . What were previously considered valuable skills slowly atrophy because they are less required [35:146].

In the school sexual abuse prevention literature, "training" teachers in the use of particular curricular models frequently seems to be emphasized over these essential teaching skills. Some descriptions of what teachers need to know to present particular predeveloped materials reduce complex concepts and interactions to a brief "laundry list" format. For example, a Bridgework Theater videotape (funded by a 1980 grant from the National Center on Child Abuse and Neglect to develop prevention resources) takes only 30 minutes to train teachers to lead a classroom discussion to accompany its prevention play. This session includes ". . . information on reporting suspected abuse, indicators of sexual abuse, prevention concepts, and guides to leading the group discussion" [36:149]. While we acknowledge that time and budget constraints can hamper the best-intentioned efforts, we believe that predeveloped materials which oversimplify the complexities of both teaching and sexual abuse are not in the best interests of either teachers or students. In addition to neglecting the wider craft of teaching, the emphasis on training teachers to use predeveloped curricular materials can overlook the importance of other school personnel—administrators, school board members, and support staff such as guidance counselors, psychologists, and nurses—in the effort to prevent sexual abuse.

Another assumption in the school child sexual abuse prevention literature seems to be that all available predeveloped programs are well-planned and can be successful if they are properly executed by the teacher, i.e., they conform to the curricular model. Thus, the presenter rather than the curriculum itself is more likely to be blamed for unanticipated, potentially damaging long-term effects on children such as instilling fear and guilt [6, 9, 14]. For example, one cautionary description of such problematic outcomes for children is preceded by the notation:

These examples are not necessarily critiques of the materials used or of the programs, but may reflect on *how* the materials were used or misused [9:70].

The issue of quality assurance thus revolves around the quality of the presenter, not the materials themselves. It is seen as best addressed by "careful training and ongoing monitoring of personnel who actually deliver the training to children" or the development of "narrative scripts" for teachers to follow [6:327], solutions that may contribute to further teacher deskilling. Instead, the question should address the materials themselves and whether young children are capable of grasping the subtle and complex concepts around sexual abuse prevention that may "make sense to adults but which are consistently misunderstood by children" [13:259].

A brief training session focused on the use of predeveloped curricular materials seems particularly inadequate in dealing with the topic of child sexual abuse, an emotional and confusing issue for most people. In particular, there is a real possibility that elementary teachers themselves may have been victims of such abuse, since the vast majority of them are women and prevalence studies suggest that as many as 64% of women may have had this experience. In this context, "training" teachers so they do not "pass on their own fears, biases or misunderstandings" [9:96] to children is a worthy but monumental task, one that certainly cannot be accomplished in 30 minutes or a few hours. Because child sexual abuse prevention has arisen so recently as an educational issue, inservice work with teachers is necessary. Such systematic efforts as the previously mentioned Wisconsin Legislation's mandate of protective behaviors training programs and technical assistance for educators [12] are to be applauded. However, brief sessions that simply train teachers to use predeveloped materials are woefully insufficient and may actually contribute to overall teacher deskilling. As a long-range strategy to help teachers deal with the issue of child sexual abuse, attention needs to be devoted to the topic at the preservice level of teacher education, where it is currently given only superficial treatment [23, 37, 38].

Brief interventions. We must also be aware that these predeveloped curricular materials are commodities designed to be sold for profit in the lucrative school market. Given the myriad demands on a teacher's time and the organizational constraints of the school, materials that take up little teacher and student time are more likely to sell. Thus, "brief intervention" [31] is an accurate generic description for most of the available curricular materials. For example, of the 18 preschool and elementary programs described in the recent *Educator's Guide to Preventing Child Sexual Abuse* [39], the number of specified sessions with children ranged from one to four. (Five of the described programs do not specify number of sessions.) Eight programs involve only one session, and three involve two sessions. The longest teacher/student contact time specified is two and one-half hours. Worse yet, some schools simply show a film with no discussion at all or buy a coloring book or comic for all students and call it a prevention program [9]. Cordelia Anderson suggests that teaching the complex and subtle issues involved in sexual abuse prevention requires, among other things, sufficient contact time between teacher and student for interaction and clarification [15], something unlikely to be accomplished in one, two, or even three sessions. The small allotment of time suggested in most programs may actually serve to exacerbate student confusion. The same simplistic assumption seems to be frequently made about training children to protect themselves and training teachers for sexual abuse prevention: A brief intervention will suffice to deal with complex concepts.

Avoiding controversy. Avoiding controversy is another selling point for curricular materials. Since explicitness is the biggest area of controversy in child sexual abuse prevention [15], most material geared toward young children refers vaguely to "underneath your swim suit" or private parts, rather than using such explicit words as penis, vagina and vulva to define areas where touch can constitute sexual abuse [18]. This can convey the following double message to children:

You can talk to me about sexual abuse, it's not your fault, there's nothing wrong with you. But your body is so bad that I can't even say what is underneath your swimming suit [15:21].

At best, such a message is incomplete; at worst, it is dangerous because:

Prevention means we've got to have a healthier understanding of what is appropriate sexuality. If we are so fearful of sexuality, of our bodies, that we can't say breast, penis, vulva, vagina, anus, we are perpetuating the fear at the same time we are going full force talking about what's abusive and what's unhealthy [15:22].

As part of the attempt to avoid controversy, many materials are marketed under the title of safety education, facilitating their use where sexuality education is not accepted. This is not to suggest that sexual abuse prevention is totally inappropriate in a safety education curriculum. For children, the issues around feeling safe can encompass a broad range of areas, including sexual abuse prevention. However, in the United States, the labeling of these programs as safety education is often based on marketing strategies rather than on curricular or pedagogical needs. This strategy assumes that school administrators, who constituted much of the early resistance to prevention programs because of fear of negative parental response [15] and who are ultimately responsible for school expenditures, are more likely to find these less explicit safety education materials "in good taste" [36:149]. This separation from sexuality education can become a problem when sexual abuse prevention, with vague allusions to private parts and emphasis on saying no, constitutes the first or only classroom reference to sexuality; young children then learn that sexuality is essentially secretive, negative, and even dangerous. For example, a proposed safety mini-unit geared toward protecting elementary children from molestation has the scary title, "Staying Alive" [40]. The time has come for prevention proponents to venture beyond the more acceptable, narrow domains of safety education and sexual abuse and to become visible advocates for K-12 school sexuality education.

Mandatory Reporting

The educator's ability to identify child sexual abuse victims, either through noticing possible indicators or by actual child disclosure, is central to school prevention efforts. Some proponents argue that identification should not be a primary goal of these programs [9, 15], while others assert that programs failing to identify abused children "appear to be doing something wrong in view of the fact that somewhere around 20% of the girls and 10% of boys will be abused before they reach eighteen" [6:328]. Whether seen as a primary goal or not, disclosure and the attendant issue of reporting are logical possible outcomes of school sexual abuse prevention programs. It has been reported that one-sixth of the children attending a particular classroom presentation subsequently revealed a prior sexual assault; of these, one-half had never reported the incident previously [41].

Furthermore, personal experience in working with teachers indicates that concerns over mandatory reporting are widespread and are behind a great deal of reluctance to get involved with prevention (and sexuality education) programs. Yet, the assumption seems to be made among many prevention proponents that providing teachers with information is sufficient to alleviate these concerns. Thus, the reporting issue is most frequently addressed by informing teachers of possible indicators of sexual abuse, their legal mandate to report, and the procedures for doing so. This rational, "objective" depiction of the reporting process glosses over several dilemmas that arise for teachers as they are faced with identifying and reporting sexual abuse. First, it obscures both the ongoing controversy surrounding mandated reporting and the ethical decisions inherent in the process. Secondly, it sets forth a truncated view of the overall process and assumes consistently positive outcomes after reporting. Finally, it neglects the context in which the teacher works and minimizes the emotional impact of the process on the reporter.

Obscuring the ethical nature of decisions. Mandatory reporting is presented as a noncontroversial given in the sexual abuse prevention literature when, in fact, such laws have been decidedly controversial ever since their passage [2]. All 50 U.S. states passed new child maltreatment reporting laws (most including neglect and sexual abuse) in the 1960s and 1970s. Although there is variation among states, people in an expanded number of job categories are now mandated to report if they have "reasonable cause to suspect" actual or, in some states, potential harm to a child. Nevertheless, the reality is that many mandated professionals do not fully comply with the reporting requirements. Overall, only an estimated 44% of sexual abuse cases known to professionals are reported [2:205], although school personnel (including nurses and social workers) appear to have a higher reporting rate (76%) than other groups of child welfare professionals [2:217].

Precisely what constitutes reasonable cause for suspicion or potential harm is open to varying interpretations, and the lists of possible indicators offered to educators are frequently so general as to be of minimal use. For example, one writer suggests that two or more of the following appearing simultaneously may indicate sexual abuse:

Personality change; change from being outgoing to clingy; regression in toilet-training habits; signs of being uncomfortable with someone formerly trusted; withdrawal from self; sophisticated sexual knowledge, beyond what is expected for age group; moodiness, excessive crying; changes in eating, sleeping habits; increased activity; behavior problems; unusual shyness; sudden unfounded fears; unusual need for reassurance, need to be told "You're okay"; unnatural interest in own or other's genitals; poor peer relations or absence of friends; gender role confusion; consistently arriving early for school and leaving late; inappropriate sexual self-consciousness [24:174].

Furthermore, since legal definitions of sexual abuse are also rather general, the reality is that professionals are frequently left to their judgment in deciding whether a particular situation fits the definition [42:64]. In other words, there are ethical judgments involved in decisions to report child sexual abuse. (One such judgment involves the legal age of consent. In Wisconsin, for example, anyone under age 16 is legally incapable of consenting to sexual activity. Thus, if a teacher became aware of such activity between two 15-year-olds, perhaps by being sought out for contraceptive advice, the teacher is legally mandated to report.) When these judgments are reduced to lists of indicators and legal definitions, teachers are misled and insulted.

Assuming positive outcomes of reporting. Instead of illuminating the complex dilemmas around reporting, materials directed at educators most frequently advise them that their role is simply to report suspected cases of child sexual abuse to the designated authorities, not to launch their own investigations or to judge whether abuse has actually occurred [11, 25]. Essentially their involvement ends with the report. What happens after the report is made is depicted as a neutral, objective process, sometimes simplified to a flow chart [11], with the assumption that the investigation will be handled promptly, thoroughly, and fairly, e.g., "Trained investigators will ascertain whether abuse has, in fact, occurred" [11:176]. However, the reality is that institutional insularity and lack of consensus on handling sexual abuse frequently contribute to delay and confusion in dealing with the situation [2:211-213]. To further exacerbate the problem, expanded reporting requirements have led to large increases in the number of cases reported nationally; for example, there has been a 91% increase in the annual figures between 1976 and 1980. At the same time, Reagan administration funding cutbacks in social services have resulted in a smaller number of staff to investigate these increasing numbers of reports [42]. A realistic assessment of the local process for investigating child sexual abuse reports is essential information for educators.

Contrary to the assumption of positive outcomes after reporting, the impact of an investigation (even one that is unsubstantiated) on a family can be devastating, sometimes actually increasing the level of stress and placing the child at greater risk than before [42]. Given the reduced number of staff and the current emphasis within child protective services on short-term crisis intervention rather than ongoing services and support for families when reports of abuse are substantiated, monitoring is frequently all the worker is able to do [42].

Neglecting the school context. In urging teacher to fulfill their ethical and legal obligations in reporting child sexual abuse, proponents can lose sight of the context in which teachers work. Creating an atmosphere of openness and trust [25:120] and finding time to be available for one-to-one talks during which a child might disclose sexual abuse is difficult, given the organizational constraints of the school. Nevertheless, teachers are routinely exhorted to assure children of their availability, e.g., "encourage the children to approach him or her privately to discuss any personal concerns and to seek additional information" [31:89]. One proponent even suggests that "the teacher should be available to the child *and her or his family* for emotional support" (emphasis added) after the report is made [25:121].

For a child to disclose sexual abuse is usually an emotionally stressful experience. Reporting is also stressful, especially if the accused is a parent with whom the teacher has developed a relationship or if the teacher lives and works in a small community where professional, family, and friendship links are interconnected. The whole process is even more painful if the teacher has experienced such abuse in her or his own past. To obscure these possibilities with legal imperatives seems misleading and dishonest.

For the teacher, support from others within the school is crucial, but not always available. Because many state departments of education and school districts do not have policies for reporting child sexual abuse [25], the teacher may be isolated in dealing with a child's disclosure. In some districts reporting policy differs from legal requirements of the state, e.g., teachers are required to report to an administrator, not social services or a law enforcement agency. Some teachers experience this situation as a conflict between keeping their jobs and fulfilling their legal responsibility, particularly when an administrator is reluctant to report. The reporting philosophy of the school principal has been found to exert an important influence on teacher reporting. Where a principal encourages it, teachers are more likely to report; where principals are reluctant to report (frequently for reasons related to maintaining good parental relations and school image), teachers report less often [44]. Thus, proponents of school prevention programs must also inform and cultivate the support of administrators, school board members, and other school personnel [33]. If these decision makers see school sexual abuse prevention as a priority, they can lend personal and material support to the efforts of teachers.

While mandatory reporting is an important way to help prevent child sexual abuse, teachers deserve a more realistic portrayal of the complexity of the situation. The issue is simply too complex to be reduced to lists and legal obligations.

CONCLUSION

Recognition of the seriousness and prevalence of child sexual abuse, extensive research increasing our knowledge in the area, and major efforts toward prevention have all been important recent developments. Much effort has been expended in a short time in working towards possible solutions. Given the rapid proliferation of materials, those involved in the school sexual abuse prevention movement need to constantly and critically examine the assumptions and consequences inherent in this work. To point out some of the dilemmas that school sex education prevention programs can create for classroom teachers is not to imply that all programs are problematic. These issues are raised so that such dilemmas, where they exist, may be better addressed. Critiques must be brought to the attention of those influencing policy on child sexual abuse education, including legislators, school board members, school and social service administrators. School personnel alone cannot solve the problem of child sexual abuse but may serve as part of a larger network, including parents, that must function cooperatively and supportively to deal with this issue.

No matter how good curricular materials and programs are, the problem of child sexual abuse will not be solved without dealing with the issues on a broader social level as Conte and his associates have pointed out:

Many professionals involved in sexual abuse prevention programs recognize that ultimately all materials and programs should be viewed as temporary efforts to help children resist and escape abuse until such time as other activities can be successful in changing the conditions which cause and support abuse of children [45].

The problem cannot be solved by teaching children to resist and escape; the real battle lies in making fundamental changes in a society that allows and even encourages child sexual abuse.

NOTES AND REFERENCES

1. FINKELHOR, D. *Sexually Victimized Children*. Free Press, New York (1979).
2. FINKELHOR, D. *Child Sexual Abuse: New Theory and Research*. Free Press, New York (1984).

3. RUSSELL, D. E. H. The incidence and prevalence of intrafamilial and extrafamilial sexual abuse of female children. *Child Abuse & Neglect* 7:133-146 (1983).
4. WYATT, G. E. The sexual abuse of Afro-American and white American women in childhood. *Child Abuse & Neglect* 9:507-519 (1985).
5. WYATT, G. E. and PETERS, S. D. Issues in the definition of child sexual abuse in prevalence research. *Child Abuse & Neglect* 10:231-240 (1986).
6. CONTE, J. R., ROSEN, C., SAPERSTEIN, L. and SHERMACK, R. An evaluation of a program to prevent the sexual victimization of young children. *Child Abuse & Neglect* 9:319-328 (1985).
7. WATSON, R. A hidden epidemic. *Newsweek* May 14, pp. 30-36 (1984).
8. BRASSARD, M. R., TYLER, A. H. and KEHLE, T. J. School programs to prevent intrafamilial child sexual abuse. *Child Abuse & Neglect* 7:241-245 (1983).
9. PLUMMER, C. A. Prevention education perspective. In: *The Educator's Guide to Preventing Child Sexual Abuse*, M. Nelson and K. Clark (Eds.), pp. 1-5. Network Publications, Santa Cruz, CA (1986).
10. RIGGS, R. S. Incest: The school's role. *Journal of School Health* 52:365-370 (1982).
11. STRINGER, G. M. An overview of reporting. In: *The Educator's Guide to Preventing Child Sexual Abuse*, M. Nelson and K. Clark (Eds.), pp. 175-177.
12. STATE OF WISCONSIN. 1985 Wisconsin Act 213, enacted April 10 (1986).
13. CONTE, J. R. and BERLINER, L. Sexual abuse of children: Implications for practice. *Social Casework* 62:601-606 (1981).
14. CONTE, J. R. Evaluating prevention education programs. In: *The Educator's Guide to Preventing Child Sexual Abuse*, M. Nelson and K. Clark (Eds.), pp. 126-129.
15. ANDERSON, C. A history of the touch continuum. In: *The Educator's Guide to Preventing Child Sexual Abuse*, M. Nelson and K. Clark (Eds.), pp. 15-25.
16. WEST, P. F. *Protective Behaviors: Anti-Victim Training for Children, Adolescents, and Adults.* Protective Behaviors, Inc., Madison, WI (1984).
17. PLUMMER, C. A. Child sexual abuse prevention: Keys to program success. In: *The Educator's Guide to Preventing Child Sexual Abuse*, M. Nelson and K. Clark (Eds.), pp. 69-79.
18. BUTLER, S. Thinking about prevention: A critical look. In: *The Educator's Guide to Preventing Child Sexual Abuse*, M. Nelson and K. Clark (Eds.), pp. 6-14.
19. KRAIZER, S. K. Rethinking prevention. *Child Abuse & Neglect* 10:259-261 (1986).
20. FINKELHOR, D. Sexual abuse: A sociological perspective. *Child Abuse & Neglect* 6:95-102 (1982).
21. KILBOURNE, J. The child as sex object: Images of children in the media. In: *The Educator's Guide to Preventing Child Sexual Abuse*, M. Nelson and K. Clark (Eds.), pp. 40-46.
22. RUSH, F. Myths, fairy tales and films. In: *The Educator's Guide to Preventing Child Sexual Abuse*, M. Nelson and K. Clark (Eds.), pp. 29-39.
23. GLADBACH, R. M. and WHEELER, V. R. Child abuse and neglect: A curriculum proposal. *The Teacher Educator* 21:9-14 (1986).
24. HERMAN, P. Educating children about sexual abuse. *Childhood Education* 61:169-174 (1985).
25. MAYER, A. *Sexual Abuse: Causes, Consequences, and Treament of Incestuous and Pedophilic Acts.* Learning Publications, Holmes Beach, FL (1985).
26. GILGUN, J. F. and GORDON, S. Sex education and the prevention of child sexual abuse. *Journal of Sex Education and Therapy* 11:46-52 (1985).
27. SMITH, T. A. and CONTE, J. R. What can offenders teach us about prevention? *Preventing Sexual Abuse* 1:1-3 (1986).
28. RYAN, W. *Blaming the Victim.* Vintage Books, New York (1971).
29. ADAMS, C. Considering children's developmental stages in prevention education. In: *The Educator's Guide to Preventing Child Sexual Abuse*, M. Nelson and K. Clark (Eds.), pp. 103-107.
30. Letter in curriculum packet from one of the prevention projects listed as a resource in the Wisconsin Department of Public Instruction publication, "Child Sexual Assault and Abuse: Guidelines for Schools," Madison, WI, May 1984.
31. WOLFE, D. A., MACPHERSON, T., BLOUNT, R. and WOLFE, V. V. Evaluation of a brief intervention for educating school children in awareness of physical and sexual abuse. *Child Abuse & Neglect* 10:85-92 (1986).
32. SWAN, H. L., PRESS, A. N. and BRIGGS, S. L. Child sexual abuse prevention: Does it work? *Child Welfare* 64:395-405 (1985).
33. DAVIS, L. L. The role of the teacher in preventing child sexual abuse. In: *The Educator's Guide to Preventing Child Sexual Abuse*, M. Nelson and K. Clark (Eds.), pp. 87-92.
34. DOWNER, A. Training teachers to be partners in prevention. In: *The Educator's Guide to Preventing Child Sexual Abuse*, M. Nelson and K. Clark (Eds.), pp. 80-86.
35. APPLE, M. W. *Education and Power.* Routledge and Kegan Paul, Boston (1982).
36. Bridgework Theater, program summary. In: *The Educator's Guide to Preventing Child Sexual Abuse*, M. Nelson and K. Clark (Eds.), p. 149.
37. GLISCZINSKI, C. The student teacher's preparation for identifying and reporting suspected cases of abuse and neglect. Unpublished master's thesis, University of Wisconsin-Madison (1982).
38. MOLNAR, A. and GLISCZINSKI, C. Child abuse: A curriculum issue in teacher education. *Journal of Teacher Education* 34:39-41 (1983).
39. NELSON, M. and CLARK, K. (Eds.). *The Educator's Guide to Preventing Child Sexual Abuse.* (1986).

40. MCNAB, W. L. Staying alive: A mini-unit on child molestation prevention for elementary school children. *Journal of School Health* 55:226-229 (1985).
41. KENT, C. Child sexual abuse prevention project: An educational program for children. Hennepin County Attorney's Office, C-2100 Government Center, Minneapolis, MN (1979).
42. FALLER, K. C. Unanticipated problems in the United States child protection system. *Child Abuse & Neglect* 9:63-69 (1985).
43. AMERICAN HUMANE ASSOCIATION. *Highlights of the 1980 National Reporting Data.* American Humane Association, Englewood, CO (1982).
44. PELCOVITZ, D. A. *Child Abuse as Viewed by Suburban Elementary Teachers.* Century 21, Saratoga, CA (1980).
45. CONTE, J. R., ROSEN, C. R. and SAPERSTEIN, L. An analysis of programs to prevent the sexual victimization of children, paper presented at the Fifth International Congress on Child Abuse and Neglect, Montreal (1984). *The Journal of Primary Prevention* (In press).

Résumé—On assiste à la prolifération des programmes de prévention des sévices sexuels dans les écoles et cette prolifération touche également les matières utilisées pour cet enseignement. Le présent article procède à un examen critique des à priori qui sont à la base de cet enseignement concernant la rôle du personnel des écoles primaires dans la prévention. Cet article se penche aussi sur les conséquences inattendues que ces hypothèses ont provoquées. Les conséquences non voulues comprennent l'accent mis sur une solution simpliste que l'on entend apporter à un problème social complexe et cela contribue à montrer du doigt la victime. Il y a des problèmes qui se posent pour les maîtres d'école. Ces problèmes sont en relation avec le matériel utilisé pour ces programmes d'enseignement et également sont en rapport avec la dénonciation obligatoire des cas. L'utilisation du matériel d'enseignement préfabriqué en quelque sorte peut limiter les qualités enseignantes du maître et réduire son intervention à des points qui ne peuvent pas être sujets à controverse et qui augmentent le mystère autour de la sexualité, ce qui effraie inutilement les écoliers. En ce qui concerne la dénonciation obligatoire telle qu'on l'impose fréquemment au maître d'école, elle peut créer des problèmes supplémentaires en masquant les décisions éthiques qui sont impliquées dans ce processus en présentant les choses comme étant forcément positives une fois que la dénonciation est faite et en négligeant le contexte dans lequel les maîtres d'école doivent travailler. Les auteurs de cet article suggèrent que les enseignants devraient être sensibilisés à ces conséquences non voulues et à ces problèmes afin qu'ils puissent garder une perspective assez large sur ces problèmes sexuels et être plus efficaces dans leurs efforts en voyant les choses avec un certain recul lorsqu'ils en parlent à leurs élèves.

Resumen—El artículo nota las posibles consecuencias negativas y no intencionales de programas para la prevención del abuso sexual del niño llevados a cabo en la escuela primaria, y los dilemas que su implementación y el reportaje del abuso sexual pueden crear para los maestros. Entre las consecuencias no intencionales y negativas para los niños se encuentran: (1) contribuir la tendencia a "culpar a la víctima," (2) reforzar—en vez de disminuir—la tendencia de los niños a culpar a sí mismos, (3) comunicar mensajes confusos/dobles a los niños. El tipo de programa de prevención escolar "pre-empacado," puede tener como resultados negativos para los maestros: (1) pérdida de habilidades, (2) el ignorar el papel de otros miembros de la escuela, (3) el culpar al maestro por consecuencias inesperadas. El reporte de la sospecha de abuso sexual del niño es emocionalmente díficil para la maestra, y la confronta con dilemas personales, empíricos y éticos.

279

Banning Corporal Punishment: A Crucial Step Toward Preventing Child Abuse

by Cindy S. Moelis

Thirty nine states currently permit schools to use corporal punishment against their students, contributing to a broader trend of using physical force against children. This trend has serious consequences for individuals and society. It impedes society's attempts to ensure freedom from bodily harm and to protect our children. The purpose of this article is to place the need for banning corporal punishment in our schools in the broader context of the need to gradually eliminate all violent actions toward our children.

Levels of Violence Toward Our Children

Too often children sustain serious injuries or death when caretakers are attempting to "discipline" them. In 1987, an estimated 2.25 million children were reported as suspected abuse or neglect victims.[1] Straus and Gelles estimated that in 1985 a minimum of one million children ages 3-17, residing in two-parent families, were subjected to serious physical child abuse.[2] Over 1,100 children died last year due to maltreatment.[3] Equally as disturbing as in-home violence is the violence children experience in schools. Over one million incidents of corporal punishment of schoolchildren were reported during the 1986-87 school year.[4] Experts estimate that 10,000-20,000 students sustained medical injuries due to this institutionalized form of physical punishment.[5] In a society that purports to value human life and human rights, this should be unacceptable.

The excessive force we use on children, which is only partially reflected by these and similar statistics, has serious individual and social consequences. Statistics such as these fail to clearly portray the long term damaging consequences of physical violence toward children. For every incidence of child abuse reported, many others go undocumented. Each child that is intimidated, punched, kicked, or beaten may have siblings, friends, or classmates who are watching the violence and learning its unavoidable message:

that this form of human interaction is acceptable and that violence can be used to control others' behavior. Children imitate behaviors acted out by those adults who are important in their lives; children who observe their parents being violent to each other are three times more likely to hit their own spouses later in life than those with nonviolent parents.[6] In addition, Strauss, Gelles and Steinmetz found that "parents who were subjected to a great deal of physical punishment have the highest rates of abusive violence toward their own children."[7] There is a good chance that every child who grows up being constantly slapped or punched for displeasing his/her caretaker will grow up to be an adult that uses violence to show displeasure with his/her children or others. Ironically, when such children mature, they will be taught that if they hit another person it is an illegal act called assault and battery — unless that person is their child or student. In these cases, the use of violence is justified in the name of discipline.

It is discouraging to note that although our society generally does not tolerate the severe cases of child abuse, public intervention in the area of maltreatment is still tempered by confusion over what actions constitute discipline rather than abuse.[8] Because of our bewilderment, we may hesitate to act or may ignore warning signs that a child is in danger.

Public outrage followed news reports of the plights of Lisa Steinberg and Eli Creekmore, children who were allegedly beaten to death by their caretakers.[9] Yet, most of us are not outraged when an anonymous child is slapped by her mother in a store. Much of society's indifference toward violence that does not result in a serious injury (e.g. slapping a child) is due to a societal understanding that we should defer to caretakers' judgment on how they manage their children.

Moreover physical punishment of children is still believed to be an acceptable method of discipline.[10] Parents and other caretakers are allowed a tremendous amount of discretion; we implicitly trust them to do what is in the best interest of the child. We intervene legally only when the child seems to be obviously, physically harmed. Yet because our society is so tolerant of physical forms of discipline which are perceived as benign, such as spanking, slapping, or yanking a child, it is difficult to stop a child from being harmed before a serious injury occurs.

Even though everyone agrees that breaking a child's arm is an excessive punishment that should be labelled abusive, there is uncertainty as to how much restraint or pressure on a child's arm society should tolerate before intervening. If we act too soon, we fear being unnecessarily intrusive. If we wait too long, a child sustains serious injury.

The Need For Prevention

If by intervening in the caretaker-child relationship we are attempting to save a child from harm or death, then our current method of interceding only after a child is damaged is ineffective. The fact that 25-50 per cent of the cases of fatal abuse and neglect occur in families previously or currently known to the child protective agency or another agency in the community indicates that our current method of child welfare assistance is extremely problematic.[11] Given our cultural acceptance of physical punishment of children, we would have to become a police state that constantly watches every interaction between caretaker and child to effectively intervene before harm occurs. Of course, in a democratic society, that solution is undesirable.

Simply put, the challenge is to prevent harm to children without unduly intruding on the concept of family and privacy. While a difficult task, such balance can be achieved through an increased public awareness campaign to convey the message that the use of violence against children by any caretaker is problematic, by educating people as to how to reduce their personal levels of violence, and by creating adequate support systems for those who become frustrated and react violently while caring for children.

A preventive approach to stopping child abuse in all its forms is advocated by the National Committee for Prevention of Child Abuse, a nonprofit organization, established in 1972. One of the organization's long range goals is to create an environment less conducive to maltreatment through education and public awareness.[12] By breaking down societal norms and values that accept physical force as a means of resolving conflict and problems with our children, we will reduce the amount of harm stemming from excessive corporal punishment. By establishing the clearer standard that physical punishment is not a socially acceptable practice, parents may talk to their child instead of slapping him/her. And a school principal may not have the opportunity to hospitalize a student by an accidentally overzealous paddling.

Changing behavior that has been an accepted practice for generations is difficult. According to a recent survey conducted for the National Committee for Prevention of Child Abuse, 72 per cent of parents believe in spanking their children.[13] Yet, in that same poll, 71 per cent of those surveyed felt that physical punishment often or occasionally lead to injury to the child.[14] According to other studies, 84 to 97 percent of all parents use physical punishment on their children at some time in their life.[15] Although we have acknowledged that this activity is potentially damaging to a child, it seems that this has not changed people's attitude or behavior. Psychologist David Gil notes that adults who were subjected to physical force and violence in their childhood may not be easily convinced that it is damaging. Moreover, children can sometimes be irritating and provocative in their behavior and may push the tolerance of adults to the limit.[16] Yet despite these obstacles, if we want to be consistent in our concerns for human rights, protect our children from harmful injury, and educate the next generation not to use physical force to control others, we must recognize these barriers and work toward removing physical force as a legitimate interaction between caretakers and children.

Banning Corporal Punishment In Our Schools

To develop a less violent but socially accepted standard of discipline for caretakers and their children, we must start educating the public by example. Our social and legal institutions should condemn violence against children instead of legitimizing it. Outlawing corporal punishment in our schools and other child care facilites would provide children with the same protection from physical attack that our legal system provides for adults. More importantly, educational institutions teach children socially acceptable behavior and set an example for families' child rearing attitudes and practices.[17] Eliminating corporal punishment in our schools would be a symbolic as well as practical step in our quest to eliminate the use of physical force against children.

Schools are the logical place to begin reeducating parents and children. As Justice Warren observed in *Brown v. Board of Education*

Today, education is perhaps the most important function of state and local governments. Compulsory school attendance laws and the great expenditures for education both demonstrate our recognition of the importance of education to our democratic society . . . It is the very foundation of good citizenship. Today it is a principal instrument in awakening the child to cultural values, . . .and in helping him to adjust normally to his environment.[18]

By allowing school personnel to control our children through violence instead of teaching them discipline through patience and rewards, we are denying all the children in the 39 states where corporal punishment is allowed the opportunity for a good, safe education.

Historically, teachers were given the right to strike a student because teachers or tutors played a role similar to that of a parent. Parental delegation of rights and duties was based on the common law rule of *in loco parentis*.[19] This doctrine gave tutors the same rights and duties as parents at a time when teachers were selected by the family and understood each child's needs and problems. Our modern education system with mandatory attendance is less personalized, class size is larger, and we no longer fully accept the concept that teachers stand in the shoes of parents. The underlying rationale of parental delegation is being replaced by the proposition that "the State itself may impose such corporal punishment as is reasonably necessary 'for the proper education of the child and for the maintenance of group discipline'." [20] Since most research concludes that the use of corporal punishment is an ineffective method of controlling behavior in a classroom, the circumstances under which it is found "reasonable or necessary" should be rare.[21] Unfortunately, as statistics show, corporal punishment is not infrequent in many areas. For example, the newspaper, *The Nashville Tennessean,* reported that 18,885 incidents of corporal punishment occurred in Nashville schools in 1986-87 despite the fact that the school population is only 8,768.[22]

It seems absurd that in a society which sets up elaborate safeguards to prevent injustice to those criminally accused, teachers in certain states are allowed to play the role of the prosecutor, judge, and jury in deciding when a child will be paddled for an alleged offense. Recent statistics show that corporal punishment is often administered in a discriminatory fashion. Minorities, poor students, and handicapped children are being disproportionately paddled.[23] For example, the National Coalition of Advocates for Students observed that "while black students represent 16% of the total in-school population, they represent 28% of those corporally punished in school."[24] Due to legal prohibitions against corporal punishment in the northeastern states, a southern student is 4000 times more likely to get paddled than his/her counterpart in the north.[25]

A ban on corporal punishment in our schools, besides creating a healthier learning environment for children and setting an example for parents, would also be beneficial to the schools. The Supreme Court's declaration in *Ingraham v. Wright,* that corporal punishment of a student should only be done if it is "reasonably necessary," establishes very little guidance for teachers and principals. A ban would set an obvious standard for teachers and limit the schools' exposure to civil liability suits resulting from the use of inappropriate or overzealous corporal punishment.

Supporting a ban on corporal punishment should not be construed as advocating the abolition of discipline in the classroom. Children need a structured, disciplined environment to learn, but it does not have to be a violent one. Lists of alternative forms of non-violent discipline have been compiled by several organizations including the National Association for Social Workers and the National Education Association.[26] Current laws eliminating the use of corporal punishment as a form of discipline still allow teachers to use physical force to prevent immediate threats of harm to property, persons, or to obtain possession of weapons or other dangerous objects.[27] Eleven states and most major cities do not permit the use of physical punishment in their public schools, and children graduate from those states and cities each year. In these states, children have successfully learned without the threat of corporal punishment.

While advocating politics that eliminate the use of violence against children, we should also develop programs and policies that support caretakers and reduce stresses that contribute to the use of violence. In the context of banning corporal punishment in our schools, we should offer suport for teachers who are forced to change their methods of discipline. Retraining in alternative forms of discipline should be made available and assistance should be obtainable from principals, other teachers, and parents in maintaining a disciplined classroom. It will also be helpful to encourage communication between students, teachers and parents during and after the transition away from corporal punishment. A Congressional study discovered that "parental involvement raises student achievement and enhances development for every age group."[28] Rewarding teachers and students for creative non-violent solutions to problems that arise in the classroom and supporting educational reforms that improve teacher-student communication (e.g, small class size) would also be valuable, supportive measures. Teachers try to use every tool they have to effectively teach children. At the same time we remove the paddle as a tool, let's replace it with more positive, supportive approaches to learning.

Stopping the use of corporal punishment in our schools will not eliminate child abuse in all its forms. It will stop a systematic, highly visible, and state-sanctioned use of physical force that is employed in an attempt to control children's behavior. While banning physical punishment from our schools will not solve the larger problem of violence against children, it will provide a safer place for children to learn and grow. It is an important step in trying to educate caretakers and children who may be future caretakers, that more appropriate methods of discipline do exist. Once the 39 states stop endorsing the use of physical force against school children, our laws will more consistently protect all individuals from harm.

Cindy S. Moelis, esq. is a senior analyst for the National Center on Child Abuse Prevention Research at the National Committee for Prevention of Child Abuse. She previously worked on the President's Child Safety Partnership, a presidential task force established to investigate child victimization issues.

Footnotes

1. D. Daro and L. Mitchel, Child Abuse Fatalities Remain High : The Results of the 1987 Annual Fifty State Survey (National Committee for Prevention of Child Abuse, 1988).
2. M. Straus and R. Gelles, *Societal Change and Change in Family Violence from 1975 to 1985 As Revealed by Two National Surveys,* Journal of Marriage and the Family, 48 (186), at 465, 475.
3. *Supra* note 1.
4. Statistics obtained from the Department of Education, Office of Civil Rights, national projected data.
5. Corporal Punishment Fact Sheet, distributed by the National Coalition to Abolish Corporal Punishment in Schools, Westerville, Ohio, 1987-88.
6. M. Straus, R. Gelles, & S. Steinmetz, Behind Closed Doors: Violence in the American Family (1980), p. 100-103.
7. *Id.* at 109.
8. D. Daro, Confronting Child Abuse: Research for Effective Program Design (1988) at 9.
9. Examples of articles include *The New York Times* Nov. 6, 1987, "Parents of Girl, 6, Charged with murder after she dies;" *The Chicago Tribune* Nov. 13, 1987, "New York Pays its Respects to Girl Fatally Beaten." CBS: Nightline Program on May 19, 1988, discussed the Eli Creekmore case.
10. *See supra* note 2 at 472.
11. Martinez, L., Illinois child fatalities: A three year statistical profile. Springfield: Illinois Department of Children and Family Services, Office of Quality Control and Reporting, Division of Child Protective Services, 1986 and Lambert, B., Amid tragedy, concern for the city's most helpless. *The New York Times,* Sunday February 1, 1987.
12. *Long Range Plan: 1985-1990,* National Committee for Prevention of Child Abuse, 1987.
13. Public Attitudes and Actions Regarding Child Abuse and Its Prevention, conducted by Schulman, Ronca, and Bucuvalas, Inc. New York, New York, conducted for National Committee For Prevention of Child Abuse, (1988) p. 3.
14. *Id.* at 4.
15. *See supra* note 6 at 13.
16. D. Gil, Violence Against Children: Physical Abuse in the United States (1970), at 143.
17. *Id.* at 143.
18. 347 U.S. 483, 493 (1954).
19. Stoneman II, Corporal Punishment in the Schools: A Time For Change, 4 Journal for Juvenile Law 155-169 (1980).
20. Ingraham v. Wright, 430 U.S. 651, 662 (1977). The Supreme Court preserved the rights of the state to develop their own rules and regulations regarding the disciplining of school children. This means that the states can reject, permit, or restrict the use of corporal punishment. The case is discussed in more detail in Alan Reitman's article in this issue of Children's Legal Rights Journal.
21. Discussion of research which demonstrates the ineffectiveness of using physical force to discipline children can be found in the articles compiled in Chapter IV of Corporal Punishment in American Education, edited by Irwin Hyman and James H. Wise, Temple University Press, Philadelphia, Pennsylvania (1979) or in Irwin Hyman's article in this issue of Children's Legal Rights Journal.
22. The Last Resort, Committee to End Violence Against the Next Generation, Inc. Vol. 16, No. 3, Spring 1988. Statistics were published in *The Nashville Tennessean* on December 28, 1987.
23. *Florida Schools Rank High for Physical Punishment",* Florida Child Advocate Vol. 1, No. 1 Careco, Inc. July-Sept 1987.
24. Observation based on data obtained from the 1984 Office of Civil Rights Survey, National Summary of Projected Data
25. Corporal Punishment Fact Sheet, distributed by the National Coalition to Abolish Corporal Punishment in Schools, Westerville, Ohio, 1987-88.
26. A. Maurer, 1001 Alternatives to Corporal Punishment, Vol. 1 and Vol. 2 (1984); Bowers, E., And Hare, E., Spare the Rod?! A Resource Guide: Alternatives to Corporal Punishment by NASW (1986) p. 67-199.
27. *See e.g.,* Cal. Civ. Code §49001(a)
28. Select Committee on Children, Youth, and Families. U.S. House of Representatives. Parents: The Missing Link in Education Reform. Washington, D.C.: U.S. Government Printing Office, 1988.

SPECIAL ARTICLES

Prevention of Child Maltreatment: What Is Known

Howard Dubowitz, MD

From the Department of Pediatrics, University of Maryland Medical School, Baltimore

ABSTRACT. There has been increasing awareness of the need to prevent child maltreatment. In this review, prevention programs that have been evaluated are critically assessed. This is based on computer searches of the relevant literature spanning the last decade and final reports regarding prevention programs to state and federal agencies. Although many programs have been implemented, relatively few have been evaluated, and of those that have been, many have serious methodologic flaws. Interventions that do appear promising include home visiting, lay counseling, group and family therapy, and education about sexual abuse. In addition, comprehensive programs that address the multiple contributory factors of child maltreatment appear to be a valuable approach. Suggestions are made as to how the practicing pediatrician might play a preventive role. Finally, there is a need for good evaluation research of prevention programs. *Pediatrics* 1989;83:570–577; *abuse, maltreatment prevention.*

There has been an increasing awareness of the need to prevent child maltreatment. A panel reiterating the 1979 US Surgeon General's report concerning health promotion and disease prevention wrote: "By 1990, injuries and deaths to children inflicted by abusing parents should be reduced by at least 25%."[1] In 1985, the National Committee for the Prevention of Child Abuse enunciated a similar goal: "We can prevent child abuse and we will prove it. Our goal is to reduce child abuse by at least 20% by 1990."[2] Both the financial and human costs associated with child maltreatment, although crudely estimated, are staggering.[3] Prevention is, therefore, attractive as a way of reducing these costs of child maltreatment. In addition, there is the possibility

that early efforts to enhance family functioning could be more effective than interventions after maltreatment has already occurred. Accordingly, a wide array of prevention programs have been developed in the United States.

Prevention is a central focus in pediatric practice, and pediatricians are well placed to intervene early in high-risk situations to prevent possible maltreatment. For this review, what is known about interventions aimed at preventing child maltreatment is examined.

Prevention is commonly categorized as primary, secondary, or tertiary. Primary prevention addresses a sample of the general population, eg, a program administered to all students in a school district regarding how to prevent sexual abuse. Secondary prevention focuses on specific subsets of the population, who are thought to be at high risk for child maltreatment. Typically, these efforts are directed at poor, single mothers or families with a new infant. Tertiary prevention, or treatment, involves situations in which child maltreatment has already occurred, and the goal is to decrease recidivism and avoid the harmful effects of child maltreatment. Five years ago, Helfer[4] evaluated what was known about the prevention of child maltreatment. He found that little scientific evaluation of interventions had been conducted and recommended that good evaluation research of prevention efforts should be conducted. The review reported here is based on a background paper prepared for the Office of Technology Assessment of the US Congress, and current knowledge of the effectiveness of programs to prevent child maltreatment is examined.

METHOD

Computer searches were conducted using the Child Abuse and Neglect computerized data base,

Received for publication Feb 23, 1988; accepted April 13, 1988.
Reprint requests to (H.D.) Division of Pediatric Medicine, 700 W Lombard St, Baltimore, MD 21201.

PsychInfo, and Medline for the last decade. Several final reports concerning major studies funded by the National Center on Child Abuse and Neglect were reviewed. The different kinds of preventive interventions and program evaluations are presented in this review. Although this is representative of current knowledge, it was not possible to describe all programs.

FINDINGS

Primary Prevention

In the United States, most social services only become available after child maltreatment has already occurred, and little primary prevention exists. In addition to the specific programs that will be discussed, there are a number of activities at the state and federal levels that probably do have a primary preventive role. Examples include legislation banning the use of corporal punishment in schools, the federal Aid to Families With Dependent Children program, and the Women, Infants, and Children nutrition program. These serve to enhance family functioning and indirectly help protect children, but their effectiveness in reducing child maltreatment has not been assessed.

Prevention of Sexual Abuse. Conte et al[5] and Finkelhor et al[6] summarized the key components of efforts to prevent child sexual abuse. Programs, mostly implemented in the school systems, have focused on teaching children about sexual abuse, how to recognize abusive situations, and how to respond assertively. Programs range in length from a single half hour to a curriculum of 38 sessions, and trainers include teachers, police officers, rape crisis counselors, mental health professionals, and community volunteers. A variety of materials have been used, including videotapes, audio tapes, printed matter, coloring books, and anatomically correct dolls. Whereas some programs focus specifically on preventing abuse, others address related areas such as child development, family and life management, parenting, and methods of seeking help.

An experimental or quasiexperimental design to evaluate their interventions was used in relatively few programs. Those that did usually used pre- and posttests to assess the effectiveness of a single prevention strategy. Different outcome measures were developed for different projects, making comparisons difficult. Typically, the child's knowledge and feelings about sexual abuse and the childs' prediction of his or her response to a hypothetical abusive situation were assessed with these measures. Actual behavior was assessed in only one study, in which one of the researchers simulated a

potentially abusive situation, and the child's response was videotaped and rated.[7] The occurrence of subsequent sexual abuse was not assessed, and outcomes were usually determined immediately or soon after the intervention.

The evaluation of child sexual abuse prevention classes revealed mixed results. Some studies have demonstrated an increase in knowledge of safety rules and awareness of local resources in the event of abuse.[8] Studies of preschool children have noted the limited retention of information after only 1 week.[9] A concern is the distinction between knowledge and actual behavior. This was illustrated in one study in which children learned the textbook definition of assertiveness but were unable to give an example of how they could act assertively (A. Downer, unpublished data). Another study demonstrated that greater self-esteem and knowledge predicted a decreased vulnerability in simulated abuse situations.[7]

There are possible untoward consequences of these programs. One study found that 93% of children recognized the potential for coercive sexual assault, and 88% for violent sexual assault, within their own families.[10] The effects on children's fearfulness, understanding of their bodies, sense of security, and family relationships have not been assessed. Anecdotal evidence suggests that research is needed to evaluate these areas.

Sexual abuse prevention programs and the evaluation of effectiveness are recent developments. Because measurement of the occurrence of subsequent sexual abuse is problematic, proximate and proxy outcomes such as knowledge and attitudinal change have been assessed in most studies. This represents a reasonable first step but does not address the critical question of whether abuse is prevented.

Community Services. Communities provide a variety of services that have a primary preventive role. One format is public education concerning child maltreatment prevention, using media announcements. Public awareness campaigns convey to parents that "parenting can be rough" and that "its OK to get help." Typically, information regarding local resources is then given. Although these services have not been evaluated, it is reasonable to expect that some benefit is accrued to those who use them.

Inter-Act: Street Theater for Parents. In this program, live theater or videotapes are used to communicate parenting information to audiences that would be difficult to reach through more traditional channels.[11] The skits portray realistic situations that demonstrate problem-solving skills, using support systems, and alternatives to physical punishment. Presentations are made in settings such as well-child clinics, shopping centers, and state fairs.

This program has been evaluated by randomly pre- or posttesting different audiences. Audiences were classified into three groups: high risk, general public, and professional, and each experimental group was compared with a control group. High-risk groups consisted of single parents waiting at an unemployment office, and the general public was targeted in shopping centers and fairs. The general audiences were found to alter their attitudes most significantly, whereas skits concerning child behavior management had most impact on the high-risk group. Longer term attitudinal and behavioral changes need to be evaluated.

Secondary Prevention

Most interventions aimed at preventing child maltreatment occur in the category of secondary prevention. These interventions are based on knowledge and assumptions concerning risk factors for child maltreatment and target groups considered to be high risk, such as teenage mothers or poor and single-parent families. The goals are to enhance parenting capabilities and family functioning, thereby enabling families to more adequately care for their children and avoid possible maltreatment.

Programs for Families With New Infants.[8,11] These programs aim to improve child care practices, to protect the infants' health and safety, to improve the parents' mental health, and to enhance parent-infant interaction and healthy family functioning. Many programs begin during the prenatal period; others begin after the birth of the baby. Possible services include pre- and postnatal medical care, psychotherapy, parenting education, and perinatal support programs to enhance parent-infant bonding. These include childbirth procedures that involve both parents, rooming-in, and unlimited visiting privileges for parents with their infants, a home health visitor, and free transportation to pediatric clinics. The duration of programs varies from a targeted intervention regarding birthing, rooming-in, and visitation procedures in the hospital to a project that offers a home health visitor for the first 2 years of the baby's life.[12]

The best evaluation of such programs has been the work of Olds and colleagues[12] in their assessment of a family support program during pregnancy and the first 2 years after birth.[12] In a randomized clinical trial, four treatment groups were provided with different combinations of the following services: developmental screening of the children, free transportation to prenatal and well-child clinics,

home visits by a nurse during pregnancy, and home visits by a nurse during the child's first 2 years of life. The sample consisted of 400 women having their first baby and who were younger than 19 years of age or single or of low socioeconomic status. The nurse-visited and comparison group of women were equivalent in all standard sociodemographic characteristics, and the few differences in psychologic and social support variables were controlled for in the analyses.

Olds et al[14] found that 19% of the comparison group at highest risk (poor, unmarried teenage mothers) maltreated their children, compared with 4% of the mothers who were visited by a nurse for the extended period ($P = .07$). The same high-risk group members who were visited by a nurse punished their infants less when assessed at 10 and 22 months of age ($P = .007$, and $P = .04$, respectively), and they had fewer emergency room visits ($P = .04$). These and other marginally significant differences constitute a clear pattern of improvements made by the highest risk group of poor, unmarried, teenage mothers. Perhaps most important was the finding of diminished maltreatment in the intervention group, supported by social service records, maternal reports, observations of maternal caregiving, the children's developmental tests, and emergency room records. Moreover, during the pregnancy phase of the study, nurse home visitation led to significant ($P \le .05$) improvements in the women's use of community services, their levels of informal social support, their dietary and smoking habits, and the birth weight and duration of gestation of babies born to young adolescents and smokers.[14]

A similar project involved intensive pediatric primary care and weekly home visits by public health nurses.[14] High-risk families were randomly selected to receive the intervention or to serve as controls. The intervention group had significantly fewer hospitalizations for injuries thought to be inflicted, but there were no differences in the other outcome measures. The sample size was small and outcomes were assessed in only half the subjects, perhaps contributing to the paucity of significant findings.

Programs for Teenage Mothers.[11] These programs aim to address the multiple problems of many teenage parents: poverty, inadequate nutrition and health care, halted education, developmental delays, and inadequate parenting skills. Programs also attempt to strengthen the parent-infant relationship and foster the infant's development. Most programs enroll teenage mothers at approximately the time of delivery, although some programs begin during the prenatal period, and a few have succeeded in including fathers. Services are offered at home and in program centers, and they include parenting education, emotional support and counseling, job training and employment services, and drop-in centers. In addition, there are special workshops and interest groups, recreational activities, group meetings, meals, leaflets, day-care and field trips. The duration of programs varies between 20 weeks and until the parent no longer has a child between 0 and 3 years of age. The intensity of programs also varies from a single weekly session to approximately ten hours per week. Generally, staff are a mix of full- and part-time lay volunteers and professionals with widely varying backgrounds. The study by Olds et al[12,13] is the best illustration of the benefits accrued by teenage mothers.

Child Care. Attempting to balance work demands, career goals, and child care responsibilities can cause anxiety and stress.[15] Day care is valuable to the stressed parent whose patience is taxed by the demands of continuous child care. In addition to offering the parents some respite, child care programs can provide the child with a rich and stimulating environment, either in day-care centers, family day-care homes, or the child's own home.

Unfortunately, the quality of child care varies enormously. Although it is evident that day care is a valuable and necessary support for many families, its effectiveness in preventing child maltreatment has not been evaluated.

Interventions for "Latch Key" Children. These are programs for school-aged children of working parents, who return home from school and no adults are present. Without supervision, these children are at increased risk of being abused and, in addition, may have important needs neglected. In a typical program, usually conducted in a school, children discuss their feelings about being left alone and they receive instruction in personal safety skills, family rules, discriminating between emergencies and nonemergencies, emergency procedures, and responsibilities for siblings. Sessions with the parents address parental concerns and potential problem situations. Participants in these programs acquire knowledge and skills,[16] but the effectiveness in reducing child maltreatment remains uncertain.

Support Groups. Support groups are a key ingredient in many programs. Such groups offer an opportunity for people in similar situations to share experiences and information, thereby facilitating friendships and social networks. Given the multiple problems many maltreating families have, a supportive group can provide a buffer and help develop coping skills.

In addition to groups led by professionals, there are self-help groups such as Parents Anonymous and similar groups for the children. Whereas many of the participants join after having maltreated their children, some who recognize their propensity for abuse use the group as a preventive intervention. It appears that substantial benefit is accrued to the high-risk families who have both the insight and motivation to seek assistance through this approach.[17]

Crisis Services. Many cities and towns have resources available on a 24-hour basis to handle crisis situations. Generally, this consists of a telephone hot (or warm) line offering comfort and guidance to a desperate parent. Additional resources that may be available are baby-sitters for use in a crisis, nurseries, and counseling. The crisis service is generally able to refer clients to longer term resources when necessary. This is another intervention that appears to be a valuable resource, but its effectiveness in preventing child maltreatment has not been evaluated.

Tertiary Prevention

Tertiary prevention refers to those interventions that aim to decrease the likelihood of further maltreatment after the problem has already been identified. This includes different strategies that are monitoring, supportive, therapeutic, restrictive, or punitive. Several of the interventions that were described for secondary prevention are also used in treatment and rehabilitative efforts. In adults, the goal is to enhance healthy functioning and thereby decrease their propensity for future maltreatment. In children, treatment aims to ameliorate the psychologic trauma associated with abuse, to foster their healthy growth and development, and to diminish the risk that they, in turn, will maltreat their own children. The effectiveness of tertiary interventions in meeting these goals has rarely been assessed.

Case Work. In all 50 states, child protection services within the states' departments of social services are designated by law to respond to reports of alleged child maltreatment, and their mandate is to ensure the protection and adequate care of children. Case work involves regular monitoring of the family and efforts to enhance family functioning, such as supportive counseling and referrals to local resources. In instances of serious injury or risk to the child, child protection services have the authority, after obtaining judicial consent, to remove children from their families and temporarily place them in substitute care.

A number of problems impede the work of child protection agencies. Given their reputation for working with maltreating families, a stigma is attached to these agencies, making client families resistant to accept their services.[18] As reporting criteria have been steadily broadened during the last two decades, the number of case reports has steadily increased, but legislators have not appropriated the funds for sufficient resources to address the identified problems. Consequently, these agencies are frequently underfunded and overwhelmed, with limited resources and demoralized staff, resulting in a poor quality of professional work.[19]

A third issue concerns the fundamental nature of the social services system. Sudia[20] described the mismatch of what these agencies offer and what clients need. Decent housing, job training, employment, and money could make a substantial difference in the functioning of many high-risk families, but these are not usually included in the armamentarium of these agencies. In addition, even counseling and therapeutic skills are often lacking, and the major responsibility has become that of policing the family. In fact, extensive collaboration with law enforcement agencies is now commonplace.

Substitute Care. Substitute care refers to care not provided by the biologic family. The most common is foster care; in 1981, 269,191 children were in foster care in the United States.[21] In 1983, More than 75% of children entering substitute care were placed because of "parent-related deficiencies" or some form of maltreatment.[22]

There might be continued visitation with the biologic family depending on the circumstances, because a goal is to work toward the eventual reunification of the family. The foster care system is required by federal law to review cases on a regular basis, assess progress, and, within 1 year of the child's placement, make a definitive "permanency" plan.[23] The juvenile justice system is also responsible for monitoring the child's placement. This legislation has led to some improvement in the system in which, all too often, children have been placed in inappropriate foster homes, where they have lingered for extended periods (mean duration 33 months), and limited services have been available to foster and biologic families.[24] If after reasonable efforts have been made it becomes evident that reunification of the family is not feasible, the child might be placed for adoption.

Psychotherapy. Although psychopathologic problems have been found to contribute only modestly to child maltreatment, psychotherapy frequently is a major component of treatment programs. For adults and children, individual, couples, family, or group therapy might be offered. For preschool children, day care, particularly therapeutic day care, where staff are skilled in helping children with their developmental and emotional problems resulting from maltreatment, appears to be a helpful intervention. In addition, counseling or psychotherapy may play a valuable preventive role for children with psychiatric disturbances who are not abused. Maltreatment might be prevented by providing their parents with an understanding of and an approach to their children's behavior problems.

Family Support Services. Family advocates, parent aides, home health visitors, and support groups are interventions that are also used in treatment programs. The goal is to enhance family functioning and thereby reduce recidivism by addressing the contributory etiologic factors of maltreatment.

Legal Approaches. Although severe forms of child abuse have long been considered crimes, there has been a trend in recent years to further criminalize the problem of child maltreatment.[25,26] Law enforcement personnel and district attorneys are increasingly willing to enforce the laws and more cases are being brought to court.

A major goal of these initiatives is to punish the perpetrator for the "crime" of child maltreatment and explicitly demonstrate that child maltreatment will not be tolerated in this society. This is intended to have a deterrent effect.

Legal approaches are also considered necessary at times to mandate that maltreating families participate in recommended interventions. Frequently, these families deny their problems and refuse to comply with social service agencies and other professional staff. Court authority and the threat of removing the child(ren) or prosecution are thought to be necessary to persuade resistant clients to accept help, and many professionals support this approach. Other professionals are less sanguine about the utility and ramifications of legal approaches that have not been evaluated.

It is evident that multiple factors contribute to child maltreatment, and consequently, most programs involve packages of different services. The following evaluations were done on such projects.

Lutzker's Project-12 Ways. This program aims to reduce recidivism of child maltreatment by providing a variety of services to families referred to the program by the Illinois Child Protective Agency.[27] The program's "ecobehavioral" approach includes parent-child training, stress reduction, self-control, social support, assertiveness training, basic skills, leisure time, health maintenance and nutrition, home safety, job placement, couples' counseling, alcoholism referral, money management, and a variety of pre- and postnatal prevention services for young and unwed mothers. Several of these services are offered in the home, and treatment plans are tailored according to the needs of individual clients.

In an evaluation of this program, 50 maltreating families were randomly selected from the client population and compared to 47 families not involved in the program.[28] All families were protective service clients who either had at least one maltreatment incident or were considered to be high risk. The researchers were able to assess the number of substantiated incidents of maltreatment. The results indicated that the project led to fewer cases of maltreatment during treatment compared to the comparison group (2% v 11%, $P < .05$), but there were similar rates following treatment (8% v 11%). Thus, it is apparent that the program's major impact occurred during treatment, when families were under surveillance, and there was little evidence of enduring program effects.

Evaluation of the National Demonstration Program in Child Abuse and Neglect, 1974 to 1977. In one of the few federally funded evaluations of child abuse programs, Berkeley Planning Associates[29] assessed 11 treatment programs between 1974 and 1977. Although called treatment programs, subjects included high-risk families who had not been identified for maltreatment. There was no random assignment to programs and typically subjects were referred to the program that was available locally.

Programs were classified into five different service models: individual counseling/social work, lay therapy, group treatment, children's program, and family treatment. Each model consisted of "basic services," such as intake and diagnosis, case management, and review, and also differing interventions making each program model unique. For example, interventions in the lay therapy programs included basic services, lay counseling and the self-help group, Parents Anonymous; the family treatment programs had basic services, a "children's program," and individual, family, and group therapy.

The key outcome measure was the clinician's judgment of the client's propensity for future maltreatment, assessed at the end of the intervention. The recurrence of maltreatment during treatment was also assessed by the primary clinician, and the child protection agencies informed program staff of clients who were reported to them.

The evaluators found that, of the 1,724 parents studied, 30% were reported to have "severely" abused or neglected their child during treatment. The severity of the case at the start of treatment was the strongest predictor of recurrence. Severity of the case was assessed by a previous history of maltreatment, recent severe maltreatment, and families rated as seriously stressed. Recurrence was lowest in projects in which highly trained workers were used to manage cases.

Of 1,190 parents assessed by clinicians at the end of treatment, 42% were judged to have a reduced potential for maltreatment. Whereas parental age, employment status, and race did not predict outcomes, improvement was more likely in clients who did not abuse alcohol or drugs. In addition, a reduced propensity for maltreatment occurred more often in cases of physical abuse than when neglect was involved.

Exploration of Client Characteristics, Services, and Outcome: Evaluation of the Clinical Demonstration of Child Abuse and Neglect.[30] A second federally funded national evaluation of 19 clinical demonstration projects was conducted by Berkeley Planning Associates between 1979 and 1981. Standardized instruments were used to gather information concerning demographic characteristics of families and individual clients, clinical assessments of client functioning at the start and end of study, the types and patterns of maltreatment involved, and a summary of services provided. The sample consisted of 986 families, comprising 1,250 adults, 710 adolescents, and 975 children. The programs offered a wide array of services including crisis intervention, remedial services for children, temporary shelter, infant stimulation, parent education, psychotherapy, and services such as assistance in finding housing or employment.

Clinical progress was assessed at termination of treatment by assessing the recurrence of maltreatment during treatment and the primary clinician's rating of the client's propensity for future maltreatment and of overall progress. Families and individuals with similar characteristics were compared to assess the effectiveness of different types of services.

Adult clients showed substantial improvement in various problem areas during treatment: 57% improved in their knowledge of child development, 55% in understanding their child's needs, 49% decreased their "excessive need" for their child to obey commands, and 47% had greater self-esteem. However, more than 50% of adult clients were judged, when leaving the program, as likely to maltreat their children in the future. Seventy percent of the adult clients in the sexual abuse treatment programs were judged by their clinicians to be "overall improved," compared with 40% in the neglect programs, with the other groups occupying intermediate positions.

Abused adolescents benefited most from skill development classes, temporary shelter, and group counseling. From start to end of treatment, adolescents improved in: sleeping problems (63%), eating problems (42%), feeling maltreatment deserved (72%), depression (70%), suicides gestures (68%), and violent behavior (58%). Children achieved maximum gains through individual or group counseling and therapeutic day care. The improvements seen in children included: wetting and soiling (66%), sleeping problems (65%), chronic health problems (54%), expressive language (62%), attention span (50%), lack of trust (67%), and vandalism (61%).

Many infants, children, and adolescents were maltreated while their families were being treated. Sexual abuse cases had the lowest recurrence of maltreatment (19%) and child neglect cases the highest (66%). No specific services were associated with reduced recidivism during treatment. At the end of treatment, only 40% of the children and adolescents were residing in the same household and with the caretaker they had at the start of treatment.

Unfortunately, these major evaluation studies suffer from several serious methodologic shortcomings. There were no comparison groups, and clients were not randomly assigned to programs. The primary source of data was the clinical staff that worked most closely with clients, and their judgments cannot be expected to be unbiased. In addition, the authors acknowledge the limitation of not having outcome data beyond the time of termination with the program.

Because of the methodologic limitations of these two studies, there is little objective evidence as to which programs are effective in preventing child maltreatment. However, the results suggest that parenting education, education and skill development, lay therapy, and peer support groups may achieve the best outcomes. Although some clients require individual therapy, family or group therapy tend to be preferable.

DISCUSSION

A broad array of prevention programs have been developed, but relatively few have been evaluated. And the majority of evaluation studies have serious methodologic shortcomings that limit an assessment of their effectiveness. However, it should be clear that the lack of evidence demonstrating the effectiveness of an intervention does not mean that the intervention is not successful. Rather, it leaves the question of effectiveness unanswered. The major conclusion of this review is that there is a critical need for rigorous scientific assessment of prevention programs, and several critiques have offered useful suggestions for such research.[36,37]

Where does this leave the practicing pediatrician? In the meantime, many children are being maltreated and their families are in serious difficulty; it is unrealistic to wait for the answers from research. There is a need to be responsive now,

using the best available knowledge and theory, and there are several services that appear to be effective.

It seems that programs that teach children about sexual abuse can transmit valuable information that might help prevent subsequent abuse. Perhaps the strongest evidence is that of the effectiveness of the home health visitor, particularly for those who are at extremely high risk for maltreatment. Some interventions such as child care can clearly benefit children and their families, although the contribution to diminishing child maltreatment is likely to be indirect. Other interventions such as criminal prosecution of offenders might have far reaching and unforeseen ramifications that make it important to examine the outcomes.

The multifactorial causes of child maltreatment suggest that comprehensive approaches such as in Project 12 Ways appear to be optimal. The lay therapy in Parents Anonymous seems beneficial, particularly to well-motivated clients. Although some need individual therapy, group or family therapy appears to be often preferable. The need to take care of "concrete" needs, housing, employment, and welfare benefits, is critical.

The pediatrician can help prevent child maltreatment by being knowledgeable of resources in the community and facilitating appropriate referrals. In addition, anticipatory guidance during visits for child health supervision might play a valuable role. For example, providing a parent with constructive disciplinary strategies in place of corporal punishment. In this way pediatricians can assist parents to improve their parenting. Finally, it is apparent that public policies and social programs that effectively enhance the functioning of families are key to protecting children. Pediatricians should be forceful advocates for children and families.

ACKNOWLEDGMENTS

This article is based on a background paper prepared by the author for the Office of Technology Assessment, US Congress, contract No. 633-3705.1.

I thank the reviewers of the Office of Technology Assessment for their helpful criticisms and Ann Lazur for preparation of this manuscript.

REFERENCES

1. US Surgeon General: Control of stress and violent behavior, in US *Surgeon General's Report on Health Promotion and Disease Prevention.* Government Printing Office, 1983
2. Garbarino J: Can we measure success in preventing child abuse? Issues and policies, programs in research. *Child Abuse Neglect* 1986;10:143–156
3. Daro D: *Confronting Child Abuse: Theory, Policy and Practice.* New York, Free Press, in press, 1989
4. Helfer R: A review of the literature on the prevention of

290

child abuse and neglect. *Child Abuse Neglect* 1982;6:251–261

5. Conte JR, et al: An analysis of programs to prevent sexual victimization of children. *J Primary Prevention*, in press, 1989

6. Finkelhor D, and associates: *A Source Book on Child Sexual Abuse.* Beverly Hills, CA, Sage Publications, 1986

7. Fryer GE, Kraizer SK, Miyoshi T: Measuring actual reduction of risk to child abuse: A new approach. *Child Abuse Neglect* 1987;11:173–179

8. *Child Abuse Prevention Project Profiles.* Chicago, National Committee for Prevention of Child Abuse, 1982

9. Borkin J, Frank C: Sexual abuse prevention for preschoolers: A pilot program. *Child Welfare* 1986;65:75–82

10. Swan HL, et al: Child sexual abuse prevention, does it work? *Child Welfare* 1985;64:395–405

11. Simmon JT: *Programs That Work: Evidence of Primary Prevention of Child Abuse.* Houston, Greater Houston Committee for Prevention of Child Abuse, 1986

12. Olds DS, Henderson CR Jr, Chamberlin R, et al: Preventing child abuse and neglect: A trial randomized of nurse home visitation. *Pediatrics* 1986;78:65–78

13. Olds D, Henderson CR Jr, Tatelbaum R, et al: Improving the delivery of prenatal care and outcomes of pregnancy: A randomized trial of nurse home visitation. *Pediatrics* 1986;77:16–28

14. Gray J, et al: Prediction and prevention of child abuse and neglect. *J Soc Issues* 1979;35:127–139

15. Brazelton TB: Issues for working parents. *Am J Orthopsychiatry* 1986;56:14–25

16. *Preventing Child Abuse: A Resource for Policymakers and Advocates.* Boston, Massachusetts Committee for Children and Youth, 1987

17. Lieber LL, Baker JM: Parents anonymous: Self-help treatment for child abusing parents: A review and evaluation. *Child Abuse Neglect* 1977;1:133–148

18. Harrison WD: Role strain and burnout in child protective services. *Soc Serv Rev* 1980;54:31–44

19. *Too Young to Run: The Status of Child Abuse in America.* Washington, DC, The Child Welfare League of America, 1986

20. Sudia CE: What services do abusive families need? in Pelton LH (ed): *The Social Context of Child Abuse and Neglect.* New York, Human Sciences Press, 1981, pp 268–290

21. Maximus Inc: *Comparative Statistical Analysis of 1983 State Child Welfare Data,* prepared for Evaluation Branch, Planning, Research and Evaluation Division, Office of Planning and Management, Administration for Children, Youth and Families, Office of Human Development Services, BOA No. 105–84–8103

22. Kusserow RP: *Interpreting Foster Care Entry Rates,* US Department of Health and Human Services publication No. OAI-85-H-035. Government Printing Office, 1985

23. *The Adoption Assistance and Child Welfare Act of 1980,* Statutes at Large, PL 96-272

24. Fanshel D, Shinn EB: *Children in Foster Care: A Longitudinal Investigation.* New York, Columbia University Press, 1978

25. *Attorney General's Task Force on Family Violence: Final Report.* Washington, DC, Author, 1984

26. Newberger EH, Bourne R: The medicalization and legalization of child abuse. *Am J Orthopsychiatry* 1978;48:593–607

27. Lutzker JR, Frame R, Rice JM: Project 12 ways: An ecobehavioral approach to the treatment and prevention of child abuse and neglect. *Educ Treat Child* 1982; 5:141–155

28. Lutzker JR, Rice JM: Project 12-ways: Measuring outcome of a large in-home service for treatment and prevention of child abuse and neglect. *Child Abuse Neglect* 1984; 8:519–524

29. Berkeley Planning Associates: *Child Abuse and Neglect Treatment Programs: Final Report and Summary of Findings From the Evaluation of the Joint OCD/SRS National Demonstration Program in Child Abuse and Neglect 1974–1977.* contract HRA 106-74-120, 1977

30. *The Exploration of Client Characteristics, Services, and Outcomes: Evaluation of the Clinical Demonstration of Child Abuse and Neglect.* Berkeley, CA, Berkeley Planning Associates, 1982

Prevention of Child Sexual Abuse

Myth or Reality

N. Dickon Reppucci and Jeffrey J. Haugaard
University of Virginia

ABSTRACT: Programs to prevent child sexual abuse have proliferated as a result of increased public awareness and professional documentation of its incidence. We describe the content and format of these prevention programs in general and examine selected programs for effectiveness. Although there is limited evidence for an increase in knowledge for program participants, most evaluations suffer from basic design problems and present few results indicative of either primary prevention or detection. Overall, we argue that self-protection against sexual abuse is a very complex process for any child and that few, if any, prevention programs are comprehensive enough to have a meaningful impact on this process. Finally, we discuss several untested assumptions that guide these programs. We conclude that it is unclear whether prevention programs are working or even that they are more beneficial than harmful.

The widespread, documented incidence of child sexual abuse (Finkelhor, 1979; Russell, 1984; Wyatt, 1985) and numerous clinical reports of harm to victims (Haugaard & Reppucci, 1988) provided the impetus for the professional development of programs to prevent its occurrence. However, the recent explosion of these programs nationwide has come about in no small part because of the vast amount of publicity that this topic has received in the past five years. In 1984, the issue of child sexual abuse was dramatically brought to public awareness with the arrest in California of Virginia McMartin and six of her employees for alleged sexual abuse of 125 children over a 10-year period at her day care center. A few months later, another highly publicized case in Minnesota resulted in indictments against 24 parents and other adults for allegedly sexually abusing over 50 children. *Newsweek* and *Life* ran cover stories on child sexual abuse. *Sixty Minutes, 20-20,* and *Nightline* featured TV reports on the topic, and the Public Broadcasting System televised a four-part series on its prevention. Moreover, the pictures of missing children that appeared on milk cartons, billboards, and telephone books were and are constant reminders that untold numbers of children have disappeared, some possibly becoming victims of sexual abuse. Although charges were subsequently dismissed against all the alleged abusers in the Minnesota case, the McMartin case was still being prosecuted in March 1988, when Judge Pounders called it the "most expensive case

in (USA) history" (Stewart, 1988, p. 3A), with $7.5 million spent so far. He justified this expense because "The case has benefited society as a whole, . . . because people have become aware of a social problem that may not have been spoken about" (Stewart, 1988, p. 3A).

Recently, we (Haugaard & Reppucci, 1988) described what is and is not known about the etiology and treatment of child sexual abuse and argued strongly for increased research and action. We also noted with concern the inadequate research base for child sexual abuse prevention programs. The purpose of this article is twofold: (a) to describe briefly the content and effects of selected sexual abuse prevention programs, and (b) to emphasize that several underlying assumptions that power these programs are frequently accepted as fact, even though they are based mainly on clinical anecdote and "best guess." Our analysis is limited to existing evaluated programs focused on teaching children vigilance either directly or indirectly through parent or teacher involvement because these are representative of the types of programs being implemented nationwide. We will not conclude, as Melton (in press) has, that the prevention of child sexual abuse is impossible, or as Finkelhor and Strapko (in press) have, that "the overwhelming and irrefutable message of the evaluation studies is that children do indeed learn the concepts they are being taught." Rather, we will conclude that caution is warranted regarding both of these positions. We will also suggest that the reporting of sexual abuse is a complex act for the child that requires cognitive and emotional maturity and understanding that many young children may not possess.

Let us begin with a vignette from the recent evaluation of a preventive intervention.

At the conclusion of a standard interview evaluating the use of the special *Spiderman* comic about the prevention of sexual abuse, a fourth grade boy said, "This is just what happened to me." And he proceeded to tell of being sexually molested by a teenage neighbor over a period of a year and a half starting when he was in the second grade. He was silent over that period to protect his mother from the harm the neighbor threatened to inflict upon her if he told. The boy concluded, "He said he would put soap suds in her eyes and put her in the washing machine and he has a black belt in karate and he said he would get her." Finally the boy was asked if having had the *Spiderman* (1984) comic at the time would have made a difference. "Yes," he replied, "I would have told my mom about it. I wouldn't have been so afraid. I would have known that it was right to tell." (Garbarino, 1987, p. 148)

The Complexity of Sexual Abuse Prevention

The process that a child must go through either to repel an abusive approach or to report an occurrence of abuse is very complex. This complexity appears not to be appreciated by many of those involved in the prevention programs currently in existence, which seem to be based on the idea that children can be taught a few facts during a one- or two- shot presentation and that the children will then both understand the issues and be able to protect themselves. The extent to which the level of a child's cognitive and emotional development will affect the ways in which he or she can be self-protective often seems neglected.

Latane and Darley's (1969) paradigm for understanding the process that an individual goes through when deciding whether to react in an emergency situation can be adapted to delineate the steps that a child must go through in order to repel or report abuse. First, the child must recognize that he or she is in an abusive situation. Then the child must believe that he or she can and should take some sort of action. Finally, the child must possess and use specific self-protective skills. Each of these issues must be addressed if a child's self-protective skills are to be enhanced. For instance, a prevention program that does not provide age-appropriate, concrete instructions for how to act in an abusive situation, or a program that gives good instruction on how to act but does not help the child identify abusive situations in an age-appropriate fashion, may be of little value to the child.

Programs must first inform a child about what sexual abuse is. However, there is a lack of firm agreement as to what constitutes an abusive act (Atteberry-Bennett, 1987; Finkelhor & Associates, 1986; Haugaard & Reppucci, 1988). Although most adults can agree that certain acts always entail sexual abuse (e.g., a parent having intercourse with a child), there is considerable disagreement about other acts (e.g., whether a 10-year-old boy is experiencing sexual abuse from his mother who cleans his genitals thoroughly each night when she gives him a bath, or whether a 10-year-old girl is experiencing sexual abuse from her father when he kisses her on the lips each morning when he goes to work; Atteberry-Bennett, 1987). If children are given a broad definition of sexual abuse that they should report, many nonabusive incidents may be reported, which may cause anger and suffering to those who are reported (Schultz, 1988) and may be frustrating and confusing to the children doing the reporting. If a narrow definition is provided, then acts that are abusive may go unreported. Yet, if definitions are vague, many children, especially younger children, may have no idea what is expected of them. Several prevention programs have dealt with the definitional issue of what sexual abuse is by trying to teach the concept of touches that feel good, bad, and confusing. Learning these concepts may be possible for older children, but younger children are very poor at making fine distinctions between abstract entities, for example, between good and confusing touches (Daro, 1988).

If a child is able to label a certain experience as sexual abuse, then the child must feel empowered to report or repel it. Many programs attempt to empower children by teaching them that they do not have to allow other people to touch them (under most circumstances) and that they have the right to say "no" to anyone who tries to touch them in ways that they do not want to be touched. However, children at different cognitive levels often find it more or less difficult to distinguish between times when an action should or should not be taken. Young children are much better at following broad and general rules (e.g., do not ever cross the street without a parent) than they are at following rules that require making distinctions (e.g., you can cross this street without a parent, but not this other street, and this third street can only be crossed during the daytime without a parent). We know very little about the ways that children react to such rules as "Doctors can touch you in your private parts, and your parents can touch you if they are helping you clean yourself or if you are hurt there, but no one, not even your parents, can touch you there at other times." Such rules may be incomprehensible to many children, who may simplify them so that anyone who is caring for them can touch them in certain places, or that no one can touch them or make them do anything they do not want to do.

If a child comprehends that a certain act is sexual abuse and knows that he or she can and should stop it or tell someone about it, the child must have a plan for doing so. Many prevention programs teach that the child should tell a parent or other adult and keep telling adults until someone believes him or her. Although this may be a good general approach, it is questionable whether it gives the child enough information to plan and implement the reporting or repelling. Many adults have been in situations in which they know that something should be done, but without a specific plan, they chose to do nothing rather than to engage in a wrong or ineffective action. Why do we think that children, who are not as cognitively or emotionally competent as adults on most tasks (Weithorn, 1984), will be able to engage in these complex behaviors in an emotionally delicate and sometimes frightening situation?

Clearly, the process of self-protective behaviors that is being taught in prevention programs must be recognized for its complexity. Keeping this complexity in mind, we now turn to an examination of extant programs.

Programs for School Children

Most of the programs to prevent child sexual abuse have been designed for use with elementary school children, although a few are for preschoolers or students in junior or senior high school. The programs tend to emphasize two goals: (a) primary prevention (keeping the abuse from ever occurring) and (b) although often mislabeled as sec-

Correspondence concerning this article should be addressed to N. Dickon Reppucci, Department of Psychology, Gilmer Hall, University of Virginia, Charlottesville, VA 22903.

293

ondary prevention, detection (encouraging disclosure of past and ongoing sexual abuse so that children can receive intervention and protection). Five years ago, Plummer (1984) suggested that nearly 500,000 children had been reached nationally by preventive education programs in schools alone. Since that time the numbers of children exposed to such programs have increased by quantum leaps.

Programs for children are generally concerned with the following themes: educating children about what sexual abuse is; broadening their awareness of the identity of possible abusers to include people they know and like; teaching that each child has the right to control the access of others to his or her body; describing a variety of "touches" that a child can experience—which are good, bad, or confusing; stressing action steps that the child can take in a potentially abusive situation, such as saying "no" to adults or leaving or running away; teaching that some secrets should not be kept and that a child is never at fault for sexual abuse; and stressing that the child should tell a trusted adult if touched in an inappropriate manner and should keep telling someone until something is done to protect the child (Conte, Rosen, & Saperstein, 1984; Finkelhor, 1986; Hazzard, Webb, & Kleemeier, 1988).

Finkelhor (1986) noted that there has been a general effort to skirt the emotionally charged topic of sexuality and sex education in prevention programs. Therefore, child sexual abuse prevention is usually approached through a protective, rather than sexual, standpoint. The concepts of good and bad touching are often approached through discussions of bullies and relatives who forcefully try to kiss a child. More intimate or long-term types of sexual abuse tend to be ignored as are specific discussions of molestation by parents. Also generally missing is the information that some "bad" touches can actually feel good. The presentations are entertaining, with occasional injections of humor. These tactics are used to increase the number of schools willing to accept prevention programs by avoiding controversy and to keep the presentations from overly frightening the children. Unfortunately, by avoiding sexuality, young children may learn that "sexuality is essentially secretive, negative, and even dangerous" (Trudell & Whatley, 1988, p. 108).

Prevention programs vary in a number of ways. Some involve only one presentation (Conte, Rosen, & Saperstein, 1984), whereas others involve as many as 38 short sessions (Committee for Children, 1983). Shorter programs generally deal with only the topic of sexual abuse prevention, whereas longer programs present a number of topics, the general theme of which is the child's right to be assertive with others in certain situations. Programs aimed at primary prevention may require more sessions than those whose major goal is case identification because some abused children will identify themselves after even brief prevention efforts (e.g., several children in Seattle identified themselves after viewing a 30-second public service announcement on television). Also, the skills and concepts for primary prevention are usually taught in the abstract and are frequently more difficult

for children to grasp because they have no concrete reference point (Conte, Rosen, & Saperstein, 1984).

Prevention programs come in many formats, including slide presentations, movies, plays, discussions, and role-play situations, as well as various types of printed material such as pamphlets or comic books. Most prevention educators recommend the use of high-interest, nonthreatening formats, such as plays and puppet shows that are often the most expensive to mount (Koblinsky & Behana, 1984).

The presenters of the programs also vary (Conte, Rosen, & Saperstein, 1984). The rationale for using particular presenters includes their familiarity with the children (e.g., teachers), their expertise in the topic (e.g., specially trained volunteers or mental health professionals), or their positions in the community as authority figures who have the children's respect (e.g., police officers). Most programs take place through the schools and attempt to make use of teachers because of their ongoing contact with the children, their possible ability to deal with a sensitive topic in the best way for their class, and their role in identifying and supporting abused children. In addition, for those programs that provide follow-up discussions with the children in small groups, teachers are potentially ideal discussion leaders. However, often there is little preparation of teachers for these roles (Trudell & Whatley, 1988).

Type and length of program format and the identity of the presenter are usually determined by the resources and predilections of whatever group is most involved in bringing the program to a community. Such groups are most often composed of community members who have become part of a task force on sexual abuse or are organized by such individuals as the health coordinator of a school district. Unfortunately, there has not been any evaluation comparing the effectiveness of format, length, or presenter, either overall or for different age children.

Preventive interventions for school children have much appeal because of their potential both to reach large numbers of children in a relatively cost-efficient fashion and to reduce the number of children affected by sexual abuse. However, having positive goals is not enough. Effectiveness of intervention is critical. Yet most programs appear to continue on the strength of their positive goals rather than on a systematic evaluation of their effectiveness.

Programs for Parents and Other Adults

Finkelhor (1986) stressed the value of prevention programs aimed at parents and professionals involved with children. Prevention programs aimed at parents, professionals involved with children, and adults in general are potentially very valuable. These programs may help parents both to identify signs indicating that their child was or is being abused and to react in a constructive manner if abuse is discovered. If parents can be encouraged to educate their children about abuse prevention, then the children may be more likely to receive repeated exposures of information from a trusted source. Moreover, a discussion about sexual abuse with a parent may make it easier for a child to talk with the parent if the child is subsequently abused. The importance of helping parents talk to their children about sexual abuse was highlighted by Finkelhor's (1984) findings. Only 29% of his random sample of 521 parents of 6- to 14-year-old children had talked with them about sexual abuse; of those parents, only 53% had mentioned that the abuser might be someone whom the child knew, and only 22% had ever suggested that a family member might be involved. In other words, only 6% of the total sample had ever suggested that a family member might be an abuser.

In spite of the possible advantages of parent education, relatively few efforts have been made to involve parents. One reason for this may be that many parents have a difficult time talking to their children about sexual topics of all sorts. In addition, Finkelhor's (1984) survey found that most parents tend to think of their own children as well supervised and able to avoid danger and that they do not want to frighten their children unnecessarily. Moreover, parents who are likely to attend such educational programs may be better informed and more likely to discuss these issues with their children anyway. For example, in the only evaluation of a parent workshop program, Porch and Petretic-Jackson (1986) found that 57% of the parents who completed pre- and postworkshop questionnaires had discussed sexual abuse with their children before the workshop took place, a percentage double that found in Finkelhor's (1984) random sample. For prevention programs to reach a broad cross-section of parents, educators may need to devise more innovative means for delivering their programs, such as providing them through places of employment or community service clubs, such as Kiwanis and Rotary. Such innovations would also have the potential advantage of reaching a greater number of men, the major perpetrators of child sexual abuse. These men might be discouraged from becoming abusers if they believed that children are more likely to tell someone of an approach (Finkelhor, 1986).

Prevention programs aimed at teachers, pediatricians, day care workers, clergy, and the police could provide information allowing these professionals to detect sexual abuse in a child more effectively and to react in a constructive manner. Although such programs exist, only three evaluations have been reported. Nevertheless, their results are encouraging. Hazzard (1984) found that elementary school teachers who participated in a six-hour training program about prevention of child abuse in general, in comparison with a control group of untrained teachers, increased significantly in knowledge about child abuse, were more likely to report talking with individual students to assess whether abuse was occurring, and discussed possible abuse situations with colleagues more often. However, they were no more likely to report cases to protective services. In a second study specifically focused on the prevention of child sexual abuse, Kleemier, Webb, Hazzard, and Pohl (1987) reported that elementary school teachers who participated in a six-hour workshop, relative to nonparticipating controls, increased in knowledge

about child sexual abuse and were better able to identify behavioral indicators of abuse and to suggest appropriate interventions. Over a six-week follow-up period, they also read more about child abuse than control teachers; however, the two groups did not differ on reporting of suspected cases. In contrast, Swift (1983) found that reporting rates from 71 trained school counselors and nurses increased 500% from 10 cases during the 12-month pretraining period to 50 cases during the 12-month posttraining period. Unfortunately, Swift did not distinguish the percentage of unfounded reports contained in the increased reporting rates. If there was not an increase in founded reports, was the increased reporting a benefit? Some would answer in the affirmative because such reporting may influence abusers for whom the accusations could not be founded to cease and desist. Others (such as Goldstein, Freud, & Solnit, 1979) would argue that more harm than good could be the result and that family privacy rights may have been invaded inappropriately.

Outcome Research for Day-Care and School-Based Prevention Programs

Several school-based prevention programs have investigated the effectiveness with which the children learned the material presented. Before beginning this discussion, we emphasize that the investigations mentioned, regardless of their shortcomings, should be commended because they are among the very few programs that have any evaluation component at all.

Conte, Rosen, Saperstein, and Shermack (1985) evaluated a program consisting of three, one-hour presentations given by specially trained deputy sheriffs at a private day-care center. The participant group consisted of 10 4- and 5-year olds, and 10 6- to 10-year-olds, with a similarly composed wait-list control group. One week before the presentation and at some unspecified time after the program, each child was interviewed by a social work graduate student, most of whom were unaware of the child's group. At the postpresentation interview, children in the participating group had significantly increased their knowledge about the concepts and skills that the authors believed would help them avoid becoming victims of child sexual abuse. The older children made a larger gain than the younger children. However, although the children's knowledge increased significantly, the average number of correct responses was only 50% for the participating group on the posttest (as contrasted to 25% on the pretest).

The program presentations by the sheriffs were tape-recorded and compared with the model by which they had been trained. Analysis indicated that assault by a stranger was stressed more than had been intended and that several presenters told "horror stories" to illustrate their points even though these were not included in the training model. This information indicates the importance of ongoing monitoring to ensure that the presenter's beliefs do not unduly modify the planned presentation by altering its strength and integrity (Reppucci, 1985; Sechrest, White, & Brown, 1979).

Borkin and Frank (1986) evaluated the retention of basic information about what to do when somebody touches you in a "not okay" way with a preschool sample. The 83, three- to five-year-old children who responded had all seen an adaptation of the play, *Bubbylonian Encounter*, enacted by hand puppets six weeks earlier. Children were asked, "What should you do if someone tries to touch you in a way that doesn't feel good?," and answers of "say no," "run away," or "tell someone" were scored as correct. Although 43% of the four- and five-year-olds answered correctly, only one three-year-old (4%) did. Moreover, because no pretesting was done, there is no way to determine what percentage of the four- and five-year-olds would have answered correctly without ever seeing the play. These results raise the question of whether a one-time presentation is useful for teaching concepts to such young children, even when done in an interesting way.

In the most extensive study to date of the impact of sexual abuse prevention programs on preschool children, the Berkeley Family Welfare Research Group (Daro, 1988; Daro, Duerr, & LeProhn, 1987) evaluated seven representative curricula (Child Assault Prevention; Children's Self-Help; Talking About Touching; Touch Safety; Child Abuse Prevention, Intervention and Education; Youth Safety Awareness Project; and SAFE—Stop Abuse through Family Education) that ranged in duration from a one-time 15-to-30 minute session to 21 15- to 20-minute sessions over a three- to six-week period. Parent meetings of one to two hours' duration were a part of each curriculum, which apparently contributed to encouraging two thirds of the parents to discuss some of the concepts with their children following the presentation. Although a detailed reporting of this investigation is beyond the scope of this article, a few findings are worth noting. Children were more likely to interpret pictures of frequently encountered interactions such as tickling and bathing as evoking a negative affect after participation in prevention training, a result that can hardly be interpreted as positive. It appears that preschoolers were unable to comprehend the concept of a mixed-up or confusing touch. Although some of the children appeared to have a rudimentary grasp of the concept that there is a connection between the physical act of being touched and the emotion that it generates, even at posttest half the children could not provide an explanation for why they selected a particular affect in response to the pictures they were shown. Given the critical nature of this connection as a building block for the prevention programs, Daro (1988) asked, "If the children cannot explain their own response, is it possibly too much to expect that they can understand the subtle nuances and emotions described and elicited either during the prevention program or in a case of actual abuse?" In addition, children found it difficult to distinguish how touches can change or how feelings regarding touches can change. They also found the concept of differentiating between types of secrets difficult to comprehend or to accept. Even the issue of "stranger danger," one of the least ambiguous ideas presented was not internalized well enough by many children so that they could apply these teachings. In summary, this investigation clearly raises questions regarding the developmental readiness of preschoolers to grasp the concepts being taught in prevention programs in any meaningful way. Furthermore, the other two studies with preschool children also indicated that important gaps in the childrens' knowledge remained even after the prevention programs were presented.

Plummer (1984) evaluated a preventive program that consisted of three one-hour presentations to 112 fifth-grade students. Sixty-nine children completed pre- and posttest 23-item questionnaires that dealt with the concepts of the program. Posttest measures were given immediately after the program and two and eight months later. More students gave correct answers at the posttest immediately following the program than on the pretest. Although a majority of the concepts were still retained at the eight-month follow-up, questions about breaking promises, whether molesters were often people whom the child knew, and who was to blame if the child was touched in a sexual way were answered incorrectly significantly more often. What is particularly disturbing about the lowering of knowledge on these three items is that they are crucial concepts in any prevention program.

Ray and Dietzel (1984) evaluated a program that consisted of a slide presentation, a movie, and the distribution of a workbook that the students were encouraged to take home and discuss with their parents. One hundred ninety-one third-grade participants answered a 12-item questionnaire covering the concepts taught in the program. Half of the students saw a follow-up film two weeks after the initial presentation, which reinforced the concepts that were taught initially. Some of the students were pretested, some were posttested immediately following the presentation, and all were posttested at one and six months following the presentation.

As a group, the students answered more questions correctly on the posttest immediately after the program than on the pretest, and those students who received the follow-up movie presentation had significantly higher scores on the one-month and six-month posttests, again indicating the importance of review sessions. These findings, when combined with those of Plummer (1984), suggest that some sort of review work after the initial presentation may be an essential component for increasing retention of the material. They also indicate that prevention researchers should employ follow-up procedures to determine durability of effects.

Another noteworthy aspect of the Ray and Dietzel (1984) study was that the average number correct on the pretest was about 9 out of the 12 questions, indicating that the students already knew many of the program's concepts before it took place. Thus, although the average correct response of 11.5 on the posttest was a statistically significant increase from the pretest, it is unclear whether this small rise in absolute terms indicates a meaningful increase in knowledge. On the other hand, the children may have learned more than was revealed because of a possible ceiling effect on this limited-item questionnaire

296

(for further discussion of this issue, see Conte, 1984; Hazzard & Angert, 1986; Kleemeier & Webb, 1986).

Only a few investigations have used a nontreatment control group. Wolfe, MacPherson, Blount, and Wolfe (1986) found that fourth- and fifth-grade children who participated in a single presentation of two five-minute skits followed by a one-hour classroom discussion showed a higher percentage of knowledge of correct actions to take in an abusive situation than a group of nonparticipating children. However, even though the differences were statistically significant, the actual percentages of children in the participating group answering each question correctly was never more than 10% higher than those in the control group.

Saslawsky and Wurtele's (1986) evaluation of the film *Touch* also used a nontreatment control group and found significant differences favoring the participating group. Again, although significant statistically, the differences between the control and participating groups were less than 2 points on both a 13-point Personal Safety Questionnaire and a 32-point scoring scale for four vignettes. It should be noted that this study did find that the gains were maintained at a three-month follow-up assessment and that these investigators were the first to report the psychometric properties of their measuring instruments, a major methodological improvement over other studies.

Swan, Press, and Briggs (1985) evaluated the effectiveness of a 30-minute presentation of the play *Bubbylonian Encounter* with a group of 63 second- through fifth-grade students. Before and soon after the play, the children were shown five videotaped vignettes depicting inappropriate and appropriate touch and were asked to identify which type of touch was in each vignette. No significant improvement was found on the posttest because of very high accuracy on the pretest for which 92% of the children correctly identified the vignettes showing sexual abuse.

Thus, the investigations by Ray and Dietzel (1984), Wolfe et.al. (1986), Saslawsky and Wurtele (1986), and Swan et. al. (1985) raise important cost–benefit questions. These studies present data indicating that many children had a high degree of knowledge about the concepts being taught even before the prevention programs were started and that any post-program increases, although statistically significant, were quite small in absolute terms. Given these results, the cost–benefit issue involves whether the changes in knowledge about actions to take in a hypothetical abusive situation justify the expense, time away from class, and possible negative consequences of the prevention program.

The investigation by Swan et al. (1985) is one of four that evaluated the play for possible negative effects. These investigators telephoned a separate sample of parents whose children had also seen the play within a week of the play's presentation and asked if they noticed any adverse reactions to the play in the children, such as loss of sleep or appetite, nightmares, or expression of fear, and if their children had discussed the play with them at home.

Only 7% of the children had said that they did not like the play, and only 5% of the parents said that their child had shown any adverse reactions; 42% of the children had discussed the play at home.

Wurtele and Miller-Perrin (1987) asked both parents and children to fill out questionnaires measuring their fear levels before and after a prevention program. Parents also assessed frequency and severity of particular behavior problems thought to be related to program participation. No significant change in negative behaviors was found, although this may have been a function of the small sample size ($N = 25$).

In a third study that examined possible negative effects, Garbarino (1987) evaluated the impact of the widely distributed special edition of the *Spiderman* comic book that contains two stories dealing with sexual abuse. Graduate students interviewed 36 boys and 37 girls in the second, fourth, and sixth grades who had read the comic in school. More than 80% of the questions dealing with sexual abuse were answered correctly by all age groups. The children were asked how the comic made them feel in terms of arousing worry or fear. Girls in the second and sixth grades reported feeling worried or scared more than their male counterparts (35% vs. 17% in second grade and 30% vs. 17% in sixth grade). Among fourth graders, 50% of both boys and girls reported these feelings. The children were concerned that "it" might happen to them. At first glance, this result might appear to be a negative side effect; certainly Garbarino interpreted it this way. However, it could also be interpreted as positive in that the comic book may have made an impression on the children that they are less likely to forget. As with fairy tales, the most enduring have frequently been those that have been somewhat disturbing to their young audience in the process of warning them about some harmful event that could happen.

Finally, Hazzard, Webb, and Kleemeier (1988) compared the responses of 286 third and fourth grade students from four schools who participated in a three-session adaptation of the *Feeling Yes, Feeling No* curriculum with those of 113 delayed-intervention control children from two other schools, who were matched for ethnic composition and achievement level. All children were assessed before, immediately after, and six weeks after the intervention on a knowledge questionnaire. The major finding was that participating children exhibited significantly greater knowledge on the posttestings than the control group, although they showed no differences on the pretesting. In addition, parents were asked several questions about the intervention's impact on their children. Although most comments were positive, 13% of the parents noted that their children had been "more fearful of strangers," whereas less than 5% noted other negative effects, such as nightmares, fear of men, reluctance to go to school, disobedience, sleeping problems, bedwetting, and changed reactions to physical affection.

These four studies indicate that even though a sizable number of children may express some worry after a prevention program, only a small percentage of school-age

297

children show some clear negative responses to participation. Unfortunately, we do not know whether such a small percentage change in negative behaviors would be typical in any group of children over a several-week period because no control groups were used. Recall, however, that Daro (1988) found that preschool children were more likely to interpret pictures of tickling and bathing as evoking a negative affect after participation in a prevention program. These results raise the possibility that different or more numerous negative consequences may appear in children of various ages.

The Hazzard et al. (1988) study deserves further note because it is the first report to provide evidence of substantial detection of children who revealed abuse experiences after participating in a prevention program. Eight children reported ongoing sexual abuse, and 20 others reported past occurrences. Although this result was a significant step beyond the often reported individual case of detection, the authors did not provide a definition of these disclosures nor of how many turned out to be founded cases. Given that these findings appear to be extraordinarily important, it is disappointing that Hazzard et al. concluded with the vague statement that "although follow-up information was not available on all disclosures, we were not made aware of any disclosures which were subsequently felt to be false allegations by school personnel or Protective Services" (p. 19).

A Related Study

Although they did not use a sexual abuse prevention program per se, Fryer, Kraizer, and Miyoshi (1987a, 1987b) used role-play techniques to reduce susceptibility to stranger abduction. In a program consisting of eight daily 20-minute sessions, children were taught four concrete rules to follow when they were approached by a stranger and were not with a caretaking adult. Twenty-three kindergarten, first-, and second-grade students participated in the program initially and formed the experimental group, and 21 nonparticipating children from the same grades formed the control group and were given the program later. The day before and after the program, each child was sent on an errand by his or her teacher and met one of the researchers (a male stranger) who asked the child to accompany him to his car to help him carry something into the school (the in vivo abduction situation). (It should be emphasized that the researchers went to extraordinary lengths before, during, and after the program to inform parents and to protect children from any anxiety associated with meeting the stranger.)

Pretest results showed that about half of the children in each group agreed to accompany the stranger. Posttest results showed that only 22% of the participating group agreed to go and that there was no change in the control group. Six months later, participating children who had failed the posttest (four children) and the children in the control group were given the training program. Children from all groups were then subjected to a similar in vivo abduction situation. All of the participating children who had passed the original posttest, all of the control children,

and two of the four "retrained" children resisted the abduction situation. The authors concluded that the testing showed that the children had developed the ability to avoid stranger abduction of the type used.

Several components that led to the success of this program may be important for developing and testing sexual abuse prevention programs. First, this program taught specific concrete rules and steps to follow. These might be easier for young children to comprehend than the less concrete "good touch/bad touch" idea (with some bad touches actually feeling good). Second, the program used active role-taking techniques rather than puppet shows or other passive learning techniques employed by most child sexual abuse prevention programs. Wurtele, Marrs, and Miller-Perrin (1987) recently provided more evidence that kindergarten children who were taught self-protective skills through modeling and active rehearsal learned them better than those in a control group who were taught the same skills by passively watching an experimenter model them. Third, the pretesting and posttesting may have served to "set up" and then reinforce the skills taught by the program. It is interesting to note that none of the control students, each of whom had been approached by a stranger two times before the program, agreed to accompany the stranger after the program. Perhaps these children were able to reflect on their own experience when taught the skills, thereby increasing their retention of them. Fourth, a few children were less able to learn the skills, and this highlights the need to assess which children may need more instruction for prevention programs to be meaningful for them. Finally, the authors showed that it is possible to provide a meaningful behavioral assessment of the effectiveness of the program. Such assessments represent the best means of estimating the strength of the behaviors being taught and should be pursued whenever appropriate.

Summary

These evaluations as a whole provide some limited support for the efficacy of sexual abuse prevention programs. The most common finding was a statistically significant, yet often slight, increase in knowledge about sexual abuse following a prevention program. The major area of knowledge gain seemed to be about the fact that family members or friends could engage in abusive activities; however, this was also the area in which the most loss of knowledge occurred on some follow-up measures. The instruments that were used to measure change often seemed to have a ceiling effect in that most children answered a high percentage of the questions accurately even before they participated in the program. Thus, it may be that the children learned more than the tests measured or that children know more of the basic concepts than the prevention educators think they do. If it is the former, better assessment instruments are needed; if the latter, the value of the programs may be questionable.

In the few studies that examined differences between older and younger children, the younger children, not surprisingly, learned significantly less. The results raise

298

questions as to whether these programs are useful for preschool children, or whether programs that are useful for school-age children are appropriate for younger children. Review sessions seemed to increase retention of knowledge for all but the youngest age groups. In fact, without such sessions, durability of learning seems so weak that it is questionable whether there is any long-term value to prevention programs, particularly those involving only one presentation, even if there are immediate knowledge gains. The one exception to this was the Fryer et al. (1987a, 1987b) role-playing program to increase self-protective behaviors.

Most of the evaluations had basic design problems. Although a few studies did use nontreatment control groups, most did not; therefore, there is no way to indicate whether the programs were responsible for any changes that might have occurred. Other flaws included small samples, interviewers who were not unaware of the assignment of groups, lack of attention to the psychometric properties of the measuring instruments, and the lack of pretesting to establish a baseline of knowledge.

Finally, even though no investigator discussed the issue, the question of cost–benefit analysis needs to be raised. Although these programs appear to have a great deal of face validity, in general, the results are meager. More attention must be paid to the effectiveness of different types of programs for children of different ages and the relative impact of each in conjunction with their costs, both in terms of financial resources of communities and of the possible negative consequences to the participants. More sophisticated research designs are necessary before we can make any claims regarding the overall positive impact of these interventions (see also, Wurtele, 1987).

Untested Assumptions

Most prevention programs have developed from a foundation of anecdotal clinical information (Conte, 1984) and therefore are based on several untested assumptions (Reppucci, 1987). One of these assumptions is that we know what types of skills will make a child less susceptible to sexual abuse. However, research into the incidence of child sexual abuse clearly shows that sexual abuse comes in many different forms (Haugaard & Reppucci, 1988). It may be that skills useful for preventing one type of abuse might not be useful for preventing another very different type, or that some skills may be useful for children of one age but not for children of another. Clarity as to the specific skills and behaviors that prevention programs should teach is needed in order to allow researchers to develop means of measuring their acquisition. This clarity should be based on assessing what actually happens in abusive situations and the techniques that abusers use to engage their victims. However, in vivo assessment situations are very difficult to construct because of various ethical problems, not the least of which is that subjecting children to sexual abuse situations in order to assess what prevention behaviors they exhibit is not acceptable.

Another assumption is that children will be able to transfer the knowledge gained from prevention programs into effective action when needed. Prevention programs are powered by the ideas that increasing children's knowledge about abuse, providing them with action alternatives such as giving them permission to say no and get help, and bringing the dangers of abuse to their attention may be important in preventing sexual victimization, but there is no evidence to demonstrate that these ideas actually prevent abuse. In fact, Downer (1984) found that although 94% of the children in her study could define assertiveness after prevention training, only 47% could provide an example of an assertive response to an abusive situation. Furthermore, even if her children had been able to reply with an effective response, there is no evidence that in a real abusive situation they would have responded appropriately. As noted previously, most individuals, including adults, are aware of situations in which they acted quite differently from the way they knew they should act.

A third assumption is that there are no negative effects of the prevention programs or at least that the negative effects are insignificant when compared with the positive effects. It is not known whether programs about the incorrectness of some forms of touching will adversely affect the children in a number of ways, including their comfort with nonsexual physical contact between them and their parents and others and with exploratory sexual play between them and other children. Although Swan et al. (1985) and Hazzard et al. (1988) did ask parents about negative consequences seen in their children, the behaviors that they asked the parents to recall would indicate extreme and immediate negative effects. Garbarino (1987) also found that a sizable percentage of his sample did express worry and fearfulness after reading the *Spiderman* comic book. Daro's (1988) finding of increased negative affect by preschoolers to scenes of bathing and tickling also may be cause for concern. In addition, anecdotal evidence suggests that at least some children have temporary negative reactions. Conte (1984) reported that some preschool children have been afraid to ride home from school with anyone but their parents. The following vignette provides another example.

A first grade child interpreted the message that she had the right to say "no" as generalizing to all realms of behavior. For several weeks following the prevention program she frequently told her parents that she had the right to say "no" to any requests that she did not like or made her feel uncomfortable. The parents reported much anguish and frustration on their part about this behavior and about the fact that they had to punish her in order to convince her that she did not have the right to disobey them whenever she wanted to.

Neither the anecdotes nor the evaluation studies measured or provided insight into any long-term or subtle effects. Although it may be unlikely that most children are adversely affected in any way, the risk of possible negative consequences, such as increased fearfulness or disruption of children's understanding of their world, warrants their investigation.

The crux of the matter is whether any of the programs have actually achieved either of their major goals—

299

primary prevention or detection. There is no evidence, not even one published case example, that primary prevention has ever been achieved. Often it is assumed that these programs work because well-meaning professionals and parents believe that they do. For example, Swan et al. (1985) found that over 99% of a sample of 225 parents and professionals rated the play *Bubbylonian Encounter* as a helpful tool in teaching prevention concepts, but then these investigators inappropriately concluded on the basis of these endorsements that the play "can be effective in teaching children sexual abuse prevention concepts" (p. 404). Finkelhor (1986) has also suggested that these programs may achieve primary prevention by acting as a deterrent to potential abusers who may be less likely to engage in abusive behaviors because of fear of detection. Unfortunately, no evidence exists regarding the deterrent effect of these programs. Moreover, if primary prevention is the major goal, then it may be more productive to develop prevention programs that are specifically geared to helping parents and other adults restrain from engaging in abusive sexual behaviors.

In contrast, there are some reported instances of successful detection (e.g., Finkelhor & Strapko, in press; Hazzard et al., 1988) in that individual cases of ongoing or past abuse have been discovered as a result of the interventions. In fact, Finkelhor and Strapko (in press), although they presented no data, argued that the "most important unambiguous finding" is that "prevention education encourages children to report abuse they have already suffered." However, they also point out that "researchers have not studied systematically the percentage of children who disclose, the types of disclosures they make, or how these disclosures vary according to type of program, age of children or type of school context." Furthermore, no information exists on the impact of the disclosure on the child and his or her family.

We began this article with a case vignette from Garbarino's (1987) assessment of the *Spiderman* comic book intervention that uncovered a case of child sexual abuse. Such cases are often cited as justifying preventive interventions. On some sort of ethical balancing scale, the judgment that must be made is whether the possible uncovering of a small number of cases of abuse compensates for the seemingly minor negative consequences that have now been documented for up to 50% of the participants (Garbarino, 1987). Are these consequences a small price to pay in order to uncover and alleviate the possible severe abuse of a few as documented by case examples?

Conclusion

Without more definitive information about these untested assumptions and more thorough evaluations of ongoing prevention programs, we cannot be sure whether preventive programs are working, nor can we be sure that they are causing more good than harm. This harm may come in two forms. As mentioned, the programs may adversely affect a child's positive relationships with meaningful people in his or her life or cause the child undue worry or fear at least in the short run. However, it may also be

that these programs can actually place some children at a greater risk for sexual abuse if we incorrectly assume that the children are protected because of these programs and consequently become less vigilant about the problem (Wald & Cohen, 1986). The fear is that parents, teachers, and others who work with children will abdicate their responsibility to protect to the abuse prevention programs. The complexity of the process that a child must go through to repel or report abuse, the variety of abusive situations that a child may encounter, and the short duration of most prevention programs virtually ensure that a child cannot be assumed to be protected simply because of participation in a program. Adults must be encouraged to continue and to increase their protective efforts rather than be reassured that children are learning to be self-protective.

Extensive investigations of the full range of effects of prevention programs must be undertaken. We cannot continue to assume that they accomplish their goals. Because the safety of children is the goal of these programs, we need to know much more about which ones work to teach which skills to which children. We must engage in more basic research with a goal of understanding the process that a child must go through in order to repel or report abuse and to determine how this process differs for children at various levels of cognitive and emotional development.

We have raised several questions about extant prevention programs, not to stop such efforts, but to encourage those involved to begin to ascertain by means of systematic evaluation whether they are really helping children. Without these evaluations, we risk developing programs that make adults feel better but do not protect children. Unless the usefulness of sexual abuse prevention programs can be demonstrated, the reality is that the prevention of child sexual abuse may indeed be only a myth.

REFERENCES

Atteberry-Bennett, J. (1987). *Child sexual abuse: Definitions and interventions of parents and professionals.* Unpublished doctoral dissertation. University of Virginia, Institute of Clinical Psychology, Charlottesville.

Borkin, J., & Frank, L. (1986). Sexual abuse prevention for preschoolers: A pilot program. *Child Welfare, 6,* 75–83.

Committee for Children. (1983). *Talking about touching: A personal safety curriculum.* (Available from the Committee for Children, P.O. Box 15190, Seattle, WA 98115)

Conte, J. R. (1984, August). *Research on the prevention of sexual abuse of children.* Paper presented at the Second National Conference for Family Violence Researchers, Durham, NH.

Conte, J. R., Rosen, C., & Saperstein, L. (1984, September). *An analysis of programs to prevent the sexual victimization of children.* Paper presented at the Fifth International Congress on Child Abuse and Neglect, Montreal, Canada.

Conte, J. R., Rosen, C., Saperstein, L., & Shermack, R. (1985). An evaluation of a program to prevent the sexual victimization of young children. *Child Abuse and Neglect, 9,* 319–328.

Daro, D. (1988). *Prevention programs: What do children learn.* Unpublished manuscript, University of California, Berkeley School of Social Welfare, Berkeley.

Daro, D., Duerr, J., & LeProhn, N. (1987, July). *Child assault prevention instruction: What works with preschoolers.* Paper presented at the

300

Third National Family Violence Research Conference, University of New Hampshire, Durham.

Downer, A. (1984). *Development and testing of an evaluation instrument for assessing the effectiveness of a child sexual abuse prevention curriculum.* Unpublished master's thesis, University of Washington, Seattle.

Finkelhor, D. (1979). *Sexually victimized children.* New York: Free Press.

Finkelhor, D. (1984). *Child sexual abuse: New theory and research.* New York: Free Press.

Finkelhor, D. (1986). Prevention: A review of programs and research. In D. Finkelhor and Associates (Eds.), *A sourcebook on child sexual abuse* (pp. 224–254). Beverly Hills, CA: Sage.

Finkelhor, D., and Associates (Eds.). (1986). *A sourcebook on child sexual abuse.* Beverly Hills, CA: Sage.

Finkelhor, D., & Strapko, N. (in press). "Sexual abuse prevention education: A review of evaluation studies." In D. Willis, E. Holden, & M. Rosenberg (Eds.), *Child abuse prevention.* New York: Wiley.

Fryer, G. E., Kraizer, S. K., & Miyoshi, T. (1987a). Measuring actual reduction of risk to child abuse: A new approach. *Child Abuse and Neglect, 11,* 173–179.

Fryer, G. E., Kraizer, S. K., & Miyoshi, T. (1987b). Measuring children's retention of skills to resist stranger abduction: Use of the simulation technique. *Child Abuse and Neglect, 11,* 181–185.

Garbarino, U. (1987). Children's response to a sexual abuse prevention program: A study of the *Spiderman* comic. *Child Abuse and Neglect, 11,* 143–148.

Goldstein, J., Freud, A., & Solnit, A. J. (1979). *Before the best interests of the child.* New York: Free Press.

Haugaard, J. J., & Reppucci, N. D. (1988). *The sexual abuse of children: A comprehensive guide to current knowledge and intervention strategies.* San Francisco: Jossey-Bass.

Hazzard, A. (1984). Training teachers to identify and intervene with abused children. *Journal of Clinical Child Psychology, 13,* 288–293.

Hazzard, A., & Angert, L. (1986, August). *Child sexual abuse prevention: Previous research and future directions.* Paper presented at the meeting of the American Psychological Association, Washington, DC.

Hazzard, A. P., Webb, C., & Kleemeier, C. (1988). *Child sexual assault prevention programs: Helpful or harmful?* Unpublished manuscript, Emory University School of Medicine, Atlanta, GA.

Kleemeier, C., & Webb, C. (1986, August). *Evaluation of a school-based prevention program.* Paper presented at the meeting of the American Psychological Association, Washington, DC.

Kleemeier, C., Webb, C., Hazzard, A., & Pohl, J. (1987, August). *Child sexual abuse prevention: Evaluation of a teacher training model.* Paper presented at the meeting of the American Psychological Association, New York City.

Koblinsky, S., & Behana, N. (1984). Child sexual abuse: The educator's role in prevention, detection, and intervention. *Young Children, 39,* 3–15.

Latane, B., & Darley, J. M. (1969). Bystander "apathy." *American Scientist, 57,* 244–268.

Melton, G.B. (in press). The improbability of prevention of sexual abuse. In D. J. Willis, E. W. Holden, & M. S. Rosenberg (Eds.), *Child abuse prevention.* New York: Wiley.

Plummer, C. (1984). *Preventing sexual abuse: What in-school programs teach children.* Unpublished manuscript.

Porch, T. L., & Petretic-Jackson, P. A. (1986, August). *Child sexual assault prevention: Evaluation of parent education workshops.* Paper presented at the meeting of the American Psychological Association, Washington, DC.

Ray, J., & Dietzel, M. (1984). *Teaching child sexual abuse prevention.* Unpublished manuscript.

Reppucci, N. D. (1985). Psychology in the public interest. In A. M. Rogers & C. J. Scheier (Eds.), *The G. Stanley Hall Lecture Series* (Vol. 5, pp. 121–156). Washington, DC: American Psychological Association.

Reppucci, N. D. (1987). Prevention and ecology: Teen-age pregnancy, child sexual abuse, and organized youth sports. *American Journal of Community Psychology, 15,* 1–22.

Russell, D. E. H. (1984). *Sexual exploitation, rape, child sexual abuse, and work place harassment.* Beverly Hills, CA: Sage.

Saslawsky, D. A., & Wurtele, S. K. (1986). Educating children about sexual abuse: Implications for pediatric intervention and possible prevention. *Journal of Pediatric Psychology, 11,* 235–245.

Schultz, L. G. (1988). *One hundred cases of wrongfully charged child sexual abuse: A survey and recommendations.* Unpublished manuscript, West Virginia University, School of Social Work, Morgantown.

Sechrest, L., White, S. O., & Brown, E. (Eds.). (1979). *The rehabilitation of criminal offenders: Problems and prospects.* Washington, DC: National Academy of Sciences.

Spiderman and power pack. (1984). New York: Marvel Comics.

Stewart, S. A. (1988, March). Molestation trial's costs hit $7.5 M. *USA Today,* p. 3A.

Swan, H. L., Press, A. N., & Briggs, S. L. (1985). Child sexual abuse prevention: Does it work? *Child Welfare, 64,* 667–674.

Swift, C. (1983). *Consultation in the area of child sexual abuse* (NIMH Report 83-213). Washington, DC: National Institute of Mental Health.

Trudell, B., & Whatley, M. H. (1988). School sexual abuse prevention: Unintended consequences and dilemmas. *Child Abuse and Neglect, 12,* 103–113.

Wald, M. S., & Cohen, S. (1986). Preventing child abuse: What will it take? *Family Law Quarterly, 20,* 281–302.

Weithorn, L. A. (1984). Children's capacities in legal contexts. In N. D. Reppucci, L. A. Weithorn, E. P. Mulvey, & J. Monahan (Eds.), *Children, mental health, and the law* (pp. 25–55). Beverly Hills, CA: Sage.

Wolfe, D. A., MacPherson, T., Blount, R., & Wolfe, U. V. (1986). Evaluation of a brief intervention for educating school children in awareness of physical and sexual abuse. *Child Abuse and Neglect, 10,* 85–92.

Wurtele, S. K. (1987). School-based sexual abuse prevention programs: A review. *Child Abuse and Neglect, 11,* 483–495.

Wurtele, S. K., Marrs, S. R., & Miller-Perrin, C. L. (1987). Practice makes perfect? The role of participant modeling in sexual abuse prevention programs. *Journal of Consulting and Clinical Psychology, 55,* 599–602.

Wurtele, S. K., & Miller-Perrin, C. L. (1987). An evaluation of side effects associated with participation in a child sexual abuse prevention program. *Journal of School Health, 57,* 228–231.

Wyatt, G. E. (1985). The sexual abuse of Afro-American and White-American women in childhood. *Child Abuse and Neglect, 9,* 507–519.

301

Primary Prevention of Child Abuse: Is It Really Possible?

MARY K. RODWELL

Virginia Commonwealth University
School of Social Work

DONALD E. CHAMBERS

University of Kansas
School of Social Welfare

Despite the growing interest in child abuse and its prevention, to date no systematic research has been conducted to determine the usefulness of instruments used to identify and predict abuse or neglect. The present study is a review and analysis of predictive instruments of abuse or neglect with the goal of identifying the predictive efficiency of the instruments. Analysis reveals a variety of problems with predictive efficiency, particularly as predicting individual risk of abuse or neglect relates to primary prevention. Implications of the findings and suggestions for practice are discussed.

Introduction

One of the ironies of social program history in the United States is that the earliest *Society For the Prevention of Cruelty to Children* (SPCC) did not engage in basic prevention. In fact, the New York SPCC was single minded in its focus on "child rescue": its mission was a form of law enforcement; its devotion was to the already abused child. The strategy was to remove the child from a dangerous environment in order to "prevent" child abuse from *recurring* (Breamer, 1974, p. 117). While that may be a secondary prevention of considerable importance, it is not basic (i.e., primary) prevention in the sense of avoiding the damage of the original assault. The SPCC, in attempting to deliver the child from further harm, was not attentive to what antecedent causes for the harm might be.[1] The concept of antecedents are crucial to primary prevention because unless basic causes can be unambiguously identified, first order consequences cannot be prevented.

Although the definitive intellectual history of child abuse has yet to be written, it appears to have taken nearly fifty years before primary prevention was actually embedded in child abuse and neglect program designs. This is of more than historical interest because this basic divergence between program designs intent on the protection of children (the child rescuers), those attending to the deficits of parents (the parental reformers) and those which have as their goal the prevention of initial abusing or neglecting events (the primary preventionists) persist to this day.[2]

For example, what is perhaps the best known concept in child abuse, the "Battered-Child Syndrome", is ideologically in the "child rescue" not the primary prevention tradition (Kempe, 1962). It is in the "child rescue" tradition because the syndrome profile is used to identify and treat those children who have already been abused. A modern example of the "parent rehabilitation" tradition in child abuse and neglect programming is Parents United. Its program design is one in which reunification of parents and children post-abuse is the central objective. Examples of the primary prevention tradition are program designs which seek to screen mothers of newborn children for "predictors" of potential child abuse and/or neglect. Healthy Start is an example of such a program.

Since funding for programs concerned with child abuse and neglect is limited, it is vital to assess the evidence for the effectiveness of these three approaches. But in what follows we focus on primary prevention, to the exclusion of secondary and tertiary prevention, because it appears to be the most difficult to evaluate. We review the existing literature, argue that there is no serious evidence supporting the efficacy of the predictors of child abuse that together create the program theories that have been used to shape prevention programs for child abuse, and then discuss the implications of that finding.

Review of the Literature

The crucial issue for primary prevention is the ability to identify predictors of child abuse; if predictors do not exist, no basis for primary prevention programs exist because one must identify an at risk population in order to properly shape and target a program of primary prevention.

In order to determine what is known about predictors of abuse or neglect, a thorough review of the empirical research and a subsequent analysis of those findings were undertaken. Efforts were made to identify major lines of inquiry that might be considered together in identifying the theoretical and conceptual issues pertaining to child abuse prediction. Unfortunately, these lines of inquiry seem to go no further than 1985, because no published studies of the type necessary for this analysis were found after that time.

Method

The literature review began with a computer search of "Dialog"[3] which netted 24 nonredundant titles. In addition, all *Child Welfare* journals from 1963 to the present and *Child Abuse and Neglect* journals from 1970 forward were reviewed for articles that included prediction or correlation in relation to child abuse and neglect. Eighteen titles were added to the review. Finally, the bibliographies of several well known child welfare books were reviewed in the same manner. This process resulted in 29 additional titles. From the total of 71 titles, we were able to locate all but three dissertations and five articles.[4] Thus, this literature review is based on 63 published works.[5] "Publication bias" is always an issue in this kind of review, since it is well documented that positive findings are much more likely to be published. The authors were prepared to use various procedures (e.g., fail-safe N, etc.) to estimate the likely effect of publication bias had the preponderance of findings been positive.

The second stage in this literature search included a review of each article for relevance. The use of "prediction" in the title meant automatic relevance. If the abstract indicated either predictive or correlational research related to either abuse or neglect, the article was included. No article was included without data-based results. All conceptual or theoretical articles were excluded. Forty-eight articles remained after this second stage screening.

These articles were then reviewed thoroughly using a formal coding sheet (a reading guide to insure the same data was consistently gathered on all studies). The coding sheet included: a.) title, author, professional discipline, date of publication; b.) criteria by which article was selected; c.) theoretical base and specific research hypotheses; d.) definitions used for abuse/neglect; e.) sampling process; f.) research design used to test hypotheses; g.) measurement procedures and issues; h.) variables contaminating findings, moderating variables and subtype issues; i.) predictive efficiency; and j.) overall quality of the research.

In the third and final stage of the review process, we eliminated all articles not containing data and analysis with potential for making the predictions of interest. Thus, to be included in the results reported here, the study had to present, for example, the results of regression or discriminant function analysis, t-tests or chi-square measures. Twenty-one studies met these criteria and were included.

It is notable that only two of these twenty-one studies concerned neglect (Giovannoni & Billingsley, 1979; Polansky & Pollane, 1975). The rest focused on child abuse. Because so few empirical studies of neglect exist, we chose, reluctantly, to drop neglect from this review. It is also notable that the selected studies differed greatly in their choice of variables related to child abuse. Approximately half of the studies identified totally different variables for investigation and half used some, not all, of the same variables. No two studies by different authors considered exactly the same, nor even a high proportion of the same variables.

Results of the Literature Review

Even with the difficulty in identifying like variables and with the problem of comparable operationalization of variables, three categories identify the general conceptual focus of the studies reviewed here. They are:

(a.) Attitudinal/personality focus on parent or child, including such variables as distress, rigidity, aggressive impulses, child behaviors, self-esteem as antecedents of child abuse.

(b.) Interactional focus on the covariance of personality or attitudinal variables of the parent with child-related variables (as noted above) and environmental variables such as social isolation, economic status, living situation, etc.

(c.) Ecological/environmental focus on socioeconomic or demographic characteristics, for example, income, race, welfare recipiency.

These categories describe the variables the investigators are prone to use in explaining and, thus, predicting child abuse. Table 1 below shows the relationship of each study to these categories. Note that more studies focused on attitude and personality variables, though as we will see later, these particular variables do not represent a higher capacity for efficiently predicting child abuse.

Analysis of Predictive Efficiency

The key question this review seeks to answer is whether there is any evidence for antecedents that can validly and efficiently predict the existence of child abuse. The prediction of future events is a complex business and a number of issues must be taken into account before an efficient predictor can be said to be available.

The analysis of predictive efficiency involves more than constructing correlation coefficients, regression equations or t-tests, although all of those summary statistics are useful. These statistical maneuvers are summarizing techniques for the purpose of contrasting groups. Here we are interested in making predictions about individual instances. When it comes to making predictions about individuals there are four different kinds of estimates that together determine predictive efficiency. They can be illustrated best by a 2x2 table which shows the possible outcomes of predictions with actual future events (see Figure 1).

"Positives" are instances where abuse *was* predicted and *did* actually occur. "Negatives" are instances where abuse *was not* predicted and *did not* occur. Both are instances of accurate prediction and, added together, are called "Total." Note that there are two ways that a prediction can go wrong. one is a "False Negative," instances where abuse was not predicted but

Table 1

Types of Antecedent Variables Used in Predictive Research in Abuse

	Attitude/ Personality	Interactional	Ecological/ Environmental
Study/Year			
(American)			
Anderson, Lauderdale/1982	x		
Cohn/1977	x		
Egelund, et al./1980	x		
Melnick, Hurley/1969	x		
Milner, et al./1984	x		
Paulson, et al./1977	x		
Seaberg/1977	x		
Schneider/1982	x		
Spinetta/1978	x		
Altemeir, et al./1984		x	
Gray, et al./1979		x	
Johnson, L'Esperance/1984		x	
Kotelchuck/1984		x	
Starr/1982		x	
Garbarino/1976			x
Spearly, Lauderdale/1983			x
(British)			
Hanson et al./1977		x	
Lealman et al./1983		x	
Lynch et al./1977		x	

actually did happen. The other is a "False Positive," instances where abuse was predicted but actually *did not* happen.

Traditionally these predictive estimates are calculated as ratios. It is important to note that in evaluating how good predictions are, the base for these ratios should be the relevant total predictions made (i.e. total positive predictions, total negative predictions, and grand total of predictions, etc.). In that way some estimate can be made of the proportion of right to wrong

Figure 1

Illustration of the types of prediction the predictive efficiency concept generates.

		Prediction	
		Abuse Will Occur	Abuse Will Not Occur
	Abuse Did Occur	positive	false negative
Actual Events			
	Abuse Did Not Occur	false positive	negative
		(total positive predictions made)	(total negative predictions made)

Figure 2

Equations for Determining Predictive Efficiency

Total positives	= positive/total positive predictions made
Total negatives	= negative/total negative predictions made
False positives	= false positive/total positive predictions made
False negatives	= false negatives/total negative predictions made

$$\text{Overall Accuracy (Total)} = \frac{\text{Total positives} + \text{Total negatives}}{\text{Grand total (positive and negative) of predictions made}}$$

predictions. We calculated the various predictive efficiencies as shown in Figure 2. In addition, the ability of a predictor to efficiently pick out abused children will be expressed by a "Missed Case" ratio, i.e., the ratio of false negatives to the total number of abused children actually (or estimated to be) in the population or sample.

Information about the relative proportion of right or wrong predictions is of practical value because, as we shall see in more detail later on, there are ways in which even a very good predictor can go wrong. For example, it is perfectly possible for a variable to be extremely good at picking out all children who will be abused in the future; but in doing so will wrongly identify an equal or even greater number of children as abused-in-the-future when in fact they will not be abused at all! (See Light, 1973; Light & Pillemer, 1984).

In addition to correlational statistics or regression analyses designed to reveal general overall relationships between variables, our study required the reporting of additional statistical maneuvers (e.g., factor analysis, discriminant functions, etc.) that tested the ability of selected variables to make advance predictions in a different data set. We found 11 of the remaining 19 articles in the original pool contained sufficient information to estimate predictive efficiencies about abuse. All eleven focus on either attitudinal/personality or interactional antecedents as predictors. It is interesting to note that no study using ecological/environmental antecedents met this criterion for inclusion.

Findings

Discussion of the results will be hampered by the unevenness of the quality of the studies on at least six counts. Most studies used sampling methods that were reflective of convenience rather than controlled comparisons which would allow generalization to a broader population. All studies, with the exception of the work by Lealman (1983) and by Altemeir and associates (1984), were retrospective. Researchers used samples of families who had already been identified as abusing. In addition, mothers only were the subjects in most studies, thus systematically excluding fathers or male caregivers. Only two studies of those included in our analysis, that by Egelund (1980) and Kotelchuck (1982), used data from a significant number of fathers. About a fourth of Egelund's and a third of the sample of the Kotelchuck study were male. Also, most studies included were conducted in hospital settings (usually public) to the exclusion of community based, private and nonmedical facilities. Possibly because of this limitation, the subjects in all studies reflect a lower socioeconomic strata, even though there are no empirical data confirming that abuse and neglect are limited in that way.[6]

Additionally, attempts to establish controlled comparisons or research designs that would rule out contaminating, intervening variables or other alternate explanations of results were only partially successful. Finally, potential treatment effects in some studies undermined the clarity of the results because data were gathered simultaneous with the provision of services to high risk or abusing families. Note that if treatments were effective, and generally they were somewhat effective, the consequence of collecting data while treating effectively is to reduce the number of abusing or neglectful incidents. This will cause a potential underestimate of the strength of an identified predictor variable. For example, if stress is a good predictor of abuse, but families in the study are learning effective stress management techniques, then stress will appear to be less robust as a predictor as the number of abuse or neglect incidents declines. Unfortunately, the studies with the potential for treatment effect do not give us clear measure of the effectiveness of treatment so that we can judge with precision the extent of this underestimation.

Given the methodological weaknesses of these predictive studies, the reader may question the usefulness of a discussion of the predictive ability of the instruments when their validity and reliability are essentially unknown. At this point it would seem that, contrary to current practice wisdom, we do not know how much we know. The results here are offered to underscore just how much we may not know and to give impetus to further refinement of capacities to predict abuse and neglect that seem to have stopped in about 1985.

The largest group of studies to be discussed (8) have been conducted in the United States. Three British studies have also been included. However, because child abuse is such a culturally defined concept, it would be misleading to summarize predictive studies across national boundaries. We would not wish to give readers the impression that the results of British studies could be utilized without replication on U.S. samples. On that account we will summarize U.S. and British studies separately. Table 2, however, arrays results of all the predictive studies simultaneously.

Table 2

Predictive Studies in Child Abuse[1]

Study (Year)	Total (%)	+ (%)	− (%)	False + (%)	False − (%)	Missed Cases (%)	N of Study
(U.S. Studies)							
Altemeir, et al. (1984)	84	5	99	95	1	34	1400
Cohn (1977)	75	66	91	34	9	10	52
Egelund et al. (1980)	78	24	91	76	9	63	267
Johnson							
L'Esperance (1984)*	74	70	81	30	19	16	39
Kotelchuck (1984)	78	80	77	20	23	25	402
Milner (1984)	54	28	85	72	15	31	190
Paulson (1977)	65	54	73	46	27	39	114
Starr (1982)	70	n.a.	n.a.	33	27	n.a.	174
(British Studies)							
Hanson, et al. (1977)	83	97	64	3	36	21	187
Lealman, et al. (1983)	84	13	99	87	1	15	2802
Lynch, et al. (1977)	80	88	75	12	25	30	100

[1] Some studies cited in this table "validated" findings using samples different from those used to initially identify predictors. Where that was the case, data on predictive efficiency is always taken from the "validation" sub-study.

* Unlike the other studies tabled, this one concerns prediction of *recurrence* of abuse.

U.S. Studies

Keeping the above caveats in mind, the seven U.S. studies show a relatively high overall accuracy rate with respect to predicting both those abused and free from abuse—71% accurate, on average (median total). There was consistency among the studies in this regard as all but one clustered within 10% of this figure. The best overall accuracy achieved in this set of studies was 84%.

Note, however, that the average (mean) false positive rate is very large—50.6%. While overall predictive accuracy is satisfactory, on average the antecedents used in these studies will falsely identify half of those it accuses of child abuse, misidentifying one child as abused for every child correctly predicted to be abused. Moreover, these studies use predictors which would routinely fail to identify a substantial proportion of abused children: one of every three children who are actually abused, since the average (median) missed case rate is about 35% (with an average deviation of 11%).

While no study reviewed here has what could be considered an acceptable false positive rate, there is substantial variation among these studies with respect to false positives. The lowest false positive rate found was 20% (the Kotelchuck study using interactional variables). This means that even the best study relative to false positives misidentified as abused one of every five children on which it made predictions. There were two studies with false positive rates in the 30% range (both with interactional variables). All others were higher. The highest false positive rate was an extremely large 95% (the Altemeir study also using interactional variables).

With respect to missed case rates, there is not as much variability among the seven studies. The lowest missed case rate was 16% (with interactional variables) while the highest was 63% (using attitude/personality variables). The average deviation among the missed case rates was 10.6%.

An interesting detail in Table 2 is whether recurrence is any easier to predict than the initial occurrence. Contrasting the predictive accuracy of the Johnson/L'Esperance 1984 study of the prediction of recurrence among adjudicated abusers against the average accuracy of the studies predicting abuse in samples with no known history of abuse, we find that predictions of recurrence are only 6% more accurate! Note also that the problem of false positives is still with us in the prediction of recurrence. Even with the advantage of knowing an initial instance of child abuse, the false positive rate in the Johnson/L'Esperance study is 30%.

However, this false positive rate is less than the 53% rate found as an average of all studies and the Johnson/L'Esperance study produces one of the *lowest* missed case rates (16%) of any in the group. While their sample is very small, it does suggest that recurrences can be predicted without overlooking a significant proportion of cases.

We could not explain the substantial variation in predictive efficiency in these U.S. studies by any obvious feature of the research process, such as sample size or method, research design, various characteristics of the subjects used, instrumentation, etc. For example, there are high and low overall accuracy, false positives and missed case rates among studies with large samples (N=1400) and studies with small samples (N=39). There are high and low overall accuracy, false positive and missed case rates among studies using matched controls, among studies using some version of random assignment, among studies using prospective and among studies using retrospective designs.

Nor is it possible to associate good predictive efficiency with any specific predictive variable or any set of them. It appears that wherever instruments or predictor variables are used with more than one sample, overall accuracy rates, false positives and missed case rates vary substantially. It is also clear that such variation in results cannot be attributed to the general type of antecedent variable used, at least with respect to the attitudinal, interactional, and ecological categories discussed earlier. Predictive efficiencies as a function of antecedent variables are presented in Table 3 below.

Our summary conclusion is that, based on existing empirical data, there is no reason to believe that child abuse in the U.S.A. can be efficiently predicted in advance. It cannot be

Table 3

Predictive Efficiencies as a Function of Antecedent Variables in U.S. Studies*

Type of Predictor Variable	Total Rate	False Positive Rate	Missed Case Rate
1. ATTITUDINAL/ PERSONALITY	66%	65%	44%
2. INTERACTIONAL	76%	45%	27%

* Recall that studies using ecological antecedents produce data that does not allow the analysis of predictive efficiencies, thus those studies are not included in this table.

predicted without an alarmingly large proportion of mislabeling of non-abusers or of missed cases. Further, the damage done by mislabeling in the indiscriminant and/or mass use of these instruments in primary prevention programs would be likely to fall disproportionately on the poor and on racial minorities.

The British Studies

All the British studies report findings with predictive efficiencies as good as or better than the U.S. studies. Of considerable interest is the 1977 Hanson, McCulloch and Hartley study which appears to have an overall predictive accuracy equal to or marginally better than any U.S. study, while simultaneously generating substantially lower false positive rates. The total rate exceeds all other predictive studies (83%). In addition, it produces the lowest false positive rate of any study we could locate—3%. Overall, these are better results than any found in the U.S. studies because, while the overall accuracy is equal to those found in the U.S. studies, the false positive rate is reduced almost to the vanishing point.

A crucial factor, however, is a high missed case rate. It may be that is order to achieve a satisfactory overall accuracy and a tolerable false positive rate in the prediction of first instances of child abuse, a high missed case rate is inevitable.

These generally improved results bear a closer look for U.S. application, for they appear to illustrate a research strategy that might be well to emulate. The Hanson, McCulloch and Hartley study clearly is directed at the high risk child abuse, overlooking the thornier "at risk" category (p. 48). They chose to target the kind of child abuse that ordinary physicians can agree *on medical grounds* is physical abuse or non-accidental injury. That same kind of clear targeting does not seem characteristic of the U.S. studies. The "at-risk" idea may be the cause of the too-wide, over-inclusive "net" that has been used by U.S. investigators in their search for predictors of child abuse.

Another strategically interesting point, the study distinguishes child abusers from others by a very simple concept: "number of adverse circumstances." Beginning with 67 correlates of abuse, the investigators analyze not for which particular set best accounts for the differences between abusers and nonabusers; but for some raw number of factors which distinguishes between the two. In this sense the explanatory and etiological question is side-stepped and the emphasis is clearly on prediction.

Discussion

This analysis of the research related to the prediction of child abuse is discouraging. We conclude that efficient prediction for the purposes of primary prevention is impossible for any practical professional purpose. What is the reason for this state of affairs? It is possible that we simply do not know enough to identify the important variables. It is also possible that the technical and methodological shortcomings in the research have obscured important findings. It is certainly true that despite earnest and skillful attempts, the research reviewed here was often disabled by errors in instrumentation, research design and sampling methods. Wherever the explanation lies, it remains quite clear that we have not come any noticeable distance in our ability to make practical predictions about child abuse. Clearly, if prediction is our goal, more and better conceived and implemented predictive studies are needed.

From another perspective, Richard Light (1973), and others after him, offer a clear clue to the reason why accurate prediction is so difficult here. Without going into the technical details of his argument, the problem is due to the relatively low incidence of child abuse. Efficient predictions of any very low incidence phenomenon require extraordinarily accurate instruments. Light shows convincingly that screening instruments for child abusers must be more than 99% accurate in order to be acceptable (Light & Nagi, 1977).

According to the results found here, it is quite impossible to predict the initial episode of child abuse without simultaneously overlooking a significant number or "scooping up" many more children than those who are really vulnerable. No set of variables, or combination, does a good enough job of early identification to allow those committed to child protection to speak thoroughly about the efficacy of primary prevention because accurate targeting is practically impossible. This review shows that any primary prevention program based on present data will be bound to intervene in many more homes than are necessary. The current potential for stigma resulting from well-intended, but unnecessary early intervention should not be overlooked.

Further, it means that protective services workers as a part of secondary or tertiary prevention could, therefore, frequently and wrongly remove children permanently or at least potentially traumatize families and children who were in no danger. The problem of false positives is not trivial for any level of prediction; even given the *best* predictors available, one of every three to five children will be misidentified as endangered.

These conclusions have important implications for future funding allocations and should be taken seriously. Given present fiscal shortages, funding of primary prevention programs should cease unless or until mass prevention efforts of the nonstigmatizing sort, such as those seen in some Latin American countries, are accepted as the norm. This would require a legislative acceptance of the potential of high frontend costs of broadly-targeted services over long-term cost savings in secondary and tertiary prevention. The alternative is to cease funding of primary prevention programs until research provides efficient antecedents necessary to implement such programs.

Given the underfunded and overburdened nature of the child welfare system, in combination with the limits of current predictive research, the priority should be funding for programs of *secondary prevention* or treatment program designs that can show effectiveness with respect to limiting the damage of the first abuse incident and/or preventing recurrence. From our perspective, family preservation projects fall into this category.

Nothing said above should be taken to indicate that the concept of primary prevention of child abuse is hopeless. In fact, the British studies show a research strategy by which efficient prediction could be accomplished. Research funding is needed to replicate those promising results here in the U.S.A. To follow this research strategy, however, requires us to be much less ambitious about the type of child abuse we will strive to predict and to prevent. It means abandoning the attempt to identify children "at risk" and to clearly target physical abuse of the kind that is medically determinable. While ideologically that may not be the most satisfying way to proceed, were we able to do primary prevention on the basis of validated predictions of even this limited scope, we would do our clients, their children and our profession a great favor.

References

Altemeir, W., O'Connor, S., Vietz, P., Sandler, H., & Sherrod, K. (1984). Prediction of child abuse. *Child Abuse and Neglect, 8,* 393–400.

Anderson, S., & Lauderdale, M. (1982). Characteristics of abusive parents: A look at self-esteem. *Child Abuse and Neglect, 6,* 285–293.

Bremner, R. (1974). *Children and youth in America* (Vol. II). Cambridge: Harvard University Press.

Cohn, M. (1977). *Assessment of risk in child abusing and neglecting parents.* Unpublished doctoral dissertation, University of California at Los Angeles.

Egelund, B., Breitenbucher, M., & Rosenberg, D. (1980). Prospective study of the significance of life stress in the etiology of child abuse. *Journal of Counseling and Clinical Psychology, 48,* 192–205.

Garbarino, J. (1976). A preliminary study of some ecological correlates of child abuse: The impact of socio-economic stress on mothers. *Child Development, 47,* 178–185.

Giovanonni, J., & Billingsley, A. (1979). Child neglect among the poor: A study of parental adequacy in families of three ethnic groups. *Child Welfare, 49,* 196–204.

Gray, J., Cutler, D., Dean, J., & Kempe, C. (1979). Prediction and prevention of child abuse and neglect. *Journal of Social Issues, 35,* 127–139.

Hanson, R., McCulloch, T., & Hartley, S. (1977). Key characteristics of child abuse. In A. Franklin (Ed.), *Child abuse prediction, prevention and follow up* (pp. 39–53). Edinburgh: Churchill Livingstone.

Johnson, W. & L'Esperance, J. (1984). Predicting the recurrence of Child Abuse. *Social Work Research and Abstracts, 20,* 21–26.

Kempe, C., Silverman, F., Droegmueller, W., & Silver, H. (1962). The battered child syndrome. *Journal of the American Medical Association, 181,* 4–11.

Kotelchuck, M. (1984). Child abuse and neglect: Prediction and misclassification. In R. Starr (Ed.), *Child abuse prediction: Policy implications* (pp. 67–104). Cambridge, MA: Ballinger Publishing Co.

Lealman, G., Hatch, D., Stone, J., Phillips, J., & Ord-Smith, C. (1983, June 25). Prediction and prevention of child abuse An empty hope? *Lancet,* 1423–1424.

Light, R. (1973). Child abuse and neglect in America: A study of alternative policies. *Harvard Educational Review, 43,* 198–240.

Light, R., & Nagi, S. (1977). *Child maltreatment in the United States.* NY: Columbia University Press.

Light, R., & Pillemer, D. (1984). *Summing up the science of reviewing research.* Cambridge, MA: Harvard University Press.

Lynch, M., & Roberts, J. (1977). Early alerting signs. In A. Franklin (Ed.),

Child abuse prediction, prevention and follow-up (pp. 75–99). Lexington, MA: Lexington Books.

Melnick, B., & Hurley, J. (1969). Distinctive personality attributes of child abusing mothers. *Journal of Consulting and Clinical Psychology, 33,* 746–749.

Milner, J., Gold, R., Ayoub, C., & Jacewitz, M. (1984). Predictive validity of the child abuse potential inventory. *Journal of Consulting and Clinical Psychology, 52,* 879–884.

Paulson, M. (1977). Parental attitude research instrument (PARI): Clinical vs. statistical inferences in understanding abusive mothers. *Journal of Clinical Psychology. 33,* 848–854.

Pelton, L. (1978) Child abuse and neglect: The myth of classlessness. *The American Journal of Orthopsychiatry, 48,* 608–617.

Seaberg, J. (1977). Predictors of injury severity in physical child abuse. *Journal of Social Service Research, 1,* 63–76.

Schneider, C. (1982). The Michigan screening profile of parenting. In R. Starr (Ed.), *Child abuse prediction: Policy implications* (pp. 157–174). Cambridge, MA.: Ballinger Publishing Co.

Spearly, J. & Lauderdale, M. (1983). Community characteristics and ethnicity in the prediction of child maltreatment rates. *Child Abuse and Neglect, 7,* 91–105.

Spinetta, J. (1978). Parental personality factors in child abuse. *Journal of Consulting and Clinical Psychology, 46,* 1409–1414.

Starr, R. (1982). A research based approach to the prediction of child abuse. In R. Starr (Ed.), *Child abuse prediction: Policy implications* (pp. 105–134). Cambridge, MA: Bollinger Publications.

Notes

1. Actually, there developed a divergence among SPCCs later in their history, some followed the New York SPCC child rescue viewpoint while others such as the Massachusetts SPCC emphasized rehabilitation of parents in order to return children to their original homes (Bremner,1974). This program strategy was, also, not one which could focus easily on primary prevention.

2. Secondary prevention is prevention of recurrence or spread of the problem (treatment) and tertiary prevention is limiting or reducing the seriousness of the problematic condition (rehabilitation). Secondary prevention or treatment programs which reduce recurrence are extremely important, but have very different costs, benefits and operating characteristics than primary prevention programs.

3. The data bases for "Dialog" were: *Psycinfo, Psycalert, Child Abuse and Neglect* and *Dissertation Abstracts.*

4. Only the most recent of the articles in the line of inquiry pursued by Altemeir (1984), Milner (1985), and Schneider (1982) were included because the latest study represented the most recent and best development of their predictive instruments.

5. The complete listing of all sixty-three articles is too large for inclusion in this article, but is available from the first author upon request.

6. For a thorough review of the argument on this issue see Pelton (1978), who concludes that child abuse and neglect must be class related since every empirical study he can find confirms that statement. Of course, all the studies he reviews involve *official abuse and neglect reports*. Since Pelton himself concedes that poor people are more likely to be reported and prosecuted, his argument that this is not a reporting bias does not convince us.

PREVENTION OF CHILD NEGLECT
Emerging Issues

DAVID A. WOLFE

University of Western Ontario and the Institute for the Prevention of Child Abuse

Research studies conducted over the past decade involving maltreating families largely confirm that the vast majority of parents lack competence in their role because of inadequate availability of resources, poor preparation and support in their role as parents, and impairment in coping due to overwhelming sources of stress present in the family and community. This article presents an overview of some of the risk factors that have been identified and that especially pertain to child neglect. Suggestions of ways to conceptualize prevention goals follow from these identified risk factors. Examples of some of the more promising programs that have emerged in recent years, based on a family support model of prevention and early intervention, are discussed. Recent programs directed at prevention of child neglect have primarily built on successful treatment approaches and applied them to a much broader segment of the parenting population at an earlier point in time. Several conclusions and suggestions for prevention planning in the area of child maltreatment follow from this discussion.

Although intervention models have greatly improved in recent years and have contributed to encouraging gains in treatment outcomes, the field of child abuse and neglect remains split between promising research findings, on the one hand, and the realities of child protection and welfare, on the other hand. Unfortunately, the dominant theme in most services to maltreating families remains that of protection, not treatment or assistance (Azar & Wolfe, 1989). Because most intervention tends to occur only after a major identified incident of abuse or neglect, parents must be identified and labeled in order to receive some level of assistance. Current laws and priorities focus

AUTHOR'S NOTE: *Correspondence may be addressed to David A. Wolfe, Department of Psychology, University of Western Ontario, London, Ontario N6A 5C2.*

CRIMINAL JUSTICE AND BEHAVIOR, Vol. 20 No. 1, March 1993 90-111 largely on the most serious indicators of risk to the child, leaving child protection agencies with few resources to assist families who have not, as yet, violated any community standard. Understandably, to offer services at an earlier point in time to the many families that could benefit requires a retooling of our priorities and procedures within the child welfare system, to encourage parents to seek assistance early on for their important role (Wolfe, 1990).

Psychological interventions with reported maltreating parents have developed gradually from an individually based pathology model to an all-encompassing ecological model, with an evolving emphasis on the importance of the parent-child relationship and its context. Simultaneously, the orientation toward the treatment issue, that is, how such behavior is viewed, has shifted gradually away from a parent-focused, deviance viewpoint and more toward one that accounts for the vast number of stress factors that impinge on the developing parent-child relationship. This shift toward a more process-oriented, contextual theory of maltreatment places greater emphasis on the importance of promoting parental competence and reducing the burden of stress on families. As Belsky (1984) explains, parental competence (i.e., sensitivity to the child's developing abilities and communications) is influenced by such factors as (a) parental resources (e.g., education, attitudes about childrearing, parents' background experiences), (b) the child's characteristics (e.g., temperament, health, developmental level), and (c) the family context (e.g., the marital relationship, the quality of social networks and supports, and community resources).

Despite theoretical advances, recent reviews of interventions with abusive and neglectful parents raise some doubt as to the effectiveness of treatment efforts (and adequacy of research efforts) that are delivered well after negative patterns of parent-child interaction have been established (Azar & Wolfe, 1989; Cohn & Daro, 1987; Fink & McCloskey, 1990; Mash & Wolfe, 1991; Videka-Sherman, 1989; Wekerle & Wolfe, 1992). Some of the prominent factors contributing to this lackluster success with tertiary treatment of child maltreatment have to do with the nature of the target population and our general tendency to miss the mark in servicing their needs. First of all, there is a marked tendency for parents to be unwilling to seek help until it is forced on them or the problem becomes major. Avoidance of services makes sense, however, in light of our current strategy for combating child maltreatment. Currently, our child welfare system functions on the basis of reaction to crises and conflicts, and consequently little effort is directed toward the "front-end" of the child welfare system. Those families who are most in need often receive very little support and assistance until they commit a major violation of childcare practices. This article explores some of the factors that could form the basis for alternative service delivery for abusive and neglectful families, and provides an overview of the more promising programs that have emerged in recent years based on a family support model of prevention and early intervention.

IDENTIFYING PREVENTION OBJECTIVES: WHO AND WHAT ARE THE TARGETS OF PREVENTATIVE SERVICES?

CRITICAL PERIODS FOR PREVENTION ACTIVITIES

Greater attention is needed to address the concern of *how* some parents gradually acquire the preconditions that lead to the rather sudden onset of abusive behavior, or the more gradual onset of neglect. Rather than focusing on observable factors that are often present once a family has been labeled or reported, this viewpoint looks at the process by which the more subtle, preexisting factors associated with the individual parent, child, or family situation become transformed over time into a high-risk or maltreating situation.

The transitional model of child maltreatment (Wolfe, 1987) was formulated to describe such a course of development in terms that have relevance to prevention and early intervention. The model is based on two presuppositions. First, the development of inappropriate child-rearing patterns is presumed to follow a somewhat predictable course in the absence of intervention or major compensatory factors. This course is described in reference to stages, which serve to underscore the contention that abuse and neglect develop from a gradual transformation in the parent-child relationship from mild to very harmful interactions. Accordingly, the initial stage is relatively benign in comparison to later stages, in that the parent has not as yet behaved in the manner that significantly interferes with the parent-child relationship. However, this viewpoint suggests that failure to deal effectively with the demands of their role early on can readily lead to increased pressure on the parent-child relationship and a concomitant increase in the probability of abusive or neglectful behavior.

The second presupposition of this model relates to the importance of psychological processes that are linked to the expression of anger, arousal, and coping reactions in adults. Specifically, these processes include operant and respondent learning principles for the acquisition or maintenance of behavior, cognitive-attributional processes that influence an individual's perception and reaction to stressful events, and emotional conditioning processes that determine the individual's degree of physiological arousal, perceived discomfort, and self-control under stressful circumstances.

The initial stage in this model, labeled "reduced tolerance for stress and disinhibition of aggression," begins with the parent's own preparation for this role (in terms of psychological and social resources, attributional style, modeling, and similar learning experiences from childhood), and his or her current style of coping with daily demands that compete with the parenting role. Parents' responses during this period, in which their roles and responsibilities are gradually being acquired, are based largely on their own family of origin and their preparation for this role by their previous childcare experiences. For those who are at risk of inappropriate childcare, training is often inadvertently accomplished over the course of childhood through the modeling of aggressive problem-solving tactics and an external attributional style, rehearsal and reinforcement of aggressive behavior with siblings and peers, the absence of opportunities to learn prosocial behavior, and/or the reliance on avoidance strategies as a means of coping with stress. For those at risk of neglectful parenting style in particular, we often see a family background of deficient maternal-child interaction, lack of maternal availability, and inconsistent parental affect and response to the child (Drotar, 1992).

Several factors may play a critical role in mediating the expression of aggressive and/or avoidant behavior once the individual becomes a parent. In particular, the degree of control, feedback, and predictability that parents perceive in relation to stressful life events can influence their behavior. For example, if they are able to achieve some success in controlling stressful aspects of their life, they are more likely to adopt a purposeful, planned approach to childrearing. In addition, compensatory factors such as a supportive spouse, socioeconomic stability, success experiences at work or school, and positive social supports that the individual can draw on for information or assistance (Belsky, 1984; Cicchetti & Rizley, 1981) may serve to buffer some parents from the effects of major stressors during this stage.

The second stage in this model, titled "poor management of acute crises and provocation," represents the hypothetical point in the development of poor parenting style in which the adult's current attempts or methods of handling life stress or child behavior begin to fail significantly. The parent often experiences feelings of losing control, and at this juncture the risk of child maltreatment (and other forms of poor coping reactions) begins to increase. A parent may step up the intensity of power-assertive methods that he or she believes are necessary to reestablish a semblance of control, or if predisposed to neglect/avoidance, he or she may develop a diminished pattern of social exchange with the child. Conditioned emotional responding (i.e., prior reactions of anger and irritation related to the child) may overtake, or impair, the parent's rational behavior at this point. Feelings of extreme agitation and irritation, which may have originated from other sources of anger besides the child (e.g., an employer, a neighbor, or a spouse) are (mis)attributed to the child, because the parent has learned (through months or years of interaction with the child) to associate feelings of discomfort or irritation with child provocation (also, the child is often the easiest party to blame for such unpleasant feelings of arousal). Consequently, when the child cries or fusses to seek attention (for example), the parent may distort the seriousness or potential harm posed by the situation. This appraisal, in turn, may lead him or her to conclude that excessive countermeasures are justified to gain control of the child's aversive behavior.

Once again, the degree of stress experienced by the parent may be offset by compensatory factors. In particular, improvement in the child's behavior or the involvement of community programs to assist parents in coping with difficult family-related issues, hold promise for reducing the acute crisis situation.

The third and most unyielding stage in the transitional model of maltreatment, titled "habitual patterns of arousal and aggression with family members," represents a chronic pattern of irritability, arousal, and/or avoidance of responsibility on the part of the parent. By this time, the parent may maintain that the use of excessive punishment and force is absolutely necessary to control the child's behavior, or (in the case of neglect), he or she may have established a pattern of inappropriate avoidance of responsibility. Provocative stimuli, such as child behavior problems, frustration, and emotional arousal are commonplace by this point, and the parent's response to such events (such as abusive interchanges or neglectful avoidance) continues to escalate in intensity, duration, and frequency.

By this third stage, parents often perceive that they are trapped into continuing to use harsh or extreme methods to control their children or to avoid the stress associated with childcare. Although this perception is somewhat accurate (due to the fact that children can habituate to the higher level of punishment and thus may not respond as well to it), this belief justifies their use of further force/avoidance. A parent is now caught in the vicious cycle of using coercive methods to diminish tension and irritation, and he or she may receive some short-term gain through such methods by the reduction of the child's aversive behavior.

Unfortunately, reversal of this process is very difficult by this stage, and is aided by very few compensatory factors. Although treatment efforts may be directed toward families at this point in time, the method of interacting with one's children has become so ingrained that it becomes very difficult to rely on anything but coercive and avoidant methods. Thus treatment providers are faced with the dilemma of introducing ways to change well-established patterns of family interaction in such a manner that the parent will recognize that the benefits (e.g., a well-behaved child, or more pleasant family interaction) outweigh the costs (e.g., efforts needed to learn different disciplinary methods, pronounced increases in child problem behavior in the short term).

The challenging task for professionals becomes one of interrupting this deterioration and intervening in such a way as to restore the family's ability to cope with external demands and provide for the

327

developmental and socialization needs of their children. According to this view, the parent-child relationship was either never well-established from the beginning, or it began to disintegrate during periods of developmental change or family stress. Therefore an overriding goal of preventing child maltreatment from the perspective of healthy child development is the establishment of positive socialization practices that are responsive to situational and developmental changes. Such healthy practices serve to buffer the child against other socialization pressures that can be stressful or negative, and reduce the need for the parent to rely on power-assertive or neglectful methods to control or avoid their childcare responsibilities.

DEVELOPING CHILD-FOCUSED PREVENTION PRIORITIES

From a developmental perspective, maltreated children's experiences with their caregivers may have their greatest significance in terms of the formation of positive relationships with others and contentment in their social environment. For example, the formation of attachment is one of the most critical early developmental tasks, which is believed to set the stage for subsequent relationship formation (Sroufe & Fleeson, 1986). In the field of child maltreatment, the attachment concept has been theoretically linked to the perpetuation of maltreatment across generations (Kaufman & Zigler, 1989), the failure of these children to form subsequent relationships with others (Erickson, Sroufe, & Egeland, 1985), and their vulnerability to additional developmental failures that rely to some extent on early attachment success (Aber & Allen, 1987). Not surprisingly, Cicchetti, Toth, and Bush (1988) report that the vast majority of maltreated infants form insecure attachments with their caregivers (70% to 100% across studies). This poor resolution of attachment may be most significant in terms of influencing a child's relationship formation with peers, future partners, and future offspring.

Such findings regarding the broad and diverse developmental disabilities of maltreated children point to the importance of studying abuse and neglect in terms of socialization practices, rather than in terms of individual acts of commission or omission. Accordingly, the impact of maltreatment on a child's development must be considered in relation to the *overall quality of care* that the child is exposed to over time.

An important challenge to our understanding of the effects of maltreatment and our concomitant response to this problem lies in our recognition that the effects are dependent on different stages of the child's development and the presence or absence of health-promoting factors (e.g., family stability, alternatives to physical punishment). Such a view provides special attention to developmental limitations and abilities of children who have experienced various forms of maltreatment, and is an optimistic framework for establishing early prevention and intervention goals.

If we accept the theoretical and philosophical argument that maltreatment is indirectly responsible for a myriad of developmental problems, then our understanding of the behavioral and emotional adjustment problems shown by maltreated children rests on an awareness of their developmental deficits (in addition to some direct effects of maltreatment or insensitive parenting). Such a position carries with it important implications for establishing intervention and prevention goals. First of all, it is important to recognize the developmental differences that may emerge as a function of maltreatment. An individual child's symptoms may be an understandable result of his or her efforts to learn social behaviors without the benefit of sensitive parenting or careful guidance. Accordingly, the identified "referral concern" may shift from one that assesses current problematic behavior alone toward one that identifies the developmental concerns that underlie such expressions. This premise directs intervention to the strengthening of developmentally relevant tasks or skills, in addition to specific presenting complaints.

A developmentally guided intervention and prevention strategy works on the principle of providing the least intrusive, earliest assistance possible, instead of relying on aversive contingencies. The focus of intervention can be shifted away from identifying misdeeds of the parent, and more toward promoting an optimal balance between the needs of the child and the abilities of the parent.

The developmental course of children from such family environments typically proceeds unabated. Maltreated children are more likely to associate with delinquent peers and engage in antisocial behaviors (Malamuth, Sockloskie, Koss, & Tanaka, 1991; Patterson, DeBaryshe, & Ramsey, 1989), which further serves to impair their ability to master important developmental tasks. Moreover, such associations perpetuate attitudes, motivations, emotions, and beliefs that encourage the likelihood of coercive behavior. This course, combined with added cultural stereotypes for men and women, may lead to both sexual and nonsexual forms of acting out during adolescence and young adulthood in attempts to control and coerce others (Dutton, 1988).

STRENGTHENING PARENTAL COMPETENCY

Most families require some degree of assistance in child rearing today, especially during the child's early years. This view derives from the simple principle that a parent who is well-prepared for the life changes associated with child rearing is less likely to succumb to the increasing stress factors that prevail. This viewpoint supports the principles of preventive mental health — skills, knowledge, and experiences that boost the individual's coping abilities (e.g., their sense of mastery and control over stressful aspects of their role) will increase their resistance to the forces that oppose their healthy adjustment (Dohrenwend, 1978). Such parents are said to be *socially competent*, in that they are able to apply interpersonal skills to meet the demands of the situation and provide positive outcomes for all persons involved. Socially competent parents display interpersonal strengths (e.g., praising, complimenting, or showing affection), and they are able to observe the demands of a situation in order to choose the appropriate response (Burgess, 1985). The parent who is socially incompetent, on the other hand, fosters incompetence in the child who, in turn, reacts aversively to the parent. A vicious cycle of rejection, depression, or low self-esteem may result, leading to child maladjustment and parent-child conflict.

Developmental research informs us that a style of cooperation tends to develop reciprocally among parents and children from a very early point in time. Parents who are themselves cooperative and attentive to their child's needs and capabilities tend to have children who are similarly cooperative and easier to manage. In sharp contrast, parents who rely on intrusive and power assertive methods of control are more likely to have offspring who reciprocate in kind with annoying and disruptive behavior, and who will fail to acquire prosocial behaviors. Thus it is important to consider the major factors associated with the development of healthy versus high-risk parent-child relationships, and to investigate intervention methods that promote such relationships from the earliest point in time.

Prenatal Factors

The importance of proper prenatal care in establishing the early beginnings of the parent-child relationship is supported by both medical and psychological research. In terms of intrauterine care, serious disturbances in fetal growth and development, as well as later disturbances of the newborn, can be affected prenatally by maternal nutrition, age, substance abuse, and viral and bacterial infections. Mother's (and perhaps father's) use of drugs, alcohol, and cigarettes have been linked to infant prematurity, low birth weight, slowed development, and the "difficult child syndrome." These health factors, in addition to genetic endowment, can lead to physical and mental handicaps that impair the mother's and child's later abilities to establish strong ties. Fortunately, there is emerging evidence that many of these problems can be prevented by proper education, medical care, and assistance provided during the prenatal period.

Maternal adjustment and preparation for parenthood are also believed to affect complications during pregnancy, labor, and delivery. This is a grave concern among mothers who experience extreme stress or depression during pregnancy, due either to exogenous conditions (such as relationship conflict or violence, financial instability) or endogenous factors (such as hormonal changes or personality functioning). In addition, how well both parents prepare for their role certainly affects their degree of success with the newborn. Prospective studies (e.g., Brunnquell, Crichton, & Egeland, 1981; Egeland, Breitenbucher, & Rosenberg, 1980) have shown that high life stress and change during pregnancy are linked to abuse and related problems, especially among mothers who were anxious, unknowledgeable about children, and ill-prepared. Once again, such negative outcomes can be prevented during this period of development. The provision of an adequate support system (e.g., family members, nurse visitors, etc.) seems to mitigate the effects of life stress and personal adaptation to a significant degree.

Postnatal/Infancy Factors

The formation of healthy infant-caregiver attachment represents a major task during this developmental period, which may have a significant effect on the quality of subsequent patterns of care. Parents who were poorly adjusted or prepared before the child's birth are more likely to have negative outcomes with their child, regardless of the child's birth status (e.g., prematurity, illness, etc.). Furthermore, children who receive poor quality of care during early infancy have been found to show interactional patterns of avoidance or anxious attachment to their caregivers, which leads to further developmental decline (Egeland & Sroufe, 1981). In contrast, the parent who is well-prepared for life changes associated with child rearing is less likely to succumb to the increasing stress factors that prevail. Skills, knowledge, experiences, and support that boost the individual's coping abilities will increase their resistance to forces that oppose their healthy adjustment. The same holds true for the infant, whose temperament and responsiveness contribute in important ways to his or her own treatment.

Infancy and Early Childhood

During this stage of development, parental resources and responses to the child, as well as the child's opportunity and ability to develop adaptive behavior, appear to be critical determinants of the parent-child relationship. Specific qualities that reflect competence in the parenting role, and thereby enhance the parent-child relationship, include such actions as verbal communication that provides information and stimulation to the infant, physical freedom for the infant to explore his or her environment, responsiveness to the infant's needs in a manner that is consistent with his or her developmental level, and positive affect that accompanies all supportive verbal and physical interactions (Cicchetti et al., 1988).

In brief, if the parent's responses to the young child are age appropriate, peer supported, and otherwise successful from the perspective of the parent's wishes and the child's needs, the risk of relying on power assertive control tactics or avoidance may be reduced, and the child's development of adaptive abilities will be enhanced. The value of early assistance and support programs for new families and disadvantaged families is apparent from these findings.

ILLUSTRATIVE PREVENTION PROGRAMS

Prevention and early intervention programs for adults and teens who have not been specifically identified as abusive or neglectful are founded primarily on the premise that promoting a *positive and responsive parent-child relationship* is both a desirable intervention target as well as a viable child maltreatment-prevention strategy. The rationale for such programs is straightforward: Many families with very young children (under 24 months of age) are not yet experiencing the serious child behavior management problems that bring their counterparts with preschool and school-age children to the attention of child protection agencies. Parent-child interactions are still relatively benign although subtle indications of future problems may be present. If parents can be assisted in their role at this early stage, the chances of influencing patterns of parenting and promoting healthier parent-infant relationships are improved. Ipso facto, the likelihood of relational failure and signs of child abuse and neglect are diminished (Wekerle & Wolfe, 1992).

A common feature in many programs aimed at early intervention of child maltreatment and/or developmental delay is the home-visitor component, in which a professional or trained lay person visits the family home to provide parenting-related instruction and to act as a liaison with other community and health care systems. Thus, chiefly through education and support, these programs strive to enhance adult competency to help parents gain control over their lives (Pransky, 1991). Family support programs may be directed at various types of parents who are at risk of maltreatment, such as parents who have been identified and referred for assistance, new parents who require or request support in their role, and teen parents who lack the maturity and resources necessary for adequate childcare.

Wekerle and Wolfe (1992) recently reviewed 24 studies that involved parents and young adults who represented various degrees of risk status regarding maltreatment and child development, and which used adequate evaluation procedures. Most of these studies fall under the heading of "family support programs," which are philosophically committed to enhancing parental competence and reducing stress factors that impair the formation of a positive and healthy parent-child relationship. In the main, family support studies of at-risk parents have found short-term positive outcomes, particularly for *parental* outcome measures and for those mothers deemed at greatest risk (e.g., poor, single, young; Booth, Mitchell, Barnard, & Spieker, 1989; Frankel, 1988; Seitz, Rosenbaum, & Apfel, 1985). Although positive gains have been found in terms of indirect measures of parental behavior (knowledge and attitudes), several studies have also found improvements in observed parental behavior and, to a lesser extent, indicators of maltreatment (e.g., child abuse reports). Also, these studies show that family support programs improve general maternal functioning rather than specific dimensions of personal adjustment (e.g., Gaudin, Wodarski, Arkinson, & Avery, 1991; Teleen, Herzog, & Kilbane, 1989).

There is initial, but persuasive, evidence to suggest that multilevel programs (i.e., offering additional services as parents require them over a longer period of time) are worth the additional effort and expense, compared to less intensive services for higher risk families (Olds & Kitzman, 1990). For example, the Resource Mother program, which provided pre- and postnatal care to disadvantaged teens (Unger & Wandersman, 1988), found that the earlier in pregnancy the teens were recruited, the more likely it was that they would continue participation once their child was born. Consistent with the principles of community mental health noted above, it is reasonable to assume that greater involvement in intervention may lead to greater identification with and ownership of the growth process set in motion by preventive efforts.

Overall, Wekerle and Wolfe (1992) conclude that those programs that span from 1 to 3 years and provide a personalized approach (e.g., home visits) stand out as most successful in achieving the desired outcomes and most successful with higher risk individuals, a conclusion shared by Roberts, Wasik, Casto, and Ramey (1991) in their review of informal and formal home visiting programs. This apparent intervention-population matching may be best understood by considering the often isolated, unskilled, and impoverished characteristics of these mothers. That is, their need for support, parenting instruction, and resource linkage seems to be fulfilled by the more personalized, outreach nature of the home visitor approach.

Findings reported in their review also generally support the utility and cost-benefit of (a) home visits, especially those begun prior to the onset of maltreatment, (b) specific skills training that addresses parental misperceptions and false expectations of young children, (c) specific skills training that promotes alternatives to physical punishment and the use of more prosocial, developmentally relevant activities for the parent to engage in with his or her child, (d) parental competency programs broadly aimed at nonidentified individuals, a strategy that reduces concerns due to labeling and detection, and (e) preschool-based programs for child victims, which emphasize developmental gains and prosocial peer interactions.

RESEARCH NEEDS AND FUTURE DIRECTIONS

SELECTION OF PARTICIPANTS

A current roadblock to the implementation of effective early intervention and prevention programming is the lack of information pertaining specifically to the nature of the population. Unfortunately, little specificity is provided by researchers that allows one to match intervention type to individual needs of persons or families.

The decision as to who should receive preventive services is often a difficult and ambiguous one. Concerns for the efficient use of funds have often popularized a narrow definition of the target population to include only those individuals having specific "risk indicators." Although understandable, this practice raises some precautions regarding the identification and participation of individuals determined to be at risk. The problem of determining risk status is complicated by the absence of clearcut guidelines for identification procedures, the lack of complete knowledge concerning risk factors, and the relatively low incidence of child maltreatment in the general population (Caldwell, Bogat, & Davidson, 1988). Thus, if identification procedures are faulty, those identified as at risk may be subjected to a variety of

adverse consequences (e.g., derogatory labels, self-fulfilling proph-
ecy, invasion of privacy).

An alternative approach to targeting subjects with specific risk
indicators should be explored, in which general indicators (e.g., first-
time parenthood) serve as entry criteria for prevention programs. An
advantage of targeting new parents is that habitual, negative patterns
of parent-child interaction have not been established (although dysfunctional parenting tendencies may be present), and prevention programs are not stigmatized by an "at-risk" label.

THE IMPORTANCE OF MATCHING SERVICES TO THE NEEDS OF PARENTS, CHILDREN, AND FAMILIES: WHAT WORKS FOR WHOM?

A major conclusion reached by Wekerle and Wolfe (1992) was that
no *particular* method of intervention is likely to lead to desirable
outcomes for even a majority of families, especially by the time child
maltreatment has been identified. From a cost-benefit perspective, the
cost of remediating serious child-rearing concerns is prohibitive.

These costs may be reduced by placing greater emphasis on preparing parents for their child-rearing role well in advance of the
emergence of problems, and having a wider range of appropriate
services available. Such a model requires staff who are trained to assist
with families at a level that is most beneficial, rather than attempting
to detect and intervene after the fact. Staff would have to be sensitive
to individual, community, and cultural preferences, as well as socioeconomic limitations, that constitute the majority of disadvantaged
families, and be willing to tolerate such differences for the purpose of
establishing a basis for improving the parent-child relationship. This
approach requires more investment in family development at an earlier
point in time, but holds considerable promise in reducing the costs and
failures of the current reactive system.

On what basis should early intervention services be provided and
matched to families? There is an urgent need to match interventions
to the needs of each family as best as possible. Although this seems
obvious, the literature shows repeated attempts to design and implement a particular strategy to any given sample of maltreating parents,
with little regard to the needs of each participant (especially cultural
and ethnic minorities; see below). Whereas some parents require

information and assistance in basic child rearing, many others require social support, childcare respite, and/or personal counseling. Yet the interventions persist in attempting to fit the patient to the cure, rather than the reverse. Although the expanding multiservice programs are promising in this regard, they lack thorough evaluation and follow-up, and tend to have weak or inadequate research designs (e.g., Project 12-Ways; Wesch & Lutzker, 1991).

Willett, Ayoub, and Robinson (1991), for example, found a sizable group of at-risk families that showed no change at all in family functioning over time, even after lengthy intervention involving parenting skills and community supports. These researchers speculate that intervention may be serving to *maintain* family functioning at its initial level and prevent decline (no untreated control group was used in this study, however). Families who respond well to structured intervention may actually be leaving the programs after a relatively brief period of time; ipso facto, families who remain in treatment are more likely to show "zero growth" and take up the majority of resources just to maintain their entry level of functioning. This conjecture, if correct, has important implications for the delivery of services to families in need, due to limited resources and the importance of reaching families at the earliest point in time.

Moreover, few prevention or intervention programs have been directed at the developmental needs of abused and neglected children. Rather, treatment has been predominately aimed at adults (Fantuzzo, 1990). Although our understanding of the developmental impact of these problems has grown, efforts to remediate and/or prevent such problems have been slow to develop. Neglected children, in particular, suffer major psychological consequences that have been inadequately addressed by current approaches.

FINDING EFFECTIVE WAYS TO ADDRESS COROLLARY FAMILY PROBLEMS

To date, the potentiating effects of socioeconomic stress, family disadvantage, and substance abuse on abuse and neglect have not received adequate attention. Although most researchers acknowledge the presence and impact of these contextual factors, few approaches have been designed to address these problems in a systematic manner. Although multiservice programs are promising in this regard, they have not as yet provided adequate evaluation data. Similarly, the influence of the parent's competing (negative) lifestyle and habits, that is often cited as a major concomitant factor among maltreating families, has been addressed only serendipitously, rather than systematically. This fact leads to the recommendation that service delivery be expanded to include multiservice capabilities to address the negative influence of major contextual stress factors on effective family functioning. Subsidized daycare and housing, respite programs, homemaker services, and so on show promise in this regard, but require systematic implementation and evaluation.

PROGRAMS TO ADDRESS THE NEEDS OF ETHNIC MINORITIES

Attention must be directed to societal influences that play a role in child abuse and neglect, especially in circumstances where families are exposed to major effects of poverty, health risks, and environmental conflict (Sipes, 1992). Research needs to identify the special risks and strengths of diverse cultural and ethnic groups, and to be sensitive to ethnic and cultural issues in the planning of services (Fantuzzo, 1990). Such a cross-cultural perspective to child abuse and neglect intervention and prevention would redirect the focus away from individuals and families, and explore societal and cultural conditions that attenuate or exacerbate these problems. Although there is a general lack of research with maltreated children from ethnic and minority communities, adequate information exists to recommend the implementation and evaluation of culturally relevant intervention and prevention methods (Sipes, 1992).

PROGRAMS AIMED AT ADOLESCENTS

Youth represent a sizable proportion of child maltreatment reports (Garbarino, 1992), but they typically receive less than adequate assistance. From an intervention perspective, there is reason to support the extension of programs that have shown effectiveness with clinically referred youth to an at-risk youth population. The most effective programs for parent-adolescent conflict, which have been in existence for several years, involve several components, such as effective communication, parent training, contingency management, and family therapy (see, for example, Foster & Robin, 1988). Although such methods may not be capable of overcoming very longstanding parent-adolescent conflict and maltreatment, they may be effective in addressing the emerging issues that accompany adolescent development, especially for families with a limited history of protective service involvement.

On a more primary level, prevention services for youth populations could integrate educational concepts (e.g., attitudes and knowledge issues affecting healthy versus violent relationships) with practical skills aimed at noncontrolling conflict resolution. Such efforts have been undertaken recently by school boards (e.g., Jaffe, Sudermann, & Reitzel, in press) and by protective service agencies (Wolfe, 1992), following from the belief that this age group offers a unique window of opportunity to challenge existing beliefs and attitudes concerning the use of power and aggression toward others. Accordingly, educationally focused prevention programs targeted to low- and high-risk adolescents merit development and evaluation in schools, communities, and service agencies, on such topics as control and power in relationships, sexual and physical violence, and family and child-rearing values.

THE NEED FOR A MULTISERVICE, PUBLIC HEALTH MODEL OF ONGOING SUPPORT FOR FAMILIES

Given its prevalence, child maltreatment can be compared to other major threats to public health, such as AIDS, childhood diseases, poverty, and home safety. Therefore, it makes sense in the long run to address the causes of this problem from a public health vantage point, rather than tertiary intervention. Evidence for the effectiveness of such a model can be found in reports from Scandinavian countries. Sweden, Finland, and Denmark all have nationwide programs that resemble the family support programs being explored in the United States. In addition, these countries have the benefits of universal insurance, free tuition for academic and vocational training, paid educational leave to upgrade skills, yearly cash allowances for each child under age 16 and for nonworking mothers for 6 months during pregnancy, maternal

child health services, subsidized primary health care, and other benefits. Pransky (1991) summarizes the results of these benefits:

- Ninety-five percent of pregnant mothers start prenatal care before the
  end of the fourth month, compared to less than 85% in the United
  States.
- Fewer than 4% of mothers are under the age of 20 at the time of their
  first birth, compared with 10% in the United States.
- Infant mortality rates and births of low birth-weight babies are among
  the lowest in the world.
- Infant death from respiratory disease rate is 22-67 per 100,000 (com-
  pared with 107/100,000 in the United States).
- Prevalence of mild mental retardation is 8-10 times lower than in the
  United States.
- **Rates of child abuse are about 8 times lower than in the United
  States.**

Expenditures for health care as a percentage of gross national
product (GNP) in these countries are less as well (7%-10% versus 11%
in the United States). The percentage of GNP spent on social services,
however, is much greater (25%-35% versus 18% in the United States).
We should keep these comparative expense figures in mind when
considering the costs of the current U.S. approach to child-rearing and
family concerns. For example, on a national basis it cost approximately $19 billion in 1987 to assist families that were started by
teenagers; nearly 66% of daughters of single women later go on
welfare; and the costs of providing high-quality prenatal care are
almost double for high-risk infants, on average, than the costs for
normal, low-risk infants ($706 vs. $476, respectively; Child Welfare
League of America, 1989).

As noted by Pransky (1991), such family support programs as those
in place in Scandinavian countries have considerable social and political appeal: "strengthening and promoting well-functioning, independent, self-supporting families that produce children who, in turn, will
become independent, self-supporting adults" (p. 59). Thus a public
health approach to the prevention of child abuse and neglect is a promising strategy that merits serious consideration (Willis, Holden, &
Rosenberg, 1992). Such a strategy would not undermine existing
efforts at treatment and early intervention, but rather would be de-

signed to approach the widespread problem of child maltreatment from a broader, more fundamental vantage point.

REFERENCES

Aber, J. L., & Allen, J. P. (1987). Effects of maltreatment on young children's socioemotional development: An attachment theory perspective. *Developmental Psychology, 23,* 406-414.

Azar, S. T., & Wolfe, D. A. (1989). Child abuse and neglect. In E. J. Mash & R. A. Barkley (Eds.), *Treatment of childhood disorders* (pp. 451-493). New York: Guilford.

Belsky, J. (1984). The determinants of parenting: A process model. *Child Development, 55,* 83-96.

Booth, C. L., Mitchell, S. K., Barnard, K. E., & Spieker, S. J. (1989). Development of maternal social skills in multiproblem families: Effects on the mother-child relationship. *Developmental Psychology, 25,* 403-412.

Brunnquell, D., Crichton, L., & Egeland, B. (1981). Maternal personality and attitude in disturbances of child rearing. *American Journal of Orthopsychiatry, 51,* 680-691.

Burgess, R. L. (1985). Social incompetence as a precipitant to and consequences of child maltreatment. *Victimology: An International Journal, 10,* 72-86.

Caldwell, R. A., Bogat, G. A., & Davidson, W. S., II. (1988). The assessment of child abuse potential and the prevention of child abuse and neglect: A policy analysis. *American Journal of Community Psychology, 16,* 609-624.

Child Welfare League of America. (1989). *Children's legislative agenda.* Washington, DC: Author.

Cicchetti, D., & Rizley, R. (1981). Developmental perspectives on the etiology, intergenerational transmission, and sequelae of child maltreatment. In D. Cicchetti & R. Rizley (Eds.), *New directions for child development: Developmental perspectives on child maltreatment* (pp. 31-55). San Francisco: Jossey-Bass.

Cicchetti, D., Toth, S., & Bush, M. (1988). Developmental psychopathology and incompetence in childhood: Suggestions for intervention. In B. B. Lahey & A. E. Kazdin (Eds.), *Advances in clinical child psychology* (Vol. 11, pp. 1-77). New York: Plenum.

Cohn, A. H., & Daro, D. (1987). Is treatment too late: What ten years of evaluative research tell us. *Child Abuse & Neglect, 11,* 433-442.

Dohrenwend, B. (1978). Social stress and community psychology. *American Journal of Community Psychology, 6,* 1-14.

Drotar, D. (1992). Prevention of neglect and non-organic failure to thrive. In D. J. Willis, E. W. Holden, & M. Rosenberg (Eds.), *Prevention of child maltreatment: Development and ecological perspectives* (pp. 115-149). New York: Wiley.

Dutton, D. G. (1988). *The domestic assault of women: Psychological and criminal justice perspectives.* Boston: Allyn & Bacon.

Egeland, B., & Sroufe, A. (1981). Attachment and early maltreatment. *Child Development, 52,* 44-52.

Egeland, B., Breitenbucher, M., & Rosenberg, D. (1980). Prospective study of the significance of life stress in the etiology of child abuse. *Journal of Consulting and Clinical Psychology, 48,* 195-205.

Erickson, M. F., Sroufe, L. A., & Egeland, B. (1985). The relationship between quality of attachment and relationship problems in preschool in a high-risk sample. In I. Bretherton &

E. Waters (Eds.), *Monographs of the Society for Research in Child Development, 50*(1-2), 147-166.

Fantuzzo, J. W. (1990). Behavioral treatment of the victims of child abuse and neglect. *Behavior Modification, 14*, 316-339.

Fink, A., & McCloskey, L. (1990). Moving child abuse and neglect prevention programs forward: Improving program evaluations. *Child Abuse & Neglect, 14*, 187-206.

Foster, S. L., & Robin, A. L. (1988). Family conflict and communication in adolescents. In E. J. Mash & L. G. Terdal (Eds.), *Behavioral assessment of childhood disorders* (2nd ed., pp. 717-775). New York: Guilford.

Frankel, H. (1988). Family-centered home-based services in child protection: A review of the research. *Social Service Review, 61*, 137-157.

Garbarino, J. (1992). Preventing adolescent maltreatment. In D. J. Willis, E. W. Holden, & M. Rosenberg (Eds.), *Prevention of child maltreatment: Developmental and ecological perspectives* (pp. 94-114). New York: Wiley.

Gaudin, J. M., Jr., Wodarski, J. S., Arkinson, M. K., & Avery, L. S. (1991). Remedying child neglect: Effectiveness of social network interventions. *Journal of Applied Social Sciences, 15*, 97-123.

Jaffe, P. G., Sudermann, M., & Reitzel, D. (in press). An evaluation of a secondary school programme on violence in intimate relationships. *Violence and Victims.*

Kaufman, J., & Zigler, E. (1989). The intergenerational transmission of child abuse and the prospect of predicting future abusers. In D. Cicchetti & V. Carlson (Eds.), *Child maltreatment: Research and theory on the causes and consequences of child abuse and neglect* (pp. 129-150). New York: Cambridge University Press.

Malamuth, N. M., Sockloskie, R. J., Koss, M. P., & Tanaka, J. S. (1991). Characteristics of aggressors against women: Testing a model using a national sample of college students. *Journal of Consulting and Clinical Psychology, 59*, 670-681.

Mash, E. J., & Wolfe, D. A. (1991). Methodological issues in research on physical child abuse. *Criminal Justice and Behavior, 18*, 8-29.

Olds, D. L., & Kitzman, H. (1990). Can home visitation improve the health of women and children at environmental risk? *Pediatrics, 86*, 108-116.

Patterson, G. R., DeBaryshe, B. D., & Ramsey, E. (1989). A developmental perspective on antisocial behavior. *American Psychologist, 44*, 329-335.

Pransky, J. (1991). *Prevention: The critical need.* Springfield, MO: Burrell Foundation.

Roberts, R. N., Wasik, B. H., Casto, G., & Ramey, C. T. (1991). Family support in the home: Programs, policy, and social change. *American Psychologist, 46*, 131-137.

Seitz, V., Rosenbaum, L. K., & Apfel, N. H. (1985). Effects of family support intervention: A ten-year follow-up. *Child Development, 56*, 376-391.

Sipes, D.S.B. (1992). *Review of the literature on cultural considerations in treatment of abused and neglected ethnic minority children.* Paper prepared for the Working Group on Treatment of Child Abuse and Neglect, American Psychological Association.

Sroufe, L. A., & Fleeson, J. (1986). Attachment and the construction of relationships. In W. W. Hartup & Z. Rubin (Eds.), *Relationships and development* (pp. 51-71). Hillsdale, NJ: Lawrence Erlbaum.

Teleen, S., Herzog, B. S., & Kilbane, T. L. (1989). Impact of a family support program on mothers' social support and parenting stress. *American Journal of Orthopsychiatry, 59*, 410-419.

Unger, D. G., & Wandersman, L. P. (1988). A support program for adolescent mothers: Predictors of participation. In D. R. Powell (Ed.), *Parent education as early childhood intervention: Emerging directions in theory, research, and practice* (pp. 105-130). Norwood, NJ: Ablex.

Videka-Sherman, L. (1989, October). *Therapeutic issues for physical and emotional child abuse and neglect: Implications for longitudinal research.* Paper presented at research forum Issues in the Longitudinal Study of Child Maltreatment, Institute for the Prevention of Child Abuse, Toronto, Canada.

Wekerle, C., & Wolfe, D. A. (1992). *An empirical review of prevention strategies for child abuse and neglect.* Manuscript submitted for publication.

Wesch, D., & Lutzker, J. R. (1991). A comprehensive 5-year evaluation of project 12-Ways: An ecobehavioral program for treating and preventing child abuse and neglect. *Journal of Family Violence, 6,* 17-35.

Willett, J. B., Ayoub, C. C., & Robinson, D. (1991). Using growth modeling to examine systematic differences in growth: An example of chance in the functioning of families at risk of maladaptive parenting, child abuse, or neglect. *Journal of Consulting and Clinical Psychology, 59,* 38-47.

Willis, D. J., Holden, E. W., & Rosenberg, M. (1992). Child maltreatment prevention: Introduction and historical overview. In D. J. Willis, E. W. Holden, & M. Rosenberg (Eds.), *Prevention of child maltreatment: Developmental and ecological perspectives* (pp. 1-14). New York: Wiley.

Wolfe, D. A. (1987). *Child abuse: Implications for child development and psychopathology.* Newbury Park, CA: Sage.

Wolfe, D. A. (1990). Preventing child abuse means enhancing family functioning. *Canada's Mental Health, 38,* 27-29.

Wolfe, D. A. (1992). *Promoting healthy, non-violent relationships among at-risk youth* (Research progress report to the Institute for the Prevention of Child Abuse). Toronto: Canada.

343

REDUCING THE LITERAL AND HUMAN COST OF CHILD ABUSE: IMPACT OF A NEW HOSPITAL MANAGEMENT SYSTEM

Eli H. Newberger, M.D., John J. Hagenbuch, A.C.S.W., Nancy B. Ebeling, A.C.S.W., Elizabeth Pivchik Colligan, A.C.S.W., Jane S. Sheehan, R.N., and Susan H. McVeigh, B.A.

From the Children's Hospital Medical Center, the Division of Family and Children's Services of the Massachusetts Department of Public Welfare, and Children's Protective Services, Boston, Massachusetts

ABSTRACT. Social service personnel from one public and two voluntary agencies were integrated into a consultation group in an academic pediatric hospital, leading to a reduction in the actual cost of medical services and the risk of reinjury subsequent to the diagnosis of child abuse. In the 1969–1970 hospital year, 62 cases of child abuse were seen, of which 39 were hospitalized. The average hospital stay was 29 days; the average hospital cost $3,000. Total hospital costs for the 39 cases were $123,000, of which bed costs made up $95,000. There were at least three subsequent incidents of child abuse in these 39 cases, and there was one subsequent death; the reinjury rate was 10% for hospitalized cases.

In September 1970 the Trauma X Group, an interdisciplinary, interagency consultation unit based in the hospital, was formed. With formal consultation and continued surveillance after discharge by the Trauma X Group, the following data were obtained from the 1970–1971 hospital year. Of 86 cases, 60 were hospitalized. The average hospital stay was 17 days; the average hospital cost $2,500. Total hospital costs for the 60 cases was $150,000, of which bed costs made up $101,000. There was one incident of reinjury and no deaths subsequent to diagnosis in these 60 cases; the reinjury rate was 1.7%. The risk of reinjury calculated from a modified life table was reduced from 8% in the year previous to the formation of the group to 7% and 2%, respectively, in the subsequent year and six-month periods, supporting the dollar-cost impression of effectiveness. Foster placement, furthermore, was infrequent and does not explain the differential impact of the Trauma X Group in the intervals under study. *Pediatrics*, 51:840, 1973, CHILD ABUSE, BATTERED CHILD SYNDROME, QUALITY OF CARE, EVALUATION OF FAMILY INTERVENTION.

T HE challenge posed by the initial recognition or suspicion of child abuse is traditionally met by the personnel of a hospital in an urban setting in a variety of ways, ranging from frank refusal to accept the diagnosis to a quick proferring of a variety of professional services.[1] Occasionally, but not always, a long-range therapeutic plan, with particular attention to continuing supportive relationships, is developed by physician, nurse, psychiatrist, and social worker as the diagnostic formulation and communication with the relevant community agencies proceeds.

Experience at our hospital and elsewhere indicates, however, that even the best-laid plans seem frequently to be frustrated by a combination of factors associated with those severe family crises where a child's life falls into jeopardy.[2] These include the personalities of his parents, for whom denial and projection often serve as principal means of ego defense[3]; his family's anxious confusion in confronting an array of clinical specialty services and social agencies working disconjugately to protect their child from themselves[4,5]; the exigencies of life in poverty, including mistrust of community

(Received November 1, 1972; revision accepted for publication January 22, 1973.)

The work reported in this paper was supported in part by grants from the Office of Child Development, Department of HEW (Project OCD-62-141), and from the Office of Justice Administration, Boston, Massachusetts (Project 70-046). It was presented in part at the Annual Meeting of the American Pediatric Society in May 1972.

ADDRESS FOR REPRINTS: (E.H.N.) The Children's Hospital Medical Center, 300 Longwood Avenue, Boston, Massachusetts 02115.

TABLE I

SOCIAL DIAGNOSTIC DATA FOR PRESENTATION AT TRAUMA X MEETING

Date
Division/Clinic
Patient's First Name
DOB _____

Social Worker: _____ Address _____
REFERRAL: _____ DATE: _____
DESCRIPTION OF INJURY: _____
FAMILY CONSTELLATION:
  Names/B.D.–Parents:
  Ethnic Group:
  Employment–Source of Income:
  Names/B.D.-Siblings:

PREVIOUS AND CURRENT COMMUNITY CONTACTS:
  Worker:
  Agency:
  When:

INTERVIEW(S) WITH PARENTS: DATES: WHERE:
  Attitude toward injury/hospitalization:
  Perceptions/Expectations of child:
  Parents' view of own upbringings:
  Family Stresses:

POTENTIAL STRENGTHS:
  1. Family
  2. Supportive personal ties:
    a. Neighborhood
    b. Agency
    c. School
    d. Church, etc.

DIAGNOSTIC IMPRESSION:

TREATMENT PLAN:

GAPS IN MANAGEMENT:

IMPRESSIONS OF OUTCOME
  1. Without intervention
  2. With recommended plan

QUESTIONS FOR DISCUSSION:

TRAUMA MEETING NOTES:

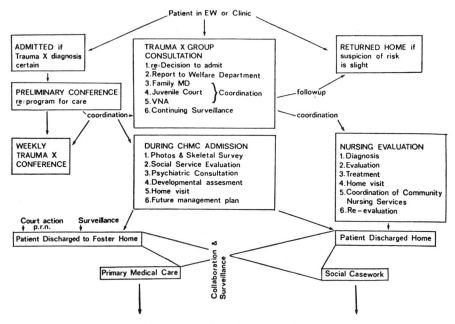

FIG. 1. Management model for Trauma X cases.

institutions, racism, unemployment, and drugs[6]; the clinical team's frustration generated by missed appointments, confrontations with angry parents, and time-consuming contacts with outside agencies; and conflicts among the responsible personnel stemming from the emotions brought forth by prolonged contact with disturbed families.[7]

No one can adequately measure the human cost of child abuse. The present study is designed to demonstrate the effectiveness of a collaborative community effort to provide more nearly adequate preventive and therapeutic help to the victims of child abuse and their families. The evaluation of dollar costs and of a very crude measure of the behavioral effectiveness of intervention —the reinjury of a child—is intended both to promote awareness of the considerable literal and human expense of these cases, and to show how this toll can be reduced by an effort to coordinate human services of a kind which in the United States are generally isolated in State Departments of Welfare and fragmented among institutions whose programs attend to specific aspects of child health, mental health, and social welfare.

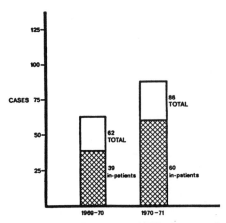

FIG. 2. Trauma X patients, Children's Hospital Medical Center, Boston, Massachusetts.

METHODS

In September 1970 an interdisciplinary, interagency consultation unit, the Trauma X Group, was formed at Children's Hospital in response to a crisis in the system for the protection of children living in Massachusetts.[8]

A shortage of personnel in the state agency designated by law to receive reports of child abuse cases and to provide protective services led to an appraisal of the prevailing method of hospital case management. Until that time, physicians had simply reported cases of suspected inflicted injury to the Department of Public Welfare, whose resources to deliver protective social services were severely limited. The number of injuries subsequent to initial diagnosis were apparently high, and our staff—as well as our colleagues in the Welfare Department—agreed that a more systematic program of case-finding, evaluation, intervention, and follow-up was necessary.

Accordingly, a group of interested individuals reviewed the problem; house management guidelines were written; and a concerted effort was made to recruit the interest and support of the chiefs of the clinical departments and the administration of the hospital. The functions of the Trauma X Group were defined as follows:

1. To become informed of each new case of inflicted injury or neglect.

2. To participate in the formulation of the plan for disposition and continuing care of the child.

3. Periodically to review the entire active hospital roster of Trauma X cases for purposes of evaluation and quality control.

4. To develop, in conjunction with the Department of Public Welfare, a unified proposal to the Juvenile Court in those cases where legal action was necessary. A designated member of the Trauma X Group would represent the hospital staff in court in such situations.

5. To educate the house staff, social service staff, and nursing staff in the pathogenesis of the problem and enlightened approaches to its control.

6. To serve as a focus at the Hospital for advancing the competence of the Boston community to deal effectively with child abuse and neglect. This function included the development of better channels of communication with other agencies and the discussion of health policy alternatives which affected the index population.

7. To carry on research into the determinants and concomitants of child abuse and neglect. This role integrated the responsibilities to monitor the clinical progress of the hospital population and to advance knowledge of the field in etiology and in the methodology of intervention.

A management model for the management of all Trauma X cases was proposed to the hospital staff at the time of the organization of the Trauma X Group (Fig. 1).

The three social agencies who regularly offer consultation on the management of

TABLE II

REINJURY AFTER DIAGNOSIS*

	1969–1970	1970–1971
Reinjuries after Trauma X diagnosis	3	1
Deaths subsequent to diagnosis	1	0
Rate of reinjury	4/39 = 10%	1/60 = 1.7%
	(data to 1/1/72)	

* Trauma X inpatients, Children's Hospital Medical Center, Boston, Massachusetts.

TABLE III

TRAUMA X CASES
CUMULATIVE LIFE TABLE DATA

	9/15/69 to 9/14/70	9/15/70 to 9/14/71	9/15/71 to 2/14/72
Person-months observed	307	648	150
Reinjuries in the interval	4	5	1
Risk of reinjury	8%	7%	2%

TABLE IV

LIFE TABLE: 9/15/69 TO 9/14/70

Month After Entry X	Observed At X	Last Anniversary at X	Observed X to (X+1)	First Reinjury X to (X+1)
0–	50	0	50	0
1–	50	3	47	2
2–	45	3	42	1
3–	41	1	40	1
4–	39	3	36	0
5–	36	8	28	0
6–	28	9	19	0
7–	19	5	14	0
8–	14	0	14	0
9–	14	5	9	0
10–	9	3	6	0
11–	6	4	2	0
12–	2			

Month After Entry X	Probability of Reinjury X to (X+1)	Probability of Survival X to (X+1)	Cumulative Probability of Survival to X
0–	0	1.00	1.00
1–	.04	.96	1.00
2–	.02	.98	.96
3–	.02	.98	.94
4–	0	1.00	.92
5–	0	1.00	.92
6–	0	1.00	.92
7–	0	1.00	.92
8–	0	1.00	.92
9–	0	1.00	.92
10–	0	1.00	.92
11–	0	1.00	.92
12–	0	1.00	.92

Risk of reinjury in the interval = 8%

TABLE V

LIFE TABLE: 9/15/70 TO 9/14/71

Month After Entry X	Observed at X	Last Anniversary at X	Observed X to (X+1)	First Reinjury X to (X+1)
0–	107	0	107	0
1–	107	6	101	3
2–	98	11	97	0
3–	87	9	78	0
4–	78	5	73	1
5–	72	16	56	0
6–	56	8	48	0
7–	48	7	41	0
8–	41	9	32	1
9–	31	14	17	0
10–	17	10	7	0
11–	7	6	1	0
12–	1			

Month After Entry X	Probability of Reinjury X to (X+1)	Probability of Survival X to (X+1)	Cumulative Probability of Survival to X
0–	.00	1.00	1.00
1–	.03	.97	1.00
2–	.00	1.00	.97
3–	.00	1.00	.97
4–	.01	.99	.97
5–	.00	1.00	.96
6–	.00	1.00	.96
7–	.00	1.00	.96
8–	.03	.97	.96
9–	.00	1.00	.93
10–	.00	1.00	.93
11–	.00	1.00	.93
12–			

Risk of reinjury in the interval = 7%.

Children's Hospital cases of child abuse, through participation in the Trauma X Group, are the Department of Public Welfare (Inflicted Injury Unit, Division of Family and Children's Services), and two voluntary agencies, Children's Protective Services and Parents' and Children's Services. Regular representation from the Children's Hospital staff at Trauma X meetings comes from the administration and from the departments of medicine, psychiatry, radiology, social service, and nursing. Legal consultation is acquired through several sources: from the hospital's own legal counsel, from a lawyer associated with the Laboratory of Community Psychiatry at the Harvard Medical School, and from a consultant retained for certain protective actions in the Juvenile Court.

A full-time Case Data Coordinator arranges case conferences, takes detailed minutes of the meetings, informs the various personnel involved in management of new developments, and reviews and updates the data on all cases in the file.

Three to five new cases are discussed at a two-hour luncheon conference each week. An effort is made to create an atmosphere which is congenial and unintimidating, both for the personnel from community clinical practice settings who come to the hospital to discuss their cases and for the benefit of our own house officers and professional staff, from whom an adequate flow of information on these cases is essential.

Systematic review of the data pertinent to the formulation of management judgments is helped by a short handout on each case, which is prepared in advance by the hospital social worker. The format of the handout is displayed in Table I.

In December 1972, a problem-oriented record keeping system was introduced for Trauma X cases. It will be reported subsequently.

RESULTS

Figure 2 summarizes the Trauma X patients seen at the Children's Hospital in the hospital years before and after the organization of the Trauma X group in September 1970.

Figure 3 summarizes the literal cost of inpatient Trauma X cases at Children's Hospital. With a reduction of the mean hospital stay from 29 to 17 days in the year following the organization of the Trauma X Group, the disproportionate contribution of the day rate to the total cost was changed appropriately, demonstrating somewhat more efficient management by this criterion of effectiveness. (These fiscal data have been particularly useful in contacts with Welfare Department officials and state legislators in an effort to improve services for these families.)

The rates of reinjury among the hospitalized cases in the hospital years before and after the formation of the Trauma X Group are summarized in Table II.

A more sensitive and accurate estimate of the risk of reinjury can be computed by constructing a life table which measures the total number of person-months contributed by the population of cases under observation in a given time interval. Table III displays the results of the life table analysis of the data from the calendar year preceding the formation of the Trauma X Group and for the subsequent year and half-year intervals. The details of the calculation of risk for the periods under evaluation (9/15/69 to 9/14/70, 9/15/70 to 9/14/71, and 9/15/71 to 2/14/72) are shown on Tables IV, V, and VI. Follow-up information complete to May 1, 1972, is included in this table. The

tests of significance of these data are summarized in Figure 4.

DISCUSSION

The impression of effectiveness in reducing the human cost of child abuse suggested by the crude rates of reinjury is supported equivocally by the life table data, which are not significant when treated by the standard method.[9] Cautious interpretation of this analysis is indicated, furthermore, because the outcome data are affected by an ascertainment bias comprising three principal elements:

1. Follow-up information was more easily available once the program of regular surveillance began.

TABLE VI

LIFE TABLE: 9/15/71 TO 2/14/72

Month After Entry X	Observed at X	Last Anniversary at X	Observed X to (X+1)	First Reinjury X to (X+1)
0–	51	0	51	1
1–	50	9	41	0
2–	41	12	29	0
3–	29	7	22	0
4–	22	15	7	0
5–	7			

	Probability of Reinjury X to (X+1)	Probability of Survival X to (X+1)	Cumulative Probability of Survival to X
0–	.02	.98	1.00
1–	0	1.00	.98
2–	0	1.00	.98
3–	0	1.00	.98
4–	0	1.00	.98
5–			

Risk of reinjury in the interval = 2%

TABLE VII

ASCERTAINMENT BIAS

	Effect on Outcome Data (+ = toward better outcome)		
	1969–1970	1970–1971	1971–1972
Adequacy of follow-up data	+	–	–
Length of follow-up interval	–	+/–	+
Breadth of definition of Trauma X	–	+	+

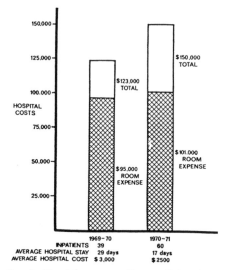

FIG. 3. Hospital expenses, Trauma X inpatients, Children's Hospital Medical Center, Boston, Massachusetts.

TABLE VIII

Presenting Symptoms: Trauma X Cases

	July 1, 1969, to June 30, 1970	July 1, 1970, to June 30, 1971	July 1, 1971, to March 30, 1972
Symptoms:			
Bruises	19	17	36
Burns	5	16	8
Skull fractures	6	6	10
Other bone fractures	11	9	12
Neglect	15	14	16
Head injuries	2	6	7
Lacerations	2	4	3
Poisonings	1	6	4
Abandonments	0	2	1
Deaths	1	2	1
Inpatients	39	60	91
Outpatients	23	26	42
Total cases	62	86	133

TABLE IX

Foster Placement: Trauma X Cases

	1969–1970	1970–1971	1971–1972 (6 months)
Patients	62	86	93
Placed in foster care	9	16	20
Rate	9/26 = 15%	16/86 = 19%	20/93 = 22%

2. Earlier cases have had more time in which to be exposed to reinjury.
3. With increasing diagnostic sophistication, cases with more subtle clinical signs have been included in the index population.

The effects on the outcome data of the bias of ascertainment are summarized on Table VII.

Were children with less serious injuries preferentially selected for inclusion in the series as time went on, the likelihood of reinjury might also have progressively diminished. The nature of the presenting symptoms in the cases in the two hospital years under study indicates that the severity of their injuries did not change. These data are summarized in Table VIII. An indirect inference of the risk to the children in the series may be drawn from the rates at which the judgment was made to separate them from their families. As shown in Table IX, these rates increased slightly. Interestingly, they approximate Kempe's estimate of the number of child abuse cases in which drastic protective intervention, placing children in foster care, is necessary.[10]

There is a discrepancy, however, between Kempe's conception of "the battered child" and our definition of "Trauma X." In his classic paper, Kempe defined the syndrome as follows: "The battered child syndrome is a term used by us to characterize a clinical condition in young children who have received serious physical abuse, generally from a parent or foster parent."[11]

The Children's Hospital euphemism, Trauma X, is defined as a *syndrome with or without inflicted injury, in which a child's survival is threatened in his home.*

This definition focuses on the risk to a child rather than on the *intentions* of a family which has not adequately been able to protect him. In distinction to the process of making a diagnosis of child abuse in the conventional sense, where the *intent* to batter is estimated from contacts with the family, this diagnostic concept tries to measure the capacity of parents to protect their children.

STANDARD ERROR OF RISK:

$$\text{Cum. Surv.} = P_k = p_0\, p_1 \cdots p_{k-1}$$

$$\frac{\partial P_k}{\partial p_i} = \frac{P_k}{p_i}$$

$$S^2 = V(P_k) = \sum_{i=0}^{k-1} \left(\frac{P_k}{p_i}\right)^2 V(p_i)$$

$$= \sum_{i=0}^{k-1} \left(\frac{P_k}{p_i}\right)^2 \frac{p_i q_i}{n_i}$$

$$= P_k^2 \sum_{i=0}^{k-1} \frac{q_i}{p_i n_i}$$

1969 – 70

$$S^2 = .0016 \qquad P_k = .92$$
$$S = .04$$

1970 – 71

$$S^2 = .0012 \qquad P_k = .93$$
$$S = .035$$

1971 – 72

$$S^2 = .0004 \qquad P_k = .98$$
$$S = .02$$

Sig. tests:

H_0 : there is no difference between (69 – 70) and (70 – 71)

$$Z = \frac{.93 - .92}{\sqrt{.0016 + .0012}} = .19 \qquad \text{not sig. } (p = .84)$$

H_0 : there is no difference between (69 – 70)(70 – 71), and (71 – 72)

$$Z = \frac{.93 + .92 - 2\,(.98)}{\sqrt{.0012 + .0016 + 4\,(.0004)}} = 1.67$$

not sig. $(p = .10)$

FIG. 4. Life table significance tests.

In making a diagnosis of child abuse, a clinician can use his technical and human skills to identify what has gone wrong in the family's ability to nurture a child and in an unpunitive way to help them solve their problem with him. Furthermore, these data seem to show that a hospital can serve as an effective portal of entry into the child health and welfare service system for disorganized families whose children's lives are in jeopardy.

REFERENCES

1. Holter, J. C., and Frideman, S. B.: Principles of management in child abuse cases. Amer. J. Orthopsychiat., 38:127, 1968.

2. Rowe, D. S., Leonard, M. F., Seashore, M. R., Lewiston, N. J., and Anderson, F. P.: A hospital program for the detection and registration of abused children. New Eng. J. Med., 282:17, 1970.

3. Steel, B. F., and Pollack, C. B.: A psychiatric study of parents who abuse infants and small children. In Helfer, R. E., Kempe, C. H., eds.: The Battered Child. Chicago, Illinois: University of Chicago Press, 1968, p. 130.

4. Helfer, R. E., and Kempe, C. H.: The child's need for early recognition, immediate care and protection. In Helping the Battered Child and His Family. Philadelphia: J. B. Lippincott, 1972, pp. 70–71.

5. Silver, L. B., Dublin, C. C., and Louris, R. S.: Agency section and interaction in cases of child abuse. Social Casework, pp. 164–71, 1971.

6. Gil, D. G.: Violence Against Children. Cambridge, Massachusetts: Harvard University Press, 1970.

7. Galdston, R.: Violence begins at home. J. Amer. Acad. Child Psych., 10:2, 1971.

8. Newberger, E., Hass, G., and Mulford, R.: Child abuse in Massachusetts. Mass. Physician, 32: 31, 1973.

9. Cutler, S. J., and Ederer, F.: Maximum utilization of the life table method in analyzing survival. J. Chronic Dis., 8:699, 1958.

10. Kempe, C. H.: Pediatric implications of the battered baby syndrome. Arch Dis. Child., 46:24, 1970.

11. Kempe, C. H., Silverman, F. N., Steele, B. F., Droegemueller, W., and Silver, H. K.: The battered child syndrome. JAMA, 181:1, 1962.

Acknowledgment

The authors wish to thank Mrs. Joanne B. Bluestone, Associate Hospital Director, Miss Elizabeth Maginnis, formerly Director, Social Service Department, and Drs. C. A. Janeway and J. B. Richmond, respectively, Chiefs, Departments of Medicine and Psychiatry, Children's Hospital Medical Center, for their enthusiastic support of this work. The able technical assistance of Ms. Ann Marshall, Ms. Anne Matthews, and Ms. Geraldine Farrell is gratefully acknowledged.

Child Abuse: Issues and Answers

By

Senator Walter Mondale

Senator Walter Mondale of Minnesota introduced the Child Care Prevention and Treatment Act which was signed into law by President Nixon January 31, 1974. Senator Mondale is also Chairman of the Senate Subcommittee on Children and Youth, which is currently investigating such problems as day care; crib death syndrome; other child health issues; and trends and pressures in American family life.

For so long the child abuser was the modern Salem witch. We were the horrible monsters who did these things to our children. Yes, the deeds were indeed monstrous but we are not monsters.

> Jolly K., founder of Parents Anonymous,
> before the Senate Subcommittee on
> Children and Youth

Perhaps more than any other witness who testified before my Subcommittee on Children and Youth, a remarkable woman named Jolly K. taught me what child abuse is about.

She made it clear that as a nation, for many years we averted our attention from the horror of child abuse. Unable to cope psychologically with the stories of burning and beating, we assured ourselves that such things didn't really happen very often. If they did happen, we told ourselves, obviously the abuser was taken care of by the criminal justice system. What happened to the child victim in such cases was a little unclear.

I and my colleagues on the Subcommittee on Children and Youth learned a lot during 1973, when we held hearings and fought for federal legislation on child abuse. We would like to think that

many other Americans—the general public as well as those professionally concerned—developed a new understanding and awareness of the scope and complexity of our national child abuse problem. We would also like to think that, with the enactment of the Child Abuse Prevention and Treatment Act, we have taken at least a first step toward addressing this problem on a national scale.

Each year in this country, more than 60,000 children are reported to have been beaten, burned, or otherwise physically abused by adults—usually their parents. I have met some of these children. In a hospital in Washington, D.C. I saw a little girl whose torso and legs had been horribly burned. I have seen pictures of children who were punctured with forks, scarred by cigarette burns, whipped with belts.

My subcommittee received testimony in Washington, Denver, New York, and Los Angeles. We heard from social workers, doctors, lawyers, lay therapists, psychologists, psychiatrists, and abusing parents. Jolly K. told us in her own words how she once threw a knife at her own daughter.

But there was a bright side. Everywhere we went, we found dedicated, concerned people who were giving freely of their time and energy to try to identify child abuse victims and prevent further abuse by rehabilitating their families.

We learned that in Denver and New York and St. Paul, multidisciplinary child abuse teams have made great strides in identification and treatment of child abuse and are working on solutions to the more elusive problem of prevention. We learned that in Hawaii and Florida, concerned officials have taken the lead in developing programs under the auspices of state government. And we learned that many potential programs were stymied for lack of funds.

Before outlining how we hope the new law will operate on the federal level, I would like to outline some of the assumptions underlying its form.

Perhaps the most important conclusion of the Subcommittee's investigation was that existing laws—on both the state and federal level—have simply not done an effective job of dealing with child abuse. We found that almost every state in the Union either passed or updated child abuse legislation in the last ten years. Yet day after day we were reading in the newspapers the sad stories of child abuse cases that were identified too late—only after the child died or suffered permanent damage. One reason the state laws are not working, we concluded, is that they often do not provide for positive programs. The focus is almost entirely on the criminal side—on reporting of cases and prosecution of abusers.

On the federal level, we learned that there was no focused program dealing with child abuse at all. In the entire federal government, not even one person was assigned to work full time on child abuse. Child welfare funds made available to the states under the Social Security Act are limited and can be used for many programs besides prevention and treatment of child abuse.

A second conclusion of the Subcommittee was that a truly effective child abuse program requires a multidisciplinary approach. The medical, legal, and social ramifications of child abuse are terribly complex. No social worker, lawyer, or doctor can or should be expected to deal with all of these problems without the cooperation and assistance of various agencies and experts in several disciplines.

The third conclusion on which the bill was based is more subtle and more controversial. Yet I think that it is the most hopeful discovery we made—that it is possible to treat child abuse, to prevent it from recurring, and to keep together many of the families whose problems have driven them to the extreme of child abuse. New findings indicate that abusers tend to be—as Jolly K. so eloquently told the Subcommittee—people under pressure from other problems. These may be re-lated to alcoholism, drug use, poverty, or marital conflict. Often the child becomes the object of the parent's frustration. And often that very parent was abused as a child.

The main thrust of the legislation is to support demonstration programs designed to prevent, identify, and treat child abuse. A wide variety of agencies, institutions, or individuals can apply for funding. Welfare departments, law enforcement authorities, hospitals, parent organizations, and state governments can all submit applications and be funded if they meet the usual criteria for federal programs. The demonstration programs can be broad—such as the creation of a regional center. Or they could deal with a specific aspect of the child abuse problem, such as training law enforcement officials or social workers to work with problem families.

A portion of the funds appropriated each year under the law will be reserved specifically for technical assistance to state governments in improving their child abuse programs. A minimum of 5 percent of the funds appropriated and a maximum of 20 percent will be reserved for this purpose. In order to qualify for these funds, states must already have in effect or be in the process of establishing a system for reporting and investigating cases of child abuse and neglect, and for ensuring cooperation among the appropriate agencies, including the courts.

The bill required the creation of a new National Center on Child Abuse and Neglect in HEW. The new center will be required to compile all the research and all the information on programs, and make it available to anyone who needs it. The center must also develop some training materials for persons in the field, provide technical assistance, and conduct a study of the causes and incidence of child abuse and neglect.

At the time this article is written, it appears that Congress will appropriate $4.5 million to get the new programs off the ground in fiscal 1974, which ends July 1. The spending level authorized for fiscal 1975 is $20 million. Authorizations for 1976 and 1977 are $25 million each year.

I have no illusion that this minimal funding will solve the problem of child abuse in this country. In the long run, it will also be necessary to strengthen our existing resources on the state and local levels. Traditionally, under the Social Security Act, the states are responsible for dealing with child abuse and neglect. But because these funds are limited, most states have not targeted them on child abuse and neglect. I think that child abuse is such a critical, immediate problem that we must do all we can to alleviate it now.

So I have also introduced amendments which

would require the states, in order to continue to receive these Social Security funds, to develop a specific procedure for dealing with child abuse. This procedure would include reporting, investigation of reports, and provision of services to affected children and their families. I have also been working to secure additional funding for the Social Security programs so that they can meet these requirements.

These amendments and the new law are only the beginning. We are only too aware of the inadequacy of these measures to address the complicated and elusive questions of child neglect and of the emotional and developmental implications of abuse.

In our continuing attempt to meet these challenges, the Subcommittee has adopted as its conscience the words of the eminent psychologist, Erik Erikson: "The most deadly of all possible sins is the mutilation of a child's spirit."

Senator Mondale has made available the following synopsis of the **Child Abuse Prevention and Treatment Act.**

I. *Legislative History*

Introduced by Senator Mondale and Representative Patricia Schroeder in March, 1973; hearings before Senate Subcommittee on Children and Youth; passed 57 to 7 by the Senate in July, 1973; hearings before House Select Subcommittee on Education; passed by House 354 to 36 in December, 1973; signed by the President January 31, 1974.

II. *Summary of Legislation*

A. Creates National Center on Child Abuse and Neglect within Office of Human Development at HEW. Center functions include compilation and dissemination of research and program information; development of training materials; technical assistance; research into causes and incidence of child abuse and neglect; and administration of demonstration grant program.

B. Creates demonstration grant and contract program for public or nonprofit private agencies or organizations for project designed to prevent, identify, or treat child abuse and neglect. Some of the activities which could be funded under this section include training; establishment of centers designed to serve a geographical area with respect to child abuse and neglect; provision of expert teams for consultation on child abuse and neglect to rural areas; self-help programs for abusing parents and other innovative programs. Legislation specifies that at least 50 percent of funds appropriated annually under the Act be spent on demonstration programs.

C. Provides grants to states for technical assistance on child abuse and neglect programs. In order to qualify for assistance under this section, states must meet a series of requirements including having in effect a child abuse reporting law with immunity provisions; procedures for investigation of reporting cases of child abuse and neglect; having in effect administrative procedures, personnel, etc. "necessary to assure that the State will deal effectively with child abuse and neglect cases"; procedures for cooperation between various agencies dealing with child abuse; and assurance that funds received under this section will not be used to reduce current level of funding for this purpose in the state. Not less than 5 percent and not more than 20 percent of funds appropriated for the Act in a given year are to be spent on this section.

D. Requires that programs or projects related to child abuse and neglect under Titles IV-A and IV-B of the Social Security Act comply with requirements related to reporting; investigation; immediate action to protect a child; confidentiality of records; and cooperation with law enforcement officials.

E. Creates an Advisory Board on Child Abuse and Neglect, composed of representatives of federal agencies with responsibilities for programs related to child abuse and neglect.

F. Authorizes $15 million for 1974; $20 million for 1975; and $25 million each for 1976 and 1977. HEW has said that it will request a supplemental appropriation to get the program underway in 1974, but has not revealed the size of the request. Senator Mondale has said he will ask the Senate Appropriations Committee for $10 million.

III. *Implications for States*

A. *States can apply for funding under two different provisions of this Act*: Sec. 4(a), the demonstration grant and contract program; and Sec. 4(b), technical assistance to states. In order to qualify for funds under Sec. 4(b), states must meet a series of requirements. States do not have to comply with those requirements to receive funding under the demonstration program.

B. States already using funds received under Titles IV-A and/or IV-B of the Social Security Act for child abuse and neglect programs, will now be required to comply with provisions of this Act relating to reporting, investigation, child protection, confidentiality, and cooperation with law enforcement officials.

The shock troops in any community's campaign against child abuse are Children's Protective Services (CPS) workers. They provide the vital surveillance lifeline for the children. Yet because of universal lack of support, both moral and financial for CPS, the "burn-out" rate among these valiant souls exceeds 100% per year in most areas. As far as I am concerned, failure to provide treatment services for child abuse victims and their families falls into the same category as withholding steroids from children with nephrosis. Like many others involved with child abuse, I naively viewed PL93-247 as the vehicle whereby funds for needed treatment would become available. It was not to be. Instead, the bulk of the money provided under *The Child Abuse Prevention and Treatment Act* has been frittered away on "research" attempts to reinvent the wheel and "educational" programs designed to enhance the incomes of public relations firms and the travel industry.

Where the Money Went

Last summer a mega-course was held in Seattle on the relationship of juvenile delinquency and child abuse. It was well advertised with multicolored brochures. A big feature was the presence of no less than 21 out-of-state "experts" flown in especially for the occasion. Each received a $200 honorarium along with travel expenses direct from the trough of John Q. Public. For those not fortunate enough to attend, a transcript of the proceedings has been promised. Similar publications emanating from the National Center of Child Abuse and Neglect (NCCAN) could probably fill the New Orleans Superdome.

A veteran in child abuse work, Vincent Fontana, says,

progress in attacking the root causes of child maltreatment in this country does not lie in our public relations firms or in model legislation or media commercialism. Inadequacy of effort and insufficient expertise at the [Child Abuse] Center and in the Office of Child Development have allowed expenditures of limited dollars to carry out needless research, collect information through additional unnecessary surveys and support conference and education programs through so-called federally funded demonstration projects.[2]

The law requires that at least 50% of appropriated funds be used for demonstration grants. Information dissemination, including operation of the Child Abuse and Neglect Clearinghouse, is performed by contract. Training and technical assistance are funded by competitive contracts and grants. State grants to improve services are

Abuse of the child abuse law

In the belief that public officials potentially can affect health more than physicians, for the past 15 years I have engaged in the part-time practice of "political medicine." When I started as a starry-eyed rookie, I viewed successful passage of some legislation as a big deal. As a scarred, and perhaps burned-out, veteran I now know that getting a law enacted by Congress is simple compared to seeing that it is implemented in the manner intended by its original sponsors. The reason is as much due to the fraility of human nature as to the constitutional separation of powers among the three branches of government. If an official of the executive branch, from the President on down, is handed a program to administer that he did not ask for in the first place, nothing short of thumb screws will cause him to consult with the authors on what they had in mind.

Rather than recount old political war stories, however, these comments concern a piece of legislation in which I was not involved: *The Child Abuse Prevention and Treatment Act* (PL93-247). My perspective is from worm's eye. I am the pediatrician for the child abuse team at my hospital. We see most of the physically abused children who require hospitalization in our population area of approximately 1 million. We average about 50 cases per year.

Treatment Resources Lacking

Our greatest frustration is the pitiful lack of treatment resources in the community after the child leaves the hospital. The pioneer studies of Kempe, Helfer, Fontana, De Francis, Steele, Pollack, and others have provided us with information both on the origins of child abuse as well made directly to "eligible" states. No less than 5% nor more than 20% of the appropriations can be used to fund state grants.

A total of $59.1 million has been spent in the four years since enactment of the law. As a tribute to the American free-enterprise system, *all* of the contract money, $8,759,461, has gone to for-profit corporations. Space does not allow a listing of the titles and amounts of money for the individual contracts and research grants. The information can be obtained by writing one's congressman. One can be assured of some fascinating reading as well as demonstrating interest. If few abused children benefited, one can hope that at least the Dow-Jones averages gained a few points.

How about research? Sixteen projects have been funded to the tune of $5.2 million, not in itself an extravagant amount. While new vistas are undoubtedly being opened by some of them, perusal of the titles does not overpower me with a sense of originality.

A consequence of all the "attention" given to child abuse is that politicians at the local, state, and national levels feel that they have actually accomplished something. Why bother funding expensive child protective services, foster homes, and mental health treatment when "media messages" provide the illusion of meaningful activity? Mandatory reporting laws are cheap. Doing something about the cases that are reported is not.

A Modest Proposal

So what can be done? Make me HEW Secretary for a day, and the following regulations would be issued without preliminary notice.

A moratorium would be placed on all conferences and publications on child abuse. The pages of established journals are available to authors with anything new to say. No more research proposals would be entertained unless the investigator submitted a term paper demonstrating familiarity with previous studies of child abuse and made a convincing case on how the proposed research would lead to improved treatment or prevention.

By far my most important move would be to require that all NCCAN administrators spend at least half of their time in the trenches as CPS workers. I doubt that many have even seen abused children, let alone worked with them. I am sure there are enough vacancies within commuting distance of D.C. If the paperwork piles up on their desks while they are away, less mischief will be perpetrated.

Precious few pediatric disorders lend them-

selves as readily to prevention as child abuse. A lot of young lives and souls will continue to be sacrificed until bureaucratic tail-chasing and public indifference are overcome.

ABRAHAM B. BERGMAN, M.D.
Children's Orthopedic Hospital
   and Medical Center;
Departments of Pediatrics and
   Health Services,
University of Washington

Box C-5371
Seattle, WA 98105

REFERENCES

1. Kempe CH, Helfer RE: *Helping the Battered Child and His Family.* Philadelphia, JB Lippincott Co, 1972.
2. Fontana VJ: Testimony before the US House of Representatives, Subcommittee on Select Education of the Committee on Education and Labor, Feb 25, 1977.

357

The Criminal Law and the Incest Offender:
A Case for Decriminalization? *

RONALD B. SKLAR **

The criminal law's attitude toward incest has been documented in two very recent papers.[1] The purpose of the present paper is not to go over this old ground. It is rather to inquire into society's rationale for criminalizing incest and then to examine the growing movement for decriminalization.

For present purposes, therefore, it is sufficient to summarize briefly the existing attitude of the criminal law:

1. Incest has been called "the universal crime."[2] But as a "crime" rather than a "taboo" or ecclesiastical offence, it is of relatively recent origin. It was not punishable in England until 1908[3] and hence was not an offence under the common law.[4] At present, however, jurisdictions which do not include it in their list of crimes represent the exception. Some do not punish incest at all (Luxembourg, Portugal and Turkey) and some punish it only in the context of broader provisions concerning sexual intercourse with children.[5] Canada[6] and the American states[7] stand with the majority in punishing incest separately. Some countries may introduce limiting factors, such as, for example, Italy, where the incest, to be criminal, must result in "public scandal,"[8] "what the offended modesty of the majority of average citizens cannot tolerate."[9]

2. For the crime of incest ("legal" incest) to occur, heterosexual sexual intercourse must take place between the parties.[10] Other forms of sexual behavior — which the clinician would consider "incestuous" — may be criminal, as well, but would have to be reached under "indecent assault," "gross indecency" or related offences. Consent of the "assaulted" party will usually be a defence in these cases, unless the party is deemed too young — in Canada, below the age of 14[11] — to give his or her consent. Such behavior may also be reached under "neglect," "corrupting children," "contributing to delinquency," "child abuse" or similar provisions (which, for that matter, can encompass "legal" incest as well). If the delinquency or child abuse route is chosen, prosecution may be diverted to other courts — in Canada, the Social Welfare or Juvenile Court, with less formal procedures and atmosphere and lower sanctions. As is evident, police and prosecutorial discretion abounds under this scheme.

3. There is redundancy between the incest provision and the general

---

*Delivered at the annual meeting of the AAPL, in Montreal, October, 1978.
**Mr. Sklar is on the Faculty of Law, McGill University, Montreal, Canada, H2W 154.

69

provisions prohibiting sexual intercourse with females under prescribed ages — in Canada, under 16 and, the more seriously punished situation (maximum of imprisonment for life), under 14 years of age. [12] Though one would expect the incest provision to be invoked in the blood-relationship situation (where the maximum penalty is 14 years of imprisonment),[13] the prosecutor, until some high court says otherwise, seems to have discretion to invoke the more general provisions.

4. Incest generally requires a blood relationship between the parties,[14] which is known at the time the act takes place. The range of blood relationships, as might be expected, varies from jurisdiction to jurisdiction. The ban generally extends as far as uncles-nieces and aunts-nephews, with penalties sometimes, though not generally, made dependent on the degree of the relationship.[15] In Canada, the relationships prohibited are parent-child, siblings full and half, and grandparent-grandchild.[16] There is no age limitation, *i.e.*, the code covers adult relationships. However, and this is not surprising, studies have indicated that prosecutions for incest between adult relatives very seldom occur.[17] Furthermore, and perhaps no more surprising, recidivism among incest offenders, both as to other sexual offences and repetitions of incest, reportedly is highest for the incest offender vs. children, less so for the incest offender vs. minors, and lowest — in fact, the lowest recidivism rate for any sexual offender — for the incest offender vs. adults.[18] In general, however, recidivism of incest after initial discovery is rare.[19]

5. Except where the younger person is below the age criminal liability can attach (in Canada, that age is still set at seven),[20] both parties to the act of incest may be criminally liable. Such is the case in Canada. The duress implicit in the situation involving a young daughter is recognized in the Canadian provision (Section 150), but only to the extent of stating that the court who is "satisfied" such duress existed "is not required to impose any punishment upon her." Even then, delinquency proceedings will remain a possibility. The trial testimony of the other party to the act, whether adult or child, may have to be "corroborated" either because of general statutory provisions requiring corroborative evidence in sexual offences (as is the case in Canada[21]) or because the other party to the act may be deemed an "accomplice" of the offender.[22]

6. In its 1978 Working Paper on Sexual Offences, the Law Reform Commission of Canada has recommended the repeal of Section 150 of the Criminal Code, the incest provision. It would be replaced by one that would retain the prohibition of sexual relations between parents and children under the age of 18 within the context of a general provision relating to sexual relations with "a young person within [the offender's] authority."[23] This, in effect, would decriminalize incest between siblings and between adults, the approach that has been proposed in Sweden.[24] Due to what it calls "the strong social and religious views held by many about incest even between adults," the Commission has solicited opinions on the wisdom of its proposal.[25]

II

It is becoming generally accepted, albeit begrudgingly, that conduct

360

should be labeled "criminal," and the actor thus subjected to the rigors of the criminal process and to criminal sanctions, *only* where such conduct meets two criteria:

1. That it be widely viewed by society as morally blameworthy; and
2. That it be harmful (there be a "victim").

This reality, it must be admitted, has not yet totally permeated our criminal codes, but conduct that lacks one or the other prerequisite has been or is presently on the carpet before most law reform commissions and, to a lesser extent (because they react more slowly), before legislative bodies. Abortion, euthanasia and the possession and/or sale of marijuana are forms of conduct which, one would have to say, now lack the first prerequisite in the eyes of a great many people, while homosexuality between consenting adults and prostitution lack the second. For this reason, they pose serious problems, even crises, for law enforcement officials, juries and sentencing judges and, when prosecuted, probably diminish the public's already fragile respect for the criminal law.

The "moral blameworthiness" requirement stems from the essential nature of the criminal law — what distinguishes it, say, from civil wrongs or "tort" law — namely, that it calls forth a "judgment of community condemnation."[26] Its "central distinguishing aspect," as one writer has put it, is its "stigmatization of the morally culpable."[27]

This notion of the offender's moral blame or "responsibility" for his conduct has, of course, been eroded by other disciplines, most notably psychology, psychiatry and philosophy. It is hard nowadays to maintain one's faith in the notion of human autonomy, the freedom to choose to do right or wrong — the essence of moral responsibility for one's actions. But the criminal law hangs tough. Except for a strictly construed defence of insanity and, in some jurisdictions (not yet Canada), a partial defence of "diminished responsibility," the criminal law persists in imputing responsibility, blame, to the offender, relegating the offender's claim of "no real choice" to the time of sentencing and, *sub rosa*, to the stage of police and prosecutorial discretion. It has to, to survive in its present form.

The second requirement, "harm," does not stem from any essential nature of the criminal law. One can, quite consistently with criminal law theory and policy, argue for the punishment of the morally wicked without regard to whether the offender has harmed anyone, including himself. The Devlin-Hart debate[28] over the criminal punishment of prostitution and homosexuality between consenting adults has confirmed this. Though he undoubtedly is fighting a losing battle, Lord Devlin's argument that society may quite properly utilize the criminal law to coerce adherence to its moral principles is hardly unrespectable.

"Harm" is an essential ingredient of criminal conduct for other reasons: expediency (not used pejoratively) and fairness. The criminal law is too expensive and cumbersome a process, its police resources and court time are in too high demand and too short supply, its effect on people's lives (not only the offender's) is too drastic, the methods its enforcement officers must use to uncover the so-called "victimless crime"[29] (entrapment, informers) are too degrading to allow its use against conduct that produces no provable harm, creates no "victim." The criminal law has justifiably been termed "a last-resort process."[30]

Does incest meet these two criteria? If "yes," then, presumptively, it is a worthy subject for the criminal sanction. It meets the first; for incest, it seems safe to say, is an abhorred crime, and the offender stands morally condemned in the eyes of the general public. The general public's view, of course, may be based on mis- or non-information about the reality and dynamics of the incest situation, and it is possible to re-educate them on the subject. Decriminalizing incest would certainly be a step, probably a substantial one, in that direction. But the question must be asked whether it should be the first.

Is incest "harmful"? Where incest between adults or between siblings is concerned, the response to this question must be "unproved." Medical evidence on alleged genetic risks for the child of an incestuous union is scanty and inconclusive.[31] Other claimed harms boil down to religious or moral arguments.[32] These, as maintained above, do not by themselves justify imposition of the criminal law, a conclusion also reached by the Law Reform Commission of Canada.

However, where the incest involves an adult, especially a parent, and a child or minor, the evidence is otherwise. Studies, mostly of father-daughter incest, have revealed, in the words of one, "depression, symptom formation, or acting-out behavior" in the children and minors seen. "[A]ll were judged to be experiencing some degree of distress, . . ."[33] The few follow-up studies that have been made generally agree that the incest "has a negative effect on the girl's development, [although] the degree and nature of the after-effects of the trauma have yet to be confirmed."[34] There is some evidence that daughters sexually abused by their fathers tend to marry physically and sexually abusive men, perhaps even repeating the incest syndrome.[35] It must be noted at this point that the criminal law's actual or threatened intervention plays no small part in the child's distress: "[M]others who were pressured by their families not to file charges experienced loss of family support and often had to sever important family ties and move in order to protect their children. For the child the series of events were bewildering, and the mother's anxiety rendered her less available to the child."[36] The daughter will suffer a more direct anxiety and guilt over her own role in initiating the criminal process, especially if she feels partly responsible for the onset of the incestuous behavior. She has "gained her liberation" through her disclosure, but it is not achieved "without emotional storm."[37] Finally, the child's "later pathology [may be] due more to the family's disorganization [an undoubted effect of the institution of criminal charges] than to the incest itself."[38] We will return to this point very shortly.

III

We have arrived at the concluding section of the paper. As noted above, incest with children or minors presumptively merits the attention of the criminal law. Are there, however, countervailing factors, forces that nonetheless militate against criminalizing this form of incest? Quite a few exist.

1. The possibility that criminal charges will be initiated will discourage (not always; for some, it might encourage) family members from seeking

help from one or more of the social agencies equipped to offer help. Likewise, a social worker made aware of the situation may, for the same reason, be reluctant to seek therapeutic help for the family — especially as the social worker knows that he or she may have to testify in court and that, as the Quebec Court of Appeal reiterated recently in a case involving incest,[39] the law still does not recognize any privilege against disclosure of communications made to the social worker by members of the family.[40] The threat of the criminal sanction thus hangs heavily over the family. A family already in crisis has to cope additionally with the decision of "what to do about it" and with the knowledge that, if outside help is sought, "daddy" or husband may have to go to jail. Whether or not the family decides to reveal the problem to outsiders, the ordeal of making that decision can only further tear the family apart.

2. If the manner has been reported out of the family and criminal proceedings have been in fact instituted, further family trauma will occur. Some of the effects of incarceration, should that be ordered, no doubt are no different for the family of the incest offender than for the family of the bank robber: separation of family members, economic hardship during and after incarceration, emotional hardship, and the like. However, the anxiety and guilt the child feels over the consequences of her accusation, greatly exacerbated by the ordeal of appearing in court against her father should the matter go to trial and, in any event, by her contact with the law enforcement machinery,[41] seems unique to the incest case. The child is victimized by the law both through its individual impact upon her and, as noted above, through its impact on her mother and on the family as a whole. The degree of trauma for the victim and the family caused by incestuous conduct which is not made public is not known.[42]

3. In most incest situations, the criminal law is anti-therapeutic, for the offender and for the family; it is not a treatment or supportive process. It "aggravates rather than aids,"[43] and may well be, for that reason, the least appropriate of societal responses.

4. The legal provisions dealing with incest are a mess. The incest crime itself pertains to a relatively small aspect of incestuous sexual behavior. There are at least a dozen provisions of most criminal codes and youth protection acts that can apply to incestuous conduct and several to "legal" incest as well. This ambiguity allows for enormous police and prosecutorial discretion both as to whether or not to prosecute criminally and as to what provisions to prosecute under (all with widely varying penalties), with inevitable disparities in treatment of like cases. This situation certainly is not unique to the incest offence or to incestuous conduct, but seems particularly acute in these areas. The answer, however, where this countervailing factor is concerned, may lie not in decriminalizing incest, but rather in clarifying the provisions dealing with incest and incestuous behavior and placing controls on the scope of police and prosecutorial discretion in the area.[44]

5. The "responsibility" argument which, as noted above, is a cornerstone for imposition of the criminal process, takes little account of the dynamics of the incest situation. Incest "definitely [is] a familial problem, . . . Legal removal of the father only causes additional stresses without ameliorating the basic family problems."[45] Incest is a symptom of "family

disorganization" as well as individual pathology.[46] It "does not take place in isolation but is carried out within the family dynamics."[47] It seems to occur most frequently in the so-called "mid-life crisis" period of the husband/father, during his late thirties and forties.[48] Overcrowding in the home has been called "a crucial factor."[49] The "mother's passivity" plays a role in contributing to the incest, and "it is generally accepted that mothers are in some degree of collusion with the incest."[50] It has even been suggested that the father's incestuous relationship with the daughter acts as a pressure valve within the marriage and that it may, in a dysfunctional family, serve to preserve the marriage.[51] The girls, according to an earlier study, may be "reacting to their mothers' unconscious desire to put them in the maternal role."[52] It is further said to be natural for the daughter to practice her flirting technique on the father, and the flirtation becomes a problem when both she and her father fail to perceive the limits of this "harmless" activity.[53] Whether it is the daughter's "promiscuity and submissiveness" or the father's "parental possessiveness" and coercion that typify the relationship depends upon which study you read.[54] Probably it is a little of both.[55] Whether or not one accepts all of the preceding, it seems clear that while only the father is declared "guilty," "all members of the family play a role in the incest drama."[56]

I am willing, for the most part, to accept these clinical assessments of the incest situation, but, as a criminal law professor, I am troubled by them — greatly. Assuming we all accept that the prevention of incest is a desired goal, what is the consequence of such assessments? The criminal law, as earlier noted, is posited on the notion of responsibility — that man is responsible, and hence accountable, for his actions. This is the principal *message* the criminal law sends out to society, to the potential offender. To the extent the decriminalization of incest with children or minors would be premised upon the view that incest is a "family problem," a "symptom of family disorganization" in which every member "plays a role," what message would *thereby* be sent out?

My concern is not for the erosion of a theory. My concern is much more pragmatic: by decriminalizing incest, we allow the incest offender to lighten the onus of his actions.[57] We tell him that his thoughts and the early stages of his conduct are symptoms of family breakdown or the result of youthful seduction and the like, and are not necessarily "guilty." We label him, too, as a "victim" and enable him, at least in his own mind, to escape society's moral disapproval.[58] The question must be asked whether this transformation of the problem will undermine the person's already weakening internal controls against such conduct. The labels we give to things count.

I do admit that we are justifiably skeptical of the criminal law's preventive powers, especially with respect to sexual offences,[59] but in making such judgments we tend to think only of prevention through conscious fear of punishment. As the Norwegian criminal law theorist, Johannes Andenaes, has written, the threat of criminal punishment may have "general-preventive effects" through "strengthen[ing] moral inhibitions," both at the conscious and unconscious levels, and through "stimulat[ing] habitual law-abiding conduct." And "even if it can be shown that conscious fear of punishment is not present in certain cases [and incest probably is such a case], this is by no means the same as showing that the secondary effects of punishment are without importance. To the lawmaker, the achievement of inhibition and habit is of greater value than mere deterrence.'[60] Anything that might impair our internal controls against undesirable conduct must be viewed with great caution.

As I see it, it is no answer to these concerns that most decriminalization proposals allow for penal-type sanctions (removal of the father or, as a "last resort,"[61] a sentence of imprisonment) through the Family Court in cases where measures more stringent than therapeutic intervention appear needed.[62] First, the great difficulty of prescribing criteria for such Family Court intervention (one study uses terms like "an extremely rigid father" or one who exhibits "poor impulse control" or is "psychotic"[63]) still further loads the system with discretion and disparities of disposition. However, the more basic objection is that Family Court, to the general public, deals with "family problems," not blameworthy acts. Social disapproval is still absent.

And so, if the arguments and points of this paper be accepted, we are left in a dilemma. The decriminalization of incest committed with children or minors would, I maintain, have a deleterious effect on the prevention of this form of incest, while the actual invocation of the criminal process does more harm than good to the offender, the young victim, and the family. Incest may not be alone in presenting this dilemma. It may be that most criminal offences could be analyzed this way.

References

1. Manchester AH: Incest and the law, in Eekelaar JM & Katz SN, (eds.): Family Violence: An International and Interdisciplinary Study. Toronto, Butterworths, 1978, p. 487; Cooper IK: Decriminalization of incest — New legal-clinical responses, in Family Violence, *op. cit.,* p. 518
2. Weinberg SK: Incest Behavior. New York, Citadel Press, 1955, p. 3
3. Punishment of Incest Act, 1908, 8 Edw. 7, ch. 45
4. Stephen L: A History of the Criminal Law of England (1883), pp. 429-430
5. For example, Belgium, France and the Netherlands. Maisch H: Incest. London, André Deutsch Ltd., 1973, pp. 66-67
6. Criminal Code, R.S.C. 1970, ch. C-34, s.150. This provision appeared in 1892 in Canada's first criminal code.
7. American Jursiprudence 2d, 41:512-513 (1968)
8. Italian Penal Code of 1930, s.564, in The American Series of Foreign Penal Codes, South Hackensack, N.J., Fred B. Rothman, 1978
9. Galeotti EM: Incest under Italian Law (unpublished). Proceedings of the Second International Conference on Family Law — Violence in the Family, 1977, p. 2
10. "Legal" incest does not, therefore, include father-son incest, *i.e.,* "homosexual incest," a form that a very recent study has suggested may be "higher [in the population] than has been assumed." Dixon KN, Arnold LE, Calestro MA: Father-Son Incest: Underreported Psychiatric Problem? Amer J Psychiat 135:835, 838 (1978)
11. Criminal Code, R.S.C. 1970, ch. C-34, s.140
12. *Id.,* s.145
13. *Id.,* s.150(2)
14. Manchester, *op. cit.,* n.1, pp. 495-497
15. Maisch, *op. cit.,* n.5, pp. 68-69
16. Criminal Code, R.S.C. 1970, ch. C-34, s.150(1), (4). As to parent-child, however, see n.10 *supra,* and accompanying text.
17. Manchester, *op. cit.,* n.1, pp. 505-506
18. Gebhard PH, Gagnon JH, Pomeroy WB, Christenson CV: Sex Offenders. New York, Harper & Row, 1965, pp. 221-222, 241-242, 264-265
19. Cormier BM, Kennedy M, Sangowicz J: Psychodynamics of father-daughter incest. Can Psychiat Assn J 7:203, 204 (1962)

20. Criminal Code, R.S.C. 1970, ch. C-34, s.12. For the child between seven and fourteen, criminal liability depends on whether "he was competent to know the nature and consequences of his conduct and to appreciate that it was wrong." *Id.*, s.13

21. *Id.*, s.139

22. "In sexual crimes [including incest], the other person — usually the woman — may or may not be an accomplice, according as she is, by the nature of the crime, a victim of it or a voluntary partner in it." 7 Wigmore, Evidence s.2060, p. 443 (Chadbourn rev. 1978). A child below the age of consent in the particular jurisdiction generally cannot be an accomplice. *Ibid.* (cases cited at n.7)

23. Law Reform Commission of Canada: Criminal Law Working Paper no. 22 — Sexual Offences, 1978, p. 32

24. Engström LG: New Penal Provisions on Sexual Offences Proposed in Sweden. Current Sweden 118:1, 7 (1976). This recommendation reportedly has not been adopted. Manchester, *op. cit.*, n.1, p. 510, n.101

25. Law Reform Commission of Canada, *op. cit.*, n.23, p. 32. The writer has been advised that to date (October, 1978) the opinions received have been strongly opposed, with favorable responses mainly from psychiatrists and gay groups.

26. Hart HM Jr: The aims of the criminal law. Law & Contemp Probs 23:401, 404 (1958)

27. Kadish SH: Some observations on the use of criminal sanctions in enforcing economic regulations. U Chicago L Rev 30:423, 437 (1963)

28. Devlin P: The Enforcement of Morals. London, Oxford University Press, 1965 (first read in 1959 as the Maccabaean Lecture in Jurisprudence at the British Academy); Hart HLA: Law, Liberty and Morality. New York, Vintage Books, 1963

29. A term if not coined then popularized in Packer HL: The Limits of the Criminal Sanction. Stanford, Stanford University Press, 1968

30. Goldstein AS, Goldstein J: Crime, Law and Society. New York, The Free Press, 1971, p. 1

31. Engström, *op. cit.*, n.24, pp. 5-6; Manchester, *op. cit.*, n.1, pp. 500-501

32. *Id.*, p. 500

33. Browning DH, Boatman B: Incest: Children at risk. Amer J Psychiat 134:69, 72 (1977)

34. Cooper, *op. cit.*, n.1, p. 520

35. Summit R, Kryso J: Sexual abuse of children, a clinical spectrum. Amer J Orthopsychiat 48:237, 248 (1978)

36. Browning and Boatman, *op. cit.*, n.33, p. 72

37. Cormier, *et al., op cit.*, n. 19, p. 214

38. Cooper, *op. cit.*, n.1, p. 520; Maisch, *op. cit.*, n.5, pp. 208-209

39. *R. v. St-Jean*, 34 C.R.N.S. 378, 387 (Que. C.A. 1976)

40. Privileges against disclosing information in court, since they do not advance the search for truth, but rather "shut out the light," are not favored by the common law of evidence. McCormick: Evidence (2nd ed., Cleary ed.), St. Paul, West Publishing Co., 1972, p. 152. In Canada, section 41 of the draft code on Evidence prepared by the Law Reform Commission (see Report, Evidence, 1975) would extend a qualified privileged communication status to the social worker — client relationship:

    A person who has consulted a person exercising a profession for the purpose of obtaining professional services by a professional person, has a privilege against disclosure of any confidential communication reasonably made in the course of the relationship if, in the circumstances, the public interest in the privacy of the relationship outweighs the public interest in the administration of justice.

41. Most reform proposals stress the importance of avoiding the psychological trauma of a courtroom appearance while still protecting the accused's rights (see Law Reform Commission of Canada, *op. cit.*, n.23, p. 33), but fail to observe that the interview with the police and the prosecutor, even if sympathetically and adroitly handled, can be almost as traumatizing for the child.

42. Manchester, *op. cit.*, n.1, p. 500

43. Gigeroff AK, *et al.*: Research Report Incest, Sexual Offences Under the Criminal Code of Canada Research Project. Law Reform Commission of Canada and Clarke Institute of Psychiatry, 1975, p. 13

44. The law in general exercises very little control over police and prosecutorial discretion. See Goldstein J: Police discretion not to invoke the criminal process: Low visibility decisions in the administration of justice. Yale Law J 69:543-594 (1960); Grosman BA: The Prosecutor: An Inquiry into the Exercise of Discretion. Toronto, University of Toronto Press, 1969

45. Gigeroff, *op. cit.*, n.43, p. 13

46. Cooper, *op. cit.*, n.1, pp. 519-520

47. *Id.*, p. 519

48. Cormier, *et al., op. cit.*, n.19, p. 204

49. Weinberg, *op. cit.*, n.2, p. 55; but see Cooper, *op. cit.*, n.1, p. 519 (according to recent studies, the claim that most cases "come from rural areas, are the result of poverty, alcoholism and over-crowding" is a "myth.") As to the role of alcoholism, however, see the recent study by

Browning and Boatman, *op. cit.*, n.33

50. Browning and Boatman, *op. cit.*, n.33, p. 69
51. Lustig N, Dresser JV, Spellman SW, Murray TB: Incest: A family group survival pattern. Arch Gen Psychiat 14:31, 39 (1966)
52. Kaufman I, Peck AL, Taguiri CK: The family constellation and overt incestuous relations between father and daughter. Amer J Orthopsychiat 24:266, 277 (1954)
53. Summit and Kryso, *op. cit.*, n.35, p. 243
54. Compare Weinberg, *op. cit.*, n.2, p. 115, with Summit and Kryso, *op. cit.*, n. 35, pp. 243-244
55. Cormier, *et al.*, *op. cit.*, n.19, p. 206
56. Cooper, *op. cit.*, n.1, p. 519
57. Gusfield JR: Moral passage: The symbolic process in public designations of deviance. Social Probs 15:175-188 (1968), writing about the effect of the movement to redefine the alcoholic as sick.
58. On the criminal law's perhaps key function of expressing the community's disapproval for the actor's conduct, see Hart, *op. cit.*, n.26; Cohen MR: Moral aspects of the criminal law. Yale Law J 49:987, 1017 (1940)
59. Andenaes J: The general preventive effects of punishments. U Pennsylvania Law Rev 114:949, 957-958 (1966)
60. Andenaes J: General prevention — illusion or reality. J Crim Law, Criminol & Pol Sci 43:176, 179-180 (1952)
61. Cooper, *op. cit.*, n.1, p. 525
62. *Id.*, pp. 524-525; Gigeroff, *op. cit.*, n.43, pp. 14-15; *cf.* Law Reform Commission of Canada, *op. cit.*, n.23, pp. 31-32
63. Cooper, *op. cit.*, n.1, pp. 524-525

Child Abuse Intervention: Conflicts in Current Practice and Legal Theory*

Barbara Markham, JD

From the Children's Hospital Medical Center, Harvard School of Public Health, and Boston University Law School, Boston

ABSTRACT. Recent litigation of child abuse cases indicates that two contradictory policies compete for court approval. One policy would reduce the amount of intervention into abusive families on grounds of privacy. The other seeks to maintain and expand channels of investigation and treatment. While attempting to prescribe a comprehensive approach to child abuse, these conflicting policies, in fact, address different problems in child protection. Without a treatment formulation that focuses on the separate issues raised by each policy, it is not clear that clinicians will be able to sustain child abuse investigatory and protective authority against the privacy attack. This treatment synthesis must entail development of standards that maximize protection of the child from caretakers at the earliest stages of risk and protection from administrative procrastination in case resolution. Protecting the child rather than the family institution should provide the central focus of policy formulation. *Pediatrics* 65:180–185, 1980; *child abuse, child protection, family intervention, legal medicine, trauma management.*

In August 1978, Greater Boston Legal Services filed a class action suit on behalf of parents acting for themselves and for their children against the Commonwealth of Massachusetts. The complaint alleges that the Department of Public Welfare violated the plaintiffs' right to family integrity in its administration of the child protective system.[1] In November 1978, in a broadcast interview with Dr. Eli Newberger on Boston station WEEI, the Massachusetts Committee on Children and Youth announced its intention to sue the Commonwealth for failure to adequately protect children endangered in their homes. In short, a suit claiming that the state intervenes too aggressively in child abuse cases is arising simultaneously with one alleging that the state fails to intervene aggressively enough. It appears that child abuse policy is rapidly approaching a directional crisis. Indeed, it is part of the emotionalism and irony of child abuse that decisions as policy-laden as those encountered in general approaches of child protection may ultimately be made by the courts.

These broadly conceived suits are the culmination of individual attacks on the inadequacies of all phases of family intervention, and decisions increasing liability for failure to intervene[2] parallel those which create greater procedural barriers to family intrusion.[3] Each suit reflects the thinking of schools of intervention that differ not only in their approach, but also in their origins. For lack of better terminology, I will refer to the family integrity advocates as the privacy model and the early intervention advocates as the medicolegal model.

The privacy model is expounded largely by those who deal with the court aspects of child protection. Lawyers who specialize in juvenile law and parent defense have martialed the privacy attack through legal teaching, writings, and the courts.[4] By contrast, the campaign for greater intervention has been led largely by physicians, lawyers, and social workers who are involved in the day to day treatment and observations of disturbed families.[5] Ironically, the juvenile justice advocates emerge as the most vociferous proponents of "parents' rights" while the family-oriented professionals most strongly advocate a policy of "children's rights."

Several questions concerning child abuse intervention must be resolved. First, what are the values each model seeks to protect? Secondly, how do the responsibilities that each group carries affect how it views the state's responsibility? Finally, to what extent do these models of intervention actually represent "parents' rights" versus "children's

* See Letter to the Editor, p 191.
Received for publication March 13, 1979, accepted April 30, 1979.
Reprint requests to (B. M.) 210 Locust St, Apt 14C, Philadelphia, PA 19106.

rights" and to what extent are they complementary?

THE NATURE OF THE PROBLEM

Between 60,000 and 2 million cases of child abuse are estimated to occur annually.[6,7] The range and divergent definitions and methods of these estimates illustrate the difficulty of identifying and treating the abused child. First, mild trauma may be confused with other pathology such as infection.[8] Moreover, observations of injury frequently occur in unsuspicious contexts, such as the parent seeking medical attention for the child.[8] This problem is intensified by the fact that, with each incident of injury, the parent may go to a different hospital to avoid the detection that might occur with physician awareness of a pattern of unexplained injuries.[9] Often the conclusive indication of abuse or neglect occurs only with the lack of recurrence of symptoms while the child is in a protected environment.[8] The highest incidence of abuse has been asserted to occur in children under the age of 3 years, which underscores the difficulty of obtaining information from the child.[9]

A characteristic of the child abuse syndrome is the likelihood of reinjury.[8] In fact, it appears that reinjury may occur on an escalating scale of frequency and intensity.[2] Morse et al[10] and Silver et al[11] reported in a follow-up study that abusive parents reinjured children in 35% of study cases, despite the fact that the problem had been identified and followed by intervention.

The escalating nature of abuse becomes more understandable, even predictable, given the environmental and psychological context in which it occurs. The most striking observation which has emerged is the degree to which abusive parents were once abused children.[8,10,11] In many cases child abuse appears to be part of a pattern of generalized family violence among parents and towards their children.[10,11] In addition to general histories of disturbed childhoods, these distressed families display a higher incidence of isolation from community organizations, financial difficulties (in spite of being substantially self-supporting), marital discord, alcoholism, and prior involvement with police agencies, usually during adolescence. In the study by Fontana et al,[9] almost 50% of the abused children were conceived prior to marriage, which suggests that these children were perceived as a source of trouble before they were born. While this description of the context of child abuse is not universally applicable, it illustrates that child abuse occurs when the substantial stress of child rearing is superimposed on already strained emotional and environmental resources.

Given the tendency of abusiveness to pass from one generation to another and for the level of violence to increase in intensity and effect, it seems obvious that some form of intervention is necessary to prevent the intergenerational cycle of pain, permanent injury, mental retardation, and death which results each year. The question remains, however: what happens to these children and families once intervention by professionals and by the state has occurred? The infliction of injury is only half the tale of the child abuse syndrome.

Existing services for distressed families include homemaker services, social and psychological counseling, visiting nurses, parenting counseling, Parents Anonymous, and foster care. Excessive reliance on foster care and inadequate exploration of in-home support services comprise the major source of dissatisfaction with state intervention.[12] The degree of administrative abuse of foster care services was demonstrated in a 1973 Massachusetts study which revealed that: 68% of children had been in foster care for four to eight years; 83% had never been returned to their parents; 33% were unsupervised by a social worker during foster placement; 33% had multiple placements; 75% of foster parents were not given information about their foster child's specific disability prior to placement.[1] Failure by state agencies to follow up on intervention through continued monitoring and reevaluation of the families' needs and progress proves a source of frustration to clinicians interacting with both the families and the state (B. Markham, JD, personal observations, 1978).

Legal analysis is now struggling to evolve a framework for intervention in what has traditionally been regarded as a medical and social problem. This struggle reflects the difficulty of defining the priority of interests to be protected by diffuse and compelling value systems.

Privacy

Protecting the family unit from control by the state has been fundamental in our legal and political processes.[13] The right of parents to raise their children as they see fit has been clearly enunciated in Supreme Court decisions.[14,15] Decisions protecting the rights of married couples to use contraceptives and women to obtain abortions enunciated zones of privacy protecting family-related decisions.[16,17] From this politically and culturally based premise of the importance of the family as a distinct institution, the privacy school proceeds:

Since our society values the principle of family autonomy and privacy, we should carefully examine any decision to coercively limit parental autonomy in raising children.[13]

The most significant assertion of parental autonomy has come from the Juvenile Justice Standards Projects (JJSP).[4] The JJSP standards represent an attempt to comprehensively reform existing family intervention law by limiting the threshold of entry and by restricting the discretion of state intervenors. The standards propose prohibiting intervention unless the child is suffering from a specifically identifiable risk of *"physical harm causing disfigurement, impairment of bodily functioning, or other serious injury"* (emphasis supplied).[4]

These proposals rest on the assumption that child protection will continue to be underfinanced, and that limitations on intervention will guarantee a more efficient use of resources for those most seriously in need.[12] The restrictions also stem from the concern over the positive harm which may be inflicted "by the state's forced intervention between parent and child."[12,18] Once the state intervenes, the JJSP standards seek to control the nature and extent of that intervention to prevent arbitrary administration and to encourage return of children to parents.[12]

The standards provide for removal only when the child cannot be adequately protected from specific serious harms at home through the delivery of services. The state would carry the burden of proving the inadequacy of in-home service.[12] Once children have been removed, the standards provide that they must be returned as soon as they can be protected at home from the original specific harm. The standards further provide for immediate termination, subject to certain exceptions, of all parental rights if the parent reinjures the child.[12] Otherwise, parental rights would be terminated in the hopes of adoption if the child could not be safely returned home within one year for a child over 3 years old and six months for a child under 3; the majority of abuse victims are in the latter category.[12] Michael Wald, a primary author of these reforms, justifies speedy termination on the grounds that de facto termination occurs in 40 to 80% of removals and that most children returned to their parents were returned within the first year.[12] The harm children suffer from temporary multiple placements provided substantial impetus to the desire to establish firm standards in the areas of removal and termination.[12] In short, the proposals operate to make state intervention more difficult at initiation and to dramatically force the cases to quick permanent resolution.

Recent judicial decisions suggest that providing greater procedural protection to parents and controlling the operation of intervention is gaining credibility. *Sims vs Texas Dept of Public Welfare,*[3] currently pending before the United States Supreme Court, reflects the concern with procedural safeguards to parents. Specifically, the court held:

(1) a court cannot order investigation of a family without notifying them; (2) centralized child abuse registries constitute a violation of parental privacy in the absence of a judicial determination of actual abuse or neglect; (3) the state must make a clear showing that continued custody beyond a ten-day emergency seizure period is necessary to protect the child from danger; (4) the state must prove the necessity by clear and convincing evidence rather than by a preponderance of evidence; (5) an attorney must be appointed for the child since the state cannot be assumed to represent the child's interest.[3] *In Re Clear* reinforced substantive parental protection by denying termination of parental rights to a child who had been in foster care for four years from birth because the state department of welfare failed to follow a program to encourage return of the child. This case was decided on statutory grounds despite evidence that early efforts at reunification precipitated severe reactions from the child including nightmares and overt rejection of the mother. The court ruled that the statute mandating efforts at reunification was so narrowly constructed that it precluded court discretion to allow adoption where reunification efforts may have been inappropriate.[19]

The goals of this approach are (1) to force accountability for efforts and results in the child protection system and (2) to force a reallocation of resources from foster care towards more services to the most urgent cases.[18] The question remains whether this model adequately protects all the values involved in child protection and whether it can, in fact, operate to protect those values to which it assigns priority.

The Medicolegal Model

Early and aggressive intervention comprises the central feature of the medicolegal model. It too rests on a well-developed body of theory, particularly the doctrine of parens patriae or the state's paternalistic right of guardianship of minors.[20] The Supreme Court has affirmed the state's legitimate interest in protecting life and the welfare of children in its decisions on abortion and on the procedural requirements of juvenile proceedings.[16,21]

The child abuse-reporting statutes represent the deference to early intervention. While there is some variation in the language of the statutes, most mandate certain professionals—physicians, social workers, school teachers—to report any suspicion of child abuse to a state agency.[22] Enacted largely between 1963 and 1967, these statutes reflect the substantial impact of Kempe's identification and description of the battered child syndrome in 1962.[23]

Protection of the child is the central priority of

the medicolegal model.[24] In *Nelson Textbook of Pediatrics*[25] immediate intervention is presented as the most appropriate management of the cases. Hospitals have been experimenting with multidisciplinary teams of physicians, lawyers, social workers, and nurse practitioners for comprehensive evaluation, counseling, formulation of treatment plans, and follow-up. In addition to the Trauma-X team at Children's Hospital in Boston, children's hospitals in Washington, DC, and Pittsburgh have comprehensive intervention programs. This comprehensive approach includes advocacy for the child in the courts and with the welfare agencies.

The early-intervention advocates are motivated primarily by the repetitive nature of abuse and the chronic nature of the environmental and psychological conditions leading to its infliction. That "the battered child is only the last phase of the spectrum of the maltreatment syndrome" provides a focal point of clinical understanding of the problem.[6,7] To counter the restrictions imposed by JJSP standards, members of the child abuse intervention team at Children's Hospital Medical Center in Boston developed a separate model for early intervention. They maintain that early limited intervention will better preserve family integrity by insuring services *before* family conditions degenerate to the point where temporary or permanent removal is required.[5]

Briefly, the model proposes intervention in cases of nonserious as well as serious harm. This would be accomplished through two distinct court jurisdictions for services and removal. Consistent with the JJSP standards, removal would only occur when the child could not be protected through administration of services at home. Counseling and services would be designed to relieve specific stresses. In order to terminate services or foster care, the burden of proving that a child will be safe from future injury would shift from the state to the parents. This burden assumes that the history of past injury disrupts the presumption that the parents are fit and that the parents have exclusive access to information about their fitness. Placing the burden on them would thus render the assessment of future endangerment somewhat less speculative. These clinicians further believe that expansion of the reporting and investigation systems will not only bring cases to attention earlier but will provide better information to prevent unnecessary intervention.[5]

Notwithstanding the disruption of the presumption of parental fitness, the authors of this model oppose a fixed time scale for termination of parental rights. They argue that adequate time must be allowed for complete rehabilitation and that parental progress towards rehabilitation rather than absolute achievement of this goal should be the key consideration. Moreover, they fear that rather than terminate relationships so abruptly, judges will fail to remove children where protection is necessary in order to avoid the operation of automatic termination. Accordingly, this model calls for court review of placements every six months to assess family progress and to consider termination.[5]

The medicolegal model also has support from the courts. *Landeros vs Flood*[2] held physicians and a hospital liable in malpractice for a subsequent reinjury of a child after the physicians failed to identify abuse in earlier treatment and initiate state involvement. The court held that the prospect of reinjury was so great that, as a matter of law, it was a predictable consequence of failure to intervene:

... one of the distinguishing characteristics of [child abuse] is that the assault ... is not an isolated, atypical event but part of an environmental mosaic of repeated beatings ....that will not only continue but will become more severe unless there is appropriate medicolegal intervention.[27]

The clinicians here were held liable independently of the reporting statute on grounds of common law negligence.[2] The case thus suggests that the duty to intervene inheres in the nature of the problem.

The goal of the medicolegal model is to protect children by improving the conditions which lead to their endangerment. Ideally, this approach benefits both children and their caretakers and better serves the family institution. As in the privacy model, the question remains whether this model overlooks significant values or adequately protects the values it considers fundamental.

DISCUSSION

On one level both models share common themes and values. In many respects, the JJSP standards serve merely as a codification of existing principles, such as the use of foster care as a tool of last resort.[18] Both models reflect a concern for the welfare of children: the JJSP standards ultimately defend family privacy as the framework "most likely to lead to decisions that help children."[5] Both models also require a great deal of speculative judgment: determining whether in-home services will adequately protect a child from future endangerment necessarily calls for subjective assessment.

Most importantly, both models are grounded in the reality of child abuse and intervention. It is the realistic orientation of the models, however, that creates their ultimate antagonism. Each model fundamentally addresses one side of the battered child syndrome: the privacy model deals with the lack of appropriate alternatives to the family, and the medicolegal model deals with the consequences of the problem of child abuse. In short, the privacy model addresses its standards to the nature of the existing solutions, while the medicolegal model directs its remedy to the nature of the precipitating problem. In so doing, the medicolegal model proves more faithful to its own stated objectives.

The JJSP standards rest on the assumption that protecting the family is the best way to protect the child. The standards thus ignore the central reality of the problem: abusive families do not function in a harmony of interests. Involuntarily or not, abused children and parents face an adversary existence. To insist that the presumption of parental fitness continue even after abuse is identified results in a de facto dominance of the parent's interest against the child's, notwithstanding the Standards' insistence that the child's interest is paramount.[4]

In order to fully evaluate the child's interest, it is necessary to weigh the consequences of intervention against the consequences of nonintervention. It is important to realize that removal and intervention are not synonymous. While citing the harms that flow from removal and intervention, the privacy advocates do not compare them to the harms which result from lack of intervention. Moreover, data on harm from service intervention are conspicuously lacking. Data on specific benefits of services are sparse, but clearly such comparative data will never be forthcoming if intervention is obstructed.

Since the data are inconclusive, the relative benefits and harms of services can only be a source of debate.[5] What is beyond debate is the degree to which children unprotected will be reinjured. This fact defeats the conclusion that while the JJSP standards may work hardship on some individual children, they will operate systematically more effectively for most children.[12] The net result of preventing early intervention will be to insure an increase in serious injury. Once a family situation has degenerated into serious abuse, the likelihood for removal increases with the inability of services, whose effect requires time, to interrupt the cycle quickly enough. The Standards thus operate both to increase risk to children and to force more traumatic forms of intervention.

The elimination of unbridled discretion comprises a central goal of the JJSP standards.[18] However, the proposals operate merely to shift discretion away from the courts and agencies and back to the clinicians. By eliminating state coerciveness in many salient cases, the Standards push evaluation and treatment formulation back to the least visible and least accountable sector of child protection—the voluntary system. Not only will these professionals possess more discretion but they will be forced to exercise it against a background of less information since they have no authority to obtain information about families. As a result, uninformed speculation in treatment formulation will increase with no indication of the inappropriateness of intervention until it fails.

Given the divergent approaches of the two models, one must examine the consequences of this conflict on the protection process, both in its legal and medical dimensions. The first consequence is that one model could be adopted to the exclusion of the other. The JJSP standards emanate from the highly credible forum of the law reform institutes of the American Bar Association. The medicolegal model sifts down from clinical observation and practice and diverse journals. Without a more comprehensive formulation of policy, it is not clear that clinicians will be able to sustain either the information systems they need or the protective ability that they exercise only with the aid of the state.

Alternatively, rather than competing for credibility, the two models could be applied so as to operate in a complementary way. Specifically, the model of early state intervention should be employed as the best means of, first, protecting victims and, second, of helping families. Thirdly, consistent with the medicolegal model of fitting the solution to the problem, the forms of intervention should be tied to specifically identifiable harms and stresses. Finally, the controls over dispositions, particularly over the criteria for termination of services, foster care, and parental rights should be based on the privacy model with the exception that parental fitness should not be presumed.

This synthesis seems reasonable because, while the medicolegal model best protects the child at the threshold of entry into the child protection system, the semiannual court review that it proposes does not sufficiently emphasize the need for finite resolution of these cases. The privacy model more effectively prevents the traditional judicial rubber stamping of administrative procrastination by requiring resolution on the basis of fixed standards. The possibility of premature separation or judicial reluctance to remove when necessary remain risks, but the existing pattern of interminable cycles of foster care presents such conspicuous harm that it must be effectively addressed. Ideally, this formulation should provide the maximum protection to the child, increase the likelihood of the family remaining intact, and create greater certainty and accountability in the administration of intervention.

Finally, in the formulation of child abuse standards, it is particularly important to dispense with euphemisms. The privacy model maintains that the best way to protect the child is to protect the family. The medicolegal model asserts that protecting the child reinforces the family. Both are right and both are ultimately irrelevant. The goal in child abuse intervention is to stop inflicted harm to the defenseless. Other values may serve that goal but they should not mitigate its priority.

ACKNOWLEDGMENT

The author thanks the Sexual Abuse and Trauma-X teams at Children's Hospital Medical Center in Boston for their inclusion of her in their team discussions, and Dr Richard B. Markham for helpful comments and criticism.

REFERENCES

1. *Lynch vs Dukakis*, CA No. 78-2152-G at 2. (DC Mass, 1978)
2. *Landeros vs Flood*, 131 Cal 69, 551 P 2d 389, 1976
3. *Sims vs Texas Department of Public Welfare*, 438 F Suppl 1179, 1977
4. Institute of Judicial Administration of the American Bar Association, Juvenile Justice Standards Project. *Standards Relating to Abuse and Neglect* (Tentative Draft). Cambridge, MA Ballinger Publishing Co, 1977
5. Bourne R, Newberger EH: Family Autonomy or Coercive Intervention? Ambiguity and Conflict in the Proposed Standards for Child Abuse and Neglect. *BU Law Review* 57: 672, 1977
6. Newberger EH, Hyde JN Jr: Principles and implications of current pediatric practice. *Pediatr Clin North Am* 22:695, 1975
7. Gelles RJ: Violence toward children in the United States. *Am J Orthopsychiatry* 48:580, 1978
8. Kempe CH, et al: The battered child syndrome. *JAMA* 181: 17, 1962
9. Fontana VJ, et al: The maltreatment syndrome in children. *N Engl J Med* 269:1391, 1963
10. Morse CW, et al: A three- year follow-up study of abused and neglected children. *Am J Dis Child* 120:445, 1970
11. Silver, et al: Does violence breed violence: Contributions from a study of the child abuse syndrome. *Am J Psychiatry* 126:405, 1963
12. Wald M: State intervention on behalf of neglected children, standards for removal of children from their homes, monitoring the status of children in foster care, and termination of parental rights. *Stanford Law Review* 28:636, 1976
13. Wald MS: State intervention on behalf of neglected children: A search for realistic standards. *Stanford Law Review* 27: 989, 1976
14. *Meyer vs Nebraska*, 262 US 390, 1923
15. *Wisconsin vs Yoder*, 406 US 207, 1972
16. *Griswald vs Connecticut* 381 US 479, 1965
17. *Roe vs Wade*, 410 US 113, 1973
18. McCathren RR: Accountability in the child protection system: A defense of the proposed standards relating to abuse and neglect. *BU Law Review* 57:710, 1977
19. *In Re Clear* 58 Misc. 2d 699, 296 NYS 2d 184
20. *Black's Law Dictionary*, Ed 4. St Paul, MN, West Publishing Co, 1968
21. *McKeiver vs Pennsylvania*, 403 US 528, 1976
22. 119 Mass. General Laws Annotated 51A
23. Thomas M: Child abuse and neglect. I. Historical overview, legal matrix and social perspectives. *NC Law Review* 50:293, 1972
24. Newberger EH: A physician's perspective on the interdisciplinary management of child abuse. *Psychiatr Opinion* 13: 13, 1976
25. Vaughn VC, McKay RJ: *Nelson Textbook of Pediatrics*, Ed 10. Philadelphia, WB Saunders Co, 1975, p 107

Child Abuse and Neglect:
Changing Policies and Perspectives

BEVERLY B. KOERIN

Editor's note: *The author's condensation of the development of society's posture toward child abuse and neglect captures the determining essentials of history, attitudes, laws and evolution of services. It provides a ready orientation to all who are new to protective services.*

Contemporary society has, within the last century, recognized certain responsibilities to its children, as indicated in the development of public school education, child labor laws, and aid to dependent children. However, recognition that society must at times protect children from their parents or guardians is a relatively new development. Child abuse reporting laws in the 50 states are the result of legislative action within the last 20 years.

The Family and Social Values

At the turn of the century, protective services for neglected and abused children in the United States were provided by private agencies, and more recently, under public auspices after the Social Security Act provided that public welfare agencies deal with these problems. Historically, the ambivalence of communities and society in general

Beverly B. Koerin, B.S., M.S.W., is Assistant Professor, Virginia Commonwealth University, Richmond.

0009-4021/80/090531-11 $01.25 © Child Welfare League of America toward handling child abuse and neglect has been reflected in the inadequacy of programs and laws designed to deal with this social problem. The reluctance of society to intervene between parent and child is not surprising in light of the dominant cultural values and norms. "The family is the fundamental unit in our society that has the responsibility for developing healthy children. It is expected to care, love, nurture, train, guide, and protect its children" [6].

United States society is based on this notion of family as an inviolable social unit, and historically many measures to protect children have been slow in gaining acceptance, especially measures to protect children from their own families. In 1874, a child in New York, Mary Ellen, was found to have been severely abused by her family, but there were no existing laws or sanctions by which the child could be protected. She was finally protected under a provision in the law relating to cruelty to animals. This led to the foundation of the New York Society for Prevention of Cruelty to Children, the first protective service agency in the nation [1]. In 1877 the American Humane Association (AHA) was established as an organization committed to encouraging legislation to protect children. The AHA was instrumental in lobbying for child labor laws, special juvenile courts, separate detention facilities, and child abuse reporting laws. The AHA has had a difficult fight to gain acceptance for child protection measures.

Societal Values

Child abuse and neglect existed long before organizations were founded in attempts to deal with the problem. However, societal values have been strong deterrents to intervention in behalf of children. The old concept of pater potestas—all power vested in the father—was firmly entrenched in the belief system of most Americans; a man's wife and children were often viewed and sometimes treated as his chattel. Gradually, the newer concept of parens patriae became more widely accepted. This doctrine held that the community had a right to intervene in family situations when the community peace was threatened. The doctrine was derived from early Germanic tribal laws and then expanded under the Norman domino doctrine, which held that the king, or state, was a parent to the citizens and had a responsibility to protect all subjects [8]. Public opinion based on values has held that the family is entitled to privacy and as little government interference as possible. Parents have a right to custody, control and immediate supervision; this right is not absolute if the parents do not assume their parental responsibilities. When parents failed to care properly for their children, they were (and often still are) viewed in a punitive light by most members of society.

The social policy developing from this kind of public opinion operated in private agencies, whereby children were removed from their homes and placed in foster care (seen as a punitive measure to parents as well as protection for the child) [11]. As social policy became translated into public policy, parents found to be neglecting or abusing their children were prosecuted under applicable criminal codes. Protective service during this era, prior to the advent of social work as a profession, was seen as law enforcement. The welfare of the child was often subordinated in the legal process of establishing parental guilt. Criminal prosecution necessitates proving blame beyond a reasonable doubt, and in child neglect or abuse, there is often a lack of evidence because of the absence of witnesses (either no one else was present or those who witnessed the abuse or neglect did not want to become involved), and the parents' desire to protect each other. If court action fails, the child may face greater danger of abuse. Also, prosecution does not affect the causes of the parental neglect—emotional and/or situational problems [5].

Public Policy and Public Awareness

During the 1930s, social workers became more influential in affecting social and public policy, and child abuse was seen—at least within the profession—as a frequent outgrowth of parental incapacities rather than primarily of willful acts or failures to act by the parents [9].

The Social Security Act incorporated a provision stating that protective services should be provided by public welfare agencies, especially in areas where this type of service was not offered under other auspices. This provision was a shift in public policy in the direction of treatment of families, rather than punishment of parents [1:8]. Thus, during the 1920s and 1930s, the social work orientation prevailed, although this was translated into public policy only in regard to the Social Security Act and in policy formation within welfare agencies providing protective services. Public opinion was not an active catalyst in policy making at that time because of public preoccupation with the economic conditions of the times, and limited media involvement. Social policy was largely formulated by social work professionals, and transformed into public policy in minimal ways.

In the last 20 years, child neglect and especially child abuse have become well publicized social problems and support from other disciplines has also been a major force in shaping public opinion and encouraging policy formation. In the 1950s and 1960s, a great deal of data was collected regarding the incidence of child abuse. The AHA and the American Medical Association (AMA) collected the information, and their accounts were widely publicized in professional journals and in popular magazines.

Dramatic material was presented by pediatricians and emergency room doctors, who were discovering alarming numbers of child abuse cases. Dr. Henry Kempe, a pediatrician at the University of Colorado School of Medicine, collected data from other doctors throughout the country and documented the shocking evidence of abuse. In July 1962, the *Journal of the American Medical Association (JAMA)* published his article "The Battered Child Syndrome," and public attention suddenly became focused on this social problem as a result of media coverage of the article. An editorial in *JAMA* in July 1962 stressed the need for the abused child to be protected from the parent and the need to protect the parent from his/her own impulses to harm the child. The editors urged that mandatory reporting laws be passed, that adequate protective services be made available, and that the medical professionals assume their responsibility in determining when a child was suffering from the battered child syndrome [7].

The AHA was also active in disseminating information regarding child abuse through its publication of *Child Abuse: Preview of a Nationwide Study*, in 1960, and *Review of Legislation to Protect the Battered Child*, in 1964. However, the *JAMA* reports on the battered child syndrome became the major source of public concern, perhaps a reflection of the public status of the social work profession relative to the medical profession. The medical profession had much greater impact than social workers or social welfare organizations. In 1960 the *Reader's Guide to Periodical Literature* began listing a topic "Cruelty to Children"; from 1962–1965 there were many articles in magazines such as *Newsweek* and *Time*, most of which referred to the AMA publication. Newspapers and television also covered the subject, and public opinion was aroused.

Members of the medical profession approached the United States Children's Bureau in the early 1960s to learn what they might do to protect children (and to protect doctors who make reports of suspected child abuse). In January 1962 the Children's Bureau convened two meetings with lawyers, doctors, social workers and judges to discuss this concern, and from these meetings developed suggested models for state legislation for child abuse reporting laws [2:202–203].

The 1960s were a fertile period for legislation relating to civil rights and children's rights. After the mild recession of 1960–1961, the economy entered an expansionary period; this prosperous period from 1961 to the late 1960s was the longest in U.S. history [4:398–399]. Many people were better able to meet their basic physical needs, and thus could focus on social needs (rights). Also, during this time there was greater public recognition, due in part to media coverage, of the problems of urban living. Mobility, transience, and reduction of daily involvement with neighbors and relatives result in reduced social control and personal influences on parental behavior toward their children. As a result of media coverage and the pressure of professional groups, primarily doctors and social workers, between 1963 and 1967, all 50 states passed child abuse reporting laws, thus formalizing the social policy that children need protection.

Punishment Versus Treatment

Much to the chagrin of the social work profession, the legislators were much more affected by outraged public opinion and by the concerns of the medical profession in drafting legislation than by social work attitudes toward child abuse. The legislators were undoubtedly shocked during public hearings by the statistics on child abuse and the pictures they saw of abused children. They also acted in response to demands of their constituents and the medical pressure groups.

The first child abuse reporting laws were protective of the professionals reporting suspected incidents and punitive in the measures dealing with abusive and neglecting families. The new laws included provisions for reporting incidents to law enforcement bodies, with an underlying stress on removal of children and prosecution of parents [1:21]. The AHA and social workers then began trying to influence revision of legislation, and between 1967–1970, most state laws were revised on the basis of research related to therapeutic work with families, on the recognition that a large majority of abuse and neglect cases are handled successfully by agencies without court action, and on the understanding of the increased damage to child and family that a punitive approach often has (especially when prosecution of parents fails and a child suffers from the parents' heightened hostility).

The laws of most states have been revised so that reports go solely to child protective agencies. Other revisions include expanding the range of professions responsible for reporting, enlarging the concept of abuse, and making reporting mandatory for those professions cited in the law. Although the medical profession is still the primary profession cited, teachers, social workers and probation officers are among the other professionals often included.

Defining Neglect and Abuse

Public opinion seems to remain largely punitive toward neglecting and abusing parents, and public policy in relation to treatment of these families often reflects compromises between conflicting forces. Legislators, by and large, share the public attitudes, and social workers are often at a disadvantage in dealing with the shock and anger of some legislators as they consider laws to protect children. Certainly legal provisions, influenced by community values, are forces in determining what will be defined as neglect or abuse. Although abuse is more easily defined, child neglect is a "value-loaded concept defined by middle class norms" [8]. Even under the law, in different states neglect refers to different things (such as behavior of parents, child's surroundings, or condition of the child). In 1968, under AFDC rules in Maryland and Florida, activities considered indices of child neglect included the mother's involvement in promiscuous behavior in or out of the home, cohabitation or pregnancy out of wedlock.

At present, these parental activities or practices are often still weighed in agency consideration as to filing a petition for custody. Although these factors do not provide proof of parental neglect, they may be damaging evidence in neglect or custody hearings, depending on the judge, the state, and the race of the AFDC or non-AFDC mother. The notion of a stable, "moral" environment is a middle class norm; parental deviation from the norm need not indicate that a child is being neglected [8]. A common-law relationship may be a warm, stable relationship for the child.

Decisions to report neglect or abuse may be based on reasons related as much to economic and ethnic factors as to actual neglect and abuse, a fact that accounts, in part, for the higher incidence of reported neglect and abuse among lower income families; thus, the community tremendously influences the working definition of neglect and abuse. Incidents of physical neglect are reported by professionals and community members to a much greater extent than incidents related to emotional neglect. This seems to reflect the prevailing, and sometimes conflicting, values that children need protection but that families have a right to privacy. In addition, emotional neglect is less easily defined and observed, more difficult to establish in court than physical neglect, and probably prevalent to a greater extent among all income groups. Social workers also influence the definition of neglect and abuse in their decisions as to which families are to receive protective services. It is hoped that social work professionals consider the child's total situation rather than the family's violation of community norms that may have no bearing on the quality of the child's care and well-being. However, social workers must operate within the sanctions of the law, the agency and the community while recognizing their responsibility to the clients.

Recent Trends: Continued Contradictions

There seem to be several factors influencing the growing interest in child abuse. Within the last few years there has been a great deal of concern about the family as a social unit. Drug abuse, runaways and alienation between parent and child have been widely publicized, and child abuse and neglect have been areas of concern to both the family and the community. In the early and middle 1960s, much of the publicity about child abuse was in documentary form and aroused the citizenry and legislators. In more recent years, child abuse has been the topic of many popular television shows, and the subject has often been handled well. The abusing parents were often portrayed as individuals unable to cope with stressful events or to control aggressive impulses or emotions; they were portrayed sympathetically as persons who felt both fear and guilt at their behavior. The professionals involved with them offered protection to the children and treatment, not punishment, to the parent. In some cases, the public attitude toward abusing parents may have undergone subtle changes toward a less punitive view.

Emotions a Factor

Thus, public opinion may be slowly changing toward parents who abuse and neglect their children. More persons (legislators included) are able to accept the ideas that mishandling of children by parents need not be willful, and that parents need help. These beliefs are more easily accepted intellectually than they are emotionally, as most persons are still shocked by reports of abuse. Thus, as a rational response, new laws of a more therapeutic and less punitive nature have been passed. However, in terms of funding and implementation of programs for protective services, and in terms of community usage of such programs, the emotional element may play a major role. People in general have a negative attitude toward child abusers and have mixed feelings about the economically dependent, including children. Historically, there has always been an effort to protect children, but at the least expense to the taxpayer, such as colonial American indenture and workhouse practices.

Though the family is regarded as the primary social unit, and it is believed that efforts should be made to maintain the family unit, the manner of funding child welfare programs defeats these goals. For example, Young noted that in 1964, 60 cents a day was allowed for each added ADC child, $2 to $3 a day for a foster child, $5 to $7 a day for a child in a congregate care institution, and $10 to $12 a day for residential treatment placement. "We do the least to maintain a child within his own home and more and more as his placement makes return to normal life in the community less and less possible" [9]. Relatively little money has been appropriated for the prevention of child abuse and neglect, which would be a deterrent to removal of children from their families and their placement in other homes or institutions.

Conclusion

Child abuse and neglect are now recognized social problems. Public opinion has been aroused, the attitudes may have become, by virtue of social conditions and mass media, less punitive, encouraging shifts in public policy. However, the emotional element of shock and anger toward the parents and ambivalence at intervention into family relations have also influenced child protective policy and practice in terms of the inadequacy of existing laws, underfunding of programs, reluctance of individuals to report incidents of abuse, and continued community pressure on protective service agencies to deal more punitively with parents. Such attitudes persist on a gut level and will probably influence the course of child protective services and laws for a considerable time. Therefore, it is important to approach the public and legislators from both ethical and pragmatic bases.

From an ethical viewpoint, social workers and members of other disciplines must continue to help the public accept, on an emotional level, the basic beliefs that are the foundation of child protective services: the dignity of the child and the child's right to good care and relationships with parents; the right of parents to fulfill their parental role; the desire of most parents to be good parents; parental neglect as an indicator of stress or disturbance; the capacity of people to change; and society's responsibility for children [3].

However, this will be a monumental task, and a pragmatic approach will probably have a greater effect at this point. It is necessary to influence public opinion and legislators' opinions on a practical basis, pointing out the expense of prosecution of parents and child placement costs as opposed to initial outlays for preventive programs that would maintain family integrity and treat, not punish, such families. Another argument for a less punitive approach is the increased danger to the child's well-being when punitive actions against the parents fail and when the child remains at home to face their increased resentment and anxiety. Finally, there is need for continued research to substantiate social work's contention that protective services are effective in protecting children and, in many cases, maintaining family integrity. ◆

References

1. American Humane Association. Speaking Out for Child Protection. Denver: AHA, 1973, pp. 10–19.

2. "Abused Children," Children X, 5 (September-October 1963).

3. Child Welfare League of America. CWLA Standards for Child Protective Services. New York: CWLA, 1960, p. 3.

4. Dauten, Carl A., and Valentine, Lloyd M. Business Cycles and Forecasting. Chicago, Southwestern, 1968.

5. De Frances, Vincent. Child Abuse Legislation in the 1970s. Denver: American Humane Association, 1970, pp. 1–4.

6. Fredericksen, Hazel, and Mulligan, R.A. The Child and His Welfare. San Francisco: W.H. Freeman, 1972, p. 204.

7. Kempe, C. Henry. "The Battered Child Syndrome," Journal of the American Medical Association CLXXXI (July 7, 1962), pp. 17–24, 42.

8. Richmond School of Social Work. Proceedings of Institutes on Protective and Related Community Services. Richmond, VA: 1968, pp. 1, 19, 79, 68.

9. Young, Leontine. Wednesday's Children. New York: McGraw-Hill, 1964; pp. 142–144.

Child Abuse and Neglect

Each year the state intervenes in the private lives of hundreds of thousands of families in this country. The grounds for intervention are allegations of abuse or neglect; the purpose, to "save" children. The past twenty years have been marked by an increased public awareness of the dimensions of child maltreatment in our society. Laws have undergone alteration as legislatures have struggled to define standards for government intervention. As knowledge about the "causes" and "cures" of child abuse and neglect grows, change will continue. This article will focus on where we are, and where we're going.

> **" The state may intervene in the parent/child relationship as a result of its parens patriae power. "**

The Interests Involved

Every child abuse or neglect proceeding involves three parties: the child, the parents, and the state. The interests of each are different.

American tradition promotes family autonomy. We cherish a belief that parents should be allowed to raise their children as they see fit. The right of parents to control their children's upbringing has been given constitutional protection. 1/ It is one of the "liberty" interests, protected by the Fourteenth Amendment of the United States Constitution. 2/

This right, however, is clearly not absolute. 3/ The state may intervene in the parent/child relationship as a result of its parens patriae power. The rationale for intervention in an abuse situation is the protection of a child. 4/ Balanced against the desire to intervene is the state's desire to promote family autonomy, both because of our history of such autonomy and because of the effectiveness of the family as an institution.5/ The state also has police power, which may be brought to bear in criminal proceedings against the parents. However, use of this authority is in direct opposition to the state's interest in preserving the family. Therein lies the dilemma.

Children's interests in these proceedings do not have the stature of legal rights as children have no legal entitlement to necessities such as adequate food or medical care. 6/ Their interests are viewed as protected by the state when it uses its parens patriae authority.

Principles Underlying Intervention

The most important task of any legislature drafting the laws relating to child abuse is to determine what principles form the basis for state intervention. Without an understanding of these principles, statutes cannot be sufficiently tailored to serve the state's interests. Major problems of neglect and abuse laws in this country have, in fact, been their vagueness and broadness. 7/ They have not sufficiently defined the acts that constitute abuse and neglect and have thereby given an incredi-

13

383

14

ble amount of discretion to agencies and courts.

Most commentators today agree that a presumption of minimal state intrusion should exist. 8/ There are several reasons for this. First, as noted above, parents have a liberty interest in raising their own children as they see fit. 9/ Second, allowing families to engage in diverse child-rearing practices promotes our political interest in individual freedom and privacy and contributes to a diversity of ideas and lifestyles. 10/ Finally, such a presumption serves the child's need for "continuity of care by autonomous caretakers."11/

In a system which is allegedly geared to protecting the child, the last reason is the most important. Goldstein, Freud and Solnit, in their highly respected book, Beyond the Best Interests of the Child, established the concept of the "psychological parent," based on the need of each child for "unbroken continuity of affectionate and stimulating relationships with an adult." 12/ Each time the law interferes in a parent-child relationship, it may disrupt whatever bond there is and cause emotional and psychological harm to the child. 13/ Therefore, before the state causes such harm, it should be sure that this emotional harm is less than that being suffered by the child in the home. The child's welfare is not served by state intervention that results in further damaging him.

The other important principle underlying intervention is that any intrusion should serve the best interests of the child. Although all states attempt to act according to this principle, the statutes enacted do not always logically reflect this goal. Thus, many statutes focus on parental unfitness, inadequacy or immorality. The motivation is often to punish parents for certain "unacceptable" behavior without determining whether such behavior is in

> **❝** *Typical abuse statutes today encompass four types of child maltreatment: 1) physical abuse, 2) sexual abuse, 3) emotional abuse, and 4) neglect.* **❞**

fact harmful to the child. 14/ Furthermore such intervention may work in direct opposition to the principle above, because the child's best interests would best be served by no state intervention.

Standards for Intervention

Typical abuse statutes today encompass four types of child maltreatment: 1) physical abuse, 2) sexual abuse, 3) emotional abuse and 4) neglect. The specificity of the law has varied with each type of abuse.

A. Physical Abuse

Physical abuse has been the most easily defined. It is generally viewed as the parental infliction of physical injury to the child. It is regarded as an act of commission by the parents. Physicians look to evidence of bruises, lacerations, broken bones caused by twisting or pulling, hemorrhaging beneath the scalp caused by shaking or hitting, internal injuries and bleeding caused by hitting or kicking, and various types of burns as indicators of physical abuse. 15/ The statutes generally require proof of physical injury coupled with a parental explanation for the injury that does not accord with the medical evidence relating to causation.

The major problem with definitions of physical abuse derives from an effort to distinguish between discipline in the form of corporal punishment and physical abuse. Parents have the duty and responsibility to discipline their children and corporal punishment is permitted, within reason. 17/

15

However, the line of "reason" varies from community to community and is subject to much discretion on the part of courts. The principle of minimal state intervention requires that intrusion be avoided where the parent is disciplining the child. 18/ The problems of inflicting pain in the name of discipline are best dealt with by public education. 19/ The American Bar Association proposes that intervention should be authorized

when a child has suffered, or there is a substantial risk that a child will imminently suffer, a physical harm, inflicted nonaccidentally upon him/her by his/her parents, which causes, or creates a substantial risk of causing disfigurement, impairment of bodily functioning, or other serious physical injury. 20/

This definition more clearly draws the line between cases of physical discipline and those of abuse. At this time, most state statutes are not as narrowly drawn.

B. Sexual Abuse

Probably nothing arouses more public outcry than sexual abuse of children. The law's response has been confused. There are myriad statutes and innumerable definitions. State laws prohibit incest, either between blood relations only or between family members related by blood or by law (ie., adoptive parents, step-parents, siblings, stepsiblings, etc.). 21/ In addition there are both civil and criminal statutes regarding the sexual assault of children. Abuse is defined in many ways; it may include incest, sodomy, sexual contact, seduction, exciting the lust of a child, oral sex perversion and other acts. 22/ Sexual abuse may be treated differently depending on the child's age. 23/ Some states merely forbid sexual abuse without defining the term at all. 24/

16

❝ *The principle problem with the entire area of child abuse is that often the result of disclosure and intervention is harm that equals or exceeds the effects of the abuse itself.* ❞

The principle problem with the entire area of child abuse is that often the result of disclosure and intervention is harm that equals or exceeds the effects of the abuse itself. 25/ Little is known about the effects of the abuse and about the treatment necessary to correct the emotional and psychological harm. 26/ Presumably, as more research is done, the legal standards will evolve to more effectively deal with this problem. One writer has suggested that we should avoid encouraging children to act provocatively. 27/ She notes that girls especially are taught early to use "feminine wiles" to get adult approval. This type of behavior by children should not be encouraged.

One other suggested method of prevention is to teach children the difference between appropriate and inappropriate physical interaction between adults and children. 28/ In essence, this is the same as telling children not to ride with strangers.

In the 1980's, courses in parenting might be more widely instituted in high schools, so that parents might realize importance of teaching their children these values.

C. Emotional Abuse

The concept of emotional abuse is relatively recent and subject to a number of criticisms. Most state laws include emotional abuse under terms such as "mental injury," or "gross neglect which would effect a child's mental or emotional well--

being." 29/ The language is vague and subject to differing interpretations. Problems arise in attempts to determine whether a child is emotionally disturbed or emotionally abused. 30/ Without the possibility of proving a causal connection existed between the inappropriate parental behavior and the child's emotional difficulty, no case exists. Often, expert witnesses are called to testify that the child is emotionally disturbed. However, if the child is emotionally disturbed, it often is difficult to determine the cause of the disturbance. 31/

Attempts have been made to more precisely define emotional abuse and thus give guidance to the courts. The ABA defines it as a situation in which:

a child is suffering serious emotional damage, evidenced by severe anxiety, depression, or withdrawal, or untoward aggressive behavior toward self or others and the child's parents are not willing to provide treatment for him/her. 32/

This definition focuses on the child's behavior and the parents' failure to attempt to cure or treat that behavior; it does not focus on parental behavior which causes the child's emotional problems. By this emphasis, the provision avoids the problem of emotional disturbance v. emotional abuse.

Few cases are ever brought to trial solely on the basis of emotional abuse as it is too difficult to prove. In the 1980's with the emphasis on nonintervention, this trend will probably continue.

D. Neglect

Neglect typically involves acts of omission by the parents. Statutory provisions are often defined in terms of parental misconduct. Neglect can include abandonment, failure to provide adequate parental care or control, food, shelter, clothing, edu-

ation or health care, and failure to prevent conditions harmful to a child's well-
being. 32/ Most include a proviso stating
that failure to provide these necessities
is not a result of lack of financial means,
thereby removing poverty as grounds for a
finding of neglect. 33/

Some provisions are much less explicit,
using terms such as lack of adequate or
proper parental care. Attempts to define
these broad terms have been made by the
courts, 34/ but there are basic problems
with these definitions. First, attention
is focused on parental misconduct and often
there is no requirement that the inadequacy relate to a specific harm suffered by
the child. 35/ Thus, intervention may frequently occur when it is contrary to the
child's best interests. Second, these statutes fail to give the parents adequate and
fair warning of the minimum level of behavior
expected of them. 36/ They encourage ad
hoc determinations and allow almost limit-
less discretion to agencies, prosecutors
and judges. One result has been discrimination against the poor and minorities. 37/
These statutes have been subject to attack on the grounds of vagueness. 38/

If statutes were drawn with regard
to the principle of minimal state intervention, they would define neglect in
terms of the actuality of harm or
the risk of serious physical harm to
the child resulting from conditions created
by the child's parents. The ABA has drafted
such a provision. 39/ It focuses on failure
of the parents to adequately prevent the
child from suffering serious physical harm.
Although the language may still be considered somewhat vague, the emphasis is on

> **Most jurisdictions do not require that counsel be appointed for the child in neglect proceedings.**

the child and the statute does not sweep as
broadly as those referring to inadequate
parental care. We may see a trend toward
the adoption of this type of provision in
the future.

The Adjudicatory Hearing

Abuse and neglect proceedings are usually
bifurcated; there is an adjudicatory hearing to determine whether or not the child
is abused, and if the child is found to be
harmed or at risk, a dispositional hearing
to determine placement is held. Due process
clearly requires that the parents have adequate and timely notice of the hearing and
of the alleged charges so that they can prepare to meet the allegations.

The government has the burden of proving
the allegations. Because an abuse proceeding
is a civil proceeding, a civil standard of
proof is used; abuse or neglect must be prov-
en by a preponderance of the evidence. (In
a criminal proceeding for physical or sexual
abuse the state would have to prove abuse beyond a reasonable doubt.) Parents have the
right to be heard on their own behalf and to
cross-examine witnesses. In all states, parents have the right to be represented by an
attorney.

A more difficult question is whether
indigent parents have a right to a court-
appointed attorney, most importantly in
those instances in which their parental
rights are at issue. 40/The Supreme Court
recently heard argument in a case involving
the right of an indigent parent to a court-
appointed attorney in a proceeding to terminate parental rights. 41/ The decision
in this case may be relevant to a neglect
proceeding as well.

Most jurisdictions do not require that
counsel be appointed for the child in neglect
proceedings. 42/ The Federal Child Abuse and
Treatment Act provides that abused children
must be represented by a guardian ad litem.

18

The child's best interests may differ from those of his/her parents or those of the state. For example, the state may feel the child should be removed from the home and be placed in foster care. The parents will wish to keep the child, while the child might do best with his grandparents who no one has investigated.

Dispositional Alternatives

There are currently two basic dispositions available. One is to leave the child in the home and provide services to the family. The other is to remove the child and place him/her elsewhere. The majority of children adjudicated neglected are separated from their families. 43/ Most children are placed in foster homes and remain there for a considerable length of time. 44/ This lengthy separation interferes with both the principle of minimal state intervention and that of promoting the child's best interests. Sometimes the child's best interest lies in the severing of parental ties and subsequent placement for adoption after substantial but unsuccessful efforts have been made to rehabilitate parents.

On the other hand, often the state will intervene and take children out of their home when they would have been better off left with their parents under the supervision of protective services. Frequently, when the child is taken out of his home and placed in the state's care and custody, little is done to remediate the situation. It has been noted that it is sheer hypocrisy for a legislature to provide for intervention, in the form of a neglect or abuse petition, to protect the child, fail to provide necessary resources and then claim that children are being protected by the state. 45/

A dispostion in accord with the principle of minimal state intervention would require that children be kept in the home and

> **"** *The very real possibility of multiple placements is probably the most damaging aspect of foster care.* **"**

that a plan for social services, designed remedy the conditions causing intervention be developed. Children could be removed only if the services could not alleviate the conditions or if there was no other way to protect the child from serious physical harm. 46/

Much of the evidence shows that placement in foster care is more harmful than leaving the child in the home. 47/ Children suffer from the disruption of ties to their parents. They may feel that placement is a punishment. Multiple placements lead to a lack of stability in the child's development and inability to form new ties with adults. 48/ Since it is the most common disposition, however, it is worth considering what should be done to assure high quality foster care.

The very real possibility of multiple placements is probably the most damaging aspect of foster care. 49/ Therefore, standards should provide for temporary foster care in a single home with provisions for return to the home or termination of parental rights and permanent placement elsewhere. 50/ While in foster care, the child's relationship with his/her parents should be encouraged.

At disposition, the social service agency should designate the specific services to be provided to the family and should inform the parents of obligations they must fulfill in order to regain custody of their children. 51/ Review hearings should be required every 3-6 months and the social service agency should be required to report explicitly on the nat-

...e of services provided, visitation be-
...een parents and child, whether additional
...rvices are needed and whether return of
...e child is expected. 52/

The child's need for continuity of care
...ould determine the length of time that he/
...e will remain in foster care before ter-
...nation of parental rights is sought. Pres-
...tly children remain in limbo for years
...thout a permanent placement. One writer
...ggests that 6 months should be the maxi-
...m period of foster care for children under
...ree years of age, and that one year
...ould be the maximum time for children
...er three. After that time, parental rights
...ould be terminated and permanent placement
...de, if the child cannot return to his/her
...rents. 53/ The ABA has adopted these
...andards in its Standards Relating to Abuse
...d Neglect. 54/ No doubt we will see a
...end toward more specific guidelines con-
...rning intervention in the 1980's.

Reporting Requirements

It appears that the incidence of child abuse
is much higher than the statistics on children brought into the system would indicate. 55/
In an effort to discover existing cases of
abuse and neglect, all 50 states and the District of Columbia have mandatory reporting
laws. Reporting incidents of suspected abuse
is required of medical professionals who are
often the first and only persons to see a
child and who are usually able to render
the most competent diagnosis. 56/ The trend
has been to expand the class of required reporters to include teachers and school officials, social workers, police, child care
workers, clergymen, coroners, and attorneys. 57/ Reporters are required to report
physical abuse, neglect, sexual abuse and
emotional abuse in most states. 58/

The majority of statutes provide criminal penalties for failure to report -- a fine
and/or jail sentence is usually mandated. 59/
However, a potentially more effective method
of encouraging reporting is being developed,
outside of the legislative arena. Two California court cases illustrate the possibility for tort suits for civil damages for
failure to report. In Robinson v. Wical,
M.D. et al, 60/ doctors, police and a hospital were sued for failure to report a
child's suspicious injuries. The child was
sent home and suffered permanent brain damage as the result of another beating. The
case was settled out of court for over half
of a million dollars.

In Landers v. Flood, 61/ the California Supreme Court held that a cause of action
for common law tort and statutory negligence
was stated in a case brought against a physician for failure to diagnose the battered
child syndrome. Plaintiff was to have the
opportunity to prove that a reasonably prudent physician would have diagnosed the child
as abused and reported such abuse.

In light of the medical procedures available for diagnosing a case of child abuse,

20

it is likely that civil suits may increase in the 1980's, at least against medical personnel. Such suits should provide an inducement for more medical professionals to comply with reporting laws. Because professionals can only be held to the level of care that would be exercised by a reasonably prudent person in their profession, and because diagnosis by persons other than medical persons seems more difficult, the use of civil suits may be less successful against other professionals.

Reporting may be improved and increased by provisions mandating rather than merely encouraging the general public to report. However, there is the possibility of inflicting a great deal of harm on parents by labeling them abusive or neglectful and storing their names as "alleged abusing parents" in central registries. 62/ Parents who are never charged or who are acquitted of charges must be able to have their names and records expunged from the registries. Safeguards of this kind have been developed in many states and will no doubt be adopted by others in the 1980's. Simple procedures must be developed for parents unjustly termed "abusers" to clear the record.

Biographical Note

The author of this article, Anne Donahue, J.D., May 1981, Georgetown University Law Center.

FOOTNOTES

1/ See e.g., Pierce v. Society of Sist[...] 268 U.S. 510 (1925); Meyer v. Nebras[...] 262 U.S. 390 (1923).

2/ Pierce, supra n.1 268 U.S. at 534 Meyer, supra n.1, 262 U.S. at 399

3/ See Prince v. Massachusetts, 321 U.S. 158 (1944).

4/ Note, "Constitutional Limitations on Scope of State Child Neglect Statutes 79 Col.L.Rev. 719,721 (1979). See a[...] Institute of Judicial Administration/ American Bar Association, Commission Juvenile Justice Standards, Standards Relating to Abuse and Neglect, 1977.

5/ Areen, Judith, "Intervention Between Parent and Child: A Reappraisal of t[...] State's Role in Child Neglect and Abu[...] Cases," 63 Geo. L.J. 887, 893 (1975).

6/ Id. at 892.

7/ 79 Col. L.Rev., supra n.4, at 719-72[...]

8/ See, e.g., IJA/ABA, supra n.4 at 37, Standard 1.1; Areen, supra n.5, at 9[...] 19; Wald, Michael I., "State Interve[...] tion on Behalf of 'Neglected' Childre[...] Standards for Removal of Children fr[...] their Homes, Monitoring the Status of Children in Foster Care, and Terminat[...] of Parental Rights," 28 Stan.L.Rev. [...] 637 (1976).

9/ See notes 1/and 2/, supra.

10/ IJA/ABA, supra n.4 at 37, Commentary to Standard 1.1.

11/ Goldstein, J., Freud, A., and Soinit [...] Before the Best Interests of the Chi[...] pp. 4-5, The Free Press, 1979.

21

Goldstein, J., Freud, A., and Solnit A., Beyond the Best Interests of the Child, p.6, The Free Press, 1973.

Goldstein, supra n.11, at 8-12.

79 Col.L.Rev., supra n.4, at 721.

U.S. Dept. of HEW and Nat. Center on Child Abuse and Neglect, Resource Materials, A Curriculum on Child Abuse and Neglect, pp. 23-24, DHEW Publ. No. (OHDS) 79-30221, Sept.1979.

Areen, supra n.5, at 922-23.

See Areen, Cases and Materials on Family Law, Foundation Press, 1978, pp.994-1000. See also State v. Fischer, 245 Iowa 170, 60 N.W.2d 105 (1953).

Goldstein, supra n.11, at 72-74.

Id.

IJA/ABA, supra n.4, at 51, Standard 2.1(A).

MacFarlane, Kee, "Sexual Abuse of Children," reprinted in Resource Materials, supra n.15, at 55,56.

Id. at 56-57.

Id.

Id.

Id. at 63; IJA/ABA, supra n.4, at 58, Commentary to Standard 2.1(D); Goldstein, supra n.11, at 62-65.

MacFarlance, supra n.21, at 62-66.

Id. at 67-68.

Id.

"Emotional Maltreatment of Children," Resource Materials, supra n.15 at 50.

30/ Whiting, Leila, "Emotional Neglect of Children," printed in Child Abuse and Neglect: Issues on Innovation and Implementation, Proceedings of the Second Annual National Conference on Child Abuse and Neglect, DHEW Pub. No. (OHDS) 78-30147, 1978, pp.209-210.

31/ Id. See also Goldstein, supra n.11, at 76-77.

32a) IJA/ABA, supra n. 4, at 55-56, Standard 2.1(C).

32b) Areen, supra n.17, at 925-927.

33/ Id.

34/ Id. at 927.

35/ IJA/ABA, supra n. 4, at 53, Commentary to Standard 2.1)B).

36/ Goldstein, supra n.11, at 16-17.

37/ Id. at 17. See also, Wald, supra n. at 629.

38/ See, e.g., Roe v. Conn, 417 F.Supp. 769 (M.D. Ala. 1976); Alsager v.District Court, 406 F.Supp. 10 (S.D. Iowa), aff'd 545 F.2d 1137 (8th Cir.1976); Linn v. Linn, 205 Neb. 218, 286 N.W. 2d 765 (1980); Davis v. Smith, ___ Ark. ___, 583 S.W.2d 37 (1979).

42/ Areen, supra n. 17, at 1125.

43/ Areen, supra n. 17, at 887.

44/ Wald, supra n. 8, at 630-33.

45/ IJA/ABA, supra n. 4, at 116 Commentary to Standard 6.3.

46/ See, e.g., Areen, supra n.17, at 935-36; Wald, supra n. 8, at 643.

47/ Wald, supra n. 8, at 644-46. See also Mnookin, "Foster Care--In Whose Best In-

22

terests," 43 Harv. Educ. Rev. 599 (1973)

48/ Wald, supra n. 8 , at 644-46.

49/ Wald, supra n. 8 , at 646, 671.

50/ See generally, Wald, supra n. 8 .

51/ Id. at 679.

52/ Id. at 681, 683. See also, Areen, supra
n. 17 , at 936-37.

53/ Wald, supra n. 17 , at 695-96.

54/ IJA/ABA, supra n. 4 , at 154, Standard
8.3.

55/ Areen, supra n. 17 , at 887, f.n.1.

56/ See DeFrancis, V., Child Abuse Legislation in the 1970's (1974 ed.).

57/ Basharov, D., "The Legal Aspects of Reporting Known and Suspected Child Abuse
and Neglect," 23 Vill. L. Rev. 458, 467-
68 (1978).

58/ Id. at 471-72.

59/ Id. at 480.

60/ Civ. N. 37607, Cal. Superior Court,
San Luis Obispo, filed Sept. 4, 1970.

61/ 17 Cal. 3d 399, 131 Cal. Rptr. 69, 551
P.2d 389 (1976).

62/ Sussman, A., "Reporting Child Abuse: A
Review of the Literature," 8 Fam.L.Q.
245, 311-12 (1974).

Child Abuse & Neglect, Vol. 9, pp. 365–372, 1985
Printed in the U.S.A. All rights reserved.

HOW EFFECTIVE IS THE MULTIDISCIPLINARY APPROACH? A FOLLOW-UP STUDY

NEIL J. HOCHSTADT, PH.D.

Director, Behavioral Science Department, La Rabida Children's Hospital and Research Center and Assistant Professor, Pritzker School of Medicine, Department of Pediatrics, University of Chicago, East 65th Street at Lake Michigan, Chicago, IL 60649

NEIL J. HARWICKE, PH.D.

Senior Psychologist, Behavioral Science Department, La Rabida Children's Hospital and Research Center, Chicago

Abstract—The multidisciplinary approach to diagnose, evaluate, and plan the treatment of victims of child abuse and neglect has been widely advocated and adopted by hospitals and community-based protective service teams. Despite the increasing prevalence of this approach, few if any studies have looked at its effectiveness. In the current study the effectiveness of the multidisciplinary approach was assessed by looking at the number of recommended services obtained by a sample of 180 children one year after evaluation by a multidisciplinary team. The results indicate that a large percentage of services recommended by the multidisciplinary team were obtained. This compares with the very low probability of service acquisition reported in samples of abused and neglected children identified by CPS teams but not having access to a multidisciplinary evaluation. The multidisciplinary team plays a central role in acquiring the services needed to reduce the deficits and sequelae suffered by the victims of child abuse and neglect.

Résumé—Les auteurs ont voulu évaluer la valeur de l'approche multidisciplinaire, ce qui n'a pas été fait souvent jusqu'à présent Cette approche est recommandée, en général, par les spécialistes de la question, mais la preuve de son efficacité manque en grande partie. Le sort de 180 enfants souffrant de mauvais traitements ou de négligence a été évalué dans le but de mesurer la valeur de l'approche multidisciplinaire. Contrairement à ce qui se passe dans les situations où ce genre de tactique n'est pas la règle, l'approche multidisciplinaire a l'avantage de mobiliser un nombre de services plus élevé et de les mettre au bénéfice des enfants. Le résultat, de ce côté-là, est donc positif. Il faut cependant faire une nuance en ce qui concerne les enfants victimes de négligence. Malgré le fait que la vie de ces enfants est en danger (en particulier les cas de déficits nutritionnel et de croissance) on a trop tendance à remettre ces enfants, une fois dépistés, entre les mains de leurs parents. Il semble que l'on assume que, dans les cas de négligence, la situation est moins dangereuse que dans les cas de mauvais traitements, ce qui est faux. Il apparaît donc que l'approche multidisciplinaire est fructueuse en ce qui concerne le nombre et la qualité des services mis à la disposition des familles, mais qu'elle n'a pas évité, jusqu'à présent, le piège qui consiste à considérer la négligence comme moins dangereuse que la violence.

Key Words—Child abuse and neglect; Multidisciplinary; Follow-up.

INTRODUCTION

IT HAS BEEN REPORTED that abused and neglected children suffer from a wide range of deficits and many sequelae of their trauma. Early treatment planning and the provision of requisite services and treatment are essential if these children are to have a chance to attain

The authors wish to thank the Schoen Family Fund and the Albert Pick, Jr. Fund for their support of this project. Our special thanks to Dr. Burton J. Grossman for his support and guidance.

normal growth and development. Recently, there has been an emphasis on the need for early diagnosis and consultation by multidisciplinary teams, but little effort has been made to determine if these efforts lead to the provision of the required services for this high risk population. In response to the lack of research in this area, the current study evaluated the effect of a multidisciplinary child abuse and neglect program on service delivery.

The multidisciplinary approach to diagnose, evaluate, and plan the treatment of victims of child abuse and neglect has been widely advocated [1–5], and has been widely adopted by hospitals and community-based protective service teams in the recent past. Despite the increasing prevalence of this model, there have been few, if any, follow-up studies of its effects on service delivery, especially in the child abuse field [6]. Follow-up studies have looked at emotional sequelae [7], intellectual deficits [8–12] and neurological impairments [8, 11, 13]. The difficulties in conducting follow-up research in this area are many, and include methodological problems (e.g., the inability to define abuse and neglect, and the choice of dependent variables), time constraints, loss to follow-up of a large number of patients, and difficulty in obtaining data due to issues of confidentiality and poor interagency cooperation [14].

One of the primary purposes of the multidisciplinary approach is to reduce the fragmentation of the service delivery system [15]; yet there are no indicators that fragmentation has decreased as the result of the increased use of the multidisciplinary approach [16]. In studies of protective service agencies and court systems, Terr and Watson [17], Purvine and Ryan [18], Burt and Balyeat [19], Polier [20], and Cain [21] found evidence of fragmented service delivery, lack of planning, duplication of services and failure to deliver the requisite services. The importance of articulating the multidisciplinary evaluation with follow-up services is highlighted by the fact that 50% of the estimated 420,000 children in foster care in the United States will spend their pre-adult lives in out-of-home placement, much of which has been attributed to the lack of adequate case planning [22].

A basic measure of the success of the multidisciplinary approach is whether the services recommended by the process are obtained. In this study we sought to determine how successful our multidisciplinary program was in obtaining the requisite services for abused and neglected children and their families.

Background

La Rabida Children's Hospital and Research Center is a 77-bed pediatric specialty hospital, affiliated with the University of Chicago and staffed by physicians from the Department of Pediatrics, University of Chicago. It provides both inpatient and outpatient services to children with chronic illnesses and rehabilitative needs. In 1977 a modest child abuse and neglect program was undertaken based on the following premises:

1. The Child Protective Service units (CPS) of the Illinois Department of Children and Family Services (DCFS), the legally mandated reporting agency in Illinois, generally lacked the data base upon which to make decisions regarding the children they serve. Decisions concerning children in need of protective services were commonly based on the expediencies of the CPS system rather than on the needs of the children.
2. Interventions made on the child's behalf must be made early in the protective service/ juvenile court system, immediately after identification of the suspected abuse, but prior to court involvement. Once court action was taken, we thought it would be difficult or impossible to make meaningful changes on behalf of the child or the family.
3. Child abuse and neglect are best viewed as long-term problems rather than as discreet episodes. Child abuse victims and their families require long-term follow-up.
4. A Diagnostic/Consultation/Community Outreach Model would be a more effective and cost efficient approach than the traditional approach that is based on counseling.

The Program

Initially the La Rabida program consisted of a comprehensive, multidisciplinary evaluation of children referred by CPS units for suspicion of abuse or neglect. The evaluation consisted of inpatient medical and psychological evaluations of the child (or evaluation of development in children under 3 years of age), documentation of the abuse/neglect (via x-rays, bone surveys, photographs, etc.), psychosocial assessment of the family, educational assessment, and extended behavioral assessments and other ancillary evaluations as indicated (e.g., psychiatric evaluations, speech, language and hearing evaluations, etc.). A case conference with the child's CPS worker and the DCFS hospital liaison in attendance was held following the completion of the multidisciplinary evaluation. Specific recommendations and treatment plans were made at this case conference. While the components of the above diagnostic program were not in themselves remarkable, to our knowledge La Rabida Children's Hospital was, and still is, the only facility in Chicago to offer these comprehensive services to abused and neglected children.

In the second year of the program, a grant from the Chicago Community Trust provided for the addition of a community outreach worker to facilitate the follow-up by home visits, serve as facilitator and ombudsman to these families in the general pediatric clinics and monitor the progress that the CPS teams were making in obtaining the specific services recommended by the multidisciplinary evaluation. Follow-up of our sample was through the community worker's liaison to the families (natural and foster) and to the CPS workers, and through pediatricians and others in the hospital's outpatient clinics.

METHODS

Procedure

One year following discharge the recommendations made by the multidisciplinary team were reviewed be the community worker who contacted the child's CPS worker, parent(s), and/or the foster parent(s) to ascertain whether the services recommended had been received. Two independent sources (e.g., case worker and parent) were required to corroborate whether services had been obtained.

Retrospective review of records identified twelve categories of recommendations (services):

- return to the natural home,
- foster placement,
- residential psychiatric placement,
- individual psychotherapy (child),
- special education classroom placement,
- family therapy,
- additional psychiatric/psychological diagnostic services,
- individual psychotherapy (family member),
- additional diagnostic services,
- infant stimulation programs (0–3 years old),
- in-home support services (e.g., homemaker services),
- visiting nurse services.

The number and type of recommendations varied from case to case, i.e., in some cases no recommendations were made regarding placement (return to natural home, foster placement or residential placement), but recommendations were made regarding other services (special education placement, additional diagnostic services, etc.). Where the hospital-based multidisciplinary team offered no recommendations regarding placement, the recommendation of the state CPS team determined the placement. This study looked only at those recommendations made by the multidisciplinary team.

Subjects

Approximately 200 children were evaluated during a two plus-year period of time, all having been reported to DCFS as *suspected* of being abused or neglected. Of this number, 180 children were located for inclusion in this study. There were no specific referral criteria to the program other than the case having been reported to the CPS unit for investigation of suspected child abuse or neglect. Individual CPS workers made the decision to refer each child to the program. Retrospective review of records revealed that children fell in one of five categories: (1) no documented medical or historical evidence of abuse or neglect (N = 36); (2) medical evidence of abuse (N = 27); (3) medical or historical evidence of neglect (N = 46); (4) medical evidence of abuse and neglect (N = 30), and (5) failure-to-thrive (FTT), children under 3 years old with a history of delayed or arrested physical growth (below the 3rd percentile for weight), with no organic etiology, who gained weight during hospitalization (N = 41). The mean age at admission for the total sample was 4.36 years. The mean age for the FTT children was 0.99 years and 5.36 years for the non-FTT sample. Ninety-seven children were male and 83 female; 13 children were white, 163 black and 4 latino.

Outcome Measures

The primary goal of the study was to ascertain the effect of the multidisciplinary team on service delivery, as measured by determining the number of recommendations that were followed/obtained by the child's CPS worker one year following the multidisciplinary evaluation. Other factors surveyed were: the legal status of the child at discharge and at follow-up (e.g., return home with full rights restored to the parents, temporary custody, ward of the state, etc.), and the place of residence of the child at follow-up. The legal status of the child and the place of residence are thought to provide an indirect measure of the effect of the multidisciplinary evaluation.

RESULTS

Follow-up after one year revealed that a surprisingly high percentage of the recommendations made by the multidisciplinary team had been obtained by the children and families (Table 1). The effectiveness of the multidisciplinary team is seen most clearly in the placement decisions (return home or foster care), where the recommendations of the multidisciplinary team were followed 100% of the time (return home) and 92% of the time (foster care). [The 10 children recommended for foster care in the no-abuse/neglect category (Table 2) represent an artifact of the evaluation process and of the protective services system. These children were being evaluated while allegations of abuse/neglect were under investigation. The retrospective review of their medical records revealed no evidence (by medical exam or history) of abuse/neglect. The protective services investigation determined that the initial allegation was not substantiated. However, during the evaluation deficits in the family's ability to care for the child were noted and foster care was recommended.]

Other services were obtained less frequently ranging from 76% (visiting nurse) to 29% (additional psychological and psychiatric assessment). In general, outpatient psychological service recommendations were not followed as frequently as other service recommendations. Family psychotherapy, individual psychotherapy (child), and additional psychological/psy-

Table 1. Percentage of Recommended Services Obtained 1 Year After Multidisciplinary Evaluation

Recommendation(s)	Number of Recommendations	% Obtained
Return Home	18	100
Foster Care	78	92
Visiting Nurse	33	76
Additional Medical Assessment	56	66
Infant (0-3) Stimulation Program	36	64
Individual Psychotherapy (family member)	28	64
Residential (Psychiatric) Treatment	17	59
In-home Supports	7	57
Special Education Class	27	52
Family Therapy	18	44
Individual Psychotherapy (child)	37	35
Additional Psychological/Psychiatric Assessment	14	29

chiatric assessment were obtained 44%, 35% and 29% of the times they were recommended, respectively. The type of abuse suffered by the child did not influence the number of recommended services obtained (Table 2), but the type of abuse/neglect suffered by the child did influence the type of service(s) recommended. For example, the multidisciplinary team was more likely to recommend additional medical assessment, infant stimulation programs and visiting nurses for the FTT group than for other groups.

Other outcome measures of the effectiveness of the multidisciplinary approach, albeit indirect, are the legal status of the child at discharge, at follow-up, and the place of residence at follow-up (Tables 3 and 4 respectively). Data related to legal status and residence was collected for the first year of the study only. The legal status at discharge differed between the groups significantly ($p < .0003$; Table 3). This difference was accounted for, in large measure, by the high number of FTT children sent home rather than being placed in temporary custody. At follow-up (Table 3) the children's legal status had shifted to guardianship from predominantly temporary custody at discharge. This legal maneuver makes the child's legal status as a ward of the state somewhat more permanent. The shift in legal status between

Table 2. Percentage of Recommended Services Obtained 1 Year After Multidisciplinary Evaluation X Type of Abuse/Neglect

	Type of Abuse				
Recommended Services	No Abuse/Neglect $n = 36$	Neglect $n = 46$	Abuse $n = 27$	Abuse and Neglect $n = 30$	F.T.T. $n = 41$
Return Home	100 (4)*	100 (2)	100 (7)	100 (1)	100 (4)
Foster Care	80 (10)	100 (17)	84 (19)	91 (22)	100 (10)
Visiting Nurse	86 (7)	66 (3)	50 (6)	100 (1)	81 (16)
Additional Medical Assessment	69 (13)	79 (14)	79 (14)	44 (9)	33 (6)
Infant (0-3 years) Stimulation Program	50 (8)	50 (4)	100 (6)	100 (2)	56 (16)
Individual Psychotherapy (family member)	50 (4)	33 (3)	66 (12)	100 (3)	66 (6)
Residential Psychiatric Treatment	100 (1)	100 (2)	50 (10)	50 (4)	—
In-home Supports	100 (1)	0 (1)	0 (1)	100 (1)	66 (3)
Special Education Class	60 (5)	75 (8)	20 (5)	44 (9)	—
Family Therapy	29 (70)	50 (2)	50 (6)	100 (2)	0 (1)
Individual Psychotherapy (child)	43 (7)	40 (5)	37 (16)	22 (9)	—
Additional Psychological/ Psychiatric Assessment	0 (1)	75 (4)	0 (1)	0 (1)	17 (6)
Total	65	64	64	65	66

Note: Number in parenthesis represents total number of recommendations made in each category

Neil J. Hochstadt and Neil J. Harwicke

Table 3. Legal Status at Discharge (Follow-up)

	Temporary Custody	Return Home	Guardianship	n
No Abuse/Neglect	7 (3)	12 (15)	0 (1)	19
Neglect	9 (3)	4 (2)	2 (10)	15
Abuse	15 (9)	5 (6)	2 (7)	22
Abuse & Neglect	10 (3)	5 (5)	5 (12)	20
F.T.T.	2 (1)	14 (12)	0 (3)	16
Total	43 (19)	40 (40)	9 (33)	$n = 92$

Note: Number in parenthesis represents follow-up data
Discharge (X^2 (8) = 29.10, $p < .0003$)
(Follow-up x^2 (8) = 35.28 $p < .00002$)
Data represents children evaluated in first year of program only

discharge and follow-up differed significantly as a function of the type of abuse/neglect ($t < .0002$). More children in the no-abuse/no-neglect group were likely to be returned home in that interval, whereas substantially more abused children were still in temporary custody at follow-up. FTT children were more likely to have been returned home than children in any of the other categories except no-abuse/no-neglect.

Residence at follow-up is largely influenced by the child's legal status. That is, the child is more likely to be living out of the home if he has been placed in guardianship than if he remains in temporary custody. Table 4 presents the child's place of residence at follow-up. This table presents data related to the the child's place of residence at follow-up as a function of the type of abuse and the place of residence. Significant differences between the groups emerged. Many more children in the no-abuse/no-neglect group were living with their parents at follow-up than in the group as a whole ($p < .0004$). More neglected children were still living in foster care at follow-up than would have been expected.

DISCUSSION

Abused children, their families, and the multidisciplinary team function within highly complex and overlapping systems (medical, social service, protective service, judicial and legal). Given the complexity of the multiple systems within which the multidisciplinary team functions, the current study demonstrates that this approach can have a very positive effect on the delivery of requisite services to abused and neglected children and their families. Although the current study did not use a control group, a previous study conducted by the New York State Assembly's Select Committee on Child Abuse [23] found that only 1.2% of the protective services cases surveyed received services beyond the initial CPS involvement.

Table 4. Residence at Follow-up

	Relative	Parents	Foster Home	Institution/ Group Home	n
No Abuse/Neglect	0	14	4	0	18
Neglect	1	2	11	1	15
Abuse	9	7	4	2	22
Abuse & Neglect	7	5	6	2	20
F.T.T.	1	12	3	0	16
Total	18	40	28	5	$n = 91$

(x^2 (12) = 41.73, $p < .00004$)
Note: Data represents children evaluated in first year of program only

Since New York and Illinois have similar child abuse laws and protective service systems, the 1.2% can provide a valuable baseline against which the current study's success can be measured. These results indicate that the multidisciplinary approach plays a central role in service acquisition for abused and neglected children. Our experience shows that the multidisciplinary team generally performs a number of functions which increase the probability of service acquisition. These functions include: providing the "clout" often necessary to dislodge services, reducing the fragmentation and duplication of efforts and providing case coordination.

The current study provides tentative answers to other questions. The finding that more FTT than abused children were returned home at discharge is very troublesome given the fact that 63% of the deaths recorded in Illinois in 1981 were due to neglect [24]. This finding suggests that more risks are being taken with a population that already is at high risk. Findings from the current study also highlight the vulnerability of these children. Of the 19 reports of re-abuse/neglect in this study (data was obtained on 117 cases), 42% (8 cases) involved children who had been previously neglected or who failed to thrive. The reasons for overestimating the safety of neglected children are unclear and warrant further investigation. It has been our impression that CPS workers and the protagonists of the juvenile justice system view frank abuse as a more serious problem than neglect. The legal system finds it easier to respond to tangible abuse than to the more intangible problems of neglect. This overestimation of the safety of neglected children, as opposed to abused children, also appears to occur on multidisciplinary teams. This is highlighted in the current study by the fact that neglected children are more likely to be returned home than abused children. The results also point to the fact that there may be an overestimation of the number of abused children who need to be removed from the home, and that we may be keeping these children in out-of-home placements longer than needed. One contributing factor may be the lack of adequate follow-up services. That is, if better follow-up services were available, CPS units and the courts would be more comfortable permitting more abused children to remain at home or return home sooner. More research is needed to ascertain risk factors which might permit more abused children to remain safely at home; or be returned home following brief, rather than extended, separations. The import of such research is self-evident in light of the known psychological sequelae of separation on children. The expansion of the role of the multidisciplinary team to encompass follow-up might aid in reintegrating families more rapidly and more successfully.

The results of the current study indicate that the multidisciplinary team can make significant contributions to the follow-up care of abused and neglected children.

REFERENCES

1. HELFER, R. E. A plan for protection: The child abuse center. *Child Welfare* **49**:486–494 (1970).
2. DE FRANCIS, V. Child Protection: A comprehensive, coordinated process. In: *Fourth National Symposium on Child Abuse*, American Humane Association (Ed.), Charleston, SC (1973).
3. DELNERO, H., HOPKINS, J., and DREWS, K. The medical center child abuse consultation team. In: *Helping the Battered Child and its Family*, C. H. Kempe and R. E. Helfer (Eds.). J. B. Lippincott, Philadelphia (1972).
4. NATIONAL CENTER ON CHILD ABUSE AND NEGLECT. *The Community Team Approach to Case Management and Prevention: Child Abuse and Neglect, the Problem and its Management*. Department of Health, Education and Welfare. Publication #OHD 75-30075, Washington DC (1975).
5. MARTIN, H. *The Abused Child: A Multidisciplinary Approach to Developmental Issues and Treatment.* Ballinger, Cambridge (1976).
6. KLINE, D. F. Educational and psychological problems of abused children. *Child Abuse & Neglect* **1**:301–307 (1977).
7. MORSE, W. SAHLER, O. G. and FRIEDMAN, G. B. A three-year follow-up study of abused and neglected children. *American Journal of Diseases of Children* **120**:439–446 (1970).
8. ELMER, E. Identification of abused children. *Children* **10**:180–184 (1963).
9. ELMER, E. and GREGG, G. Developmental characteristics of abused children. **Pediatrics 40**:596–602 (1967).

10. GILL, D. Physical abuse of children. *Pediatrics* **45**:857–864 (1970).
11. MARTIN, H. A child and his development. In: *Helping the Battered Child and His Family*, C. H. Kempe and R. E. Helfer (Eds.). Lippincott, Philadelphia (1972).
12. MORGAN, S. R. Psychoeducational profile of emotionally disturbed abused children. *Journal of Clinical Psychology* **8**:3–6 (1979).
13. KEMPE, C., SILVERMAN, F., STEELE, F., DROEGMULLER, W., and SILVER, H. The battered child syndrome. *Journal of the American Medical Association* **181**:17–24 (1962).
14. ISAACS, C. E. Treatment of child abuse: A review of the behavioral interventions. *Journal of Applied Behavior Analysis* **15**:273–294 (1982).
15. ROTH, R. *Multidisciplinary Teams in Child Abuse and Neglect Programs*, prepared by National Center on Child Abuse and Neglect. Department of HEW, Publication #HDS 78–30152 (1978).
16. STRAUS, P. and GIRODET, D. Three French follow-up studies on abused children. *Child Abuse & Neglect* **1**:99–103 (1977).
17. TERR, L. and WATSON, A. The battered child re-brutalized: Ten cases of medical-legal confusion. *American Journal of Psychiatry* **124**:126–133 (1968).
18. PURVINE, M. and RYAN, W. Into and out of a child welfare network. *Child Welfare* **48**:125–135 (1969).
19. BURT, M. R. and BALYEAT, R. A new system for improving the care of neglected and abused children. *Child Welfare* **3**:167–179 (1974).
20. POLIER, J. W. Professional abuse in children: Responsibility for the delivery of services. *American Journal of Orthopsychiatry* **45**:357–362 (1975).
21. CAIN, V. *Concern for children in placement, In: 1977 Analysis of Child Abuse and Neglect Research*, National Center on Child Abuse and Neglect. Department of HEW, Publication #OHDS 78–30139, Washington DC (1978)
22. STEIN, T. J. and GAMBRILL, E. D. The Alameda Project: A two-year report and a one-year follow-up. *Child Abuse & Neglect* **3**:521–528 (1979).
23. NEW YORK STATE ASSEMBLY, SELECT COMMITTEE ON CHILD ABUSE. *Summary Report on the Relationship between Child Abuse and Neglect and Later Socially Deviant Behavior.* New York (1978).
24. OAKES, B. Child abuse and neglect reports. In: *Annual Report for Fiscal Year 1980*. Illinois Department of Children and Family Services, Springfield, IL (1981).

Permanency Planning and the Child Abuse Prevention and Treatment Act: The Paradox of Child Welfare Policy

Mary Ann Jimenez

California State University, Long Beach
School of Social Work

The Child Abuse Prevention and Treatment Act of 1974 and the Adoptions Assistance and Child Welfare Act of 1980 have imposed conflicting mandates on the public child welfare system. CAPTA places the moral weight of the federal government behind professional intervention with troubled families, while the Adoptions Assistance Act was designed to protect the autonomy of families. As these policies currently stand, the goal of protection of vulnerable children is seriously undermined.

One of the major themes in child welfare since the Progressive Era has been a growing commitment to the emotional, social and economic dependence of children. The belief in the legitimacy of this dependence is at the center of child welfare policy, especially policies designed to prevent child abuse and neglect and those intending to provide substitute care for children. This paper presents an analysis of two policies designed to promote the goal of protection of dependent children: the Child Abuse Prevention and Treatment Act (1974) and the Adoption Assistance and Child Welfare Act (1980). The article begins by offering an historical perspective of the emergence of the belief in childhood vulnerability in the Progressive Era and discusses subsequent efforts to fashion a set of policies that would consistently insure the protection of children. The tension between family rights and the necessity for public intervention in family life has been an ongoing theme in child welfare policy since the progressive Era; this theme was sharply outlined in the debates surrounding the passage of the two landmark federal policies which currently underlie public child welfare practices.

The contradictory hypotheses of these policies has led to conflicting mandates for child protective services which constrain the best efforts of child welfare professionals to safeguard vulnerable children.

The Progressive Era and the Emergence of Child Welfare

Throughout the colonial period and well into the 19th century, all but the children of the wealthiest families were viewed largely in economic terms: as an asset to the family or, in cases where there was no viable family, a burden to the state. It is this perspective which undergirded the system of apprenticeship or "binding out" of dependent children in the 18th and 19th centuries. Public care of children was limited to almshouses, orphanages and houses of reform for much of the 19th century (Rothman, 1971). Public concern for the emotional well-being of children and their developmental and social needs awaited a confluence of factors: the emergency of the child saving movement at the end of the 19th century; the discovery of child abuse as a social problem in the same period; and the increasing demand for skilled labor facilitating the passage of child labor laws in many states around the turn of the century.

Another sign of the increased legitimacy of the conception of childhood vulnerability was the passage of laws in several states at the end of the 19th century removing children from almshouses, where many had been confined alongside adult poor, some of whom were mentally disordered (Folks, 1902; Bremner, 1972). These policies were seen as humanitarian efforts to subtract children from the economic equation of industrialization. While the child labor laws presented poorer families with severe hardships, they also set the stage for a less instrumental view of children than had existed previously.

In terms of public policy, during the Progressive Era children began to be seen as having substantially different needs than adults; vulnerability became a major characteristic of childhood. This conviction demanded that adults insure the child's protection and proper development.

White House Conference on Youth

The question of how best to protect children and insure their proper development was first addressed in a public forum at the first White House Conference on Youth in 1909. Conference participants strongly endorsed family care of poor children as a far preferable alternative to institutionalization in almshouses or orphanages. The theme of family as the most important factor in child development had not been a significant one before this Conference; its emphasis there gave an important boost to Progressive reformers crusade to provide financial assistance for widowed or abandoned mothers caring for their children in their own homes (Gibson and Lewis, 1980). By 1913, 20 states had enacted mother's pensions to enable children from poorer families to be cared for in their own homes rather than in institutions (Bremner, 1972).

The Growth of Foster Care

In highlighting the importance of a family environment for children, reformers also gave impetus to the trend toward foster care that had been evident since 1853, when Charles Loring Brace organized the Children's Aid Society in New York to send homeless children West where they were cared for by rural families. Almost 20,000 children were sent West in the first 20 years of the Society's operation (Folks, 1902; Bremner, 1972). As the creation of the Children's Bureau in 1912 focused more attention on children, foster care too gained increased legitimacy as a way to care for vulnerable children. It is important to note that during the Progressive Era, foster care originally was seen as a means of preserving family values, not as constituting a challenge to those values.

The Rise of Child Protection

The theme of protecting children from family abuse developed separately from that of promoting family life as the strongest guarantee of children's well being, but it too was linked to the emerging view of children as dependent and vulnerable. The now famous case of Mary Ellen, a child severely abused by her foster mother in 1874, has been described frequently as responsible for the creation and legitimation of protective services for children (Richett and Hudson, 1979; Nelson, 1984). As a result of this case and the subsequent creation of the New York Society for the Prevention of Cruelty to Children, the formerly private arena of parent-child relationships began to be subject to public intervention, initially from private agencies with public mandates (like the NYPCC). Progressive reformers were later to question the intrusiveness of these agencies, which they felt unfairly disrupted poor families. Instead these reformers urged a reaffirmation of the superior value of the home and family unit as the best means of insuring the child's well-being. Nevertheless, the principle of child protection had been legislated in most Eastern states by the end of the 19th century and would reemerge with vigor in the 1960s (Nelson, 1984).

During the Progressive Era the tensions evident in current child welfare policy were first formulated: what were the respective roles of the family and the state in the protection of the vulnerable child? The assumption that the child should be instrumental in meeting the needs of the family had been replaced by the conviction that the family had the duty to be instrumental in the development of the child. This duty implied a public responsibility to guarantee its fulfillment and would ultimately claim considerable public resources.

Conflicts in Contemporary Child Welfare Policy

Since the Progressive era, the power of the government to intervene in family life has increased substantially. In spite of the firmly established principle of government intervention on behalf of the child and the commitment of public resources to the goal of protection, a perception exists that public child welfare has not accomplished its mission (Besharov, 1983; Besharov, 1987; Cox and Cox, 1984; Faller, 1985). The feeling that public child welfare has not entirely succeeded in its mandate is linked to the continuing increase in reports of child abuse. In particular, the increase in the number of child fatalities due to maltreatment has quickened public interest in the protective service system (National Center on Child Abuse Prevention Research, 1987; Little Hoover Commission, 1987).

At least part of the reason for the difficulties faced by child welfare workers in their efforts to carry out their mandates to protect children lies in conflicting contemporary policies which embody the same unresolved conflicts about the family and the government originating in the Progressive Era. The Child Abuse Prevention and Treatment Act of 1974 (Public Law 93-247) positioned the federal government to assume a proactive role in the detection, and to a far lesser extent, prevention and treatment of child abuse, especially as it occurs in the family. This legislation put the moral weight of the federal government behind the necessity for *professional intervention* in the family unit in cases of suspected abuse or neglect. The Adoption Assistance and Child Welfare Act of 1980 (PL 96-272) embodied the ethos of permanency planning, and shifted the support of the federal government away from intervention in the family system, and towards placement prevention and reunification. In short, the Adoptions Assistance Act of 1980 casts the federal government in the role of *protector* of the family from *outside interference.*

Social Origins of the Two Policies

Both of these policies evolved from a new interest in children's rights that appeared as part of the wider movements of the 1970s (Pine, 1986). The movement for social equality and civil liberties of the 1960s and early 1970s, which transformed the ways members of minority groups and women defined themselves, also sought to reorder the relationship of members of these groups to the political and economic structures in the country. These movements for social equality focused attention on the rights of children, especially since the denial of these rights was perceived to be intimately tied to the oppression of women. The movement for children's rights followed logically out of these gender and ethnic based struggles for equality. The disillusionments attendant on the Vietnam War and Watergate also led to the recognition that sanctioned authority (including parental authority) could be oppressive, that its legitimacy was open to question and that advocacy on behalf of those underrepresented in systems of power was legitimate and even necessary.

The Child Abuse Prevention and Treatment Act of 1974 was fashioned out of this ethos, although it received its immediate impetus from media attention to the "battered child syndrome" in the late 1960s and early 1970s. New attention had been directed to the problem of abused children as a result of a series of investigations of childhood injuries by the medical profession in the late 1940s and 1950s. In 1962, C. Henry Kempe published "The Battered-Child Syndrome" in the *Journal of the American Medical Association*, thereby establishing a new definition of an old social problem (Kemp). The public interest in child welfare grew as a result of the publicity generated by this article, leading every state to enact legislation between 1963 and 1967 encouraging the reporting of child abuse (Richett and Hudson, 1979; Nelson, 1984).

The Adoptions Assistance Act of 1980 reflected the same interest in protecting the rights of vulnerable children as had CAPTA, but it also was a product of the more conservative climate of the Carter administration and its concern for family values (Antler, 1978). An eagerness to protect the family from outside influences, especially what were seen as the social, moral and governmental excesses of the late 1960s and early 1970s, characterized the political rhetoric of the Carter administration. This climate led to a reaction to the growth of the foster care system, which was seen as infringing on family rights. Federal support for foster care had come in the form of the Social Security Act Amendments of 1962, which appropriated money for state sponsored child welfare services and provided federal funds for foster care for the first time. The availability of these funds increased the incentives for states to place children in foster care (Gibson and Lewis, 1980). The different strategies reflected in the policies are evident in an analysis of the hearings surrounding their passage. CAPTA is based on the assumption that professionals have the duty to intervene inside the boundaries of family life in order to insure the well-being of children. The Adoption Assistance and Child Welfare Act, on the other hand, is an effort to protect the family from the interference of the child welfare professional and the policies of the child welfare establishment. CAPTA, in short, seeks to protect children from parents who would misuse their authority, while the 1980

Act seeks to protect children from policies which undermine the authority of parents.

The Child Abuse Prevention and Training Act

CAPTA authorized limited government research into child abuse prevention and treatment; created a national clearing-house for child abuse data, and established funding incentives to tighten up state reporting laws. The only provision of the 1974 law that suggested the increased role protective services were to have in the coming decade was a requirement that states must have personnel and facilities available for treatment as well as for reporting and investigating in order to receive federal funds. Since the problem of child abuse was viewed as limited to a small minority of psychologically disturbed families, the implications of this requirement for the dramatic increase in protective services was not anticipated by lawmakers. In fact, the perception that this low cost measure did not abridge any rights or forge any serious new federal commitments was critical to the passage of the act (Nelson, 11984).

After 1974 states revised their own reporting laws in line with CAPTA to qualify for federal funds. It was in this round of revisions that states added the "protective custody" provisions to mandatory reporting laws that were to have profound consequences for the growth in protective services (Nelson, 1984). Protective custody made explicit what had always been implicit in reporting laws: the necessity for direct intervention by child welfare professionals in the family system. In hindsight it is clear that the intentions of the sponsors of CAPTA and state reporting laws were confounded by their ignorance of the actual incidence of child abuse and the magnitude of reporting that would occur. By the time of the Congressional hearings on the renewal of the legislation in 1977 and 1981, however, there was a sense that the problem was far greater than had been believed in 1974, though exact figures were still elusive (House, Hearings, 1977, p. 2, 13, 134; House Hearings, 1981, pp. 44–45). In 1977 child abuse was considered to be of "epidemic" proportions, as protective service agencies in various states were flooded with reports of child abuse that overran the child welfare system (House Hearings, 1977, p. 28). In the 1981 hearings child abuse similarly was described by one witness as reaching "alarming proportions" (House Hearings, 1981, p. 45). One physician testified in 1977 that in New York City reports of child abuse had increased dramatically since 1974. He complained that "We are being flooded with case reports but we don't investigate them. The children necessarily are being sacrificed." (House Hearings, 1977, p. 43.) Several states reported a dramatic increase in the reports of child abuse since the passage of CAPTA; one Massachusetts official told of a 700% increase (House Hearings, 1977, p. 85,89). The most important response to this increase in reports of child abuse was the urgent call for more professional training and services to treat abusing families and protect abused children. Social workers were frequently cited as the most critical professionals among those working in protective services. One NASW representative argued staunchly that the "social worker is the key professional in services to abused children and their families" (House Hearings, 1977, p. 24, 68, 116, 128; House Hearings, 1981, p. 33, 124–125).

In spite of the accumulation of convincing testimony that more than reporting laws were necessary to protect at risk children, Congress did not authorize any significant increase in funding for social services to vulnerable families. Instead, the blind faith that mandatory reporting would solve the problem of child abuse was reiterated in 1977 and in subsequent extensions of the original bill. Legislative myopia notwithstanding, it. is not surprising that CAPTA and its extensions had the net effect of increasing professional and government intervention in family life, given the theme of professional expertise and intervention that was a *leitmotif* of the hearings. The perception of this interference has provoked several critics. One child welfare expert, Theodore Stein, characterized the legislation as providing for "coercive intervention into family life that is unprecedented in American history," and noted that it "jeopardizes the values that we place on family privacy and on parental autonomy" (1984, p. 302). Douglas Besharov, who has written extensively on issues of child protection, similarly pointed out "an unprecedented increase in the level of state intervention into private family matters over the past twenty years" (1985, p. 19). Governmental intervention into the family has come from police officers, lawyers and judges; all are caught up increasingly in the nexus of family life.

The profession most concerned with child abuse and the one which has attracted the most public criticism is social work. Since public agencies mandated to receive child abuse reports were staffed with social workers, the connection in the public mind between child abuse and the social work profession was axiomatic. This connection was strengthened by the insistence of the lawmakers that the connection between poverty and child abuse be ignored. Lawmakers instead preferred to support what has been called the "myth of classlessness" in order to limit the scope of the problem to the individual, psychological realm (Pelton, 1981).

This emphasis implied a casework approach, one that was seen to be the domain of the profession of social work. This perspective on the problem precluded a critical look at child care services, nutrition, economic inequality, joblessness, and other factors impacting children at risk for abuse. Such a perspective, completely missing in the assumptions underlying CAPTA, would have revealed that the absence of public goods such as child care, prenatal and family nutrition programs were at least as significant in placing children at risk as the psychological problems presented by some parents. Failure to look at wider issues, such as joblessness and serious structural inequality that impact on the well-being of families, was a fundamental constraint on any policy attempt to protect children from abuse.

In spite of this narrow emphasis on the casework approach to the problem of child abuse, one unanticipated consequence of CAPTA was an adversarial relationship that tended to develop between the child welfare worker and the family. Due to the requirement for reporting and the consequent necessity of investigating incidents of suspected child abuse, child welfare workers have sometimes functioned more as detectives than as emphathetic caseworkers or change agents (Faller, 1985). Since federal funding has not kept pace with the number of families who need services as a result of reporting laws, the ability of the child welfare professional to offer casework to clients has been seriously compromised (Stein, 1984). Under these circumstances, it is not surprising that momentum gathered among policy makers for another look at public child welfare.

Adoptions Assistance and Child Welfare Act

The discontent with public child welfare in the wake of CAPTA was growing at the same time as the social work profession was taking another look at foster care, especially at the problem of "drift" and the consequent sense of instability and impermanence that seemed to be experienced by many children placed in foster homes (Maas and Engler, 1959). The clear implication of the problem of drift was that children were suffering in foster homes. Foster care itself emerged as a public issue two years after the passage of CAPTA. The ultimate result of the public concern expressed about the problems of foster care was the passage of the Adoptions Assistance and Child Welfare Reform Act of 1980 (PL 96–272).

During the several rounds of hearings in the late 1970s that preceded the enactment of the law, it became clear that foster care, which had been upheld in the Progressive Era as an important means of protecting family values, was now viewed as antithetical to those values. An important argument of those testifying before Congress was that the child welfare system was to blame for allowing this "drift" to take place by ignoring the biological parents, failing to monitor children in foster placements, and most importantly failing to work toward the goal of reunification of parents and children. One HEW official in 1979 summed up these problems as the "crisis of foster care" (House Hearings, 1979, p. 3). There was a strong sense that child welfare professionals were interferring unnecessarily in family life. An influential report prepared for the Subcommittee on Children and Youth of the Senate Committee on Labor and public Welfare in 1975 argued that preference should be "ordinarily given first to preserving the biological family; second to creating adoptive families; and third to placing children in stable foster homes" (Mott, 1975, p. 6). The priorities had shifted away from foster care because: "Central to the rights of a child are the rights to permanence, stability, continuity, and nurture during childhood." Foster care was not seen as able to provide for these needs, partly because "Discussions between biological parents and case workers about the care children receive are likely to be infrequent and one-sided." The report went on to explain that mothers have complained that "they were not consulted about alternatives to foster care for their children and that they had no say in the selection of the foster home for the child." Furthermore, families were discouraged from seeing their children by "the caseworkers, the foster parents, or the distance they would have to travel to see them." Caseworkers were criticized for prohibiting foster parents from "developing close emotional ties with the children placed in their care." One of the major recommendations of the report was to "Limit intervention by the case worker wherever practical" (Mott, 1975, p. 1, 37). This assault on the competency of the casework was a dramatic reversal from the reliance on the professional intervention of the social worker that was a continuing theme in the CAPTA hearings.

In the 1976 House hearings the capriciousness of public child welfare was emphasized. Any possibility that professional skill and judgment were at the heart of the placement process was wholly eliminated: "The welfare department can place the child in virtually any licensed foster home or institution at its whim." Voluntary placements were criticized; one witness argued that they are 'informally coerced' and that these placements should be outlawed for they provide "no independent check of a social worker's determination that placement is necessary..." The entire child welfare establishment was assailed:" welfare departments are typically not accountable to anyone for what happens to these children, children who are voluntarily placed are quite often the orphans of the living;"and "Individual social workers and judges...make highly discretionary decisions" (House Hearings, 1976, p. 102, 37,75, 83). In 1979 one representative of the Children's Defense Fund testified in House Hearings that "an antifamily bias...pervades the policies and practices of the child welfare system." Furthermore children in "child welfare systems are in double jeopardy because they are also subject to neglect by public officials who have responsibility for them." The federal role "exacerbates both the antifamily bias and the public neglect of these children" through the support of the foster placement system (House Hearings, 1979, pp. 135–136). A spokeswoman from the APWA sounded a dissident note when she argued that caseworkers in public child welfare were largely inexperienced; she suggested that money be spent on training and services, rather than solely on regulation of the child welfare departments (House Hearings, 1976, pp. 92–93). Yet regulations were far less costly than mounting elaborate training programs for caseworkers or funding comprehensive services for families at risk, a truism demonstrated by CAPTA.

Foster care itself was characterized as "long term confinement;" children were to be "deinstitutionalized." Congressmen were reminded of "illustration after illustration where foster care parents have abused children..." (House Hearings, 1976, pp. 37, 41). During the hearings that ultimately led to the passage of the 1980 act, there was some emphasis on economic and social problems of families at risk for foster placement. Some who testified made dramatic pleas for federally funded services for these families to prevent foster placement, including homemaker, child care and counseling services (Hearings, 1976, pp. 86, 93). Yet the commitment to provide these services was undermined by another more important theme: the cost saving that was anticipated with the contraction of the foster care system (Hearings, 1976; Hartley, 1984). Not surprisingly, while federal mechanisms for funding preventive and reunification services were built into the 1980 legislation, the amount appropriated has been far short of what was authorized. This failure to authorize funds has led many to question how many services are being provided to families, despite the requirement that "reasonable efforts" must be made to prevent the removal of the child from the home and to return those that have been removed (House Hearing, 1985, p. 169; Pine, 1986; Seaberg, 1986). Several observers have voiced concern that the low level of funding for services may be undermining the best intent of the law to provide for the welfare of children (Senate Hearings, 1985, pp. 37–39; House Hearings, 1985, pp. 84–85; Cox and Cox, 1984; Hartley, 1984; Faller, 1985).

Thus the 1980 legislation served a conservative purpose by fashioning a more laissez-faire approach to child welfare services and family life than had existed previously. The assumption behind the 1980 Adoptions Assistance and Child Welfare Act was that protecting the family from outside interference was the best way to safeguard the interests of the child. This new form of child protection was often called child advocacy, partly in order to distinguish it from the more traditional and in some ways less credible child welfare (Richett and Hudson, 1979).

The 1980 Act did have several important consequences; one has apparently been to increase the number of children being discharged from foster homes, although this trend is apparently being offset by high reentry rates of children into foster care (Rzepnicki, 1987). Another important consequence has been the establishment of a system of review of foster placements by each state, necessary in order to qualify for foster care reimbursement. The requirements for periodic review, development of case plans and other tracking mechanisms, along with those provisions for due process for families, have no doubt served to help insure that children are less likely to 'drift' in foster care without the attention of caseworkers and the courts and so to promote the goal of permanency planning. But such regulations have also multiplied the paperwork of public child welfare workers and, combined with the increasing number of reports of child abuse received by state agencies, may have served to move them further away from the provision of services which would insure that children return home to families who are able to care for them (National Center on Child Abuse Prevention Research). In fact, the ambiguous position of the child welfare professional interfering (as a result of the CAPTA mandate) with the privacy of the family has led to resentment among those who are the subject of child abuse investigations and has led to the formation of a powerful group known as VOCAL or Victims of Child Abuse Legislation. VOCAL was a powerful force in the passage of a recent law in California (SB243) which limits the authority of the protective service system to remove the child from the home in cases of physical abuse. The resentment felt by some clients of the protective services system compromises the ability of the caseworker to offer services and some argue may increase the risk for the child (Faller, 1985; Christopherson, 1983).

Foster Care and Protection of Children

Ironically, neither the temporary nature nor the detrimental effects of foster care assumed by policy makers have been supported by research. In reviewing studies of the effects of permanency planning on children, Seltzer and Bloksberg found that "no differences in adjustment have been found between children who were in permanent placements and those who are in temporary placements." They also found that adoption proved to be a more stable situation for children than did returning them to their biological homes from foster care (1987). In fact, recent evidence strongly suggests that children who are returned to their own homes are more likely to reenter foster placement than are those discharged to adoptive placements (Rzepnicki, 1987). Regarding the issue of "drift," one study found that a majority of foster children studied in a "large national sample experienced a low number of placements, suggesting they had a stable relationship with their foster parents" (Pardeck, 1984). A study of children placed in Pennsylvania between 1978 and 1979 found that "The majority of children who enter foster care return to their families within a relatively short time." The researchers added "Our findings also bear out those of others that the foster care experience is a relatively stable one for children with the majority having one or two placements while in care" (Lawder *et al.*, 1986).

It is questionable whether foster care in itself is harmful to children. Trudy Festinger's study of the outcomes of foster care for emancipated young adults found that "most are functioning in society in about the same way as others their age." Festinger's results moved her to ask question why so many "dire predictions" are made for children in foster care (1983).

In a recent review of research, Barth and Berry found that children who are returned to their own homes are more at risk than those who are placed in adoptive homes or with foster families (1987). The authors noted that abused children who remain in their own homes and whose families receive services are five times more likely to be reabused than children placed with foster families. They concluded that "Of all placement options, in-home services or reunification with birth families, as it presently operates, fails most often to free from abuse and to yield developmental well-being" (Barth and Berry, 1987).

To perhaps oversimplify the thrusts of these two federal policies: the first sought to protect children from child abuse; the second to protect them from foster care. Why have few policy makers recognized that children in foster care and children from abusing homes are often one and the same? Children who are at risk for abuse may need temporary and even permanent respite from their biological families. In the absence of national child care, homemaker services and the full complement of other services that would allow us to claim a real national family policy, foster care is likely to be a very viable solution for many of these children. Child welfare professionals must be able to call on a wide range of resources to effectively accomplish their mandate to protect children. If a substantial amount of critical services are not to be made available to families, foster care takes on added significance in the effort to protect children. Barth and Berry argue that a longer service period of 2 to 3 years is necessary to protect children returned to their families, notwithstanding the family's right to privacy. Based on their review of research, the authors conclude that "Foster care, the recent whipping boy of child welfare services, appears to offer considerable developmental advantages to children and is often regarded favorably and as sufficiently permanent by them" (1987).

Conclusion

The best interests of children are not served by the confluence of these two policies. Reporting and regulations cannot by themselves provide the necessary help to children in danger of abuse or neglect. Instead substantial services to troubled families, including child care, homemaker services, widely available health care *and* foster care services should accompany a commitment to professional intervention in the form of casework services. Equally as important to the well-being of children is a domestic policy that would promote work and economic equality. With clear evidence that the despair of poverty is a serious contributing factor to the abuse and neglect of children, it is unlikely that either of these two policies by themselves can do more than transform personal tragedy into bureaucratic disorder.

Along with the growing public commitment to protect children, the belief in the importance of the family as the primary source of children's well being has remained an important theme in child welfare policy, indeed in American values generally. Child welfare professionals are suffering from the same conflicting mandates today that emerged in the Progressive Era: protect children by protecting the integrity of the family, and protect children from parental abuse. Under current conditions these goals may be too often mutually exclusive.

References

Antler, S. (1978). Family policy and the Carter administration. *Social Thought, 14*, 15–22.

Barth, R. and Berry, M. (1987). Outcomes of child welfare services under permanency planning. *Social Services Review, 61*, 71–89.

Besharov, D. J. (1985). Right versus rights. the dilemma of child protection. *Public Welfare, 43*, 19–27

Besharov, D. J. (1983). Protecting abuse and neglected children: can law help social work? *Child Abuse and Neglect, 7*, 421–434.

Besharov, D. J. (1987). Contending and overblown expectations. *Public Welfare, 45*, 7–12.

Bremner, R. (1972). *From the depths.* NY: New York University Press.

Cox, M. and Cox, R. (1984). Foster care and public policy. *Journal of Family Issues, 5*, 182–196.

Christopherson, R. J. (1983). Public perception of child abuse and the need for intervention: are professionals seen as abusers? *Child Abuse and Neglect, 7*, 435–438.

Faller, K. C. (1985). Unanticipated problems in the United States child protection system. *Child Abuse and Neglect, 9*, 63–69.

Festinger, T. (1983). *No one ever asked us.* NY: Columbia University Press.

Gibson, T. and M. R. Lewis (1980). Sowing the seeds of trouble: an historical analysis of compliance structures in child welfare. *Journal of Sociology and Social Welfare, 7*, 679–701.

Folks, H. (1902). *Care of destitute, dependent and delinquent children.* NY: J.B. Lyon Co.

Hartley, E. K. (1984). Government leadership to protect children from foster care 'drift'. *Child Abuse and Neglect, 8*, 337–342.

Kempe, C. H. (1962). The battered child syndrome. *The Journal of the American Medical Association, 181*, 17–24.

Lawder, E., Poulin, J. & Andrews, R. (1986). A Study of 185 Foster Children 5 Years After Placement. *Child Welfare, 65*, 241–251.

Little Hoover Commission Report. (1987). The Children's Services Delivery System in California. Sacramento, California: Unpublished Report.

Maas, H. and R. Engler (1959). *Children in need of parents.* NY: Columbia University Press.

Mott, P. (1975). Foster care and adoptions: some key policy issues. Prepared for the Subcommittee on Children and Youth of the Committee on Labor and Public Welfare, United States Senate.

National Center on Child Abuse Prevention Research of the National Committee for Prevention of Abuse. (1987). A summary report on preventing child maltreatment deaths: a meeting of the states. Washington, DC: Unpublished Report.

Nelson, B. J. (1984). *Making an issue of child abuse.* Chicago: University of Chicago Press.

Pardeck, J. (184). Multiple placement of children in foster family care: an empirical analysis. *Social Work, 29,* 506–508.

Pelton, L. H. (1981). Child abuse and neglect: the myth of classlessness. In L. H. Pelton (Ed.), *The social context of child abuse and neglect.* NY: Human Sciences Press.

Pine, B. (1986). Child welfare reform and the political process. *Social Service Review, 60,* 339–359..

Rzepnicki, T. (1987). Recidivism of foster children returned to their own homes: a review and new directions for research. *Social Service Review, 61,* 56–69.

Richett, D. and Hudson, J. (1979). The socio-legal history of child abuse and neglect: An analysis of the policy of children's rights. *Journal of Sociology and Social Welfare, 6,* 849–871.

Rothman, D. (1971). *The discovery of the asylum.* Boston: Little Brown.

Seltzer, M. M. and Bloksberg, L. M. (1987). Permanency planning and its effects on foster children: a review of the literature. *Social Work, 32,* 65–68.

Stein, T. (1984). The child abuse prevention and treatment act. *Social Services Review, 58,* 302–314.

U.S. House Hearings. (1976). Foster care: problems and issues. Hearings Before the subcommittee on Select Education of the Committee on Education and Labor. House of Representatives, Ninety-Fourth Congress, Second Session. September 8,1976. Washington, D.C.: Government Printing Office.

U.S. House Hearings. (1977). Hearings on the proposed extension of the Child Abuse Prevention and Treatment Act. Committee on Education and Labor. House of Representatives. Ninety-Fifth Congress, First Session. March 11, 1977. Washington, D.C.: Government Printing Office.

U.S. House Hearings. (1981). Hearings on the reauthorization of the Child Abuse Prevention and Treatment and Adoption Reform Act. Committee on Education and Labor. Ninety-Seventh Congress. First Session. March 9 & 12, 1981. Washington, D.C.: Government Printing Office.

U.S. House Hearings. (1979). Hearings on amendments to social services, foster care, and child welfare programs. Subcommittee on Public Assistance and Unemployment Compensation of the Committee on Ways and Means. Ninety-Sixth Congress. First Session. March 22 and 27, 1979. Washington, D.C.: Government Printing Office.

U.S. House Hearings. (1985). Hearings on amendments to the Foster Care and
    Adoption Assistance Program. Subcommittee on Public Assistance and
    Unemployment Compensation. Committee on Ways and Means. Ninety-
    Ninth Congress. First Session. September 19, 1985. Washington, D.C.:
    Government Printing Office.
U.S. Senate Hearings. (1985). Hearings on Foster Care and Adoption Assis-
    tance Program. Subcommittee on Social Security and Income Maintenance
    Programs of the Committee on Finance. Ninety-Ninth Congress. First Ses-
    sion. June 24, 1985. Washington, D.C.: Government Printing Office.

Acknowledgments

Komisaruk, Richard. "Clinical Evaluation of Child Abuse-Scarred Families: A Preliminary Report." *Juvenile Court Judges Journal* 17 (1966): 66–70. Reprinted with the permission of the National Council of Juvenile and Family Court Judges. Courtesy of Yale University Law Library.

Gil, David G. "A Sociocultural Perspective on Physical Child Abuse." *Child Welfare* 50 (1971): 389–95. Reprinted with the permission of Transaction Publishers.

Spinetta, John J., and David Rigler. "The Child Abusing Parent: A Psychological Review" *Psychological Bulletin* 77 (1972): 296–304. Copyright (1972) by the American Psychological Association. Reprinted by permission.

Gelles, Richard J. "Child Abuse as Psychopathology: A Sociological Critique and Reformulation." *American Journal of Orthopsychiatry* 43 (1973): 611–21. Copyright (1973) by the American Orthopsychiatric Association Inc. Reprinted by permission.

Blumberg, Marvin L. "Psychopathology of the Abusing Parent." *American Journal of Psychotherapy* 28 (1974): 21–29. Reprinted with the permission of the Association for the Advancement of Psychotherapy.

Davidson, Arthur T. "Child Abuse: Causes and Prevention." *Journal of the National Medical Association* 69 (1977): 817–20. Reprinted with the permission of the National Medical Association. Courtesy of Yale University Medical Library.

Jayaratne, Srinika. "Child Abusers as Parents and Children: A Review." *Social Work* 22 (1977): 5–9. Reprinted with the permission of the National Association of Social Workers.

Martin, Michael J. "Family Circumstances in Child Maltreatment: A Review of the Literature." *Family Perspective* 12 (1978): 167–75. Reprinted with the permission of *Family Perspective*. Courtesy of *Family Perspective*.

Spinetta, John J. "Parental Personality Factors in Child Abuse." *Journal of Consulting and Clinical Psychology* 46 (1978): 1409–14. Copyright (1978) by the American Psychological Association. Reprinted by permission.

Gruber, Kenneth J. "The Child Victim's Role in Sexual Assault by Adults." *Child Welfare* 60 (1981): 305–11. Reprinted with the permission of Transaction Publishers.

Friedrich, William N., and Karen K. Wheeler. "The Abusing Parent Revisited: A Decade of Psychological Research." *Journal of Nervous and Mental Diseases* 170 (1982): 577–87. Reprinted with the permission of Williams & Wilkins.

Friedrich, William N., and Alison J. Einbender. "The Abused Child: A Psychological Review." *Journal of Clinical Child Psychology* 12 (1983): 244–56. Reprinted with the permission of Lawrence Erlbaum Associates Inc.

Wolfe, David A. "Child-Abusive Parents: An Empirical Review and Analysis." *Psychological Bulletin* 97 (1985): 462–82. Copyright (1985) by the American Psychological Association. Reprinted by permission.

Gelles, Richard J. "The Family and Its Role in the Abuse of Children." *Psychiatric Annals* 17 (1987): 229–32. Reprinted with the permission of Slack, Inc. Courtesy of University of California, San Francisco, Library.

Stewart, Cyrus, Mary Margaret Senger, David Kallen, and Susan Scheurer. "Family Violence in Stable Middle-Class Homes." *Social Work* 32 (1987): 529–31. Reprinted with the permission of the National Association of Social Workers.

Hegar, Rebecca L. and Jeffrey J. Yungman. "Toward a Causal Typology of Child Neglect." *Children and Youth Services Review* 11 (1989): 203–20. Reprinted with the permission of Elsevier Science, Ltd. Courtesy of *Children and Youth Services Review*.

Salzinger, Suzanne, Richard S. Felman, Muriel Hammer, and Margaret Rosario. "Risk for Physical Child Abuse and the Personal Consequences for Its Victims." *Criminal Justice and Behavior* 18 (1991): 64–81. Reprinted with the permission of Sage Publications, Inc.

Westcott, Helen. "The Abuse of Disabled Children: A Review of the Literature." *Child Care, Health and Development* 17 (1991): 243–58. Reprinted with the permission of Blackwell Scientific Publications Ltd.

Milner, Joel S., and Chinni Chilamkurti. "Physical Child Abuse Perpetrator Characteristics: A Review of the Literature." *Journal of Interpersonal Violence* 6 (1991): 345–66. Reprinted with the permission of Sage Publications, Inc.

Menard, Janet L. and Genevieve M. Johnson. "Incest: Family Dysfunction or Sexual Preference?" *Family Therapy* 19 (1992): 115–22. Reprinted with the permission of Libra Publishers, Inc.

Ney, Philip G., Tak Fung, and Adele Rose Wickett. "Causes of Child Abuse and Neglect." *Canadian Journal of Psychiatry* 37 (1992): 401–5. Reprinted with the permission of the *Canadian Journal of Psychiatry*. Courtesy of Yale University Medical Library.

Gil, David G. "Unraveling Child Abuse." *American Journal of Orthopsychiatry* 45 (1975): 346–56. Copyright (1975) by the American Orthopsychiatric Association Inc. Reprinted by permission.

Gil, David G. "Primary Prevention of Child Abuse: A Philosophical and Political Issue." *Psychiatric Opinion* 13 (1976): 30–34. Reprinted with the permission of the author. Courtesy of Stanford University, Lane Medical Library.

Swift, Carolyn. "The Prevention of Sexual Child Abuse: Focus on the Perpetrator." *Journal of Clinical Child Psychology* 8 (1979): 133–36. Reprinted with the permission of Lawrence Erlbaum Associates Inc.

Helfer, Ray E. "A Review of the Literature on the Prevention of Child Abuse and Neglect." *Child Abuse & Neglect* 6 (1982): 251–61. Reprinted with the permission of Elsevier Science Ltd. Courtesy of Yale University Law Library.

McMurtry, Steven L. "Secondary Prevention of Child Maltreatment: A Review." *Social Work* 30 (1985): 42–48. Reprinted with the permission of the National Association of Social Workers.

Myers, John E.B. "The Streetlight Over the Courthouse." *Journal of Juvenile Law* 10 (1986): 103–10. Reprinted with the permission of LaVerne Law Review, Inc. Courtesy of Yale University Law Library.

Trudell, Bonnie, and Mariamne H. Whatley. "School Sexual Abuse Prevention: Unintended Consequences and Dilemmas." *Child Abuse & Neglect* 12 (1988): 103–13. Reprinted with the permission of Elsevier Science Ltd. Courtesy of Yale University Law Library.

Moelis, Cindy S . "Banning Corporal Punishment: A Crucial Step Toward Preventing Child Abuse." *Children's Legal Rights Journal* 9 (1988): 2–5. Reprinted with the permission of William S. Hein & Co., Inc. Courtesy of *Children's Legal Rights Journal.*

Dubowitz, Howard. "Prevention of Child Maltreatment: What Is Known." *Pediatrics* 83 (1989): 570–77. Reprinted by permission of *Pediatrics.*

Reppucci, N. Dickon, and Jeffrey J. Haugaard. "Prevention of Child Sexual Abuse: Myth or Reality." *American Psychologist* 44 (1989): 1266–75. Copyright (1989) by the American Psychological Association. Reprinted by permission.

Rodwell, Mary K., and Donald E. Chambers. "Primary Prevention of Child Abuse: Is It Really Possible?" *Journal of Sociology and Social Welfare* 19 (1992): 159–76. Reprinted with the permission of Western Michigan University, School of Social Work.

Wolfe, David A. "Prevention of Child Neglect: Emerging Issues." *Criminal Justice and Behavior* 20 (1993): 90–111. Reprinted with the permission of Sage Publications, Inc.

Newberger, Eli H., John J. Hagenbuch, Nancy B. Ebeling, Elizabeth Pivchik Colligan, James S. Sheehan, and Susan H. McVeigh. "Reducing the Literal and Human Cost of Child Abuse: Impact of a New Hospital Management System." *Pediatrics* 51 (1973): 840–8. Reprinted by permission of *Pediatrics.*

Mondale, Walter. "Child Abuse: Issues and Answers." *Public Welfare* 32 (1974): 9–11. Reprinted with the permission of the American Public Welfare Association.

Bergman, Abraham B. "Abuse of the Child Abuse Law." *Pediatrics* 62 (1978): 266–67. Reprinted by permission of *Pediatrics.*

Sklar, Ronald B. "The Criminal Law and the Incest Offender: A Case for Decriminalization?" *Bulletin of the American Academy of Psychiatry and the Law* 7 (1979): 69–77. Reprinted with the permission of the Bulletin of the American Academy of Psychiatry and the Law. Courtesy of Yale University Law Library.

Markham, Barbara. "Child Abuse Intervention: Conflicts in Current Practice and Legal Theory." *Pediatrics* 65 (1980): 180–85. Reprinted by permission of *Pediatrics.*

Koerin, Beverly B. "Child Abuse and Neglect: Changing Policies and Perspectives." *Child Welfare* 59 (1980): 542–50. Reprinted with the permission of Transaction Publishers.

Donahue, Anne. "Child Abuse and Neglect." *Children's Legal Rights Journal* 2 (1981): 13–22. Reprinted with the permission of William S. Hein & Co., Inc. Courtesy of Harvard Law Library.

Hochstadt, Neil J., and Neil J. Harwicke. "How Effective is the Multidisciplinary Approach? A Follow-Up Study." *Child Abuse & Neglect* 9 (1985): 365–72. Reprinted with the permission of Elsevier Science Ltd. Courtesy of Yale University Law Library.

Jimenez, Mary Ann. "Permanency Planning and the Child Abuse Prevention and Treatment Act: The Paradox of Child Welfare Policy." *Journal of Sociology and Social Welfare* 17 (1990): 55–72. Reprinted with the permission of Western Michigan University, School of Social Work.

Series Index by Author

Please Note: Numbers at the end of each entry refer to the volume in which the article appears.